READINGS IN Marketing Strategy

SECOND EDITION

READINGS IN Marketing Strategy

SECOND EDITION

Victor J. Cook, Jr.
Tulane University

Jean-Claude Larréché
INSEAD

Edward C. Strong
Tulane University

The Scientific Press • 507 Seaport Court • Redwood City, CA 94063-2731 • (415) 366-2577

READINGS IN MARKETING STRATEGY, Second Edition
Victor J. Cook, Jr., Jean-Claude Larréché, and Edward C. Strong

Printed in the United States of America

10 9 8 7 6 5 4 3

ISBN 0-89426-139-8

Publisher: The Scientific Press
Text design & production editor: Gene Smith
Cover design by Rogondino & Associates
Cover photo by Glen Wexler

CONTENTS

PREFACE

In the 1990s, strategic marketing has come to embrace more than the traditional concepts of product life cycles, market segmentation, product positioning, and product portfolio analysis. While these classic ideas have endured the test of time and remain at the core of strategic marketing thinking, new dimensions have been born in the crucible of the worldwide competitive marketing wars of the 1980s.

As the first edition of this volume was being assembled in the late 1970s, a *customer orientation* was becoming less and less a *sufficient* condition for marketing success. While it certainly was then, and remains today, a *necessary* condition for success, *competitive analysis* has emerged as a new and crucial element to be considered in parallel with customer behavior. In the 1990s strategic marketing continues to build on the solid foundations of customer and competitor analyses, but has taken on a new and equally important role.

The new role of strategic marketing is to *lead* the various functions of a business to adopt a market oriented perspective and to coordinate the company's actions in all areas that influence market position. For example, marketing and financial planning should be more closely coordinated. The strategic impact on market position of accounting conventions in a company should be identified. The relationship between competitive strategy and corporate strategy should be articulated. Many factors traditionally considered to be outside the domain of marketing, like capital spending, inventories and receivables, plant and equipment, and engineering, have a profound and enduring impact on a company's competitive market position. Strategic marketing must lead in the coordination of these decisions to achieve a cohesive, market focused strategy. Finally, corporate culture and organizational design must be modified to contribute most effectively to the company's competitive market position.

The leadership challenge to strategic marketing, combined with the now traditional customer and competitor analyses, suggests the general definition of "strategic marketing" that was used in the development of this second edition. We take a marketing strategy to be the *manner* in which *resources* are put at *risk* in the search for *competitive market advantages* that will *maximize long-run shareholder value*. The key words in this definition of marketing strategy are in italics. The "manner" in which a strategy is implemented refers to the three fundamental determinants of a strategic marketing plan. These are the timing in the product life style, the segments selected as targets, and the positioning with which a strategy is executed. In this definition the word "resources" refers to all lines on a company's balance sheet and income statement which affect competitive market position, as well as intangible assets such as people and brand names. The resources of interest include the traditional marketing elements of advertising, sales force, distribution, public relations, product design, and brand equity. In addition, strategic marketing decisions also affect labor, plant and equipment, logistics, management, manufacturing processes, inventory levels, and receivables.

In its leadership role a major concern of strategic marketing is the riskiness of a strategy. The financial risk of the company is an important part of overall risk, but equally important are the marketing dimensions of risk based upon the rate of change in primary demand and anticipated market position. A focus of strategic marketing is the search for competitive market advantages. This encompasses both the creation of new advantages, as well as ways of improving competitive position along established dimensions. Finally, strategic marketing takes as a general objective the maximization of long-run shareholder value. In some cases this goal is achieved with maximum market share. In other cases it may be achieved by withdrawal from a market. And in still other instances, shareholder value may be maximized by holding a stable market share position. Working under the umbrella of this broad definition of strategic marketing, which blends contingency theory with the principles of maximum market value, we believe great strides will be taken in the leadership role of this discipline in the 1990s.

The purpose of this book is to provide students and teachers with a comprehensive set of readings useful in understanding and designing successful marketing strategies. The volume is organized into the following six sections:

1. Strategic marketing problems
2. Strategic marketing objectives
3. Product market strategies
4. Product portfolio strategies
5. The strategic marketing spirit
6. Perspectives on action learning in marketing

A total of 41 articles by 49 authors are included. A number of factors were considered in making the final selection. We have, first, tried to cover systematically the key areas that follow from our definition of marketing strategy. Second, only articles published since 1980 were included, unless they were of such enduring value as to warrant republication. An example of the latter is Professor Levitt's "Marketing Myopia." Third, from among the broad array of current articles, we attempted to select those which we believe will endure throughout the decade of the 1990s. An example of this selection criteria is the 1988 paper on "Assessing Advantage: A Framework for Diagnosing Competitive Superiority," by Professors Day and Wensley. Fourth, we have attempted to pick articles which rise above specific industry differences and idiosyncrasies. Finally, since strategic marketing is such an action oriented discipline, the second edition concludes with a special section on action learning in marketing. We believe this final section serves to focus the concepts of the preceding sections on the *Markstrat2* environment. Many of the questions that are asked by students and professors alike about the behavior, validity, and usefulness of *Markstrat2* as a learning environment, are addressed with articles in this final section.

The articles in the second edition came from 15 sources which we gratefully acknowledge: Abt Books, *Academy of Management*, Association for Business Simulation and Experiential Learning, *Business Horizons*, *Fortune*, The Free Press, *Harvard Business Review*, *Journal of Business*, *Journal of Business Research*, *Journal of Consumer Marketing*, *Journal of Marketing*, *Journal of Marketing Research*, McGraw Hill Book Company, Penguin Books, and the *Strategic Management Journal*.

We believe you will find the second edition a comprehensive blend of the best state-of-the-art thinking by strategic marketing scholars with classic ideas that have stood the test of time. This edition is targeted to three specific market segments. First, users of the *Markstrat2* simulation will find this book ideally suited to the special interests of their students. Second, beyond the special interests of *Markstrat2* users, this edition provides an ideal product for those instructors interested in a state-of-the-art readings book. A third segment of the market which this product was designed to serve is those looking for a companion reader to case books and other strategic marketing simulations.

SECTION I

Strategic Marketing Problems

In the 25 years since Professor Levitt introduced us to the problem of marketing myopia, we have come better to understand and to articulate more comprehensively the nature of strategic marketing problems. Among these, marketing myopia remains, perhaps, the most profound and pervasive. The belief that growth is assured by an expanding market, that no competitive substitutes exist, an unlimited faith in mass production economies, and a commitment to product technology are sources of myopia which still afflict a broad cross-section of management. The inward looking company viewpoint is so natural and the blindness it produces is so complete as to prevent consideration of the other major problems in strategic marketing.

The Marketing Concept and Mix

The "marketing concept" was one of the first cures applied to the affliction Levitt called marketing myopia. But, as Professor Webster implies in his description of the strategic problem of changing corporate culture, corporate immune systems have been actively rejecting the cure for myopia for as long as the disease has been known. Achieving a customer orientation runs into organizational difficulties, functional road blocks, and conventional planning techniques which effectively neutralize many attempts to achieve a market oriented perspective. Of all the cures applied to marketing myopia, the marketing concept and its firm customer orientation, remain one of the most potent weapons available.

In recent years it has become fashionable to proclaim that the "marketing mix" and the management of the four Ps are not strategic marketing problems. Some have claimed these are merely tactical issues, not deserving the attention of a serious strategic thinker. Professor Shapiro's paper is a timely and effective reminder that the management of the marketing mix, so contingent upon market segment selection, remains a vital element in the design and implementation of positioning strategies. In fact, a positioning strategy cannot be designed without explicit reference to product, promotion, distribution, and pricing.

Strategic Marketing Objectives

Lurking in the shadows of every discussion of marketing strategy is the problem of which objective or objectives should lead the firm. In his comprehensive review of marketing, strategic planning, and the theory of the firm, Professor Anderson offers several answers to this question. He presents three main alternatives. First is the objective of maximizing the risk adjusted, long-run net present value of the firm. Second, and apparently at odds with the first, is the more behaviorally oriented objective of satisfying aspiration-level constraints within the firm. Third, and arguably more at odds with the first, is the view that the objective of an organization should be to adapt to external resource constraints in order to insure its survival. The view that value maximizing objectives are somehow inconsistent or incompatible with behavioral objectives is, of course, a red herring. If the behavioral objective of a firm is to survive through the specialized negotiation of resource exchanges with external interests, as the contingency theorist would argue, surely management must seek in these negotiations the best price and value outcomes. The economic and behavioral viewpoints are not mutually exclusive. In fact, they are eternally interdependent. We can ignore the interest of either points of view only at great peril.

The External Environment

Negotiation for resource exchanges that maximize the long run value of a firm takes place in an intensely competitive environment. And this competitive environment is constantly under threat from the power of customers and suppliers on the one hand the possibility of new entrants and competitive substitutes on the other hand. Professor Porter's article identifies and explains in detail the problems of industry competition and the forces that drive competitors. Then, in the next article, Mr. Ohmae captures the complexity of industry competition with a concept he calls the "strategic triangle." In doing so, he highlights the strategic marketing problem of *relativity* in the use of skills and resources. In his view the three major players in the strategic game are Customers, Competitors, and the Company, or the 3 Cs. Competition is expressed in terms of key segment selection, key marketing functions performed, and the key attributes of an offering. On each of these dimensions, strategic marketing is an "US ÷ (US + THEM)" game.

The Search for Competitive Advantages

In the last selection of this section Professors Day and Wensley describe the problem of strategic marketing as finding new edges in the market while slowing the erosion of present advantages. The authors argue that superior skills and resources represent the ability of a business to do more or do better than its competitors. *Superior skills* are the distinctive capabilities of a firm's management and employees that set them apart from the personnel of competing organizations. *Superior resources* are the tangible requirements for achieving competitive market advantage. These may stem from scale efficiencies and manufacturing, location advantages, breadth of the sales force, number of distributors, brand equity and many more. These *sources* of advantages may lead to positional gains in basically two ways, both of which are part of the value chain. Skills and resources may create high perceived value, yielding higher selling prices and margins, or they may be applied to achieving lower relative costs. Of course, the most successful strategy will produce both lower delivered costs and higher perceived values. Finally, the authors propose that performance be measured by customer satisfaction, loyalty, market share, and profitability. The process by which skills and resources may be converted into superior market positions and performance outcomes is developed in detail. The authors conclude that any attempt to understand or assess competitive advantages must account for the three defining features of the concept: sources of advantage, positional advantages, and performance outcomes. These three elements of competitive advantage must be linked to the investment profiles of individual competitors in order to sustain existing and create new competitive market advantages.

Combined, the seven selections in Section I leave very few rocks uncovered or dark corners unilluminated. We believe most of what we have learned about strategic marketing problems is captured in this selection of readings. ■

1

Marketing Myopia [HBR Classic]

Theodore Levitt

Shortsighted managements often fail to recognize that in fact there is no such thing as a growth industry

How can a company ensure its continued growth? In 1960 "Marketing Myopia" answered that question in a new and challenging way by urging organizations to define their industries broadly to take advantage of growth opportunities. Using the archetype of the railroads, Mr. Levitt showed how they declined inevitably as technology advanced because they defined themselves too narrowly. To continue growing, companies must ascertain and act on their customers' needs and desires, not bank on the presumptive longevity of their products. The success of the article testifies to the validity of its message. It has been widely quoted and anthologized, and HBR has sold more than 265,000 reprints of it. The author of 14 subsequent articles in HBR, Mr. Levitt is one of the magazine's most prolific contributors. In a retrospective commentary, he considers the use and misuse that have been made of "Marketing Myopia," describing its many interpretations and hypothesizing about its success.

EVERY MAJOR INDUSTRY was once a growth industry. But some that are now riding a wave of growth enthusiasm are very much in the shadow of decline. Others which are thought of as seasoned growth industries have actually stopped growing. In every case the reason growth is threatened, slowed, or stopped is *not* because the market is saturated. It is because there has been a failure of management.

At the time of this article's publication, Theodore Levitt was lecturer in business administration at the Harvard Business School. Now a full professor there, he is the author of six books and many other articles for HBR.

Fateful Purposes

The failure is at the top. The executives responsible for it, in the last analysis, are those who deal with broad aims and policies. Thus:

- ☐ The railroads did not stop growing because the need for passenger and freight transportation declined. That grew. The railroads are in trouble today not because the need was filled by others (cars, trucks, airplanes, even telephones), but because it was *not* filled by the railroads themselves. They let others take customers away from them because they assumed themselves to be in the railroad business rather than in the transportation business. The reason they defined their industry wrong was because they were railroad-oriented instead of transportation-oriented; they were product-oriented instead of customer-oriented.
- ☐ Hollywood barely escaped being totally ravished by television. Actually, all the established film companies went through drastic reorganizations. Some simply disappeared. All of them got into trouble not because of TV's inroads but because of their own myopia. As with the railroads, Hollywood defined its business incorrectly. It thought it was in the movie business when it was actually in the entertainment business. "Movies" implied a specific, limited product. This produced a fatuous contentment which from the beginning led producers to view TV as a threat. Hollywood scorned and rejected TV when it should have welcomed it as an opportunity—an opportunity to expand the entertainment business.

Today TV is a bigger business than the old narrowly defined movie business ever was. Had Hollywood been customer-oriented (providing entertainment), rather than product-oriented (making movies), would it have gone through the fiscal purgatory that it did? I doubt it. What ultimately saved Hollywood and accounted for its recent resurgence was the wave of new young writers, producers, and directors whose previous successes in television had decimated the old movie companies and toppled the big movie moguls.

There are other less obvious examples of industries that have been and are now endangering their futures by improperly defining their purposes. I shall discuss some in detail later and analyze the kind of policies that lead to trouble. Right now it may help to show what a thoroughly customer-oriented management *can* do to keep a growth industry growing, even after the obvious opportunities have been exhausted; and here there are two examples that have been around for a long time. They are nylon and glass—specifically, E. I. duPont de Nemours & Company and Corning Glass Works.

Both companies have great technical competence. Their product orientation is unquestioned. But this alone does not explain their success. After all, who was more pridefully product-oriented and product-conscious than the erstwhile New England textile companies that have been so thoroughly massacred? The DuPonts and the Cornings have succeeded not primarily because of their product or research orientation but because they have been thoroughly customer-oriented also. It is constant watchfulness for opportunities to apply their technical know-how to the creation of customer-satisfying uses which accounts for their prodigious output of successful new products. Without a very sophisticated eye on the customer, most of their new products might have been wrong, their sales methods useless.

Aluminum has also continued to be a growth industry, thanks to the efforts of two wartime-created companies which deliberately set about creating new customer-satisfying uses. Without Kaiser Aluminum & Chemical Corporation and Reynolds Metals Company, the total demand for aluminum today would be vastly less.

Error of Analysis

Some may argue that it is foolish to set the railroads off against aluminum or the movies off against glass. Are not aluminum and glass naturally so versatile that the industries are bound to have more growth opportunities than the railroads and movies? This view commits precisely the error I have been talking about. It defines an industry, or a product, or a cluster of know-how so narrowly as to guarantee its premature senescence. When we mention "railroads," we should make sure we mean "transportation." As transporters, the railroads still have a good chance for very considerable growth. They are not limited to the railroad business as such (though in my opinion rail transportation is potentially a much stronger transportation medium than is generally believed).

What the railroads lack is not opportunity, but some of the same managerial imaginativeness and audacity that made them great. Even an amateur like Jacques Barzun can see what is lacking when he says:

> I grieve to see the most advanced physical and social organization of the last century go down in shabby disgrace for lack of the same comprehensive imagination that built it up. [What is lacking is] the will of the companies to survive and to satisfy the public by inventiveness and skill.[1]

Shadow of Obsolescence

It is impossible to mention a single major industry that did not at one time qualify for the magic appellation of "growth industry." In each case its assumed strength lay in the apparently unchallenged superiority of its product. There appeared to be no effective substitute for it. It was itself a runaway substitute for the product it so triumphantly replaced. Yet one after another of these celebrated industries has come under a shadow. Let us look briefly at a few more of them, this time taking examples that have so far received a little less attention:

☐ *Dry Cleaning*. This was once a growth industry with lavish prospects. In an age of wool garments, imagine being finally able to get them safely and easily clean. The boom was on.

Yet here we are 30 years after the boom started and the industry is in trouble. Where has the competition come from? From a better way of cleaning? No. It has come from synthetic fibers and chemical additives that have cut the need for dry cleaning. But this is only the beginning. Lurking in the wings and ready to make chemical dry cleaning totally obsolescent is that powerful magician, ultrasonics.

☐ *Electric Utilities*. This is another one of those supposedly "no-substitute" products that has been enthroned on a pedestal of invincible growth. When the incandescent lamp came along, kerosene lights were finished. Later the water wheel and the steam engine were cut to ribbons by the flexibility, reliability, simplicity, and just plain easy availability of electric motors. The prosperity of electric utilities continues to wax extravagant as the home is converted into a museum of electric gadgetry. How can anybody miss by investing in utilities, with no competition, nothing but growth ahead?

But a second look is not quite so comforting. A score of nonutility companies are well advanced toward developing a powerful chemical fuel cell which could sit in some hidden closet of every home silently ticking off electric power. The electric lines that vulgarize so many neighborhoods will be eliminated. So will the endless demolition of streets and service interruptions during storms. Also on the horizon is solar energy, again pioneered by nonutility companies.

Who says that the utilities have no competition? They may be natural monopolies now, but tomorrow they may be natural deaths. To avoid this prospect, they too will have to develop fuel cells, solar energy, and other power sources. To survive, they themselves will have to plot the obsolescence of what now produces their livelihood.

☐ *Grocery Stores*. Many people find it hard to realize that there ever was a thriving establishment known as the "corner grocery store." The supermarket has taken over with a powerful effectiveness. Yet the big food chains of the 1930s narrowly escaped being completely wiped out by the aggressive expansion of independent supermarkets. The first genuine supermarket was opened in 1930, in Jamaica, Long Island. By 1933 supermarkets were thriving in California, Ohio, Pennsylvania, and elsewhere. Yet the established chains pompously ignored them. When they chose to notice them, it was with such derisive descriptions as "cheapy," "horse-and-buggy," "cracker-barrel storekeeping," and "unethical opportunists."

The executive of one big chain announced at the time that he found it "hard to believe that people will drive for miles to shop for foods and sacrifice the personal service chains have perfected and to which Mrs. Consumer is accustomed."[2] As late as 1936, the National Wholesale Grocers convention and the New Jersey Retail Grocers Association said there was nothing to fear. They said that the supers' narrow appeal to the price buyer limited the size of their market. They had to draw from miles around. When imitators came, there would be wholesale liquidations as volume fell. The current high sales of the supers was said to be partly due to their novelty. Basically people wanted convenient neighborhood grocers. If the neighborhood stores "cooperate with their suppliers, pay attention to their costs, and improve their service," they would be able to weather the competition until it blew over.[3]

It never blew over. The chains discovered that survival required going into the supermarket business. This meant the wholesale destruction of their huge investments in corner store sites and in established distribution and merchandising methods. The companies with "the courage of their convictions" resolutely stuck to the corner store philosophy. They kept their pride but lost their shirts.

Self-Deceiving Cycle

But memories are short. For example, it is hard for people who today confidently hail the twin messiahs of electronics and chemicals to see how things could possibly go wrong with these galloping industries. They probably also cannot see how a reasonably sensible businessman could have been as myopic as the famous Boston millionaire who 50 years ago unintentionally sentenced his heirs to poverty by stipulating that his entire estate be forever invested exclusively in electric streetcar securities. His posthumous declaration, "There will always be a big demand for efficient urban transportation," is no consolation to his heirs who sustain life by pumping gasoline at automobile filling stations.

Yet, in a casual survey I recently took among a group of intelligent business executives, nearly half agreed that it would be hard to hurt their heirs by tying their estates forever to the electronics industry. When I then confronted them with the Boston streetcar example, they chorused unanimously, "That's different!" But is it? Is not the basic situation identical?

In truth, *there is no such thing* as a growth industry, I believe. There are only companies organized and operated to create and capitalize on growth opportunities. Industries that assume themselves to be riding some automatic growth escalator invariably descend into stagnation. The history of every dead and dying "growth" industry shows a self-deceiving cycle of bountiful expansion and undetected decay. There are four conditions which usually guarantee this cycle:

1. The belief that growth is assured by an expanding and more affluent population.
2. The belief that there is no competitive substitute for the industry's major product.
3. Too much faith in mass production and in the advantages of rapidly declining unit costs as output rises.
4. Preoccupation with a product that lends itself to carefully controlled scientific experimentation, improvement, and manufacturing cost reduction.

I should like now to begin examining each of these conditions in some detail. To build my case as boldly as possible, I shall illustrate the points with reference to three industries —petroleum, automobiles, and electronics—particularly petroleum, because it spans more years and more vicissitudes. Not only do these three have excellent reputations with the general public and also enjoy the confidence of sophisticated investors, but their managements have become known for progressive thinking in areas like financial control, product research, and management training. If obsolescence can cripple even these industries, it can happen anywhere.

Population Myth

The belief that profits are assured by an expanding and more affluent population is dear to the heart of every industry. It takes the edge off the apprehensions everybody understandably feels about the future. If consumers are multiplying and also buying more of your product or service, you can face the future with considerably more comfort than if the market is shrinking. An expanding market keeps the manufacturer from having to think very hard or imaginatively. If thinking is an intellectual response to a problem, then the absence of a problem leads to the absence of thinking. If your product has an automatically expanding market, then you will not give much thought to how to expand it.

One of the most interesting examples of this is provided by the petroleum industry. Probably our oldest growth industry, it has an enviable record. While there are some current apprehensions about its growth rate, the industry itself tends to be optimistic.

But I believe it can be demonstrated that it is undergoing a fundamental yet typical change. It is not only ceasing to be a growth industry, but may actually be a declining one, relative to other business. Although there is widespread unawareness of it, I believe that within 25 years the oil industry may find itself in much the same position of retrospective glory that the railroads are now in. Despite its pioneering work in developing and applying the present-value method of investment evaluation, in employee relations, and in working with backward countries, the petroleum business is a distressing example of how complacency and wrongheadedness can stubbornly convert opportunity into near disaster.

One of the characteristics of this and other industries that have believed very strongly in the beneficial consequences of an expanding population, while at the same time being industries with a generic product for which there has appeared to be no competitive substitute, is that the individual companies have sought to outdo their competitors by improving on what they are already doing. This makes sense, of course, if one assumes that sales are tied to the country's population strings, because the customer can compare products only on a feature-by-feature basis. I believe it is significant, for example, that not since John D. Rockefeller sent free kerosene lamps to China has the oil industry done anything really outstanding to create a demand for its product. Not even in product improvement has it showered itself with eminence. The greatest single improvement—namely, the development of tetraethyl lead—came from outside the industry, specifically from General Motors and DuPont. The big contributions made by the industry itself are confined to the technology of oil exploration, production, and refining.

Asking for Trouble

In other words, the industry's efforts have focused on improving the *efficiency* of getting and making its product, not really on improving the generic product or its marketing. Moreover, its chief product has continuously been defined in the narrowest possible terms, namely, gasoline, not energy, fuel, or transportation. This attitude has helped assure that:

☐ Major improvements in gasoline quality tend not to originate in the oil industry. Also, the development of superior alternative fuels comes from outside the oil industry, as will be shown later.

☐ Major innovations in automobile fuel marketing are originated by small new oil companies that are not primarily preoccupied with production or refining. These are the companies that have been responsible for the rapidly expanding multipump gasoline stations, with their successful emphasis on large and clean layouts, rapid and efficient driveway service, and quality gasoline at low prices.

Thus, the oil industry is asking for trouble from outsiders. Sooner or later, in this land of hungry inventors and entrepreneurs, a threat is sure to come. The possibilities of this will become more apparent when we turn to the next dangerous belief of many managements. For the sake of continuity, because this second belief is tied closely to the first, I shall continue with the same example.

Idea of Indispensability

The petroleum industry is pretty much persuaded that there is no competitive substitute for its major product, gasoline—or if there is, that it will continue to be a derivative of crude oil, such as diesel fuel or kerosene jet fuel.

There is a lot of automatic wishful thinking in this assumption. The trouble is that most refining companies own huge amounts of crude oil reserves. These have value only if there is a market for products into which oil can be converted—hence the tenacious belief in the continuing competitive superiority of automobile fuels made from crude oil.

This idea persists despite all historic evidence against it. The evidence not only shows that oil has never been a superior product for any purpose for very long, but it also shows that the oil industry has never really been a growth industry. It has been a succession of different businesses that have gone through the usual historic cycles of growth, maturity, and decay. Its overall survival is owed to a series of miraculous escapes from total obsolescence, of last-minute and unexpected reprieves from total disaster reminiscent of the Perils of Pauline

Perils of Petroleum

I shall sketch in only the main episodes. First, crude oil was largely a patent medicine. But even before that fad ran out, demand was greatly expanded by the use of oil in kerosene lamps. The prospect of lighting the world's lamps gave rise to an extravagant promise of growth. The prospects were similar to those the industry now holds for gasoline in other parts of the world. It can hardly wait for the underdeveloped nations to get a car in every garage.

In the days of the kerosene lamp, the oil companies competed with each other and against gaslight by trying to improve the illuminating characteristics of kerosene. Then suddenly the impossible happened. Edison invented a light which was totally nondependent on crude oil. Had it not been for the growing use of kerosene in space heaters, the incandescent lamp would have completely finished oil as a growth industry at that time. Oil would have been good for little else than axle grease.

Then disaster and reprieve struck again. Two great innovations occurred, neither originating in the oil industry. The successful development of coal-burning domestic central-heating systems made the space heater obsolescent. While the industry reeled, along came its most magnificent boost yet—the internal combustion engine, also invented by outsiders. Then when the prodigious expansion for gasoline finally began to level off in the 1920s, along came the miraculous escape of a central oil heater. Once again, the escape was provided by an outsider's invention and development. And when that market weakened, wartime demand for aviation fuel came to the rescue. After the war the expansion of civilian aviation, the dieselization of railroads, and the explosive demand for cars and trucks kept the industry's growth in high gear.

Meanwhile, centralized oil heating—whose boom potential had only recently been proclaimed—ran into severe competition from natural gas. While the oil companies themselves owned the gas that now competed with their oil, the industry did not originate the natural gas revolution, nor has it to this day greatly profited from its gas ownership. The gas revolution was made by newly formed transmission companies that marketed the product with an aggressive ardor. They started a magnificent new industry, first against the advice and then against the resistance of the oil companies.

By all the logic of the situation, the oil companies themselves should have made the gas revolution. They not only owned the gas; they also were the only people experienced in handling, scrubbing, and using it, the only people experienced in pipeline technology and transmission, and they understood heating problems. But, partly because they knew that natural gas would compete with their own sale of heating oil, the oil companies poohpoohed the potentials of gas.

The revolution was finally started by oil pipeline executives who, unable to persuade their own companies to go into gas, quit and organized the spectacularly successful gas transmission companies. Even after their success became painfully evident to the oil companies, the latter did not go into gas transmission. The multibillion dollar business which should have been theirs went to others. As in the past, the industry was blinded by its narrow preoccupation with a specific product and the value of its reserves. It paid little or no attention to its customers' basic needs and preferences.

The postwar years have not witnessed any change. Immediately after World War II the oil industry was greatly encouraged about its future by the rapid expansion of demand for its traditional line of products. In 1950 most companies projected annual rates of domestic expansion of around 6% through at least 1975. Though the ratio of crude oil reserves to demand in the Free World was about 20 to 1, with 10 to 1 being usually considered a reasonable working ratio in the United States, booming demand sent oil men searching for more without sufficient regard to what the future really promised. In 1952 they "hit" in the Middle East; the ratio skyrocketed to 42 to 1. If gross additions to reserves continue at the average rate of the past five years (37 billion barrels annually), then by 1970 the reserve ratio will be up to 45 to 1. This abundance of oil has weakened crude and product prices all over the world.

Uncertain Future

Management cannot find much consolation today in the rapidly expanding petrochemical industry, another oil-using idea that did not originate in the leading firms. The total United States production of petrochemicals is equivalent to about 2% (by volume) of the demand for all petroleum products. Although the petrochemical industry is now expected to grow by about 10% per year, this will not offset other drains on the growth of crude oil consumption. Furthermore, while petrochemical products are many and growing, it is well to remember that there are nonpetroleum sources of the basic raw material, such as coal. Besides, a lot of plastics can be produced with relatively little oil. A 50,000-barrel-per-day oil refinery is now considered the absolute minimum size for efficiency. But a 5,000-barrel-per-day chemical plant is a giant operation.

Oil has never been a continuously strong growth industry. It has grown by fits and starts, always miraculously saved by innovations and developments not of its own making. The reason it has not grown in a smooth progression is that each time it thought it had a superior product safe from the possibility of competitive substitutes, the product turned out to be inferior and notoriously subject to obsolescence. Until now, gasoline (for motor fuel, anyhow) has escaped this fate. But, as we shall see later, it too may be on its last legs.

The point of all this is that there is no guarantee against product obsolescence. If a company's own research does not make it obsolete, another's will. Unless an industry is especially lucky, as oil has been until now, it can easily go down in a sea of red figures—just as the railroads have, as the buggy whip manufacturers have, as the corner grocery chains have, as most of the big movie companies have, and indeed as many other industries have.

The best way for a firm to be lucky is to make its own luck. That requires knowing what makes a business successful. One of the greatest enemies of this knowledge is mass production.

Production Pressures

Mass-production industries are impelled by a great drive to produce all they can. The prospect of steeply declining unit costs as output rises is more than most companies can usually resist. The profit possibilities look spectacular. All effort focuses on production. The result is that marketing gets neglected.

John Kenneth Galbraith contends that just the opposite occurs.[4] Output is so prodigious that all effort concentrates on trying to get rid of it. He says this accounts for singing commercials, desecration of the countryside with advertising signs, and other wasteful and vulgar practices. Galbraith has a finger on something real, but he misses the strategic point. Mass production does indeed generate great pressure to "move" the product. But what usually gets emphasized is selling, not marketing. Marketing, being a more sophisticated and complex process, gets ignored.

The difference between marketing and selling is more than semantic. Selling focuses on the needs of the seller, marketing on the needs of the buyer. Selling is preoccupied with the seller's need to convert his product into cash, marketing with the idea of satisfying the needs of the customer by means of the product and the whole cluster of things associated with creating, delivering, and finally consuming it.

In some industries the enticements of full mass production have been so powerful that for many years top management in effect has told the sales departments, "You get rid of it; we'll worry about profits." By contrast, a truly marketing-minded firm tries to create value-satisfying goods and services that consumers will want to buy. What it offers for sale includes not only the generic product or service, but also how it is made available to the customer, in what form, when, under what conditions, and at what terms of trade. Most important, what it offers for sale is determined not by the seller but by the buyer. The seller takes his cues from the buyer in such a way that the product becomes a consequence of the marketing effort, not vice versa.

Lag in Detroit

This may sound like an elementary rule of business, but that does not keep it from being violated wholesale. It is certainly more violated than honored. Take the automobile industry.

Here mass production is most famous, most honored, and has the greatest impact on the entire society. The industry has hitched its fortune to the relentless requirements of the annual model change, a policy that makes customer orientation an especially urgent necessity. Consequently the auto companies annually spend millions of dollars on consumer research. But the fact that the new compact cars are selling so well in their first year indicates that Detroit's vast researches have for a long time failed to reveal what the customer really wanted. Detroit was not persuaded that he wanted anything different from what he had been getting until it lost millions of customers to other small car manufacturers.

How could this unbelievable lag behind consumer wants have been perpetuated so long? Why did not research reveal consumer preferences before consumers' buying decisions themselves revealed the facts? Is that not what consumer research is for—to find out before the fact what is going to happen? The answer is that Detroit never really researched the customer's wants. It only researched his preferences between the kinds of things which it had already decided to offer him. For Detroit is mainly product-oriented, not customer-oriented. To the extent that the customer is recognized as having needs that the manufacturer should try to satisfy, Detroit usually acts as if the job can be done entirely by product changes. Occasionally attention gets paid to financing, too, but that is done more in order to sell than to enable the customer to buy.

As for taking care of other customer needs, there is not enough being done to write about. The areas of the greatest unsatisfied needs are ignored, or at best get stepchild attention. These are at the point of sale and on the matter of automotive repair and maintenance. Detroit views these problem areas as being of secondary importance. That is underscored by the fact that the retailing and servicing ends of this industry are neither owned and operated nor controlled by the manufacturers. Once the car is produced, things are pretty much in the dealer's inadequate hands. Illustrative of Detroit's arm's-length attitude is the fact that, while servicing holds enormous sales-stimulating, profit-building opportunities, only 57 of Chevrolet's 7,000 dealers provide night maintenance service.

Motorists repeatedly express their dissatisfaction with servicing and their apprehensions about buying cars under the present selling setup. The anxieties and problems they encounter during the auto buying and maintenance processes are probably more intense and widespread today than 30 years ago. Yet the automobile companies do not *seem* to listen to or take their cues from the anguished consumer. If they do listen, it must be through the filter of their own preoccupation with production. The marketing effort is still viewed as a necessary consequence of the product, not vice versa, as it should be. That is the legacy of mass production, with its parochial view that profit resides essentially in low-cost full production.

What Ford Put First

The profit lure of mass production obviously has a place in the plans and strategy of business management, but it must always *follow* hard thinking about the customer. This is one of the most important lessons that we can learn from the contradictory behavior of Henry Ford. In a sense Ford was both the most brilliant and the most senseless marketer in American history. He was senseless because he refused to give the customer anything but a black car. He was brilliant because he fashioned a production system designed to fit market needs. We habitually celebrate him for the wrong reason, his production genius. His real genius was marketing. We think he was able to cut his selling price and therefore sell millions of $500 cars because his invention of the assembly line had reduced the costs. Actually he invented the assembly line because he had concluded that at $500 he could sell millions of cars. Mass production was the *result* not the cause of his low prices.

Ford repeatedly emphasized this point, but a nation of production-oriented business managers refuses to hear the great lesson he taught. Here is his operating philosophy as he expressed it succinctly:

> Our policy is to reduce the price, extend the operations, and improve the article. You will notice that the reduction of price comes first. We have never considered any costs as fixed. Therefore we first reduce the price to the point where we believe more sales will result. Then we go ahead and try to make the prices. We do not bother about the costs. The new price forces the costs down. The more usual way is to take the costs and then determine the price; and although that method may be scientific in the narrow sense, it is not scientific in the broad sense, because what earthly use is it to know the cost if it tells you that you cannot manufacture at a price at which the article can be sold? But more to the point is the fact that, although one may calculate what a cost is, and of course all of our costs are carefully calculated, no one knows what a cost ought to be. One of the ways of discovering . . . is to name a price so low as to force everybody in the place to the highest point of efficiency. The low price makes everybody dig for profits. We make more discoveries concerning manufacturing and selling under this forced method than by any method of leisurely investigation.[5]

Product Provincialism

The tantalizing profit possibilities of low unit production costs may be the most seriously self-deceiving attitude that can afflict a company, particularly a "growth" company where an apparently assured expansion of demand already tends to undermine a proper concern for the importance of marketing and the customer.

The usual result of this narrow preoccupation with so-called concrete matters is that instead of growing, the industry declines. It usually means that the product fails to adapt to the constantly changing patterns of consumer needs and tastes, to new and modified marketing institutions and practices, or to product developments in competing or complementary industries. The industry has its eyes so firmly on its own specific product that it does not see how it is being made obsolete.

The classical example of this is the buggy whip industry. No amount of product improvement could stave off its death sentence. But had the industry defined itself as being in the transportation business rather than the buggy whip business, it might have survived. It would have done what survival always entails, that is, changing. Even if it had only defined its business as providing a stimulant or catalyst to an energy source, it might have survived by becoming a manufacturer of, say, fan belts or air cleaners.

What may some day be a still more classical example is, again, the oil industry. Having let others steal marvelous opportunities from it (e.g., natural gas, as already mentioned, missile fuels, and jet engine lubricants), one would expect it to have taken steps never to let that happen again. But this is not the case. We are now getting extraordinary new developments in fuel systems specifically designed to power automobiles. Not only are these developments concentrated in firms outside the petroleum industry, but petroleum is almost systematically ignoring them, securely content in its wedded bliss to oil. It is the story of the kerosene lamp versus the incandescent lamp all over again. Oil is trying to improve hydrocarbon fuels rather than develop *any* fuels best suited to the needs of their users, whether or not made in different ways and with different raw materials from oil.

Here are some things which nonpetroleum companies are working on:

☐ Over a dozen such firms now have advanced working models of energy systems which, when perfected, will replace the internal combustion engine and eliminate the demand for gasoline, The superior merit of each of these systems is their elimination of frequent, time-consuming, and irritating refueling stops. Most of these systems are fuel cells designed to create electrical energy directly from chemicals without combustion. Most of them use chemicals that are not derived from oil, generally hydrogen and oxygen.

☐ Several other companies have advanced models of electric storage batteries designed to power automobiles. One of these is an aircraft producer that is working jointly with several electric utility companies. The latter hope to use off-peak generating capacity to supply overnight plug-in battery regeneration. Another company, also using the battery approach, is a medium-size electronics firm with extensive small-battery experience that it developed in connection with its work on hearing aids. It is collaborating with an automobile manufacturer. Recent improvements arising from the need for high-powered miniature power storage plants in rockets have put us within reach of a relatively small battery capable of withstanding great overloads or surges of power. Germanium diode applications and batteries using sintered-plate and nickel-cadmium techniques promise to make a revolution in our energy sources.

☐ Solar energy conversion systems are also getting increasing attention. One usually cautious Detroit auto executive recently ventured that solar-powered cars might be common by 1980.

As for the oil companies, they are more or less "watching developments," as one research director put it to me. A few are doing a bit of research on fuel cells, but almost always confined to developing cells powered by hydrocarbon chemicals. None of them are enthusiastically researching fuel cells, batteries, or solar power plants. None of them are spending a fraction as much on research in these profoundly important areas as they are on the usual run-of-the-mill things like reducing combustion chamber deposit in gasoline engines. One major integrated petroleum company recently took a tentative look at the fuel cell and concluded that although "the companies actively working on it indicate a belief in ultimate success . . . the timing and magnitude of its impact are too remote to warrant recognition in our forecasts."

One might, of course, ask: Why should the oil companies do anything different? Would not chemical fuel cells, batteries, or solar energy kill the present product lines? The answer is that they would indeed, and that is precisely the reason for the oil firms having to develop these power units before their competitors, so they will not be companies without an industry.

Management might be more likely to do what is needed for its own preservation if it thought of itself as being in the energy business. But even that would not be enough if it persists in imprisoning itself in the narrow grip of its tight product orientation. It has to think of itself as taking care of customer needs, not finding, refining, or even selling oil. Once it genuinely thinks of its business as taking care of people's transportation needs, nothing can stop it from creating its own extravagantly profitable growth.

'Creative Destruction'

Since words are cheap and deeds are dear, it may be appropriate to indicate what this kind of thinking involves and leads to. Let us start at the beginning—the customer. It can be shown that motorists strongly dislike the bother, delay, and experience of buying gasoline. People actually do not buy gasoline. They cannot see it, taste it, feel it, appreciate it, or really test it. What they buy is the right to continue driving their cars. The gas station is like a tax collector to whom people are compelled to pay a periodic toll as the price of using their cars. This makes the gas station a basically unpopular institution. It can never be made popular or pleasant, only less unpopular, less unpleasant.

To reduce its unpopularity completely means eliminating it. Nobody likes a tax collector, not even a pleasantly cheerful one. Nobody likes to interrupt a trip to buy a phantom product, not even from a handsome Adonis or a seductive Venus. Hence, companies that are working on exotic fuel substitutes which will eliminate the need for frequent refueling are heading directly into the outstretched arms of the irritated motorist. They are riding a wave of inevitability, not because they are creating something which is technologically superior or more sophisticated, but because they are satisfying a powerful customer need. They are also eliminating noxious odors and air pollution.

Once the petroleum companies recognize the customer-satisfying logic of what another power system can do, they will see that they have no more choice about working on an efficient, long-lasting fuel (or some way of delivering present fuels without bothering the motorist) than the big food chains had a choice about going into the supermarket business, or the vacuum tube companies had a choice about making semiconductors. For their own good the oil firms will have to destroy their own highly profitable assets. No amount of wishful thinking can save them from the necessity of engaging in this form of "creative destruction."

I phrase the need as strongly as this because I think management must make quite an effort to break itself loose from conventional ways. It is all too easy in this day and age for a company or industry to let its sense of purpose become dominated by the economies of full production and to develop a dangerously lopsided product orientation. In short, if management lets itself drift, it invariably drifts in the direction of thinking of itself as producing goods and services, not customer satisfactions. While it probably will not descend to the depths of telling its salesmen, "You get rid of it; we'll worry about profits," it can, without knowing it, be practicing precisely that formula for withering decay. The historic fate of one growth industry after another has been its suicidal product provincialism.

Dangers of R&D

Another big danger to a firm's continued growth arises when top management is wholly transfixed by the profit possibilities of technical research and development. To illustrate I shall turn first to a new industry—electronics—and then return once more to the oil companies. By comparing a fresh example with a familiar one, I hope to emphasize the prevalence and insidiousness of a hazardous way of thinking.

Marketing Shortchanged

In the case of electronics, the greatest danger which faces the glamorous new companies in this field is not that they do not pay enough attention to research and development, but that they pay *too much* attention to it. And the fact that the fastest growing electronics firms owe their eminence to their heavy emphasis on technical research is completely beside the point. They have vaulted to affluence on a sudden crest of unusually strong general receptiveness to new technical ideas. Also, their success has been shaped in the virtually guaranteed market of military subsidies and by military orders that in many cases actually preceded the existence of facilities to make the products. Their expansion has, in other words, been almost totally devoid of marketing effort.

Thus, they are growing up under conditions that come dangerously close to creating the illusion that a superior product will sell itself. Having created a successful company by making a superior product, it is not surprising that management continues to be oriented toward the product rather than the people who consume it. It develops the philosophy that continued growth is a matter of continued product innovation and improvement.

A number of other factors tend to strengthen and sustain this belief:

1. Because electronic products are highly complex and sophisticated, managements become top-heavy with engineers and scientists. This creates a selective bias in favor of research and production at the expense of marketing. The organization tends to view itself as making things rather than satisfying customer needs. Marketing gets treated as a residual activity, "something else" that must be done once the vital job of product creation and production is completed.
2. To this bias in favor of product research, development, and production is added the bias in favor of dealing with controllable variables. Engineers and scientists are at home in the world of concrete things like machines, test tubes, production lines, and even balance sheets. The abstractions to which they feel kindly are those which are testable or manipulatable in the laboratory, or, if not testable, then functional, such as Euclid's axioms. In short, the managements of the new glamour-growth companies tend to favor those business activities which lend themselves to careful study, experimentation, and control—the hard, practical realities of the lab, the shop, the books.

What gets shortchanged are the realities of the *market*. Consumers are unpredictable, varied, fickle, stupid, shortsighted, stubborn, and generally bothersome. This is not what the engineer-managers say, but deep down in their consciousness it is what they believe. And this accounts for their concentrating on what they know and what they can control, namely, product research, engineering, and production. The emphasis on production becomes particularly attractive when the product can be made at declining unit costs. There is no more inviting way of making money than by running the plant full blast.

Today the top-heavy science-engineering-production orientation of so many electronics companies works reasonably well because they are pushing into new frontiers in which the armed services have pioneered virtually assured markets. The companies are in the felicitous position of having to fill, not find markets; of not having to discover what the customer needs and wants, but of having the customer voluntarily come forward with specific new product demands. If a team of consultants had been assigned specifically to design a business situation calculated to prevent the emergence and development of a customer-oriented marketing viewpoint, it could not have produced anything better than the conditions just described.

Stepchild Treatment

The oil industry is a stunning example of how science, technology, and mass production can divert an entire group of companies from their main task. To the extent the consumer is studied at all (which is not much), the focus is forever on getting information which is designed to help the oil companies improve what they are now doing. They try to discover more convincing advertising themes, more effective sales promotional drives, what the market shares of the various companies are, what people like or dislike about service station dealers and oil companies, and so forth. Nobody seems as interested in probing deeply into the basic human needs that the industry might be trying to satisfy as in probing into the basic properties of the raw material that the companies work with in trying to deliver customer satisfactions.

Basic questions about customers and markets seldom get asked. The latter occupy a stepchild status. They are recognized as existing, as having to be taken care of, but not worth very much real thought or dedicated attention. Nobody gets as excited about the customers in his own backyard as about the oil in the Sahara Desert. Nothing illustrates better the neglect of marketing than its treatment in the industry press.

The centennial issue of the *American Petroleum Institute Quarterly,* published in 1959 to celebrate the discovery of oil in Titusville, Pennsylvania, contained 21 feature articles proclaiming the industry's greatness. Only one of these talked about its achievements in marketing, and that was only a pictorial record of how service station architecture has changed. The issue also contained a special section on "New Horizons," which was devoted to showing the magnificent role oil would play in America's future. Every reference was ebulliently optimistic, never implying once that oil might have some hard competition. Even the reference to atomic energy was a cheerful catalogue of how oil would help make atomic energy a success. There was not a single apprehension that the oil industry's affluence might be threatened or a suggestion that one "new horizon" might include new and better ways of serving oil's present customers.

But the most revealing example of the stepchild treatment that marketing gets was still another special series of short articles on "The Revolutionary Potential of Electronics." Under that heading this list of articles appeared in the table of contents:

- "In the Search for Oil"
- "In Refinery Processes"
- "In Production Operations"
- "In Pipeline Operations"

Significantly, every one of the industry's major functional areas is listed, *except* marketing. Why? Either it is believed that electronics holds no revolutionary potential for petroleum marketing (which is palpably wrong), or the editors forgot to discuss marketing (which is more likely, and illustrates its stepchild status).

The order in which the four functional areas are listed also betrays the alienation of the oil industry from the consumer. The industry is implicitly defined as beginning with the search for oil and ending with its distribution from the refinery. But the truth is, it seems to me, that the industry begins with the needs of the customer for its products. From that primal position its definition moves steadily backstream to areas of progressively lesser importance, until it finally comes to rest at the "search for oil."

Beginning & End

The view that an industry is a customer-satisfying process, not a goods-producing process, is vital for all businessmen to understand. An industry begins with the customer and his needs, not with a patent, a raw material, or a selling skill. Given the customer's needs, the industry develops backwards, first concerning itself with the physical *delivery* of customer satisfactions. Then it moves back further to *creating* the things by which these satisfactions are in part achieved. How these materials are created is a matter of indifference to the customer, hence the particular form of manufacturing, processing, or what-have-you cannot be considered as a vital aspect of the industry. Finally, the industry moves back still further to *finding* the raw materials necessary for making its products.

The irony of some industries oriented toward technical research and development is that the scientists who occupy the high executive positions are totally unscientific when it comes to defining their companies' overall needs and purposes. They violate the first two rules of the scientific method—being aware of and defining their companies' problems, and then developing testable hypotheses about solving them. They are scientific only about the convenient things, such as laboratory and product experiments.

The reason that the customer (and the satisfaction of his deepest needs) is not considered as being "the problem" is not because there is any certain belief that no such problem exists, but because an organizational lifetime has conditioned management to look in the opposite direction. Marketing is a stepchild.

I do not mean that selling is ignored. Far from it. But selling, again, is not marketing. As already pointed out, selling concerns itself with the tricks and techniques of getting people to exchange their cash for your product. It is not concerned with the values that the exchange is all about. And it does not, as marketing invariably does, view the entire business process as consisting of a tightly integrated effort to discover, create, arouse, and satisfy customer needs. The customer is somebody "out there" who, with proper cunning, can be separated from his loose change.

Actually, not even selling gets much attention in some technologically minded firms. Because there is a virtually guaranteed market for the abundant flow of their new products, they do not actually know what a real market is. It is as if they lived in a planned economy, moving their products routinely from factory to retail outlet. Their successful concentration on products tends to convince them of the soundness of what they have been doing, and they fail to see the gathering clouds over the market.

Conclusion

Less than 75 years ago American railroads enjoyed a fierce loyalty among astute Wall Streeters. European monarchs invested in them heavily. Eternal wealth was thought to be the benediction for anybody who could scrape a few thousand dollars together to put into rail stocks. No other form of transportation could compete with the railroads in speed, flexibility, durability, economy, and growth potentials.

As Jacques Barzun put it, "By the turn of the century it was an institution, an image of man, a tradition, a code of honor, a source of poetry, a nursery of boyhood desires, a sublimest of toys, and the most solemn machine—next to the funeral hearse—that marks the epochs in man's life."[6]

Even after the advent of automobiles, trucks, and airplanes, the railroad tycoons remained imperturbably self-confident. If you had told them 60 years ago that in 30 years they would be flat on their backs, broke, and pleading for government subsidies, they would have thought you totally demented. Such a future was simply not considered possible. It was not even a discussable subject, or an askable question, or a matter which any sane person would consider worth speculating about. The very thought was insane. Yet a lot of insane notions now have matter-of-fact acceptance—for example, the idea of 100-ton tubes of metal moving smoothly through the air 20,000 feet above the earth, loaded with 100 sane and solid citizens casually drinking martinis—and they have dealt cruel blows to the railroads.

What specifically must other companies do to avoid this fate? What does customer orientation involve? These questions have in part been answered by the preceding examples and analysis. It would take another article to show in detail what is required for specific industries. In any case, it should be obvious that building an effective customer-oriented company involves far more than good intentions or promotional tricks; it involves profound matters of human organization and leadership. For the present, let me merely suggest what appear to be some general requirements.

Visceral Feel of Greatness

Obviously the company has to do what survival demands. It has to adapt to the requirements of the market, and it has to do it sooner rather than later. But mere survival is a so-so aspiration. Anybody can survive in some way or other, even the skid-row bum. The trick is to survive gallantly, to feel the surging impulse of commercial mastery; not just to experience the sweet smell of success, but to have the visceral feel of entrepreneurial greatness.

No organization can achieve greatness without a vigorous leader who is driven onward by his own pulsating *will to succeed*. He has to have a vision of grandeur, a vision that can produce eager followers in vast numbers. In business, the followers are the customers.

In order to produce these customers, the entire corporation must be viewed as a customer-creating and customer-satisfying organism. Management must think of itself not as producing products but as providing customer-creating value satisfactions. It must push this idea (and everything it means and requires) into every nook and cranny of the organization. It has to do this continuously and with the kind of flair that excites and stimulates the people in it. Otherwise, the company will be merely a series of pigeonholed parts, with no consolidating sense of purpose or direction.

In short, the organization must learn to think of itself not as producing goods or services but as *buying customers*, as doing the things that will make people *want* to do business with it. And the chief executive himself has the inescapable responsibility for creating this environment, this viewpoint, this attitude, this aspiration. He himself must set the company's style, its direction, and its goals. This means he has to know precisely where he himself wants to go, and to make sure the whole organization is enthusiastically aware of where that is. This is a first requisite of leadership, for *unless he knows where he is going, any road will take him there.*

If any road is okay, the chief executive might as well pack his attaché case and go fishing. If an organization does not know or care where it is going, it does not need to advertise that fact with a ceremonial figurehead. Everybody will notice it soon enough.

Retrospective Commentary

Amazed, finally, by his literary success, Isaac Bashevis Singer reconciled an attendant problem: "I think the moment you have published a book, it's not any more your private property. . . . If it has value, everybody can find in it what he finds, and I cannot tell the man I did not intend it to be so." Over the past 15 years, "Marketing Myopia" has become a case in point. Remarkably, the article spawned a legion of loyal partisans—not to mention a host of unlikely bedfellows.

Its most common and, I believe, most influential consequence is the way certain companies for the first time gave serious thought to the question of what businesses they are really in.

The strategic consequences of this have in many cases been dramatic. The best-known case, of course, is the shift in thinking of oneself as being in the "oil business" to being in the "energy business." In some instances the payoff has been spectacular (getting into coal, for example) and in others dreadful (in terms of the time and money spent so far on fuel cell research). Another successful example is a company with a large chain of retail shoe stores that redefined itself as a retailer of moderately priced, frequently purchased, widely assorted consumer specialty products. The result was a dramatic growth in volume, earnings, and return on assets.

Some companies, again for the first time, asked themselves whether they wished to be masters of certain technologies for which they would seek markets, or be masters of markets for which they would seek customer-satisfying products and services.

Choosing the former, one company has declared, in effect, "We are experts in glass technology. We intend to improve and expand that expertise with the object of creating products that will attract customers." This decision has forced the company into a much more systematic and customer-sensitive look at possible markets and users, even though its stated strategic object has been to capitalize on glass technology.

Deciding to concentrate on markets, another company has determined that "we want to help people (primarily women) enhance their beauty and sense of youthfulness." This company has expanded its line of cosmetic products, but has also entered the fields of proprietary drugs and vitamin supplements.

All these examples illustrate the "policy" results of "Marketing Myopia." On the operating level, there has been, I think, an extraordinary heightening of sensitivity to customers and consumers. R&D departments have cultivated a greater "external" orientation toward uses, users, and markets—balancing thereby the previously one-sided "internal" focus on materials and methods; upper management has realized that marketing and sales departments should be somewhat more willingly accommodated than before; finance departments have become more receptive to the legitimacy of budgets for market research and experimentation in marketing; and salesmen have been better trained to listen to and understand customer needs and problems, rather than merely to "push" the product.

A Mirror, Not a Window

My impression is that the article has had more impact in industrial-products companies than in consumer-products companies—perhaps because the former had lagged most in customer orientation. There are at least two reasons for this lag: (1) industrial-products companies tend to be more capital intensive, and (2) in the past, at least, they have had to rely heavily on communicating face-to-face the technical character of what they made and sold. These points are worth explaining.

Capital-intensive businesses are understandably preoccupied with magnitudes, especially where the capital, once invested, cannot be easily moved, manipulated, or modified for the production of a variety of products—e.g., chemical plants, steel mills, airlines, and railroads. Understandably, they seek big volumes and operating efficiencies to pay off the equipment and meet the carrying costs.

At least one problem results: corporate power becomes disproportionately lodged with operating or financial executives. If you read the charter of one of the nation's largest companies, you will see that the chairman of the finance committee, not the chief executive officer, is the "chief." Executives with such backgrounds have an almost trained incapacity to see that getting "volume" may require understanding and serving many discrete and sometimes small market segments, rather than going after a perhaps mythical batch of big or homogeneous customers.

These executives also often fail to appreciate the competitive changes going on around them. They observe the changes, all right, but devalue their significance or underestimate their ability to nibble away at the company's markets.

Once dramatically alerted to the concept of segments, sectors, and customers, though, managers of capital-intensive businesses have become more responsive to the necessity of balancing their inescapable preoccupation with "paying the bills" or breaking even with the fact that the best way to accomplish this may be to pay more attention to segments, sectors, and customers.

The second reason industrial-products companies have probably been more influenced by the article is that, in the case of the more technical industrial products or services, the necessity of clearly communicating product and service characteristics to prospects results in a lot of face-to-face "selling" effort. But precisely because the product is so complex, the situation produces salesmen who know the product more than they know the customer, who are more adept at explaining what they have and what it can do than learning what the customer's needs and problems are. The result has been a narrow product orientation rather than a liberating customer orientation, and "service" often suffered. To be sure, sellers said, "We have to provide service," but they tended to define service by looking into the mirror rather than out the window. They *thought* they were looking out the window at the customer, but it was actually a mirror —a reflection of their own product-oriented biases rather than a reflection of their customers' situations.

A Manifesto, Not a Prescription

Not everything has been rosy. A lot of bizarre things have happened as a result of the article:

☐ Some companies have developed what I call "marketing mania"—they've become obsessively responsive to every fleeting whim of the customer. Mass production operations have been converted to approximations of job shops, with cost and price consequences far exceeding the willingness of customers to buy the product.

☐ Management has expanded product lines and added new lines of business without first establishing adequate control systems to run more complex operations.

☐ Marketing staffs have suddenly and rapidly expanded themselves and their research budgets without either getting sufficient prior organizational support or, thereafter, producing sufficient results.

☐ Companies that are functionally organized have converted to product, brand, or market-based organizations with the expectation of instant and miraculous results. The outcome has been ambiguity, frustration, confusion, corporate infighting, losses, and finally a reversion to functional arrangements that only worsened the situation.

☐ Companies have attempted to "serve" customers by creating complex and beautifully efficient products or services that buyers are either too risk-averse to adopt or incapable of learning how to employ—in effect, there are now steam shovels for people who haven't yet learned to use spades. This problem has happened repeatedly in the so-called service industries (financial services, insurance, computer-based services) and with American companies selling in less-developed economies.

"Marketing Myopia" was not intended as analysis or even prescription; it was intended as manifesto. It did not pretend to take a balanced position. Nor was it a new idea—Peter F. Drucker, J. B. McKitterick, Wroe Alderson, John Howard, and Neil Borden had each done more original and balanced work on "the marketing concept." My scheme, however, tied marketing more closely to the inner orbit of business policy. Drucker—especially in *The Concept of the Corporation* and *The Practice of Management*—originally provided me with a great deal of insight.

My contribution, therefore, appears merely to have been a simple, brief, and useful way of communicating an existing way of thinking. I tried to do it in a very direct, but responsible, fashion, knowing that few readers (customers), especially managers and leaders, could stand much equivocation or hesitation. I also knew that the colorful and lightly documented affirmation works better than the tortuously reasoned explanation.

But why the enormous popularity of what was actually such a simple pre-existing idea? Why its appeal throughout the world to resolutely restrained scholars, implacably temperate managers, and high government officials, all accustomed to balanced and thoughtful calculation? Is it that concrete examples, joined to illustrate a simple idea and presented with some attention to literacy, communicate better than massive analytical reasoning that reads as though it were translated from the German? Is it that provocative assertions are more memorable and persuasive than restrained and balanced explanations, no matter who the audience? Is it that the character of the message is as much the message as its content? Or was mine not simply a different tune, but a new symphony? I don't know.

Of course, I'd do it again and in the same way, given my purposes, even with what more I now know—the good and the bad, the power of facts and the limits of rhetoric. If your mission is the moon, you don't use a car. Don Marquis's cockroach, Archy, provides some final consolation: "an idea is not responsible for who believes in it."

References

1. Jacques Barzun, "Trains and the Mind of Man," *Holiday*, February 1960, p. 11.
2. For more details see M. M. Zimmerman, *The Super Market: A Revolution in Distribution* (New York, McGraw-Hill Book Company, Inc., 1955), p. 48.
3. Ibid., pp. 45–47.
4. *The Affluent Society* (Boston, Houghton Mifflin Company, 1958), pp. 152–60.
5. Henry Ford, *My Life and Work* (New York, Doubleday, Page & Company, 1923), pp. 146–47.
6. Jacques Barzun, "Trains and the Mind of Man," *Holiday*, February 1960, p. 20.

2

The Rediscovery of the Marketing Concept

Frederick E. Webster, Jr.

The marketing concept helped American businesses gain dominant positions in the world's economy. Yet, the rush to strategic planning forced out the marketing concept at many companies. Now, as American firms lose their positions, the marketing concept is back in vogue.

This article will explore the reasons for the decline *and* resurgence of management interest in the marketing concept. It will also highlight some of the basic requirements for the development and maintenance of a customer focus. In the process, we will consider briefly the origins and essential features of the marketing concept, its evolution into corporate strategic planning, the current swing in emphasis from strategic *planning* to strategic *management*, and some basic issues of management values.

THE MANAGEMENTS of many American companies have rediscovered the marketing concept, a business philosophy first developed more than three decades ago. In the process, they have found it difficult to develop the customer focus that is central to a market-driven enterprise. Among the barriers to developing that market orientation are:

- An incomplete understanding of the marketing concept itself;
- The inherent conflict between short-term and long-term sales and profit goals;
- An overemphasis on short-term, financially-oriented measures of management performance; and
- Top management's own values and priorities concerning the relative importance of customers and the firm's other constituencies.

Many of these barriers have their roots in formal strategic-planning systems, with their emphasis on financial criteria for management action, which had their heyday in the 1970s. These systems are now being substantially modified in many companies.

Frederick E. Webster, Jr., is the E. B. Osborn Professor of Marketing at the Amos Tuck School of Business Administration, Dartmouth College, Hanover, N.H. He is also the executive director of the Marketing Science Institute.

The Changed Business Environment

It is widely noted that American industry has lost competitiveness in world markets in the last decade. At the same time, it has not been able to defend its domestic markets against foreign competitors. The country's huge trade deficit (which reflects a strong U.S. dollar and, most importantly, the tremendous affection the American market has for foreign suppliers) is only part of the evidence of American manufacturers' failure to respond effectively to changes in their markets. More recently, the declining dollar has intensified foreign competition in many markets, such as automobiles and computer chips, while demand in both the manufacturing and consumer-goods sectors shows little or no real growth. Changing competition, continuing technological innovation, and evolving customer preferences, the basic forces driving business and product life cycles, are not new challenges by any means. These have been facts of life for business managers as long as there have been markets. What has apparently happened is that many businesses, and even whole industries, have suffered a substantial, sometimes fatal, impairment of their ability to respond to these forces. In many companies, the most serious weaknesses have been a loss of customer and market orientation and a basic inability to offer competitively-priced products that are responsive to customers' current needs and preferences.

Strategic planning, once thought to be part of the way to cope with a changing competitive environment and evolving product life cycles, has actually led to problems for many firms. Formal, centralized strategic planning systems, often accompanied by a heavy emphasis on product-portfolio frameworks and the seductive logic of the experience curve, are now recognized to have caused many businesses to lose sight of what is required to remain competitive in their industries. The basic problem is not with strategic planning *per se* but with the ways in which it has been implemented and misunderstood in many firms. One result of this misunderstanding has been that the basic requirements for effective marketing are not always seen as key ingredients in the development and implementation of sound business strategy.

The Development of the Marketing Concept

Until the mid-1950s, the business world equated "marketing" with "selling." Under this traditional view of marketing, the key to profitability was greater sales volume, and marketing's responsibility was to sell what the factory could produce. The focus was on products, not customers, and products were taken as given—what the factory was currently producing was what the sales force had to sell. The emphasis within marketing was short-term and tactical, focusing on the selling process itself (personal selling, advertising, and sales promotion including short-term price inducements). The marketing job was to convince prospects that they needed what the firm was producing.

As the American economy matured into a consumer society in the 1950s, and as post-war conditions of scarcity were replaced by an abundance of manufacturers and brands scrambling for the patronage of an increasingly affluent consumer, the marketing concept evolved. Volume, price, and promotional orientations were seen to be less profitable than an orientation that focused on the needs of particular sets of customers. This customer orientation offered carefully tailored products and an integrated mix of marketing elements —products, prices, promotion, and distribution. A short-term, tactical viewpoint was replaced by a long-term, strategic orientation. The key to profitability was not current sales volume but long-term customer satisfaction and the then-new strategic concepts of market segmentation and product differentiation.[1] The firm that analyzed its markets carefully, selected groups of customers whose needs matched up best with its capabilities, and tailored its product offering to do the best job of satisfying those needs was rewarded. This firm realized not only better profit margins and repeat purchases but also the cost efficiencies of more focused marketing efforts.

One of the first statements of the marketing concept as a management philosophy was made by Peter Drucker, who remains to this day one of its strongest defenders. Drucker argued that marketing was a *general management* responsibility:

> There is only one valid definition of business purpose: to create a satisfied customer. It is the customer who determines what the business is. Because it is its purpose to create a customer, any business enterprise has two—and only these two—basic functions: marketing and innovation . . . . Actually marketing is so basic that it is not just enough to have a strong sales force and to entrust marketing to it. Marketing is not only much broader than selling, it is not a specialized activity at all. It is the whole business seen from the point of view of its final result, that is, from the customer's point of view.[2]

Within the business community, forward-thinking executives such as John B. McKitterick of General Electric were developing similar thoughts:

> So the principal task of the marketing function in a management concept is not so much to be skillful in making the customer do what suits the interests of the business as to be skillful in conceiving and then making the business do what suits the interests of the customer.[3]

From the academic community, Theodore Levitt's seminal statement of the marketing concept argued that customer needs must be the central focus of the firm's definition of its business purpose:

> . . . the organization must learn to think of itself not as producing goods and services but as buying customers, as doing the things that will make people want to do business with it. And the chief executive himself has the inescapable responsibility for creating this environment, this viewpoint, this attitude, this aspiration.[4]

All of these expressions of the marketing concept emphasize that marketing is first and foremost a general management responsibility. Executives must put the interests of the customer at the top of the firm's priorities. Under the marketing concept, as opposed to the traditional sales orientation, the product is not a given but a variable to be tailored and modified in response to changing customer needs. Marketing represents the customer to the factory as well as the factory to the customer.

Despite the marketing concept's apparent wisdom and importance, it has always had to struggle for continued acceptance—even in those firms that embraced it. The reasons for this are never simple or obvious. At its roots, the marketing concept calls for constant change as market conditions evolve, and change is usually difficult for organizations. Beyond that, American industry's well-known preoccupation with quarterly financial performance (a reflection of the short-term concerns of institutional investors, among other things), and the parallel growth in the importance and sophistication of financial management in the 1960s and 1970s, contributed to putting marketing in the back seat in many firms. It also has been observed by some chief executives that marketing managers in their firms have not developed the analytical tools and other skills necessary to understand the customer and represent customer needs and preferences persuasively in management discussions.[5]

Instead of marketing, the orientation in many firms (especially industrial firms and others that do not sell frequently purchased products directly to the consumer) continues to be the traditional one toward sales. The top marketing executive may even be called the sales manager, and it is clear that sales volume is the most important marketing objective. With a sales orientation, more is better, every order is a good order, and every customer is a good customer, despite the conflicting demands made on the firm's limited capabilities. The focus is on current products, not the continuous development of new ones. If marketing exists, it is as a staff function. The emphasis within marketing is short-term and tactical, focused on selling more today rather than developing new markets and responding to changing customer needs and competition.

There are also several good indicators of a true marketing orientation. The top marketing executive reports to the chief executive officer and has line responsibility for both the sales function and other marketing activities such as market research, product development, distribution, advertising, and sales promotion. There is a marketing-research or market-information system that fulfills marketing's fundamental responsibility of being an expert on the customer. In market-oriented firms, sales management is guided by and tied to marketing strategy; it does not operate as an autonomous management function. The company's business strategies have a clear and strong marketing component built around precise definitions of market segments and careful analysis of target segments, customers, and the firm's unique competitive advantages in those segments. There is an organized and active product-development function, and R&D is guided by good market information and marketing direction. There are key-account strategies for dealing with major customers and distributors, who are regarded as business assets and managed as long-term relationships. In a marketing-oriented company, management is seeking profitability, not just sales volume. It consistently articulates the importance of being a customer-focused and market-driven enterprise, putting the interests of the customer ahead of all other claimants on the company's resources.

From Marketing to Strategic Planning

The marketing concept that was developed in the 1950s and 1960s fit nicely into the evolving emphasis on corporate strategy and long-range strategic planning in the 1960s and 1970s. Corporate strategy and formal strategic-planning systems were completely consistent with the strategic orientation of the marketing concept and the emphasis on marketing as a general management responsibility. The development of a customer-oriented business required long-term planning and product and market development to make the business grow.

Figure 1
Ansoff's Growth Vectors

		Products: Old	Products: New
Markets	Old	Market Penetration	Product Development
	New	Market Development	Diversification

Marketing planning and the broader area of long-range planning began to merge and evolved into the broader concept of corporate strategic planning. Strategic planning focuses on the two key, strategic choices that any firm makes—which customer markets to serve and which products to offer in those markets.

One of the most important contributions to the establishment of corporate strategic planning as a separate management discipline was that of H. Igor Ansoff, who has been called "The Father of Strategic Planning."[6] Building on the base established in marketing, Ansoff argued that Levitt's mandate to define the business mission in terms of customer needs was too broad. It did not consider the basic fact that a firm's technical competence and its ability to respond to customer needs had to be factored into the definition of strategy and the selection of markets served and products offered. Ansoff proposed four strategic options, called growth vectors, defined by the cells in a two-by-two matrix of old/new products/markets: market penetration; market development; product development; and diversification (see Figure 1). Each defined a direction in which the firm could elect to grow, depending upon its basic capabilities and market opportunities. The problem was to allocate the firm's efforts and resources among competing growth opportunities, finding the best growth vectors. Ansoff also developed the concept of "competitive advantage" (sometimes called "distinctive competence"), the idea that every firm has a certain thing that it does especially well in particular market segments and that gives it an edge over its competition. The firm must find market niches that value, and provide further opportunities to develop, its competitive advantage. Finally, there was the concept of strategic "synergy," the argument that each new venture (product or market) should benefit from, be consistent with, and help to develop some aspect of the firm's competitive strengths and distinctive competence.

Ansoff's three concepts of strategy—growth vectors, competitive advantage, and synergy—have intuitive appeal and make a good deal of sense. Less obviously, this strategic-planning framework presents an implicit argument for a softening of the customer orientation of the marketing concept. The basic premise is that customer needs must be balanced against what the firm can do well and what is consistent with its strategy given competitive realities. Customer orientation is certainly not inconsistent with the concept of corporate strategy. But the strategic-planning framework subtly shifts the focus of management attention away from customers and toward competitors and market dominance.

As strategic planning gained in popularity, firms developed large central staffs to implement a strategic planning system. Annual planning cycles were established to create and update one-, three-, and five-year plans for achieving some carefully defined corporate objectives, which very often emphasized growth and return-on-investment criteria. Strategic-planning management positions were regarded as among the most attractive for MBAs and other "fast-trackers." It was where the action was, the control room of the enterprise. As one CEO put it when reflecting on this era of management in his firm, "All the good marketing guys wanted to become strategic planners."

The strategic-planning boom also fueled growth in management consulting. Among the most popular products to come out of this industry were the product-portfolio and experience-curve models developed by the Boston Consulting Group, the growth-share matrix developed by McKinsey & Company in its work with General Electric, the Arthur D. Little generic-strategies model based on the product's life-cycle stage and market position, and the PIMS (Profit Impact of Marketing Strategy) studies of the Strategic Planning Institute, originated at General Electric by Sidney Schoeffler.[7] All of these approaches tended to view market opportunities in terms of the market's growth rate and the firm's ability to dominate its chosen market segments. Market share (defined relative to the share of the largest competitor) became the key strategic variable, especially when the PIMS studies showed that market share, among 37 variables examined, was most strongly correlated with business profitability measured by return on investment.[8]

The Biases of Strategic Planning

The formal strategic-planning approaches and portfolio models brought analytical rigor and a higher order of financial discipline to the task of developing corporate strategy. They also brought a definite set of priorities and biases to the task of managing a business. Underlying the approaches and models was a kind of optimism about the economy and an assumption of sustained economic growth. Management's principal strategic problem became one of choosing among competing growth opportunities. Product/market opportunities were evaluated by the market's growth rate and the firm's ability to achieve a dominant position in that market. Market niching, a strategic concept growing out of the general notion of market segmentation, was seen as a way of isolating oneself from head-to-head competition with well-entrenched competitors. The search was for high-growth markets and well-protected niches in which the firm could achieve the highest rates of growth and returns on investment. As market share and high-growth markets received strategic emphasis, and management-performance evaluation focused more sharply on relatively short-term financial measures (especially return on investment and return on assets), there was a subtle reversion to the traditional sales orientation that had preceded the marketing concept. Mergers and acquisitions, as means of both achieving large market share and dominant position and moving into growth markets more quickly, gained greatly in importance relative to the slower and less certain internal development of new products and markets around the core of existing businesses. Diversification into new, high-growth products and markets was seen as a very attractive growth vector for the firm wishing to move away from its traditional, mature, low-growth businesses.

Market-niching strategies gained in popularity as firms searched for opportunities to match more precisely their distinctive competences with customer needs in the absence of strongly entrenched competitors. One inevitable consequence of market niching is that markets are individually smaller than less carefully defined segments would be. The firm could easily become stronger and stronger in smaller and smaller segments. By itself, this is not bad. The firm that has successfully positioned itself in a number of related market niches may be strongly protected against competitive threats. The problem is that the firm may lose sight of the forest for the trees by misdefining and misreading its competition, especially if management has defined its served market too narrowly—which it could be easily deceived into doing to make sure it has a dominant position in the served market.

Market niching, product differentiation, and low-cost leadership have been presented by some authors as three distinct strategic options. Either the firm can strive for high market share and low-cost leadership through exploiting the experience curve (it is often assumed that this firm also needs to have the lowest prices), or it can define a distinct and well-protected market niche, or it can attempt to build a loyal following of customers willing to pay more for a highly differentiated product (high quality and high price, which are implicitly assumed to go together). Some analysts argued that the firms that had the highest return on investment were those that had either a cost-leadership (low-price) position or a highly differentiated (high-price) product, while the lowest returns were earned by those that were neither fish nor fowl, stuck in the middle with neither low cost nor high quality. The empirical evidence to support these arguments was, at best, anecdotal.[9]

What Strategic Planning Left Out

The points of emphasis in these strategic-planning frameworks may not be as significant as the points that were left out. Most importantly, the customer seemed to be largely out of the picture. Markets were defined as aggregations of competitors, not customers. Product positioning and product quality were barely mentioned when defining markets and thinking about opportunities for building market share. The internal development of new businesses, driven by consistent commitments to research and development, played second fiddle to growth through mergers and acquisitions. The building and maintenance of marketing channels and distribution arrangements received little strategic attention, as did the development of a long-term customer franchise. Expenditures on R&D to achieve process and productivity improvements in established businesses often seemed less attractive than the redeployment of funds into new ventures, especially as tax-driven asset-revaluation opportunities provided large positive cash flows. A new breed, "conglomerateurs," became role models for managers in a broad variety of industries. Large, stable, mature, traditional markets lost their luster, and some of America's largest manufacturing enterprises could see little point in defending their historical positions in those slow-growth businesses.

Meanwhile, foreign competitors saw American industry not responding to customer needs in many evolving markets, avoiding investment in its mature businesses, and abandoning some of its traditional market strongholds, and moved in. The U.S. market, with only about 15 percent of the world's population, accounts for approximately 40 percent of the world's consumption. A producer in a smaller country with growth aspirations and a limited domestic market for things it has learned to make very well is likely to look first at the U.S. market because of its size, homogeneity, affluence, and accessibility. In a number of cases, American businesses were clearly not offering products that American consumers wanted (such as small, economical, and reliable automobiles, farm tractors, and motorcycles), had lost their technological leadership (watches, consumer electronics, and tires), or had simply not invested in the continued product and process improvement required to maintain competitiveness (appliances, steel, and automobiles).

Foreign (especially Asian) competitors entering the U.S. market frequently gained toeholds in relatively unexplored market niches, often at the low-price end of the market. They then built customer and trade loyalty through offering high quality and favorable prices and margins, and gradually expanded out of those niches into adjoining market segments, picking off additional customers and competitors. They continued to offer superior customer value, often incorporating product features that domestic suppliers offered only as extra-cost options or not at all, and eventually dominated the total market, not just a few carefully defined segments. In many instances, they destroyed the "nichers," who had created their own vulnerability by defining their businesses and their sets of competitors too narrowly.

Strategic planning tended (unintentionally) to drive out attention to customers and their needs, the central thrust of the marketing concept, as the primary requirement for long-term profitability. By shifting attention to competitors, growth, and short-term return on investment, and by regarding mature businesses as primarily sources of cash rather than as key contributors to future profitability, the strategic-planning models weakened the ability of some of this country's most important companies and industries to respond to evolving customer needs, new technology, and changing competition, especially from overseas competitors. By concentrating management's attention on *corporate* strategy, they weakened the *functional* strategies, especially marketing strategy, necessary to implement the higher-level strategies successfully.

Levels of Strategy

As strategic planning evolved out of long-range planning and the marketing concept, there was a blurring of the distinctions among various levels of strategy. One useful classification[10] describes five types of strategy: enterprise, corporate, business, functional, and subfunctional. *Enterprise* strategy defines the mission of the company in society, often as a mission statement that expresses management values and relates the firm to the society it serves. *Corporate* strategy answers the question, "What business are we in?" and integrates the various businesses within the product portfolio. *Business* strategy answers the question, "How do we want to compete in our chosen businesses?" *Functional* strategies—in marketing, production, finance, R&D, purchasing, and human resources/organizational development—implement the business strategy. *Subfunctional* strategies, such as those for market segmentation and targeting, product development and management, pricing, distribution, personal selling, advertising and sales promotion, and publicity, implement the functional strategies.

Clearly, the formal strategic-planning approaches and product-portfolio models emphasized corporate and business strategies while downplaying, if not ignoring, the functional and subfunctional strategies necessary to implement them. Attention to strategic planning drove out attention to good marketing. On the other hand, there certainly is nothing in the total concept of strategic planning that requires inattention to marketing; in fact, a planning process that focuses only on corporate- and business-level strategies and leaves out the functional and subfunctional levels of strategy is simply incomplete. Strategic planning took its toll primarily in the marketing, R&D, and production areas because financial strategy grew in importance and often dominated the others, an emphasis consistent with the cash-flow and investment orientation of the product-portfolio view of corporate strategy.

From Strategic Planning to Strategic Management

By the early 1980s, management practitioners and academic advocates of strategic planning had realized something had gone wrong. Many firms with the most elaborate and expensive strategic-planning systems saw their management spending an inordinate amount of time preparing and reading planning documents while their operating business lost competitive effectiveness. In many cases, means had become ends; the planning process became a dominating influence, taking a significant portion of management time away from actually running the business. Some very large and well-known companies that had pioneered formal strategic-planning systems, such as General Electric, began to scale back their corporate planning organizations and push planning responsibility back into the operating units. A new focus on implementation began to develop. Articles began to appear, both in the popular business press and in academic journals, arguing that there was more to strategic *management* than strategic *planning*.[11]

Strategic management has been defined as a six-part process, including goal formulation, environmental analysis, strategy formulation, evaluation of strategic options, strategy implementation, and strategic control.[12] Corporate strategic planning tended to end before implementation and control. Perhaps people assumed that operating management would worry about strategies at the functional and subfunctional levels even if top management did not. It is fair to conclude that most divisional managers assumed that the planning process was complete after top management had accepted their business plans. Business unit managers were often forced to spend most of their energies fighting for and defending capital allocations for their businesses rather than on the work of operating the business. Once the planning job had been done, operating management had to turn quickly to hitting the targets for sales volume, current profitability, return on investment, and cash flow called for by the annual plan. There was little time for attention to the details of strategy implementation.

Strategic management begins to redress the balance by bringing a renewed focus on implementation and the search for long-term, sustainable, competitive advantages over competitors serving the needs of a carefully defined set of customers. It can be seen in a new concern for quality, innovation, productivity, entrepreneurship, and internal development of new businesses instead of mergers and acquisitions. In many instances, it is manifested in a divestiture of related businesses acquired in the diversification boom of the 1960s and 1970s. It is a case of going back to basics, including solid marketing.[13]

Marketing Rediscovered

Current business publications are full of examples of firms that are rediscovering the marketing concept. Several years ago, General Electric appointed its first corporate vice president of marketing in over a decade and charged him with responsibility for bringing about a "marketing renaissance." Apple Computer hired a new president from PepsiCo, hoping he would bring the marketing skills that the firm needed to develop so urgently.

The 1986 GTE Corporation annual report highlights, on its cover, "Market Sensitivity: Reaching Out to Customers." We read about "an aggressive new consumer drive" at 3M Corporation, where the "key weapon in its arsenal" is a "separate marketing group."[14] Hewlett-Packard's president, John Young, is quoted as saying "Creating a personal computer group was . . . a way of communicating to everyone that marketing was okay. . . ."[15] Chairman Donald Peterson of Ford Motor Company may not have realized that he was repeating company history *and* Henry Ford's original dream when he observed, in 1985, "My single greatest desire is to develop Ford Motor Company as a customer-driven company . . . If you do that, everything else falls into place."[16] Ford's recent new-car successes and reported gains in market share and profitability are strong evidence that Ford is achieving this objective. In a recent presentation to the Marketing Science Institute, the director of corporate marketing research at DuPont reported efforts to develop "a marketing community." He outlined a series of specific actions being taken under the leadership of the company's CEO "to make sure that everyone clearly understands that serving customers and markets is the first priority for all functions."[17]

Management thinking about marketing appears to be coming back to the basic marketing concept articulated in the mid-1950s. A major study of business planning by Yankelovich, Skelly, and White for Coopers and Lybrand concluded that "CEOs have indicated that development and implementation of more innovative and cost-effective marketing strategies will indeed be their highest operational priority in the latter half of the 1980's."[18] We are learning once again that marketing is not sales, it is not corporate strategy, and it is not business strategy, and market share and profitability are not objectives that stand by themselves. Marketing strategy is an extension and implementation of corporate and business strategies. It focuses on the definition and selecting of markets and customers to be served and the continual improvement, in performance and cost, of products to be offered in those markets. In a market-driven, customer-oriented business, the key element of the business plan will be a focus on well-defined market segments and the firm's unique competitive advantage in those segments.

Developing a Customer-Oriented Firm

Having identified both the need for and the difficulty of developing a market-driven, customer-focused business, we can outline some of the basic requirements for achieving this goal. These include:

- Customer-oriented values and beliefs supported by top management;
- Integration of market and customer focus into the strategic-planning process;
- The development of strong marketing managers and programs;
- The creation of market-based measures of performance; and
- The development of customer commitment throughout the organization.

Each of these is vital to the development of a customer-oriented firm, and weakness in any area is sufficient to scuttle the whole effort.

Values and Beliefs

At the base of all organizational functioning is the core of values and beliefs, the culture shared by members of the organization. Organizational culture is only barely understood, especially in the context of marketing, but interest among managers and researchers is growing rapidly.[19]

An organizational belief in the primacy of the customer's interests as the beacon for all of the firm's activities must be at the heart of a market-oriented business. The customer-focused definition of the business must originate with top management, including the CEO and the heads of strategic operating units. Not only must the business be defined by the customer needs it is committed to serving, but it must also define its distinctive competence in satisfying those needs, its unique way of delivering value to the customer. These beliefs and values must include a commitment to quality and service as they are defined by customers in the served markets.

Customer-oriented values and beliefs are uniquely the responsibility of top management. Only the CEO can take the responsibility for defining customer and market orientation as the driving forces, because if he doesn't put the customer first he has, by definition, put something else, the interests of some other constituency or public, first. Organization members will know what that is and behave accordingly. CEOs must give clear signals and establish clear values and beliefs about serving the customer.

Marketing's Role in Strategic Planning

The next step is to integrate marketing into the strategic-planning process. The business plan should stress market information, market-segment definition, and market targeting as key elements. All activities of the business should be built around the objective of creating the desired position with a well-defined set of customers. Separate market segments should be the subject of separate business plans that focus on the development of relationships with customers that emphasize the firm's distinctive competence. Marketing's first responsibility in this context is to be truly expert on the customer's problems, needs, wants, preferences, and decision-making processes. Competitor analysis is also an important part of understanding the firm's position and opportunities in all targeted market segments.

This obviously is the role of marketing called for by the marketing concept. Marketing does not simply find markets and create demand for what the factory currently produces. Its contribution to strategic planning and implementation begins with the analysis of market segments and the assessment of the firm's ability to satisfy customer needs. This includes the analysis of demand trends, competition, and, in industrial markets, the competitive conditions faced by firms in those segments. Marketing also plays a key role by working with top management to define business purpose in terms of customer-need satisfaction.

In this market-oriented view of the strategic-planning process, financial goals are seen as results and rewards, not the fundamental purpose of the business. The purpose is customer satisfaction, and the reward is profit, as noted by Peter Drucker in the original statement of the marketing concept. The relationship between marketing objectives and financial results should be made clear in the formal strategic-planning document.

Developing Marketing Managers and Programs

The development of marketing-management competence requires detailed programs, with the CEO's active involvement, for recruiting and developing professional marketing managers. It also requires programs for recognizing and rewarding superior marketing performance, not just by marketing managers but by all managers, to bring their contributions to the attention of other managers, develop strong role models, and reinforce the basic commitment to customer-oriented beliefs and values. All of the organization's communications and management-development resources are potential vehicles for accomplishing this purpose, including in-company and on-campus executive-development programs, management meetings and seminars, and company publications. Top-management involvement in these activities can substantially enhance the credibility of the marketing-management effort.

With competitive marketing management, the rest of the firm can expect superior quality in the development and execution of marketing programs. The basic purpose of all of the firm's activities should be the delivery of superior value in products and services. Marketing should be given the resources necessary to develop a first-class marketing-information system. Marketing management must be held responsible for being expert on the customer. The company must be willing to invest in the customer-service systems necessary to establish market leadership. Similarly, there must be investment in the development of a leadership position in marketing channels. Finally, top management must insist upon the very best planning and creativity in the development of marketing communications and in the training and deployment of the sales force. These details are crucial to the delivery of an effective marketing strategy, something that has been overlooked in formal strategic-planning systems and models.

Market-Based Measures of Performance

Perhaps the key to developing a market-driven, customer-oriented business lies in the way managers are evaluated and rewarded. The effort will come to naught if, in the final analysis, managers are evaluated solely in terms of sales volume and short-term profitability and rate-of-return measures. While one of the hallmarks of a marketing-oriented firm is a striving for profitability rather than sales volume or market share alone, it is *long-term* profitability and market position that are the objectives. The question of balancing short- and long-term profit objectives is one of the most difficult challenges to top management in any business.

It is significant that the Coopers and Lybrand study gave top priority to the development of market-based measures of managerial performance. It observed that financial management should be part of the marketing team. In addition to such measures of marketing performance as indices of customer satisfaction and service levels, it was suggested by some managers involved in the study that new market-based financial measures such as rate of return by channel of distribution, type of account, and type of media expenditure, be developed. One of the respondents noted that financial management will be much more integrated with marketing than in the past as it is driven more by marketing goals than by cost-control goals.

Measurement and reward systems are critical in the development of a market-oriented business. Just as managers will emphasize those things on which top management's statements of values and beliefs focus their attention, they will also do those things for which they are evaluated and rewarded.

Developing Customer Commitment Throughout the Organization

In the final analysis, as Drucker and Levitt noted, marketing is not something that can be delegated to a small group of managers while the rest of the organization goes about its business. Rather, it is the whole business as seen from the customer's viewpoint. Managers at General Electric have captured this idea with the phrase, "Marketing is too important to be left to the marketing people!" One of the principal responsibilities marketing management has is to make the entire business market-driven and customer-focused. This advocacy role is a key one for the corporate marketing staff.

The task is to be sure that everyone in the firm works toward that overriding objective of creating satisfied customers. Each individual, and especially those who have direct contact with the customer in any form, is responsible for the level of customer service and satisfaction. The product is defined by each interaction the customer has with any company representative. An important role for marketing management is to be sure that information about customer service and satisfaction is gathered and sent to all parts of the organization on a regular basis. For industrial marketers, it may be extremely useful to have management representatives of customer companies talk with the marketer's personnel, from top management to production and service workers, on a regular basis to explain the challenges and problems they face and how the marketer will be called upon to help find solutions.

Many spokesmen for American top management express the belief that the rediscovery of marketing may provide an important boost to their firm's competitiveness at home and abroad. The marketing concept, emphasizing the importance of satisfying customer needs as the key to long-term profitability, is now expressed in such new phrases as "close to the customer," but the basic idea is more than 30 years old. Once again, we see firms committing resources to marketing, focusing on and nurturing their traditional businesses, and building long-term relationships with their customers. Customer-service programs are receiving increased attention, and market-based measures of performance are becoming parts of management-evaluation systems. Focus on the customer is once again seen as the fundamental requirement for company survival and competitive effectiveness. With proper attention to such basic issues as top-management support and corporate culture, the integration of marketing into the planning process, the development of highly competent marketing-management personnel, market-based management evaluation and reward systems, and making sure the total organization understands and accepts the basic commitment to customer satisfaction, we can hope that the marketing concept will at last be firmly entrenched in American business.

References

1. See, for example, Wendell R. Smith, "Product Differentiation and Market Segmentation as Alternative Marketing Strategies," *Journal of Marketing,* July 1956, pp. 3–8.
2. Peter F. Drucker, *The Practice of Management* (New York: Harper & Row, 1954): p. 37.
3. John B. McKitterick, "What Is the Marketing Management Concept?" *The Frontiers of Marketing Thought and Action* (Chicago: American Marketing Association, 1957): pp. 71–82.
4. Theodore Levitt, "Marketing Myopia," *Harvard Business Review,* July–August 1960, pp. 45–56.
5. Frederick E. Webster, Jr., "Top Management's Concerns About Marketing: Issues for the 1980s," *Journal of Marketing,* Summer 1981, pp. 9–16.
6. H. Igor Ansoff, *Corporate Strategy* (New York: McGraw-Hill, 1965).
7. For a review of these various product-portfolio models and strategic-planning approaches, see Derek F. Abell and John S. Hammond, *Strategic Market Planning: Problems and Analytical Approaches* (Englewood Cliffs, N.J.: Prentice-Hall, 1979).
8. Robert D. Buzzell, Bradley T. Gale, and Ralph G. M. Sultan, "Market Share—Key to Profitability," *Harvard Business Review,* January–February 1975, pp. 97–106.
9. Michael E. Porter, *Competitive Strategy* (New York: The Free Press, 1980), pp. 34–46.
10. Dan E. Schendel and Charles W. Hofer (eds.), *Strategic Management: A New View of Business Policy and Planning* (Boston: Little, Brown and Company, 1979), pp. 11–13.
11. See, for example, Frederick W. Gluck, Stephen P. Kaufman, and A. Steven Walleck, "Strategic Management for Competitive Advantage," *Harvard Business Review,* July–August 1980, pp. 154–63.
12. Schendel and Hofer (see note 10).
13. "Do Mergers Really Work?" *Business Week,* June 3, 1985, pp. 88–100.
14. "3M's Aggressive New Consumer Drive," *Business Week,* July 16, 1984, p. 114.

15. Bill Saporito, "Hewlett-Packard Discovers Marketing," *Fortune,* October 1, 1984, p. 51.
16. "Now That It's Cruising, Can Ford Keep Its Foot on the Gas?" *Business Week,* February 11, 1985, p. 48.
17. H. Paul Root, "Marketing Practices in the Years Ahead: The Changing Environment for Research on Marketing," presentation to the Trustees Meeting, Marketing Science Institute, November 7, 1986, p. 2.
18. Coopers & Lybrand/Yankelovich, Skelly, and White, "Business Planning in the Eighties: The New Marketing Shape of American Corporations," 1985, p. 7.
19. See, for example, Mark G. Dunn, David Norburn, and Sue Birley, "Corporate Culture: A Positive Correlate with Marketing Effectiveness," *International Journal of Advertising,* 1985: 4, pp. 65–73; and A. Parasuraman and Rohit Deshpande, "The Cultural Context of Marketing Management," in R. W. Belk (ed.), *Proceedings* of the 1984 Educators' Conference of the American Marketing Association, pp. 176–79.

3

Getting Things Done —Rejuvenating the Marketing Mix

Benson P. Shapiro

An effective marketing program blends elements of the mix so that they harmonize powerfully.

The marketing mix concept is an essential part of marketing theory. But describing the concept and putting it to effective use are two different things. In this article, the author reviews the elements of the marketing mix and lends insight into how these elements interact. Applying such ideas as consistency, integration, and leverage, he demonstrates how a marketing program must fit the needs of the marketplace, the skills of the company, and the vagaries of the competition. To meet such disparate demands, the elements of the marketing mix must (among other attributes) make the most effective use of company strengths, take aim at precisely defined segments, and protect the company from competitive threats.

THE MARKETING MIX CONCEPT is one of the most powerful ever developed for executives. Since just after World War I, it has been the essential organizing theme of many MBA marketing courses. It is now the main organizing concept for countless corporate marketing plans as well as for most marketing textbooks and many courses and executive education programs. It has endured because it is both effective and simple.

Now there are several ways to add even more strength to the concept while maintaining its simplicity. This article examines the marketing mix as an integrated whole, presents criteria for explaining why some programs prosper and others fail, and can help improve your ability to predict which programs will succeed and which will not. It then restates some of the more important themes behind the marketing mix concept and suggests several ways to add more power to it.

First, though, a review of the basic marketing mix concept is in order. The marketing mix is the "tool kit" that marketers use to do their job. It consists of four elements:

1. Product (or product policy)
2. Pricing
3. Communication (the most visible element of the mix, which includes advertising and personal selling)
4. Distribution

The marketing mix gives executives a way to ensure that all elements of their program are considered in a simple yet disciplined fashion. One can describe the essence of almost any marketing strategy by presenting the target market segment and the elements of the mix in brief form. IBM's personal computer strategy might, for example, be described as follows:

- *Target market segment*. Managers and professionals (not hobbyists or technical specialists).
- *Product*. Parity technology, fairly easy to use.
- *Price*. Reasonable (not high enough to provide an umbrella for competition but high enough to yield healthy profits for IBM).
- *Communication*. Personal sales to large customers through IBM's powerful sales force; heavy advertising stressing friendliness and broad applicability of the product.

Benson P. Shapiro is Professor of Business Administration and Senior Associate Dean at the Harvard Business School, and has been head of the school's required MBA marketing course.

- *Distribution*. Directly through the sales force to major customers; mainly through independent full-service dealers to smaller customers.

Most companies would benefit from the discipline of a similar description of their marketing strategy's core. It helps ensure that the plan is clear and that the details do not obscure the strategy.

A few examples will quickly make apparent the wide variety of marketing approaches available. A big difference exists between the marketing approaches of companies that sell toothpaste and those that sell huge coal-fed boilers for electric generation. Such a difference is, of course, natural and to be expected. Toothpaste costs little, and companies can sell it in small quantities to many consumers for whom it is more than a trivial but less than a major purchase decision. Coal-fed boilers cost tens of millions of dollars and few people buy them; producers sell them to companies where many people labor over the choice of a unit for a long time.

More surprising are the variations among marketers of the same product categories. Cosmetics, for example, are sold in many different ways. Avon has a sales force of several hundred thousand who call directly on individual consumers. Charles of the Ritz and Estée Lauder use selective distribution through department stores. Cover Girl and Del Laboratories emphasize chain drugstores and other mass merchandisers. Cover Girl does a great deal of advertising, while Del emphasizes personal selling and promotions. Redken sells through beauticians. Revlon's strategy encompasses a wide variety of brands and selling approaches.

These variations are more than anomalies. They represent fundamental strategies in the war for a distinctive, comparative advantage and competitive success.

Interaction Within the Mix

The marketing mix concept emphasizes the fit of the various pieces and the quality and size of their interaction. There are three degrees of interaction. The least demanding is "consistency"—a logical and useful fit between two or more elements. It would seem generally inconsistent, for example, to sell a high-quality product through a low-quality retailer. It can be done, but the consumer must understand the reason for the inconsistency and respond favorably to it. Even more difficult is maintaining such an apparent inconsistency for a long time.

The second level of positive relationship among elements of the mix is "integration." While consistency is a coherent fit, integration is an active, harmonious interaction among the elements of the mix. For example, heavy advertising is sometimes harmonious with a high selling price because the added margin from the premium price pays for the advertising and the heavy advertising creates the brand differentiation that justifies the high price. National brands of consumer package goods such as Tide laundry detergent, Campbell soup, and Colgate toothpaste use this approach. This does not mean, however, that heavy advertising and high product pricing are always harmonious.

Exhibit I
The Sales Response Curve

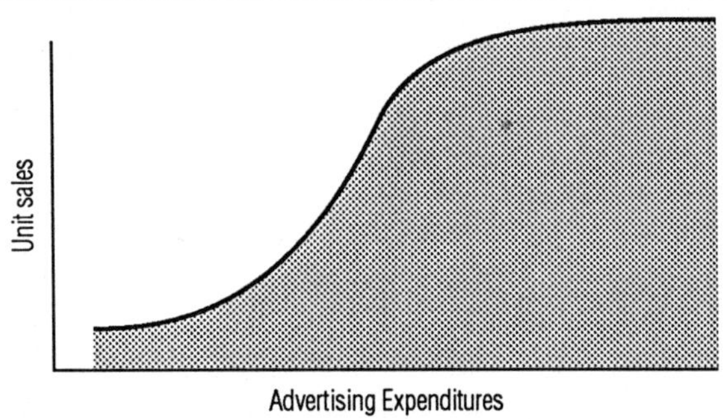

The third—and most sophisticated—form of relationship is "leverage," whereby each element is used to the best advantage in support of the total mix. The sales response curve helps answer this question (see Exhibit I). In its simplest form, the curve shows the relationship between sales, usually measured in units but sometimes in dollars, and a marketing input measured in either physical or financial terms.

The relationship between advertising expenditures and sales is shown in Exhibit I. This relationship can often be represented by a mathematical formula or by a chart listing unit sales and advertising expenditures. But the graphical representation of the sales response curve is more meaningful to most people.

Sales response curves enable a marketer to study the relationship between a given level of expenditure of one or more marketing variables and the likely level of sales. More powerful, however, is the ability to look at the changes in sales related to changes in expenditure level. Exhibit I, for example, implies that as advertising expenditures increase, they have little impact initially, then a great deal of impact, and, finally, little impact again from additional expenditures. In the same way, the marketer can understand the dynamics of the relationships and interactions of two elements in a three-dimensional graph.

It would not be sensible to invest additional advertising dollars in the flat part of the curve (upper end) to generate sales, but rather to invest dollars in other elements of the mix. Products with heavy advertising would then benefit more from improved distribution than from an overkill of advertising.

I now go beyond the relationships of the elements of the mix with one another to consider the relationship of the total program with the market, the company, and the competition.

Program-Market Fit

Product policy discussions both in business schools and in real life invariably put great emphasis on the product-market fit. An important question in new product development, for example, is whether the product concept fits market needs. Some years ago, when J. M. Smucker considered the introduction of a thick catsup in a wide-mouthed jar, the company's executives agonized over whether consumers would respond positively to the new concept. When Loctite Corporation introduced the Bond-A-Matic 2000, a dispenser for its industrial adhesive line, a serious concern was how the dispenser would fit into the prospective customer's manufacturing operation. Managers can expand the concept of product-market fit to encompass the relationship between the total program and the market. The idea is to develop a program that fits well the needs of the target market segments the company is exploiting.

Such a program builds logically on consistency, integration, and leverage. To leverage you use the most efficient tools for the market segment being emphasized. (Efficiency, in this sense, relates to the engineering concept of output per unit of input. Thus we might look at unit sales generated per dollar of advertising or personal selling to determine which was more efficient, or what combination of the two was most efficient.) It is probably best to approach the price-sensitive, brand-insensitive consumer, for example, with price promotions instead of expensive advertising programs or elaborate packaging.

One of the first steps in marketing-program development is to completely, carefully, and explicitly delineate the market. One of the last steps before launching a program is to review the impact of each element and of the total mix on the target consumers. The review should include tests for consistency, integration, and leverage.

Program-Company Fit

A good program-market fit and a consistent, integrated, and leveraged program are not enough for success. The program must fit the company. Just as each individual has certain strengths and weaknesses, so do organizations.

A marketing program must be symbiotic with the company or operating unit implementing the program. A marketing organization with extensive mass advertising experience and expertise, for instance, is more likely to be able to carry out a program that depends heavily on advertising than an organization with less strength in that area.

Over time, these behavioral or cultural attributes can change. But the rate of change is limited. It usually takes quite a long time for a company to develop a strength in advertising if it has little understanding of the field. For example, it is not easy for novices to identify and hire advertising experts from other companies. Such an approach takes time and, often, several trial-and-error cycles. Sometimes the beginners hire the wrong people; even when they hire the right people, the newcomers they select are often so alien to the culture of the company that the "transplant" is "rejected." One executive usually cannot change a whole culture, particularly in a large organization. Over time, strong leaders can change the culture, but not with ease and great speed. Thus the behavioral fit between the program and the company must be carefully considered.

The marketing program must fit the company's overall capabilities as well. A price-oriented strategy works well in a company that stresses efficient manufacturing and distribution along with administrative austerity. An account-oriented marketing program is much more likely to thrive in a customer-oriented culture that has responsive operating and logistics people than in a manufacturing-oriented culture that stresses efficiency to the detriment of customer service. The large plant geared to long production runs is well suited to a strategy of a narrow product line with intense price orientation. And the company with a strong balance sheet and low cost of capital can much more easily provide generous credit terms than can a financially limited competitor.

Market position can also help to determine the most sensible marketing program. The market share leader, for example, gains when it encourages competition on a fixed-cost basis via elements like national advertising, company-owned distribution, or heavy research and development. Its position enables it to spread the costs over a large volume, reducing its cost per unit sold far below that of smaller competitors. Anheuser-Busch, for example, spends less on advertising per barrel of beer sold than its major competitors because it spreads its huge advertising budget over many more units than do its smaller competitors.

Small unit-share competitors or niche marketers, on the other hand, should emphasize marketing programs that stress variable costs so that their cost-per-unit-sold is equal to that of their largest competitors. Thus small companies often stress intensive price promotions, a commission sales force, and independent distributors.

The consumer's or distributor's image of the company can also have a big impact on program-company fit. In the early 1980s, Levi Strauss & Company introduced a line of men's suits in which the jacket, vest, and pants were displayed and sold separately in department and specialty stores. The product line included matched items meant to look like a tailored suit. Although the concept met success for some competitors, it failed for Levi Strauss because the stores and the target consumers viewed the company not as a credible source of "suits" but as a jeans and sportswear manufacturer.

Executives cannot develop or review a program in isolation; they can assess it only in relation to the company using it.

Competitor-Program Fit

How should the program deal with competition? Your company's program should be such that it builds well on your strengths and avoids stressing your weaknesses, all the while protecting you from the competition. Your company derives strength from a program that evades your competitors' strengths, capitalizes on their weaknesses, and in total builds a unique market personality and position.

Accomplishing this set of related tasks requires meticulous analysis and honest introspection. Perhaps the most serious danger, other than neglecting the competitor-program fit altogether, is to underestimate the competition's strengths. Don't be too proud or too uninformed to see your competition's good points and your own company's weaknesses.

Too many companies display their disregard for the competition when they wonder, particularly about market leaders, "Why can't we emulate them?" The answer is twofold. First, the strengths of the leading competitor are almost certainly so distinctive that any attempt at imitation would fall short of the mark. Second, the current leading competitor in all likelihood took command when the market was quite different—when a leading competitor with similar strengths and capabilities did not exist. Thus, in a sense, the leader expanded into a "vacuum" that no longer exists. Companies that blindly attempt to imitate the leader usually fall, often very painfully

Companies compete with one another by emphasizing different elements of the marketing mix and by using different mixtures of those elements. The competitive response or reaction matrix is a useful table for visualizing the alternative action-reaction pattern.[1] A simple matrix might include two companies and three subelements of the marketing mix such as price, product quality, and advertising (see Exhibit II).

Exhibit II
Competitive Response Matrix

		Company A Action		
		Price	*Quality*	*Advertising*
Company B Reaction	*Price*	$C_{p,p}$	$C_{q,p}$	$C_{a,p}$
	Quality	$C_{p,q}$	$C_{q,q}$	$C_{a,q}$
	Advertising	$C_{p,a}$	$C_{q,a}$	$C_{a,a}$
	Total	1.0	1.0	1.0

The vertical columns represent action taken by our company, Company A. We might, for example, cut price (left-hand column), increase quality, or increase advertising. The reactions of Company B, our competitor, are represented by the horizontal rows. The coefficients (numbers indicated by the "Cs" in the matrix) represent the probability of Company B responding to Company A's move. The subscript "p" is for price, "q" for quality, and "a" for advertising; the first subscript is Company A's action and the second is Company B's response. The coefficient $C_{a,p}$ (upper right-hand corner), then, represents the probability of Company B responding to Company A's increase in advertising (right-hand column of the matrix) with a price cut (top row of the matrix). The diagonal ($C_{p,p}$,$C_{q,q}$,$C_{a,a}$) represents the likelihood of Company B responding to a move by Company A with the same marketing tool (by, say, meeting a price cut with a price cut). We can estimate the coefficients by studying past behavior and/or by seeking management's judgment. The coefficients must, of course, add to a total probability of one (or 100%).

Once we have developed the matrix, we can review each of our potential marketing actions, here, for example, with regard to price, quality, and advertising in light of probable competitor response. If we expect that there is a 70% chance that the competitor will meet our price cut but only a 20% chance that it will meet a quality increase, we might reason that a quality increase helps us to develop a more unique marketing approach than the price cut, which is more likely to be imitated. We can also continue our disciplined conjecture by asking how we (Company A) should respond to the competition's (Company B's) most likely reaction to each of our actions. If we cut price, and it is 70% likely to meet our new price, what should we plan to do when it does meet our new price?

The competitive response matrix is a flexible analytical approach. One can add more columns representing many marketing tools, add more rows for delayed responses (for example, will the competition cut price immediately, in a month, in a quarter?), and add rows for additional competitors. The discipline of the approach is exceedingly valuable.

The competitive response matrix is useful in helping to develop a distinctive approach to the market. It enables a competitor to understand more easily how it can differentiate itself from the marketing programs of other competitors.

Formal competitive analysis programs are particularly important for making large capital commitments. The essence of these programs is to play the role of the competitor or of a group of major competitors. Some companies even go so far as to have their own executives play competitive games built around their industry, with one or several company executives representing each competitor. The response matrix can be incorporated into these elaborate, formal approaches.

The Expanded Mix

Like most concepts, the marketing mix is an abstraction from reality. And real marketing programs don't always fit the product, price, communication, and distribution paradigm perfectly For instance, several aspects of the total mix really involve combinations of the four basic elements. These combinations include:

- Promotion
- Brand
- Terms and conditions

Strictly defined, "promotion" includes short-term price cuts to the trade and consumer incentives like coupons, contests, and price allowances; it involves price and communication. In many industries and companies, trade and consumer promotion account for a larger share of the budget than advertising or personal selling. There is certainly no need to expend much effort trying to categorize consumer promotion as price or communication. The important thing to note is that it is useful and fits into the mix.

Often viewed as part of the product, "brand" is also part of communication. In fact, it can serve as a useful, integrative force to bring product policy and communication closer together.

"Terms and conditions" relate to a myriad of elements of a contractual nature that are closely related to price (payment terms, credit, leasing, delivery schedules, and so on). But they are so close to personal selling that I think they should be viewed as an interface between price and communications. Elements like service support and logistical arrangements also approach product policy. The important thing is not necessarily to categorize these issues but to consider them as marketing tools.

In conclusion, I suggest you use the marketing mix concept to answer the following questions:

Are the elements consistent with one another?

Beyond being consistent, do they add up to form a harmonious, integrated whole?

Is each element being given its best leverage?

Are the target market segments precisely and explicitly defined?[2]

Does the total program, as well as each element, meet the needs of the precisely defined target market segment?

Does the marketing mix build on the organization's cultural and tangible strengths, and does it imply a program to correct weaknesses, if any?

Does the marketing mix create a distinctive personality in the competitive marketplace and protect the company from the most obvious competitive threats?

Use these questions to help focus on the most important aspects of the marketing mix and its fit.

References

1. Jean Jacques Lambin, in *Advertising, Competition and Market Conduct in Oligopoly Over Time* (Amsterdam: North Holland Publishing, 1976), describes the approach in great depth. I am indebted to my colleague, Robert J. Dolan, for introducing me to it.
2. See my article with Thomas V. Bonoma, "How to Segment Industrial Markets," HBR May–June 1984, p. 104, and our book, *Segmenting the Industrial Market* (Lexington, MA: Lexington Books, 1983), which explains that marketing segments can be defined by such attributes beyond customer demographics as urgency of need or personality type.

With Professors Robert J. Dolan and John A. Quelch, Professor Shapiro developed a three-volume marketing management series based on the Harvard Business School MBA required marketing course. This article is adapted from the material in the marketing mix chapter (Part Six) of *Marketing Management: Principles, Analysis and Applications* (Richard D. Irwin, Inc., 1985), the first of the three volumes.

4

Marketing, Strategic Planning & the Theory of the Firm

Paul F. Anderson

The process of goal formulation must operate prior to, but also be interactive with, the process of strategy formulation.

The strategic planning process is inextricably linked with the issue of corporate goal formulation. It is argued that greater progress will be made in understanding marketing's participation in strategic planning if marketing's role in the goal formulation process can be explicated. Unfortunately, the extant theories of the firm are inadequate in varying degrees for this purpose. A new theory of the firm is proposed that attempts to specify the role of marketing and the other functional areas in the goal setting and strategic planning process.

Would you tell me, please, which way I ought to go from here? asked Alice.
That depends a good deal on where you want to get to, said the Cat.
I don't much care where, said Alice.
Then it doesn't matter which way you go, said the cat.
LEWIS CARROL—*Alice's Adventures in Wonderland*

THE OBVIOUS WISDOM of the Cheshire's statement reveals an important fact concerning strategic planning: without a clear set of objectives, the planning process is meaningless. Two authorities on the subject refer to strategy as "the major link between the goals and objectives the organization wants to achieve and the various functional area policies and operating plans it uses to guide its day-to-day activities" (Hofer and Schendel 1978, p. 13). Other strategy experts generally agree that the process of goal formulation must operate prior to, but also be interactive with, the process of strategy formulation (Ackoff 1970, Ansoff 1965, Glueck 1976, Newman and Logan 1971). Given the growing interest of marketers in the concept of strategic planning, it would appear fruitful to assess the current state of knowledge concerning goals and the goal formulation process.

Over the years, this general area of inquiry has fallen under the rubric of the "theory of the firm." One objective of this paper is to review some of the major theories of the firm to be found in the literature. The extant theories have emerged in the disciplines of economics, finance and management. To date, marketing has not developed its own comprehensive theory of the firm. Generally, marketers have been content to borrow their concepts of goals and goal formulation from these other disciplines. Indeed, marketing has shown a strange ambivalence toward the concept of corporate goals. The recent marketing literature pays scant attention to the actual content of corporate goal hierarchies. Even less attention is focused on the normative issue of what firm goals and objectives ought to be. Moreover, contemporary marketing texts devote little space to the subject. Typically, an author's perspective on corporate goals is revealed in his/her definition of the marketing concept, but one is hard pressed to find further development of the topic. There is rarely any discussion of how these goals come about or how marketing may participate in the goal formulation process.

This is not to say that received doctrine in marketing has been developed without regard for corporate objectives. The normative decision rules and procedures that have emerged always seek to attain one or more objectives. Thus it could be said that these marketing models implicitly assume a

Paul F. Anderson is a Professor of Marketing at Penn State University.

theory of the firm. However, the particular theory that serves as the underpinning of the model is rarely made explicit. More importantly, marketing theorists have devoted little attention to an exploration of the nature and implications of these theories. For example, the product portfolio (Boston Consulting Group 1970, Cardozo and Wind 1980), and PIMS (Buzzell, Gale and Sultan 1975) approaches that are so much in vogue today implicitly assume that the primary objective of the firm is the maximization of return on investment (ROI). This objective seems to have been accepted uncritically by many marketers despite its well-documented deficiencies (e.g., its inability to deal with timing, duration and risk differences among returns and its tendency to create behavioral problems when used as a control device; Hopwood 1976, Van Home 1980). However, the concern expressed in this paper is not so much that marketers have adopted the wrong objectives, but that the discipline has failed to appreciate fully the nature and implications of the objectives that it has adopted.

As a result, in the last sections of the paper the outline of a new theory of the firm will be presented. It will be argued that the theories of the firm developed within economics, finance and management are inadequate in varying degrees as conceptual underpinnings for marketing. It is asserted that the primary role of a theory of the firm is to act as a kind of conceptual backdrop that functions heuristically to guide further theory development within a particular discipline. As such, the proposed model is less of a theory and more a Kuhnian-style paradigm (Kuhn 1970). Moreover, for a theory of the firm to be fruitful in this respect it must be congruent with the established research tradition of the field (Laudan 1977). It will be demonstrated, for example, that the theories emerging from economics and finance are inconsistent with the philosophical methodology and ontological framework of marketing. However, the proposed model is not only fully consonant with marketing's research tradition, but, unlike existing theories, it explicitly considers marketing's role in corporate goal formulation and strategic planning. Thus it is hoped that the theory will be able to provide a structure to guide future research efforts in these areas.

Economic Theories of the Firm

In this section three theories of the firm are reviewed. The first, the neoclassical model, provides the basic foundation of contemporary microeconomic theory. The second, the market value model, performs a similar function within financial economics. Finally, the agency costs model represents a modification of the market value model to allow a divergence of interests between the owners and managers of the firm. In this sense, it operates as a transitional model between the economically oriented theories of this section and the behavioral theories of the section to follow. However, all three may be classified as economic models since they share the methodological orientation and conceptual framework of economic theory. Note that each postulates an economic objective for the firm and then derives the consequences for firm behavior under different assumption sets.

The Neoclassical Model

The neoclassical theory of the firm can be found in any standard textbook in economics. In its most basic form the theory posits a single product firm operating in a purely competitive environment. Decision making is vested in an owner-entrepreneur whose sole objective is to maximize the dollar amount of the firm's single period profits. Given the standard assumptions of diminishing returns in the short run and diseconomies of scale in the long run, the firm's average cost function will have its characteristic U-shape. The owner's unambiguous decision rule will be to set output at the point where marginal costs equal marginal revenues. The introduction of imperfections in the product market (such as those posited by the monopolistically competitive model) represent mere elaborations on the basic approach. The objective of the firm remains single period profit maximization.

The neoclassical model is well known to marketers. Indeed, it will be argued below that the profit maximization assumption of neoclassical economics underlies much of the normative literature in marketing management. It will be shown that this is true despite the fact that neoclassical theory is inconsistent with the basic research tradition of marketing. Moreover, the neoclassical model suffers from a number of limitations.

For example, the field of finance has challenged the profit maximization assumption because it fails to provide the business decision maker with an operationally feasible criterion for making investment decisions (Solomon 1963). In this regard, it suffers from an inability to consider risk differences among investment alternatives. When risk levels vary across projects, decision criteria that focus only on profitability will lead to suboptimal decisions (Copeland and Weston 1979, Fama and Miller 1972, Van Horne 1980). As a result of these and other problems, financial economists have generally abandoned the neoclassical model in favor of a more comprehensive theory of the firm known as the market value model.

The Market Value Model

Given the assumptions that human wants are insatiable and that capital markets are perfectly competitive, Fama and Miller (1972) show that the objective of the firm should be to maximize its present market value. For a corporation this is equivalent to maximizing the price of the firm's stock. In contrast to the profit maximization objective, the market value rule allows for the consideration of risk differences among alternative investment opportunities. Moreover, the model is applicable to owner-operated firms as well as corporations in which there is likely to be a separation of ownership and control.

The existence of a perfectly competitive capital market allows the firm's management to pursue a single unambiguous objective despite the fact that shareholders are likely to have heterogeneous preferences for current versus future income. If, for example, some stockholders wish more income than the firm is currently paying in dividends, they can sell some of their shares to make up the difference. However, if other shareholders prefer less current income in favor of more future income, they can lend their dividends in the capital markets at interest. In either case shareholder utility will be maximized by a policy that maximizes the value of the firm's stock.

The value maximization objective is implemented within the firm by assessing all multiperiod decision alternatives on the basis of their risk-adjusted net present values (Copeland and Weston 1979, Fama and Miller 1972, Van Horne 1980):

$$NPV_j = \sum_{i-1}^{n} \frac{A_i}{(1 + k_j)^i} \qquad (1)$$

where NPV_j equals the net present value of alternative j, A_i equals the net after-tax cash flows in year i, n is the expected life of the project in years, and k_j is the risk-adjusted, after-tax required rate of return on j. In the absence of capital rationing, the firm should undertake all projects whose net present values are greater than or equal to zero. Assuming an accurate determination of k_j, this will ensure maximization of the firm's stock price. The discount rate k_j should represent the return required by the market to compensate for the risk of the project. This is usually estimated using a parameter preference model such as the capital asset pricing model or (potentially) the arbitrage model (Anderson 1981). However, it should be noted that there are serious theoretical and practical difficulties associated with the use of these approaches (Anderson 1981; Meyers and Turnbull 1977; Roll 1977; Ross 1976, 1978).

From a marketing perspective this approach requires that all major decisions be treated as investments. Thus the decision to introduce a new product, to expand into new territories, or to adopt a new channel of distribution should be evaluated on the basis of its risk-adjusted net present value. While similar approaches have been suggested in marketing (Cravens, Hills and Woodruff 1980; Dean 1966; Howard 1965; Kotler 1971; Pessemier 1966), it has generally not been recognized that this implies the adoption of shareholder wealth maximization as the goal of the firm. Moreover, these approaches are often offered in piecemeal fashion for the evaluation of selected decisions (e.g., new products), and are not integrated into a consistent and coherent theory of the firm.

Despite the deductive logic of the market value model, there are those who question whether corporate managers are motivated to pursue value maximization. An essential assumption of the market value theory is that stockholders can employ control, motivation and monitoring devices to ensure that managers maximize firm value. However, in the development of their agency theory of the firm, Jensen and Meckling (1976) note that such activities by shareholders are not without cost. As a result, it may not be possible to compel managers to maximize shareholder wealth.

The Agency Costs Model

The separation of ownership and control in modern corporations gives rise to an agency relationship between the stockholders and managers of the firm. An agency relationship may be defined as "a contract under which one or more persons (the principal(s)) engage another person (the agent) to perform some service on their behalf which involves delegating some decision making authority to the agent" (Jenson and Meckling 1976, p. 308). In any relationship of this sort, there is a potential for the agent to expend some of the principal's resources on private pursuits. As such, it will pay the principal to provide the agent with incentives and to incur monitoring costs to encourage a convergence of interests between the objectives of the principal and those of the agent. Despite expenditures of this type, it will generally be impossible to ensure that all of the agent's decisions will be designed to maximize the principal's welfare. The dollar value of the reduction in welfare experienced by the principal along with the expenditures on monitoring activities are costs of the agency relationship. For corporate stockholders these agency costs include the reduction in firm value resulting from management's consumption of nonpecuniary benefits (perquisites) and the costs of hiring outside auditing agents.

The tendency of managers of widely held corporations to behave in this fashion will require the stockholders to incur monitoring costs in an effort to enforce the value maximization objective. Unfortunately, perfect monitoring systems are very expensive. Thus the stockholders face a cost-benefit trade-off in deciding how much to spend on monitoring activities. Since it is unlikely that it will pay the shareholders to implement a "perfect" monitoring system, we will observe corporations suboptimizing on value maximization even in the presence of auditing activities. This leads to implications for managerial behavior that are quite different from those predicted by the market value model. For example, the Fama-Miller model predicts that managers will invest in all projects that will maximize the present value of the firm. However, the agency costs model suggests that management may actually invest in suboptimal projects and may even forego new profitable investments (Barnea, Haugen and Senbet 1981).

The recognition that a firm might not pursue maximization strategies is a relatively new concept to the literature of financial economics. However, in the middle 1950s and early 1960s, various economists and management specialists began to question the neoclassical assumption of single objective maximization on the basis of their observations of managerial behavior. This led directly to the development of the behavioral theory of the firm.

Behavioral Theories of the Firm

In this section two behaviorally oriented theories of the firm will be reviewed. While other approaches could also be included (Bower 1968, Mintzberg 1979), these models will lay the foundation for the development of a constituency-based theory in the last sections of the paper. The first approach is the behavioral model of the firm that emerged at the Carnegie Institute of Technology. The behavioral model can best be understood as a reaction against the neoclassical model of economic theory. The second approach is the resource dependence model of Pfeffer and Salancik (1978). The resource dependence perspective builds on a number of ideas contained in the behavioral model. For example, both approaches stress the coalitional nature of organizations. Moreover, both models emphasize the role of behavioral rather than economic factors in explaining the activities of firms.

The Behavioral Model

The behavioral theory of the firm can be found in the writings of Simon (1955, 1959, 1964), March and Simon (1958), and especially in Cyert and March (1963). The behavioral theory views the business firm as a coalition of individuals who are, in turn, members of subcoalitions. The coalition members include "managers, workers, stockholders, suppliers, customers, lawyers, tax collectors, regulatory agencies, etc." (Cyert and March 1963, p. 27).

The goals of the organization are determined by this coalition through a process of quasi-resolution of conflict. Different coalition members wish the organization to pursue different goals. The resultant goal conflict is not resolved by reducing all goals to a common dimension or by making them internally consistent. Rather, goals are viewed as "a series of independent aspiration-level constraints imposed on the organization by the members of the organizational coalition" (Cyert and March 1963, p. 117).

As Simon (1964) points out, in real world decision making situations acceptable alternatives must satisfy a whole range of requirements or constraints. In his view, singling out one constraint and referring to it as the goal of the activity is essentially arbitrary. This is because in many cases, the set of requirements selected as constraints will have much more to do with the decision outcome than the requirement selected as the goal. Thus he believes that it is more meaningful to refer to the entire set of constraints as the (complex) goal of the organization.

Moreover, these constraints are set at aspiration levels rather than maximization levels. Maximization is not possible in complex organizations because of the existence of imperfect information and because of the computational limitations faced by organizations in coordinating the various decisions made by decentralized departments and divisions. As a result, firm behavior concerning goals may be described as satisficing rather than maximizing (Simon 1959, 1964).

Cyert and March (1963) see decentralization of decision making leading to a kind of local rationality within subunits of the organization. Since these subunits deal only with a small set of problems and a limited number of goals, local optimization may be possible, but it is unlikely that this will lead to overall optimization. In this regard, the firm not only faces information processing and coordination problems but is also hampered by the fact that it must deal with problems in a sequential fashion. Thus organizational subunits typically attend to different problems at different times, and there is no guarantee that consistent objectives will be pursued in solving these problems. Indeed, Cyert and March argue that the time buffer between decision situations provides the firm with a convenient mechanism for avoiding the explicit resolution of goal conflict.

Thus in the behavioral theory of the firm, goals emerge as "independent constraints imposed on the organization through a process of bargaining among potential coalition members" (Cyert and March 1963, p. 43). These objectives are unlikely to be internally consistent and are subject to change over time as changes take place in the coalition structure. This coalitional perspective has had a significant impact on the development of management thought. Both Mintzberg (1979) and Pfeffer and Salancik (1978) have developed theories of the firm that take its coalitional nature as given. In the following section the resource dependence approach of Pfeffer and Salancik is outlined.

The Resource Dependence Model

Pfeffer and Salancik (1978) view organizations as coalitions of interests which alter their purposes and direction as changes take place in the coalitional structure. Like Mintzberg (1979) they draw a distinction between internal and external coalitions, although they do not use these terms. Internal coalitions may be viewed as groups functioning within the organization (e.g., departments and functional areas). External coalitions include such stakeholder groups as labor, stockholders, creditors, suppliers, government and various interested publics. Pfeffer and Salancik place their primary emphasis on the role of environmental (i.e., external) coalitions in affecting the behavior of organizations. They believe that "to describe adequately the behavior of organizations requires attending to the coalitional nature of organizations and the manner in which organizations respond to pressures from the environment" (Pfeffer and Salancik 1978, p. 24).

The reason for the environmental focus of the model is that the survival of the organization ultimately depends on its ability to obtain resources and support from its external coalitions. Pfeffer and Salancik implicitly assume that survival is the ultimate goal of the organization and that to achieve this objective, the organization must maintain a coalition of parties willing to "legitimize" its existence (Dowling and Pfeffer 1975, Parsons 1960). To do this, the organization offers various inducements in exchange for contributions of resources and support (Barnard 1938, March and Simon 1958, Simon 1964).

However, the contributions of the various interests are not equally valued by the organization. As such, coalitions that provide "behaviors, resources and capabilities that are most needed or desired by other organizational participants come to have more influence and control over the organization" (Pfeffer and Salancik 1978, p. 27). Similarly, organizational subunits (departments, functional areas, etc.) which are best able to deal with critical contingencies related to coalitional contributions are able to enhance their influence in the organization.

A common problem in this regard is that the various coalitions make conflicting demands on the organization. Since the satisfaction of some demands limits the satisfaction of others, this leads to the possibility that the necessary coalition of support cannot be maintained. Thus organizational activities can be seen as a response to the constraints imposed by the competing demands of various coalitions.

In attempting to maintain the support of its external coalitions, the organization must negotiate exchanges that ensure the continued supply of critical resources. At the same time, however, it must remain flexible enough to respond to environmental contingencies. Often these objectives are in conflict, since the desire to ensure the stability and certainty of resource flows frequently leads to activities limiting flexibility and autonomy. For example, backward integration via merger or acquisition is one way of coping with the uncertainty of resource dependence. At the same time, however, this method of stabilizing resource exchanges limits the ability of the firm to adapt as readily to environmental contingencies. Pfeffer and Salancik suggest that many other activities of organizations can be explained by the desire for stable resource exchanges, on the one hand, and the need for flexibility and autonomy on the other. They present data to support their position that joint ventures, interlocking directorates, organizational growth, political involvement and executive succession can all be interpreted in this light. Other activities such as secrecy, multiple sourcing and diversification can also be interpreted from a resource dependence perspective.

Thus the resource dependence model views organizations as "structures of coordinated behaviors" whose ultimate aim is to garner the necessary environmental support for survival (Pfeffer and Salancik 1978, p. 32). As in the behavioral model, it is recognized that goals and objectives will emerge as constraints imposed by the various coalitions of interests. However, the resource dependence model interprets these constraints as demands by the coalitions that must be met in order to maintain the existence of the organization.

Research Traditions and the Theory of the Firm

In reflecting on the various theories of the firm presented herein, it is important to recognize that one of their primary roles is to function as a part of what Laudan calls a "research tradition" (Laudan 1977). A research tradition consists of a set of assumptions shared by researchers in a particular domain. Its main purpose is to provide a set of guidelines for theory development. In so doing it provides the researcher with both an ontological framework and a philosophical methodology.

Machlup, in a closely related argument, notes that much of the criticism of neoclassical theory arises because of a confusion concerning the purposes of the theory (1967). He points out that the "firm" in neoclassical analysis is nothing more than a theoretical construct that is useful in predicting the impact of changes in economic variables on the behavior of firms in the aggregate. For example, the neoclassical model performs well in predicting the *direction* of price changes in an industry that experiences an increase in wage rates or the imposition of a tax. It does less well, however, in explaining the complex process by which a particular firm decides to implement a price change. Of course, this is to be expected since the theory of the firm was never intended to predict the real world behavior of individual firms.

Thus the question of whether corporations really seek to maximize profits is of no concern to the economic instrumentalist. Following Friedman, the only consideration is whether such assumptions lead to "sufficiently accurate predictions" of real world phenomena (1953, p. 15). Similarly, the financial economist is unmoved by criticism related to the lack of reality in the market value and agency cost models. The ultimate justification of a theory from an instrumental viewpoint comes from the accuracy of its predictions.

In contrast to the instrumentalism of the first three theories of the firm, the behavioral and resource dependence models have been developed from the perspective of realism. The realist believes that theoretical constructs should have real world analogs and that theories should describe "what the world is really like" (Chalmers 1978, p. 114). Thus, it is not unexpected that these models are essentially inductive in nature. Indeed, in describing their methodological approach Cyert and March state that they "propose to make detailed observations of the procedures by which firms make decisions and to use these observations as a basis for a theory of decision making within business organizations" (1963, p. 1).

Thus it can be seen that the theories of the firm that have been developed in economics and financial economics emerged from a very different research tradition than the behaviorally oriented theories developed in management. This fact becomes particularly significant in considering their adequacy as a framework for marketing theory development. For example, the discipline of marketing appears to be committed to a research tradition dominated by the methodology of inductive realism, yet it frequently employs the profit maximization paradigm of neoclassical economic theory. Despite the recent trend toward the incorporation of social objectives in the firm's goal hierarchy, and the recognition by many authors that firms pursue multiple objectives, profit or profit maximization figures prominently as the major corporate objective in leading marketing texts (Boone and Kurtz 1980, p. 12; Markin 1979, p. 34; McCarthy 1978, p. 29; Stanton 1978, p. 13). More significantly perhaps, profit maximization is the implicit or explicit objective of much of the normative literature in marketing management. While the terms may vary from return on investment to

The ontology of the research tradition defines the kinds of entities that exist within the domain of inquiry. For example, in the neoclassical model such concepts as middle management, coalitions, bureaucracy and reward systems do not exist. They fall outside the ontology of neoclassical economics. Similarly, the concepts of the entrepreneur, diminishing returns, and average cost curves, do not exist (or at least are not used) in the resource dependence model. The ontology of the research tradition defines the basic conceptual building blocks of its constituent theories.

The philosophical methodology, on the other hand, specifies the procedure by which concepts will be used to construct a theory. Moreover, it determines the way in which the concepts will be viewed by theorists working within the research tradition. For example, the neoclassical, market value and agency costs models have been developed in accordance with a methodology that could be characterized as deductive instrumentalism. The models are deductive in that each posits a set of assumptions or axioms (including assumptions about firm goals) from which implications for firm behavior are deduced as logical consequences (Hempel 1965, p. 336). The models are also instrumentalist in that their component concepts arc not necessarily assumed to have real world referents. Instrumentalism views theories merely as calculating devices that generate useful predictions (Feyerabend 1964, Morgenbesser 1969, Popper 1963). The reality of a theory's assumptions or its concepts is irrelevant from an instrumentalist point of view.

It is essentially this aspect of economic instrumentalism that has drawn the most criticism from both economists and noneconomists. Over 30 years ago concerns for the validity of the theory among economists emerged as the famous "marginalism controversy" which raged in the pages of the *American Economic Review* (Lester 1946, 1947; Machlup 1946, 1947; Stigler 1946, 1947). More recently, much of the criticism has come from proponents of the behavioral theory of the firm (Cyert and March 1963, Cyert and Pottinger 1979). Perhaps the most commonly heard criticism of the neoclassical model is that the assumption of a rational, profit-maximizing decision maker who has access to perfect information is at considerable variance with the real world of business management (Cyert and March 1963, Simon 1955). Moreover, these critics fault the "marginalists" for concocting a firm with "no complex organization, no problems of control, no standard operating procedures, no budget, no controller, [and] no aspiring middle management" (Cyert and March 1963, p. 8). In short, the business firm assumed into existence by neoclassical theory bears little resemblance to the modern corporate structure.

Concerns with the realism of assumptions in neoclassical theory have been challenged by Friedman (1953) and Machlup (1967). In Friedman's classic statement of the "positivist" viewpoint, he takes the position that the ultimate test of a theory is the correspondence of its predictions with reality. From Friedman's perspective the lack of realism in a theory's assumptions is unrelated to the question of its validity.

Machlup, in a closely related argument, notes that much of the criticism of neoclassical theory arises because of a confusion concerning the purposes of the theory (1967). He points out that the "firm" in neoclassical analysis is nothing more than a theoretical construct that is useful in predicting the impact of changes in economic variables on the behavior of firms in the aggregate. For example, the neoclassical model performs well in predicting the *direction* of price changes in an industry that experiences an increase in wage rates or the imposition of a tax. It does less well, however, in explaining the complex process by which a particular firm decides to implement a price change. Of course, this is to be expected since the theory of the firm was never intended to predict the real world behavior of individual firms.

Thus the question of whether corporations really seek to maximize profits is of no concern to the economic instrumentalist. Following Friedman, the only consideration is whether such assumptions lead to "sufficiently accurate predictions" of real world phenomena (1953, p. 15). Similarly, the financial economist is unmoved by criticism related to the lack of reality in the market value and agency cost models. The ultimate justification of a theory from an instrumental viewpoint comes from the accuracy of its predictions.

In contrast to the instrumentalism of the first three theories of the firm, the behavioral and resource dependence models have been developed from the perspective of realism. The realist believes that theoretical constructs should have real world analogs and that theories should describe "what the world is really like" (Chalmers 1978, p. 114). Thus, it is not unexpected that these models are essentially inductive in nature. Indeed, in describing their methodological approach Cyert and March state that they "propose to make detailed observations of the procedures by which firms make decisions and to use these observations as a basis for a theory of decision making within business organizations" (1963, p. 1).

Thus it can be seen that the theories of the firm that have been developed in economics and financial economics emerged from a very different research tradition than the behaviorally oriented theories developed in management. This fact becomes particularly significant in considering their adequacy as a framework for marketing theory development. For example, the discipline of marketing appears to be committed to a research tradition dominated by the methodology of inductive realism, yet it frequently employs the profit maximization paradigm of neoclassical economic theory. Despite the recent trend toward the incorporation of social objectives in the firm's goal hierarchy, and the recognition by many authors that firms pursue multiple objectives, profit or profit maximization figures prominently as the major corporate objective in leading marketing texts (Boone and Kurtz 1980, p. 12; Markin 1979, p. 34; McCarthy 1978, p. 29; Stanton 1978, p. 13). More significantly perhaps, profit maximization is the implicit or explicit objective of much of the normative literature in marketing management. While the terms may vary from return on investment to contribution margin, cash flow or cumulative compounded profits, they are all essentially profit maximization criteria. Thus such widely known and accepted approaches as product portfolio analysis (Boston Consulting Group 1970), segmental analysis (Mossman, Fischer and Crissy 1974), competitive bidding models (Simon and Freimer 1970), Bayesian pricing procedures (Green 1963), and many others all adhere to the profit maximization paradigm. It may seem curious that a discipline that drifted away from the research tradition of economics largely because of a concern for greater "realism" (Hutchinson 1952, Vaile 1950) should continue to employ one of its most "unrealistic" assumptions. In effect, marketing has rejected much of the philosophical methodology of economics while retaining a significant portion of its ontology.

It would seem that what is required is the development of a theory of the firm that is consistent with the existing research tradition of marketing. Such a theory should deal explicitly with the role of marketing in the firm and should attempt to explicate its relationship with the other functional areas (Wind 1981) and specify its contribution to the formation of corporate "goal structures" (Richards 1978). In this way it would provide a framework within which marketing theory development can proceed. This is particularly important for the development of theory within the area of strategic planning. It is likely that greater progress could be made in this area if research is conducted within the context of a theory of the firm whose methodological and ontological framework is consistent with that of marketing.

Toward a Constituency-Based Theory of the Firm

The theory of the firm to be outlined in this section focuses explicitly on the roles performed by the various functional areas found in the modern corporation. There are basically two reasons for this. First, theory development in business administration typically proceeds within the various academic disciplines corresponding (roughly) to the functional areas of the firm. It is felt that a theory explicating the role of the functional areas will be of greater heuristic value in providing a framework for research within these disciplines (and within marketing in particular).

Second, a theory of the firm that does not give explicit recognition to the activities of these functional subunits fails to appreciate their obvious importance in explaining firm behavior. As highly formalized internal coalitions operating at both the corporate and divisional levels, they often share a common frame of reference and a relatively consistent set of goals and objectives. These facts make the functional areas an obvious unit of analysis in attempting to explain the emergence of goals in corporations.

The proposed theory adopts the coalitional perspectives of the various behaviorally oriented theories of the firm and relies especially on the resource dependence model. As a matter of analytical convenience, the theory divides an organization into both internal and external coalitions. From a resource dependence perspective, the task of the organization is to maintain itself by negotiating resource exchanges with external interests. Over time the internal coalitions within corporate organizations have adapted themselves to enhance the efficiency and effectiveness with which they perform these negotiating functions. One approach that has been taken to accomplish this is specialization. Thus certain coalitions within the firm may be viewed as specialists in negotiating exchanges with certain external coalitions. By and large these internal coalitions correspond to the major functional areas of the modern corporate structure.

For example, industrial relations and personnel specialize in negotiating resource exchanges with labor coalitions; finance, and to a lesser extent, accounting specialize in negotiating with stockholder and creditor groups; materials management and purchasing specialize in supplier group exchanges; and, of course, marketing specializes in negotiating customer exchanges. In addition, public relations, legal, tax and accounting specialize to a greater or lesser extent in negotiating the continued support and sanction of both government and public coalitions. In most large corporations the production area no longer interacts directly with the environment. With the waning of the production orientation earlier in this century, production gradually lost its negotiating functions to specialists such as purchasing and industrial relations on the input side and sales or marketing on the output side.

The major resources that the firm requires for survival include cash, labor and matériel. The major sources of cash are customers, stockholders and lenders. It is, therefore, the responsibility of marketing and finance to ensure the required level of cash flow in the firm. Similarly, it is the primary responsibility of industrial relations to supply the labor, and materials management and purchasing to supply the matériel necessary for the maintenance, growth and survival of the organization.

As Pfeffer and Salancik point out, external coalitions that control vital resources have greater control and influence over organizational activities (1978, p. 27). By extension, functional areas that negotiate vital resource exchanges will come to have greater power within the corporation as well. Thus the dominance of production and finance in the early decades of this century may be attributed to the fact that nearly all vital resource exchanges were negotiated by these areas. The ascendance, in turn, of such subunits as industrial relations and personnel (Meyer 1980), marketing (Keith 1960), purchasing and materials management (*Business Week* 1975) and public relations (Kotler and Mindak 1978) can be explained in part by environmental changes which increased the importance of effective and efficient resource exchanges with the relevant external coalitions. For example, the growth of unionism during the 1930s did much to enhance the role and influence of industrial relations departments in large corporations. Similarly, the improved status of sales and marketing departments during this same period may be linked to environmental changes including the depressed state of the economy, the rebirth of consumerism, and a shift in demand away from standardized "Model-T type products" (Ansoff 1979, p. 32). More recently, the OPEC oil embargo, the institutionalization of consumerism, and the expansion of government regulation into new areas (OSHA, Foreign Corrupt Practices Act, Affirmative Action, etc.) has had a similar impact on such areas as purchasing, public relations and legal.

Thus the constituency-based model views the major functional areas as specialists in providing particular resources for the firm. The primary objective of each area is to ensure an uninterrupted flow of resources from the appropriate external coalition. As functional areas tend to become specialized in dealing with particular coalitions, they tend to view these groups as constituencies both to be served and managed. From this perspective, the chief responsibility of the marketing area is to satisfy the long-term needs of its customer coalition. In short, it must strive to implement the marketing concept (Keith 1960, Levitt 1960, McKitterick 1957).

Of course, in seeking to achieve its own objectives, each functional area is constrained by the objectives of the other departments. In attempting to assure maximal consumer satisfaction as a means of maintaining the support of its customer coalition, marketing will be constrained by financial, technical and legal considerations imposed by the other functional areas. For example, expenditures on new product development, market research and advertising cut into the financial resources necessary to maintain the support of labor, supplier, creditor and investor coalitions. When these constraints are embodied in the formal performance measurement system, they exert a significant influence on the behavior of the functional areas.

In this model, firm objectives emerge as a series of Simonian constraints that are negotiated among the various functions. Those areas that specialize in the provision of crucial resources are likely to have greater power in the negotiation process. In this regard, the marketing area's desire to promote the marketing concept as a philosophy of the entire firm may be interpreted by the other functional areas as a means of gaining bargaining leverage by attempting to impress them with the survival value of customer support. The general failure of the other areas to embrace this philosophy may well reflect their belief in the importance of their own constituencies.

Recently, the marketing concept has also been called into question for contributing to the alleged malaise of American business. Hayes and Abernathy (1980) charge that excessive emphasis on marketing research and short-term financial control measures has led to the decline of U.S. firms in world markets. They argue that American businesses are losing more and more of their markets to European and Japanese firms because of a failure to remain technologically competitive. They believe that the reliance of American firms on consumer surveys and ROI control encourages a low-risk, short run investment philosophy, and point out that market research typically identifies consumers' current desires but is often incapable of determining their future wants and needs. Moreover, the short run focus of ROI measures and the analytical detachment inherent in product portfolio procedures tends to encourage investment in fast payback alternatives. Thus Hayes and Abernathy believe that American firms are reluctant to make the higher risk, longer-term investments in new technologies necessary for effective competition in world markets. They feel that the willingness of foreign firms to make such investments can be attributed to their need to look beyond their relatively small domestic markets for success. This has encouraged a reliance on technically superior products and a longer-term payoff perspective.

From a resource dependence viewpoint the Hayes and Abernathy argument seems to suggest that the external coalitions of U.S. firms are rather myopic. If the survival of the firm is truly dependent on the adoption of a longer-term perspective, one would expect this to be forced on the firm by its external coalitions. Indeed, there is ample evidence from stock market studies that investor coalitions react sharply to events affecting the longer run fortunes of firms (Lev 1974, Lorie and Hamilton 1973). Moreover, recent concessions by government, labor and supplier coalitions to Chrysler Corporation suggest a similar perspective among these groups.

However, the real problem is not a failure by internal and external coalitions in recognizing the importance of a long-run investment perspective. The real difficulty lies in designing an internal performance measurement and reward system that balances the need for short run profitability against long-term survival. A number of factors combine to bias these reward and measurement systems in favor of the short run. These include:

- Requirements for quarterly and annual reports of financial performance.
- The need to appraise and reward managers on an annual basis.
- The practical difficulties of measuring and rewarding the long-term performance of highly mobile management personnel.
- Uncertainty as to the relative survival value of emphasis on short-run versus long-run payoffs.

As a result of these difficulties, we find that in many U.S. firms the reward system focuses on short run criteria (Ouchi 1981). This naturally leads to the use of short-term financial control measures and an emphasis on market surveys designed to measure consumer reaction to immediate (and often minor) product improvements. In some cases the marketing area has adopted this approach in the name of the marketing concept.

However, as Levitt (1960) noted more than two decades ago, the real lesson of the marketing concept is that successful firms are able to recognize the fundamental and enduring nature of the customer needs they are attempting to satisfy.

As numerous case studies point out, it is the *technology* of want satisfaction that is transitory. The long-run investment perspective demanded by Hayes and Abernathy is essential for a firm that focuses its attention on transportation rather than trains, entertainment rather than motion pictures, or energy rather than oil. The real marketing concept divorces strategic thinking from an emphasis on contemporary technology and encourages investments in research and development with long-term payoffs. Thus, the "market-driven" firms that are criticized by Hayes and Abernathy have not really embraced the marketing concept. These firms have simply deluded themselves into believing that consumer survey techniques and product portfolio procedures automatically confer a marketing orientation on their adopters. However, the fundamental insight of the marketing concept has little to do with the use of particular analytical techniques. The marketing concept is essentially a state of mind or world view that recognizes that firms survive to the extent that they meet the real needs of their customer coalitions. As argued below, one of the marketing area's chief functions in the strategic planning process is to communicate this perspective to top management and the other functional areas.

Implications for Strategic Planning

From a strategic planning perspective, the ultimate objective of the firm may be seen as an attempt to position itself for long-run survival (Wind 1979). This, in turn, is accomplished as each functional area attempts to determine the position that will ensure a continuing supply of vital resources. Thus the domestic auto industry's belated downsizing of its product may be viewed as an attempt to ensure the support of its customer coalition in the 1980s and 1990s (just as its grudging acceptance of the UAW in the late 1930s and early 1940s reflected a need to ensure a continuing supply of labor).

Of course, a firm's functional areas may not be able to occupy all of the favored long run positions simultaneously. Strategic conflicts will arise as functional areas (acting as units at the corporate level or as subunits at the divisional level) vie for the financial resources necessary to occupy their optimal long-term positions. Corporate management as the final arbiter of these disputes may occasionally favor one area over another, with deleterious results. Thus, John De Lorean, former group executive at General Motors, believes that the firm's desire for the short run profits available from larger cars was a major factor in its reluctance to downsize in the 1970s (Wright 1979). He suggests that an overwhelming financial orientation among GM's top executives consistently led them to favor short-run financial gain over longer-term marketing considerations. Similarly, Hayes and Abernathy (1980) believe that the growing dominance of financial and legal specialists within the top managements of large U.S. corporations has contributed to the slighting of technological considerations in product development.

Against this backdrop marketing must realize that its role in strategic planning is not preordained. Indeed, it is possible that marketing considerations may not have a significant impact on strategic plans unless marketers adopt a strong advocacy position within the firm (Mason and Mitroff 1981). On this view, strategic plans are seen as the outcome of a bargaining process among functional areas. Each area attempts to move the corporation toward what it views as the preferred position for long-run survival, subject to the constraints imposed by the positioning strategies of the other functional units.

This is not to suggest, however, that formal-analytical procedures have no role to play in strategic planning. Indeed, as Quinn's (1981) research demonstrates, the actual process of strategy formulation in large firms is best described as a combination of the formal-analytical and power-behavioral approaches. He found that the formal planning system often provides a kind of infrastructure that assists in the strategy development and implementation process, although the formal system itself rarely generates new or innovative strategies. Moreover, the study shows that strategies tend to emerge incrementally over relatively long periods of time. One reason for this is the need for top management to obtain the support and commitment of the firm's various coalitions through constant negotiation and implied bargaining (Quinn 1981, p. 61).

Thus, from a constituency-based perspective, marketing's role in strategic planning reduces to three major activities. First, at both the corporate and divisional levels it must identify the optimal long-term position or positions that will assure customer satisfaction and support. An optimal position would reflect marketing's perception of what its customers' wants and needs are likely to be over the firm's strategic time horizon. Since this will necessarily involve long run considerations, positioning options must be couched in somewhat abstract terms. Thus the trend toward smaller cars by the domestic auto industry represents a very broad response to changing environmental, social and political forces and will likely affect the industry well into the 1990s. Other examples include the diversification into alternative energy sources by the petroleum industry, the movement toward "narrowcasting" by the major networks, and the downsizing of the single family home by the construction industry. The length of the time horizons involved suggests that optimal positions will be determined largely by fundamental changes in demographic, economic, social and political factors. Thus strategic positioning is more likely to be guided by long-term demographic and socioeconomic research (Lazer 1977) than by surveys of consumer attitudes.

Marketing's second major strategic planning activity involves the development of strategies designed to capture its preferred positions. This will necessarily involve attempts to gain a competitive advantage over firms pursuing similar positioning strategies. Moreover, the entire process is likely to operate incrementally. Specific strategies will focus on somewhat shorter time horizons and will be designed to move the firm toward a particular position without creating major dislocations within the firm or the marketplace (Quinn 1981). Research on consumers' current preferences must be combined with demographic and socioeconomic research to produce viable intermediate strategies. For example, Detroit's strategy of redesigning all of its subcompact lines has been combined with improved fuel efficiency in its larger cars (*Business Week* 1980).

Finally, marketing must negotiate with top management and the other functional areas to implement its strategies. The coalitional perspective suggests that marketing must take an active role in promoting its strategic options by demonstrating the survival value of a consumer orientation to the other internal coalitions.

Marketing's objective, therefore, remains long run customer support through consumer satisfaction. Paradoxically, perhaps, this approach requires marketers to have an even greater grasp of the technologies, perspectives and limitations of the other functional areas. Only in this way can marketing effectively negotiate the implementation of its strategies. As noted previously, the other functional areas are likely to view appeals to the marketing concept merely as a bargaining ploy. It is the responsibility of the marketing area to communicate the true long run focus and survival orientation of this concept to the other interests in the firm. However, this cannot be accomplished if the marketing function itself does not understand the unique orientations and decision methodologies employed by other departments.

For example, the long run investment perspective implicit in the marketing concept can be made more comprehensible to the financial coalition if it is couched in the familiar terms of capital budgeting analysis. Moreover, the marketing area becomes a more credible advocate for this position if it eschews the use of short-term ROI measures as its sole criterion for internal decision analysis. At the same time, an appreciation for the inherent limitations of contemporary capital investment procedures will give the marketing area substantial leverage in the negotiation process (Anderson 1981).

In the final analysis, the constituency model of the firm suggests that marketing's role in strategic planning must be that of a strong advocate for the marketing concept. Moreover, its advocacy will be enhanced to the extent that it effectively communicates the true meaning of the marketing concept in terms that are comprehensible to other coalitions in the firm. This requires an intimate knowledge of the interests, viewpoints and decision processes of these groups. At the same time, a better understanding of the true nature of the constraints imposed by these interests will allow the marketing organization to make the informed strategic compromises necessary for firm survival.

The author wishes to thank George Day, Larry Laudan and two anonymous referees for their very helpful comments and suggestions. He also wishes to thank his colleagues at Virginia Tech's Center for the Study of Science in Society for their many helpful suggestions.

Bibliography

Ackoff, Russell (1970), *A Concept of Corporate Planning*, New York: John Wiley & Sons.

Anderson, Paul F. (1981), "Marketing Investment Analysis," in *Research in Marketing*, 4, Jagdish N. Sheth, ed., Greenwich, CT: JAI Press, 1–37.

Ansoff, Igor H. (1965), *Corporate Strategy*, New York: McGraw-Hill.

——— (1979), "The Changing Shape of the Strategic Problem," in *Strategic Management: A View of Business Policy and Planning*, Dan E. Schendel and Charles W. Hofer, eds., Boston: Little Brown and Company, 30–44.

Barnard, Chester I. (1938), *The Functions of the Executive*, London: Oxford University Press.

Barnea, Amir, Robert A. Haugen and Lemma W. Senbet (1981), "Market Imperfections, Agency Problems and Capital Structure: A Review," *Financial Management*, 10 (Summer), 7–22.

Boone, Louis E. and David L. Kurtz (1980), *Foundations of Marketing*, 3rd ed., Hinsdale, IL: Dryden Press.

Boston Consulting Group (1970), *The Product Portfolio*, Boston: The Boston Consulting Group.

Bower, Joseph L. (1968), "Descriptive Decision Theory from the 'Administrative' Viewpoint," in *The Study of Policy Formation*, Raymond A. Bauer and Kenneth J. Gergen, eds., New York: Collier-Macmillan, 103–48.

Business Week (1975), "The Purchasing Agent Gains More Clout," (January 13), 62–63.

——— (1980), "Detroit's New Sales Pitch," (September 22), 78–83.

Buzzell, Robert D., Bradley T. Gale and Ralph G. M. Sultan (1975), "Market Share: A Key to Profitability," *Harvard Business Review*, 53 (January–February), 97–106.

Cardozo, Richard and Yoram Wind (1980), "Portfolio Analysis for Strategic Product-Market Planning," working paper, The Wharton School, University of Pennsylvania.

Chalmers, A. F. (1978), *What Is This Thing Called Science?* St. Lucia, Australia: University of Queensland Press.

Copeland, Thomas E. and J. Fred Weston (1979), *Financial Theory and Corporate Policy*, Reading, MA: Addison-Wesley Publishing Company.

Cravens, David W., Gerald E. Hills and Robert B. Woodruff (1980), *Marketing Decision Making*, rev. ed., Homewood, IL: Richard D. Irwin,

Cyert, Richard M. and James G. March (1963), *A Behavioral Theory of the Firm*, Englewood Cliffs, NJ: Prentice-Hall.

——— and Garrel Pottinger (1979), "Towards a Better Microeconomic Theory," *Philosophy of Science*, 46 (June), 204–22.

Dean, Joel (1966), "Does Advertising Belong in the Capital Budget?" *Journal of Marketing*, 30 (October), 15–21.

Dowling, John and Jeffrey Pfeffer (1975), "Organizational Legitimacy," *Pacific Sociological Review*, 18 (January), 122–36.

Fama, Eugene and Merton H. Miller (1972), *The Theory of Finance*, Hinsdale, IL: Dryden Press.

Feyerabend, Paul K. (1964), "Realism and Instrumentalism: Comments on the Logic of Factual Support," in *The Critical Approach to Science and Philosophy*, Mario Bunge, ed., London: The Free Press of Glencoe, 280–308.

Friedman, Milton (1953), "The Methodology of Positive Economics," in *Essays in Positive Economics*, Chicago: University of Chicago Press.

Glueck, William (1976), *Policy, Strategy Formation and Management Action*, New York: McGraw-Hill.

Green, Paul E. (1963), "Bayesian Decision Theory in Pricing Strategy," *Journal of Marketing*, 27 (January), 5–14.

Hayes, Robert H. and William J. Abernathy (1980), "Managing Our Way to Economic Decline," *Harvard Business Review*, 58 (July–August), 67–77.

Hempel, Carl G. (1965), *Aspects of Scientific Explanation*, New York: Macmillan Publishing Co.

Hofer, Charles W. and Dan Schendel (1978), *Strategy Formulation: Analytical Concepts*, St. Paul, MN: West Publishing Company.

Hopwood, Anthony (1976), *Accounting and Human Behavior*, Englewood Cliffs, NJ: Prentice-Hall.

Howard, John A. (1965), *Marketing Theory*, Boston: Allyn and Bacon.

Hutchinson, Kenneth D. (1952), "Marketing as a Science: An Appraisal," *Journal of Marketing*, 16 (January), 286–93 .

Jensen, Michael C. and William H. Meckling (1976), "Theory of the Firm: Managerial Behavior, Agency Costs and Ownership Structure," *Journal of Financial Economics*, 3 (October), 305–60.

Keith, Robert J. (1960), "The Marketing Revolution," *Journal of Marketing*, 24 (January), 35–38.

Kotler, Philip (1971), *Marketing Decision Making*, New York: Holt, Rinehart and Winston.

——— and William Mindak (1978), "Marketing and Public Relations," *Journal of Marketing*, 42 (October), 13–20.

Kuhn, Thomas S. (1970), *The Structure of Scientific Revolutions*, 2nd ed., Chicago: University of Chicago Press.

Laudan, Larry (1977), *Progress and Its Problems*, Berkeley, CA: University of California Press.

Lazer, William (1977), "The 1980's and Beyond: A Perspective," *MSU Business Topics*, 25 (Spring), 21–35.

Lester, R. A. (1946), "Shortcomings of Marginal Analysis for Wage-Employment Problems," *American Economic Review*, 36 (March), 63–82.

——— (1947), "Marginalism, Minimum Wages, and Labor Markets," *American Economic Review*, 37 (March), 135–48.

Lev, Baruch (1974), *Financial Statement Analysis: A New Approach*, Englewood Cliffs, NJ: Prentice-Hall.

Levitt, Theodore (1960), "Marketing Myopia," *Harvard Business Review*, 38 (July–August), 24–47.

Lorie, James H. and Mary T. Hamilton (1973), *The Stock Market: Theories and Evidence*, Homewood, IL: Richard D. Irwin.

Machlup, Fritz (1946), "Marginal Analysis and Empirical Research," *American Economic Review*, 36 (September), 519–54.

——— (1947), "Rejoinder to an Antimarginalist," *American Economic Review*, 37 (March), 148–54.

——— (1967), "Theories of the Firm: Marginalist, Behavioral, Managerial," *American Economic Review*, 57 (March), 1–33.

March, James G. and Herbert A. Simon (1958), *Organizations*, New York: John Wiley & Sons,

Markin, Rom (1979), *Marketing*, New York: John Wiley & Sons.

Mason, Richard 0. and Ian I. Mitroff (1981), "Policy Analysis as Argument," working paper, University of Southern California.

McCarthy, E. Jerome (1978), *Basic Marketing*, 6th ed., Homewood, IL: Richard D. Irwin.

McKitterick, J. B. (1957), "What is the Marketing Management Concept?" in *Readings in Marketing 75/76*, Guilford, CT: Dushkin Publishing Group, 23–26.

Meyer, Herbert E. (1980), "Personnel Directors Are the New Corporate Heros," in *Current Issues in Personnel Management*, Kendrith M. Rowland et al., eds., Boston: Allyn & Bacon, 2–8.

Meyers. Stewart C. and Stuart M. Turnbull (1977), "Capital Budgeting and the Capital Asset Pricing Model: Good News and Bad News," *Journal of Finance*, 32 (May), 321–36.

Mintzberg, Henry (1979), "Organizational Power and Goals: A Skeletal Theory," in *Strategic Management*, Dan E. Schendel and Charles W. Hofer, eds., Boston: Little, Brown and Company.

Morgenbesser, Sidney (1969), "The Realist-Instrumentalist Controversy," in *Philosophy, Science and Method*, New York: St. Martin's Press, 200–218.

Mossman, Frank H., Paul M. Fischer and W. J. E. Crissy (1974), "New Approaches to Analyzing Marketing Profitability," *Journal of Marketing*, 38 (April), 43–48.

Newman, William H. and James P. Logan (1971), *Strategy, Policy and Central Management*, Cincinnati: South-Western Publishing Company.

Ouchi, William G. (1981), *Theory Z*, Reading, MA: Addison-Wesley.

Parsons, Talcott (1960), *Structure and Process in Modern Societies*, New York: Free Press.

Pessemier, Edgar A. (1966), *New-Product Decisions: An Analytical Approach*, New York: McGraw-Hill.

Pfeffer, Jeffrey and Gerald R. Salancik (1978), *The External Control of Organizations*, New York: Harper and Row.

Popper, Karl R. (1963), *Conjectures and Refutations*, New York: Harper & Row.

Quinn, James Brian (1981), "Formulating Strategy One Step at a Time," *Journal of Business Strategy*, 1 (Winter), 42–63.

Richards, Max D. (1978), *Organizational Goal Structures*, St. Paul: West Publishing Company.

Roll, Richard (1977), "A Critique of the Asset Pricing Theory's Tests: Part I," *Journal of Financial Economics*, 4 (March), 129–76.

Ross, Stephen A. (1976), "The Arbitrage Theory of Capital Asset Pricing," *Journal of Economic Theory*, 13 (December), 341–60.

——— (1978), "The Current Status of the Capital Asset Pricing Model (CAPM)," *Journal of Finance*, 33 (June), 885–901.

Simon, Herbert A. (1955), "A Behaviorial Model of Rational Choice," *Quarterly Journal of Economics*, 69 (February), 99–118.

——— (1959), "Theories of Decision Making in Economics and Behavioral Science," *American Economic Review*, 49 (June), 253–83.

——— (1964), "On the Concept of Organizational Goal," *Administrative Science Quarterly*, 9 (June), 1–22.

Simon, Leonard S. and Marshall Freimer (1970), *Analytical Marketing*, New York: Harcourt, Brace & World.

Solomon, Ezra (1963), *The Theory of Financial Management*, New York: Columbia University Press,

Stanton, William J. (1978), *Fundamentals of Marketing*, 5th ed., New York: McGraw-Hill.

Stigler, G. J. (1946), "The Economics of Minimum Wage Legislation," *American Economic Review*, 36 (June), 358–65.

——— (1947), "Professor Lester and the Marginalists," *American Economic Review*, 37 (March), 154–57.

Vaile, Roland S. (1950), "Economic Theory and Marketing," in *Theory in Marketing*, Reavis Cox and Wroe Alderson, eds., Chicago: Richard D. Irwin.

Van Horne, James C. (1980), *Financial Management and Policy*, 5th ed., Englewood Cliffs, NJ: Prentice-Hall.

Wind, Yoram (1979), "Product Positioning and Market Segmentation: Marketing and Corporate Perspectives," working paper, The Wharton School, University of Pennsylvania.

——— (1981), "Marketing and the Other Business Functions," in *Research in Marketing*, 5, Jagdish N. Sheth, ed., Greenwich, CT: JAI Press, 237–64.

Wright, Patrick J. (1979), *On A Clear Day You Can See General Motors*, Grosse Pointe, MI: Wright Enterprises.

5

Industry Structure & Competitive Strategy: Keys to Profitability

Michael E. Porter

The focus of structural analysis is on identifying the stable, underlying characteristics of an industry—its economic and technological structure—that shape the arena in which competitive strategy must be set.

The first step in structural analysis is an assessment of the competitive environment in which the company operates—the basic competitive forces and the strength of each in shaping industry structure. The second is an assessment of the company's own strategy—of how well it has positioned itself to prosper in this environment. Taken together, these steps are the key to forecasting a company's earning power

THE SUCCESS OF A COMPANY'S competitive strategy depends on how it relates to its environment. Although the relevant environment is very broad, encompassing social as well as economic forces, the key aspect of the company's environment is the industry or industries in which it operates. Industry structure has a strong influence in defining the rules of the competitive game as well as the strategies potentially available to the company.

The intensity of competition in an industry is not a matter of luck. Rather, competition is rooted in underlying industry economics and goes well beyond the established competitors. Not all industries have equal potential. They differ fundamentally in their ultimate profit potential as the collective strength of the forces of competition differs; the forces range from intense in industries like tires, paper and steel, where no firm earns spectacular returns, to relatively mild in industries such as oil field equipment and services, cosmetics and toiletries, where high returns are common.

The essence of competitive strategy for a company is to find a position in its industry where it can best cope with these competitive forces or can influence them in its favor. Knowledge of the underlying sources of competitive pressure can reveal the basic attractiveness of an industry, highlight the critical strengths and weaknesses of a company, clarify the areas where strategic changes may yield the greatest payoff and pinpoint the industry trends that promise the greatest significance as either opportunities or threats.

Structural Determinants of Competition

Competition in an industry continually works to drive down the rate of return on invested capital toward the competitive floor rate of return, or the return that would be earned by the economist's "perfectly competitive" industry. This competitive floor, or "free market," return is approximated by the yield on long-term government securities adjusted upward by the risk of capital loss. Investors will not tolerate returns below this rate for very long before switching their investment to other vehicles, and firms habitually earning less than this return will eventually go out of business.

The presence of rates of return higher than the adjusted free market return serves to stimulate the inflow of capital into an industry either through new entry or through additional investment by existing competitors. The strength of the competitive forces in an industry determines the degree to which this inflow of investment drives the return down to the free market level, hence the ability of firms to sustain above-average returns.

Michael Porter is a Professor of Business Administration at the Harvard Business School.

Figure 1
Forces Driving Industry competition

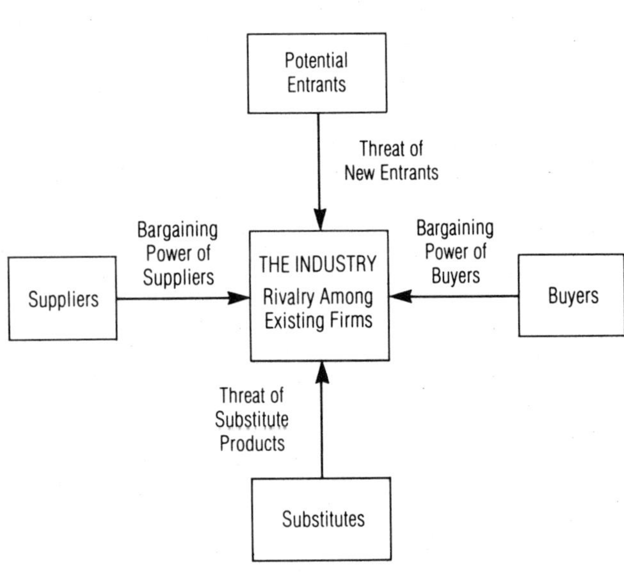

The state of competition in an industry depends on five basic competitive forces, illustrated in Figure 1. The collective strength of these forces determines the ultimate profit potential in the industry, where profit potential is measured in terms of return on invested capital. As Figure 1 demonstrates, competition extends well beyond the established players. Customers, suppliers, substitutes and potential entrants are all competitors and may be more or less prominent depending on the particular circumstances.

All five competitive forces jointly determine the intensity of industry competition and profitability, but the strongest force or forces become crucial from the point of view of strategy formulation. For example, even a company with a very strong market position in an industry where potential entrants are no threat will earn low returns if it faces a superior, lower cost substitute. Even with no substitutes and blocked entry, intense rivalry between existing competitors will limit potential returns.

Different forces take on prominence, of course, in shaping competition in each industry. In the ocean-going tanker industry the key force is probably the buyers (the major oil companies), while in tires it is powerful original equipment market buyers coupled with tough competitors. In the steel industry, the key forces are rivalry with foreign competitors and substitute materials.

The underlying *structure* of an industry, reflected in the strength of its five competitive forces, should be distinguished from the many short-run factors that can affect competition and profitability in a transient way. Fluctuations in economic conditions over the business cycle can influence the short-run profitability of nearly all firms in an industry, as can material shortages, strikes, spurts in demand and the like. While such factors have tactical significance, the focus of structural analysis is on identifying the stable, underlying characteristics of an industry—its economic and technological structure—that shape the arena in which competitive strategy must be set.

Industry structure can shift gradually over time, and firms will have unique strengths and weaknesses in dealing with structure. Yet understanding industry structure must be the starting point for strategy analysis. The key economic and technological characteristics critical to the strength of each competitive force are discussed below.

Threat of Entry

New entrants to an industry bring new capacity, the desire to gain market share and often substantial resources. They can bid down prices or inflate costs, reducing profitability. Companies diversifying through acquisition into an industry from other markets often apply their resources to cause a shake-up, as Philip Morris did with Miller beer. Thus acquisition into an industry with intent to build position should probably be viewed as entry, even if it doesn't add a competitor in the literal sense.

Most often, the decision whether or not to enter or diversify into an industry will depend on the *entry deterring price*. The entry deterring price is that which, adjusted for product quality and service, just balances the potential rewards from entry (forecast by the potential entrant) against the expected costs. Of course, incumbent firms may eliminate the threat of entry by pricing below the hypothetical entry deterring price. If they price above it, gains in terms of profitability may be short-lived, since potential entrants will forecast above-average profits from entry, and will enter.

The cost of entry into an industry will depend in part on the *probable reaction from existing competitors*. If a potential entrant expects the incumbents to respond forcefully to make its stay in the industry a costly and unpleasant one, it may well decide not to enter. If the industry has a history of vigorous retaliation to entrants, if the incumbent firms have substantial resources to fight back (including excess cash and unused borrowing capacity, excess productive capacity or great leverage with distribution channels or customers), or if the industry's growth is sufficiently slow that entry of a new competitor would depress the sales and financial performance of established firms, then potential entrants are likely to meet strong retaliation from incumbents.

The cost of entry will also depend importantly on *barriers to entry* into the industry. Entry barriers are features of an industry that give incumbents inherent advantages over potential entrants. A number of industry characteristics commonly lead to such barriers.

The *need to invest large financial resources in order to compete* creates a barrier to entry, whether those resources must be raised in the capital markets or not. While today's major corporations have the financial resources to enter almost any industry, the huge capital requirements in fields like computers and mineral extraction limit the pool of likely entrants. Capital may be required not only for production facilities, but also for things like customer credit, inventories or covering start-up loses. Xerox created a major barrier to entry in copiers, for example, when it chose to rent copiers rather than sell them outright.

Potential entrants will generally be at a disadvantage in the *capital markets*. Unless a company is entering an industry through diversification, the newcomer is in an inherently riskier position than the established firms, and this will be reflected in the risk premiums it will have to pay to attract capital.

A potential entrant will face barriers if the industry is characterized by *economies of scale*—declines in unit costs of a product (or operation or function that goes into producing a product) as the absolute volume produced per period increases.[1] Scale economies deter entry by forcing the entrant either to come in at large scale and risk strong reaction from existing firms or to accept a cost disadvantage, both undesirable options. Scale economies can be present in nearly every function of a business—production, research and development, marketing, service network, sales force utilization or distribution. For example, scale economies in production, research, marketing and service are probably the key barriers to entry in the mainframe computer industry, as Xerox and GE sadly discovered.

Scale economies may relate to an entire functional area, as in the case of a sales force, or they may stem from particular operations or activities. In television set manufacturing, economies of scale are large in color tube production but less significant in cabinetmaking and set assembly. Each component of costs must be examined separately to determine the extent of economies of scale.

Scale economies may form a particularly significant entry barrier if the companies in an industry are generally diversified or vertically integrated. A company that is part of a multibusiness firm may be able to achieve scale economies if it is able to *share operations or functions* subject to economies of scale with other companies in the firm. Consider, for example, a company that manufactures small electric motors that go into industrial fans, hairdryers and cooling systems for electronic equipment assembled by other divisions of the firm. If its economies of scale in motor manufacturing extend beyond the number of motors needed in any one market, it will reap economies in motor manufacturing that exceed those available if it only manufactured motors for use in, say, hairdryers. Thus related diversification around common operations or functions can remove restraints imposed by limited volume of a given market.[2] The prospective entrant must be appropriately diversified or face a cost disadvantage.

The benefits of sharing are particularly potent when a company can incur *joint costs*. Joint costs occur where a firm producing product A (or an operation or function that is part of producing A) must inherently produce product B. For example, technological constraints limit the amount of space airline passenger services can devote to passengers, but make available cargo space and payload capacity. Since it can spread the cost of putting the plane into the air over both passengers and freight, the firm that competes in both passenger and freight may have a substantial advantage over the firm competing in only one market. A similar advantage accrues to businesses whose manufacturing processes result in by-products. The entrant that cannot capture the highest incremental revenue from the by-products will face a disadvantage if incumbent firms can.

The potential entrant also faces the possibility of foreclosure of inputs or markets for its product if most established competitors in the industry are *integrated* (operate in successive stages of production or distribution). In such cases, incumbents purchase from in-house units or sell their inputs in-house. The unintegrated entrant will face a difficult time getting comparable prices and may get "squeezed" if integrated competitors offer it different terms from those offered their captive units.

Entry can be deterred by an entrant's need to secure *distribution channels* for its products. Existing competitors may have ties with channels based on long relations, high quality service or even exclusive contracts whereby the channel is solely identified with a particular manufacturer. To the extent that logical distribution channels for the product are served by established firms, the newcomer must persuade the channels to accept its product, using price breaks, cooperative advertising allowances and other measures that generally cut into profits. A new food product, for example, must displace others from the fiercely competitive supermarket shelf via promotions, intense selling efforts or heavy advertising to create consumer pull. Sometimes this barrier to entry is so high that, to surmount it, a new firm must create an entirely new distribution channel in order to get into the industry.

Newcomers will find it particularly difficult to compete with established firms for distribution channels and buyers if the industry is characterized by *product differentiation*. Product differentiation means that established firms have brand identification and customer loyalties stemming from past advertising, customer service and product differences. Not infrequently, these firms can benefit from economies of scale as a result. The cost of creating a brand name, for instance, need only be borne once; the name may then be freely applied to other products of the company, subject only to any costs of modification. A newcomer, on the other hand, must spend heavily to overcome existing distributor and customer loyalties. Investments in building a brand name are particularly risky, since they are unrecoverable.

Product differentiation is perhaps the most important entry barrier in baby care products, over-the-counter drugs, cosmetics, investment banking and public accounting. In the brewing industry, product differentiation is coupled with economies of scale in production, marketing, and distribution to create high barriers.

Entry can also be deterred if *switching costs* are high. Switching costs are one-time costs of switching brands or switching from one supplier's product to another's. Switching costs may include such things as employee retraining costs, the cost of new ancillary equipment, the cost and time needed to test or qualify a new source or to redesign a product or even the psychic costs of severing a relationship. If such costs are high, the entrant must offer a major improvement in cost or performance to induce the buyer to switch. For example, suppliers of intravenous solutions and kits for use in hospitals have different procedures for attaching solutions to patients, and the hardware for hanging the solution bottles are not compatible. This industry is characterized by relatively high returns.

Government policy may also represent a substantial entry barrier in some industries. Government can consciously or unconsciously limit or even foreclose entry into industries, using such controls as licensing requirements or limits on access to raw materials (e.g., coal lands or mountains suitable for ski areas). Government regulation restricts entry to such industries as trucking, railroads, liquor retailing, broadcasting and freight forwarding.

More subtle restrictions on entry can stem from government subsidies to incumbents or from governmental controls such as air and water pollution standards or product safety and efficacy regulations. Pollution control requirements can raise capital needed for entry and can increase required technological sophistication and even optimal scale of facilities. Standards for product testing, common in industries like food and other health-related products, can impose substantial lead times on getting into an industry, not only raising the cost of entry but giving established firms ample notice of impending entry and, sometimes, full knowledge of competitor products. Government policy in such areas certainly may have social benefits, but it often has second-order consequences for entry that go unrecognized.

While the barriers mentioned so far can perhaps be surmounted by entrants willing to invest the capital, established firms may have other *cost advantages* not replicable by potential entrants no matter what their size and attained economies of scale. For instance, some industries are characterized by *proprietary product technology*—know-how or techniques that are kept proprietary through patents or secrecy. In others, the established firms may have locked up the most *favorable raw material sources*, or tied up foreseeable raw material needs early at prices reflecting a lower demand for them than currently exists. For example, Frasch sulphur firms like Texas Gulf Sulphur gained control of some very favorable salt dome sulphur deposits many years ago, before mineral right holders were aware of their value as a result of the Frasch mining technology. Discoverers of sulphur deposits were often disappointed oil companies exploring for oil. Similarly, established firms in some industries may have cornered *favorable locations* before market forces bid up prices to capture their full value. Potential newcomers will enter at a permanent competitive disadvantage.

Experience Curve

Another important factor that creates cost advantages is the *experience curve*. In some businesses, unit costs tend to decline as the firm gains more cumulative experience in production. Experience is just a name for certain kinds of technological change. Workers become more efficient (the classic learning curve), layout improves, equipment and processes become specialized. Changes in product design techniques and operations control make manufacturing easier.

Cost declines with experience seem to be most significant in businesses involving a high labor content and/or complex assembly operations (aircraft, shipbuilding). They are nearly always greatest in the early and growth phases of a product's development, diminishing in later phases.

In some ways, cost declines with experience operate in the same manner as scale economies. Experience can lower costs in marketing, distribution and other areas as well as production or operations within production, and each component of costs must be examined for experience effects. Diversification can enhance cost declines due to experience, since diversified firms can share operations or functions subject to experience cost declines and units in diversified firms can benefit from the experience gained by other related units. In the case where an activity like raw material fabrication is shared by multiple business units, experience obviously accumulates faster than it would if the activity were used solely to meet the needs of one company.

Economies of scale are often cited as one of the reasons costs decline with experience, But economies of scale are dependent on volume per period, not cumulative volume, and are very different analytically from cost declines with experience. Economies of scale and experience also have very different properties as entry barriers. The presence of economies of scale *always* leads to cost advantage for the large-scale or properly diversified firm, presupposing that the large firm has the most efficient facilities, distribution systems, service organizations and other functional units for its size.

Experience is a more ethereal entry barrier than scale. The mere presence of an experience curve does not ensure an entry barrier. The experience must be proprietary—i.e., not available to competitors and potential entrants through (1) copying, (2) hiring competitors' employees or (3) purchasing the latest machinery from equipment suppliers or the relevant know-how from consultants or others.

If the experience curve can be kept proprietary by established firms, then they can erect an entry barrier. Newly started firms, with no experience, will have inherently higher costs than established firms and will have to incur heavy start-up losses from below or near-cost pricing before they can gain the experience requisite to cost parity with established firms. Because of their lower costs, established firms (particularly the market share leader) will have higher cash flows to invest in new equipment and technique. New entrants will never catch up. A number of firms (notably Texas Instruments, Black and Decker and Emerson Electric) have built successful strategies based on the experience curve through aggressive investments to build cumulative volume early in the development of their industries, often by pricing in anticipation of future cost declines.

Many times, however, experience cannot be kept proprietary. Even when it can, it may accumulate more rapidly for the second and third firms in the market than it did for the pioneer. The later firms can observe some aspects of the pioneer's operations. In situations where experience cannot be kept proprietary, new entrants may actually have an advantage if they can buy the latest equipment or adapt to new methods unencumbered by having operated the old way in the past.

An experience barrier can be nullified by product or process innovations leading to a substantially new technology that creates an entirely new experience curve.[3] New entrants can leapfrog the industry leaders and alight on the new experience curve, to which the leaders may be poorly positioned to jump. Similarly, technological change may penalize the large-scale firm if facilities designed to reap economies of scale are specialized, hence less flexible in adapting to new technologies.

Commitment either to achieving scale economies or to reducing costs through experience has some potential risks. It may cloud the perception of new technological possibilities, or of other ways of competing less dependent on scale or experience. Emphasis on scale over other valuable entry barriers such as product differentiation may work against image or responsive service. Hewlett-Packard has erected substantial barriers based on technological progressiveness in industries like calculators and minicomputers, where other firms are following strategies based on experience and scale.

Properties of Entry Barriers

All entry barriers can and do change as conditions in the industry change. The expiration of Polaroid's basic patents on instant photography, for instance, greatly reduced its absolute cost entry barrier built by proprietary technology; it is not surprising that Kodak plunged into the market. Product differentiation in the magazine printing industry has all but disappeared, reducing barriers. Conversely, in the auto industry economies of scale increased enormously with post-war automation and vertical integration, virtually stopping successful new entry.

While entry barriers sometimes change for reasons largely outside a company's control, company strategic decisions can have a major impact on entry barriers. In the 1960s, many U.S. wine producers stepped up product introductions, raised advertising levels and expanded distribution nationally, increasing entry barriers by raising economies of scale and product differentiation and making access to distribution channels more difficult. Similarly, decisions by members of the recreational vehicle industry to integrate vertically have greatly increased the economies of scale there.

Finally, some firms may possess resources or skills that allow them to overcome entry barriers into an industry more cheaply than most other firms. Gillette, with well developed distribution channels for razors and blades, faced lower costs of entry into disposable lighters than many other potential entrants would have faced.

Rivalry Between Existing Competitors

Rivalry between existing competitors takes the familiar form of jockeying for position—using tactics like price competition, advertising battles, product introductions and increased customer service or warranties. Rivalry occurs because one or more competitors either feel pressured or see the opportunity to improve position. In most industries, competitive moves by one firm have noticeable effects on its competitors and thus may incite retaliation. Firms are consequently *mutually dependent*.

A sequence of actions and reactions may or may not leave the initiating firm and the industry as a whole better off. If moves and countermoves escalate, then all firms in the industry may suffer and be worse off than before. Some forms of competition (notably price competition) are highly unstable and likely to leave the entire industry worse off from a profitability standpoint. Price cuts are quickly and easily matched by rivals and, once matched, lower revenues for all firms unless industry price elasticity of demand is very great. Advertising battles, on the other hand, may well expand demand or raise the level of product differentiation in the industry, to the benefit of all firms.

Rivalry in some industries is characterized by such phrases as "warlike," "bitter" or "cut-throat," while in other industries it is termed "polite," or "gentlemanly." The intensity of rivalry can be traced to the presence of a number of interacting structural factors.

When the *competitors in an industry are numerous*, the likelihood of mavericks that will touch off rivalry is great, since some firms may believe they can make moves without being noticed. Even if there are relatively few firms, if they are *relatively balanced* in terms of the resources for sustained and vigorous retaliation, they may be prone to take each other on. On the other hand, when an industry is highly concentrated or dominated by one or a few firms, relative power will be stable and apparent to everyone, and the leader or leaders will be able to impose discipline through devices like price leadership.

Slow industry growth is generally a destabilizing force for rivalry, since it can turn competition into a market share game for firms seeking expansion. When industry growth is rapid, firms can improve results just by keeping up with the industry; in fact, all their financial and managerial resources may be consumed by expanding with the industry.

High fixed costs create strong pressures for all firms to fill capacity, which often leads to rapidly escalating price cutting. Many basic materials like paper and aluminum suffer from this problem. The key is fixed costs relative to value added, rather than the absolute level of fixed costs. Firms purchasing a high proportion of costs in outside inputs (low value added) may feel enormous pressures to fill capacity to break even, even if the absolute proportion of fixed costs is low. A similar situation faces industries whose products are very difficult or costly to store. Here firms will be vulnerable to temptations to shade prices in order to ensure sales. This sort of pressure keeps profits low in lobster fishing and in industries that manufacture certain hazardous chemicals.

When the industry *product is perceived as a commodity or near-commodity,* buyer choice will largely be dictated by price and service, creating strong pressures for price and service competition. Differentiation, on the other hand, creates layers of insulation against competitive warfare because buyers have preferences and loyalties to particular sellers. Similar insulation against rivalry is provided by *switching costs* (defined earlier).

Rivalry is increased by pressures that lead to *chronic overcapacity.* For example, where economics dictate that capacity can be augmented only in large increments, capacity additions can be chronically disruptive to the industry supply-demand balance, particularly when there is a risk of bunching of capacity additions. The industry may face chronic periods of the kind of overcapacity and price cutting that afflict chlorine, vinyl chloride and ammonium fertilizer.

Competitors that are diverse in strategies, origins, personalities and relationships to their parent companies create volatile rivalry because they have differing goals and differing ideas about how to compete and are continually colliding head-on in the process. They have a hard time accurately reading each others' intentions and agreeing on the rules of the game for the industry. Strategic choices "right" for one competitor will be "wrong" for the others.

Foreign competitors often add a great deal of diversity to industries because of their differing circumstances and often differing goals. Owner-operators of small manufacturing or service firms may be willing to accept subnormal rates of return on their investment capital in exchange for independence; such low returns may appear unacceptable or irrational to a large publicly held competitor. In such an industry, the posture of the small firms may limit the profitability of the larger concern. Similarly, firms viewing a market as a dumping outlet for excess capacity will adopt policies contrary to those of firms that view the market as their main business.

Differences in the way companies competing in an industry relate to their corporate parents is another important source of diversity. A company that is one part of a vertical chain of businesses within its corporate organization may well adopt goals very different from those of a free-standing company competing in the same industry. A company that represents a "cash cow" in its parent company's portfolio of businesses will behave differently from one being developed for long-run growth.

Industry rivalry becomes even more volatile if a number of firms in the industry have *high stakes in achieving success*. For example, a diversified firm may place great importance on achieving success in a particular industry in order to further its overall corporate strategy. Or a foreign firm like Bosch, Sony or Philips may perceive a strong need to establish a solid position in the U.S. market in order to build global prestige or technological credibility. Such firms may be willing to sacrifice profitability for the sake of expansion.

Finally, industry rivalry can be volatile when an industry faces high *exit barriers*—factors that keep companies competing in businesses even though they may be earning low or even negative returns on investment. Excess capacity does not leave the industry, and companies that lose the competitive battle do not give up. Rather, they hang on grimly and, because of their weakness, sometimes resort to extreme tactics that can destroy the profitability of the entire industry.

Exit barriers may be high when assets are highly specialized to a particular business or location, hence difficult to liquidate; when labor agreements, resettlement costs or spare parts maintenance create fixed costs of exit; when interrelationships between one company and others in a multi-business firm in terms of image, marketing ability, access to financial markets, shared facilities and so on lend the business broader strategic importance; when government denies or discourages exit because of job loss and regional economic effects (particularly common outside the U.S.); or when managements are unwilling to make economically justified exit decisions because of loyalty to employees, fear of the consequences for their own careers, pride or other emotional reasons.

While exit barriers and entry barriers are conceptually separate, their combination is an important aspect of the analysis of an industry. Exit and entry barriers often rise and fall together. The presence of substantial economies of scale in production, for example, usually implies specialized assets, as does the presence of proprietary technology. Figure 2 illustrates the possible combinations. The best case from the viewpoint of industry profits is where entry barriers are high but exit barriers are low. Here entry will be deterred and unsuccessful competitors will leave the industry. Where both entry and exit barriers are high, profit potential is high but is usually accompanied by more risk. Although entry is deterred, unsuccessful firms will stay and fight in the industry.

While the case of low entry and exit barriers is unexciting from a profitability standpoint, the worst case is where entry barriers are low and exit barriers are high. Here entrants will be attracted by upturns in economic conditions or other temporary windfalls. They will not leave the industry, however, when results deteriorate. As a result, industry capacity will stack up and profitability will usually be chronically poor.

Shifting Rivalry

Industry features that determine the intensity of competitive rivalry can and do change. As an industry matures, its growth rate declines, resulting in intensified rivalry, declining profits and (often) a shakeout. In the booming recreational vehicle industry of the early 1970s, nearly every producer did well; but slow growth since then has eliminated the high returns to all except the strongest members. The same story has been played out in industry after industry—snowmobiles, aerosol packaging and sports equipment, to name a few.

Rivalry can also shift when an acquisition introduces a very different personality into an industry. This has been the case with Philip Morris' acquisition of Miller Beer and

Figure 2
Exit and Entry Barriers Combine

		EXIT BARRIERS	
		Low	High
ENTRY BARRIERS	Low	Low Returns	Worst Case
	High	Best Case	High Returns but Risky

Procter & Gamble's acquisition of Charmin Paper Company. Also, technological innovation can boost the level of fixed costs in the production process and raise the volatility of rivalry, as it did in the shift from batch to continuous-line photofinishing in the 1960s.

While a company must live with many of the factors determining the intensity of industry rivalry that are built into industry economics, it may have some latitude to influence rivalry through its choice of strategy. A company may try to raise buyers' switching costs by designing its product into its customers' operations or by making its customers dependent for technical advice. A company can attempt to raise product differentiation through new kinds of service, marketing innovations or product changes. Focusing selling efforts on the fastest growing segments of the industry or on market areas with the lowest fixed costs can reduce the impact of industry rivalry. If it is feasible, a company can try to avoid confrontation with competitors having high exit barriers, thus sidestepping involvement in bitter price cutting.

Pressure from Substitute Products

All firms in an industry are competing, in a broad sense, with industries producing substitute products. Substitutes limit the profit potential of an industry by placing a ceiling on the prices firms in the industry can charge. The more attractive the price-performance tradeoff offered by substitutes, the tighter the lid on industry profits. Sugar producers confronted with the large-scale commercialization of high fructose corn syrup, a sugar substitute, are learning this lesson today, as are producers of acetylene and rayon, who face tough competition from lower cost alternatives.

Substitutes not only limit profits in normal times, but also reduce the bonanza an industry can reap in boom times. In 1978, the producers of fiberglass insulation enjoyed unprecedented demand as a result of high energy costs and severe winter weather. But the industry's ability to raise prices was tempered by the plethora of insulation substitutes, including cellulose, rock wool and styrofoam. These substitutes are bound to become an even stronger force once the current round of plant additions by fiberglass insulation producers has boosted capacity enough to meet demand (and then some).

Identifying substitute products entails searching for other products that can perform the same *function* as the product of the industry. Sometimes this can be a subtle task, one that takes the analyst into businesses seemingly far removed from the industry in question. Securities, for example, face increasing competition from alternative investments such as real estate, insurance and money market funds.

Government regulations, subsidies and tax policies should also be considered in the search for substitutes. The U.S. government is currently promoting solar heating, for example, using tax incentives and research grants. Government decontrol of natural gas is quickly eliminating acetylene as a chemical feedstock. Safety and pollution standards also affect relative cost and quality of substitutes.

Attention should focus on substitute products that (a) are enjoying steady improvement in price-performance tradeoff with the industry's product, (b) would entail minimal switching costs for prospective buyers or (c) are produced by industries earning high profits. In the latter case, substitutes often come rapidly into play if some development increases competition in their industries and causes price reduction or performance improvement.

Effective defense against substitute products may require *collective industry action*. While advertising by one firm in an industry does little to bolster the industry's position against a substitute, heavy and sustained advertising by all industry participants may well improve the industry's collective position against the substitute. Similar arguments apply to collective industry response through industry groups and other means in areas such as product quality improvement, marketing efforts and product distribution.

Trend analysis can be important in deciding whether company strategy should be directed toward heading off a substitute strategically or accepting the substitute as a key competitive force. Electronic alarm systems, for example, represent a potent substitute in the security guard industry. Electronic systems can only become more important as a substitute since labor-intensive guard services face inevitable cost escalation, while electronic systems are highly likely to improve in performance and decline in cost. Here the appropriate response of security guard firms is probably to offer packages of guards and electronic systems, with the security guard redefined as a skilled operator, rather than attempt to compete against electronic systems with a traditional guard service.

Bargaining Power of Buyers

Buyers represent a competitive force because they can bid down prices, demand higher quality or more services, and play competitors off against each other—all at the expense of industry profitability. The power of each important buyer group depends on a number of characteristics of its market situation and on the relative importance of its purchases from the industry compared with the industry's overall business.

A buyer group will be powerful if it *purchases large volumes relative to seller sales*, so that retaining its business is financially important to the seller. Large volume buyers are particularly potent forces if heavy fixed costs characterize the industry (as in corn refining and bulk chemicals) and raise the stakes to keep capacity occupied.

Buyer power is enhanced if the products purchased from the industry *represent a significant fraction of total purchases*. In this case, the buyer will be prone to expend the resources necessary to shop for a favorable price and to purchase selectively. If the product sold by the industry is a small fraction of the buyer's costs, the buyer will usually be much less price sensitive. Similarly, a buyer suffering from *low profits* has great incentive to lower purchasing costs. Suppliers to Chrysler, for example, are complaining that they are being pressed for superior terms. Highly profitable buyers are generally less price sensitive and more concerned about the long-run health of their suppliers (that is, unless the purchase represents a large fraction of their costs). Buyer power is also increased if buyers have a lot of *information* about market conditions, supplier costs and offers to other buyers.

If buyers are either already partially integrated or *pose a strong threat of backward integration*, they are in a position to demand bargaining concessions. Major automobile producers like General Motors and Ford frequently use this bargaining lever. They engage in the practice of *tapered integration*, or producing some of their needs for a given component in-house and purchasing the rest from outside suppliers. Not only is their threat of further integration particularly credible, but partial manufacture in-house gives them detailed knowledge of costs, which is a great aid in negotiation. Buyer power can be partially neutralized when firms in the industry offer a threat of forward integration into the buyer's industry.

Finally, the *impact of the supplier's product* on the buyer's business will help determine the bargaining power of purchasers. If the quality of the buyer's product is very much affected by the quality of the industry's product, the buyer will generally be less price sensitive. In oil field equipment, for instance, a malfunction can lead to large losses (as witness the enormous cost of the recent failure of a blowout preventer in a Mexican offshore oil well); the quality of enclosures for electronic medical and test instruments can greatly influence the user's impression about the quality of the equipment inside.

Finally, *switching costs* (defined earlier) lock the buyer to particular sellers and mitigate buyer power. On the other hand, if the industry's products are standard or undifferentiated, buyers, sure that they can always find alternative suppliers, may play one company against another, as they do in aluminum extrusion.

Most sources of buyer power apply to consumer as well as to industrial and commercial buyers. For example, consumers tend to be more price sensitive if they are purchasing products that are undifferentiated or expensive relative to their incomes.

The power of wholesalers and retailers is determined by the same rules, with one important addition. Retailers can gain significant bargaining power over manufacturers if they can *influence consumer's purchasing decisions*, as they do in audio components, jewelry, appliances and sporting goods. Similarly, wholesalers can gain bargaining power if they can influence the decisions of the retailers or other firms to which they sell.

Altering Buying Power

The power of buyers can rise or fall as the underlying factors creating buyer power change with time or as a result of a company's strategic decisions. In the ready-to-wear clothing industry, for example, the buyers (department stores and clothing stores) have become more concentrated and control has passed to large chains; as a result, the industry has come under increasing buyer pressure and suffered failing profit margins. So far the industry has been unable to differentiate its products or to engender switching costs that would lock its buyers in sufficiently to neutralize these trends.

A company's choice of the buyer group it sells to is a crucial strategic decision. A company can improve its strategic posture by finding buyers who possess the least power to influence it adversely—in other words by *buyer selection*. Rarely do all the buyer groups a company sells to enjoy equal power. Even if a company sells to a single industry, there are usually segments within that industry that exercise less power (and that are less price sensitive) than others. For example, the replacement market for most products is less price sensitive than the original equipment market.

Bargaining Power of Suppliers

Suppliers can exert a competitive force in an industry by raising prices or reducing the quality of the goods they sell. Such price increases can squeeze profitability out of an industry unable to recover cost increases in its own prices. By raising their prices, for example, chemical companies have contributed to the erosion of profitability of contract aerosol packagers because the packagers, facing intense competition from self-manufacture by their customers, have limited freedom to raise their prices.

The conditions making suppliers powerful are largely the inverse of those making buyers powerful. If a supplier group is *dominated by a few companies and more concentrated than the industry it sells to*, it will be able to exert considerable influence on prices, quality and terms. On the other hand, the power of even large powerful suppliers can be checked if they have to compete with *substitutes*. Industries producing alternative sweeteners, for example, compete sharply for many applications even though individual suppliers are large relative to individual customers.

If suppliers sell to a number of industries, so that one particular *industry does not represent a significant fraction of sales*, they will be much more prone to exert pricing pressure. If the industry is an important customer, suppliers' fortunes will be closely tied to the industry, and suppliers will want to protect the industry through reasonable pricing and assistance in activities like research and development and lobbying.

Differentiation and switching costs cut off buyers' options in playing one supplier off against another and raise supplier power. And a *credible threat of forward integration* provides a check against an industry's ability to improve the terms on which it purchases.

It is important to recognize *labor* as a supplier, and one that exerts great power in many industries. There is substantial empirical evidence that scarce, highly skilled employees (e.g., engineers and scientists) and/or tightly unionized labor can bargain away a significant fraction of potential profits in an industry. The features that determine the potential power of employees as a supplier include those outlined above plus labor's *degree of organization* and the ability of the supply of scarce varieties of employees to *expand*. Where labor is strongly organized and supply of scarce employees constrained from expansion then can be a factor in competition. Where labor is strongly organized and supply of scarce employees constrained from expansion they can be a factor in competition.

Government, which has been discussed primarily in terms of its possible impact on entry barriers, must also be recognized as a potentially powerful buyer and supplier. In these roles, government can often influence industry competition by the policies it adopts. Government plays a crucial role as a buyer of defense-related products and as a supplier of timber through the Forest Service's control of vast timber reserves in the western United States. Many times government's role as a supplier or buyer is determined more by political factors than by economic circumstances, and this is probably a fact of life.

The conditions determining supplier power are frequently beyond a company's control. However, as with buyer power, the firm can sometimes improve its situation through strategy. It can promote a threat of backward integration, seek to eliminate switching costs and the like.

Structural Analysis and Competitive Strategy

Once the forces affecting competition in an industry and their underlying causes have been diagnosed, a company is in a position to identify its strengths and weaknesses relative to the industry. The crucial strengths and weaknesses from a strategic standpoint are the company's posture vis-à-vis the underlying causes of each competitive force. Where does it stand against substitutes? Against the sources of entry barriers? In coping with rivalry from established competitors?

Competitive strategy is taking offensive or defensive action in order to strengthen a company's position in relation to the five competitive forces—positioning the company so that its capabilities provide the best defense against the existing array of competitive forces, influencing the balance of forces through strategic moves that improve the company's relative position or anticipating shifts in the factors underlying the forces and responding so as to exploit change by choosing a strategy appropriate to the new competitive balance before rivals recognize it.

A *positioning strategy* takes the structure of the industry as given and matches the company's strengths and weaknesses to it, building defenses against the competitive forces or finding positions in the industry where the forces are weakest. Knowledge of the company's capabilities and of the causes of the competitive forces will highlight the areas where the company should confront competition and where it should avoid competition. If the company is a low-cost producer, for example, it may choose to confront powerful buyers while it takes care to sell them only products not vulnerable to competition from substitutes.

Alternatively, a company can take an offensive approach by developing *strategies designed to influence the balance of competitive forces*. Innovations in marketing can raise brand identification or otherwise differentiate the company's product. Capital investments in large-scale facilities or vertical integration can bolster entry barriers. Structural analysis can be used to identify the factors driving competition that will be most susceptible to strategic actions.

Industry evolution is important strategically because evolution can present opportunities to *exploit changes in the sources of competition*. In the familiar product life cycle pattern of industry development, for example, growth rates change as the business matures, advertising declines and companies tend to integrate vertically.

These trends are not so important in themselves; what is critical is whether they affect the structural sources of competition. For example, extensive vertical integration, both in manufacturing and in software development, is taking place in the maturing minicomputer industry. This very significant trend has greatly increased economies of scale as well as the amount of capital necessary to compete in the industry. This in turn has raised entry barriers and threatens to drive some smaller competitors out of the industry.

Obviously, the trends carrying the highest priority from a strategic standpoint are those that affect the most important sources of competition in the industry and those that elevate new structural factors to the forefront. In contract aerosol packaging, for instance, the dominant trend toward less product differentiation has increased the power of buyers, lowered the barriers to entry and intensified competition.

The task of structural analysis in the long run is to examine each competitive force, forecast the magnitude of each underlying cause and construct a composite picture of the likely profit potential of the industry. Of course, this picture may differ considerably from present realities. Today, the solar heating business is populated by dozens and perhaps hundreds of companies, none with a major market position. Entry is easy and competitors are battling to establish solar heating as a superior substitute for conventional heating methods.

The potential of solar heating will depend largely on the shape of future barriers to entry, the improvement of the industry's position relative to substitutes, the ultimate intensity of competition and the power that will be captured by buyers and suppliers. These characteristics will, in turn, be influenced by such factors as the establishment of brand identities, the creation of significant economies of scale or experience curves in equipment manufacture, the ultimate capital costs and the eventual importance of fixed costs in production.

Of course, no structural analysis can be complete without a diagnosis of how present and future government policy, at all levels, may affect competitive conditions. For purposes of strategic analysis it is usually more illuminating to consider how government affects competition through the five competitive forces than to consider it as a force in and of itself. However, strategy may well involve treating government as a factor to be influenced.

Structural Analysis and Diversification

The framework for analyzing industry competition is obviously useful in setting diversification strategy, since it provides a guide for answering the extremely difficult question inherent in diversification decisions. What is the potential of this business? The framework may allow a company to spot an industry with a good future before this potential is reflected in the prices of acquisition candidates. It will also help a company identify industries where its strengths will allow it to overcome entry barriers more cheaply than other firms. And the framework can help in identifying acquisitions that can take advantage of existing operations—for example, acquisitions that would allow a firm to overcome key entry barriers by providing shared functions or pre-existing relations with distribution channels.

References

1. To avoid needless repetition, the term "product," rather than "product or service," is used throughout to refer to the output of an industry. The principles of structural analysis will apply equally to product and service businesses. They also apply to industry competition in any country or international market, although some of the institutional circumstances may differ.
2. For this entry barrier to be significant, it is crucial that the shared operation or function be subject to economies of scale that extend beyond the size of any one market. If this is not the case, cost savings of sharing can be illusory. A company may see its costs decline after entering a related business as overhead is spread, but this depends solely on the presence of excess capacity in the operation or function in the base business. Such economies are short-run, and once capacity is fully utilized the true cost of the shared operation will become apparent.
3. For an example of this drawn from the history of the automobile industry, see William J. Abernathy and Kenneth Wayne. "The Limits of the Learning Curve," *Harvard Business Review*, September–October 1974, p. 109.

6

The Strategic Triangle

Kenichi Ohmae

The job of the strategist is to achieve superior performance, relative to competition, in the key factors for success of the business.

IN THE CONSTRUCTION of any business strategy, three main players must be taken into account: the corporation itself, the customer, and the competition. Each of these "strategic three C's" is a living entity with its own interests and objectives. We shall call them collectively, the "strategic triangle."

Seen in the context of the strategic triangle, the job of the strategist is to achieve superior performance, relative to competition, in the key factors for success of the business. At the same time, the strategist must be sure that his strategy properly matches the strengths of the corporation with the needs of a clearly defined market. Positive matching of the needs and objectives of the two parties involved is required for a lasting good relationship; without it, the corporation's long-term viability may be at stake.

But such matching is relative. If the competition is able to offer a better match, the corporation will be at a disadvantage over time. If the corporation's approach to the customer is identical to that of the competition, the customer will be unable to distinguish between their respective offerings. The results could be price war, which may bring short-term benefits to the customer but will hurt the corporation as well as its competitors. A successful strategy is one that ensures a better or stronger matching of corporate strengths to customer needs than is provided by competitors.

In terms of these three key players, strategy is defined as the way in which a corporation endeavors to differentiate itself positively from its competitors, using its relative corporate strengths to better satisfy customer needs (Figure 1).

Kenichi Ohmae is Director of McKinsey & Co. and this article is excerpted from his book, *The Mind of the Strategist*.

Figure 1
The strategic three C's.

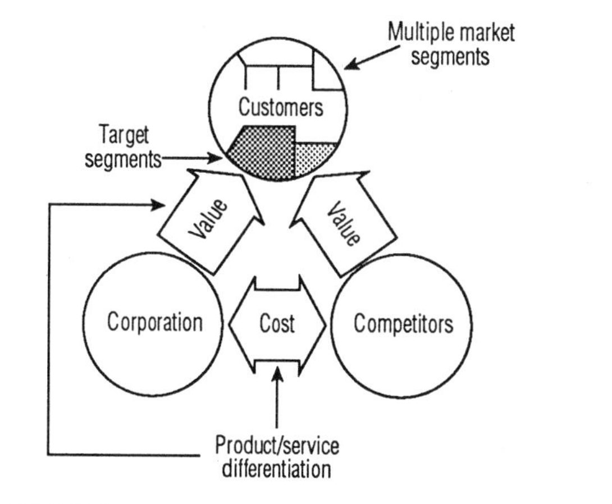

Strategic Planning Units

For a large company made up of a number of different businesses selling to different customer groups, there is clearly more than one strategic triangle to be dealt with and more than one strategy to be developed. The question is, how many? At what level in the organization does it make sense to try to develop a strategy?

To develop and implement an effective strategy, a business unit needs to have full freedom of operation vis-à-vis each of the three key players. With respect to customers, it must be able to address the total market, not just its sections. If the strategic planning unit is defined too narrowly—i.e., placed too low in the organization—it may lack the authority to take a total market perspective. This will be a handicap if the competitors' perspective takes in the entire needs of the customer, including some that cannot be detected through the limited lens of a business unit. For example, if a customer is looking for integrated electronic components, the supplier who offers only a specialized switch will be at a disadvantage.

In order to be able to respond with maximum freedom to the total needs of the customer, the strategic planning unit (SPU) needs, in terms of the corporation itself, to encompass all the critical functions. These functions might range all the way from procurement, design and engineering, manufacturing, and sales and marketing to distribution and service. This is not to say that the SPU may not share certain resources—e.g., R&D—with other units. Rather, it means that a good business unit strategy must address all the functional aspects of customer needs and competition. A conventional organizational unit may not have every key function reporting to it, but in strategic planning one needs to explore every possibility of utilizing the corporation's relative strengths to achieve differentiation from the competitor. Such differentiation comes only from differences in functional strengths, singly or in combination.

Unable to achieve competitive differentiation by strengthening its distribution and service network, a Japanese manufacturer of air-conditioning equipment decided to do so by developing a line of sturdy, highly reliable, but expensive home air-conditioners. Being an engineering-oriented company, it could do this very well. What it couldn't do, it turned out, was sell the product.

In fact, it failed to achieve a share of even 1 percent, and for a reason that had never entered management's head. Distributors, the real decision makers when it comes to brand selection, rejected the new line completely. Why? The units were too heavy to be lifted by an ordinary two-person installation crew. Instead of thinking through the strategic implications of all the key functions, this manufacturer had resorted to its favorite solutions—engineering—prematurely.

Existing functional strengths can, of course, often be successfully exploited to gain the desired differentiation. Another company, a maker of plain-paper copiers, was handicapped by a relatively weak servicing network compared with that of its dominant competitor. Recognizing its functional weakness, this company decided to compensate by exploiting its strengths: engineering, manufacturing efficiency, and quality control. It developed a line of machines that had just two advantages over the competitor's offerings: they were relatively service-free and slightly cheaper. This combination enabled the company to increase its market share rather quickly.

Broad Perspective Needed

In addition to surveying all the corporation's critical functions, the strategist must be able to look at competition in its totality, including such critical strategic elements as the competitor's R&D capabilities, shared resources in procurement, manufacturing, sales and service, or other sources of profit (including all the other businesses in which the competitor may be engaged). He must also be able to put himself mentally in the place of a strategic planner in the rival company and thus ferret out the key perceptions and assumptions on which the competitor's strategy is based.

Faced with a major worldwide shipbuilding crisis, Mitsubishi Heavy Industries has been able gradually to shift its permanently employed excess shipbuilding labor to its other businesses and subsidiaries, such as automobiles, chemical plants, power plants, and its other metal-forging and fabrication operations. Because its competitors lacked Mitsubishi's flexibility, their shipbuilding became extremely uncompetitive and unprofitable.

Strategic planning units, then, are best established at a level where they can freely address (1) all key segments of customer groups that are similar in needs and objectives, (2) all key functions of the corporation so that they can deploy whatever functional expertise is needed to establish a positive differentiation from the competition in the eyes of the customer, and (3) all key aspects of the competitor (see Figure 2) so that the corporation can seize an advantage when opportunity offers—and conversely, so that the competitors will not be able to catch the corporation off balance by exploiting unsuspected sources of strength.

Figure 2
Essential dimensions of a strategic planning unit

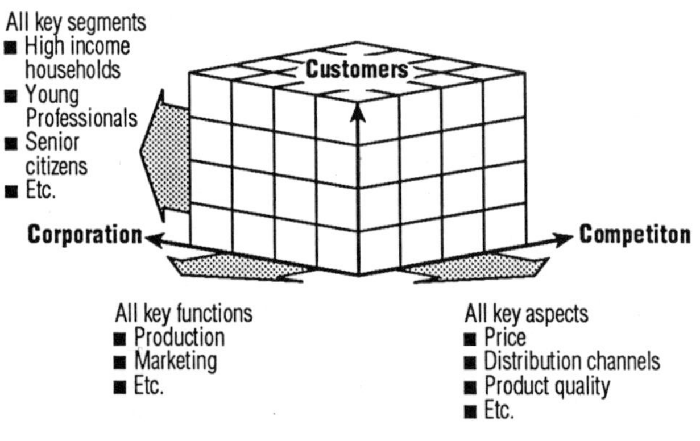

Definitional Problems

Strategic planning units should not be defined so narrowly that they lack the required degree of freedom vis-à-vis the strategic three C's. For example, a strategy for farm tractor engines would be ineffective because the strategic unit is at too low a level in the organization to (1) consider product applications and customer groups other than farmers, or (2) cope with competitors manufacturing engines for marine, truck, and/or construction equipment applications, or even with general-application original equipment manufacturer (OEM) specialists, who might enter the farm tractor market at almost any time with products having a totally different set of boundary conditions. A better choice for this strategic business unit might be small diesel engines, because such units would potentially have a broad enough perspective and adequate strategic degrees of freedom.

By the same token, a strategic planning unit that is too broadly defined cannot develop a really effective strategy. For example, a strategy for medical care would embrace equipment, service, hospitals, education, self-discipline, and even social welfare. Each of the three key players—the strategic three C's—might consist of dozens of totally different elements with different objectives and functions, making the interaction matrix a nightmare of complexity. Such a strategy would have to be expressed in the most general terms or developed in very great depth at enormous effort, to permit a reasonable understanding of the strategic thrust for the corporation. A more sensible strategy could be constructed for an intermediate unit making related kinds of equipment, e.g., blood analyzers, tomographic scanners, and back-room electronic data processing (EDPO) systems. The reason is simply that at this level, where a fairly consistent group of customers and competitors with similar needs and wants appears, functional differentiation—be it in terms of technology or distribution—becomes possible.

We see other examples of wrongly defined strategic business units in the likes of a "strategy" for hospital supply logistics, a "strategic plan" for the XYZ Company's purchasing department, or an Agriculture Ministry's "strategy" for its irrigation program. The problems addressed in these examples lack one or more critical dimensions of strategy. When no competition exists, there is no need to strategize; the need is rather to think about how to make operational improvements in the service provided to the customers or recipients. Another weakness in such strategies is the lack of sufficient degrees of freedom in the planning unit. The scope of the strategy is restricted to one or two functional departments, which may be unable to respond to the total needs of the customer, let alone to a comprehensive attack by competitors.

Testing the Decision

Business unit definition always leaves room for dispute. Halfway into the process of strategy development, therefore, when the basic parameters of the three key players have become clear, it is a good idea to reassess the legitimacy of the unit originally chosen by asking three key questions:

1. Are customer wants well defined and understood by the industry, and is the market segmented so that differences in those wants are treated differently?
2. Is the business unit equipped to respond functionally to the basic wants and needs of customers in the defined segments?
3. Do competitors have different sets of operating conditions that could give them a relative advantage over the business unit in question?

If the answers give reason to doubt the business unit's ability to compete effectively in the market, the unit should be redefined to better meet customer needs and competitive threats.

In the next three chapters [in *The Mind of the Strategist*] we will be surveying the broad categories of strategy, with each chapter focusing on a particular point of the strategic triangle: the customer and the market environment, the corporation itself, and the competition.

Nothing is more self-contradictory than to talk about "creative" strategic thinking and, in the next breath, to give codified recipes for developing strategies of various sorts. Rather than that, my purpose will be to show that an initial focus on any one of the three key players must eventually lead back to its strategic tie-in with the others. Accordingly, the shrewd strategist will always try to view the strategic three C's in perspective and try to influence the dynamics of the relationships among them so as to expand the corporation's relative advantage.

7

Assessing Advantage: A Framework for Diagnosing Competitive Superiority

George S. Day & Robin Wensley

Management must understand the reasons for the current advantages or deficiencies of the business and the vulnerability of the advantages to copying or leap-frogging by competitors.

Strategy is about seeking new edges in a market while slowing the erosion of present advantages. Effective strategy moves are grounded in valid and insightful monitoring of the current competitive position coupled with evidence that reveals the skills and resources affording the most leverage on future cost and differentiation advantages. Too often the available measures and methods do not satisfy these requirements. Only a limited set of measures may be used, depending on whether the business starts with the market and uses a customer-focused approach or alternatively adopts a competitor-centered perspective. To overcome possible myopia, the evidence of advantage should illuminate the sources of advantage as well as the manifestations of superior customer value and cost superiority, and should be based on a balance of customer and competitor perspectives.

THE NOTION that superior performance requires a business to gain and hold an advantage over competitors is central to contemporary strategic thinking. Businesses seeking advantage are exhorted to develop distinctive competences and manage for lowest delivered cost or differentiation through superior customer value. The promised payoff is market share dominance and profitability above average for the industry.

George S. Day is Magna International Professor of Business Strategy, University of Toronto. Robin Wensley is Professor of Marketing, University of Warwick, UK.

This advice is sound, but usually difficult to follow. Management first must understand the reasons for the current advantages or deficiencies of the business and the vulnerability of the advantages to copying or leap-frogging by competitors. Without a proper diagnosis, managers cannot choose the best moves to defend or enhance the current position. For many reasons the prevailing approaches to understanding competitive advantages are unlikely to yield valid and insightful diagnoses. We therefore evaluate the current approaches and methods within an organizing framework that clarifies the nature of competitive advantage. Our primary objective, however, is to use this framework to propose a process that can be used to ensure a thorough and balanced assessment of the reasons for the competitive position of a business.

Perspectives on competitive position. Little is known about how managers decide what advantages distinguish their business and how those advantages were gained. Two distinct approaches have been identified; one starts with the market and is customer-focused and the other is primarily competitor-centered.

Competitor-centered assessments are based on direct management comparisons with a few target competitors. This approach often is seen in stalemated industries where the emphasis is on "beat the competition." The key question is, "How do our capabilities and offerings compare with those of competitors?" These businesses watch costs closely, quickly match the marketing initiatives of competitors, and look for their sustainable edge in technology. Managers keep a close watch on market share and contracts won or lost to detect changes in competitive position.

Customer-focused assessments start with detailed analyses of customer benefits within end-use segments and work backward from the customer to the company to identify the actions needed to improve performance. This "market back" orientation is found in service-intensive industries such as investment banking where new services are easily imitated, cost of funds is the same, and entry is easy (Bhide 1986). Relatively little attention is given to competitors' capabilities and performance—the emphasis is on the quality of customer relationships. Evidence of continuing customer satisfaction and loyalty is more meaningful than market share.

Why should it matter how managers view the arena in which they compete? The reason is that market environments are not unambiguous realities. They are given meaning in the minds of managers through processes of selective attention and simplification (Pfeffer and Salancik 1978). Otherwise managers could not possibly cope with the myriad of trends and events that must be organized, analyzed for patterns, and acted upon. Managers therefore adopt a customer-focused or competitor-centered perspective to help simplify their environment and decide what information is to be gathered and how it is to be screened and interpreted.

Simplification comes at a cost, which is the risk that only a partial and biased picture of reality is created. A competitor-centered perspective leads to a preoccupation with costs and controllable activities that can be compared directly with corresponding activities of close rivals. Customer-focused approaches have the advantage of examining the full range of competitive choices in light of the customers' needs and perceptions of superiority, but lack an obvious connection to activities and variables that are controlled by management. Clearly a balance of the two characteristic perspectives is needed. In practice most businesses tilt—in some cases very sharply—toward one or the other.

A significant complication in the search for a balanced perspective is the confusing welter of overlapping meanings of "competitive advantage." Because there is no agreement on what elements to include or how they are related, information gaps cannot be identified. We address this problem with an organizing framework that distinguishes the sources of advantage from their consequences for relative competitive position and performance superiority. We then use this framework to guide an evaluation of the many ways in which competitive advantages have been measured. For example, we examine the merits of management judgments of strengths and weaknesses and how they compare with measures of market share, comparisons of the relative size of resource commitments, and customer comparisons of competitors on their purchase criteria. Eleven distinct measurement approaches are evaluated for (1) *conceptual validity* (is the measure compatible with the framework?), (2) *measurement feasibility* (does the measure employ readily available inputs that are likely to provide reliable and unbiased information?), and (3) *diagnostic* insights (will the measure yield information that can guide strategic choices to enhance the long-run value of the business?). Finally, we propose steps that can be taken to reorient marketing research to offer a balanced view of present and prospective advantages. The payoff for management is better insights into the actions that promise the greatest effect on the competitive position of a business.

The Concept of Competitive Advantage

There is no common meaning for "competitive advantage" in practice or in the marketing strategy literature. Sometimes the term is used interchangeably with "distinctive competence" to mean relative superiority in skills and resources. Another widespread meaning refers to what we observe in the market—positional superiority, based on the provision of superior customer value or the achievement of lower relative costs, and the resulting market share and profitability performance.

Neither of these meanings gives a complete picture, but taken together they describe both the state of advantage and how it was gained.[1] This integrated view is based on positional and performance superiority being a consequence of relative superiority in the skills and resources a business deploys. These skills and resources reflect the pattern of past investments to enhance competitive position. The sustainability of this positional advantage requires that the business set up barriers that make imitation difficult. Because these barriers to imitation are continually eroding, the firm must continue investing to sustain or improve the advantage. Thus, the creation and sustenance of a competitive advantage are the outcome of a long-run feedback or cyclical process (Figure 1).

Underlying the simple, sequential determinism of the source → position → performance framework is a complex environment fraught with uncertainty and distorted by feedbacks, lags, and structural rigidities. Before introducing these complexities, we descfibe each of the primary elements of the framework.

Figure 1
The elements of competitive advantage

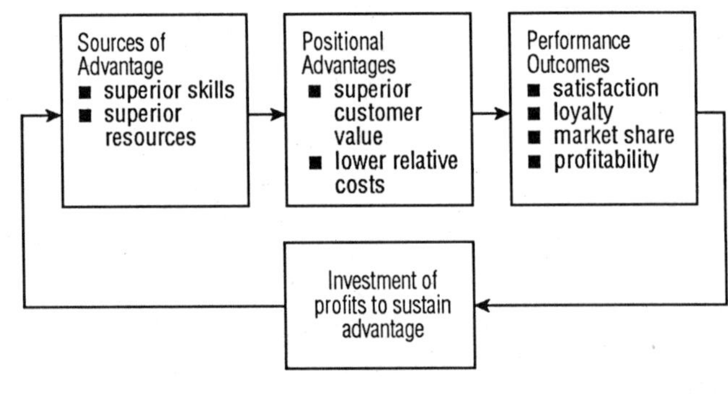

Sources of Advantage

Superior skills and resources, taken together, represent the ability of a business to do more or do better (or both) than its competitors.

Superior skills are the distinctive capabilities of personnel that set them apart from the personnel of competing firms. Some of the benefits of superior skills arise from the ability to perform individual functions more effectively than other firms. For example, superior engineering or technical skills may lead to greater precision or reliability in the finished product. Other skills are derived from the systems and organization structure that enable a firm to adapt more responsively and faster to changes in market requirements.

Superior resources are more tangible requirements for advantage that enable a firm to exercise its capabilities. They may reside in the scale of the manufacturing facility, the location, the breadth of salesforce and distribution coverage, the availability of automated assembly lines, or the family brand name.

The distinction between the antecedent *sources* of advantage and the *positional* advantages that result when they are deployed adroitly is seen readily in successful turnaround strategies such as that of Foremost-McKesson in drug retailing. The management recognized that their skills—derived from an in-depth knowledge of their suppliers' and customers' businesses and the myriad of products they handle—could be parlayed into something more than a delivery and billing service. By enhancing these skills with heavy investments in data processing hardware and systems resources, the firm sharply reduced the costs of the many activities between the suppliers' finished goods and the pharmacy shelf. These actions made the firm so efficient that its suppliers could not possibly do as well on their own. The resulting information was used to offer unique value-added services to both suppliers and customers. Foremost now can help manufacturers manage inventories, analyze marrket data, and plan new product development efforts. Retailers are tied more closely through leases of electronic ordering equipment, shelf management plans, and even the provision of price labels.

Positions of Advantage

The positional advantages of a business are directly analogous to competitive mobility barriers that could deter a firm from shifting its strategic position. They are understood best within the value chain or business system framework attributed to McKinsey and Co. but largely developed into a management tool by Porter (1985). A value chain first classifies the activities of the firm into the discrete steps performed to design, produce, market, deliver, and service a product. Supporting these specific value-creation activities are firm-wide activities such as procurement, human resource management, and technology development as well as the infrastructure of systems and management that ties the value chain together. Only activities with a great impact on differentiation, that account for a large or growing proportion of costs, need be considered.

Lowest delivered cost positions. An overall cost edge is gained by performing most activities at a lower cost than competitors while offering a parity product. NUCOR, for example, has achieved an enviable steel cost position by making extensive use of scrap metal instead of iron ore and producing all its steel by the efficient continuous-casting method, which eliminates the intermediate step of making ingots. This strategy also can be focused on a distinct market segment. For example, Fort Howard Paper uses only recycled pulp, rather than the more expensive virgin pulp, to make toilet paper and other products. The quality, however, is acceptable only to the away-from-home market (office buildings, hotels, and restaurants), so the company does not try to sell to the home market through grocery stores.

Differentiated positions. A business is differentiated when some value-adding activities are performed in a way that leads to perceived superiority along dimensions that are valued by customers. For these activities to be profitable, the customers must be willing to pay a price premium for the benefits and the premium must exceed the added costs of superior performance. A business or its products can be distinguished favorably in a myriad of ways: providing superior service, using a strong brand name, offering innovative features, and providing superior product quality are some of the favored routes. Thus Procter & Gamble is regaining lost share in the disposable diaper market with a new super-absorbent contoured model; Salomon has gained a dominant position in the ski bindings market with a stream of innovations such as step-in bindings that meet the needs of average rather than expert skiers; Digital Equipment has enhanced its position in the minicomputer market with an artificial intelligence system that dramatically reduces the time required to fill orders and increases accuracy. This view of differentiation as perceived superiority—and possibly uniqueness—on some attributes that are important to customers is consistent with the position taken by Dickson and Ginter (1987). It goes beyond physical product attributes to embrace all activities and linkages of the business, including the kind of comprehensive support that Salomon provides its dealers to ensure they actively promote the superior features of its boots and bindings.

Performance Outcomes

The most popular indicators of marketing effectiveness and competitive advantage are market share and profitability. Is this popularity due to their ready availability, strong track record, or conceptually superior insights? Alternative measures such as customer satisfaction and the value of the customer franchise are little used, even though they afford the considerable benefit of reflecting customer responses to positional advantages and thus should precede the market share and profitability outcomes.

Market share. The premise of this measure is that we can distinguish winners from losers by the market shares they achieve, just as the outcome of a horse race is given by the final standings. This view of competition is simplistic; in reality competition is played out over many time periods within evolving markets. There is a strong temptation to extend the use of market share from a measure of past performance to a reliable indicator of future advantages. Is this a reasonable extension? Though there are few markets in which current share does not have a strong relationship to future share, we seldom find an exact mapping of current market shares onto future shares. Instead a significant "regression toward the mean" effect has been found in the analysis of market share changes in the PIMS database (Buzzell 1981; Wagner 1984).[2] This phenomenon raises some fundamental questions about the interpretation of market shares.

Market share and profitability. There are several compelling reasons why the usual causal explanation is partially or completely wrong. Possibly the direction of causality is from profit to share: businesses that are lucky or uniquely endowed select initially defensible and profitable positions, then reinvest the profits so they can grow faster than their less fortunate rivals. The most persuasive explanation is that both causal mechanisms are operating over time to yield the association of share and profit observed at any point in time.

Early in the evolution of the market, first-mover advantages dominate. As the market matures, the question is whether management can capitalize on the initially strong position and build new skills and resources to keep abreast of changes in technology and market requirements. This multiple-mechanism view has support from several studies of changes in the PIMS database (Jacobson and Aaker 1985; Rumelt and Wensley 1981).

What does this emerging view of market share, as largely an outcome of strategic moves to secure cost and differentiation advantages (Gale and Buzzell 1988), imply for the relevance of market share as an indicator of advantage? If it is to serve as more than simply an outcome measure we need to be sure that the observed share

- was gained in a way that competitors will have difficulty imitating and
- refers to a market with relatively stable boundaries. A dominant share of a market in which competitive forces are evolving rapidly affords little assurance of future advantage.

The last caveat points up a further difficulty with market share measures due to the ambiguity of market definitions. The answer to the question "share of what market?" often forces difficult compromises (Day 1981). A useful market definition should reflect the strategic choices of the business. To be a valid measure of competitive forces, however, it also should relate to ways the competitors define the market and should reflect emerging commonalities and differences in market segment behavior. A single market share measure is unlikely to satisfy these requirements.

Profitability. Current profitability is the reward from past advantages after the current outlays needed to sustain or enhance future advantages have been paid. Because profitability is influenced by actions taken in many previous time frames, it is unlikely to be a complete reflection of current advantage. When the environment is turbulent it may be a misleading indication. Consequently, the same arguments used to conclude that market share should be interpreted as an outcome can be applied to profitability.

The interpretation of profitability is complicated further by limitations in the prevailing modes of valuation. The cost-based approaches that underlie most accounting results are fundamentally different from approaches that estimate financial value from the stream of future benefits (Alberts and McTaggart 1984; Rappaport 1981, 1986). Accounting conventions oriented to allocating historic and current costs to satisfy tax requirements are ill-suited to the valuation of the sources of advantage. The consequences of the accounting mindset are most evident in the treatment of intangibles. Goodwill becomes an arithmetic necessity rather than a genuine commercial asset with future value. Similarly, investments in the skill and knowledge base are treated as current overhead, without consideration of their contribution to long-run performance. However, the future value of an asset depends critically on how it is used and whether the stream of benefits can be protected from competitive forces. Thus we return full circle to the question of how investments in sources of advantage yield positional advantages and superior performance outcomes.

Converting Skills and Resources into Superior Positions and Outcomes

Information on the relative standing of a business on the sources, positions, and performance dimensions of its competitive advantage is only a means to an end. What managers really want to know is how to get the greatest improvement in performance for the least expenditure. To do so requires identification of the skills and resources that exert the most leverage on positional advantages and future performance, then selective allocation of resources toward those high leverage sources. These are the key success factors of the business that "must be applied or controlled for the business to be successful" (Ohmae 1982). They are tailored closely to the type of business; the key success factors for machine tools do not apply to college book publishing, as we see in Table 1.

The conversion of sources of advantage into payoffs has been addressed only in a piecemeal way. The strategy literature generally asks how superior skills and resources are converted into positional advantages. These are the structural determinants or "drivers" of cost or differentiation advantages (Porter 1985). In contrast, marketers—as represented by those building decision calculus and market share attraction models—generally skip the intervening positional stage. The modeling is confined to the relationship of the input sources of advantage (relative advertising, sales, and

Table 1
The Nature of Key Success Factors*

Market	Skill and Resource Factors that Create Value or Lower Costs	Important Aspects of Value to the Customer
College book publishing	Relationships with quality authors Strong editorial capabilities Publisher strength in discipline Backlist depth Sales per title	Quality of published books Publisher reputation Fit with other published works
Machine tools	Design and manufacturing quality Simplification of parts variability Instant response from central depots Raw material stock	Tool quality Parts availability

*Adapted from MacAvoy (1987).

promotion expenditures, for example) with the performance outcomes of market share or profit. Neither the marketing nor strategy approach gives much attention to the conversion of positional advantages into superior outcomes. This is a serious gap, for the intervening stage does much to mediate the relationship of inputs to outputs. The remainder of this section examines the conversion steps in detail.

Converting Sources into Positions of Advantage

The drivers of positional advantages are the high leverage skills and resources that do the most to lower costs or create value to customers. Each activity in a firm's value chain is influenced by the combined effect of these drivers (Porter 1985).

Cost drivers are the structural determinants of the cost of each activity that are largely under a firm's control. The primary drivers are (1) the scale economies or diseconomies for each activity, (2) learning that improves knowledge and processes independently of scale, (3) the pattems of capacity utilization, and (4) the linkages that are present when the way one activity is performed affects another activity. Linkages act as cost drivers when, for example, higher quality materials and more costly product designs are used to reduce service costs.

Drivers of differentiation are analogous to cost drivers but represent the underlying reasons why an activity is executed in a unique or superior way. They correspond directly to the sources of advantage that reside in superior skills or resources when mobilized by an effective strategy. The principal drivers are (1) policy choices about what activities to perform and how intensely to perform them, including features, performance, level of advertising spending, extent of services provided, and the skills and experience of personnel employed in the activity, (2) linkages within the value chain, such as coordination between sales and service to improve the speed of order handling or with suppliers and distributors, and (3) timing that gains first-mover advantages. Other drivers include location, interrelationships with other businesses, learning, and scale that permits an activity to be performed in a unique way not possible at smaller volumes. Different combinations of drivers interact to determine the extent to which an activity is unique or superior to that of competitors.

The usefulness of the notion of drivers is difficult to assess. At best it is a descriptive tool, lacking any theory to clarify how drivers work or even how they can be isolated. It is not even apparent that they all mean the same thing. For example, some drivers of differentiation correspond directly to sources of advantage such as location, scale, or level of integration. However, "policy choices," the most prominent driver of differentiation, are discretionary decisions about activities to perform and how to perform them. Though such decisions are critical, they are not sources of advantage. Instead they are mediating events that determine the degree of leverage an investment in a particular skill or resource has on cost or differentiation.

Converting Sources Directly to Performance

The characteristic work on this conversion has been done by marketers with models that are variants on the "fundamental theorem of market share determination." The theorem holds that the market shares of various competitors are proportional to their shares of total marketing effort (Kotler 1984). This relationship is a pivotal feature of the so-called market share attraction models (Little, Bell, and Keeney 1975) and has been integrated into the STRATPORT portfolio model by Larréché and Srinivasan (1982). The basic notion also has been applied directly to a game-theoretic analysis of monopolistic competition assessing a firm's competitive strength as the product of its functional expenditures and competencies (Karnani 1982). A recent effort (Varadarajan 1985) to classify strategic variables into success producers or failure preventers (where an increased level of effort above a threshold level will not increase performance) also relies on the notion that relative effort levels roughly correspond to competitive advantages.

The most extensive application of the theorem is by Cook (1983) in the "new paradigm of marketing strategies." In this model, a firm has an advantage when its capacity to supply products is greater than the market demand for its output. The resulting slack can be applied to exploiting opportunities to gain share. The size of this advantage is estimated by subtracting the firm's share of strategic investments from its share of units sold. The central premise is that an equilibrium is reached when the firm's share of spending on conventional mix investments is the same as the market share. If the share of strategic marketing investments falls below the current share of units sold, share of units eventually will decline in search of a new balance in consumer preferences.

Though the structure of the Cook model can be faulted on many grounds,[3] the flaws in the valuation mechanism are potentially more damaging. The basic valuation model proposed by Cook—and implicitly endorsed in many marketing models—presumes the *current* level of investment in terms of annual cash outlays is the proper basis for assessing the level of market share a business can sustain. The resulting market share has a net present value that relates current outlays to the discounted value of the future revenue stream (Cook 1985). In reality this model provides only a partial picture of the potential value of past and current strategic investments. A complete picture must reflect (1) the link between today's investments and opportunities to execute tomorrow's options, (2) the value of first-mover advantages, and (3) the strategic choice of when and how the profit potential of a positional advantage will be realized.

Valuing options to be exercised in the future. Why do firms invest in manifestly unprofitable projects to establish a toehold in a potentially attractive market or technology (Ohmae 1985)? In effect they are buying an option to make a later move, because the first move does not commit them to proceed further (Wensley, Barwise, and Marsh 1984). If the first stage fails or the market sours, the firm can stop after the initial investment and cut its losses. However, especially in the case of new technologies, the first investment often is a necessary condition to learning enough to be in a position to make further investments. Options of this kind are intangible assets and in growth markets may account for a large fraction of the value of a business. Conventional discounted cash flow analysis is unable to value such options properly (Meyers 1984).

First-mover advantages are derived from the opportunity pioneers have to shape the rules of subsequent competition to their advantage. These advantages are achieved through preemption of competition, access to scarce resources, proprietary experience effects, the image of leadership that is not available to followers, and customer loyalty that is gained when switching costs are high.

Why should relative timing enhance or detract from the value of a marketing investment? The fundamental reason is an irreducible ambiguity as to which combination of factors was responsible for superior or inferior performance, which acts as a powerful inhibitor to direct imitation.[4] In the presence of uncertainty, the performance that prospective imitators can expect to achieve varies greatly. If a large nonrecoverable cost also is associated with such a move, prospective entrants are further deterred from imitating the best firm in the market. Instead they are forced to develop different market positions or appeals, or leap-frog with new technologies, if they are to achieve acceptable returns. Strong evidence supports the notion that pioneering consumer brands gain long-run market share rewards as a result of the difficulty of emulating their success (Urban, Carter, and Mucha 1985). Similarly, a recent study of mature industrial businesses found the average market share at maturity was 30% for the pioneers that survived, 21% for followers, and only 15% for late entrants (Robinson 1984).

The Payoff from Positional Advantages

A differentiation or cost advantage eventually should be rewarded with share and/or profitability superior to those of competitors. The size and duration of the superior payoff will depend on

- whether the value perceived by the customer and the resulting price premium are greater than the extra cost of the activities that create differentiation.
- the objectives of the business in terms of the tradeoff between higher immediate profit (realized by taking the maximum feasible price premium) and increased market share gained with a penetration price.
- the difficulty the competitors will have in matching or leap-frogging the advantage. Not all industries afford equal opportunities to sustain an advantage. Those with durable, irreversible, and market-specific assets and a slow pace of technological change are much more likely to promise enduring profitability (Ghemawat 1986).

These considerations usually are overlooked in marketing models based on simple response functions that relate a change in marketing expenditures to a change in share or sales. The message is clear: to understand how a competitive advantage is created and sustained we must understand the intermediate stage of positional advantages. Otherwise the exercise is devoid of diagnostic value.

Toward an Integrated Concept of Competitive Advantage

The various extensions to the basic source-position-performance framework that are needed to portray better the realities of competitive strategy formulation are summarized in Figure 2.

☐ Superior skills and resources are not automatically converted into positional advantages, nor is there a certain performance payoff from superior cost or differentiation

Figure 2
A framework for assessing advantage

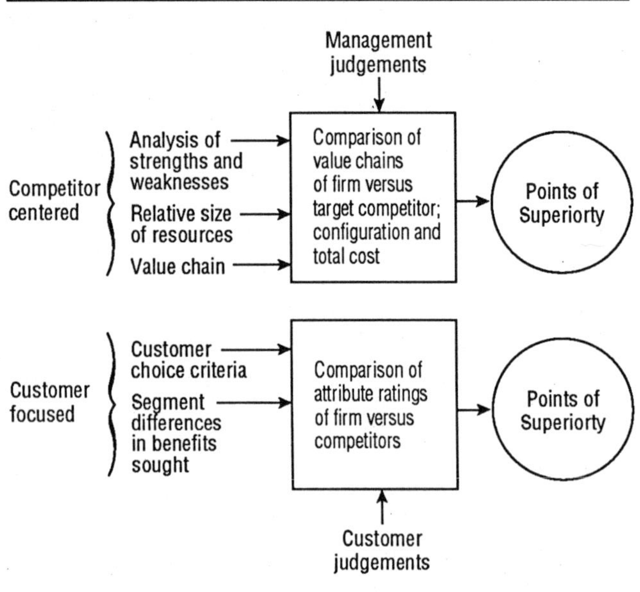

positions. Both conversions are mediated jointly by strategic choices, including objectives and entry timing and the quality of tactics and implementation.

☐ The managerial usefulness of any effort to assess advantage comes from the accurate identification of the handful of skills and resources that have the greatest leverage on position and performance. These are the key success factors that must be managed obsessively to ensure long-run competitive effectiveness.

☐ This framework describes the performance of a business in relation to that of its competitors. The absolute performance also depends on the attractiveness of the overall market as determined by competitive structure and behavior.

The next issue is the ability of the available methods to yield valid and insightful measures of the competitive standing of a business as required by each of the constructs in the framework.

Methods for Assessing Advantage

The possible measurement methods are classified in Table 2 by their place in the conceptual framework and whether they take the vantage point of customers or competitors. The immediate message of this table is that each of the many methods for assessing advantage has a specific and limited role that gives only a partial picture of the complete framework. Thus customers have little to say about how a business has gained an advantage they value (e.g., which skills and resources created and sustained superior customer service). Conversely, analyses of competitive superiority in skills and resources are made by people within the firm using competitors as the standard of comparison. The findings do not tell whether the firm will be distinguished favorably in the eyes of customers or end users. A comprehensive diagnosis can be gained only with a combination of methods. The purpose of the following sections is to guide the selection of the appropriate methods.

Table 2
Methods of Assessing Advantage

Competitor-Centered	Customer-Focused
A. Assessing Sources (Distinctive Competences)	
1. Management judgments of strengths and weaknesses	
2. Comparison of resource commitments and capabilities	
3. Marketing skills audit	
B. Indicators of Positional Advantage	
4. Competitive cost and activity comparisons	5. Customer comparisons of attributes of firm vs. competition
a. Value chain comparisons of relative costs	a. Choice models
b. Cross-section experience curves	b. Conjoint analysis
	c. Market maps
C. Identifying Key Success Factors	
6. Comparison of winning vs. losing competitors	
7. Identifying high leverage phenomena	
a. Management estimates of market share elasticities	
b. Drivers of activities in the value chain	
D. Measure of Performance	
	8. Customer satisfaction surveys
	9. Loyalty (customer franchise)
10. a. Market share	10. b. Relative share of end-user segments
11. Relative profitability (return on sales and return on assets)	

Competitor-Centered Methods

The essence of these methods is a direct comparison with target competitors. Because the departure point for this comparison is the business, the frame of reference usually is confined to direct rivals. Hence the emphasis is on relative skills and resources and the resulting cost position. The search is directed toward finding those activities the firm does better than its competitors.

The most common competitor-centered method is judgmental identification of distinctive competences, which are based on "unique levels and patterns of both skills and resources, deployed in ways that cannot be duplicated by others" (Hofer and Schendel 1978). However, a firm can have a distinctive competence without gaining a competitive advantage if what it does best is relatively unimportant to customers or competitors. Key success factors therefore have an important role in disciplining the competitive analysis process, for they direct attention to high leverage competences. Several methods such as value chain analysis can be adapted to help identify key success factors.

Identifying Distinctive Competences

Neither planning practice nor the strategic management literature has advanced much beyond *ad hoc* judgments of strengths and weaknesses for this purpose. The present state of the art reflects the original formulations of the distinctive competences notion by Selznick (1957) and Learned et al. (1969). Current discussions, such as those of Glueck and Jauch (1984) and Hitt and Ireland (1985), add little other than longer lists of factors to consider.

Judgmental analyses of strengths and weaknesses (Table 2, A1). The virtues of this general framework are also its drawback. It is deliberately broad and generalized to encompass an almost limitless array of potentially influential factors, which means it can be used in most situations. Conversely, it gives no guidance on how to avoid simply creating an indiscriminate listing of competences that does not isolate those few that are especially important.

There are several reasons why the usual enumeration of strengths and weaknesses provides little guidance. First, the judgments commonly are made without an explicit reference point (are distinctive competences relative to competitors or relative to other lesser capabilities of the business?). Second, there is often no distinction between what the business does well that is valued by customers and what it does well that is unimportant to customers. Too often the identification of competences is based solely on internal considerations. Third, the judgments tend to be based on historical data or simple trend extrapolations. Because they primarily reflect past successes they are unlikely to produce insights into future possibilities for advantage. One way to overcome these problems is to employ a participative process involving taskforces to set priorities (King 1983). This process will not be effective unless it is guided by a conceptual framework to facilitate strategic thinking. The Porter (1980) model of the five forces that determine industry profitability often is used for this purpose.

Direct comparisons of resource commitments and capabilities (Table 2, A2). Disproportionate weight tends to be given to "hard" data about competitors because it is accessible and in a format that invites direct comparison. Such tangible and visible factors as size of salesforce, number of dealers, and plant capacity generally are used to estimate the relative size of resource commitments. These data may be analyzed in terms of share of marketing effort and strategic investments as proposed by Cook (1983) in the model described before. Not only is this model limited, but this type of data gives a narrow view of the relative size of competitive capabilities and commitments. A complete assessment would also consider

- functional capabilities as reflected in such measures as the number of new products successfully developed, speed of response to service calls, the flexibility of processing equipment, and the union situation;
- forecasts of competitors' investment priorities and patterns of spending (Rothschild 1984) as an indication of the capacity to grow;
- capability to respond quickly to moves by others, as determined by uncommitted cash reserves, excess plant capacity, and new products on the shelf;
- ability to adapt to change, as a consequence of exit barriers, cost of unused capacity, and the structure of fixed versus variable costs.

Assessing superiority in skills: The role of the marketing skills audit (Table 2, A3). An old adage in planning circles holds that hard numbers drive out soft impressions. Skills are "the most distinctive encapsulation of the organization's way of doing business" (Peters 1984), but may be simply too subtle to measure. Distinctive skills may be what really matters in the long run for they are the essence of adaptive organizations (Mintzberg 1978; Quinn 1980), but how is one to identify competitive superiority on each of the following three skill sets that Peters identifies as essential?

1. A focus on total customer satisfaction.
2. A focus on continuous innovation.
3. A widespread commitment from all levels of the organization to the first two orientations.

For these skills to make an enduring difference, they must pervade all activities of the business. Unless they are nurtured continually they come to be taken for granted and performance erodes. However, it is very difficult to detect slippage in the exercise of these skills before superiority is lost. Even IBM—a paragon of excellence—recently has admitted that it got out of touch with its customers (Loomis 1987). According to the chairman, John Akers, IBM persisted in trying to sell its products rather than solutions to the problems of integrating computer systems, wringing out productivity gains, and using information systems for competitive advantage. One vehicle for assessing such a "slippery" skill as a focus on total customer satisfaction is the most generic of all forms of assessment—the marketing audit. It is a "comprehensive, systematic, independent and periodic examination of a business unit's marketing environment, objectives, strategies and activities. . . ." (Kotler, Gregor, and Rodgers 1977). Depending on who does it, for what reasons, and with which data sources, such audits might reveal this skill factor. None of the available literature, however, identifies a customer orientation or focus on customer satisfaction as an overriding theme in guiding an audit or offers guidance on how to identify this package of skills. In principle, an audit does have the breadth of concern and capacity to address these issues. We suspect that few audits give adequate attention to such manifestations of customer orientation as the integration of management functions toward serving customer needs and the willingness to invest in and act on customer research or reward employees on the basis of customer satisfaction. Such information, coupled with evidence of competitors' performance on these dimensions, would give a powerful insight into the ability of the business to respond to changing market requirements.

Biases in management judgments. In the absence of objective and comparative measures of subtle skills, the only recourse is to the knowledge of the business unit managers. However, their assessments often are subverted by myopia. Subjective judgments are readily biased by selective perceptions and dominated by facts and opinions that are easy to retrieve. Often "hard" evidence of the past or current success of a strategy is given more weight than "soft" assessments of future threats (Barnes 1984; Hogarth and Makridakis 1981). This problem is particularly insidious with performance measures such as share and profitability, which reflect the payoff from past competitive advantages. Further bias stems from differences across organizational levels in the perceptions of which skill and resource factors are important. The problem has received little consideration, despite one study that found senior managers emphasized personnel and financial capabilities whereas middle managers based their judgments of strengths and weaknesses on technical and marketing attributes (Stevenson 1976). This study also found a persistent pattern of unwarranted optimism at higher levels in the organization. Such divergent opinions are difficult to reconcile without external points of reference for validation.

Some progress has been made by marketing researchers on understanding (Chakravarti, Mitchell, and Staelin 1981) and overcoming the problems of managerial bias in judgments (Larréché and Moinpour 1983). This work has concentrated on improving managerial estimates of the parameters of decision calculus models. Better overall judgments result when an external measure of expertise can be used confidently to pick the best expert for an issue. The results are even better than those of the Delphi method often proposed as a solution. Unfortunately even the "best" expert is not immune to the biasing effects of selective perception.

Indicators of Positional Advantages

Competitor-centered approaches to identifying positional superiority help managers to answer the question, "How do we compare with our competitors?" The answers usually are framed in terms of observable differences in value chains, including (1) the choice of activities undertaken, (2) the way the activities are performed, and (3) consequences for the cost of each activity as well as total cost. Because it is difficult to say without recourse to customer judgments whether an activity is being performed better by a competitor, the emphasis of competitor-centered methods is inevitably on cost differences. The nature of the available methods also reinforces this cost emphasis.

Value chain comparisons of relative costs (Table 2, B4a). A firm's cost position depends on the configuration of the activities in its value chain versus that of competitors and its relative location on the cost drivers of each activity. A cost advantage is gained when the cumulative cost of performing all the activities is lower than the competitors' costs. The first step in determining the relative cost position is the identification of each competitor's value chain. Ideally, costs and assets then should be assigned to each of these activities. In practice this step is extremely difficult because the business does not have direct information on the costs of the competitors' value activities. Some costs can be estimated from public data or interviews with suppliers and distributors, whereas others can be derived by reverse engineering and similar techniques. For example, it is usually possible to determine the size of a competitor's salesforce and its expense and compensation arrangments. The result is a partial picture based on accurate data that can be filled out with informed judgment.

Cross-sectional experience curves (Table 2, B4b) provide a comparison of the current total cost positions of the competitors in a market according to their cumulative experience base (Day and Montgomery 1983). With such a curve it is possible to estimate the relative profitability of each competitor at the prevailing price. These comparisons are appropriate only when all significant competitors are similar in scope, strategy, and value chain configuration. Outside these restrictive circumstances the slope of the curve is too difficult to estimate with confidence, so it is better to resort to direct estimates of costs.

Identifying Key Success Factors

Numerous methods have been proposed for identifying key success factors (Leidecker and Bruno 1984). Most involve *ad hoc* judgments of industry experts and management. Though the results may be very insightful, testing their validity is usually difficult and they lack obvious action implications. For example, how useful is it to know that the key success factors in the food processing industry are new product development, good distribution, and effective advertising? For ice cream two very different factors have been identified: the ability to control seasonal variations and the ability to ensure economic refrigeration capacity throughout the distribution process (Ohmae 1982). Though these factors seem plausible, it is not clear that there are big differences in them among competitors or that changes in them will have a significant impact on either costs or perceived value.

More defensible insights come from explicitly relating current *sources* of advantage to the achievement of advantageous competitive *positions* or superior *performance*. To do so requires a feedback of information about the outcomes of the competitive advantage process back to the antecedents of advantage. Two adaptations of this approach have been proposed in the strategy literature: (1) discover what distinguishes winning companies from losers and (2) look for high leverage phenomena. Unfortunately, there is no evidence of the validity of either of these methods, nor have they been subjected to comparative tests. Some progress has been reported in applying these methods to specific functional areas such as information systems (Boynton and Zmud 1984).

Comparison of winning versus losing competitors (Table 2, C6). Key success factors are inferred from an analysis of differences in performance among competitors. For this approach to yield useful insights, three difficult questions must be answered. First, which competitors should be included in the comparison set? Second, what criteria should be used to distinguish the winners from the losers (e.g., profitability, growth, market share, creation of new markets)? Third, what are the reasons for the differences in performance? Rothschild (1984) identifies four categories of reasons: uniqueness of the vision or strategy, the resources possessed, differences in assumptions about the environment, and fortuitous factors such as good timing or location. There is no evidence that these reasons are either mutually exclusive or exhaustive, so their contribution to insight is speculative.

Overall, this procedure is a worthwhile starting place. For example, comparisons of firms that have succeeded in the deregulating transportation and communications markets with their weaker rivals that are being bought up show that ownership of a large facilities network—whether a long-distance network or a railroad track network—gives a larger than expected cost advantage. This advantage results from economies of flow or density, which behave like economies of scale in that average costs decline as network traffic increases. What is worrisome to many observers is that these advantages will be difficult to contest in the future, so the prognosis is for continued high levels of industry concentration.

Identifying high leverage phenomena (Table 2, C7). Carroll (1982) argues that the typical key success factors are too superficial to be actionable because they identify "things" such as customer service and access to resources, rather than relationships between desired outcomes and controllable inputs. Better insights come from thorough knowledge of the "strategic phenomena" of the business (Carroll 1982; MacAvoy 1983). Ideally these are causal relationships describing how controllable variables such as plant scale, production run length, and salesforce density affect desirable outcomes such as manufacturing and sales costs per unit. A representative relationship is between distance shipped and distribution cost per unit. The reported relationships suggest a bias toward cost-based advantages, though some have very indirect impacts on costs (e.g., the relationship of brand purchases per period and brand loyalty).

The analysis task is formidable, for a myriad of potential relationships must be examined but only a few will be found to have significant leverage. Then the current position of each leading competitor is located for each significant relationship and an estimate is made of how these competitors will change their positions. No guidelines are offered on how to find the key relationships, other than to use line management to hypothesize a number of possibilities and then test them with data. The reliance on situational knowledge does not ensure either completeness or validity.

Management estimates of market share elasticities (Table 2, C7a). The problems of finding high leverage phenomena are seemingly no worse than the difficulties inherent in the elasticity analysis proposed by Hofer and Schendel (1978) for a similar purpose. The analysis measures the degree to which the total revenues of a business will be increased or decreased by changes in marketing activities such as pricing, sales effort, and service levels. A variant of this approach has a long and successful history in decision calculus models (Little 1979) applied at the brand or product line level. It is unclear whether the concept of elasticities or response coefficients can be generalized meaningfully to the business level in the absence of any reported applications. Such applications would be susceptible to the usual problems of estimation of response coefficients by means of time series data or management judgment.

Drivers of activities on the value chain (Table 2, C7b) are analogous to strategic phenomena. The difference is that drivers are estimated for each relevant activity in the value chain. Because this is a more systematic procedure, important strategic relationships between sources and outcomes are less likely to be overlooked. Even so, the procedure is better suited to cost drivers than to differentiation drivers, because the former are based on relationships that can be identified largely from internal data obtained by:

- examining the basic economics of the business, for example, the effect of local market share on salesforce costs,
- analyzing the performance consequences of past fluctuations in costs,
- asking "what if" questions of line managers on the effects of changing a parameter such as line speed on yield,
- comparisons of the firm's costs with competitors' cost for each activity.

Regrettably, the notion of drivers has the same problems as other methods of identifying key success factors. All are better at cataloging the possibilities than isolating the few areas where superior execution or increased investment will have the greatest impact. In short, much progress must be made before the notion of key success factors fulfills its promise.

Customer-Focused Measures

A customer perspective means the comparison of competitors is made by customers rather than by the management team, as summarized in Figure 3. Emphasis is shifted

Figure 3
Comparing competitors

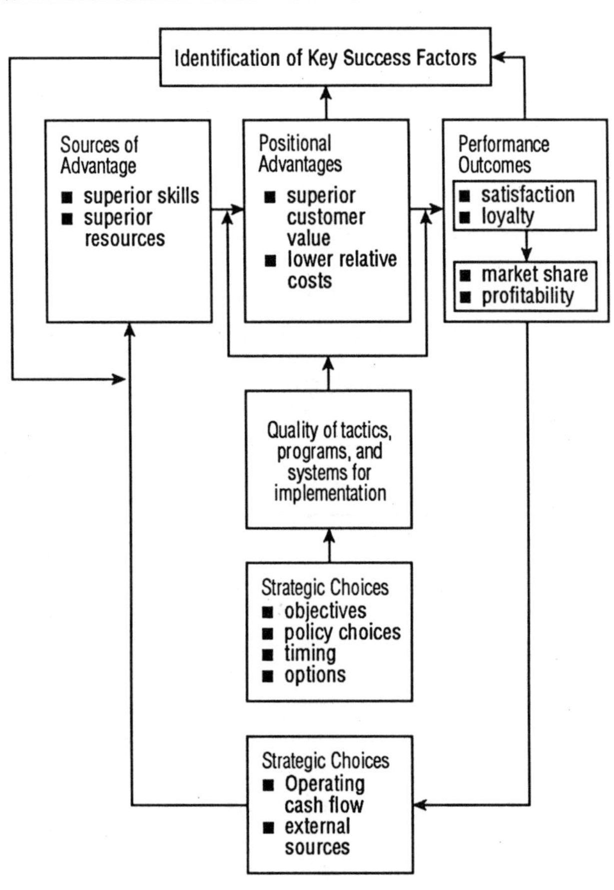

from the cost factors and the internal value chain activities addressed in the competitor-centered approaches to segment differences and differentiation advantages.

Perspectives on Positional Advantages

Choice models (Table 2, B5a). Most methods that use customer judgments are variations on the basic multiattribute choice model. All ask the same question—"Why are competitive altematives selected from a consideration set?"—and employ the same model structure to answer the question. A customer's beliefs about the performance of each supplier on the attributes that correspond to their purchase criteria are multiplied by the relative importance of each attribute, then summed to obtain an overall attitude score. The most common version is the linear compensatory model (Wilkie and Pessemier 1973), so called because good performance on one attribute can offset or compensate for poor performance on another attribute.

Diagnostic insights are gained from the importance weights. Perceived differences between alternatives on the important attributes provide direct evidence of advantage. The importance weights can be measured directly (by using a constant sum scale, for example) or derived by regressing the attribute ratings against an overall preference judgment for each alternative. The estimated regression weights then serve as proxies for importance. The first stage of analysis is often a grid plot of the importance rating of each attribute against the comparative performance rating for the business (Martilla and James 1977). Attention is directed to important attributes on which the business is judged not to be performing well.

Though this approach to assessing advantage has long been used by consumer goods companies, it is equally relevant to industrial and service markets. DuPont has undertaken dozens of such studies to good effect (Root 1986). The company has found the overall ratings of competitive standing correlate well with market share, so managers have confidence in the approach. The payoff comes from the attribute-by-attribute comparisons between DuPont's performance and that of specific competitors in specific market segments. To counteract the belief of DuPont managers that they already know the most important attributes, the researchers ask all members of the business team to list and rank the attributes. The internal list is invariably incomplete. More significant is the wide variation in importance rankings found within the team. The salesforce has one view, whereas operations and R&D often hold very different views.

All successful (reported) applications of customer-judgment methods share two features. First, they specify the attributes precisely (e.g., does better service mean repair capability, response time, or delivery time?). Specificity comes at a cost, as the attributes are often highly correlated, but the diagnostic insights are certainly superior.

The second feature of effective applications is customer or product segmentation based on similarities in attribute judgments. Gensch (1984) used this criterion to identify segments of the market of a heavy electrical equipment manufacturer according to their degree of relative preference and loyalty.[5] This information was used to target "switchable" customers for whom the firm was the second choice by only a narrow margin. Doyle and Saunders (1985) clustered all products in a highly differentiated specialty chemical market according to similarity of purchase attributes. The strategic insights came from evaluation of the attractiveness of each product segment in terms of size, growth, strength of competition, and fit with the firm's capabilities. The results dissuaded management from the risks of the "majority fallacy" by showing that niches away from the middle of the market were less competitive as target segments for a late entrant.

The full payoff from choice models will come when they can incorporate the effect of controllable marketing variables as well as product attributes on the choice among competitive alternatives. Progress in this direction has been reported by Carpenter and Lehmann (1985). They formulated a multinomial logit model to explain brand switching probabilities as a function of each competitor's marketing mix, product features, and their interactions. The output of the model reveals groups of competing brands based on their features and the impact of marketing mix elements on these groupings.

Conjoint analysis (Table 2, B5b). Most choice models lack a mechanism for recognizing tradeoffs among levels of attributes, and seldom is it possible to calculate the value of satisfying each choice criterion by estimating how it affects buyers' cost or performance. As a result the relative importance weights do not necessarily reflect the amount of buyer value that accrues from improvements in performance on each attribute. On the surface, conjoint analysis appears to overcome these problems. The procedure has the capacity to decompose an overall preference or value for money measure into utility scores, or part worths, for each level of each attribute (Green and Srinivasan 1978; Green and Wind 1975). However, it is apparently little used for assessing competitive advantage (Cattin and Wittink 1982). Among the barriers to usage are burdensome and specialized data collection procedures (Urban and Hauser 1980), which sharply limit the number of attributes that can be analyzed. Also, the models yield unreliable estimates of part worths if the choice alternatives are so close in performance that fine distinctions among altematives are obscured. In mature markets where differentiation advantages have been eroded to very thin edges, the ability to tease out subtle perceived differences is an essential feature of any useful method.

Market mapping (Table 2, B5c). The maps compress the information from customer judgments about related attributes to a few composite dimensions. Their main advantage is the pictorial representation of the relationships among competitors from the customers' point of view. They serve the same function as the "war board" used by military strategists to understand the geographic location and type of enemy emplacements, as well as targets of opportunity (Shocker and Stewart 1983). Market maps are very helpful for revealing the general pattern perceived competitive differences and also for identifying submarket boundaries. Thus they provide a useful context for undertaking fine-grained analyses of the specific reasons why customers prefer one competitor over another. Such analyses must be done separately, for the compression of attribute data into a few dimensions obscures the details of individual attributes and the action implications are lost.

Customer Evidence of Relative Performance

Three performance measures require direct customer input because the insights they provide cannot be inferred from historical evidence of market share, sales volume, or profitability.

Customer satisfaction (Table 2, D8). High on the list of strategic priorities is the achievement of long-un customer satisfaction. Few firms routinely monitor satisfaction, however, and when they do the information usually lacks relevance to issues of competitive advantage. One exception is BM, where all marketing activities (including service, sales, and software support) as well as equipment performance are directly evaluated and compensated on the basis of measures of satisfaction collected in blind surveys.

Why has the potential of this measure not been realized? Obviously, commitment to the concept is a problem, but the limitations of the usual survey measures are also an impediment. Satisfaction surveys typically are limited to assessing overall satisfaction and intentions to repurchase to reveal problems experienced by recent buyers. The measures are seldom comparative, as they focus only on the brand or product most recently purchased, and may not isolate the contribution of each product or service attribute to overall satisfaction. These are correctable problems that should be addressed in the light of research on the determinants of satisfaction (Churchill and Surprenant 1982). Satisfaction once was believed to derive from a disconfirmation process; if performance as experienced measured up to prior expectations, satisfaction ensued. This view is too simplistic. Actual product performance relative to the perceived performance of the competitive options appears to have a greater influence on satisfaction.

Customer loyalty (Table 2, D9). Many measures of competitive advantage are attempts to quantify the depth and quality of the customer franchise of the firm's products. Strong brand loyalty is the most common indicator of a valuable customer franchise, but how is such a measure to be interpreted? Economists (Porter 1976) assert that there is loyalty when the costs a consumer would incur in searching for further information exceed the benefits from the search.[6] Though this model may be correct, it is not very revealing because it does not indicate how perceptions are formed or changed. Behavioral measures such as share of purchase requirements satisfied by a brand (Johnson 1984) are equally flawed. These measures overlook the crucial aspect of loyalty as a tendency or bias toward a particular brand that may or may not be evidenced by actual purchase behavior. A customer who has a loyalty bias toward brand A may encounter a purchase decision in which brand B is heavily priced-promoted and therefore may choose brand B. In effect, the perceived superiority of the preferred brand is not sufficient to offset the price disadvantage. To understand loyalty in this setting, one must supplement the purchase behavior measure with knowledge of intermediate attitudes.

Relative share of end-user segments (Table 2, D10b). A single market share measure obscures as much as it reveals. A 20% share could reveal either a strong competitive position (e.g., if no other competitor has more than a 10% share) or a weak position (e.g., if the dominant competitor has 50% of the market). Hence it is always better to use a measure of relative market share, obtained by dividing the share of the firm by the share of the top three competitors (Capon and Spogli 1976).

Further diagnostic insights result from examining the variability in relative market share across end-user segments within the served market. If a business has the same share in every possible segment, it probably does not have a differentiated position. No brand can be equally competitive across segments that reflect very different patternof benefits sought unless it lacks a distinct need-satisfying capability. Conversely, a business with considerable variability of shares across end-use segments or customer groups is sharply positioned to satisfy a distinct pattern of needs in one or two segments. Moran (1984) has evidence that well-positioned consumer brands are more profitable because they face a lower demand elasticity within their target segments that can be converted into higher prices. Additional incremental profit comes from marketing efficiencies due to higher repeat purchase rates and customer loyalty.

The validity of the diagnostic insights from segment share differentials rests on the assumption that a more sharply focused brand or business can compete more effectively than a less focused one. Whether this assumption is true depends on the overall balance between the cost savings from economies of scope, achieved by breadth of participation in many adjacent segments (Teece 1980), and the enhanced profitability from focus on a few market segments. The choice of scope versus focus will depend in turn on the degree of segmentation in the market, for minor differences between segments will not impede larger firms from eventually entering as the "niche" grows and becomes more attractive.

Summary and Implications

An effective competitive strategy begins with the timely and actionable diagnosis of the current and prospective advantages of the business within the served market. How do managers know whether the available assessments are aiding the search for advantage or hindering it with misleading and partial information? The answer depends on how well the evidence of advantage satisfies the following requirements:

1. There is adequate illumination of the sources of advantage, as well as their manifestations of superior customer value or lowest delivered cost and superior performance.
2. There is a balance of customer-focused and competitor-centered methods so the risk of myopia due to selective attention and simplification is minimized.
3. The results have credibility while being more than a simple confirmation of prior prejudice and industry conventional wisdom. Proprietary information about the sources that exert the most leverage on positional advantages and future performance is itself a competitive advantage.

Taken together, these requirements are the basis for a process for assessing the effectiveness and quality of the performance analysis in a business.

The Nature of Advantage: The SPP Framework

Any attempt to understand a specific competitive situation must account for three defining features of the concept of competitive advantage. First, competitive advantage is a high level notion that is inherently ambiguous until it is separated into its component parts: the sources, positions, and performance outcomes (SPP). None of these elements can serve in the place of the others. Thus, an integrative multiple measures perspective is required before a full picture can be drawn.

Second, though advantages reside in superior skills and resources, they are revealed in competitive product markets. A point of advantage can be exploited profitably only when it offers significant benefits that are perceived and valued by customers and are difficult for competitors to emulate. The appropriate unit of analysis to reveal such an advantage is a market segment characterized by a distinct profile of benefits.

Third, superior skills and resources are not automatically converted into positional advantages—nor is there a certain performance payoff from superior cost or differentiation positions. Both these conversions are mediated jointly by strategic choices, including the tradeoffs among objectives and the timing of entry and the quality of implementation.

Seeking Diagnostic Insights: Information as Advantage

The usual test of a measurement approach is whether the results are credible (believable) and add insights beyond the confirmation of past beliefs. What this test overlooks is a possibility that the new and valid insights may be unavailable to or unappreciated by managers in competing firms. Early information about the emergence of a new market segment, the side effects of a new technology, or the limitations of a new material becomes a potent competitive advantage for the first mover able to capitalize on the implications.

The notion of asymmetries in insights about how to compete for future advantage requires managers in competing firms to hold significantly different perceptions and beliefs. However, individual firms appear to share the same assumptions about their market environment. In fact, an informal but often crucial validity test is whether a diagnostic insight conforms to a consensual "industry" understanding. This conformity is a plausible explanation for why new entrants, unencumbered by conventional wisdom, "can change the rules of the competitive game" even when they can be seen to have been acting on widely available information.

There is likely to be an inverse relationship between the ready availability of a particular measure and its capacity to generate new and valuable insights. The widespread familiarity with such proxy measures of competitive advantage as market share and return on sales means they already have been incorporated into managerial perceptions of advantage within most competitors. They have become explanations without diagnostic power and as such virtual tautologies: "IBM has a competitive advantage because it has the highest worldwide market share." Hence they become merely descriptive rather than diagnostic.

In practice, the readily available evidence of advantage is likely to be not only descriptive, but also historical, distorted, and incomplete. The evidence is *historical* because of the convenience of using readily available measures being collected on a routine basis to monitor past performance and serve other needs. It is *distorted* because most available measures are linked to the control and reward system, and the alternative measures tend to rely on management judgments of relative competence and positional advantages of their business, which are biased by selective perceptions and recall of past successes. Finally, the available measures are usually *incomplete* because they are derived from inappropriate conceptual frameworks.

Balancing Customer and Competitor Perspectives

Lack of completeness is a result of a reactive posture toward the assessment of advantage. By simply relying on evidence that is available or customary in the industry, firms may evolve passively toward an unbalanced reliance on either customer-focused or competitor-centered measures, to the possible neglect of the other perspective.

Limits to competitor-centering. When market demand is predictable, the competitive structure is concentrated and stable, and there are a few powerful customers, the emphasis is necessarily on competitors. Even in this setting, solely competitor-centered measures have drawbacks. The preoccupation with costs and internal activities may obscure opportunities for differentiation through creative linkages of seller, distributor, and buyer value chains. Such a perspective also deflects attention from changes in market segment structures or customer requirements that might shift attribute judgments. Further, the competitors are assumed to be doing a proper marketing job. Managers with this mindset are more likely simply to emulate their competitors when they select strategies. Such an approach reduces the likelihood of experiments with innovative strategies to alter the basis of competition. This situation is unfortunate, for strategies that "change the game" with new types of service, new delivery systems, or new production systems are the surest way to gain a sustainable edge.

Managerial or other "expert" judgment is needed in all competitor-centered methods to specify the competitors to watch and to judge the relative performance of the business and its competitors. Even seemingly firm measures of market share are a matter for judgment and debate about the appropriate served market. The susceptibility of these judgments to bias should be minimized by validation from market sources and triangulation with other ways of measuring the same variable.

Limits of customer-focusing. In dynamic markets with shifting mobility barriers, many competitors, and highly segmented end-user markets, a tilt toward a customer focus is mandatory. Unfortunately, most of the customer-focused measures are remote from the activities of the business. It is seldom apparent how the attributes that are important to the customer are influenced by activities in the value chain. A perception of superior service gained by faster delivery of orders can be influenced by manufacturing processes, the choice of technology, shipping methods, or order-handling activities. These relationships are not available from customer-focused measures, nor are there any clues as to the sustainability of the advantages. Are competitors willing and able to match the strategic move? In short, neither perspective on advantage gives a complete picture to decision makers.

Appraising the Measurement System

The specific measures of competitive advantage a business should use depend on the situation. The measures appropriate or even feasible for a semiconductor or auto parts manufacturer differ from those suited to a retail banker or apparel manufacturer. This fact does not exempt the monitoring system—comprising the measures used and the composite picture they give of the competitive position—from having to meet the basic requirements of any attempt to assess advantages. These requirements are posed as the critical questions in Table 3 that form the basis of an appraisal audit.

First, an explicit effort must be made to achieve a degree of balance and interaction between the customer-focused and competitor-centered perspectives. Though one domain of measurement may be emphasized over the other, there must be a mechanism for comparing the results of the different perspectives. Seldom are marketing research data or available methods used as effectively as possible. In practice, most marketing research is descriptive (what is the potential of this market?), tactical (what is the sales impact of this quarter's couponing program?), or motivated by curiosity about the complexities of consumer behavior or market structures. Generally the research is not directed toward understanding fundamental relationships between the sources of advantage and the resulting positional advantage and performance. As a result, the linkage between the variables marketing researchers measure and the factors managers control and manipulate is poor. To overcome this problem, researchers must give more attention to measuring customer value explicitly and must undertake clinical studies of the impact of the firm's activities on buyer costs and performance.

Second, we must audit the coverage the specific measures give of the source-position-performance framework. We would look for the use of measures at different stages as well as explicit attempts to compare and contrast them. In practice, it is critical to know whether the judged superiority in skills and resources can continue to support the observed positional superiority in the market. If it cannot, how long can a positional advantage be sustained and what needs to be done to stop the erosion? To attack these questions with any confidence we must test for inconsistencies between individual measures and also between elements of advantage. For instance, it is useful to compare managers' judgments of attribute importance with customer judgments.

Third, we must look more closely at the way each specific measure is obtained. How well does it satisfy the criteria of validity, feasibility, and diagnostic value? Further, the fact that all measures depend on some degree of judgment is no excuse for not challenging the assumptions, particularly historic ones, incorporated in the measurement approach. In many cases, performance aspects such as market share are measured in terms of historic market structures with inadequate recognition of emerging competitors and channels.

Finally, we must look critically at the overall measurement process and its development and impact within the organization. Are we learning and developing as the situation changes? How is the system designed to recognize the need for change? What potentially contradictory measures are being used to ensure the current system is adequate? Finally, any measurement system will be of commercial value only if it is linked adequately to the strategy formulation, resource allocation, and tactical planning processes of the firm.

References

1. Though our focus is on understanding how to compete better in a chosen product-market arena, this can be achieved only if the context is properly defined. The choice of product-market arena is partly a matter of strategic choice, reflecting the definition of the business (Abell 1980) and the capabilities of the business, and partly an empirical question of whether the competing alternatives arc perceived to be substitutes (Day, Shocker, and Srivastava 1979). It is possible that the choice of where to compete actually follows assessment of how to compete.
2. In more technical terms, this is merely the problem of distinguishing between random walk behavior and a more complex causal structure. Some analysts who have looked at market

share data have argued a strong and pure random walk interpretation (Mancke 1974). In so doing they have had to assume some complete form of capital market failure so that the firms failing (relatively speaking) in earlier rounds have no access to additional funds (even though they face exactly the same opportunity set as their competitor). Others have attempted to isolate the random walk component either by inference (Caves, Gale, and Porter 1977) or the application of more tightly specified models (Rumelt and Wensley 1981). The fact remains that the mere autocorrelation between current and past market share is in itself equally consistent with a pure random walk model.

3. The fundamental theorem as applied by Cook has numerous restrictive assumptions. Relaxing them renders the theorem virtually unmanageable for diagnostic or prescriptive purposes. To be fully specified, a model based on this theorem should incorporate (1) differences between firms in their ability to spend marketing dollars effectively, (2) the likelihood of diminishing returns to additional investments, (3) the carryover effects of past investments, and (4) synergistic effects of the marketing mix variables. None of these considerations are included in the Cook model. Further problems stem from the assumptions about the function relating market share responsiveness to changes in share of investments (Chattopadhyay, Nedungadi, and Chakravarti 1985).
4. Lippman and Rumelt (1982) have developed a theory of "uncertain imitability" to explain how initial advantages can be sustained when competitors are faced with this uncertainty.
5. A multivariate logit model was used to translate the customer's judgments of the relative *importance* of nine product and service attributes (such as price, warranty, quality, energy losses, financial strengths, and ability to meet delivery dates) and the *perceived value* ratings of each supplier on these attributes (on good to poor scale) into a prediction of the probability of each supplier's being chosen. This model is noteworthy because it incorporates the notions of thresholds, diminishing returns to scale, and saturation levels (Rao and Winter 1978). Individual respondents were grouped into homogeneous segments prior to the estimation of the logit coefficients. These segments had very different weightings of the attributes in their preference functions.
6. In fact, Porter goes further to characterize a detailed process of evaluation depending not only on the nature of the information itself, but also on the relevant source. Though the model presented remains plausible, it is important to recognize that little empirical evidence (and no first-hand evidence) is provided to support the model itself.

Bibliography

Abell, Derek F. (1980), *Defining the Business: The Starting Point of Strategic Planning*. Englewood Cliffs, NJ: Prentice-Hall, Inc.

Alberts, William W. and James M. McTaggart (1984), "Value-Based Strategic Investment Planning," *Interfaces*, 14 (January–February), 138–51.

Barnes, J. H. (1984), "Cognitive Biases and Their Impact on Strategic Planning," *Strategic Management Journal*, 5 (April–June), 129–38.

Baumol, William J. and Robert D. Willig (1981), "Fixed Costs, Sunk Costs, Entry Barrier and Sustainability of Monopoly," *Quarterly Journal of Economics*, 96 (August), 405–31.

Bhide, Amar (1986), "Hustle as Strategy," *Harvard Business Review*, 64 (September–October), 59–65.

Boynton, Andrew C. and Robert W. Zmud (1984), "An Assessment of Critical Success Factors," *Sloan Management Review*, 25 (Summer), 17–27.

Buzzell, Robert D. (1981), "Are There 'Natural' Market Structures?" *Journal of Marketing*, 45 (Winter), 42–51.

Capon, Noel and Joan Robertson Spogli (1976), "Strategic Market Planning: A Comparison and Critical Examination of Two Contemporary Approaches," in *Educators' Proceedings*. Chicago: American Marketing Association, 219– 23.

Carpenter, Gregory S. and Donald R. Lehmann (1985), "A Model of Marketing Mix, Brand Switching, and Competition," *Journal of Marketing Research*, 22 (August), 318–29.

Carroll, Peter J. (1982), "The Link Between Performance and Strategy," *Journal of Business Strategy*, 2 (Spring), 3–20.

Cattin, Philippe and Dick R. Wittink (1982), "Commercial Use of Conjoint Analysis: A Survey," *Journal of Marketing*, 46 (Summer), 44–53.

Caves, Richard E. (1984), "Economic Analysis and the Quest for Competitive Advantage," *AEA Papers and Proceedings* (May), 124–32.

———, Bradley T. Gale, and Michael E. Porter (1977), "Interfirm Profitability Differences: Comment," *Quarterly Journal of Economics*, 91 (November), 667–76.

Chakravarti, Dipankar, Andrew Mitchell, and Richard Staelin (1981), "Judgment Based Marketing Decision Models: Problems and Possible Solutions," *Journal of Marketing*, 45 (Fall), 13–23.

Chattopadhyay, Amitava, Prakash Nedungadi, and Dipankar Chakravarti (1985), "Marketing Strategy and Differential Advantage: A Comment," *Journal of Marketing*, 49 (Spring), 129–36.

Churchill, Gilbert A., Jr. and Carol Surprenant (1982), "An Investigation into the Determinants of Customer Satisfaction," *Journal of Marketing Research*, 19 (November),491–504.

Cook, Victor J., Jr. (1983), "Marketing Strategy and Differential Advantage," *Journal of Marketing*, 47 (Spring), 68–75.

——— (1985), "The Net Present Value of Market Share," *Journal of Marketing*, 49 (Summer), 49–63.

Day, George S. (1981), "Strategic Market Analysis and Definition: An Integrated Approach," *Strategic Management Journal*, 2, 281–99.

——— (1984), *Strategic Market Planning: The Pursuit of Competitive Advantage*. Minneapolis: West Publishing Co.

——— and David B. Montgomery (1983), "Diagnosing the Experience Curve," *Journal of Marketing*, 47 (Spring), 44–58.

———, Allan D. Shocker, and Rajendra K. Srivastava (1979), "Customer-Oriented Approaches to Identifying Product-Markets," *Journal of Marketing*, 43 (Fall), 8–19.

Dickson, Peter R. and James L. Ginter (1987), "Market Segmentation, Product Differentiation and Marketing Strategy," *Journal of Marketing*, 51 (Spring), 1–10.

Doyle, Peter and John Saunders (1985), "Market Segmentation and Positioning in Specialized Industrial Markets," *Journal of Marketing*, 49 (Spring), 24–32.

Forbis, John L. and Nitin L. Mehta (1982), "Value-Based Strategies for Industrial Products," *Business Horizons* (Summer), 32–42.

Gale, Bradley T. and Robert D. Buzzell (1988), "Market Position and Competitive Strategy," in *The Interfaces of Marketing and*

Strategy, George S. Day, Barton Weitz, and Robin Wensley, eds. Greenwich, CT: JAI Press, Inc.

Gensch, Dennis H. (1984), "Targeting the Switchable Industrial Customer," *Marketing Science*, 3 (Winter), 41–54.

Ghemawat, Pankaj (1986), "Sustainable Advantage," *Harvard Business Review*, 64 (September–October), 55–58.

Glueck, William F. and Lawrence R. Jauch (1984), *Strategic Management and Business Policy*, 2nd ed. New York: McGraw-Hill Book Company.

Green, Paul E. and V. Srinivasan (1978), "Conjoint Analysis in Consumer Research: Issues and Outlook," *Journal of Consumer Research*, 5 (September), 103–23.

——— and Yoram Wind (1975), "New Way to Measure Consumers' Judgements," *Harvard Business Review*, 53 (July–August), 107–17.

Hitt, Michael A. and R. Duane Ireland (1985), "Corporate Distinctive Competence, Strategy, Industry and Performance," *Strategic Management Journal*, 6 (July–September), 273–93.

Hofer, Charles W. and Dan Schendel (1978), *Strategy Formulation: Analytical Concepts*, Minneapolis: West Publishing Co.

Hogarth, Robin M. and Spyros Makridakis (1981), "Forecasting and Planning: An Evaluation," *Management Science*, 27 (February), 115–38,

Jacobson, Robert and David A. Aaker (1985), "Is Market Share All That It's Cracked Up to Be?" *Journal of Marketing*, 49 (Fall), 11–22.

Johnson, Tod (1984), "The Myth of Declining Brand Loyalty," *Journal of Advertising Research*, 24 (February–March), 9–17.

Kamani, Aneel (1982), "Equilibrium Market Share—A Measure of Competitive Strength," *Strategic Management Journal*, 3 (January–March), 43–51.

King, William R. (1983), "Integrating Strength-Weakness Analysis into Strategic Planning," *Journal of Business Strategy*, 4 (Spring), 475–87.

Kotler, Philip (1984), *Marketing Management: Analysis, Planning and Control*, 5th ed. Englewood Cliffs, NJ: Prentice-Hall, Inc.

———, William Gregor, and William Rodgers (1977), "The Marketing Audit Comes of Age," *Sloan Management Review*, 18 (Winter), 25–43.

Larréché, Jean-Claude and Reza Moinpour (1983), "Management Judgment in Marketing: The Concept of Expertise," *Journal of Marketing Research*, 20 (May), 110–21.

——— and V. Srinivasan (1982), "STRATPORT: A Model for the Formulation of Business Portfolio Strategies," *Management Science*, 28 (September), 979–1001.

Learned, E. P., C. R. Christensen, K. R. Andrews, and W. D. Guth (1969), *Business Policy: Text and Cases*, Homewood, IL: Richard D . Irwin, Inc.

Leidecker, Joel K. and Albert V. Bruno (1984), "Identifying and Using Critical Success Factors," *Long Range Planning*, 17 (February), 23–32.

Lippman, S. A. and R. P. Rumelt (1982), "Uncertain Imitability: An Analysis of Interfirm Differences in Efficiency Under Competition," *Bell Journal of Economics*, 418–38.

Little, John D. C. (1979), "Decision Support Systems for Marketing Managers," *Journal of Marketing*, 43 (Summer) , 9–27.

———, David E. Bell, and Ralph E. Keeney (1975), "A Market Share Theorem," *Journal of Marketing Research*, 12 (May), 136–41.

Loomis, Carol J. (1987), "IBM's Big Blues: A Legend Tries to Remake Itself," *Fortune* (January 10), 34–54.

MacAvoy, Robert E. (1983), "Corporate Strategy and the Power of Competitive Analysis," *Management Review* (July), 9–19.

——— (1987), "Establishing Superior Performance Through Competitive Analysis," in *Strategic Planning and Management Handbook*, William R. King and David I. Cleland, eds. New York: Van Nostrand.

Mancke, R. B. (1974), "Causes of Interfirm Profitability: A New Interpretation of the Evidence," *Quarterly Journal of Economics*, 88 (May), 181–93.

Martilla, John A. and John C. James (1977), "Importance-Performance Analysis," *Journal of Marketing*, 51 (January), 77–79.

Mehrotra, Sunil (1984), "How to Measure Marketing Productivity," *Journal of Advertising Research*, 24 (June–July), 9–15.

Meyers, Stewart C. (1984), "Finance Theory and Financial Strategy," *Interfaces*, 14 (January–February), 126–37.

Mintzberg, Henry (1978), "Patterns in Strategy Formulation," *Management Science*, 24, 934–48.

Moran, William T. (1984), "Research on Discrete Consumption Markets Can Guide Resource Shifts," *Marketing News* (May 15), 4.

Moriarty, Rowland T., Ralph Kimball, and John H. Gay (1983), "The Management of Corporate Banking Relationships," *Sloan Management Review*, 24 (Spring), 3–16.

Ohmae, Kenichi (1982), *The Mind of the Strategist*. New York: McGraw-Hill Book Company.

——— (1985), *Triad Power*. New York: McGraw-Hill Book Company.

Peters, Thomas J. (1984), "Strategy Follows Structure: Developing Distinctive Skills," *California Management Review*, 26 (Spring), 111–25.

Pfeffer, Jeffrey and Gerald R. Salancik (1978), *The External Control of Organizations: A Resource Dependence Perspective*. New York: Harper and Row Publishers, Inc.

Porter, Michael E. (1976), *International Choice, Strategy and Bilateral Market Power*. Cambridge, MA: Harvard University Press.

——— (1980), *Competitive Strategy*. New York: The Free Press.

——— (1985), *Competitive Advantage: Creating and Sustaining Superior Performance*. New York: The Free Press.

Quinn, James Brian (1980), *Strategies for Change: Logical Incrementalism*. Homewood, IL: Richard D. Irwin, Inc.

Rao, Vithala and Frederick W. Winter (1978), "An Application of the Multivariate Probit Model to Market Segmentation and Product Design," *Journal of Marketing Research*, 15 (August), 361–68.

Rappaport, Alfred (1981), "Selecting Strategies That Create Shareholder Value," *Harvard Business Review*, 59 (May–June), 139–49.

——— (1986), *Creating Shareholder Value: The New Standard for Business Performance*. New York: The Free Press.

Robinson, William T. (1984), "Market Pioneering and Sustainable Market Share Advantages in Industrial Goods Manufacturing Companies," Krannert School, Purdue University (November).

Root, H. Paul (1986), "Industrial Market Intelligence Systems: A Source of Competitive Advantage," presentation to the Business-to-Business Marketing Conference, American Marketing Association, New Orleans (April).

Rothschild, William E. (1984), *How to Gain (and Maintain) the Competitive Advantage*. New York: McGraw-Hill Book Company.

Rumelt, R. P. and J. R. C. Wensley (1981), "Market Share and the Rate of Return: Testing the Stochastic Hypothesis," Working Paper MGL-03, University of California, Los Angeles.

Selznick, Philip (1957), *Leadership in Administration*. New York: Harper & Row Publishers, Inc.

Shocker, Allan D. and V. Srinivasan (1979), "Multiattribute Approaches to Product Concept Evaluation and Generation: A Critical Review," *Journal of Marketing Research*, 16 (May), 159–80.

——— and David W. Stewart (1983), "Mapping Competitive Relationships: Practices, Problems and Promise," Working Paper 83–115, Vanderbilt University (September).

Smith, Wendell (1956), "Product Differentiation and Market Segmentation as Alternative Marketing Strategies," *Journal of Marketing*, 21 (July), 3–8.

South, Stephen (1981), "Competitive Advantage: The Cornerstone of Strategic Thinking," *Journal of Business Strategy*, 1 (Spring), 15–25.

Stevenson, Howard H. (1976), "Defining Strengths and Weaknesses," *Sloan Management Review*, 17 (Spring), 51–68.

Stigler, George J . (1968), *The Economics of Industry*. Homewood, IL: Richard D. Irwin, Inc.

Teece, David J. (1980), "Economies of Scope and the Scope of the Enterprise," *Journal of Economic Behavior and Organization*, 223–47.

Urban, Glen L., Theresa Carter, and Zofia Mucha (1985), "Market Share Rewards to Pioneering Brands: An Exploratory Empirical Analysis," in *Strategic Marketing and Management*, H. Thomas and D. Gardner, eds. New.York: John Wiley & Sons, Inc., 239–52.

——— and John R. Hauscr (1980), *Design and Marketing of New Products*. Englewood Cliffs, NJ: Prentice-Hall, Inc.

Varadarajan, V. R. (1985), "A Two-Factor Classification of Competitive Strategy Variables," *Strategic Management Journal*, 6 (October–December), 357–76.

Wagner, Harvey M. (1984), "Profit Wonders; Investment Blunders," *Harvard Business Review*, 62 (September–October), 121–35.

Wensley, Robin, Patrick Barwise, and Paul Marsh (1984), "Strategic Investment Decisions," *Research in Marketing*, 8.

Wernerfelt, Birger (1984), "A Resource-Based View of the Firm," *Strategic Management Journal*, 5 (April–June), 171–80.

Wilkie, William L. and Edgar A. Pessemier (1973), "Issues in Marketing: Use of Multiattribute Attitude Models," *Journal of Marketing Research*, 10 (November), 428–41.

SECTION II

Strategic Marketing Objectives

The Market Share—ROI Controversy

Everyone agrees that market share, profitability, and return on investment are different and important strategic marketing objectives. But this agreement conceals a controversy which has raged in the marketing literature for nearly 20 years. The controversy surrounds the relationship between market share and ROI. One school of thought holds that there is a strong and positive relationship between return on investment and market share. A second school of thought holds that there is no association between market share and return on investment, except that which can be attributed to luck and other chance-causes. Professor Buzzell and Mr. Gale present evidence from 15 years of studying the Profit Impact of Market Strategy (PIMS) data in the first article in this section. The authors take the position that large market share is both the reward for providing better value to the customer and a means of realizing lower costs. They also investigate the arguments of those who believe that market share is not all its cracked up to be.

The second article in this section, by Simon Majaro asks the question "what *is* market share?" The author articulates the view that there are not only many alternate measures of market share of *demand*, which lead to many different conclusions, but that a whole range of measures of market share of *supply factors* has been entirely overlooked. Which of these measures are "most applicable" as strategic marketing objectives? The author concludes that it depends on the purpose to which the measure is to be put.

The Dynamics of Market Share

Of course, both supply and demand measures of market share play a vital role in strategic marketing. The paper by C. Davis Fogg on planning gains in market share was the first to explain the links between demand measures and supply measures of market share. The author presents a simplified competitive analysis in which we find competitive dimensions specified for both sides of the market. On the demand side, for each of three different product lines, the rate of growth in each market segment and competitors' market share of dollar demand are presented. These are followed by supply side measures of pricing strategy, new product policy, overall sales force strength by territory, number of distributors, delivery norms, and probable reactions for the company and its three main competitors. In this way Mr. Fogg demonstrates explicitly how gains in market share of demand follow directly from commitments to share of supply-side factors.

One of the two principle arguments supporting the position that higher market share leads to higher return on investments is that higher share leads to larger

cumulative production volumes which lead to lower average unit costs. In diagnosing the experience curve concept, Professors Day and Montgomery document the theory of the experience curve, discuss experience curve effects, and trace its competitive implications over the product life cycle. They also raise key questions and provide answers on the measurement and interpretation of the experience curve. They conclude that there are significant risks in strategies based on experience curve effects because of the potential for misleading signals.

Market Share & Profit Potential

In her article on profit potential as a martingale process, Professor Marjorie Utsey explores the ability of experienced managers to allocate resources in a way that maximizes the net present value of future profits to the firm, in an intensely competitive simulated market environment. In the process, the author formally investigates the relationship between share of demand and share of supply under four different model specifications. Specifically, she estimates the relationship between current market share of demand and lagged market share, share of advertising dollars, share of research dollars, share of units available for sale, share of sales force dollars, and share of perceived value in the *Markstrat* environment. She concludes that management did not fall short of profit potential, either for the simulated industries as a whole or for individual firms within each industry. In other words, the difference between actual profit potential and maximum profit potential tended to be zero, not negative.

A "martingale" is a statistical process in which the expected change in a value of interest from one year to the next is constant, but in which the current values in the series are dependent to some extent on previous values. Once a firm is pointed in a direction, achieving either more than or less than maximum profit potential, the momentum of the market will tend to sustain that direction for several years at a time. Based on this evidence, the author concluded that profit potential *is* a martingale process.

The implications of this finding for strategic marketing, if duplicated in the real world, are significant. Simply put, no one firm can expect to win all the time. There will be runs of good fortune and good management, sometimes over long periods. But inevitably the winners will be bested either by bad luck or by newcomers if profit potential is a martingale process.

The article by Professor Cook attempts to identify the specific process by which gains and losses in market share occur, and how they can be sustained over long periods of time. In short, the author evaluates the dynamic interaction of market share and profit. The concepts of the value and cost of market share are introduced and operational measures of both supply and demand side values are described. The concept of "weighted average market share" is defined and used to explain how long-run share of demand and long-run share of supply are equated. Then the author investigates the theoretical effects of market share and profit in a variety of dynamic market scenarios. These scenarios cover market growth, maturity and decline strategies. They also include competitive attack, price leadership and heavy user strategies. The theoretical effects of market share on profit, and of profit on market share, are examined in concrete terms in a ten-year simulation of the wine market. It is found that vastly different results in ROI, market share, and net present values occur for the *same* firm, with the *same* cost structures, in the *same* market, with the *same* objective: to maximize the net present value of market share. The simulated differences in profitability are due to changes in the rate of market growth, the ambitions of competitors, and the imagination of management. The author concludes that the three different performance factors are not substitutes for one another. Market share, ROI, and net present value each serve a special purpose, and marketing management should incorporate all three measures in its strategic plans. ■

8

Market Position & Profitability

Robert D. Buzzell & Bradley T. Gale

A study of 57 companies reveals a link between ROI and market share—the bigger the better.

LARGE MARKET SHARE is both a reward for providing better value to the customer and a means of realizing lower costs. Under most circumstances, enterprises that have achieved a large share of the markets they serve are considerably more profitable than their smaller-share rivals. This connection between market share and profitability has been recognized by corporate executives and consultants, and it is clearly demonstrated in the results of our research over the last fifteen years.

Yet, despite all the published evidence, even well-known experts on business strategy have offered the business community widely diverging, often shifting and conflicting, interpretations about the link between market position and profitability.

Granted that high rates of return usually accompany large market share. But the mere knowledge that large share and high returns go together isn't enough for planning purposes. You need answers to these questions:

- How much do profit margins differ between small-share and large-share businesses?
- Why is high market share profitable?
- Why do strategy consultants and academics disagree on their interpretations of the share/profitability relationship? Do the differences matter?
- Can the share/profitability relationship be quantified? Can it be calibrated to take into account specific business situations?
- What does the relationship imply for formulating strategy?

Robert D. Buzzell is Professor of Business Administration, Harvard Business School. Bradley T. Gale is a director of the Strategic Planning Institute.

In this chapter we shall attempt to answer these questions by presenting evidence on the nature, importance, and implications of the links between market position and profit performance.

Measures of Market Position

We use several measures of market position—absolute market share, market-share rank, and relative market share. Each measure captures a particular nuance of market position, but their similarities far outweigh their differences.

Absolute market share compares a business unit's sales to the sales of its served market. The served market's boundaries must realistically reflect customers' feelings about which companies, products, and services actually compete head-to-head in the marketplace.

Since businesses compete in many different kinds of served markets, an absolute market share of 15 may represent the market leader in a fragmented market or the number 4 competitor in a concentrated market. In light of this, we use market-share rank to make comparisons across the many served markets in the data base. Even in situations where the size of the served market (and therefore absolute market shares) cannot be determined accurately, managers typically have a good feel for the market-share *rank* of each competitor. For purposes of comparing a portfolio of businesses that compete in many different served markets, market-share rank is the simplest measure to use. But, a market-share rank of number 1 may represent a dominant leader with seventy percent of the market, or a first-among-equals position.

Two widely used measures of *relative* market share, which contrast a business's absolute share to the structure of its market, refine the concept of share rank. Share relative to the *single* largest competitor has been used by the Boston Consulting Group in their attempts to relate the "experience curve" to competitive advantage. Share relative to *three* largest competitors has been shown by our research to be the most useful measure of relative share for calibrating competitive advantage.[1] We have applied all of these measures in this chapter to diagnose the relationship between market position and profitability and to compare our interpretation of the relationship with the views of other authors.

Market Position and Profitability

There is no doubt that market share and return on investment are strongly related (Exhibit 1). On average, market leaders earn rates of return that are three times greater than businesses with a market-share rank of fifth or worse.

We can put these typical performance levels in perspective by comparing them to a pretax profit "hurdle rate" of 20%. We find that, on average, businesses ranked number one in market share beat this hurdle by 10 percentage points, but businesses ranked fifth or worse fall short by 10 percentage points.

The PIMS data base is the world's most extensive and detailed source of information on the share/profitability relationship, but additional evidence helps to confirm its existence. For instance, companies enjoying strong competitive positions in their primary product markets tend to be highly profitable. Consider, for example, such major companies as IBM, Gillette, Kellogg, and Coca-Cola, as well as smaller, more specialized corporations like Dr. Scholl (foot care products), Dexter (specialty chemicals and materials), and Sonoco Products (industrial packaging). Research on the Federal Trade Commission's line-of-business data base also supports the share/ profitability relationship.[2] The FTC's 1975 analysis of results for some 3000 lines of businesses in 258 manufacturing industry categories in 1975 indicates a significant positive relationship between pretax return on sales and absolute market share.

Exhibit 1
ROI Increases with Market Share Rank

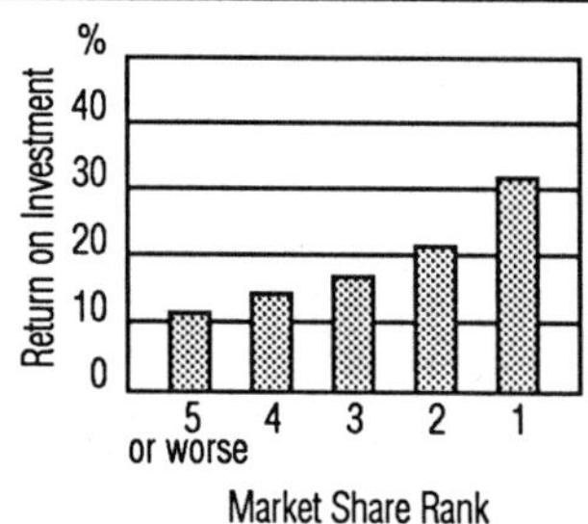

Why Is Market Share Profitable?

The data demonstrate that market leaders and small-market-share businesses have very different ROI (Exhibit 1). This evidence that the relationship exists, doe not, however, tell us *why* there is a link between market share and profitability. There are at least four possible reasons:

- Economies of scale
- Risk aversion by customers
- Market power
- A common underlying factor

The most obvious rationale for the high rate of return enjoyed by large-share businesses is that they have achieved economies of scale in procurement, manufacturing, marketing, R&D, and other cost components. A business with a 40% share of its served market is simply twice as big as one with 20% of the same market, and it can attain, to a much greater degree, more efficient methods of operation within a particular type of technology. The effects of economies of scale represent the primary direct causal mechanism that links share to profitability. Related to scale economics is the so-called "experience curve" phenomenon widely publicized by the Boston Consulting Group (BCG). Interpretation of the experience curve will be discussed in a later section of this chapter.

If a business has achieved (or is expected to achieve) the leading market-share position, risk-averse buyers may favor its products because they don't want to take the chances sometimes associated with buying from a smaller-share competitor. The customer preference comes as a direct consequence of share: a person placing an order with a dominant supplier feels he/she won't be challenged to defend that decision. IBM enjoys this kind of advantage in many of its business units. Many household consumers have the same kind of confidence in Kodak film, Gillette razor blades, and Bayer aspirin.

Many economists, especially in the antitrust field, believe that economies of scale have relatively little importance in most industries. These economists argue that if large-scale businesses earn higher profits than their smaller competitors, it is a result of their greater market power: their size permits them to bargain more effectively, "administer" prices, and, in the end, realize significantly higher prices for a particular product.[3]

The simplest of all explanations for the share/profitability relationship suggests that both share and ROI reflect a common underlying factor, for example, the quality of management. Good managers (including, perhaps, lucky ones!) succeed in achieving large shares of their respective markets; they are also skillful in controlling costs, getting maximum productivity from employees, and so on. Moreover, once a business achieves a leadership position—possibly by developing a new field—it is much easier for it to retain its lead than for others to catch up.

These varied explanations of why the share/profitability relationship exists are not mutually exclusive. To some degree, a large-share business may benefit from all four kinds of relative advantages. It is important, however, to understand how much of the increased profitability that accompanies large market share comes from each of these or other sources.

Exhibit 2
How Market Leaders Differ from Small-Share Businesses

Financial and Operating Ratios	Market Share Rank (%) *#5 or worse*	*#4*	*#3*	*#2*	*#1*
Capital Structure:					
Investment/Sales	54.9	51.4	52.5	52.1	46.3
Receivables/Sales	15.3	14.8	14.7	14.7	14.7
Inventory/Sales	22.3	20.6	20.5	19.6	18.5
Operating Ratios:					
Pretax Profit/Sales	4.5	5.5	7.1	9.1	12.7
Purchase/Sales	51.3	48.9	45.8	43.4	41.8
Manufacturing/Sales	24.5	26.5	26.8	26.8	26.0
Marketing/Sales	9.2	9.3	9.5	9.5	8.9
R&D/Sales	1.9	1.8	1.9	2.3	2.1
Capacity Utilization	73.1	73.7	75.8	75.7	77.1

Dissecting the Relationship

Analyzing the PIMS data base sheds light on the driving forces behind the strong relationship between market share and ROI. The data base allows us to observe real-life relationships between share and financial and operating ratios (Exhibit 2) and between share and measures of relative prices and relative quality (Exhibit 3). As you examine these figures, remember that the PIMS sample of businesses includes a wide variety of products and industries. Consequently, when we compare businesses with market-share rank of five or worse, say, with those having the number one share position, we are *not* observing difference in costs and profits within a single industry. Each subgroup contains a diversity of industries, types of products, kinds of customers, and so on.

The data reveal important differences between large-share businesses and those with smaller shares. ROI depends, of course, on both the rate of net profit on sales and the amount of investment required to support a given volume of sales. Differences in ROI can result from differences in return on sales, investment to sales, or both.

The data show that the major reason for the share/profitability relationship is the dramatic difference in pretax profit margins on sales (Exhibit 2). Market leaders average a return on sales of 12.7%, while businesses with market-share ranks of five or worse earn only 4.5%. In the PIMS sample, the average return on sales exhibits a strong, smooth, upward trend as market share increases. By contrast, the ratio of investment to sales declines only slightly with increased market share.

Exhibit 3
Market Leaders Have Higher Perceived Quality and Command Higher Prices

	Market Share Rank *#5 or worse*	*#4*	*#3*	*#2*	*#1*
Relative Quality (Percentile)	43	45	47	51	69
Relative Price (Percent)	103.0	103.2	103.4	103.8	105.7
Number of Businesses	301	240	347	549	877

Market Position and Relative Cost

Why do profit margins on sales increase with market share? The PIMS and BCG strategic paradigms take two very different approaches to understanding and calibrating the effect of market position on profit margins. The PIMS approach observes operating expense ratios, relative quality, and capital intensity in different market positions, and quantifies their effect on profit margins. The BCG "experience curve" approach uses data on how unit costs and cumulative volume have moved together *over time* to infer what the cost ratios are among competitors at any given point in time. Those cost ratios are then translated into profit differences.

The PIMS and BCG approaches agree on the *direction* of the share/profitability relationship. But, to assess alternative market-share strategies, executives need to quantify the *magnitude* of the profit benefit normally associated with capturing a larger share of the market served. How much will our profitability go up after scoring a 10-point gain in market share? If our market share is twice that of a competitor, will our net profit margin on sales probably be two percentage points higher or ten percentage points higher than theirs?

Back in the heyday of the experience curve, cost reduction was touted as the primary reason for pursuing a share-building strategy. As explained in a 1973 Boston Consulting Group publication, "The growth-share matrix is directly derived from the experience curve. The experience curve is the means of measuring probable cost differentials. A difference (i.e., a ratio) in market share of 2 to 1 should produce about 20 percent or more differential in pretax cost on value added."[4]

How important are economies of scale (relative *current* output) and "experience" (relative *cumulative* output) in explaining the share-profitability relationship? We can shed some light on this issue by comparing the actual experiences of the PIMS data base businesses with the cost and profit differentials implied by the experience curve approach. In the early 1970s, as just quoted, BCG claimed that a 2-to-1 market share advantage should produce a 20% (or greater) advantage in "cost of value added." By this they presumably meant all *internal* costs, as opposed to the costs of purchased materials and services. Later on (in 1978) BCG revised their earlier estimates, stating that the cost advantage associated with a 2 to 1 share ratio is only about half (10% instead of 20%) of what would be expected based on the experience curve.[5]

We can use the BCG estimates of share-related cost differentials to derive expected differences in profit margins. For this purpose, suppose that the base case is a business with a relative share (i.e., relative to the largest competitor) of 1.0. Based on average PIMS results, this base case business would have the following cost structure:

Selling Price	100%
Purchases	44
Internal Costs	46
Pretax Profit	10

Using the more widely disseminated 20% differential in internal costs that is supposed to be associated with a doubling of market share, we can calculate the internal costs of businesses that are larger or smaller than the base case:

	Share Relative to Largest Competitor				
Percent of Sales	*0.25×*	*0.5×*	*1.0×*	*2.0×*	*4.0×*
Internal Costs	72	57	46	37	29
Purchases	44	44	44	44	44
Total Costs	116	101	90	81	73
Implied Profit Margin	−16	−1	10	19	27
PIMS Actual Average Profit Margin	6	8	10	12	14

Over the range of relative shares shown, the experience curve approach to calibrating competitive advantage implies a difference of 43 points (+27 versus −16) of pretax profit margin per 4 doublings of relative share. By this approach one would expect a business that is half as big as its leading competitor to earn a profit margin that is 11 points less! (The "modified experience curve" approach implies 5 points per doubling.) But the actual experience of the PIMS businesses with the indicated relative share positions shows only a 2-point difference in pretax profit margins. As some critics have suspected, the experience curve approach leads to exaggerated estimates of the effects of relative scale and experience.

Why are the share-related cost differentials so much smaller than the proponents of the experience curve claimed? There are, we believe, two primary explanations for this:

- Relative *current* market shares are often not accurate measures of relative *long-term* experience. If market positions have shifted over time, a business with a 2-to-1 current share advantage may have a much smaller advantage in cumulative output.
- Rather than the effects of "learning," many of the declines in costs over time that occur as cumulative volume builds are the result of scale increases and technological advances, often made by people outside the industry. These cost declines are not proprietary but available to *all* competitors who can use the new technology or gain in size. And even where learning or internally developed technology result in lower costs, what is learned can be transferred to competitors by equipment suppliers, departing employees, and competitive intelligence.

The share-profitability relationship *is* due in part to cost differences that reflect economies of scale and, perhaps, differences in experiences. But these cost differences are usually much smaller than what was claimed by overenthusiastic advocates of so-called experience curve pricing strategies.

Because the PIMS data base and BCG's Growth-Share classification scheme both indicate a strong positive relationship between market share and profitability, many executives apparently believe that the action implications of the two are the same. This is not necessarily so. As the data show, the experience curve approach to calculating probable cost differentials dramatically underestimates the viability of smaller-share businesses. We agree with the assumptions of the Growth-Share portfolio system about the *direction* of the impact of market share, but not about its *magnitude*. The difference is an important one, especially in situations where the key issue is whether one should stay in a particular business, or how much a gain in market share is worth.

Because it can take into account the important differences among competitors, the PIMS data base is a useful tool for calibrating the cost and margin differentials normally associated with differences in market share (and other key drivers of profitability) not only in general, as shown above, but also in an individual business's specific competitive environment, as we shall see.

Decline of the Experience Curve

Although Bruce Henderson's views of how to calibrate competitive advantage shifted dramatically during the 1970s, he never really understood the PIMS approach. According to *Forbes*,

> To Henderson, PIMS merely confirms much of what he knew all along from a combination of intuition and experience.[6]

In 1979, Michael Porter wrote a column in *The Wall Street Journal* pointing out the limitations of the experience curve as a device for formulating strategy.[7] By 1981, Walter Kiechel III was writing about "The Decline of the Experience Curve" in a *Fortune* series that examined some of the major concepts being used to formulate corporate strategy at that time. According to Kiechel,

> The news for the 1980s isn't that the experience curve has been proved wrong. Indeed, its logic has been refined, its implications plumbed for new ideas such as shared costs and the life cycle of technologies. What's happening now, though, is that the curve is being consigned to a much reduced place in the firmament of strategic concepts. With it is going a good bit of the importance originally attached to market share.[8]

Since the differences between SPI/PIMS and BCG still had not been clearly stated at that time, the PIMS baby (a multi-market data base useful as a tool for calibrating competitive advantage and for strategy analysis) was thrown out with the BCG bath water, the misnamed "experience" curve.

In retrospect, it is ironic that BCG, the pioneering firm, and Bruce Henderson, its founder, who made a major contribution by bringing economic analysis and strategy formulation to the consulting business, turned out to be using a tool that was better suited "to project normal or potential cost declines of a given competitor" than it was for measuring competitive advantage.[9]

Other Factors Affect Relative Costs

Based on early (and even later) interpretations of the experience curve, one would never have expected Japanese companies to crack the North American market in autos or steel. Clearly General Motors, Ford, and U.S. Steel were cumulative volume leaders in the 1970s. Yet they have been forced to surrender a great deal of market share to Japanese companies who had less cumulative volume. Why didn't "experience" save the U.S. auto and steel industries from Japanese competitors?

First, as we have just discussed, the competitive effects of cumulative volume were misunderstood and overstated. And while market share has been and is still important, its measurement must be refined to capture effective share in a global context.

Relative cost is driven by other factors as well as market share:

- Relative effectiveness in statistical process control,
- Relative productivity,
- International comparative advantage (relative costs of wages, materials, energy and capital), and
- Inventory and logistics costs associated with the proliferation of models and of options.

The globalization of competition over the last decade has increased the importance of these factors, relative to cumulative output, as determinants of relative costs. Unfortunately for the U.S., Japanese companies seem to have the edge over Detroit and Pittsburgh on many of these cost drivers.

International comparative advantage has played a major role in the capital intensive auto and steel industries. Relative to the U.S., Japan has lower costs of capital and labor. Relative to Japan, the U.S. has lower costs of energy and materials. The difference in relative capital and energy costs is the main reason why the Japanese have had great success in exporting steel but little success in aluminum, which is energy intensive.

Market Position, Quality and Prices

Perhaps the key reason why Japan is currently so successful in automobiles is that customer-perceived quality often outweighs price (cost) in the customer's purchase decision. The cumulative volume framework remains silent on relative customer-perceived quality and could not have helped to predict this quality effect.

By contrast, the PIMS framework explicitly charts the key steps through which perceived quality drives business performance. A study by Phillips, Chang, and Buzzell traced the linkages from superior relative quality to higher relative prices, market-share gain, lower relative costs, and higher profitability (Exhibit 4).[10] Their results showed that the PIMS measures of relative quality and other strategy variables are highly reliable indicators of the concepts represented. They concluded that relative quality does play a causal role in influencing business performance.

Exhibit 4
Winning with superior perceived quality.

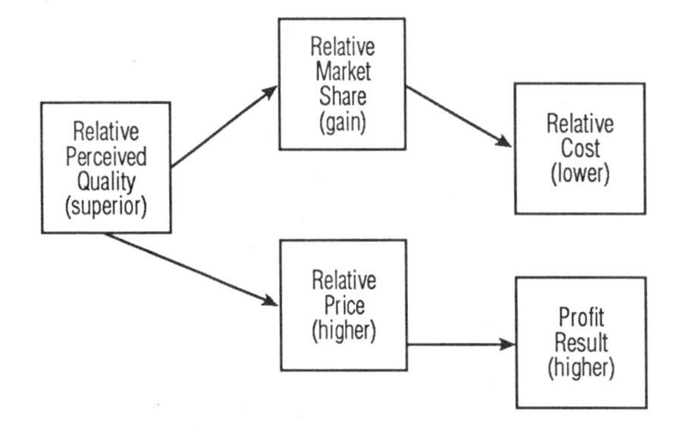

Quality is extremely important to market leaders. Looking back at Exhibits 2 and 3, the data do not always show smooth, continuous relationships between market share and the various components of quality, price, cost, and investment. Indeed, it appears that one pattern operates as share rank moves from 5 or worse to number 2, but a somewhat different pattern applies to market leaders. In particular, there are substantial differences in relative *quality* (and also in relative *prices*) between market leaders and followers (Exhibit 3). Market leaders not only command higher prices but also maintain their leadership position by offering products and services that are superior relative to those offered by their competitors.

Here is how Tom Peters summarized this subject in his best-selling book, *A Passion For Excellence*.

> The PIMS paradigm is diametrically opposite to the experience curve from a cause-and-effect standpoint: It says, First achieve a "relative perceived product-quality" edge over your competitors. If you do so, you will gain share. By gaining share (via relatively higher perceived product quality) you can, indeed, then take advantage of economies of scale as appropriate, and achieve low-cost distinction.
>
> The difference is radical. By the PIMS logic, you start from quality and achieve low cost as a result. According to the traditional experience curve approach, you buy your way in with low prices, achieve low cost, and may or may not have acceptable service and quality. If you don't have them, then you're constantly vulnerable to any higher-quality attacker who comes your way; the edge you scrambled so hard for is not likely to be sustainable. We call the distinction "earning your way in" (via quality and service) versus "buying your way in" (via heavy discounting). Only the former, it would appear, is sustainable.[11]

In the experiences of PIMS businesses, attaining a superior quality position does not seem to involve many of the strategic tradeoffs, such as higher relative direct costs or marketing expenditures, that business analysts often attribute to quality strategies. Superior quality does, however, support higher prices. . . .

Procurement Economies

In our discussion of market position and relative costs, we focused on economies of scale in value-added costs and assumed there were no procurement economies. If we had built procurement economies into the analysis, the "experience" curve's expected profit margin differentials per doubling of relative share (which were already way too large) would have been even further off the mark.

Are there economies of scale in purchased costs of materials and energy? We believe that the answer is yes, but the empirical test is not as straightforward as you might think, even with the PIMS data base at hand.

It is difficult to get a clear look at purchased cost economies (or at manufacturing economies, for that matter) because large-share businesses tend to be more vertically integrated than small-share businesses. They tend to carry out more stages of the value adding chain that results in their final sales dollar. They do more "make" and less "buy," and this clouds our ability to examine economies of scale by looking at expense ratios to sales as a function of market share. Having said this, let's examine how expense ratios to sales are related to market share, and interpret the results with care.

For small-share businesses—those ranked number five or worse—purchases represent 53% of sales, compared with only 42% for market leaders (Exhibit 2). The decline in the purchases-to-sales ratio is quite a bit less, however, if we control for the level of vertical integration.

While the vertical integration explanation of the decline in purchases to sales is probably valid for some of the businesses in the sample, we believe that the decline in costs of purchased materials usually also reflects economies of scale in buying and, perhaps, bargaining power in dealing with suppliers. Economies of scale in procurement arise from lower costs of manufacturing, marketing, and distributing when suppliers sell in large quantities. For really large-scale buyers, custom-designed components and special formulations of materials that are purchased on long-term contracts may offer very large economies.

The shift toward "make" versus "buy" as market share increases also clouds our view of economies of scale in manufacturing. If there were no economies of scale in manufacturing, greater vertical integration ought to result in a higher level of manufacturing or operational costs.[12] But the data show little or no connection between manufacturing expense as a percentage of sales, and market share (Exhibit 2), probably because the rise in cost associated with the increase in vertical integration is offset by economies of scale.

Efficient Use of Investment

While the bulk of the ROI difference between market leaders and those ranked 5 or worse is due to differences in return on sales, some twenty percent of the ROI difference is due to differences in investment intensity. On average, market leaders support their higher margins with more efficient use of investment than do followers.

If there were no scale-related economies in inventories, receivables, or fixed capital, the vertical integration phenomenon would cause us to expect investment to sales to *increase* with market share. But the investment-to-sales ratio actually *declines* slightly with increased market share (Exhibit 2). If we control for vertical integration, the decline in investment to sales is even more pronounced. Market leaders clearly benefit from economies of scale in inventories. The data show, too, that capacity utilization is slightly greater for large-share businesses.

Can Small-Share Businesses Prosper?

The fact that market share and profitability generally go hand in hand (as shown in Exhibit 1) led some consultants and corporate executives to adopt the extreme position that small-share businesses *cannot* be profitable. Reacting to this, several investigators have demonstrated that some small-share competitors can and do earn very attractive returns. Two articles in the *Harvard Business Review* have reported these studies:

> Richard Hamermesh, M. J. Anderson, and J. E. Harris analyzed the performance of companies whose results are published in the annual *Forbes* magazine financial surveys. They found "numerous successful low-share businesses" and discussed three examples of this phenomenon in some detail. One of these, Burroughs, was praised for focusing on selected segments of the computer market. As a result, the company's profits grew during the early 1970s at a rate faster than IBM's despite a huge disadvantage in *overall* market share.[13]
>
> Carolyn Woo and Arnold Cooper examined the performance of low-share businesses in the PIMS data base. They identified 40 low-share businesses that enjoyed pretax ROI's of 20% or more and compared their strategies with those of "ineffective" low-share businesses. Among other things, the successful low-share businesses were found to be characterized by high relative quality, narrow product lines, and low total costs.[14]

As these two studies show, small-share businesses can indeed be profitable. This is hardly surprising in light of the fact, noted earlier, that share is just one of approximately two dozen key profit influences that have been documented in PIMS-based research—and that other profit determinants, such as "corporate culture," also play important roles. A small-share business that is favorably positioned on most other key strategic dimensions *should* earn satisfactory profits. PIMS research shows, for example, the average ROI of small-share businesses whose products or services ranked in the top third in terms of relative quality was 18%. If a business in this group also benefited from low investment intensity, high labor productivity, and rapid market growth, its expected rate of return could easily be 25% or better. But it should be emphasized that *most* small-share businesses don't fit this description. Of the 641 businesses in the PIMS data base with shares of 10% or less, only about one in four achieved an ROI of 20% or more. In contrast, three-fourths of the businesses with shares of 40% or more had rates of return over 20%. It is useful to recognize and understand the exceptions to the general rule—but it is also important to remember that they *are* exceptions.

Is It Better To Be Small Than "Stuck in the Middle?"

The examples of profitable small-share businesses cited by Hamermesh et al. and by Woo and Cooper don't contradict the general rule that share and profitability usually go together. A stronger dissent, however, has been expressed by Michael Porter in his best-selling book, *Competitive Strategy*. Porter suggests that while there may be a positive share-profitability relationship in "some" industries, in others the relationship is inverse and in still others it is U-shaped, i.e., high on both ends and low in the middle. Citing the automobile and electric motor industries as examples of the U-shaped pattern, he warns of the dangers of being "stuck in the middle."[15] The clear implication is that in such industries, it is better to have a small share than to be, say, the second or third-ranked competitor. In the industries where the relationship is inverse, it would even be better to be a small-share competitor than to be the market leader!

Can Porter's views be reconciled with the positive share-profitability relationship shown in Exhibit 1? We should note, first, that there is an important conceptual difference between Porter's concept of share and ours. He defines "share" as a business unit's sales in relation to a broadly-defined industry such as computers or automobiles. (Hamermesh et al. followed the same approach, defining the Burroughs Corporation's market share as its fraction of total computer industry shipments.) In contrast, all of our market-share figures are measured in relation to each business unit's *served market*. The served market is defined as that part or segment of an industry (in terms of products, kinds of customers, and geographic areas) in which a business actually competes. For most businesses, the market defined in this way is considerably smaller than the overall industry in which it participates. For example, one of the successful small-share competitors cited by Porter is Mercedes-Benz. This highly-profitable firm has a very small share of total worldwide automobile sales. But, applying our concept of its relevant served market, Mercedes-Benz has a *large* share of the luxury car market. Put another way, we don't believe that Mercedes-Benz really competes with Honda, Toyota, or Volkswagen, and only to a very limited extent with General Motors. Its sales relative to these much larger producers is not, therefore, a meaningful measure of Mercedes-Benz's competitive position.

By defining market share in relation to a business unit's actual served market, we do *not* mean to encourage executives to limit their attention only to current customers, products, and geographic markets. Competitors operating in

Exhibit 5

A business that is "caught in the corner" is in an extemely poor strategic position.

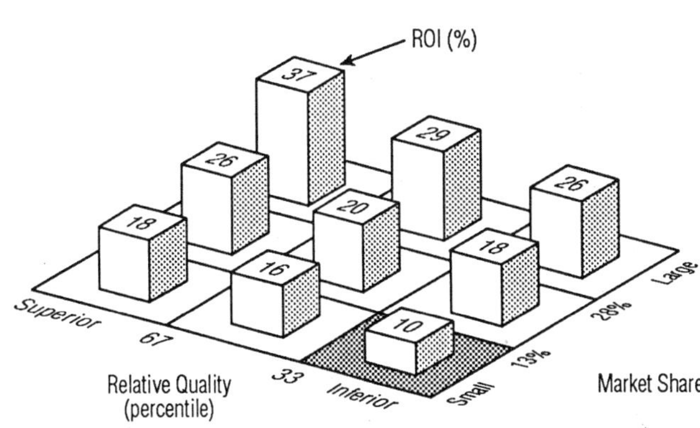

neighboring markets often can enter a market and overcome even the strongest incumbent, especially when capabilities developed in one sector are easily transferred to another. For example, Briggs & Stratton Corporation has long dominated the U.S. market for small engines of the types used in lawn mowers and garden tractors. Beginning in 1984, Honda began an aggressive campaign to promote its line of lawn and garden equipment in the U.S., utilizing its experience in manufacturing engines for motorcycles.[16] If Briggs & Stratton had been oblivious to the possibility of Honda's entry into its served market (which they were not), they could have been highly vulnerable. Thus, having a large share of a particular served market is not a guarantee of invulnerability to competition. But, we believe, a business unit's share of its served market is nevertheless a better measure of its *current* competitive position than its share of a broad and heterogeneous industry.

There is a more fundamental flaw in Porter's notion of a U-shaped relationship between share and profitability. By suggesting that small-share businesses typically earn high rates of return, he implies that this performance is *caused* by having a small share. In fact, the examples he cites illustrate how successful product differentiation can *offset* the disadvantages of a low share. As Exhibit 5 demonstrates, high quality can indeed yield high profits, even for small-share competitors—but it yields even bigger returns for those with strong market positions, and the latter is a much more common combination. A PIMS-based study by Lynn Phillips, Dae Chang, and Robert Buzzell showed that in the majority of cases superior quality, large share, *and* low costs relative to competition go together.[17] This contradicts the idea that so-called "generic strategies" aimed at low cost are incompatible with those based on product differentiation.

Even if market share *is* defined and measured in relation to industries rather than served markets, the available evidence shows that share is generally positively related to profitability. If the relationship really varied from positive to negative to U-shaped, we would expect the *average* of a broad sample of industries to show a very weak connection, if any, between share and profit performance. But this is not the case: in the Federal Trade Commission's Line of Business research program, the profitability of business segments was related to a variety of factors including each segment's "share of industry sales." The results showed a strong, *positive* relationship between share and profits.[18] This is hardly what we would expect if there were an appreciable number of industries characterized by U-shaped or down-sloping share-profitability relationships.

An analogy may help to put the seeming anomaly of successful small-share businesses into perspective. In 1985 a nationally-televised "slam dunk" competition featured some of the most talented players in the National Basketball Association. Almost all of the contestants were at least 6′8″ tall. But the winner, incredibly, was 5′5″ Spud Webb of the Atlanta Hawks! Webb's performance certainly showed that small people can win at a big person's game. But no one, presumably, would conclude from it that small players are usually or even often better at slamdunking than tall players. In the same way, we find the occasional success of small-share competitors unconvincing as the basis for any general argument for preferring a weak market position.

Other Views of Cause and Effect

While our purpose in this chapter is to focus on the strategic interpretations of the share/profitability relationship, we will briefly discuss the market power and random process interpretations.

Some economists believe concentrated market structures facilitate "oligopolistic coordination," a rather friendly, nonaggressive kind of competition, resulting in lower output, higher prices, and thereby higher rates of return than are typical in "competitive" markets. Therefore, they expect to see a direct relation between "industry concentration" (the combined market share of the top four companies) and profitability.

The PIMS business unit data base provides a straightforward approach to comparing the relative power of market share and concentration in explaining differences in profitability. The result: market share shows a far more dramatic effect on ROI than concentration when they are looked at together (Exhibit 6). Concentration actually does little to explain the structure-profit relationship. Our findings are supported by research on the Federal Trade Commission's line-of-business (LOB) data base. When analyzed in the LOB data base, share has a strong positive relation to profitability, but concentration has a weak negative relation to profitability.

We conclude that even though market share and concentration usually go together, it is the share that matters, not the concentration.[19] Put another way, the market power interpretation of the share/profitability relationship doesn't have much empirical support.

Is the share/profitability relationship all a matter of luck? Many academic technicians are attracted to a random-process interpretation of the share/profitability relationship. They reason, for example, that if many small-share competitors start out on equal terms, the lucky ones will probably gain both share and profitability. They focus their attention on change in share and change in profitability, rather than on how share differences affect profit differences in more stable market environments. Often they forget that many served markets are created by a pioneer rather than by a horde of small-share competitors awaiting the start of a random process. The pioneer starts with 100 percent share and subsequently faces challenges from early followers and late entrants.

We don't dispute that the assumptions of random process are logically sufficient to explain a dynamic share/profitability relationship. Indeed, one can find examples of businesses that (by skill or luck) were in the right place at the right time and gained in both share and profitability. But the random process view is not very interesting from a strategy perspective. If random events cause the share/profitability relationship, the action implication is to "be lucky." That advice is easy to understand, but hard to implement. Still, it is useful to know to what extent the observed share/profitability relationship is due to economies of scale versus random events.

In 1977 Caves, Gale, and Porter demonstrated that the random-process hypothesis is probably not the primary explanation for the observed relationship.[20] Here we will present a simplified update of one of their tests.

If the share/profitability relationship is due mostly to luck, it would show up more strongly in unstable markets where shares are shifting dramatically. Changing shares suggest that investment decisions by competing suppliers carry a great deal of risk. And the very fact that market shares are changing indicates that investments that succeed are capable of increasing a business's market share as well as its profit rate.

If the share/profitability relationship is stronger in markets where shares are stable, however, it is difficult to credit this result to the random-process view that luck causes share and profit to move together.

The evidence? The share/profitability relation turns out to be stronger where shares are stable as Caves, Gale, and Porter found in their 1977 study. In stable markets, market leaders on average reap 25 percentage points more ROI than

Exhibit 6

Which determines profitability – industry concentration or market share?

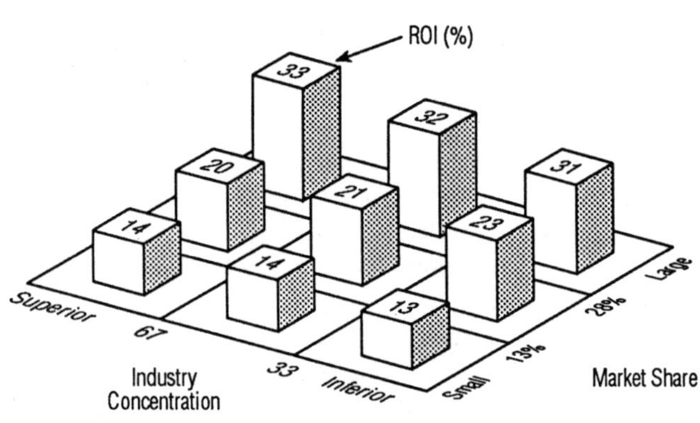

small-share businesses. In markets where shares are unstable, the ROI difference is significantly less—only 17 percentage points. These results contradict the random process interpretation of the share/profitability relationship. We conclude, therefore, that the random process hypothesis not only offers little help from a strategy perspective, but also doesn't explain much of the relationship between profitability and market share.

The whole question of "spurious" versus "causal" relationships between share and profit performance is, we believe, a red herring. Market share *in itself* doesn't "cause" anything. How can it? A business unit's market share is nothing more than a measurement. It reflects two kinds of forces, however, that *do* cause high or low profits: (1) relative scale and/or experience-based cost advantages or disadvantages and (2) relative success or lack of it in designing, producing, and marketing products that meet the needs of the customers in a particular served market. In this chapter we have shown that both factors are important—large-share businesses *do* typically have lower costs, and they also typically have product quality advantages that translate into bigger profit margins.

Our interpretation of how the share-profitability relationship typically works is summarized in these key steps:

- Superior relative quality is achieved by a combination of skillful product or service design and proper selection of market(s) to serve,
- Providing superior quality enables a successful business to charge premium prices (within reason, of course) *and* to gain market share,
- By gaining share, the business attains scale and/or experience-based cost advantages over its competitors (as noted earlier, these kinds of cost advantages are *not* generally incompatible with successful differentiation),
- Higher profitability follows as a result of premium prices, costs equal to or lower than those of competitors, and advantages in procurement and utilization of invested capital, as noted earlier.

If this is a valid picture of the typical linkage between share and profitability, then the key "causal" factors operating are scale and quality. Market share is, in effect, a convenient kind of shorthand that reflects some combination of these underlying profit influences.

Change in Profit Versus Level of Profit

In a recent study, "Is Market Share All That It's Cracked Up to Be?" Robert Jacobson and David Aaker suggest that the observed correlation between share and profitability might be due to a third factor (perhaps luck) rather than a direct effect of market share on ROI.[21] But then, to control for such third factors, they included past profitability as a factor to explain current profitability. In effect they related *change* in ROI to the *level* of market share.

Since share accounts for about 14 percent of the dispersion in ROI among businesses, we need to take more factors into account, even if they are not correlated with share.

Exhibit 7
Interpreting the relationship between ROI and market share

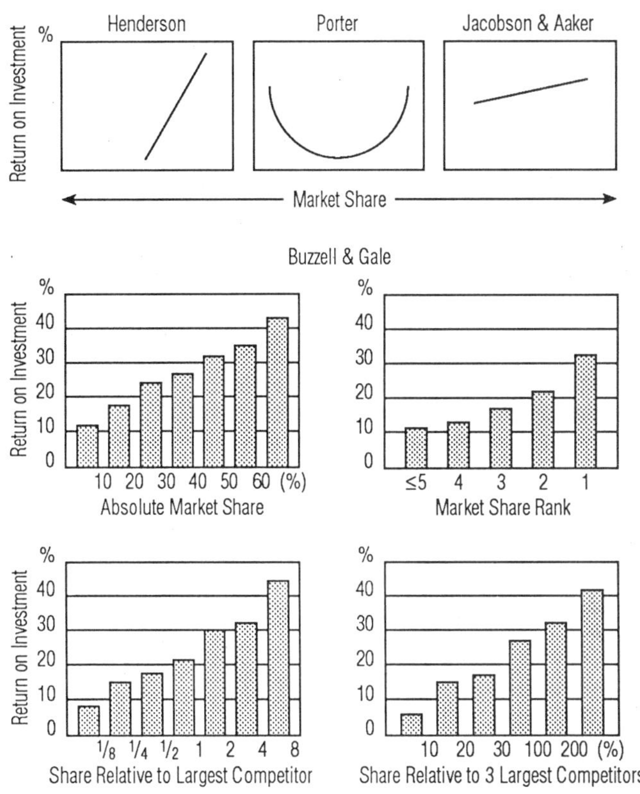

SPI's Par ROI model controls for many factors in addition to relative share and relative quality. These other drivers of profitability include capacity utilization, real market growth, purchase amount by immediate customer, investment intensity, and productivity.

Summarizing the Different Views

Exhibit 7 contrasts the ROI/share relationships depicted by Henderson, Porter, and Jacobson and Aaker, and compares them to the empirical relationships summarized by Buzzell and Gale. Relative to the actual experience of businesses in the marketplace:

1. Henderson overstates the relationship between ROI and share.
2. Jacobsen and Aaker understate the relationship between ROI and share.
3. Porter is stuck in the middle. He confuses the separate effects of market share and perceived quality on ROI.

Reductio ad Absurdum

While no analogy is perfect, the relationship between height and weight can take us a long way toward understanding these different interpretations of the ROI/share relationship and it may provide some comic relief. How would the Henderson, Porter, and Jacobson and Aaker approaches come

Exhibit 8

Reductio ad absurdum: speculations about interpreting the relationship between weight and height

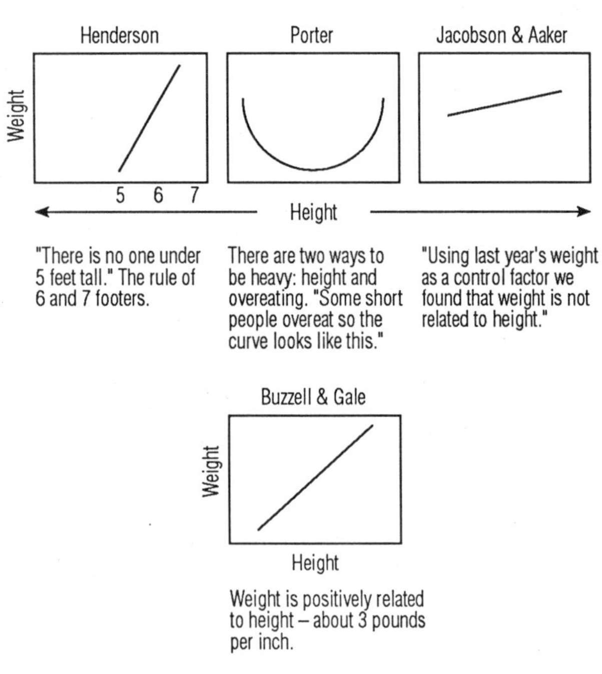

out if applied to the relationship between weight and height rather than profitability and share? Speculation has resulted in the relationships shown in Exhibit 8.

Applying the PIMS approach, we find that weight is positively related to height—about three pounds per inch. This general differential can be calibrated to reflect a person's sex and body frame.

When Henderson thought that the ROS differential per doubling of relative market share was 11 points (5 times greater than it actually is) he wrote a perspective on "The Rule of Three or Four." He reasoned that if smaller-share competitors were at a tremendous disadvantage, there would only be room for a handful of suppliers to any served market.

Suppose Henderson had similarly misgauged the weight/height relationship by a factor of 5. Observing from empirical data that the average six footer weighs about 180 pounds and believing that the weight differential was 15 pounds per inch, he might have concluded that "There Is No One Under Five Feet Tall."

Here's how Michael Porter's reasoning might be applied to the weight/height relationship. There are at least two ways to be heavy: height and overeating. Some short people overeat so the curve looks U-shaped. But what about the short people that don't overeat and the medium-height people who do overeat?

Applying Jacobson and Aaker's methodology, it is a good idea to control for factors other than height which might cause the observed weight/height relationship. Using last year's weight as a control factor we would be studying *change* in weight versus *level* of height and we would find that "weight is not strongly related to height."

When Is Market Share Most Important?

Given that market leaders have a large relative market share and thus the profitability that goes with it, it is natural to question whether the share and profitability relationship shifts from industry to industry. What kinds of businesses will find market share most critical to their success? What industries need to think most carefully about share position?

Our analyses of the PIMS data base clearly demonstrate a strong general relationship between ROI and market share. But while these general findings are interesting, more specific analyses are necessary if you wish to reposition your business so that it will outperform its competitors. The importance of share does vary considerably from one type of industry or market situation to another. We have already seen that share is more important in stable markets than it is in unstable markets. Two other interesting variations focus on the functional components of value added and the degree of investment intensity.

R&D and Marketing Versus Manufacturing

High-tech industries are characterized by heavy doses of R&D and marketing. Others carry out most of their value adding activities in the manufacturing function. Is market share more important in high-tech or smokestack industries?

People who follow the experience curve explanation of the share/profitability relationship invariably answer that share is most important in manufacturing-intensive industries. By contrast, those who believe that economies of scale are the main reason behind the share/profitability relationship feel that share matters more in industries where fixed costs are large relative to variable costs.

We used the ratio of R&D and marketing costs relative to manufacturing costs, to split the PIMS data base into two groups. For R&D and marketing intensive businesses the ROI of the average market leader is 26 percentage points greater than the ROI of the average small-share business (Exhibit 9). For manufacturing-intensive businesses the corresponding ROI differential is only 12 points. So, we conclude that market share is more important in high-tech industries.

Why? Compared to manufacturing costs, R&D and marketing costs tend to be relatively relaxed. In most markets

Exhibit 9

Market share is more important in high-tech or marketing-intensive industries.

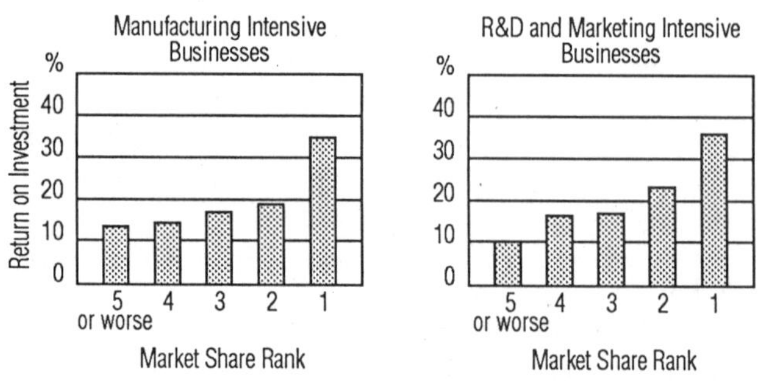

you need a certain amount of expenditure on innovation and marketing to remain a viable competitor. R&D and marketing activities are thus more subject to scale effects than are manufacturing costs.

Initially one might, therefore, expect R&D and marketing costs to decline as we move from small-share businesses to large-share businesses. But, we find that R&D-to-sales and marketing-to-sales ratios are about the same for large-share and small-share businesses (Exhibit 2). There are two reasons why we don't observe a decline. First, as noted earlier, large-share businesses are more vertically integrated (they "make" rather than "buy"). Second, and related, since R&D and marketing costs are more subject to scale effects, market leaders often pursue competitive strategies of developing product and service superiority and of introducing new products that are R&D and marketing intensive. This strategy makes it difficult for small-share competitors to keep pace. The vertical integration and innovation activities that tend to increase the R&D and marketing-to-sales ratios of large-share businesses are offset by economies of scale in marketing and R&D. This yields the flat pattern of average cost ratios we have observed (Exhibit 2).

Heavy Versus Light Investment Intensity

Market leadership has a greater payoff in industries that are not very investment intensive. For businesses with low investment to sales the ROI of the average market leader soars 25 percentage points above the ROI of the average small-share business. For investment intensive businesses the corresponding ROI differential is only 11 points.

Why? Market share helps return on sales (ROS) via economies of scale that reduce unit costs. Since

$$ROI = ROS \times (Sales/Investment),$$

the ROS differential between share leaders and followers is greatly leveraged in industries where investment-to-sales is very low.

In investment-intensive industries, on average, only the market leaders come close to earning a 20% pre-tax ROI . . . and even they fall a little short (Exhibit 10). By contrast, in low-investment situations all but the smallest-share competitors average returns well above 20%, and even the smallest-share competitors come close.

In addition to these industry differences (high-tech versus low-tech, investment-intensity light versus heavy) we have noted previously that the positive effect of absolute market share on ROI diminishes as market share gets larger because the drops in unit costs don't come as fast when market share is already large.

Market Share and Competitive Strategy

The importance of market share has, no doubt, been exaggerated by some commentators, especially those who linked the advantages of a large share to experience-based cost differentials. But the available evidence from PIMS and other sources clearly shows that share and profitability are strongly related. The relationship has been confirmed repeatedly, in analyses of the actual experiences of businesses in different kinds of industries, different time periods, and various parts of the world. Market share is not the only key to profitability, but it is certainly one of the most important. In light of this, how should market share be treated in the process of developing and evaluating competitive strategies?

First, the pursuit of market share is not in itself a strategy. It is often an important strategic objective; but it is much easier to state such a goal than it is to determine how it can be attained. In this chapter we have emphasized the importance of relative quality, both as a means of staking out a strong market position and, later, of maintaining or improving one. Other important weapons in competing for market share include product innovation and spending levels for sales forces and advertising and sales promotion. All of these play a role: the special appeal of quality is that, in many cases, it offers a means of building share without incurring any short-term penalty.

When a business doesn't have a significant quality advantage over its rivals, adopting a share-building strategy can be very costly. We have already cited an example of this in Chapter 1 [in *The PIMS Principles*]—Yamaha's disastrous effort in the early 1980s to overtake Honda as the leader in motorcycle production. Yamaha's president, Hisao Koike, adopted the slogan "Take the Lead" and pursued an aggressive program of new model introductions. By April 1983 the company was heavily in debt to finance its inventories and more than 2,000 workers had been laid off. Koike was removed as president and the "kamikaze attack" was called off.

Efforts to wrest market share away from a well-established leader are unlikely to pay off unless the leader is complacent or distracted by other problems. Considerable attention has therefore been given to the question of alternative strategies for market followers. Several of the critics of the share-profitability relationship have cited the successes of small

Exhibit 10

Market leadership pays off most in industries that are not investment intensive.

competitors who focused their efforts on particular market segments or niches. There is no doubt that this kind of market focusing is an important strategic option for many enterprises, especially those that have no possibilities of becoming leaders in more broadly-defined industries. It is for this reason that we, in the PIMS research program, have so strongly emphasized the idea of carefully defining and selecting a business unit's *served market*. Making the proper choices of products or services to offer, types of customers to serve, and geographic areas in which to operate are among the most important decisions that managers make.

Defining the served market is not, however, something that managers can control completely. Who competes with whom is an issue that is also affected by what other companies do and, ultimately, by the underlying economics of an industry. Consider, for example, the three examples of successful small-share competitors cited by Hamermesh et al. in 1978: the Burroughs Corporation (computers), Crown Cork & Seal (metal containers), and Union Camp (paper). All three had outstanding records of growth and profitability in the early 1970s. A decade later, the picture had changed considerably. During the years 1981–85, Crown Cork & Seal's average return on equity (ROE) was 11.3%; it ranked 12th among 13 companies in the packaging industry. Union Camp, with an ROE of 14.8%, placed near the middle of the rankings in the paper industry. Burroughs' ROE had declined to 7.1% (23rd out of 24 computer manufacturers) and the company was attempting to acquire Sperry in an effort to create a viable competitor to IBM in the large-computer business.

These illustrations suggest that what constitutes a distinct submarket within an industry at one time may not be so distinct at a later time. A particular product variation or customer group may, for example, simply have been neglected by larger competitors, leaving it available to a smaller rival despite the latter's inherently inferior cost position or technology. Serving such a niche may be highly profitable for some years, but eventually it is likely to become much less so. The moral would appear to be: either take steps to accentuate the differences between a submarket and the overall market (for instance, through product development) or be prepared to move on to another one.

Many of the criticisms of the market-share profitability relationship stem from the perception that it was being used, a decade ago, as a basis for overly simplistic strategic formulas. This is unfortunate; the share-profitability relationship is a fact of life that should be recognized and understood. It does not, in itself, provide any general prescriptions for management, but it does yield insights into the likely consequences of strategic choices.

The strategic implications of the market-share/profitability relationship do vary according to the circumstances of the individual business. But there is no doubt that the relationship can be translated into dynamic strategies for all companies trying to set market share goals. The PIMS data base is often used to calibrate the cost of growing against the benefits of growing, with some precision, for specific business situations and then translate this knowledge into action plans.

One example of a company pursuing strategic objectives that are consistent with the concepts and findings of this chapter is General Electric under the leadership of John F. Welch, Jr. He has said that

> . . . Our strategic aim is to evolve into a company that's either number one or number two in its arenas . . . [23]

Major steps in this evolution include the disposition of Utah Mining and the acquisition of RCA and some financial service companies. GE is shifting its portfolio away from investment-intensive arenas toward high-tech and service arenas. Welch is attempting to become number one or number two in situations where being number one or number two matters most.

Once market position is established, market leaders and followers typically need to pursue different strategies. Coming up with these different strategies is the subject of Chapter 9. [in *The PIMS Principles*].

References

1. See Appendix B for a comparison of these two measures of relative market share.
2. David J. Ravenscraft, "Structure-Profit Relationships at the Line of Business and Industry Level," *Review of Economics and Statistics*, February 1983, pp. 22–31.
3. This general argument has been made in numerous books, articles and speeches dealing with antitrust economics; see, for example, Joe S. Bain, *Industrial Organization*, 2nd edition (New York: John Wiley & Sons, 1968), especially Chapter 6.
4. Boston Consulting Group, "The Experience Curve—Reviewed," *Perspective*, No. 135 (Boston: 1973).
5. Boston Consulting Group, "The Experience Curve Revisited," *Perspective*, No. 229 (Boston: 1978).
6. "Unless You Can Be a Winner, Don't Play," *Forbes*, October 15, 1977.
7. Michael E. Porter, "Experience Curve," *The Wall Street Journal*, October 22, 1979.
8. Walter Kiechel III, "The Decline of the Experience Curve," *Fortune*, October 5, 1981.
9. Bruce D. Henderson, "Cross-Sectional Experience Curves," *Perspective*, No. 208, The Boston Consulting Group, 1978.
10. Lynn W. Phillips, Dae Chang, and Robert D. Buzzell, "Product Quality, Cost Position, and Business Performance: A Test of Some Key Hypotheses," Harvard Business School working paper #83-13 (1982) and *Journal of Marketing*, Vol. 47 (Spring 1983) pp. 26–43.
11. Tom Peters' quoted passage summarizes key points from a Brad Gale speech on "Quality as a Strategic Weapon: Getting Closer to the Customer Than Your Competitors." Tom Peters and Brad Gale helped to kick off Milliken's fourth annual

planning conference on quality at Pine Isle, Georgia, on a Saturday morning, February 1984. Whereas *In Search of Excellence* (1982) had only one chapter on quality, *A Passion for Excellence* (1985) by Tom Peters and Nancy Austin has five chapters on quality.

12. For the nonmanufacturing businesses in the PIMS sample, "manufacturing" was defined as the primary value-creating activity of the business. For example, processing transactions is the equivalent of manufacturing in a bank.
13. Richard G. Hamermesh, M. J. Anderson, Jr., and J. E. Harris, "Strategies for Low Market Share Businesses," *Harvard Business Review,* May–June 1978, pp. 95–102.
14. Carolyn Y. Woo and Arnold C. Cooper, "The Surprising Case for Low Market Share," *Harvard Business Review,* November–December 1982, pp. 106–13. In a sequel to this study, Woo compared the strategies of 41 market leaders with poor profitability and 71 high-profit leaders. See "Market-Share Leadership—Not Always So Good," *Harvard Business Review,* January–February 1984, pp. 2–4.
15. Michael E. Porter, *Competitive Strategy* (New York: The Free Press, 1980), pp. 42–43. Porter's U-shaped curve was reproduced in *Fortune* with the caption "Means to the Ends."
16. See 'We Are the Target, *Forbes*, April 7, 1986, p. 54.
17. Lynn W. Phillips, Dae R. Chang, and Robert D. Buzzell, "Product Quality, Cost Position, and Business Performance: A Test of Some Key Hypotheses," *Journal of Marketing*, Vol. 47 (Spring 1983), pp. 26–43.
18. See FTC study cited in footnote 2. For an earlier study that also measured share in relation to industry data and also found a significant *positive* relation between share and profitability see Bradley T. Gale, "Market Share and Rate of Return," *The Review of Economics and Statistics*, November 1972, pp. 412–423.
19. For an in-depth treatment of this topic, see Bradley T. Gale and Ben S. Branch, "Concentration vs. Market Share: Which Determines Performance and Why Does It Matter," *The Antitrust Bulletin*, Spring, 1982.
20. For the full load, see Richard E. Caves, Bradley T. Gale, and Michael E. Porter, "Interfirm Profitability Differences: Comment," *Quarterly Journal of Economics*, November, 1977, and Bradley T. Gale, "The Existence and Direction of Causality in Cross-Section Analysis of Hypotheses: A Paper in Research Strategy," *Proceedings of the American Statistical Association*, 1972.
21. Robert Jacobsen and David A. Aaker, "Is Market Share All That It's Cracked Up to Be?" *Journal of Marketing*, Vol. 49 (Fall 1985).
22. For a more technical discussion of the Jacobsen and Aaker study, see Appendix B.
23. *General Electric Monogram*, September–October 1981.

9

Market Share: Deception or Diagnosis

Simon Majaro

Market Share is invariably accepted without question as a valid measure of marketing success. Here Simon Majaro argues that it can be positively misleading, but that if shares of a given market are measured in a number of different ways, then the results can be used to diagnose weaknesses. He proves it with two cases.

IT IS WIDELY SUGGESTED by marketing oriented companies that one of the main criteria of business success is the market share that a firm is able to achieve and maintain. The assumption is made that the attainment of a high market share indicates an effective marketing effort. By the same token, a poor market share suggests that the enterprise has performed badly. If this is true one cannot escape from the simple axiom that in order to be successful a firm needs to direct its full attention to the maximization of market share.

In a very interesting article in the *Harvard Business Review* (January–February 1975), "Market Share—A Key to Profitability." a group of American academics reported on an ongoing project of 57 companies sponsored by the Marketing Science Institute and the Harvard Business School. The main purpose of the project was to determine the profit impact of market strategies. In the article the authors come up with a positive correlation between market share and return on investment (ROI). The authors go on to discuss why a high market share is profitable, listing economies of scale, market power and quality of management as possible contributors to such results. They specifically suggest that as market share increases, a business is likely to have a higher profit margin, a declining purchases-to-sales ratio, a decline in marketing costs as a percentage of sales, higher quality, and higher priced products. (See Figure 1.)

The findings of the team are obviously quite dramatic and cannot be ignored. Nonetheless, to the more practical marketer they present major problems: Are the companies in the sample successful because they have attained a high market-share or do they have a high market-share because they are successful? Moreover the implications of the conclusions are quite alarming for small and medium-size firms—are they all doomed to a poorer performance simply because they are unable to muster an important share of their respective markets? Finally when we talk about 'market share' we inevitably assume that we always know what

Figure 1
Market Share and Pretax Return on Investment

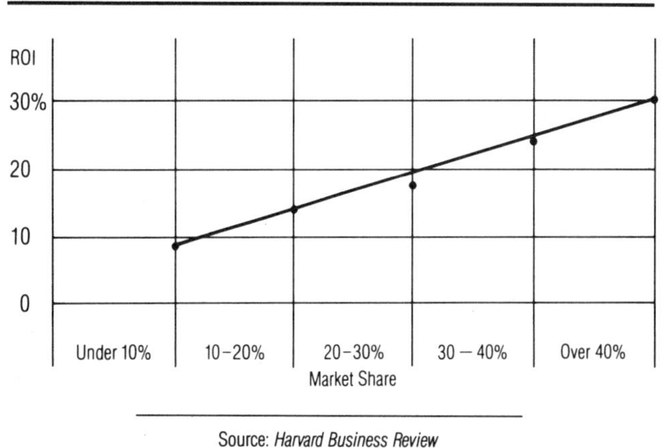

Source: *Harvard Business Review*

At the time of this writing Simon Majaro was head of the Strategic Management Learning training center in Great Britain.

market we are in. This latter point presents the biggest pitfall of the market-share concept.

Share of Which Market?

On the face of it market share is an uncomplicated concept. I manufacture electric shavers; the annual market for new electric shavers is around one million units a year; I sell 100,000 units a year and therefore my market share is 10%. I can now also investigate my performance during the last five years and monitor changes in my share of the market during that period. I can attempt to plan the future after analyzing my strengths, weaknesses and general resources and specify new objectives including a market share objective for the future. This may be more than 10% or less than 10%, depending on my assessment of my capabilities and the potential market environment. All this is fine and logical, but, it might be asked:

- What is the share in terms of money?
- What is the share of shavers for men and shavers for women?
- What is the share of the total market, i.e., all those who shave? After all electric shavers do exactly the same task as other razors and you need to know your share of the total business.
- No doubt shavers are bought either by the future owner himself for his own use or as a gift. These are two important segments. What is the share of each?
- Shavers are sold through a myriad of channels. A few cater for the AB market; others cater for the C1 and possibly C2 segments, and others cater for the lower socio-economic segments. What is the market share of each of these?

I recognize that these are fairly valid questions but I am thoroughly confused and am very tempted to abandon the market share criterion. If it is so multifaceted it is of no relevance to a simple-minded businessman like me.

Let us now explore two other examples to illustrate the danger of selecting a market share criterion without sufficient thought about which market is the most relevant for the purpose of gauging company performance. Whilst the facts and figures are hypothetical they are both based on real-life case studies.

Case 1: Stanton Pharmaceuticals

Stanton manufactures an ethical drug which alleviates the discomforts of asthma. Its performance has been good in terms of profit and return on investment. However the firm's marketing personnel fear that aggressive competition may place pressure on the performance of their product. In an attempt to lay down criteria of performance for the future they undertook a thorough study of the drug's share of the market in terms of a variety of parameters. The following results emerged:

- The market for anti-asthma drugs is around 5 million (in terms of retail prices). Stanton's share of this market is 1 million, i.e., 20%.
- Recognizing that the main decision maker in the field of drugs is the doctor who prescribes specific preparations they measured the firm's share of the total number of prescriptions issued for anti-asthma drugs. Here Stanton's share appeared to be much higher at 30%. In other words, whilst Stanton's share of the 'prescriptions market' is 30%, its share of the 'turnover market' was only 20%.
- A further complication was that the number of doctors who actually prescribed Stanton's brand represented only 18% of the total number of doctors in the market.
- At the specific request of the marketing director some research was conducted to measure how many people suffered from asthma and how many of them had been treated by Stanton's brand. Here the results indicated that 40% of those suffering from asthma were being treated with Stanton's product.

This brief case illustrates how misleading the market share analysis can be. Four ways for measuring the firm's market share in a specific and well-defined market yielded seemingly contradictory and confusing results. The findings are summarized in Figure 2 which sets out the various market shares.

Each one of the pie-charts shown is valid but the second chart shows a market share of 30% and represents good

Figure 2
Stanton's Shares of the Market for Anti-Asthma Drugs

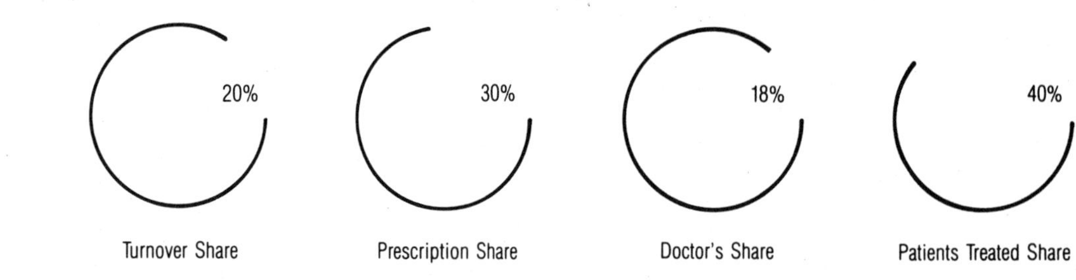

news in accordance with the *Harvard Business Review* project, whilst the third chart is bad news by the same reckoning. Yet both charts represent the identical company, the identical product, and the identical market.

Case 2: Eldorado Shipping Company

This case is a highly simplified version of a fairly typical situation in service organizations such as transport, banking, and insurance. It is very easy to measure market share in relation to the misleading parameter. Eldorado operates a regular shipping service between the UK and Eldorado (a fictitious island in the Pacific). The firm is quite successful in terms of profit, growth, ROI, and, as the management optimistically believes, in terms of market share. Whilst the company's capacity represents 60% of the tonnage on that route, its market share in terms of tons carried is respectively 67% of the tonnage carried from Eldorado to the UK, and 59% of the tonnage carried from the UK to Eldorado. The management considers such a performance fairly satisfactory, although some pressure is being placed on the sales force to increase the market share of the UK outward cargo to represent at least 60%.

Now comes the crunch: an in-depth analysis of the firm's market share in terms of revenue indicates that it is only 48% on the inward business and 46% of the outward route. Once again, a number of pie charts (Figure 3) helps to illustrate these significant disparities.

Was the management unwise in selecting tonnage as the parameter of market measurement, or should one always seek to measure market performance in a number of different ways?

Market Share as a Diagnostic Tool

These two cases seek to illustrate how dangerous it is to base objectives on the nebulous criterion known as market share. In spite of this, market share has a very important role to play in the management of a firm's marketing activities. Its real value is seldom recognized or used. The market-share approach to measuring levels of performance represents one of the most potent diagnostic tools available to a good marketer. If used correctly it can alert the imaginative manager to areas of weakness in marketing strategy of a specific product or service. The best way to illustrate the principle is to cast our minds back to the cases we have already discussed.

Initial Conclusion Wrong

We saw how Stanton Pharmaceuticals could identify different market shares in relation to different markets. On the face of the facts the conclusion that one comes to is that the market-share findings are of doubtful value, but let us look at the diagnostic implications of the four market shares identified.

1. The fact that the 'turnover share' is only 20% and the 'patients share' is 40% suggests that Stanton's product is either under-priced, or much more effective in use than competitors' products, or both. The facts can be verified, but the basic conclusion is that something is wrong with the firm's pricing policy. This is undoubtedly an important area for diagnostic investigations.
2. The disparity between the 'prescriptions share' and the 'doctors share' is of course puzzling and needs further examination. Nonetheless it seems to suggest that the firm has managed to 'convert' too few doctors to its preparation, but managed to turn these few into very 'heavy users' of Stanton's product. This indicates a patchy penetration of the general practitioner market. If this is correct, the market-share analyses have yielded a most useful payoff insofar as the firm is diagnosing an important weakness in its overall penetration strategy.
3. The enormous difference between the 'those treated' market share and the 'doctors' share points to another significant conclusion, namely that a large number of asthma sufferers are treated by a relatively small number of doctors. If this conclusion is correct it would suggest that the company must reconsider its promotional strategies and regear them to a smaller segment of the 'doctors' market. Obviously this will help to utilize available promotional and selling resources more effectively.

These reflections are examples of the kind of readings that a multidimension market-share analysis can yield. They

Figure 3
Eldorado's Shares of the UK/Eldorado Freight Market

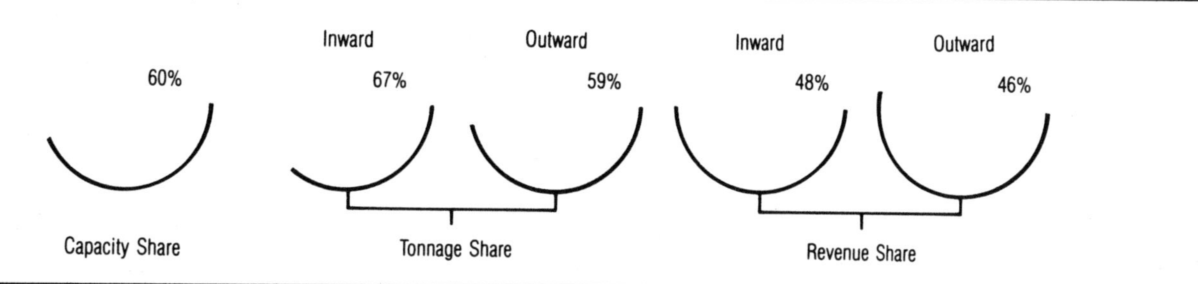

are much more useful than a single market-share study. And in the case of the Eldorado Shipping Company once again we saw the dramatic difference in market share between the 'tonnage' market and 'revenue' market. An analytic approach reveals vital clues about this firm. Having concentrated its marketing effort on the acquisition of tonnage, the firm has lost sight of the fact that some types of shipping tonnage are less valuable in terms of revenue per unit of capacity than others. In other words, Eldorado got landed with the cheaper freight whereas its competitors were content to carry a smaller tonnage of the more revenue-oriented cargoes. This is a very useful insight: Eldorado must now increase its revenue share of the market. All cargoes must be segmented in terms of the revenue to space ratio. Such analysis can form the basis of promotional and selling concentration. In other words, salesmen can be redirected towards the attainment of sales to specific types of customers with the right cargoes. They can be alerted to what represents an attractive cargo and what does not.

The examples given above were very simple. More complicated studies can be undertaken by the creative diagnostician. He can ring the changes in a variety of ways: he can measure market shares in accordance with a large number of unusual albeit logical parameters and manipulate the results to identify relevant strengths and/or weaknesses in marketing variables. In some cases marketing results could be improved whilst ostensibly reducing market share.

Market Oriented Share

We saw how markets can be defined in many ways and how the measurement of market share in relation to each market thus defined can yield different results. Unfortunately it is not always easy to measure a firm's market share in relation to a given parameter. The information required to undertake such a study is either not available or is too costly to obtain. Obviously it is necessary to be selective in the kind of market share exploration attempted, and there is absolutely no point in spending a lot of time and money measuring the firm's market share in relation to a market which is simply not measurable.

There are also instances where all the variables measured indicate a constant market share. This is particularly true of oligopolistic industries, such as cement, where a small number of manufacturers dominate the market and where price leadership is strongly adhered to. In such cases one normally finds that the market share in terms of tons, turnover or bags will be more or less the same. Yet with some imagination one can find useful disparities in relation to specific segments of the market served. Whilst the market share of the total market may be constant, variations may exist in relation to specific segments. This, of course, is extremely valuable to the marketing strategist.

Markets must always be identified in a marketing-oriented way. We must recognize that we are moving towards an era when the cost-benefit to the customer or the consumer is the criterion that will matter. Thus a carpet manufacturer whose carpets last longer than his competitors' products and has only 10% of the carpet market could specify his market share in terms of 'year/sq. ft. floor covering' and this is likely to be more than 10%. After all this is what people buy carpets for and this is how consumer satisfaction is gauged. Moreover this is how the *Which?*-type analysts evaluate the product. (*Editor's note:* the British *Which?* magazine performs product evaluations similar to those of *Consumer Reports* in the U.S.) By simply saying that the market share is 10% of the total yardage sold one is being highly production-orientated. Surely it is wrong to assume that the firm that sells 50% of the yardage produced in the country is automatically a successful company. This is what the Harvard study seems to imply.

Marketing Relevance

Referring once again to the Stanton Pharmaceuticals case mentioned earlier, we can now ascribe some marketing relevance to the various market shares listed: the 'turnover' share is, of course, production-orientated; the 'doctors' share is slightly more marketing orientated, but does not relate directly to the real market, namely those who suffer from asthma. The 'prescriptions' share is useful but once again is not truly consumer-orientated. Let us imagine that as a result of over-prescription the average patient gets 100 tablets, uses 70 and throws the other 30 away. This may be good for business, but to the firm that believes wholeheartedly in the marketing concept such an arrangement is anathema. To the marketing perfectionist the starting point for measuring market share in such circumstances is the identification of how many people suffer from asthma and how many of this well-defined segment derive solace and health from his product, and, in the most cost-beneficial way to them and to society. This sounds idealistic, but the firm that follows this simple path wins in the end.

10

Planning Gains in Market Share

C. Davis Fogg

A comprehensive approach to the process and problems of planning share gains.

GAINING MARKET SHARE is a key factor in reaching a leadership or number one position in any industry. It is particularly important to the achievement of a high volume of profits that can be used to expand a firm's business and pay dividends to stockholders, and to the attainment of leadership profit performance as measured by return on sales and return on investment. It is well documented that the higher a firm's market share the larger its cumulative production of a product, the lower its costs, and the higher its profitability.[1]

However, gaining significant share requires careful planning, thoughtful, well-executed market strategies, and specific account-by-account tactical plans. It requires a comprehensive, well-thought-out, and well-planned program. The purpose of this article is to present such a comprehensive program for gaining market share: to examine ways of increasing share, the key steps in planning market share gains, and the pitfalls that must be anticipated in implementing such a program.

When to Plan Market Share Gains

Typical situations where a business manager should seriously consider a plan to gain market share include: *poor market position*—share must be gained to increase profitability and profit volume; *new products* are being launched head-on against competition; significant *losses in share* have been suffered at the hands of competitors; a *new acquisition* is justified only if sales, profits, and market share can be significantly increased; *competition becomes vulnerable* by virtue of a strike, poor customer service, product shortage, financial difficulties, and the like.

At the time of this writing C. Davis Fogg was manager of market planning for the Electronic Products Division of the Corning Glass Works.

When Share Gains Are Difficult

It should be noted, based on the author's experience, that gains in market share are particularly difficult under several key circumstances. One such situation would be when a firm has low share, is coming from behind, and is attempting to take share away from the leaders. It's easier to grow with the market than take share away from someone who "owns" it. Secondly, it's more difficult to gain share in a commodity market where there is little or no opportunity for a unique product and significant product differentiation. Finally and obviously, share gains are tougher when there is significant competition—competition with an adequate product offering and good distribution channels and methods.

Means of Increasing Market Share

The author has found the following five key strategies to be most important for gaining market share in an industrial market.

1. *Price*—lower prices below competitive levels to take business away from competition among price-conscious customers.
2. *New Products*—introduce product modifications or significant innovations that meet customer needs better and displace existing products or expand the total market by meeting and stimulating new needs.
3. *Service*—offer more rapid delivery than competition to service-conscious customers; improve the type and timeliness of information that customers need from the

service organization, information such as items in stock, delivery promise dates, invoice and shipment data, and the like.

4. *Strength and Quality of Marketing*—field a larger, better-trained, higher-quality sales force targeted at customers who are not getting adequate quality or quantity of attention from competition; build a larger or more effective distribution network.
5. *Advertising and Sales Promotion*—increase advertising and sales promotion of superior product, service, or price benefits to under-penetrated or untapped customers; advertise new or improved benefits to all customers.

Competitive price, new products, and service are all tangible benefits that are needed by, and can be evaluated by, customers. The marketing organization is a means of both communicating benefits and facilitating service. Advertising and sales promotion are means of communicating benefits to customers and increasing their awareness of a particular manufacturer's product line.

In addition to the five key strategies for gaining share, there are a number of lesser strategies that may be important in select markets and can be considered. These strategies include improving product quality, expanding engineering assistance offered customers, offering special product testing facilities, broadening the product line to offer a more complete range of products, improving the general corporate image, offering the facilities to build special designs quickly, and establishing inventories dedicated to serving one customer.

There are several key considerations that should be taken into account in using these methods to gain market share. First, one or more of these methods should be used only when significant (to the customer) distinct product, price, or service advantages over specific competitors can be found. The advantage must be sustainable for a sufficient period of time to gain targeted share and significant enough to cause target customers to shift their business from a competitor to the firm attempting the market share gain. If a distinct sustainable advantage cannot be found or if competition is extremely competent, aggressive, and expected to counter any attempt to gain share, then the cost of gaining share may far exceed the benefits. Under these circumstances, a firm should look for another business or product line in which to invest for share gain. Second, gains in market share will not only increase sales and profit volume, but will incur significant costs—the "cost" of decreased gross margins as prices are lowered, the cost of developing new products, the cost of new plant capacity to permit decreased delivery time, and the like.

Finally, the time that it takes to implement each method varies from strategy to strategy. Pricing changes can be quickly implemented. Improving delivery may take six to eighteen months if new plant capacity must be added. Strengthening, upgrading, and training of the sales force may take six to twelve months, and developing and launching a new product may take one or more years depending upon the extent and difficulty of technical innovation required. A plan to gain share may, therefore, involve a number of different moves over a relatively long period of time.

Table I summarizes the circumstances under which each strategy can be used, how the strategy is applied in the marketplace, and the detailed cost implications of each strategy.

The Process of Planning Share Increases

There are eight key steps in the process of planning share increases. They are:

1. *Information Collection*—collect critical market and competitive information necessary to establish market share goals and strategies for reaching them.
2. *Competitive Analysis*—define which competitors are vulnerable to specific strategies, why, and what their likely reaction will be to attempts to gain share by different methods.
3. *Product Line Segmentation*—divide current (or proposed) product lines into groups where there is room for: (a) no gain in share; (b) share gain using nonproduct strategies—such as price, service, or strengthened marketing; and (c) new product and product innovations to gain share.
4. *Establish Overall Share-Gain Goals and Strategies* for each product line marketed.
5. *Key Account Analysis*—identify where competition is particularly vulnerable at specific key accounts; establish key account goals and share-gain policies, particularly if they deviate from general policies applied nationally throughout the market.
6. *Cost/Benefit Analysis*—calculate the expected share and profit gains, the costs of achieving these gains; judge whether or not the cost/benefit ratio is satisfactory; repeat steps 1 through 6 until the cost/benefit ratio is acceptable.
7. *Execute the Plan.*
8. *Monitor Results* and modify goals and action, if necessary, to combat competitive reaction or to react effectively to changes in the marketplace.

Figure 1 graphically depicts the planning process. The remainder of the article is devoted to methods of obtaining and analyzing information necessary to implement the process of planning share gains.

Information Collection

The two types of information required to properly plan share gains are: "bottom-up" information typically obtained from salesmen, sales representatives, and industrial distributors; and "top-down" information typically obtained by market research and competitive intelligence activities.

Bottom-up research will accomplish three objectives. First, it will establish overall national competitive practices and patterns, including competitive pricing policies, product line strengths and weaknesses, sales force type, strength and quality, strength of distribution, market penetration, and the

Table I
Strategies for Gaining Market Share

Strategy	When to Use	How to Apply in Marketplace	Cost Implications
1. Price	To gain share in a product line (a) where there is room for growth; (b) in launching a new product, preferably in a growth market	A. Set general market price level below average ("catch share generally" strategy) B. Lower prices at specific target accounts where reduced prices will capture high volume accounts and where competition is vulnerable on a price basis; lower prices enough to keep the business C. Lower prices against specific competitors who will not or cannot react effectively	• Will lower gross margin by decreasing spread between cost and price for a period of time • Will lower cost as cumulative volume increases and costs move down the experience curve
2. New Product	When a new product need (cost or performance) can be uncovered and a new product will (a) displace existing products on a cost or performance basis, or (b) expand the market for a class of product by tapping previously unsatisfied demand	A. Develop and launch the new product, generally B. Target specific customers and market segments where the need for the product is strongest and competition most vulnerable, and immediate large gains in share can be obtained	• Cost of R & D necessary to develop product • Capital expenditures on plant to manufacture the product • Start-up operating losses • Promotion costs of launching the new product
3. Service	To gain share for specific product lines when competitive service levels do not meet customer requirements	A. Improve service generally beyond competitive levels by increasing capacity for specified product lines B. Target specific accounts where improved service will gain share and the need for superior service is high C. Offer additional services required in general or at specific customers—information, engineering advice, etc. D. Expand distribution system by adding more distribution points	• Cost of adding capacity and/or bolstering service systems • Cost of expanding the distribution system, including additional inventories required
4. Quality/Strength of Marketing	When a market segment or specific customers are getting inadequate sales force coverage (too few calls/month) or inferior quality of coverage (poor salesmen or insufficient information conveyed by salesmen)	A. Add salesmen or sales representatives to call frequency above competitive levels in target territories or at target accounts B. Sales training programs to improve existing sales skills, product knowledge, and territorial and customer management abilities C. Sales incentive program with rewards based on share increases at target customers or in target markets or products	• Salary and overhead cost of additional salesmen or representatives • Cost of training or retraining • Cost of incentive program
5. Advertising and Sales Promotion	(a) When a market segment or specific customers are getting inadequate exposure to product, service, or price benefits compared to competition (b) A change in the benefits offered is made and needs to be communicated	A. Select appropriate media to reach target customer groups B. Set level and frequency of exposure of target customers high enough to create adequate awareness of benefits and counter level of competitive efforts	• Cost of creative work to create campaign • Production and media costs

like. Second, it will define how vulnerable each key competitor is to moves against him and the extent to which share can be taken away for each distinct product line. Third, it will identify key large volume accounts where business is held by competition, and estimate how much business can be taken away from competition by what means.

In a bottom-up survey, salesmen basically are asked what they feel is needed in price, service, nonproduct benefits, or new products to gain and maintain share in their district or territory. This information can be effectively obtained—either by drawing on the salesman's prior knowledge of, or having him conduct a direct field survey of, a specified sample of accounts. The survey sample normally will include all key large accounts and distributors and a random sample of moderate to small accounts. Salesmen are then asked to identify what each competitor's share is, at which key accounts, what strategies can be effective in taking share away and keeping it for each product line, and how much (for example, in price) is necessary to effect a change in share. They are also asked, based on previous experience or speculation, to predict what each competitor's probable reaction will be to specified moves such as price cuts, new products, increased field sales coverage, and the like. Such surveys require excellent sample design, a good information-processing system, and careful design of questionnaires to be administered to salesmen in the field and to be administered by salesmen to sample accounts. The number of accounts to be sampled and the amount of information requested must be kept small to avoid overburdening the sales force with information collection.

Top-down research is also important. Professionally conducted surveys of select customers, distributors, and key salesmen can both identify key new product concepts that can be developed and used against competition and confirm or expand on findings from the bottom-up survey. Normal competitive intelligence activities can monitor a competi-

Figure 1
Schematic Diagram of the Process of Planning Market Share Gains

(1) INFORMATION COLLECTION	(2) COMPETITIVE ANALYSIS	(3) PRODUCT LINE SEGMENTATION	(4) ESTABLISH OVERALL OBJECTIVES AND STRATEGIES	(5) SET SPECIFIC ACCOUNT TARGETS	(6) CALCULATE COST/BENEFIT	(7) IMPLEMENT
BOTTOM-UP Information from sales force survey		LINES TO MILK (Dominant position or no gain possible) Act to keep share, manage for cash. Probable cost of gaining share greater than benefit gained	Define, maintain competitive price, service, product innovation	Normal sales budgeting		Continue to manage business normally
	• Define competitive price, service selling effort and advertising level for each line • Establish where key competitors are vulnerable • Define what share gain strategies may work against each competitor	LINES SUBJECT TO SHARE GAIN (Low share, preferably growing market, don't have dominant position, competition considered vulnerable)	• Establish overall share gain goals for product lines, distribution channels, etc. • Set key overall strategies including • Price decrease and differential to be maintained for specified period of time • Service improvement • Increased selling effort • Increased advertising and promotion effort necessary to gain share • Key accounts to take away from competition	Establish sales territory and specific account targets where competition vulnerable to lower price, improved service or selling effort beyond overall policies	Establish cost/benefits of gaining additional share over "do nothing" or "maintain competitive standards" policy	Execute program for product lines where gains satisfactorily outweigh cost Reiterate process if proposed result unsatisfactory Establish strategy for lines where cost of gains outweigh benefits and lines not subject to share gain
TOP-DOWN information from market research and competitive intelligence		LINES SUBJECT TO PRODUCT INNOVATION (Unfilled customer need, subsequent new product opportunity or need for substantial improvement of existing products)	Define and develop needed innovation Establish introductory price, service, and distribution policies	Define normal new product launch strategy including • Establishing specific accounts where competition specifically vulnerable to new products or where lower pricing, improved service or selling effort beyond overall policies will gain share	Cost/benefit analysis	Execute program if justified

tor's financial condition and ability to respond to an attack on his market, his probable new product policy, and his probable reaction, based on historical information, to each type of share-gain move being contemplated.

Competitive Analysis

An in-depth analysis of competition based on survey results is required to identify those product lines where share gain is thought possible and pinpoint where and how much each competitor is vulnerable to specific share-gain strategies. Table II provides a simplified example of such an analysis and the key conclusions derived from the data.

Product Line Segmentation

Management judgment based on the competitive analysis should tentatively divide product lines into three basic categories—product lines where there is:

- No room for share gain
- Room for product innovation and subsequent share gain
- No room for product innovation but room for share gain with existing products

In general, there is *little room for share gain* when competition is highly competent—is equal or superior in strength and ability to penetrate the market, and has significant or dominant market share. There is often little room for gain when a firm has achieved dominant stable market share (usually 35% to 70% of the market) or the market for a product line is stable or declining. In each of these circumstances, the cost of gaining market share will probably outweigh the additional benefits provided by a gain in share. The principal strategy under these circumstances is to manage the product line to produce cash: price only to maintain market share and make only the minimum required investments in product changes, plant and equipment, and marketing. If there is some doubt that a product line falls into this category it should be treated as a product where share gain is possible, and a detailed plan and calculations should be prepared to substantiate whether or not share gains are worth the cost.

Table II
Simplified Competitive Analysis

Competitive Dimensions		Us	Competitors A	Competitors B	Competitors C	Comments on Data
1. Product Position	Growth Per Year		Market Share			
Line / Market Size						
1 — $15 Million	0%	65%	20%	10%	5%	1. Not subject to share gain, manage for cash.
2 — $30 Million	10%	25%	40%	15%	20%	2. Subject to share gain, A most vulnerable, B, C less so.
3 — $20 Million	15%	10%	25%	30%	35%	3. Subject to share gain, A, B, C equally vulnerable. Substantial unfilled need for a new product.
2. Pricing Strategy	Line					
H = Price for margin	1	C	C	C	H	B and C will be easiest to take share away from on price, and it will be least expensive to maintain share taken away. A is more competitive, will require larger price differentials to gain and maintain share, and it is therefore more costly to take share away.
C = Price with market	2	C	L	C	C	
L = Price leader or very aggressive	3	C	L	C	C	
3. New Product Policy	Line					
	1	L	L	F	F	Expect new products first from A, monitor market carefully to identify what they're working on—expect A to imitate earliest any new products introduced.
L = Leader	2	F	L	F	F	
F = Follower	3	L	L	L	F	
4. Overall Marketing Strength						
Number of Representatives		5	10	15	15	A strongest and equal to us. B and C vulnerable to more intensive selling effort offered by us.
Number of Distributors		40	35	30	30	
Number of Salesmen		25	20	10	7	
5. Geographic Strength	Territory					
Number of Salesmen and Representatives	E	9	7	7	6	We may be weak in district G and should consider adding salesmen, otherwise are equal or superior to competition.
	F	7	7	6	6	
	G	5	8	7	6	
	H	9	8	6	4	
6. Distributor Strength	Territory					
Number of Distributors	E	12	10	8	7	A approximately equal in strength. B and C weaker and definitely vulnerable.
	F	10	9	7	8	
	G	10	9	7	7	
	H	8	7	6	6	
7. Delivery Norm (Weeks)	Product					
	1	6	6	4	7	Delivery improvements necessary in 1, 2 to be competitive. Improvement beyond competitive levels will not gain share. Improvement in product 3 will gain advantage against A, B, and C according to sales force survey.
	2	6	3	4	4	
	3	6	6	7	9	
8. Penetration by Account Size %						
Dollar Market—All Products						
$40 Large		40%	30%	15%	15%	We're weak in medium and small accounts, need program to improve penetration and coverage there.
15 Medium		15%	30%	25%	30%	
10 Small		10%	30%	20%	40%	
$65 Million						

9. Probable Reaction to:

	Reaction	Comments on Data
• Lower Price	A—Immediate retaliation, continued price reduction to gain share back. B, C—Weaker response. Will try to hold large accounts.	Cost in taking share away from A on price will be high. B and C more vulnerable.
• New Product	A—Will immediately match new product offering. B—Eventually match. C—May match immediately.	B and to some extent C vulnerable to new product offering.
• Increased Sales Coverage	A—Will match. B, C—Some increase.	B and C vulnerable in some measure to sales coverage, particularly if a new product is launched.

Key Strategic Conclusions

1. Product Policy: Focus on lines 2 and 3 where gain is possibly by increased penetration and growth with the market and product modification for product 3.
2. Competitive Strategy: Focus on taking share away from B and C, who are vulnerable to lower pricing and a new product innovation requested by salesmen. Selectively take business away from competitor A—only up to the point where expensive price retaliation is expected.
3. Marketing Strategy: Add three salesmen to territory G and one to F to build strength against key targets—B and C. Shift call pattern and develop marketing programs or medium to small accounts where penetration is poor. Develop distribution promotion program to capitalize on advantage over B and C.
4. Service: Invest in capacity to lower delivery time in product 2 to level competitive with B and C. Maintain competitive standards in other lines.

There is room to gain share by *product innovation* where significant unfilled needs can be identified in the market, where it is technically feasible to develop a product to meet those needs, and where the product advantage in the market is sufficient to gain substantial share. In this case, the strategy is to undertake prototype product development and prove that the product is technically feasible before developing a plan to launch the product and gain share.

Finally, there is generally *room for a share gain* when a firm has less than dominant share and survey information indicates that a competitive advantage can be obtained in price, service, or selling and distribution methods and systems. This is particularly true where the product market is rapidly growing and competition is weak, fragmented, or known to be sluggish in reaction to aggressive moves by competitors. In this instance, a detailed plan for gaining share is called for as outlined below.

Establishing Share-Gain Goals and Strategies

The competitive analysis will permit establishment of overall share-gain goals and the strategies to be implemented in general in the marketplace and against each key competitor.

After preliminary overall strategies have been established, the two most difficult subsequent tasks are to establish how much change must be made (in price and service, for example) to gain share and approximately how much share gain a given change will produce. Estimates of the sensitivity of market share to proposed changes can be obtained in several ways. First, historical records document share changes based on previous moves by or against competition. Second, and perhaps best, salesmen can estimate the sensitivity of share in their territories and indicate the amount of change necessary to take business away at specified key accounts. Finally, knowledge of competitors, judgment of their probable reactions, and the percentage of share they will permit to be taken away before retaliation should put a limit on expected share gains.

How much share a competitor will allow to be taken away is a function of several factors. The first is his financial condition and ability to retaliate by building additional capacity or investing cash in other means of gaining back share. Second is his business philosophy concerning the product lines in question: does he want profits and incoming cash now or is he willing to defer current financial return for future larger returns resulting from a maintained or increased share? Finally, the importance of the product line under attack to the firm's total business will influence a competitor's reaction. If the product is of minor importance in the competitor's business, attempts to maintain share are less likely than if the product line constitutes a major portion of his business.

It is important, in addition, to realize that all of the share initially gained during an assault on competition probably cannot be maintained indefinitely, and a portion of the share may have to be "given back" to stabilize the market.

Table III is a typical objective and strategy matrix showing overall share-gain goals by product line and detailed strategies by type of product for products sold direct to original equipment manufacturers. Each cell in a strategy matrix will normally include:

- Share (or sales) to be taken away from competition
- Specific accounts where share is to be gained
- Key strategies—price, product, promotions, change in call patterns, and the like

The simple product line vs. competition matrix in Table III assumes that strategy will vary only by competitor and product line. A more complex analysis will be necessary

Table III
Competitive Matrix for Products Sold Direct to Original Equipment Manufacturers*

Product	Competitor A	Competitor B	Competitor C	Overall Goals
1	No change	No change	No change	Maintain 65% share, competitive pricing. Manage for cash. Improve service to competitive levels.
2	Take away 3% Focus on accounts X, Y, and Z with below average pricing	Take away 6% Focus on accounts L, M, and N —below average pricing	Take away 6% Focus on accounts Q, R, and S	Increase share from 25%–40 by: • Establishing competitive service and capacity • Price 3%–7% lower than market
3	Take away 5% Focus on accounts X and Y where need for product modification great	Take away 10% Focus on accounts L, M, N, and X with lowered pricing on conventional product	Take away 10% Focus on accounts Q, R, S, and M—mix of modified product and low price on conventional product	Increase share from 10%–35% by: • Product modification • Cutting price on established product 3%–7% • New plant with superior service

Overall Strategies for All Products

1. Add salesmen to territories F and G where weak.
2. Shift call patterns to call on more medium to small size accounts.
3. Increase overall advertising level 25% during share-gain period.
4. Maintain competitive service in all lines.

*The same type matrix could also be used for products sold through different distribution channels.

Figure 2
Schematic Flow of Calculation to Compute ROI and Cash Flow of a Share-Gain Plan

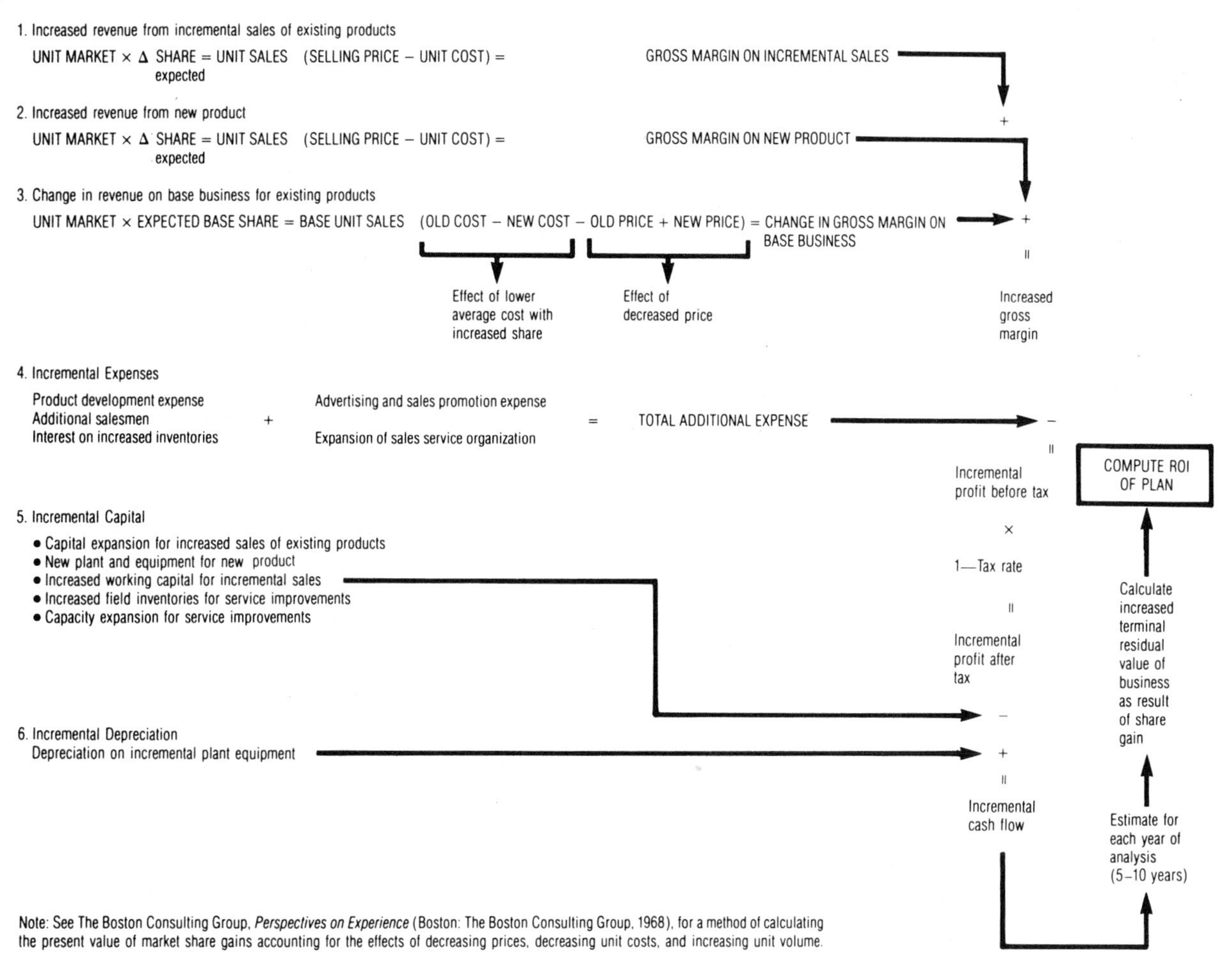

Note: See The Boston Consulting Group, *Perspectives on Experience* (Boston: The Boston Consulting Group, 1968), for a method of calculating the present value of market share gains accounting for the effects of decreasing prices, decreasing unit costs, and increasing unit volume.

when share-gain strategy is expected to vary along other dimensions such as size of customer, customer's end market (industrial, consumer, computer, etc.), different distribution channels, and the like.

Territory Goals

Specific goals are then set for each territory and for key accounts that salesmen have targeted for share gain. The potential share gains are totaled and discounted to factor in probability of success to see if reasonable account and territory goals add up to the overall share-gain goals established in the previous step. These goals become territory and account action steps if the share-gain program is accepted.

Cost Evaluation and Analysis

Once program goals are established, the costs and benefits of the proposed plan must be carefully evaluated. Figure 2 is a simplified flow diagram for calculating the incremental costs, benefits, cash flow, and return on investment (ROI) for a firm intending to gain share by a combination of lowered prices on existing products, introduction of a new product, additional field sales coverage, and improved service. The chart lists most of the key items that will have a positive or negative effect on cash flow. The analysis isolates both the gain in profits from newly acquired share and the change in profitability of the base business—that business that would have been obtained without a share-gain plan—as a result of decreased prices and lowered costs as production costs move down the experience curve with increased cumulative volume. This type of analysis is easily adapted for computer calculation.

Assessing Risk

A "source of sales analysis" is useful in assessing the risk and realism of a share-gain plan. In general, the higher the portion of a firm's five- to ten-year cumulative sales expected to come from disruptive moves against competition—lowered price, improved service, and new products—the higher the risk of the plan and the greater the advantage over competitors necessary to succeed.

Monitoring and Follow-Up

An intricate share-gain plan requires careful monitoring and control if it is to be effective. It is particularly important to insure that key account sales targets are being met, and that cost goals are on target and new product introductions are on schedule. Timing is also important. Once implementation begins, competitors will be aware of the threat to their market share; rapid, timely implementation of share-gain plans can catch competitors unaware, and share gain can take place before competitive retaliation.

It is also important to monitor competitive reaction to moves to gain share. Competitive moves should have been anticipated in the plan, figured into the market share targets, and calculations and plans prepared to defend held or gained share with continued price and cost reductions and product innovation.

Finally, it is important to recognize when attempts to stabilize competitive market shares should take place. When it is apparent that goals have been met, and/or the costs of gaining additional share obviously outweigh the benefits, it is important to attempt to stabilize shares by reverting to competitive—not aggressive—price, product, and service policies.

Pitfalls

There are five key pitfalls in implementing a plan to gain share. They are:

1. *Moving Too Slowly* and giving competition time to regroup and retaliate. Pricing, product, and service moves must be made quickly.

2. *Not Doing Enough* and being timid and conservative in moves against competition. Price cuts must be more than adequate, product advantage great and clear, and so on. It does not pay to do "just a little bit" to see if it works.

3. *No Follow Through*—neglecting the tools necessary to sustain share once gained, such as sustained cost reduction and ability to lower price or sustain excellent service or develop new products. One must be willing to stick with the battle to gain share over a long period of time.

4. *Underestimating Competition* and their ability to react, resulting in higher than forecast costs of gaining share; forgetting to figure the costs of combating competitive reaction in the share-gain financial plan.

5. *Don't Know When to Quit*—sometimes competitive reaction will be too strong; it is too costly to gain share, and giving up and concentrating on another business is the best policy.

Legal Implications of Market Share

Finally, before planning significant market share gain and seeking a dominant industry position, plans should be reviewed with legal counsel to insure that planned action is within established antitrust laws and government guidelines. In general, the government will not challenge high market share if it is attained by internal growth and legal competitive activity in the marketplace. The government may challenge market dominance if it is thought to significantly lessen competition in the industry in question or if significant share gains are obtained by acquisition rather than by internal growth.

If one attains a dominant position in a given market, the strategies appropriate to maintain or augment that position must be carefully scrutinized from the legal point of view. Aggressive, competitive action permissible for a firm seeking to improve its position in a fragmented market may be viewed quite differently by the Justice Department if undertaken by a dominant firm seeking to augment or merely defend its position in a concentrated market. A firm that dominates must guard against the possibility that in defending its dominant position, it is accused of predatory conduct that constitutes an abuse of an alleged monopoly position.

Summary

Gaining and keeping significant market share is considered by many to be the single most important key to high, long-term profitability and substantial profit volume. Market share gains must be carefully planned. The vulnerability of competition to changes in price, product, service, marketing and distribution methods, and advertising must be assessed. Potential advantages vis-à-vis competition must be identified and the costs and potential benefits of a plan to gain share carefully evaluated. Overall share-gain goals and strategies must then be translated into sales territory and individual sales account goals for implementation. Although the process of planning share gains is time consuming and costly, the profit rewards can be substantial.

Reference

1. See The Boston Consulting Group, *Perspectives on Experience* (Boston, MA: The Boston Consulting Group, 1968). Additional unpublished work by The Boston Consulting Group concerning the automotive, brewing, aluminum, cosmetics, and mobile home industries, and using public data, conclude that the higher a firm's market share, the higher its profitability, and that the leader in market share in an industry is usually the most profitable.

11

Diagnosing the Experience Curve

George S. Day & David B. Montgomery

There is now much better appreciation of the various types of experience curves that are available and the conditions under which they yield meaningful strategic insights.

Few strategy concepts are more likely to give misleading insights than the experience curve. As a result there is considerable disenchantment with the simplistic market share prescriptions that marked the early applications. Nonetheless, the experience curve remains an extremely useful organizing framework when scale, technology and learning effects are influential forces in the environment. This article reviews the measurement and interpretation problems that have to be overcome before the experience curve can be productively applied. Conclusions provide rewarding topics for further research.

FEW STRATEGY CONCEPTS have gained wider acceptance than the notion underlying the experience curve, that value-added costs net of inflation decline systematically with increases in cumulative volume. The logic is appealing, the empirical support seems persuasive and the strategic implications are often profound. Yet despite these advantages, acceptance is waning. The application problems were always formidable, but now there is a growing suspicion that some of the key strategic implications may be delusions (Kiechel 1981).

Fortunately, strategic concepts also continue to improve with cumulative research and applications activity. As a result, there is now much better appreciation of the various types of experience curves that are available and the conditions under which they yield meaningful strategic insights. Concurrent progress has been made in identifying the source of observed experience effects and clarifying the measurement and estimation problems. This paper evaluates this progress as a guide for both analysts and managers to the state of the art and suggests productive directions for further work. Before turning to specific applications issues, we will first review the basic concept and the supporting empirical evidence.

George S. Day is Professor of Marketing, University of Toronto, and David B. Montgomery is Robert A. Magowan Professor of Marketing, Stanford University.

The Concept of the Experience Curve

The antecedent of the experience curve is the production learning curve, first observed in the 1930s as a systematic decline in the number of labor hours required to produce an airplane (Yelle 1979). It was only in the mid-1960s that the notion of the learning curve was generalized by the Boston Consulting Group (1972) to encompass the behavior of all value-added costs and prices as cumulative volume or experience increase.

The usual form of the experience curve[1] is:

$$C_n = C_1 n^{-\lambda} \tag{1}$$

where

C_n = cost of the nth unit,
C_1 = cost of the first unit,
n = cumulative number of units,
λ = elasticity of unit costs with respect to cumulative volume.

The form of the function reflects a constant elasticity λ and the cost (price) will fall by

$$1 - k = 1 - 2^{-\lambda} \tag{2}$$

percent each time experience doubles. If $k = 80$, then cost will fall by $1 - 80 = 20\%$ as experience doubles and the experience curve is said to be an 80% curve or have an 80% slope. This slope will only be observed if the effects of inflation have been removed and all costs and prices are stated in real terms. Also, it should be emphasized that the curves apply to cumulative experience and not to calendar time. Experience will tend to cumulate faster in calendar time during periods of rapid growth and relatively early in the product life cycle.

Supporting Evidence

Thousands of experience curves have been plotted during the past 15 years by staff of the Boston Consulting Group (Henderson 1980b). These analyses have ranged from the direct costs of U.S. long distance calls, integrated circuits and life insurance policies, to the prices of bottle caps in Germany, refrigerators in Britain and polystyrene molding resin in the U.S. A typical example is the set of price experience curves for different sizes of Japanese motorcycles, prepared by BCG (1975) as part of a study of the British motorcycle industry, shown in Figure 1.

Figure 1[a]
Japanese motorcycle industry: price experience curves (1959-1974)

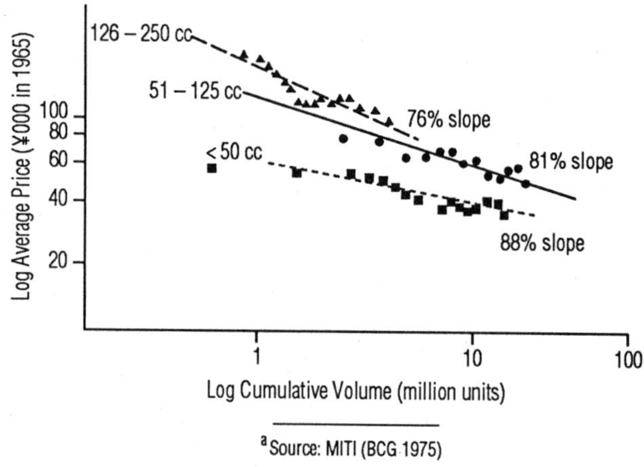

[a]Source: MITI (BCG 1975)

Unfortunately, the bulk of the evidence in support of the experience curve phenomenon has been graphical in nature and has not focused on the measurement and econometric issues, which would be required for a more scientific assessment. However, several studies that are more carefully prepared also lend credence to the experience phenomenon. Wooley (1972) obtained cost data for 18 products from 10 companies using BCG case files. His sample was carefully selected to avoid most of the difficult application issues discussed in the next section and encompassed products in the chemical, paper, steel, electronic, knit product and mechanical goods industries. His results strongly support the experience phenomenon with over 80% of the R^2 values exceeding .8 and over 80% of the λs significant at the .01 level. The median experience slope in his sample was 77.5%, with over 75% of the slopes between 70 and 90%, which is the usual range suggested by BCG based upon their client studies.

Rutenberg (1976) cites three rigorous econometric studies that support the experience curve and illustrate its robustness with respect to variations in factor input conditions. The first was a study by Rapping (1965) analyzing the output of WW II liberty ships being manufactured at different sites, each with different rates of cumulative production. His results indicated that with each doubling of accumulated output a ship required 17% less input. At the other extreme were two studies in which the factor inputs were held constant, and yet the rate of output per unit of input improved due to experience. In Arrow's (1961) classic paper on learning by doing, he cites the Horndal iron works in Sweden which experienced productivity increases in output per man hour of 2% per annum even though there had been no new capital investment in 15 years. Similarly, Barkai and Levhari (1973) found that experience steadily increased productivity by 0.4 to 0.6% per annum on an Israeli kibbutz even though capital and labor inputs were held constant. Here the gains came from changes in the output, as experience revealed which crops were best suited to the growing conditions.

Evidence to support the existence of price experience curves comes from studies by Stobaugh and Townsend (1975) and Lieberman (1981). In the former study price changes over intervals of one, three, five and seven years were estimated as a function of number of producers (competition), degree of product standardization, cumulative industry experience and static scale economies. The data were for 82 petrochemicals. Of the four explanatory variables, cumulative experience was the most important in predicting price changes. Further, when the products were divided into 13 homogeneous subsets, adding the other three variables to the experience variable was significant at the .05 level in only three of the 13 instances. For these products at least, the experience effect appears to have a dominant effect on price.

The Lieberman (1981) study analyzed three-year price changes for 37 products in the chemical processing industries. Price changes were postulated to be a function of market concentration, short run imbalances between supply and demand, experience effects, scale economies, capital embodied technological improvements and changes in factor costs. The results indicated that cumulative experience was very significant, with a coefficient corresponding to a 72% slope.

Although there are several fairly rigorous studies supporting the existence and importance of the experience effect, econometric issues have received scant attention. For example, what should be the specification in terms of variables and functional form?[2] How should the errors be specified? What about errors in the variable measures? What is the potential for simultaneous equations bias?

Sources of the Experience Curve Effect

Given evidence to support the existence of an experience curve effect, the question arises as to why this effect appears. There are three major sources: learning by doing, technological advances, and scale effects.

Learning encompasses the increasing efficiency of *all* aspects of labor input as a result of practice and the exercise of ingenuity, skill and increased dexterity in repetitive activities. Learning includes the discovery of better ways to organize work via improved methods and work specialization (for example, doing half as much twice as often). Similarly, the performance of production equipment will improve as personnel become better acquainted with their operation. For example, the capacity of a fluid catalytic cracking unit typically "grows" about 50% over a ten-year period as operators, engineers and managers gain experience in operating the unit (Hirchmann 1964). Similarly, Joskow and Rozanski (1979) found that learning by doing increases the effective capacity or output of a particular piece of nuclear equipment by approximately 5% per year. The reason is that with experience workers were more effective in using and maintaining the equipment and various technical "bugs" were identified and corrected.

Marketing activities also benefit from learning by doing. A recent survey of 13,000 new products in 700 companies (Booz, Allen and Hamilton 1981) found that cost of introduction of new products declined along a 71% slope.

Technological improvements also contribute to the experience curve effect. New production processes, especially in capital intensive industries, often contribute substantial economies. For example, Golden Wonder's introduction of continuous flow potato chip manufacture versus the traditional batch frying mode enabled them to achieve substantial economies in heating and quality control and played an important part in Golden Wonder's achievement of market share parity with the formerly dominant firm (Beevan 1974). Changes in the resource mix, such as automation replacing labor, also provide a technology driven basis for the experience effect. Process and product changes that produce yield improvements are yet another source of experience effects. Product standardization and redesign are also sources of the effect, as with the economies achieved in the automobile industry by modularization of the engine, chassis and transmission production.

Economies of scale, from the increased efficiency due to size, are another source of the experience curve effect. These scale effects apply to the majority of investment and operating costs. Seldom does an increase in throughput require an equivalent increase in capital investment, size of sales force or overhead functions. Scale is also an enabling condition for other cost reduction activities. Thus, scale creates the potential for volume discounts, vertical integration and the division of labor, which in turn facilitate learning.

Figure 2
Cost experience for steam turbine generators

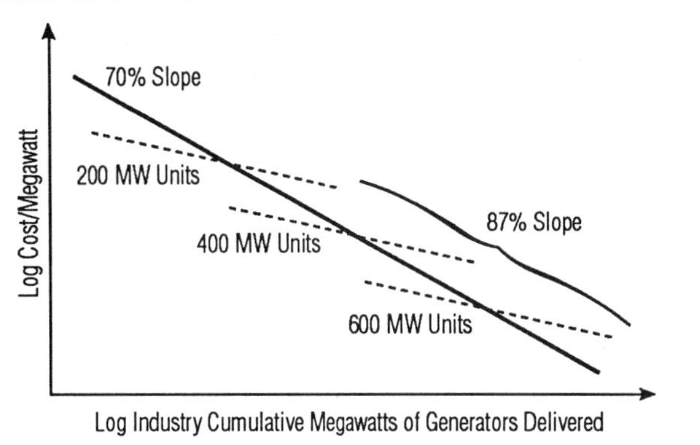

Decomposing the Experience Curve

Most experience curves reflect the joint effects of learning, technological advances and scale.[3] For example, Sultan (1974) found that the costs per megawatt of output of steam turbine generators followed a 70% slopes because of (a) practice in making units of each size, which followed an 87% slope, (b) scale economies by building larger units, 600 MW rather than 200 MW units, and (c) technological improvements in turbine bucket design, bearings and high strength steels for rotor shafts, which made possible the designs for larger units.

Normally it is difficult to distinguish the separate contributions of scale, learning and technology, in part because the process of learning usually coincides with the expansion of scale. Only a few efforts have been made to measure the relative importance of the three basic effects, and they only apply to the chemical industry. Hollander (1965) in a study of the sources of efficiency increases at DuPont rayon plants concluded that only 10–15% of the efficiency gains were due to scale effects, whereas the remainder was accounted for by technology and learning. Of this remainder between 32 and 75% (depending on the plant) was ascribed to learning. Hence scale seems relatively less important, while technology and learning have major impact. Interestingly, Hollander found that the largest proportion of the technology-driven cost reductions were due to a series of minor technical changes based on a broad consensus that continuous cost reduction action was a high priority.

Similar results for price experience were found by Stobaugh and Townsend (1975) and Lieberman (1981). Stobaugh and Townsend report that static scale economies did not account for price changes to the same extent that the confounded experience variables of learning, technology and dynamic scale did. Lieberman found a 71% experience curve when scale, new plant introductions and new competitive entry were confounded with cumulative volume, while the slope rose to 77% when these variables were separately analyzed. Thus, while scale plays an obvious role, in these instances it does not appear to be a dominant component of the experience effect.

Despite the difficulty of decomposing the experience curve to understand the underlying sources, the effort is critical to informed strategic application because:

- Cost reductions due to learning and technology are the result of continuous, planned efforts by management. Cumulative experience does not guarantee that costs will decline but simply presents management with an opportunity to exploit.
- Where the cost reductions are being achieved primarily from economies of scale through more efficient, automated facilities and vertical integration (Porter 1979), then cumulative experience may be unimportant to the relative cost position. In these situations a new entrant may be more efficient than more experienced producers.

Types of Experience Curves

Within a specific market environment a variety of experience curves can be found, depending on whether one is concerned with:

- costs or prices,
- total costs or elements of cost,
- the effect of industry or company accumulated experience,
- dynamic (time-dependent) or static (cross-sectional) comparisons.

Three combinations of these variables are of particular interest, for they lead to experience curves that are interdependent but offer very different strategic insights. The first is the company cost compression curve that relates changes in the company's costs to accumulated company experience. The second is the competitive cost comparison curve that shows the current costs of all direct competitors as a function of their respective levels of cumulative experience at that point in time. The third curve describes the behavior of industry prices and average costs as total industry experience cumulates. This last curve has a close relationship to the product life, which we will discuss at the end of this section.

Company Cost Compression Curves

This is the easiest curve to establish, for it is derived from internal cost and production records. To be sure there are many hurdles to overcome in establishing the cost corresponding to each level of company production experience with a specific product, service or cost element. Short-term discontinuities will be found due to revisions in accounting procedures, changes in the product and cost variances from fluctuations in the level of capacity utilization. Nonetheless it is usually possible to develop a meaningful company cost curve, which has immediate application as a cost control tool. Standard costs can be set, based on continuing or improving past patterns of reductions with experience, and management can be held to these targets. Abell and Hammond (1979) argue that the discontinuities that occur render the experience curve less useful for short run cost control. In light of the ambiguities of other kinds of experience curves, some would argue that this is the most useful of all the experience curves.

Competitive Cost Comparison Curves

These are cross-sectional experience curves that relate the relative cost positions of the competitors in an industry (Henderson 1978). With this curve it is possible to estimate the profitability of each of the competitors at the prevailing price. While potentially the most useful experience curve, it is also the most difficult to obtain.

We usually know the slope of our own cost curve and can reasonably estimate the cumulative experience of the relevant competitors from their market shares. Unfortunately we cannot immediately jump to the next step, which is to locate each of these competitors on our cost curve according to their relative experience. This will invariably overstate the cost differences. For example, the real price per unit of a split system central air conditioner (CAC) has been declining about 20% with each doubling of industry experience. Yet a cross-sectional experience curve relating the costs of the major competitors has a 92% slope (Biggadike 1977). There are many reasons why the slope of the cross-section curve is likely to be shallower than other experience curves:

1. Followers into a market usually have lower initial costs than the pioneer:

- The follower has an opportunity to learn from the pioneer's mistakes by hiring key personnel, "tear-down" analysis of the competitor's product and conducting marketing research to learn the problems and unfulfilled expectations of customers and distributors;
- A follower may leap frog the pioneer by using more current technology or building a plant with a larger current scale of operations;
- There may be opportunities for followers to achieve advantages on certain cost elements by sharing operations or functions with other parts of the company.

2. All competitors should benefit from cost reductions achieved by outside suppliers of components or production equipment. For example, in the spinning and weaving industry most of the advances in technology come from textile machinery manufacturers who share these improvements with their customers.

3. One competitor may have lower factor costs than another for reasons that are independent of experience, such as location advantages, the benefits of government subsidies, and reduced susceptibility to cost element inflation because of differences in cost structure (McLagan 1981).

4. Another problem that clouds cross-sectional analyses is differences between overhead rates of competitors. A large multidivision company with heavy corporate overhead allo-

cations to each strategic business unit may be at a disadvantage against a specialist producer with very lean and efficient management. Whether there is a disadvantage depends on the ability of the diversified firm to exploit opportunities for shared experience gains through corporate coordination.

5. Finally, if there have been significant changes in market position, current market shares may not be good measures of relative cumulative output.

The net effect of these factors is a cross-sectional experience curve with shallow slope, masking steeper company cost curves that are often approximately parallel to one another, as in Figure 3. Of course, it is not necessary that the various company cost curves be parallel, since this implies equivalence in both ability to exploit cost reduction opportunities and access to the necessary technology.

Figure 3
Competitive cost comparison curves

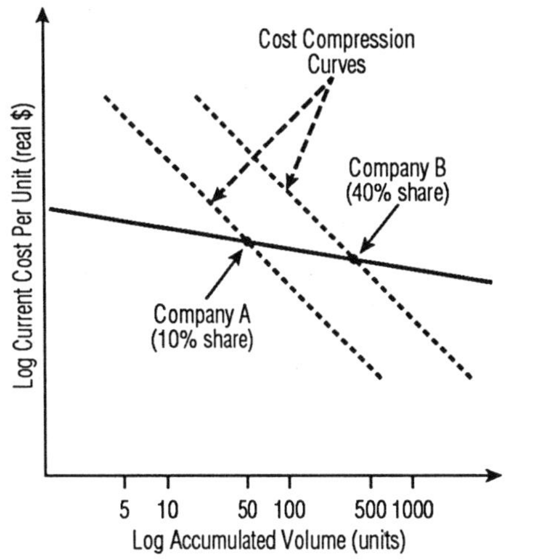

Narrowing of Competitive Cost Differentials

As markets mature and the forces acting on the cross-sectional experience curve continue to operate, competitive cost differences tend to narrow. The extent of this narrowing, has been documented in the PIMS data base (Buzzell 1981).

Further narrowing of competitive cost differentials may be triggered by changes in industry structure. In some industries the full line manufacturer is also a full service manufacturer, with concomitant high overheads and short production runs with many items in the product line. But as markets mature, an increasing proportion of customers have less need for technical service, engineering and lab support, and applications assistance. Thus the full line, full service manufacturers may be vulnerable to competitors with less experience but who incur fewer cost elements and are attacking specific segments. Indeed, the increasing fragmentation of markets during the maturity stage is a serious challenge to the full line manufacturer, for it creates a pressure for a proliferation of products to satisfy the needs of different segments. The ensuing costs may dissipate the advantages of experience.

Industry Price Experience Curves

This curve relates the industry average price to industry cumulative experience. It may be difficult to establish for two reasons. The first question is, what is or was the price prevailing at the time corresponding to an industry cumulative volume? List prices are notoriously unrealistic, given the fluctuating discount structures (hidden and otherwise) that exist to cope with changes in the industry supply picture (Burck 1972). A single price may be misleading if it requires averaging across disparate models, features and accessories, or if different competitors use different marketing mixes. When some competitors are full service high quality suppliers, and others provide minimal technical support or applications engineering while selling components, there will be a high variance in observed prices. It must always be remembered that the customer is paying for value in use. This value can be enhanced not only by a real price cut but also by adding benefits and services without corresponding price increases. The offer of a warehousing plan that permits customers to lower their component inventories is surely a price reduction.[4]

A meaningful industry price curve also requires we know the industry cumulative volume. This may be a problem simply because good industry data are unavailable or cannot be trusted. The problem is aggravated when different competitors use different strategies. This is one aspect of the question of defining industry boundaries to which we will return shortly.

The captive manufacturing issue. In some component markets the process of vertical integration is so far advanced that more than 50% of total output is "in-fed" (Wilson and Atkin 1976). If this output is purely captive it may be possible to ignore it. This would be dangerous, however, if the practice is to sell excess output on the open market to ensure optimum capacity utilization. If a beer company periodically sells 20–30% of their output of cans to other companies (especially during nonpeak periods), the long run price patterns in the industry will eventually reflect the impact of these high volume, low cost producers.

Costs, Prices and the Product Life Cycle

The average industry price curve frequently does not decline as fast as the cost curve in the early stages of the life cycle (Hedley 1976). Since the widening gap is inherently unstable, there is a sharp readjustment during a shake-out period and prices eventually establish a stable margin relationship with costs.[5] This pattern is juxtaposed on an idealized product life cycle in Figure 4, as there is often a correspondence of the stages (Day 1981a).

Introductory period. During this period prices are held below current costs in expectation of lower costs in the future and to expand the market for the product by increasing the cross-elasticity of demand with existing substitutes. A steep cost compression curve suggests a penetration price,

Figure 4
Product life cycle stages and the industry price experience curve

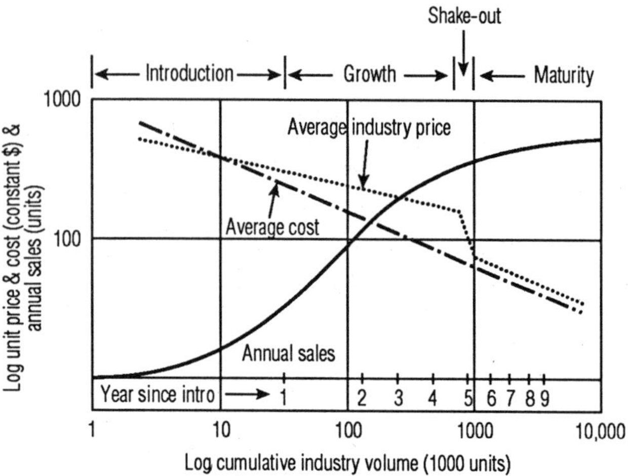

substantially below current costs (Dean 1976). Such a pricing strategy is even more attractive when (1) there is little prospect of creating and maintaining product superiority over competitors, (2) when there are few barriers to entry and expansion by competitors, or (3) when the lower price will significantly expand the current market. When and if the product takes off, the period of negative margins will eventually come to an end. Robinson and Lakhani (1975) have shown that for a new product without direct competition and in the presence of imitative consumer demand, an optimal price policy would be a penetration price substantially below initial costs.[6] The demand stimulus provided by this very low price coupled with experience based cost declines were found to lead to profits several times greater than those generated by a myopic price policy that sets price to equate marginal revenue and marginal cost each period.

In an economic analysis of the impact of the experience effect on competitive entry into new products, Spence (1981) found that the experience curve could create substantial entry barriers by conveying substantial cost advantages on the early entrants. Surprisingly, his analysis demonstrated that moderate experience slopes create a greater entry barrier than do very small or very large slopes. With small slopes experience gives little advantage to the pioneers, while steep slopes make it relatively easy for late entrants to catch up with the early entrants. Entry was found to cease after three or four firms had entered under conditions of a moderately sloped experience curve. Interestingly, Spence found that market performance improved sharply from monopoly to two or three entrants but rather slowly thereafter. Hence experience-generated concentration may not prove substantially harmful.

Growth period: building an umbrella. The germanium transistor market is a good illustration of what can happen during the growth period. As demand surged, the overriding problem was obtaining product supply. Certainly there was no incentive to cut prices. However, the combination of rising average margins and rapid growth soon attracted a number of new entrants. These new entrants were able to survive profitably because the price umbrella was still high enough to cover their high initial costs. Because of their narrow margins these new entrants were motivated to gain share at the expense of the market leader and thereby reduce costs more rapidly than the leader.

During the growth period the market leader who condones a high umbrella is trading long run market share for current profits. There are many reasons for electing this choice. The current profits are often needed to fund the still rapid growth in capacity, working capital, R&D and market development activity. The reward system often puts a premium on immediate profits. This also reduces the incentive to build capacity beyond short run needs, since poor capacity utilization will penalize profit performance. If market growth is underestimated the market leader may be forced to give up further share because of capacity constraints.

The shake-out period. The number of competitors attracted by the growth opportunities and high umbrella margins can be quite amazing. In industries such as housewares with modest barriers to entry, it is not uncommon to find 20 to 40 hopefuls entering during the growth period. Sooner or later the umbrella folds, for one or all of the following reasons:

- Growth slows or declines because the market is close to saturation or a recession has intervened;
- Aggressive late entrants buy into the market by cutting prices (a variant is the acquisition of an also-ran by a cash rich outsider that creates a competitor who can afford to invest in market share gains);
- The market leader attempts to stem the previous erosion of market share or regain previous share levels by cutting price;
- Retailers or wholesalers have limited space or capacity and decide to limit their offerings to the top three or four competitors that have a strong customer franchise.

The observable result is a sharp break in the price trend. The severity of the break will depend on the number of competitors, the size of the umbrella and the abruptness of the slowdown. In the meantime, there are still expansion plans in the pipeline that come into production during this period. The ensuing excess capacity puts further downward pressure on prices. The shake-out period becomes aptly named as marginal producers are eventually squeezed out of the market.

All these factors are currently operating in the personal computer market, where at least 150 companies build computers and another 300 have been formed to cater to the aftermarket for peripherals, software, service and support. Most of these aspirants entered the market within a two-year period. It is now clear that the market cannot support most of these companies, and so it is predicted that by 1986 there could be only a dozen companies offering microcomputer lines (*Business Week* 1982).

Toward maturity and beyond. We have already seen that competitive cost differentials steadily narrow as the market matures. At the same time the effect of experience on real unit costs and prices becomes less evident. Doubling times are longer, so year to year cost reductions tend to be swamped by cost fluctuations induced by the economic situation, availability of materials and so on.

Eventually the product progresses into late maturity and decline, with unpredictable consequences for the experience curve. For example, one manufacturer of industrial gases observed that the cost compression curve for their bottled oxygen had not only flattened but was turning up somewhat. This was not happening with either liquified or pipelined oxygen supplied by the same manufacturer. The two latter forms of oxygen supply were newer and their success had pushed bottled oxygen into the decline stage of the life cycle. Despite the drop in industry sales, no competitors had dropped out, which meant everyone was suffering reduced levels of capacity utilization and higher production costs.

Measurement and Interpretation Questions

The insights gained from the three types of experience curves depend on numerous judgments as to the treatment of costs, inflation, shared experience and the definition of the units of analysis. These put significant limitations on the strategic relevance of experience curve analysis.

Which Costs?

Although it is claimed that the experience effect applies to all costs, it is misleading to consider only total costs. Total costs decline from the effect of experience on the cost elements that combine to make up the product, including components, assembly, packaging, distribution and so on. Only some of these costs can be influenced by management. Also the amounts of experience accumulated in each cost element may be very different, as a result of shared experience, and the slopes of the experience curves may also vary between elements. For these reasons, special attention must be given to the controllable elements of value-added costs that have been adjusted for inflation.

Cost component analysis. When the slopes of the experience curves of major elements are different, the relative importance of each component changes as experience with the total product accumulates. As Table 1 shows, this may also lead to a change in the slope of the overall experience curve. In this hypothetical example, cost component B with the shallowest cost curve rapidly becomes the most important cost component. While this is an extreme circumstance, the same general effect is logically at work whenever the experience curves for major cost components have very different slopes. A similar evolution in cost structure would be revealed if component B had a more steeply sloped experience curve, but the total company experience with that component was extensive. This would be another reason for the costs of component B to decline at a much slower rate than the costs of A.

Table 1
Changes in Cost Structure as Experience Cumulates

	Cost per component at each level of cumulated experience		
	2000 units	8000 units	32,000 units
Cost component A (70% slope)	$1.00	$0.49	$0.24
Cost component B (90% slope)	1.00	0.81	0.66
	$2.00	$1.30	$0.90
Average slope of total cost curve	80%		85%

Another implication of the example of Table 1 is that products are likely to exhibit shallower total cost experience curves as they mature. In effect the slope of the total cost curve is increasingly influenced by the cost element which is declining the slowest with each doubling of total experience. But when the cost components each follow equation (1) with separate elasticities, the total cost function does not have the form of equation (1) and is no longer linear in the logarithms. Thus, what often appears as a straight line on log paper may actually be a poor fit that obscures a gradual flattening of the experience curve. For further elaboration see Montgomery and Day (1983).

Value-added costs. The experience effect is largely felt on those costs that contribute to the value added during manufacturing or when providing the service. Inclusion of all costs and especially raw materials costs may mask the desired effect. This was the problem in an analysis of the evolution of costs of insulated wire and cable. The total cost was dominated by raw materials elements, notably aluminum and copper, which are commodities subject to wide price swings. Only when the raw material costs were excluded was any pattern evident. Whether cost elements outside of the value-added portion are included in the analysis depends on the ability of the company to influence the purchase price through scale and experience. For example, significant influence would be implied if a supplier dedicated most of the output of a component to a particular customer. When in doubt, it is always desirable to break total costs into elements.

If value-added costs decline faster than other costs with increasing experience, the industry price experience curve is likely to have a smaller slope than the industry value-added experience curve. In the U.S. brewing industry between 1950 and 1976, value-added costs (payroll, advertising, capital) declined on a 76% curve while prices declined on an 87% curve. Since value-added costs were only about 32% of per barrel costs in the early 1970s, it appears likely that other costs such as taxes, raw materials, freight and containers were not declining as rapidly.

Controllable costs. Process industries such as chemicals and metal refining, which are subject to rigorous safety and environmental regulations, find that the costs of these regulations behave like an unproductive "add-on." The consequence is most noticeable with the company cost compression curve, which has a dismaying habit of turning up, perhaps with a jump discontinuity, as in Figure 5. It is less clear what impact a regulation has on relative cost positions within an industry, for regulatory burdens often fall most heavily on smaller producers. This has become very noticeable in the auto industry, as GM spreads the costs of mandated downsizing across many units. Similarly the cost of label changes in the food industry is proportionately greater for small volume packers.

Identifying relevant costs. Most cost accounting systems are designed to serve many purposes and the resulting costs are often wildly inappropriate for experience curve analysis. The major problems are with the allocation of costs, the treatment of joint costs, and the deferred recognition of actual costs until revenue is realized. Cost allocations may be made of departments or profit centers rather than to specific products. Shared resources, such as pooled sales force, researcher and support staff, may be allocated as a percentage of total sales accounted for by the product rather than reflecting the actual use of the resources. There is always the possibility that unit costs are not comparable over time because the allocation of joint costs has been arbitrarily changed or different accounting conventions have been used. Consequently, the analysis should be based on cash inputs rather than costs as recorded by cost accountants (Henderson 1980a).

Choosing the unit of analysis. When costs are averaged across a broad product line, a change in the total cost may be observed simply as a result of a change in the sales mix. For example, refrigerator manufacturers have been producing larger units on average. Here the solution is to define the product as a cubic foot of usable refrigeration space and observe the evolution of costs on this basis. This will only partially control for a shift in the mix of sizes, as the cost of a cubic foot is cheaper in a larger refrigerator. A related problem is the treatment of product variations and modifications, especially where the aim is to enhance the value of the product to the customer. At the extreme the product may have changed so much that it no longer resembles the original.

Which Deflator?

There is no single rate of inflation (Wilson 1982). For example, during 1980 when the GNP deflator was 9.0% and the implicit price deflator for producers' durable equipment was 6.5%, the following industry inflation rates were observed:

Textile machinery	10.2% per year
Underground mining machinery	2.5% per year
Accounting machines and calculators	0.6% per year

On balance the GNP deflator is a poor representation of inflation in any particular industry, although it may be adequate to evaluate long-term shifts in strategy. For shorter-term cost analysis it is better to choose a deflator that reflects the inflation of factor costs within the industry. However, care must be taken that the deflator is not so closely allied with the specific industry that the slope is defined away.

Figure 5
Discontinuities in the cost compression curve

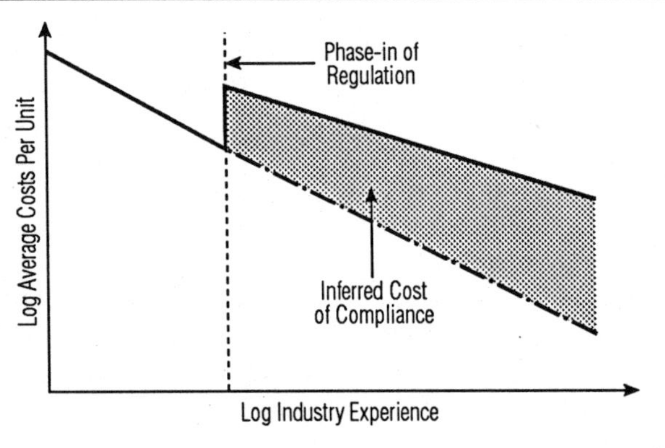

What About Shared Experience?

Cost differences between competitors are often less than we would expect from our knowledge of relative market shares and the slope of the company cost compression curve. A major reason is the effect of shared experience between two or more products using a common resource. The experience gained with one of the products can be applied to a reduction of the costs of related products.

For example, suppose company A and company B both produce product X using the same three steps. However, whereas company A only produces product X using these three steps, company B makes two other products, both of which use the same first two steps as product X. Company B then should have the advantage of the volume generated by these other products, all contributing to its cumulative experience in the first two steps. In this circumstance, if companies A and B have similar cumulative volumes for product X, company B would have lower costs on the first two steps and thereby should have lower costs and higher profits on product X than company A. Company B might well still have a cost advantage even if company A has more experience with product X because of company B's shared experience with the other two products.

Shared experience comes in many guises:

- manufacturer of semi-conductor components for calculators utilize many of the same capabilities to produce random access memories;
- textile fiber manufacturers use similar polymerization and spinning processes for polyesters and nylon;
- the same assembly operation may produce high torque motors for oil exploration and low torque motors for conveyors;
- major appliance manufacturers use the same sales and service organization for a variety of products;
- Procter and Gamble was able to overcome a lack of experience in manufacturing paper products by being far along the experience curve in selling packaged consumer products when it entered the disposable diaper market.

Although a common effect of shared experience is to reduce cost differentials between competitors, a useful way to treat shared experience operationally is as an increment to the accumulated output of the specific product or processes of which the product is comprised. The hypothetical example in Table 2 helps to illustrate this point. The cost position of company B is weakened by the lack of transferable experience with related products. Rutenberg (1976) suggests adding factors to equation (1) which reflect the impact of shared experience.

As illustrated in Table 2, the assessment of competitor's shared experience as well as the company's own shared experience is important to understanding the relative economies of the various competitors. One fiber producer has noted that since most competitors in the textile industry produce several fibers, it is necessary to estimate the unique, shared experience base of each competitor in order to understand relative cost positions. This company claims this approach has been used successfully on several occasions and has produced insights into competitive positions that otherwise would have eluded them.

How can the amount of the carryover from shared experience be estimated? As with the basic experience effect, shared experience merely presents an opportunity to reduce costs but does not guarantee it will happen. If a company has two plants making identical products that were constructed independently, and the plants do not exchange cost reduction information, then the shared experience effect will be negligible. To assess whether experience has been shared it is usually necessary to apply expert judgment to each cost element. For example, manufacturing personnel can be asked to estimate where cost reduction projects for individual products have originated in the past. Similar approaches can be used to determine the effect on sales and distribution costs of a pooled sales force and warehousing facility. Needless to say, this kind of analysis represents a formidable amount of work, which possibly accounts for the paucity of published research on this topic.

Which Product-Market?

Few issues create more uncertainty than the choice of product-market boundary for the experience curve analysis. Published evidence suggests that industry-wide cost compression effects are most evident when broad, product-market definition is used:

- kilowatt hours of electricity generated,
- silicon transistors,
- gallons of beer, or
- pounds of viscose rayon.

Such broad definitions work because they are able to encompass most sources of shared experience.

Yet, as Abell and Hammond (1979) observe, a definition that is too broad may mean that an opportunity for cost leadership in a specialized market may be overlooked:

Table 2
Effect of Shared Experience

	Accumulated Experience with Product X	Shared Experience from Production of Related Products	Total Accumulated Experience
Company A	1,000,000 units	600,000 units	1,600,000 units
Company B	600,000	——	600,000
Company C	200,000	350,000	550,000

> . . . the grinding wheel industry produces hundreds of thousands of different kinds of wheels, each particularly suited for certain industrial applications. Production of a given type of wheel requires development and control of a "recipe" consisting of quantity, type and size of abrasives, bonding agents, filters, wetting agents, etc.; the timing of adding these to the "mix," baking times and temperatures; finishing techniques and so on. Likewise a firm can gain important experience advantages in the selling and servicing of wheels to a particular application. Experience advantages on a given type of wheel can yield important cost advantages. Here the unit of analysis should be the type of wheel on the application; if it were simply "grinding wheels" significant cost advantages due to specialization would be missed . . . .

The dilemma of the breadth of product and market boundaries may be resolved if segments can be found such that cost sharing *between* segments is less important than competitive cost differentials that are dependent on the relative position within the segment (Day 1981b). This will yield a useful definition if most competitors approach the market in the same way. However, there are many situations where different competitors define their business very differently. Laboratory ovens, for example, can be manufactured and sold by oven specialists or by laboratory equipment specialists. Whether laboratory ovens constitute a distinct segment depends on whether manufacturing or selling and servicing have the greater influence on total costs. When in doubt it may be necessary to repeat the experience curve analysis using several different definitions of both products and markets.

A recurring problem is the treatment of new technologies. For example, should there be a single experience curve for tire cord, or separate curves for rayon and nylon tire cord? In general, if the consequence of the new technology is primarily to reduce production costs without a change in the functions provided to customers, then a new curve is not necessary. However, if the new technology offers significant new functions, as happened when cash registers became electronic, then a separate curve is necessary.

What Strategic Relevance?

The experience curve seemingly speaks directly to the long run strategic concerns of management. According to the Boston Consulting Group (Hedley 1976), the basic strategic message of the experience curve is:

1. The largest competitor in a particular business area should have the potential for the lowest unit costs and hence greatest profits.

   If he is unprofitable he is probably either being "out-segmented" by more focused competitors or he is defective in experience curve cost control.

2. Smaller competitors in a business area are likely to be unprofitable, and they will remain so unless a strategy can be devised for gaining dominant market share at reasonable cost.

   If achieving overall dominance is not feasible, then the smaller competitor should seek to identify an economically distinct segment of the business in which he can dominate the relevant experience bases sufficiently to attain a viable cost position overall.

These implications focus on market position relative to competitors and lead inexorably to the pursuit of dominance as a strategic imperative. However, the broad conclusions must be carefully hedged for there are many reasons why the experience curve may be inaccurate and many situations where the effects are unimportant relative to other variables. We have already seen that competitive cost differentials are dependent on the rate of value added. Thus, most of the successful applications have been within high value-added, continuous processing, capital intensive industries that are usually highly concentrated,

By contrast there is little point in looking for experience effects in custom industries such as tool and die making, which have traditionally been very fragmented (although numerical control machine tools are slowly changing that situation). Service industries have been especially resistant to experience analysis. According to Carman and Langeard (1980), the effect of learning on total costs has never been demonstrated in a service situation. There is also uncertainty as to whether economies of scale exist. Larréché (1980) found a negative association of return on assets and market share among French private commercial banks. However, this may not be true in the U.S. with the advent of new banking services, such as automated teller systems or daily interest checking accounts, which utilize capital-intensive computer systems. Indeed, preliminary PIMS findings from a sample of 85 financial service businesses reveal relationships of share and rate of return that are even stronger than those reported for consumer and industrial product business. Clearly, a great deal of work is needed before the applicability of the experience curve is established.

Risks of a Cost Reduction Strategy

All-out dedication to cost reduction efforts requires maximizing the scale of operations and pursuit of opportunities for specialization of work force, production processes and organizational arrangements. This approach confers a number of advantages, as smaller companies will attest. Unfortunately these cost reduction efforts introduce rigidities that may make the organization slower and less flexible in response to shifts in customers' requirements or competitive innovations (Abernathy and Wayne 1974). Ford recently had this problem when it closed its large, supposedly efficient Flat Rock plant because it was inflexible for conversion to the new types and sizes of engines being demanded by today's energy conscious consumer. Further, a large scale plant is vulnerable to significant changes in process technology.

A more subtle risk of an experience based strategy is a "definition of the business" that is distorted by an excessive commitment to a particular technology, rather than to satisfying customer needs. This, in turn, may lead to a preoccupation with competitors who make products with similar functions, materials and so on, and a lack of sensitivity to threats from other technologies with capacity to serve the same customer needs. The paper industry, for example, was slow to recognize the threat to paper grocery bags from plastics. Now that a plastic grocery bag is cost competitive, with the bonus of greater strength and reusability, the paper grocery bag is experiencing a competitive setback.

Summary and Conclusions

The simplistic market share dominance prescriptions that marked the early experience curve applications have been replaced with a growing sensitivity to the complexities of this concept. While its appeal as an organizing framework remains high, there is a realization that the experience curve effect is itself a product of underlying scale, technology and learning effects. Whether the experience curve is strategically relevant depends initially on whether these three effects are influential features of the strategic environment. Beyond this there is a growing recognition that there is a family of experience curves, each addressing different strategic issues, from cost component analyses to price forecasting to competitive cost comparisons. One consequence is that the earlier broad generalizations have been replaced with focused applications, where experience curve analysis plays a supportive role as one of a number of analytical methods.

An Agenda for Research

There are significant risks in analyses based on the experience curve concept because the potential for misleading signals is high. Yet when the insights are valid, they are highly valuable. These are conditions where the payoff to research is high. The following topics are judged especially rewarding.

Theory development. Few well-supported generalizations can be made about the conditions in which experience effects are significant. Specifically, what are the variables that dictate the slope of both the price curve and the competitive cost compression curve? Numerous hypotheses as to the effects of type of industry, rate of value added, competitive structure and mechanisms for technology diffusion need to be explored. A key unanswered question is the relationship of the experience curve with the product life cycle.

Both theory and practice would benefit from further research on the sources of the experience effect. Many strategic implications are derived from assumptions as to the relative contribution of learning, technology and scale. Yet published work is presently limited to three studies within the chemical industry.

Measurement sensitivity. Virtually no work has been reported on the impact of the measures on the results. What are the consequences of different assumptions about inflation, errors in the data or significant discontinuities in data series? When there is shared experience available to new products, how should the base of experience be estimated? How should "augmented" products, including technical service support, inventory financing and other services be treated?

Model specification and evaluation. In general, model specification issues have been ignored in the literature. Indeed, most of the reported analyses are straight lines fitted on a graphical plot. Other models than the log linear need to be tested for their econometric characteristics and forecasting accuracy. Forecasting tests are especially important for the industry price curve because of the hypothesized pattern of departure from the underlying cost curve. Finally, the consequences of aggregating a number of cost curves for individual components to obtain a total cost curve are not well understood.

A major area for further development is the integration of product life cycle and experience curve models that incorporate competitive behavior patterns. A recent paper by Harrell and Taylor (1981) illustrates the strategic relevance of such a model in the housewares industry. As with the other research suggested above, the payoff in improved strategic decision making and better understanding of dynamic market processes is substantial.

References

1. Equation (1) is of the Cobb-Douglas production function and is linear in the logarithm. A form similar to equation (1) is postulated for price, but the elasticity λ may differ from the elasticity corresponding to cost experience.
2. More attention has been given to these issues in the learning curve literature. Yelle (1979) describes four models other than the log linear, that provide better fits to the data in certain circumstances. See Montgomery and Day (1983) for a further discussion of these issues.
3. Some authors, such as Abell and Hammond (1979), prefer to keep scale effects separate from experience effects. Others, such as Pessemier (1980) prefer to distinguish static scale effects from dynamic scale effects that are achieved over time.
4. Hedonic price studies may prove helpful in disentangling the impact of different product features (Griliches 1961).
5. Seldom is an average industry cost curve available for this purpose, as it requires knowledge of individual company costs, weighted by the unit production for each competitor, that correspond to each level of industry cumulative volume (Conley 1970).
6. Dolan and Jeuland (1981) also have developed a model that derives an optimal pricing policy, which depends on the nature of the demand and experience curves and the type of product, whether a durable or a repeat purchase item.

Bibliography

Abell, Derek F. and John S. Hammond (1979), *Strategic Market Planning: Problems and Analytical Approaches*, Englewood Cliffs, NJ: Prentice-Hall.

Abernathy, William J. and K. Wayne (1974), "Limits of the Learning Curve," *Harvard Business Review*, 52 (September–October), 109–19.

Arrow, Kenneth J. (1961), "The Economic Implications of Learning by Doing," in *Review of Economic Studies*, 155–73.

Barkai, Haim and David Levhari (1973), "The Impact of Experience in Kibbutz Farming," *Review of Economics and Statistics*, 55 (February), 56–63.

Beevan, Alan (1974), "The U.K. Potato Crisp Industry, 1960–1972: A Study of New Entry Competition," *Journal of Industrial Economics*, 22 (June), 281–97.

Biggadike, Ralph (1977), *Scott-Air Corporation (B)*, working paper, Colgate Darden School, University of Virginia.

Booz, Allen and Hamilton (1982), *New Products: Best Practices—Today and Tomorrow*, New York: Booz, Allen.

Boston Consulting Group (1972), *Perspectives on Experience*, Boston: BCG.

——— (1975), *Strategy Alternatives for the British Motorcycle Industry*, London: Her Majesty's Stationery Office.

Burck, Gilbert (1972), "The Myths and Realities of Corporate Pricing," *Fortune*, 96 (April).

Business Week (1982), "The Coming Shakeout in Personal Computers," (November 22), 72–83.

Buzzell, Robert D. (1981), "Are There Natural Market Structures?" *Journal of Marketing*, 45 (Winter), 42–51.

Carman, James M. and Eric Langeard (1980), "Growth Strategies for Service Firms," *Strategic Management Journal*, 1 (January–March), 7–22.

Conley, Patrick (1970), "Experience Curves as a Planning Tool," *IEEE Spectrum*, 7 (Spring), 63–68.

Day, George S. (1981a), "The Product Life Cycle: Analysis and Application Issues," *Journal of Marketing*, 45 (Fall), 60–67.

——— (1981b), "Strategic Market Analysis and Definition: An Integrated Approach," *Strategic Management Journal*, 2 (July–September), 281–99.

Dean, Joel (1976), "Pricing Policies for New Products," *Harvard Business Review*, 54 (November–December), 141–53.

Dolan, Robert J. and Abel P. Jeuland (1981), "Experience Curves and Dynamic Demand Models: Implications for Optimal Pricing Strategies," *Journal of Marketing*, 45 (Winter), 52–73.

Griliches, Zvi (1961), "Hedonic Price Indices for Automobiles: An Econometric Analysis of Quality Change," *Government Price Statistics*, U.S. Congress Joint Economic Committee, U.S. Government Printing Office (January), 173–96; reprinted in *Readings in Economic Statistics and Econometrics*, A. Zellner, ed., Boston, MA: Little-Brown and Co., 1968, 103–30.

Harrell, Stephen G. and Elmer D. Taylor (1981), "Modeling the Product Life Cycle for Consumer Durables," *Journal of Marketing*, 45 (Fall), 68–75.

Hedley, Barry (1976), "A Fundamental Approach to Strategy Development," *Long Range Planning*, 9 (December) 2–11.

The authors wish to thank Professors Donald G. Morrison, David Rutenberg, V. Srinivasan, the section editor, and a *JM* referee for helpful comments on an earlier draft of this paper.

Henderson, Bruce D. (1978), *Cross-Sectional Experience*, Boston, MA: Boston Consulting Group.

——— (1980a), "Caution Based on Experience," in *Shifting Boundaries Between Regulation and Competition*, Betty Bock, ed., New York: Conference Board.

——— (1980b), *The Experience Curve Revisited*, Boston, MA: Boston Consulting Group.

Hirschman, Winifred B. (1964), "Profit from the Learning Curve," *Harvard Business Review*, 42 (January–February).

Hollander, S. (1965), *The Sources of Increased Efficiency: A Study of DuPont Rayon Manufacturing Plants*, Cambridge, MA: MIT Press.

Joskow, Paul L. and George A. Rozanski (1979), "The Effect of Learning by Doing on Nuclear Plant Operating Reliability," *Review of Economics and Statistics*, 61 (May), 161–68.

Kiechel, Walter (1981), "The Decline of the Experience Curve," *Fortune*, 105 (October), 139–46.

Larréché, Jean-Claude (1980), "On Limitations of Positive Market Share–Profitability Relationships: The Case of the French Banking Industry," unpublished working paper, Fontainebleau, France: INSEAD.

Lieberman, Marvin B. (1981), "The Experience Curve, Pricing and Market Structure in the Chemical Processing Industries," unpublished working paper, Harvard University.

McLagan, Donald L. (1981), "Market Share: Key to Profitability," *Planning Review*, 9 (March), 26–29.

Montgomery, David B. and George S. Day (1983), "Experience Curves: Evidence, Empirical Issues and Applications," in *Strategic Marketing and Strategic Management*, D. Gardner and H. Thomas, eds., New York: John Wiley.

Pessemier, Edgar A. (1977), *Product Management: Strategy and Organization*, New York: John Wiley.

Porter, Michael E. (1979), "How Competitive Forces Shape Strategy," *Harvard Business Review*, 57 (March–April), 137–45.

Rapping, Leonard (1965), "Learning and World War II Production Functions," *Review of Economics and Statistics*, 47 (February), 81–86.

Robinson, Bruce and Chet Lakhani (1975), "Dynamic Price Models for New Product Planning," *Management Science*, 21 (June), 1113–22.

Rutenberg, David (1976), "What Strategic Planning Expects from Management Science," working paper 89-75-76, Carnegie-Mellon University (December).

Spence, A. Michael (1981), "The Learning Curve and Competition," *The Bell Journal of Economics*, 12 (Spring), 49–69.

Stobaugh, Robert B. and Philip L. Townsend (1975), "Price Forecasting and Strategic Planning: The Case of Petro Chemicals," *Journal of Marketing Research*, 12 (February), 19–29.

Sultan, Ralph (1974), *Pricing in the Electrical Oligopoly*, Vols, I and II, Cambridge, MA: Harvard Graduate School of Business Administration.

Wilson, Aubrey and Bryan Atkin (1976), "Exorcising the Ghosts in Marketing," *Harvard Business Review*, 54 (September–October), 117–27.

Wilson, Robert G. (1982), "Strategies to Fight Inflation," *Journal of Business Strategy*, 2 (Winter), 22–31.

Wooley, Robert (1972), "Econometric Analysis of the Experience Effect," unpublished Ph.D. dissertation, Stanford University.

Yelle, Louis E. (1979), "The Learning Curve: Historical Review and Comprehensive Survey," *Decision Sciences*, 10 (March), 302–28.

12

Profit Potential as a Martingale Process

Marjorie Fox Utsey

This study uses data from the *Markstrat* simulation to explore the relation of actual to potential profit

The hypothesis of systematic shortfall from profit potential is rejected by applying a theoretical definition of potential to data from the *Markstrat* environment. Profit potential is defined as the NPV of the net marketing contribution resulting from realization of the optimal market share. Firms are found to be equally likely to exceed potential or to fail to reach it. This pattern is modeled by a martingale process. Factors that impact achievement of profit potential are explored.

MORE RESEARCH on the achievement of profit potential is needed. Accounting and financial ratios allow the firm to compare its performance to industry or national averages. However, this analysis does not relate performance to the firm's own potential. The current study uses data from the *Markstrat* simulation to explore the relation of actual to potential profit.

Although production managers have typically thought in terms of resource allocation for profit maximization, this way of thinking is comparatively new to marketers. The Profit Impact of Marketing Strategy (PIMS) project is barely 15 years old [2]. Yet marketing managers and scholars must cope with a world in which resources are limited, competitors are unrelenting, and profits are constrained by the extent of the market. Given these harsh realities, the marketing manager should seek to allocate resources in the way that maximizes the profits of the firm.

Marjorie Fox Utsey is Assistant Professor of Marketing at the University of New Orleans.

Background

Marketers have used market-share models to study the marketing mix and its relation to profits for several years. (Comparative summaries of market-share models are found in [6] and [10].) Several recent articles have focused on the empirical relation of market share to profit. (See [4, 12, 19].) These articles serve as a conceptual base throughout this article.

Theories of Profit Potential

The PIMS/Strategic Look-Alike Approach

Buzzell and Chussil [3] use a sample of firms from the PIMS data base to explore potential profit. They define full potential performance as achievement of the greatest possible combination of discounted cash flows and discounted future market value a firm (or strategic business unit) can be expected to attain given its current strategic position. This definition allows for the fact that some firms are in a much stronger position ex ante than others.

Potential is estimated by comparing the firm's performance to the results of top performing firms that are strategically similar. Comparison with this standard permits estimation of the improvements in return on investment and cash flow than can be expected if the firm raises its performance to match the better firm. A range of strategies is tested for each firm; the strategy that results in maximum discounted cash flow plus future market value is selected. Potential discounted cash flow plus discounted future market value is calculated for each firm over a five-year period. The result is then compared to discounted cash flow plus discounted future market value actually achieved by the firm over the same five-year period. On the basis of this comparison, 90% of firms covered by the study performed below potential; 10% exceeded potential. The typical firm performed at less than 50% of potential.

Firms may exceed computed potential if the forecasts on which estimates were based prove to be unduly pessimistic. For example, if market growth or selling price increase more than expected or costs decrease more than expected during the planning period, actual performance will exceed forecasted potential. Alternatively, "unexpected changes such as the collapse of a significant competitor, could yield 'serendipitous' benefits" [3, p. 6].

This definition of full potential is empirically based and thus relatively simple to operationalize, but it is a relative rather than an absolute standard. What if the top performer could also achieve better results? What if achievements of the top firm are attributable in part to good luck (a factor other firms cannot logically be expected to replicate)? Buzzell himself notes that windfalls can produce market-share gains, and suggests analyzing "lucky," "unlucky," and "normal" cases to create "a range of realistic profit expectations" [2, p. 8]. Finally, the marketing process may contain enough ambiguity to create an uncertainty firms cannot reduce, even when trying to imitate outcomes they can observe.

The Net Present Value of Market Share Approach

These questions lead to the search for a theoretical definition of potential that is independent of the performance of a yardstick firm. Such a definition is provided by Cook [6], in the net-present-value-of-market-share model. This linear-optimization (profit-maximization) model enables marketing managers to select the pattern of resource allocation that leads to achievement of long-run profit potential, and calculate the net present value of the resulting net marketing contribution. Rappaport offers an additional explanation of the superiority of the value-based approach to strategy evaluation compared with traditional accounting-oriented measures [18].

The value of a market-share point is calculated by multiplying the relevant level of primary demand by the firm's unit contribution and dividing the result by 100 [6]. Total gross marketing contribution is the product of this value (v) and the number of market-share points the firm possesses.

On the supply side, accurate identification of the marketing-decision variables relevant for the pursuit of market share is important. The goal is to define a parsimonious, yet complete set of descriptors. The absolute level of resource use for each factor may be translated into the firm's share of marketing capacity with respect to that resource [6].

In the model, long-run expected share of output is a linear-weighted average of capacity shares of inputs according to:

$$m = w_1x_1 = w_2x_2 + \ldots w_jx_n \qquad 0 \leq m \leq 1.0$$

where

$$0 \leq w \leq 1.0$$
$$0 \leq x \leq 1.0$$

$$\sum_{j=1}^{n} w_j = 1.0$$

The x's in the above equation represent the capacity shares of inputs; for example, the firm may choose to deploy an amount equal to 35% of industry spending on media advertising. The w's (weights) specify the effectiveness of each marketing-mix variable in producing share of output, and n is the number of marketing-mix variables employed by the firm. These w's may be provided by the judgment of the experienced marketing manager, estimated statistically as they are in the current study, or determined by subjecting statistically estimated weights to management review for fine tuning. Dawes and Corrigan [9] found that statistical estimation using a linear model produced better results than human judgment.

This process involves trial and error. Such judgments are difficult, particularly the first time they are formulated. However, one should not let the rigor of the task or fear of producing estimates that are less than perfect prevent one from attempting to model the market. A first approximation for many industries may be the default assumption that all variables have equal importance. Dawes and Corrigan [9, p. 103] have shown linear models to be "robust over deviations from optimal weightings." In particular, models employing equal weightings were shown to predict the dependent variable nearly as well as optimally weighted linear models.

The profit-maximizing share of output obtains when the optimal-capacity share of each input is put in place. The net present value (NPV) of net marketing contribution resulting from the realization of this optimal market share over the relevant time period represents the maximum potential profit to the firm in the theoretical model. The particular combination of resources that leads to achievement of this profit potential depends on factor costs for the resources, planned capacities of competitors, and primary demand. This definition requires that the firm make correct forecasts of primary demand, costs, and competitors' investments over the planning horizon. To the extent demand forecasts and competitive anticipations are incorrect, resources will be over- or underdeployed.

The cost to the firm of this combination of resources is the sum of expenditures on each of the optimal nonprice capacities. Net marketing contribution is then gross marketing contribution minus total expenditures of the firm on the relevant capacities. Net present value of marketing contribution is determined by applying a risk-adjusted discount rate to the net marketing contribution stream [8].

Methodology

Why Markstrat?

The model just described is applied to data generated by the *Markstrat* simulation, a computer-generated model based on a set of relationships that closely simulate real marketing phenomena. The model is constructed in a way that directs the attention of subjects to the major marketing-decision variables. The simulation furnishes all the data needed to implement the net present value of market-share model.

A controlled environment has the advantage of minimizing measurement error. Furthermore, it is unlikely businessmen would permit observation of similar decision making in their own boardrooms. (The advantages associated with using data generated by a simulation in general and *Markstrat* in particular are discussed further in [11, 13, 14, 15, 16]).

The Data

Fifty high-level executives of a billion dollar multinational corporation were divided in two subsamples of approximately 25 subjects. Each subsample was divided into five groups. Each subsample played an eight-period *Markstrat* simulation. One data set (London) was composed mainly of British marketing and sales executives; the other was composed of South African executives from several functional areas. Thus, the decision makers in this study were the executives who would customarily make key marketing decisions for their firms.

All brand data were aggregated and analyses were conducted at the firm level. The *Markstrat* world was treated as a single market in which the selection of sonite target segments and the trade-off between sonites and vodites were the product-line decision. There were two major advantages: (1) The net-present-value-of-market-share model is designed to deal with a single market—it has not yet been extended to include product portfolio decisions; and (2) several decision variables in *Markstrat* (R&D, salesforce, and marketing-research expenditures) are reported on a firm rather than a brand basis. Allocation of these expenditures to brands would contain arbitrary elements that could distort the data and bias the results. (For a more complete description of the rationale for aggregation, see [20].)

Model Specification and Parameter Estimation

The next task was the modeling of weighted average market share as a function of the relevant *Markstrat* variables to secure estimates of the relative importance (effectiveness in generating share of output) of each of these variables. Parameters thus calculated are used later with data from the *Markstrat* simulation to calculate profit potential for each firm.

In the real world, these parameters (the w's) may be supplied by judgment or estimated statistically. In *Markstrat*, managerial judgments were not available. Recovery of the weights from the simulation itself was not feasible because the weights were determined jointly by interaction of the players with the model. The weights estimated in each game described the relative importance of the mix variables in that particular run. Weights may vary substantially from game to game, so that each game may be regarded as a separate "industry."

The independent variables considered were the decision variables of the *Markstrat* world and the lagged value of the dependent variable. They included assortment (number of brands), physical characteristics of brands (power and design), dollar R&D, units of product available for sale (units produced plus inventory), dollar advertising, salesforce dollars, retail price (which affects the economy dimension of the perceptual map), and last year's market share.

The nature of the perceptual map in *Markstrat* made it difficult to separate price from the dimensions of economy, power, and design. Therefore, a composite variable "perceived value," was used. *PV* represented the "share of (inverted) volume-weighted interpoint distances between each brand in the firm's portfolio and all segment ideal points" [8, p. 525]. It incorporated price and product attribute effects and assortment as well, since the scores of each brand marketed by the firm were summed to create this variable.

The nature of the underlying response of market share is complex, since *Markstrat* is driven by a system of 18 equations rather than by a single response function. [See 15, p. 148–159.] Even if the underlying function is nonlinear, a linear approximation should yield adequate results because we are dealing with small intervals of the domain of the function. Furthermore, Dawes and Corrigan [9, p. 98] report "a high degree of fit between [nonlinear] models and linear approximations." Since linear functions are inherently simpler and statistical properties of the estimators are stronger, the response function in this article is fit with a linear-additive model. (See [17] for another recent instance in which a linear model of market share and change in share produces a good fit.)

The Shazam package [22] was used to perform ordinary least squares regression analysis with the sum and range constraints required by the net-present-value-of-market-share model. These constraints required that parameter values summed to 1 and that no parameters had negative values. Negative parameter values would be illogical in a marketing-resource-allocation sense.

As Table 1 shows, Models 1 and 2, which include both the *B1* (share of units produced available for sale) and *LAG* (previous period market share) variables fail to satisfy the range constraint. Model 4 does not satisfy the range constraint. These models are therefore rejected in favor of Model 3, which does satisfy both constraints.

The correlation matrix of the independent variables revealed high collinearity between *B1* (share of units available for sale) and *LAG* (previous period market share). Both were also somewhat collinear with advertising and salesforce expenditures. (In fact, *B1* by itself had an R^2 with market share of .9651.) When *B1* was omitted in Model 3, positive coefficients were obtained for all independent variables, although salesforce and *PV* still had weak *T* statistics. The parameters of Model 3 were used as input for the calculation of the profit-potential model.

Several tests were performed to validate the appropriateness of ordinary least squares and the adequacy of the linear-

Table 1
Alternative Specifications Considered

	Model 1	Model 2	Model 3[a]	Model 4	Correlation of *B1* and *m1*
LAG[b]	−0.0689	−0.0356	0.5543	0.5916	
	(−0.86)[c]	(−0.487)[c]	(3.89)[c]	(3.84)[c]	
B1[b]	1.066	1.05			1.125
	(13.45)	(13.49)			(32.9)
ADV[b]	0.1167	0.1149	0.3397	0.3314	
	(2.07)	(2.02)	(2.58)	(2.49)	
SLSF[b]	0.0308	0.0168	0.0269	0.0052	
	(0.35)	(0.199)	(0.13)	(1.025)	
RD[b]	0.0167			−0.0257	
	(1.04)			(−0.667)	
PV[b]	−0.1616	−0.1463	0.079	0.0973	
	(−3.05)	(−2.87)	(0.67)	(0.805)	
Adj R^2	0.969	0.0689	0.8168	0.8140	0.9651
F ratio	305.52	406.14	87.93	57.88	1079.72
df[b]	4.35	3.36	2.37	3.36	1.38

[a]Only Model 3 satisfies both the range and sum constraints of our theoretical model.
Model 1: *m1* = *LAG, B1, ADV, SLSF, RD, PV*
Model 2: *m1* = *LAG, B1, ADV, SLSF, PV*
Model 3: *m1* = *LAG, ADV, SLSF, PV*
Model 4: *m1* = *LAG, ADV, SLSF, PV, RD*
Correlation: *m1* = *a* + *B1*

[b]*LAG* = lagged market share; *B1* = share of units produced available for sale
ADV = share of media dollars; *SLSF* = share of salesforce dollars
RD = share of research dollars; *PV* = share of perceived value
df = degrees of freedom

[c]*T* ratios are presented in parentheses beneath their coefficients.

additive model. Plots and histograms of relevant variables were constructed. Plots of the residuals showed no discernible heteroscedasticity, or linear or nonlinear trends. The histogram of the residuals of Model 3 was roughly normal in shape. The Durbin's H statistic for the model was −2.6836, indicating autocorrelation was not present.

Each model form was estimated three times; the London data alone, the South African data alone, and the pooled set of 80 observations. If estimates differed substantially (the equivalent of coming from different real-world industries), the separate parameter estimates would be used as input to the profit-potential model.

The null hypothesis of no difference between pooled estimates and individual data-set estimates was tested for each model and could not be rejected for any model. The pooled estimates would usually be considered more reliable. However, in this case, the estimates from the London data appeared to be more appropriate. The London data exhibited a high ratio of explained to unexplained market share, while the South African data exhibited much unexplained share. (See [12] for definitions of explained and unexplained share.) Because the net-present-value-of-market-share model explains the workings of anticipated market share, it seemed appropriate to estimate the relative importance of marketing variables in a less "noisy" environment in which they explained a relatively large amount of the variation in share of output. Thus the estimates in Table 1 are for the London data set.

Calculation of Profit Potential

The net-present-value-of-market-share model allows management to calculate the maximum profit-potential market share for the firm, the weighted average-capacity share of each marketing-mix input associated with that share of output and the net-present-value-of-marketing contribution resulting from that market share. (Optimal price is calculated outside the model.)

Once price is entered, the model determines the best capacity shares for the nonprice variables. The model is operationalized in an Interactive Financial Planning System subroutine, VMS.IFPS [7]. Managers forecast primary demand, mix weights, factor costs, and retail price for the firm and for the market, and markup and estimates of competitors' mix investments. The subroutine then calculates market share, marketing contribution, and risk-adjusted net present value for each year.

A program similar to VMS.IFPS was written to conform to the set of decision variables found in the *Markstrat* world. The new program is called MAR.IFPS. The equivalent of supplying optimal price to VMS .IFPS is supplying optimal *PV* capacity to MAR.IFPS. We define this quantity by assuming the firm modifies its existing brands to match the characteristics desired by consumers at the closest ideal point. Retail prices used are those the firm should have charged to make all brands exhibit an ideal economy characteristic.

The forecasts of primary demand and competitors' actions used in VMS.IFPS are replaced with actual data from the *Markstrat* printouts in MAR.IFPS. The measurement error associated with forecasts is thus avoided. Maximum potential profit for company 1 in year 4 is calculated by entering actual primary demand for year 4, the weights just estimated, optimal *PV* and retail price based on the position of the ideal points in year 4, and competitors' actual expenditures on each mix variable in year 4. The subroutine then calculates profit-maximizing market share and associated net marketing contribution for company 1 in year 4. The process is repeated for each firm in each year.

Hypothesis Testing

It was originally expected that shortfalls in potential similar to those observed by Buzzell and Chussil [3] would be found in this data. Hypotheses were specified accordingly.

1. Do managers fall short of potential in general?

$$H_o\colon \overline{NMC^A} - \overline{NMC^P} = 0 \qquad H_a\colon \overline{NMC^A} - \overline{NMC^P} < 0$$

The null hypothesis stated that there was no difference between mean actual net marketing contribution (NMC^A) and mean potential net marketing contribution (NMC^P) for the 10 firms over the eight years. A paired t test was conducted in which actual *NMC* for each firm in each year was paired with potential *NMC* for the same firm and year. The

Figure 1
London deviation from potential

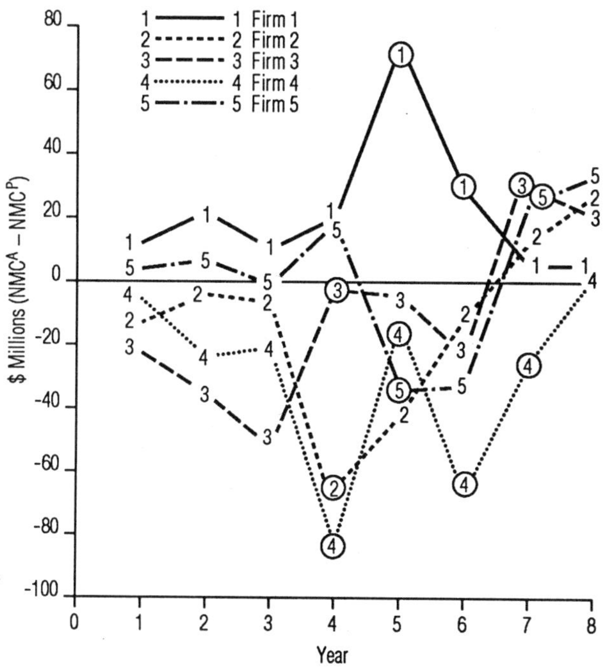

Figure 2
South African deviation from potential

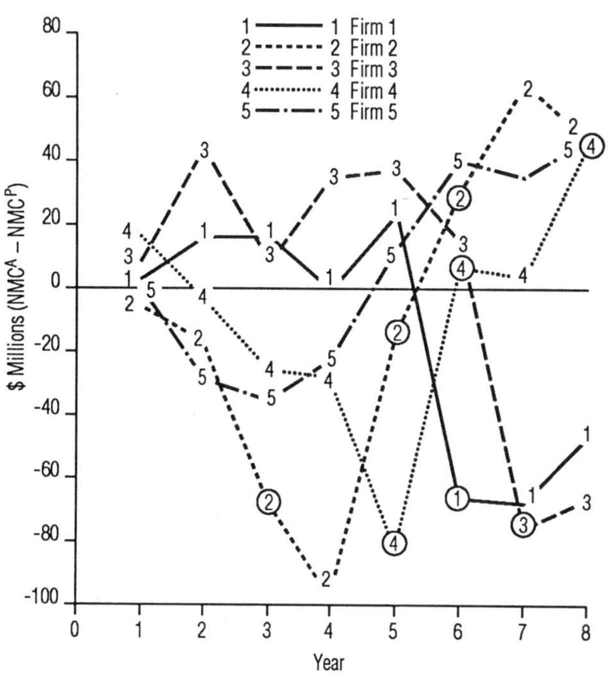

null hypothesis could not be rejected at the alpha = .05 level. This result does not mean there were no instances in which actual and potential *NMC* were unequal, but rather these inequalities tended to balance out instead of clustering on the negative side. Management did not fall short of potential in general terms.

2. Do individual firms fall short of potential?

H_o: $(\overline{NMC^A} - \overline{NMC^P})_j = 0$

H_A: $(\overline{NMC^A} - \overline{NMC^P})_j < 0$, $\quad j = 1,2,3,4,5$ firms

The null hypothesis stated that for each firm, mean *NMC* actually achieved over the eight-year period did not differ from the potential mean *NMC* the firm could have achieved. Tpothesis retested hypothesis 1 on a firm-by-firmsis. For each firm, a paired *t* test was conducted. The null hypothesis could not be rejected for 8 of the 10 firms at alpha = .05. In the London data set, firm 1 consistently achieved greater-than-potential profits, and firm 4 consistently fell short of potential.

Given that results did not produce findings of a systematic shortfall from profit potential, the next step was to explore hypotheses designed to model the behavior that in fact obtained. Following the line of reasoning developed by Rumelt and Wensley [19], we sought answers among stochastic processes.

3. Fair-Coin-Toss Hypothesis

H_o: $Pr(G_{ij} = 1) = .5 \qquad G_{ij} = 1$ if $NMC^A \geq NMC^P$,

H_a: $Pr(G_{ij} = 1) \neq .5 \qquad G_{ij} = -1$ if $NMC^A \leq NMC^P$

A new variable (G_{ij}) was created that assumed a value of 1 if performance exceeded potential and a value of −1 if performance was less than potential. The variable thus sorted the 80 observations into an overachievement group and an underachievement group. The null hypothesis implied the sizes of these two groups was not significantly different.

This hypothesis tested the proposition firms in general were equally likely to overachieve or underachieve with respect to profit potential. This was a probability test conducted with no prior knowledge of firm performance. It was equivalent to the standard introduction to probability theory in which balls of differing colors are drawn from an urn. Here, observations of deviations from potential were drawn from a sample of 80 observations.

A *z* test was conducted. The null hypothesis could not be rejected at the alpha = .05 level. (In the $N = 40$ London observations, 45% were classified as $G_{ij} = 1$. In the $N = 40$ South African observations, 55% were classified as $G_{ij} = 1$. For the total set of $N = 80$ observations, 50% were classified as $G_{ij} = 1$.) Given no prior information on firm performance, an observation drawn from the sample was as likely to exceed potential as it was to fall short.

Further clarification of this result is provided by Figures 1 and 2. Figure 1 presents the difference between actual and potential *NMC* over time for each firm in the London data set. Numbers are used to depict the data points so that the reader can follow the progress of each firm. The same information for the South African firms appears in Figure 2. The horizontal axis of each graph represents equality of actual and potential *NMC*. It is clear that approximately half of the observations fall to each side of the horizontal axis in both figures.

The fair-coin-toss hypothesis simply implied the overachievement and underachievement groups were of equal size. The hypothesis said nothing about the pattern of observations. For example, were low observations mainly found in early years while high values clustered in later years? The next hypothesis tested for the presence of a process (or pattern) in the data.

4. Martingale Hypothesis

H_o: $\overline{D_{ij}} = 0$ $\qquad D_{ij} = (NMC^A - NMC^P)_{ij+1} - (NMC^A - NMC^P)_{ij}$

H_a: $\overline{D_{ij}} > 0$

A martingale is a statistical process in which the expected variation of the value in question from one year to the next is constant. In other words, the series (as a whole, without prior knowledge) tends toward a constant value over time. Here the series is $NMC^A - NMC^P$, and the constant toward which it tends is zero. An inability to reject the null hypothesis would indicate the pattern observed above (half the observations above potential and half below) is an ongoing process rather than a composite of some years in which all firms do badly and some years in which all do well.

A paired *t* test was conducted on 70 observations. (Since D_{ij} is a difference, the first five observations of each data set were lost.) The null hypothesis could not be rejected at the alpha = .05 level. The test was repeated for each set of 35 observations. Once again, the null hypothesis could not be rejected. These findings support the conclusion that the pattern observed represents a continuing process. Reference to Figures 1 and 2 confirms this pattern visually. In most years, some firms overachieve while others do poorly.

The next logical question is whether a random-walk process can accurately describe the data. Does $NMC^A - NMC^P$ tend toward zero regardless of the past performance of the firm?

5. Random-walk hypothesis

$$H_o: Pr(G_{ij+1} = 1 | G_{ij} = 1) = .5$$
$$H_a: Pr(G_{ij+1} = 1 | G_{ij} = 1) \neq .5$$

A random walk is a process that exhibits the constant expected variation over time of a series that tends toward a constant value, *and* in which current values of the series are independent of prior values. The null hypothesis states that the sign of the current deviation of actual from potential performance is independent of the sign of last year's deviation. Even if we know a firm under- or overachieved last year, the probabilities of over- or underachievement this year remain equal. The alternative hypothesis implies a consistency of sign over the two-year period.

A *z* test was conducted and the null hypothesis was rejected. For the London data, the fraction of years with G_{ij} = 1 followed by another year with G_{ij} = 1 was .846. For the South African data, the fraction was .842. For the total data set, the fraction was .844. The *z* value was 3.91. This result implies that if we know a firm has exceeded (performed below) potential in one time period, that firm is likely to exceed (perform below) potential in the following year.

Figures 1 and 2 provide visual confirmation of this result. Although few firms remain consistently above or below the line of equality for all eight years, there are many instances in which behavior is consistent for three years or more. This result parallels the findings of Buzzell [2, p. 4]. His analysis of the PIMS data base shows a tendency for the direction of changes in market share to continue over two or three years. A firm with successful management techniques tends to continue its success (perhaps until disturbed by an environmental shock), while a firm that is performing badly usually requires more than one year to correct its problems. Furthermore, this result is logical in view of the importance of lagged market share in the *Markstrat* simulation (and in the real world). Once a firm is pointed in a direction, the momentum of the market will tend to sustain that direction for short periods of time.

Discussion

The existence of stochastic processes does not necessarily mean that results are attributable entirely to chance or luck, in *Markstrat* or in the real world. An exogeneous variable or variables could be driving the stochastic process. Isolating and understanding these factors should make it possible for firms to improve their performance. Therefore, the next task is to examine factors that impact the placement of the data points in Figures 1 and 2. Do management decision processes differ at points above the horizontal axis from those at points below? Do accurate forecasts of primary demand, careful attention to costs, and deft handling of competition enable the firm to realize or exceed potential, while failure to attend to these variables relegates the firm to a shortfall position?

Analysis of decision processes in the current study has meaning beyond the scope of the *Markstrat* world. In fact, it is the decision processes of top executives (in an oligopoly that produces a consumer durable) that are under consideration. The roles of primary demand, costs, and competition in determining profit potential are not idiosyncratic to the *Markstrat* world; they are of general importance to decision makers at large.

Several hypotheses were specified to measure the amount of the variance in profit performance that could be attributed to primary demand, costs, and competition. Unfortunately, none of these hypotheses were supported by the data. It is possible that these factors do not explain a significant proportion of the variance in profit potential, although theory [2, 21] would lead us to consider them important. It is more likely that small sample size and weak measures of the independent variables prevented verification of relationships that do exist.

For example, the demand forecasts used by the teams were not available, and the measure of the impact of cost reducing R&D was impeded by the fact that there were few projects undertaken. Specific data on the management decision processes were not collected. These data could only have been obtained by taping the sessions or placing a trained observer with each group. At data-collection time, neither seemed practical, and neither seemed necessary given the expected results. Given the results actually obtained, it would appear critical to collect such data in the future.

Figures 1 and 2 contain 19 data points that depart sharply from prior performance. (These points are circled.) A qualitative consideration of these points supports the existence of explanatory factors. For example, the existence of adequate product capacity in the form of inventory available for sale seems related to sharp increases in performance. Eighty percent of sharp increases are associated with stockouts of a competitor. Thus, firms that have the foresight to keep sufficient product on hand are able to capitalize on competitor's mistakes.

Borrowing and subsequent careful deployment of extra resources for additional marketing capacity appear to improve performance. Seventy percent of the sharp increases in performance are associated with such borrowing. These results are consistent with theoretical prescriptions to base resource allocation on capacities needed to accomplish goals rather than on preset budgets [5, 6]. Finally, it is likely that a significant portion of performance will continue to be attributable to chance (luck). For example, 8 of the 19 sharp changes in Figures 1 and 2 are associated with an unusually large change in target-segment primary demand of the same sign. These shifts in demand represent windfall profits or excess inventories for the firm depending on the direction of the change. These lucky firms gain unexplained market share and profit while seeming to follow a harvest strategy. Buzzell notes that this would appear to be ideal, but comments "no one has yet devised a foolproof way to implement this advice" [2, p. 7].

Jacobsen and Aaker [12] also distinguish between anticipated and unanticipated market share. Anticipated market share is the share we would expect the firm to realize as the result of its deployment of marketing resources (given deployments of competitors). Unanticipated share results from exogeneous events (such as windfalls from the unexpected withdrawal of a competitor, or the losses associated with a fire at the factory). The point here is that management will always be subject to events that defy forecasting and modeling techniques. Furthermore, it appears that the occurrence of such events is more frequent in current complex business environments than in earlier, simpler times. If such an element of chance can be substantiated, it implies that an important managerial skill will be the ability to quickly and accurately diagnose unexpected events and promptly formulate appropriate responses.

A critical difference between this study of profit potential and the previous one [3] concerns definitions. The strategic look-alike definition is equivalent to moving the horizontal axis in Figure 1 upward to the average level of performance achieved by company 1. Obviously, doing this would cause the other four firms to fall short of defined potential in most of the years.

Conclusions and Directions for Future Research

This study was undertaken with the expectation of observing profits below potential for most of the firms in most of the years. In fact, only 1 of the 10 firms performed consistently below potential, while 1 firm performed consistently above potential. The other 8 firms were below potential in some years and above potential in others. The initial hypothesis of systematic shortfall from potential was not supported. Clearly, a great deal of good forecasting and decision making was taking place among the executives in this simulated, but realistic example. This finding would lead us to believe a similar lack of shortfall from potential exists in many real-world industries, although this belief remains to be tested.

Future research should build on the results of this exploratory study by (1) testing the validity of the findings in a variety of settings, and (2) isolating the decision processes most likely to lead to success. This analysis should be replicated using data from real-world markets. Markets at all stages of the product life cycle should be studied to encompass the interaction of the product life cycle with resource-allocation strategies.

There is a need to study decision rules, decision processes, and the particular factors that lead to strong performance when considered. An observation of behavioral as well as economic variables should be made. Mental sets of participants should be scrutinized. Measures of quality of management should be developed. Causal modeling could help to put all the relationships together.

Markstrat is well suited to this work. In addition to providing an environment with low measurement error, *Markstrat* is easily manipulated to facilitate a variety of laboratory experiments. Teams of confederates could apply prescribed rules, while the decision processes of the other teams were observed and performances compared. Alternatively, a fully computerized *Markstrat* study could create a perfect information environment. Five sets of decision rules could be programmed to drive the 5 firms through 8 to 10 years of play. We could then observe which decision rules resulted in the best performance. Availability of information and budgets could also be manipulated.

Research that facilitates the understanding of factors and decision processes that lead to achievement of profit poten-

This research was funded by the A. B. Freeman School of Business. Subjects were executives with International Computers, Ltd. The author wishes to thank Professor Victor J. Cook, Jr. and Professors William A. Mindak, Edward C. Strong, and Donna Mohr for reviewing earlier drafts of this manuscript. The article is based on the author's dissertation, which received an honorable mention in the 1986 Marketing Science Institute marketing-strategy dissertation competition.

tial could mean improved profit performance for individual firms and the business community as a whole.

References

1. Alderson, Wroe, *Marketing Behavior and Executive Action.* Richard D. Irwin, Homewood, Ill., 1957.
2. Buzzell, Robert, "Calibrating the Cost (?) of Gaining Market Share," *The PIMSletter on Business Strategy,* 37 (1986): 1–8.
3. Buzzell, Robert, and Chussil, Mark J., "Managing for Tomorrow," *Sloan Management Review,* 26 (1985): 3–14.
4. Buzzell, Robert, Bradley, R.D., Gale, T., and Sultan, R., "Market Share—A Key to Profitability," *Harvard Business Review,* 53 (1975): 97–106.
5. Cook, Victor J., Jr., "Marketing Strategy and Differential Advantage," *Journal of Marketing,* 47 (1983): 68–75.
6. Cook, Victor J., Jr., "The Net Present Value of Market Share," *Journal of Marketing,* 49 (1985): 49–63.
7. Cook, Victor J., Jr., and Cook, William R., "VMS.IFPS—A Value of Market Share Model for the Interactive Financial Planning System," working paper, A. B. Freeman School of Business, 1984.
8. Cook, Victor J., Jr., and Page, John R., "Assessing Marketing Risk," *Journal of Business Research,* 6 (1987): 519–530.
9. Dawes, Robyn M., and Corrigan, Bernard, "Linear Models in Decision Making," *Psychological Bulletin,* 81 (1974): 95–106.
10. Eliashberg, Jehoshuha, and Chatterjee, Rabikar, "Analytical Models of Competition with Implications for Marketing: Issues, Findings, and Outlook," *Journal of Marketing Research,* 22 (1985): 237–261.
11. Green, Paul E., Robinson, Patrick J., and Fitzroy, Peter T., *Experiments on the Value of Information in Simulated Marketing Environments.* Allyn and Bacon, Boston, 1967.
12. Jacobsen, Robert, and Aaker, David A., "Is Market Share All That It's Cracked Up To Be?" *Journal of Marketing,* 49 (1985): 11–22.
13. Kinnear, Thomas C., "Problems and Opportunities in Using MARKSTRAT for Experimental Research in Marketing Management Decision," paper presented to the *AMA Educators' Conference,* August 1986.
14. Larréché, Jean-Claude, and Gatignon, Hubert, *MARKSTRAT: A Marketing Strategy Game, Player's Manual.* The Scientific Press, Palo Alto, Calif., 1977.
15. Larréché, Jean-Claude, and Gatignon, Hubert, *MARKSTRAT: A Marketing Strategy Game, Instructor's Manual.* The Scientific Press, Palo Alto, Calif., 1977.
16. Larréché, Jean-Claude, "On Simulations in Business Education and Research," *Journal of Business Research,* 6 (1987): 559–571.
17. Lilien, Gary L., and Yoon, Eunsang, "An Oligopoly Market Model When Capacity and Price Are Decision Variables: A Case Study of the Titanium Dioxide Industry," working paper, ISBM, May 1985.
18. Rappaport, Alfred, "Selecting Strategies that Create Shareholder Value," *Harvard Business Review,* 59 (May–June, 1981): 139–49.
19. Rumelt, R. P., and Wensley, J.R.C., "Market Share and the Rate of Return: Testing the Stochastic Hypothesis," working paper, University of California at Los Angeles, 1981.
20. Utsey, Marjorie F., "A Study of the Achievement of Profit Potential in a Simulated Environment," unpublished Ph.D. Dissertation, Tulane University, New Orleans, La., 1985.
21. Utsey, Marjorie F., and Cook, Victor J., Jr., "A Marketing Strategy Paradigm for Case Analysis," in the *AMA Educators' Proceedings.* Russell W. Belk et al., eds., American Marketing Association, Chicago, 1984, pp. 96–100.
22. White, Kenneth J., "Shazam, An Econometrics Computer Program," Rice University, Houston, 1980.

13

The Net Present Value of Market Share

Victor J. Cook, Jr.

This article evaluates the dynamic interaction of market share and profit.

The determinants of market share are compared with published empirical research and illustrated in a consumer product industry. The effects of market growth, maturity and decline, competitive attack, price leadership, and heavy user strategies on market share and profit are analyzed theoretically and simulated over a 10-year period.

The pursuit of market share for profit is hotly debated. At the heart of the debate lies the relationship between market share and profitability (Wind and Mahajan 1981). Evidence shows a 10-point increase in share of market is associated, on the average, with a five-point increase in return on investment (Buzzell, Gale, and Sultan 1975). Yet, the exceptions to the rule are convincing (Hamermesh, Anderson, and Harris 1978; Jacobson and Aaker 1985; Woo and Cooper 1982). Adding heat to the debate is the prospect that profitability is a random walk among market shares (Caves, Gale, and Porter 1977; Mancke 1974; Rumelt and Wensley 1981). A resolution seems to require placing a price tag on the value of a change in market share and evaluating the corresponding return on investment (Henderson 1979).

In search of a resolution, this article will outline the determinants of market share, based on the principles of causal analysis. Market share and profit studies published over 20 years are then compared with the determinants of market share to gauge the reach of past empirical research. The value and cost of market share are introduced, to illustrate how a price tag is placed on market share in a consumer product industry. The theoretical effects of market share and profit are examined for growth, maturity, and declining market strategies, as well as competitive attack, price leadership, and heavy user strategies. To demonstrate the theory, a simulation of market share and profit over a 10-year period in a dynamically competitive environment is presented. The pursuit of market share for profit is discussed, in an effort to provide new direction for scholars and managers.

The Determinants of Market Share

Market share is a consequence of interactions between demand and supply. Demand factors determine the extent of the market. Supply factors define the manner in which resources are put at risk. Performance factors measure the outcomes. Method factors influence the validity of conclusions. A path diagram (Bagozzi 1984) of the determinants of market share is presented in Figure 1. Each major concept appears at the center of the cluster of factors it represents. Demand, for example, appears at the center of a cluster of the five factors. Leading from each factor, an operational measure appears in a box. Market definition is operationalized by combining a specific product technology with a defined user segment. Measurement error is represented by a lower case epsilon.

Demand factors are antecedent concepts that reveal the behavior of buyers in consummating exchanges (Hunt 1983): market definition, primary demand, demand elasticity, heavy users, and brand equity. *Supply factors* are focal concepts that reveal the behavior of sellers in consummating

Victor J. Cook, Jr., is Professor of Marketing Strategy, A. B. Freeman School of Business, Tulane University.

Figure 1
The net present value of market share

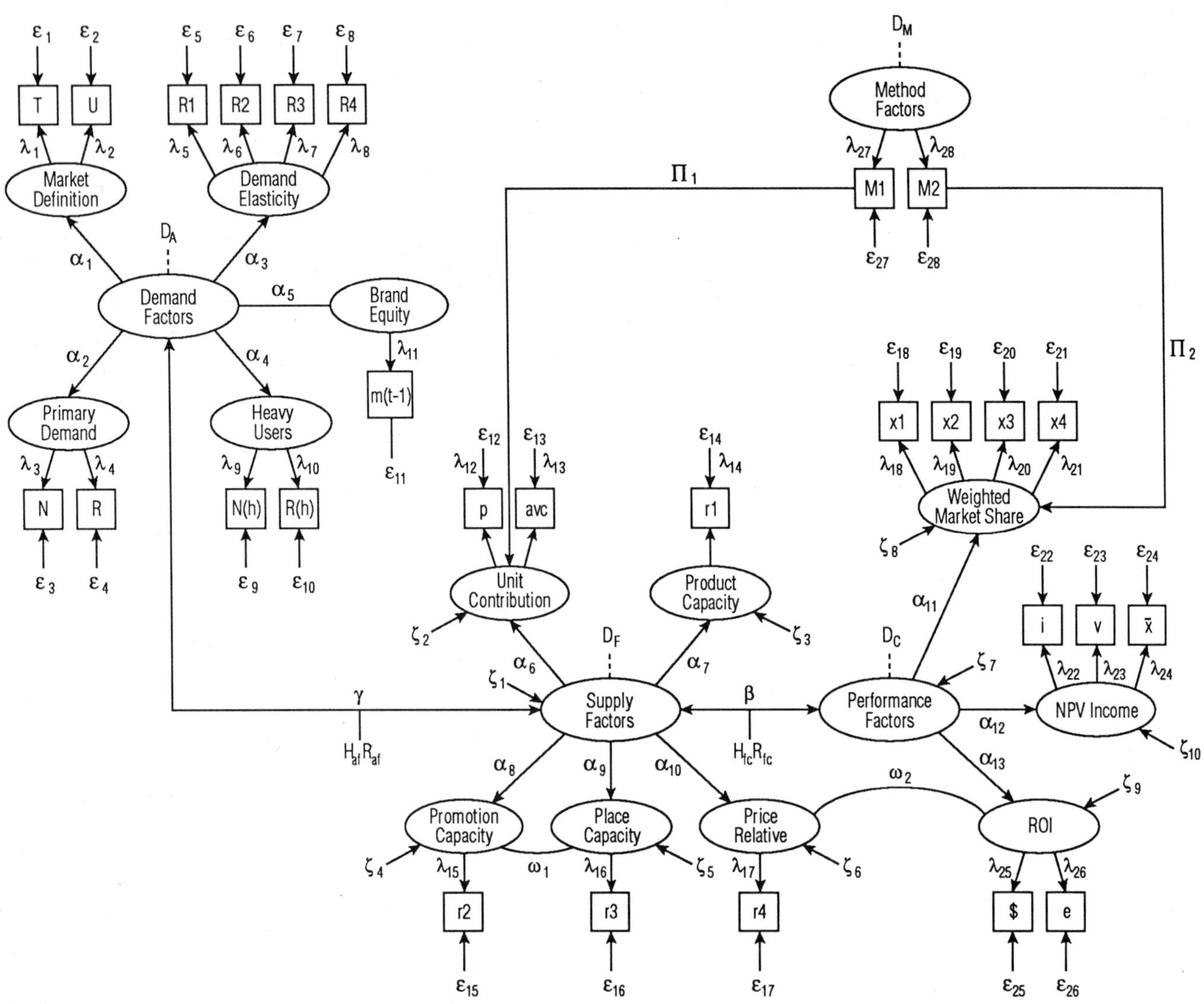

Concept	Definition of Measurements
Demand	T = Technology; U = Uses; N = Number of users; K =per capita consumption; h = heavy users; R1 = capacity of market to produce, R2 = market capacity to promote, R3 = market capacity to deliver, R4 = average market price; m(t − 1) residual brand equity measured by lagged market share.
Supply	p = company sel;ling price; avc = company average variable cost; r1 = company product capacity, r2 = company capacity to promote, r3 = company capacity to deliver, r4 = ratio of company retail price to average market price.
Performance	x1 = company share of product capacity, x2 company share of promotion capacity, x3 = company share of delivery capacity, x4 = 1 − r4; i = company's opportunity cost of capital; v = value of next market share point; $\bar{x}$ = weighted average market share; \$ = profit impact; e = total company expenditures on marketing capacity.

exchanges: unit contribution, product capacity, promotion capacity, and relative price. *Performance factors* are the consequence of demand and supply interactions: market share, NPV of income, and ROI.

Method factors affect the validity of conclusions regarding the value and cost of market share. Two method factors are the assumed maximization rule and market response function. The maximization rule specifies the objectives implicit in resource allocations, and the response function determines market share weightings.

Market Share and Profit Studies

Several studies of the relationship between market share and profit published in the marketing literature are compared with the determinants of market share in Figure 2. The determinants of market share are displayed in the rows. Twenty empirical studies of market share and profit are cited in the columns.

Market definition determines the extent of a market; this was missing, however, from most of these market share and

Figure 2
Market share and profit studies[a]

	Telser 1962	Buzzell 1964	Weiss 1968	Simon 1969	Lambin 1970	Schultz 1971	Beckwith 1972	Lambin 1972	Clarke 1973	Wildt 1974	Houston and Weiss 1974	Buzzell, Gale, and Sultan 1975	Moriarty 1975	Prasad and Ring 1976	Horsky 1977	Wittink 1977	Hanssens 1980	Naert and Weverbergh 1981	Woo and Cooper 1982	Phillips, Chang, and Buzzell 1983
Demand Factors	CIG	FGP	FGP	LIQ	RAZ	AIR	FGP	GAS	FGP	IGP	FGP	PIM	FGP	FGP	CIG	FGP	AIR	GAS	PIM	PIM
Market definition	Y					Y		Y				Y							Y	Y
Primary demand	Q			Q		Q		Q	Q			$					Q		$	$
Demand elasticity	Y					Y		Y	Y								Y			
Heavy user												Y								
Brand equity	Y	Y		Y	Y	Y	Y	Y	Y	Y	Y		Y	Y	Y	Y	Y	Y		
Supply Factors																				
Unit contribution	Y			Y	Y	Y	Y	Y	Y	Y										Y
Product capacity	r			r	r	r				r		r							r	r
Promotion capacity	e	r	e	e	e	e	e	e	e	e	e	e	e	r	e	e	e			e
Place capacity					r	r		r									r	r		
Price relative			Y		Y	Y		Y		Y	Y	Y	Y	Y		Y		Y	Y	
Performance Factors																				
Market share	m	m	m	m	m	m	m	m	m	m	m	m$	m	m	m	m	m	m	m$	m$
Income	Y					Y						Y								
ROI					Y			Y				Y			Y		Y	Y		
Method Factors																				
Response function	L	L	M	M	M	M	L	L	L	M	M	L	M	L	M	M	M	A	L	L
Maximization rule	PV			PV	PV	SR	PV	PV	SR	SR					PV					

[a]Q = quantity of primary demand, Y = yes, r = company's real capacity, e = expense of company capacity, m = market share, A = attraction, L = linear additive, M = multiplicative, PV = net present value, SR = short run.

profit studies. Primary demand was frequently omitted and sometimes confounded by monetary measures that masked the effects of demand elasticity. The impact of heavy users and other bases of market segmentation were overlooked in all but one of these market share and profit studies. Brand equity, measured by lagged market share, appeared as a determinant of market share in nearly every study.

Unit contribution was linked with market share in half the studies. The remaining authors expressed concern over the absence of direct cost estimates. The marketing mix is a key factor in a firm's strategy, yet only two of twenty studies included all four mix variables. Eight papers included measures of a company's capacity to produce. Nearly every study measured promotional capacity in terms of media expenditures, but only four incorporated place capacity as a factor. Relative price appeared in 12 of the studies listed in Figure 2.

Market share was the key performance factor in all the studies, and most were based on share of quantity. Six papers reported ROI and three included income. Maximization rules were incorporated in less than half the studies. Six of these adopted net present value solutions. Linear response functions appeared in nine, multiplicative forms in ten, and the attraction function in one of the studies.

The record of research on market share and profit is mixed. Important steps have been taken toward incorporating all of the determinants of market share listed in Figure 2. Yet, achievements to date remain limited. Key determinants of market share were routinely overlooked or assumed away. *Research has focused primarily on the form of the response function relating brand equity and advertis-*

ing expenses to market share. A more comprehensive analysis that demonstrates the long run relationship between all key demand, supply, and performance factors is needed (Anderson 1980).

The Value and Cost of Market Share

The value and cost of market share depend on assumptions about future demand, supply, performance, and method factors. Managers and scholars should be explicit in the development of these assumptions. To document the effect of strategic assumptions on a firm's market share and profit, a benchmark illustration is presented for Wineco, a beverage industry leader.

Demand Factors

Market definition influences the value and the cost of market share. A product-market is "the *set of products* judged to be substitutes, within those *usage situations* in which similar patterns of benefits are sought, and the *customers* for whom such usages are relevant" (Day, Shocker, and Srivastava 1979, p. 10). The set of substitute product technologies available to satisfy the human need for beverages ranges from those that stimulate (coffee and tea), to those that provide nutritional needs (water and milk), to those that relax (beer and wine). Usage situations vary from routine consumption at home, to parties and sporting events (Impact Research 1984).

Primary demand is measured in gallons of per capita consumption. The population base contained 55 million adults who drank wine. Within the wine market, "still wines" involved quite different technologies and uses compared with sparkling party wines, vermouth, or dessert wines. Not counting the latter three types, consumers drank an average of seven gallons each in the benchmark year. Primary demand in the U.S. market for the still wine segment was 390 million gallons. Demand elasticities with respect to industry capacity and price were assumed to be greater than one.

The heavy user segment was a significant force in the domestic still wine market. The heavy user group totaled 17 million adults, or 31% of users, and consumed 18 gallons per year per capita. Total heavy user demand was 306 million gallons, or 78% of total still wine demand.

The carryover effect of brand equity generated by previous capital outlays on the firm's capacity to produce, distribute, and promote its brand was estimated to be 6.7% in the benchmark year. These demand factors are summarized in Table 1.

Table 1
Wineco Demand and Supply Factors

DEMAND

Wine population	55 million
Wine per capita	× 7 gallons*/year
Still wine demand	385 million gallons
Heavy users	17 million
Heavy per capita	× 18 gallons*/year
Heavy user demand	306 million gallons
Wineco brand equity	6.7%

*Rounded to nearest gallon.
Gavin-Johnson 1982, Simmons 1981.

SUPPLY

	Competitors	Wineco	Wineco Factor Cost
Average retail price/gallon	$13.85	$13.85	
Average selling price/gallon	—	6.93	
Variable cost/gallon	—	4.00	
Unit contribution	—	2.93	
Capacity to produce:			
Varieties	62	24	$2.4 million
Share	72%	28%	
Capacity to deliver:			
Linear feet	13.2 million	8.1 million	$8.32/foot
Share	62%	38%	
Capacity to promote:			
Impressions	12.4 billion	2.1 billion	$16.60/000
Share	85%	15%	

Gavin-Johnson 1982.
Leading National Advertisers 1981.
Impact Research company reports 1984.

Supply Factors

Wineco sold to wholesalers as well as directly to retail outlets. Taxes and dealer markup were charged several times in the channels of distribution. A gallon of wine selling at retail for an average price of $13.85 entered Wineco's books at an average price of $6.93. The company's variable cost of grapes, bottles, materials, and other supplies totaled $4.00. The considerably greater experience of Wineco yielded a variable cost lower than its closest competitor. Unit contribution to profits was $2.93 per gallon in the benchmark year.

Capacity levels are among the most significant strategic decisions made by management (Porter 1980, p. 324). Product assortment is one dimension of the firm's capacity to meet consumer demand (Alderson 1965, pp. 78–83). It is particularly important in the wine market where consumer search for variety is legendary. Wine assortment is measured by the number of varieties offered. In the benchmark year, competitors offered a total of 62 and Wineco 24 varieties of still wine. Capacity expansion through the creation of a new product variety at Wineco's current level of operation was estimated to incur a factor cost of $2.4 million.

Place or distribution capacity in the wine trade varied with linear feet of shelf space available. Wineco occupied 8.1 and its competitors a combined total of 13.2 million linear feet. The factor cost of place capacity to Wineco was $8.32 per linear foot of shelf space.

Promotion capacity may be measured in a number of different ways. One measure relevant in the wine market is the number of impressions a firm can deliver to the target audience through available media vehicles. Measured by the number of media impressions, competitors' promotional capacity was 12.4 and Wineco's was 2.1 billion messages in the base year. Wineco's media factor cost was $16.60 per thousand impressions. Wineco and competitors' prices were equal in the benchmark year. These supply-side assumptions are summarized in Table 1.

Performance Factors

Weighted average market share is a link between profit and fixed costs. It is an average of an organization's capacity to produce, distribute, and promote the product, weighted by its effectiveness and relative price (Utsey and Cook 1984, p. 97). The average may be either an arithmetic or geometric mean, depending on whether the relationships are linear and additive or multiplicative and interactive. Computation of both an arithmetic and a geometric weighted average share of market for Wineco in the benchmark year is illustrated in Figure 3. Wineco's shares of industry capacity to produce, deliver, and promote wine the U.S. market appear as dotted horizontal bars. To the left of each bar (in parentheses) are the effectiveness weightings used if one assumes they are equal to 0.25 among the four marketing variables and competitors. It appears to the right of each bar as the weighted linear effect of marketing capacity on market share.

Share of product varieties offered by Wineco was 28% of the market total with an effectiveness weighting of 0.25. Thus, the (linear) weighted average share of product capacity for Wineco was 7.0% (0.25 × 28.0) in the benchmark year. Wineco's share of capacity to deliver wine measured by its retail share of shelf was 38%. Its share of capacity to promote measured by media advertising impressions was 15%. Wineco's lagged market share was 26%. Current distribution and promotion capacity thus contributed 9.5 and 3.7 points respectively to Wineco's 26.9% market share. Weighted brand equity added 6.7 points to Wineco's share. This is a linear weighted average. By comparison, the expected value of a geometric mean was 25.4%. The difference of 1.5 market share points is not trivial, but knowledge of which response function will best represent future long-run market behavior is arguable. Management should begin with simpler linear assumptions and equal elasticities among competitors, adding complexity as it proves necessary (Cook 1985).

Marketing contribution is the arithmetic product of the value of market share and weighted average market share. It is the task of marketing management to invest in market share points of known worth so as to maximize their long run net present value. The marginal value of a market share point in a segment may be approximated from accounting records. Unit contribution margin is multiplied by the quantity of primary demand and divided into 100 parts (Cook 1971). The use of unit contribution (price less average variable cost) in computing the marginal value of a share point

Figure 3
Weighted average share of market

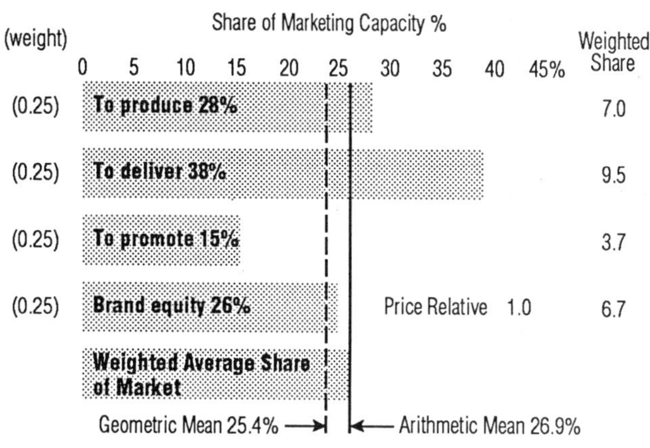

assumes the total revenue and unit cost functions are linear over the feasible decision interval. As a consequence, marginal and average values are equal. The value of a market share point to Wineco was:

$$\text{vms} = (\text{p} - \text{avc})(\text{Q})/100.$$
$$\$11.4 = (\$6.93 - \$4.00)(390)/100. \qquad (1)$$

Primary demand for wine was 390 million gallons; contribution margin was $2.93. The total contribution value of the market from Wineco's perspective was thus $1.14 billion, and each market share point was worth .01 of the total.

Given its marketing capacities and assuming a linear response function, Wineco's weighted average market share and its value of market share are the bases for estimating the company's future marketing contribution:

$$\text{z} = (\text{vms})(\bar{\text{x}}) \qquad (2)$$
$$\$307 = (\$11.4)(26.9).$$

Each share point had a value of $11.4, and Wineco put marketing capacity in place sufficient to capture 26.9 market share points.

The managerial implications of *marketing* contribution are somewhat different from a traditional *accounting* contribution (Hulbert and Toy 1977). Unit output no longer appears in the profit function. The difference between traditional accounting and marketing contribution is the valuation of market share. Marketing contribution is adjusted for competitive effects, and it is inherently future as well as customer oriented. Accounting contribution is historical and company oriented. A proof that marketing and accounting contributions are financial equivalents is presented in Appendix 1.

Return on investment is measured by the ratio of net marketing contribution to the sum of current charges against the price adjusted replacement value of depreciable assets and the current costs of other fixed investments. Whether market share is worth the risk of company resources depends on the cost of achieving that share (Boyd 1973). The costs of market share are the total of fixed investments dedicated

Figure 4
Theoretical value and cost of market share[a]

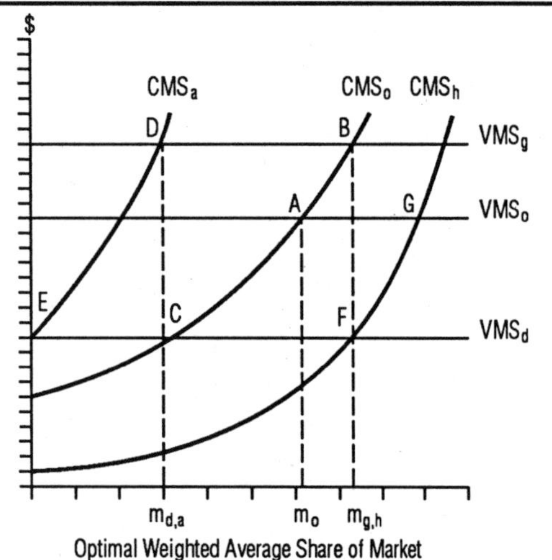

[a]Value of Market Share (VMS), Cost of Market Share (CMS), g = growth, o = equilibrium, d = decline, a = attack, h = heavy user.

to achieving capacities to produce, promote, and deliver a product, discounted for the effects of inflation (Webster, Largay, and Stickney 1980). It includes all costs of serving the market that do not change with volume. Research and development expenses, current charges for plant and equipment, product management and salesforce salaries, media advertising, warehouses, delivery trucks, insurance, and interest are some of the fixed costs of marketing capacity. The strategic marketing cost function applies to these fixed investments (Cook 1983, p. 72).

The relationship between market share and profit is now focused on two dimensions. From the demand side, what is the future value of market share? From the supply side, at what total cost must how much marketing capacity be deployed in order to achieve a long run profit maximizing allocation of resources? The final question is, what response function and maximizing rule should be assumed?

Method Factors

The maximization rule is that the marginal cost of the last share of marketing capacity should equal the marginal contribution value revenue of the last share point acquired for all marketing variables over all relevant future time periods. The initial capacity shares reported for Wineco in Figure 3 were calibrated to reflect these profit maximizing conditions under linear response assumptions. Computation of the linear maximum net present value of market share for any marketing capacity factor is described in Appendix 2, which shows that the share of market that maximizes the net present value of future earnings depends on the firm's marketing factor costs, effectiveness weightings, selling price, primary demand, and competitors' capacities.

Market response may be formulated as a linear additive, multiplicative, or attraction function. Each has its theoretical as well as its practical strengths and weaknesses (Barnett 1976; Beckwith 1972; Brodie and de Kluyver 1984; Ghosh, Neslin, and Shoemaker 1984; Karnani 1983; Leeflang and Reuyl 1984; McGuire and Weiss 1976; McGuire et al. 1968; Naert and Bultez 1973; Naert and Weverbergh 1981). Additive functions have the benefit of computational simplicity but are known to be biased in several ways, particularly in their failure to account for interactions among marketing variables. Multiplicative functions have the benefit of accounting for interactions but are computationally more complex and, like additive models, have a tendency to yield inconsistent results. Multiplicative forms also have the drawback that market share predictions fall to zero if a firm eliminates its investments in only one of the many mix factors on which its market share depends. The market share attraction function is logically consistent, yet is operationally cumbersome. For these reasons, a linear additive market response function was adopted to illustrate the theoretical relationship between market share and profit.

Theoretical Effects of Market Share and Profit

The net present value of market share is the difference between long run marginal share value and share cost, discounted at the organization's cost of capital. The goal of marketing strategy is to maximize this value.

The theoretical implications of equating the marginal value and cost of market share in a dynamically competitive market are portrayed in Figure 4. The firm may adopt a number of different marketing strategies in response to changing market and competitive conditions. The theoretical effects of six alternative strategies on the net present value of market share are assessed (for the linear case) in this figure. The six strategies are market growth, maturity, decline, competitive attack, price leadership, and heavy user.

Market Growth, Maturity, and Decline Strategies

How should a business adjust its weighted average share of marketing capacity to achieve maximum net present values over the product life cycle? The three value of market share (VMS) schedules in Figure 4 represent different stages in the product life cycle (Polli and Cook 1969, p. 391). The marginal value schedule VMS_g represents the upward shifting value of market share in the growth stage of a product's life cycle. VMS_o represents the stable value of market share in the mature stage of the product life cycle. The lower schedule, VMS_d, is the downward shifting marginal value of market share in a declining market. Suppose for the moment the firm's marginal cost of market share (CMS) schedule is in equilibrium at CMS_o.

Market growth drives management to build market share because the marginal value of the next share point increases faster than its marginal cost. In Figure 4, the firm will attempt to build share of market from m_o to m_g in order to maximize the net present value of its future position. It will move from point A to point B, and in the process, its share of investment will exceed its (current) share of market. These conditions produce what is known as a *building* strategy. A growing market pushes up the value of market share faster than the cost of market share increases at the margin.

Market maturity, with constant marginal costs, leads the firm to a *holding* strategy. Profits are maximized at $VMS_o = CMS_o$, and management holds market share at m_o until disequilibrium is induced by changes in technology, competitive actions, or the company's own initiatives.

Market decline leads to a downward adjustment in market share if the firm's marginal cost schedule remains constant. Marginal share value falls faster than marginal share costs, driving the firm to disinvest in market share. As the value of market share falls from VMS_o to VMS_d, the firm will reallocate its resources to more profitable market opportunities. It may not seem intuitively obvious that a business should purposely decrease its share of a declining market, but it is rational. The firm will move over time from point A to point C, seeking to maximize the net present value of its future position in a declining market at m_d. In the process, its share of marketing capacity will be less than its share of market. This is one set of conditions that gives rise to a *harvesting* strategy.

Competitive Attack, Price Leadership, and Heavy User Stategies

A dynamic market calls on management to make rapid adjustments of market share in response to changing competitive positions, as well as to the company's own initiatives. Over the long run, management attempts to equate the changing marginal cost of market share with its shifting marginal value. This task is complicated by the unexpected behavior of competitors.

Competitive attack dramatically alters a firm's value maximizing market share. Assume the product life cycle is in its growth stage, represented by schedule VMS_g in Figure 4. Competitive attack raises the table stakes by rapidly shifting fresh resources into play and thereby sharply increasing the marginal cost of market share. Without warning, the victim's cost of market share schedule shifts upward from CMS_o, with optimal market share at m_o, to CMS_a, with optimal market share at m_g. The shift induced by competitive attack leads to a significant decrease in the firm's optimal market share. The firm should move its resources out of this market to achieve a lower optimal weighted average share of market. In other terms, if marginal share value holds at VMS_g, management should moderate its ambitions and move from point B to point D in Figure 4. Otherwise, it is maintaining a high market share position that carries a significant opportunity loss. The firm in a declining market, facing the VMS_d schedule, is subject to even more significant shocks from competitive attack. If optimal net present value is achieved at the intersection of CMS_o and VMS_d, the firm would be at point C. Competitive attack in this declining market shifts the firm's marginal cost schedule to CMS_a, driving its optimal share of market to zero, at point E. In this event, management should withdraw from the market. A product in this position is labeled a "dog" and should be put quietly to sleep unless conditions are expected to improve in the longer term.

Price leadership offers an interesting perspective on the effects of company-initiated strategies. The first effect of a price cut is to reduce the firm's value of market share by shifting the VMS_o schedule downward. Initially, a price cut has the same effect on optimal market share as a decline in primary demand. Both act to depress the value of market share and, hence, optimal weighted average share declines. In response to its own price cut, the firm should shift its target market share from point A to point C in Figure 4. This result is nonintuitive. It follows logically from the fact that a price cut devalues market share at the margin, while short-run factor costs, primary demand, and competitive resources remain unchanged. Price leadership anticipates either *long-run* increases in primary demand, which shift the VMS schedule upward, or increased market share, which reduces factor costs and shifts the CMS schedule downward.

Segmentation strategies focus the firm's resources on smaller segments of the market that exhibit relatively homogeneous demands (Alderson 1965, p. 186). If the firm, for example, adopts a *heavy user* segmentation strategy, the result is a downward shift in the marginal cost schedule from CMS_o to CMS_h in Figure 4. The downward shift is due to the improved efficiency of reaching a smaller, more richly endowed market segment. (In the special case where heavy users can exert price pressure on the supplier, the VMS schedule shifts downward at the same time.) Heavy user strategies differentially affect a firm's capacity to produce, promote, and distribute. In the limit, the CMS schedule may shift downward in proportion to the number of heavy users in the population. Such a dramatic shift may apply to every form of marketing capacity except production. For example, if all competitors allocate distribution resources without regard to the shopping habits of heavy users, a significant opportunity exists to deploy resources dedicated exclusively to this target. The cost function for distribution shifts down in proportion to the heavy user population, while the value of market share is reduced only in proportion to their share of total demand. If 30% of users are in the heavy segment, distribution capacity may be reduced by as much as 70%. If marginal value remains constant at VMS_o, a heavy user strategy would shift the firm's optimal market share from point A to point G in Figure 4. Since dedication of distribution resources to the heavy segment may ignore medium and light user demand, the value of market share may shift downward in proportion to the quantity of heavy user consumption. Should heavy users account for 80% of unit volume, VMS may decline only 20% if this segment is isolated by channels of distribution. In this event, optimal share under a heavy user strategy would shift from point A to point F with market share at m_h in Figure 4. Experience and scale effects on factor cost have precisely the same result—a downward shift in the CMS curve—leading man-

Table 2
Performance Factors

	I	II	III	IV	V	VI	Vii
		Ten-Year Cumulative Value of Strategy in Millions*					
		Market Volatility		Market Maturity			
	Stable + Equilibrium	Growth + Attack	Decline + Retreat	Product Attack	Price Leader Solo	Price Leader + Match	Heavy User Solo
Primary demand	3,900	6,473	2,362	4,308	4,018	4,303	3,900
Market share	26.9%	30.0%	24.7%	24.8%	16.1%	12.6%	44.1%
Cost of capacity	$1,609	$2,766	$897	$1,599	$492	$591	$1,669
Net present value	$829	$1,299	$541	$847	$459	$316	$1,907
Return on investment	91%	94%	90%	96%	151%	79%	202%

Based on maximizing net present value of Wineco's (linear) weighted average market share, following the conditions in Table 1 and solutions in Appendix 2. Stable equilibrium was set at 1.0(Q) and 1.0(r'). *Growth + Attack* was set to 1.05(*Q*) and 1.1(*r'**) for all marketing factors, and *Decline + Retreat* at 0.95(*Q*) and 0.90(*r'**), both with factor elasticities of 1.05. *Product Attack* was set at 1.1(*r'**) for product capacity. *Price Leadership* by the firm was set at 0.90(*p*) for the first two years in both solo and competitive matching cases, with price elasticity at 1.20 in both years. The solo heavy user strategy set primary demand faced by Wineco at 0.8(*Q*), with competitive capacity dedicated to heavy users at 0.3(*r'**) for all marketing factors. A listing of the IFPS.m subroutine and detailed inputs are available from the author.

agement to build toward higher optimal share of market.

The behavior of demand, factor costs, and competitive resource deployments dramatically alter the market share value and cost schedules faced by a firm. These shifting and discontinuous demand and supply curves reveal the link between market share and profit.

A Simulation of Market Share and Profit

The theoretical effects of market share on profit, and of profit on market share, are examined in more concrete terms in a 10-year simulation of the wine market. The benchmark data summarized in Table 1 are characteristic of industry records. The behavior of Wineco is a composite of wine competitors and not intended to represent a particular firm.

The results of the simulation appear in Table 2. The columns present results for each of seven different strategies over a 10-year interval. In the rows are five basic measures of market and company behavior. These are reported as 10-year cumulatives of primary demand, optimal market share, cost of marketing capacity, net present value of marketing contributions, and return on investment. The specific conditions defining each strategy are summarized in the footnote to Table 2. In addition to stable equilibrium, two general classes of market behavior are examined: market volatility and market maturity.

Stable Equilibrium

Strategy I in Table 2 reflects the 10-year results of extending the benchmark year conditions. Competitive market capacity remains constant, along with prices, unit contribution, and factor costs. Primary demand is unchanged as well. Wineco maintains an optimal market share at 26.9% and incurs a cumulative cost of market capacity totaling $1,609 million. The net present value of market share is $829 million, and the company earns a return on its marketing investment of 91.2% before taxes.

Market Volatility

The effects of a volatile market are portrayed in Strategies II and III. Strategy II illustrates the effects of management efforts to maximize the net present value of market share in the face of aggressive competition in a market that is both factor and price elastic and, due to exogenous causes, growing at 5%. The strategy is labeled *Growth + Attack*. Strategy III, on the other, hand, reflects management's efforts to maximize the net present value of market share in the face of a factor and price elastic market, with primary demand declining at a rate of 5% per year due to exogenous causes and a field of competitors, each seeking to retreat in the face of the unfavorable demand trend. This strategy is labeled *Decline + Retreat*. The long-run cumulative net present value of market share for Wineco ranges from $1,299 million, in the case of Strategy II, to $541 million in Strategy III. Yet, between these two results, Wineco made no changes in its basic stance. The company simply adapted its investments to changing market conditions. Management did not try to build or hold or harvest market share. It sought to maximize the net present value of its marketing assets over the long run in a dynamic market driven by forces over which the firm had no control. Marketing factor costs were held constant over the period. Competitive selling prices and margins were equal and constant. Variable costs, unit contributions, and market response weights did not change. Optimal long run share of market for Wineco under Strategy II was 30.0%, while it was 24.7% under Strategy III.

Strategies II and III illustrate the case for both "high" and "low" relative share companies, depending on market and competitive conditions. Strategy II appears to be the high relative share (1.2) case, with a net present value over twice that of Strategy III because an elastic, growing market with vigorous competition generates increasing market share values. Strategy III is the low relative share (0.8) case. This follows from an elastic, declining market, with competitors in retreat and falling market share values. The long-run cumulative return on marketing assets for both

Strategy II and III are nearly equal to the 91% realized under conditions of stable equilibrium. Clearly, these are neither high nor low share strategies. Market shares are the *result* of seeking to maximize net present values over the 10-year period under alternative circumstances.

Market Maturity

The maturity stage of the product life cycle offers a rich tapestry of strategic alternatives. A few of these are illustrated in Table 2. One is the impact of competitive attack on a single mix factor, product variety (IV). Another is the effect of price leadership by Wineco when competitors fail to follow (V) and when they match Wineco price cuts (VI). Finally, the impact of a solo heavy user strategy (VII) on market share and profit is presented in the last column of Table 2.

Wineco's cumulative 10-year cost of marketing capacity reflects the intensity of resource utilization required by each of these mature market strategies. In the case of solo price leadership (V), a lower optimal share is realized on a smaller asset base, leading to a much higher return on investment with reduced NPV of income. The solo heavy user of strategy (VII) leads to a much higher share of market, more intense use of a larger asset base, and still higher return on investment and net present values. In each case the marketing asset base is measured by the cost of marketing capacity. It ranges from a low of $492 million when Wineco's solo price leadership remains unmatched by competitors for two years (V), to a high of $1,669 million with a solo heavy user strategy (VII). Primary demand remains roughly constant under each of these strategies, responding to changes in only one mix variable in each case.

The results of the Wineco simulation are arrayed in a more familiar cross-sectional format in Figure 5. On the lower axis is Wineco's optimal share of market for each of the seven strategies identified in the columns of Table 2. The company's optimal long run market share ranges from a low of 12.6% when competitors match its price leadership in a mature market, to a high of 44.1% when Wineco becomes the preferred brand among heavy users. On the vertical axis are the before-tax ROIs due to each strategy, ranging from a low of 79% to a high of 202%. The cumulative 10-year net present value of market share in millions of dollars is reported beside each strategy. These results are for the same firm, with the same cost structure, in the same market, following the same basic long-term marketing strategy: maximize the net present value of market share in a dynamic competitive market. The differences are due to changes in market growth, the ambitions of competitors, and the imagination of Wineco management.

The Pursuit of Market Share for Profit

The strategic marketing objective of the firm is to maximize the long run net present value of market share. To achieve this objective, management must be disciplined in making marketing investments. It should make changes in its capacity to produce, promote, and distribute in accord with shifts in primary demand, changes in competitive capacity and prices, and movements in its own unit contribution and marketing factor costs. Each of these have significant effects on the long run net present value of market share. Likewise, management's own initiatives in price leadership and target marketing can dramatically change its optimal long run course of action. Viewed in this light, both high and low share companies are snapshots of firms seeking to maximize the net present value of future marketing investments.

Successful strategic planning is vastly more complex than rule-of-thumb would imply. Detailed anticipations must be outlined of the dynamic effects of demand, supply, performance, and method factors in future competitive markets. Many will argue management cannot anticipate the future course of demand, does not know about competitive resource levels, and will not adjust market share to its most profitable point. Each of these reservations is valid. But the effort should be made to anticipate demand, reveal competitive resource commitments, and design company strategies to account for the determinants of market share. Lack of data is not an acceptable excuse for myopic marketing plans.

Demand Factors

A marketing strategy puts shareholder assets at risk in the search for differential advantage (Cook 1985). If a strategy is to succeed, it should methodically define the product technologies to be put to known end uses. Market definition cannot be ignored. Marketing plans should be expressed in real units of primary demand to avoid confounding volume with value. Future primary demand is the starting point in marketing planning, and plans that begin and end with

Figure 5
Marketing strategy, market share, and profitability[a]

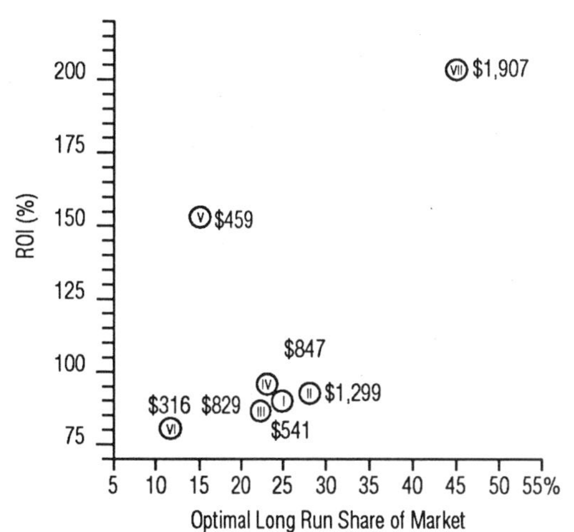

[a] Circled numerals are references to the simulation results in Table 2. ROI values are return on fixed marketing costs before taxes. The dollar entries are the cumulative 10-year net present values of market share at a capital cost of 12%.

company sales forecasts are shortsighted. Primary demand response to the combined resources of the market, or factor elasticity, should be incorporated in long run strategic plans. Failure to design marketing strategies to serve the interests of specific market segments, like heavy users, can incur large opportunity losses. Brand equity is an important asset. Its value accrues from all strategic mix investments, not just media promotion. The lagged value of brand equity directly influences the need for current and future investments in marketing capacity and should become a guideline for establishing depreciation rates on fixed assets.

Supply Factors

Unit contribution is the yardstick for measuring the value of a market to each competitor. Combined with anticipated primary demand, this traditional profit measure leads to an unambiguous indicator of the value to each competitor of changes in market share. The value of market share naturally varies among competitors, according to their scope, scale, and experience in the market. It is the job of the marketing manager to invest in market shares of known worth. Marketing capacity with known factor costs should be put in place in such a way as to achieve maximum long run marketing contribution. Management should not selectively consider only those capacities for which data are readily available or where its strengths are to be found. It is dangerous to conclude the capacity to deliver is unimportant because the firm is weak in distribution. It is risky to assume one product will be good enough to sweep a market with 12 vigorous competitors, however superior management may believe it to be. The marketing mix is at the core of a firm's strategy. Marketing management should be able to explain why a given level of production capacity is needed, when the product line is to be extended, what level of inventory is required, and what product performance characteristics are expected by the consumer. Marketing management should be able to explain why millions will be invested in media and salesforce capacity and what return on investment in delivery capacity is anticipated. If the number of outlets is to be expanded, shelf facings increased, or display advantages otherwise improved, the factor costs of these efforts should be estimated. If selling prices are to be altered, the competitive effects of the change on short and long run market share values should be anticipated. It is insufficient to claim either ignorance or hardship if company resources are misused in the search for differential advantage.

Performance Factors

Market share is a goal of marketing strategy because it is an informative and useful intermediate performance factor. Market share of quantities sold is the result of a natural weighting by users of the effectiveness of a competitor's share of capacity to produce, promote, deliver, and price its products. It is both a summary of past successes and an indicator of future events. It is a key to profitability. ROI adds a dimension of the relative quality and intensity of marketing investment. Net present value relates the income stream to time and to the opportunity costs of capital. These different performance factors are not substitutes for one another. Each serves a special purpose, and marketing management should learn to incorporate all three performance measures in its strategic plans. With the application of this discipline, marketing risk can be managed successfully in dynamic competitive environments.

Conclusions

The pursuit of market share for profit has been hotly debated. A resolution to the debate can be found by placing a price tag on the value of changes in market share and evaluating the corresponding changes in performance. The array of strategic alternatives appears to be richer than previously reported. Studies have focused too much on the form of the response function relating brand equity and advertising expense to market share. Critical factors like market definition and segmentation are routinely overlooked. Placing a price tag on a change in market share should shift management's attention from internal company performance toward customer needs and competitive positions. The concept of marketing capacity may broaden our understanding of nonprice factors in a competitive market. The price-adjusted replacement value of fixed investments dedicated to creating the capacity to produce, promote, and distribute a product are the costs of market share. Adjusted for its selling price, a firm's weighted average long run share of marketing capacity should be identical to its long run share of market.

Company oriented planning and accounting methods are the innocent purveyors of marketing myopia. A market-led company should lay its plans from market segments, backward through competitive commitments, to achieve a realistic assessment of company resources and expected performance. Balancing marketing risk with return is not a random walk. It is a challenging management responsibility. Meeting the challenge demands management assess the long run net present value of its market share.

Appendix 1

Marketing and Accounting Contribution Are Equal

Proof:

Marketing contribution from Equation 2 is $Z = (v)(m)$, where m is a discrete percentage between 0 and 100, and v is the value of market share.

Market share $m = 100(q/Q)$, where q is company unit sales and Q is primary demand.

Accounting contribution is $Z = (p - avc)(q)$.

Then $\quad (v)(m) = (p - avc)(q)$,

and $\quad v(100)(q/Q) = (p - avc)(q)$.

Solving for v gives:

$$v = (Q)(p \pm avc)/100.$$

Appendix 2

Computation of Linear Maximum Net Present Value of Market Share

To achieve a given share of capacity (designated by a row vector) x' when rivals have committed real resources at a rate r'^*, a firm must deploy its own resources (r') at a rate given by Cook (1983, p. 72),

$$r' = [x'/(100 - x')]r'^*; \quad 0 < x' \leq 100. \qquad (2.1)$$

operating in turn on each element in a vector of capacity shares.

Capacity input requirements increase exponentially with the share of capacity to produce, distribute, or promote. The marginal increase in resources with respect to a share of capacity is found by differentiating equation 2.1:

$$dr'/dx' = [100/(100 - x')^2]r'^*; \quad 0 < x' \leq 100. \qquad (2.2)$$

To equate the marginal costs of capacity with the marginal value of market share, factor costs are assigned to each real marketing capacity variable. Define a vector of factor costs c' to correspond with the resources needed to produce, promote, and distribute a product or service. A general rule for linear profit maximization of any marketing capacity variable where $f(x')$ is the optimal ratio of marginal share value to marginal share cost is

$$f(x') = dr'/dx'$$
$$= [(w'(v)]/[(c')(r'^*)/100]; \quad 0 < x' \leq 100. \qquad (2.3)$$

and w' are effectiveness weightings on each input, with prices exogenous. The arithmetic product $(c')(r') = e'$ is the firm's total expenditure on a given marketing capacity. For current charges against depreciable assets, the price adjusted replacement cost of marketing capacity defines e'. The function $f(x')$ defines the. ratios of marginal share revenue $(w')(v)$ to standardized marginal share cost $(c')(r'^*)/100$ which equate VMS with CMS. These ratios are computed in Appendix 3. Cumulative marketing contribution, less the fixed costs of optimal capacity, discounted at the cost of capital, is the net present value of market share.

Appendix 3

Optimal Ratios of Value of Market Share (VMS) to Cost of Market Share (CMS)

Capacity Share x'	VMS/CMS Ratio $f(x')$	Capacity Share x'	VMS/CMS Ratio $f(x')$	Capacity Share x'	VMS/CMS Ratio $f(x')$
1.0	1.020	31.0	2.100	61.0	6.575
2.0	1.041	32.0	2.163	62.0	6.925
3.0	1.063	33.0	2.228	63.0	7.305
4.0	1.085	34.0	2.296	64.0	7.716
5.0	1.108	35.0	2.367	65.0	8.163
6.0	1.132	36.0	2.411	66.0	8.615
7.0	1.156	37.0	2.520	67.0	9.183
8.0	1.181	38.0	2.601	68.0	9.766
9.0	1.208	39.0	2.687	69.0	10.406
10.0	1.235	40.0	2.778	70.0	11.111
11.0	1.262	41.0	2.873	71.0	11.891
12.0	1.291	42.0	2.973	72.0	12.755
13.0	1.321	43.0	3.078	73.0	13.717
14.0	1.352	44.0	3.189	74.0	14.793
15.0	1.384	45.0	3.306	75.0	16.000
16.0	1.417	46.0	3.492	76.0	17.361
17.0	1.452	47.0	3.560	77.0	18.904
18.0	1.487	48.0	3.968	78.0	20.661
19.0	1.524	49.0	3.845	79.0	22.676
20.0	1.563	50.0	4.000	80.0	25.000
21.0	1.602	51.0	4.165	81.0	27.701
22.0	1.644	52.0	4.340	82.0	30.864
23.0	1.687	53.0	4.527	83.0	34.602
24.0	1.731	54.0	4.726	84.0	39.063
25.0	1.778	55.0	4.938	85.0	44.444
26.0	1.826	56.0	5.165	86.0	51.020
27.0	1.877	57.0	5.408	87.0	59.172
28.0	1.929	58.0	5.669	99.0	69.444
29.0	1.984	59.0	5.949	89.0	82.645
30.0	2.041	60.0	6.250	90.0	100.000

The author thanks William Cook for his programming, and is indebted to Harvey Dodgson, William Mindak, Robert Rothberg, Edward Strong, and Marjorie Utsey for reviewing early drafts of this article, John Beckman for basic industry research, and the *JM* editors and reviewers for their direction.

Bibliography

Alderson, Wroe (1965), *Dynamic Marketing Behavior*, Homewood, IL: Irwin, 78–83.

Anderson, Paul F. (1980), "Market Share, ROI, and the Market Value Rule," *Theoretical Developments in Marketing*, Charles W. Lamb, Jr., and Patrick M. Dunne, eds., Chicago: American Marketing, 91–95.

Bagozzi, Richard P. (1984), "A Prospectus for Theory Construction in Marketing," *Journal of Marketing*, 48 (Winter), 11–29.

Barnett, Arnold I. (1976), "More on a Market Share Theorem," *Journal of Marketing Research*, 13 (February), 104–109.

Beckwith, Neil E. (1972), "Multivariate Analysis of Sales Responses of Competing Brands to Advertising," *Journal of Marketing Research*, 9 (May), 168–176.

Boyd, Harper W. (1973), "Market Share as a Critical Determinant of Corporate Strategy," unpublished working paper, Stanford University.

Brodie, Roderick and Cornelis A. de Kluyver (1984), "Attraction versus Linear and Multiplicative Market Share Models: An Empirical Evaluation," *Journal of Marketing Research*, 21 (May), 194–201.

Buzzell, Robert D. (1964), "Predicting Short-Term Changes in Market Share as a Function of Advertising Strategy," *Journal of Marketing Research*, 1 (August), 27–31.

———, Bradley T. Gale, and Ralph G. M. Sultan (1975), "Market Share—A Key to Profitability," *Harvard Business Review*, 53 (January/February), 97–106.

Caves, R. E., B. T. Gale, and M. E. Porter (1977), "Interfirm Profitability Differences: Comment," *The Quarterly Journal of Economics*, 91 (November), 667–673.

Clarke, Darral G. (1973), "Sales-Advertising Cross-Elasticities and Advertising Competition," *Journal of Marketing Research*, 10 (August), 250–261.

Cook, Victor J. (1971), "The Economic Meaning of Marketing Communications," unpublished working paper, University of Chicago.

——— (1983), "Marketing Strategy and Differential Advantage," *Journal of Marketing*, 47 (Spring), 68–75.

——— (1985), "Understanding Marketing Strategy and Differential Advantage," *Journal of Marketing*, 49 (Spring), 137–142.

Day, George S., Allan D. Shocker, and Rajendra Srivastava (1979), "Customer-Oriented Approaches to Identifying Product-Market Strategies," *Journal of Marketing*, 43 (Fall), 8–19.

Gavin-Jobson Associates (1982), *The Wine Marketing Handbook*, New York: Gavin-Jobson Assoc.

Ghosh, Avijit, Scott Neslin, and Robert Shoemaker (1984), "A Comparison of Market Share Models and Estimation Procedures," *Journal of Marketing Research*, 21 (May), 202–210.

Hamermesh, R. G., M. J. Anderson, Jr., and J. E. Harris (1978), "Strategies for Low Market Share Businesses," *Harvard Business Review*, 56 (January/February), 95–102.

Hanssens, Dominique M. (1980), "Market Response, Competitive Behavior, and Time Series Analysis," *Journal of Marketing Research*, 17 (November), 470–485.

Henderson, Bruce D. (1979), *Henderson on Corporate Strategy*, Cambridge, MA: Abt Books.

Horsky, Dan (1977), "Market Share Response to Advertising: An Example of Theory Testing," *Journal of Marketing Research*, 14 (February), 10–21.

Houston, Franklin S. and Doyle L. Weiss (1974), "An Analysis of Competitive Market Behavior," *Journal of Marketing Research*, 11 (May), 151–155.

Hunt, Shelby D. (1983), "General Theories and the Fundamental Explananda of Marketing," *Journal of Marketing*, 47 (Fall), 9–17.

Impact Research (1984), *Beverage Trends in America 1960–2000*, New York: M. Shanken Communications, Inc.

Jacobson, Robert and David A. Aaker (1985), "Is Market Share All That It's Cracked Up To Be?" unpublished working paper, University of California, Berkeley.

Karnani, Aneel (1983), "Minimum Market Share," *Marketing Science*, 2 (Winter), 75–93.

Lambin, Jean-Jacques (1970), "Optimal Allocation of Competitive Marketing Efforts: An Empirical Study," *Journal of Business*, 43 (October, 468–484.

——— (1972), "Is Gasoline Advertising Justified?" *Journal of Business*, 45 (October), 585–619.

Leading National Advertisers (1981), *Ad $ Summary*, New York: LNA, Vol. 9.

Leeflang, Peter S. H. and Jan C. Reuyl (1984), "On the Predictive Power of Market Share Attraction Models," *Journal of Marketing Research*, 21 (May), 211–215.

McGuire, Timothy W. and Doyle L. Weiss (1976), "Logically Consistent Market Share Models II," *Journal of Marketing Research*, 13 (August), 296–302.

———, John U. Farley, Robert E. Lucas, Jr., and L. Winston Ring (1968), "Estimation and Inference for Linear Models in which Subsets of the Dependent Variable Are Constrained," *American Statistical Association Journal*, 63 (December), 1201–1213.

Moriarty, Mark (1975), "Cross-Sectional, Time-Series Issues in the Analysis of Marketing Decision Variables," *Journal of Marketing Research*, 12 (May), 142–150.

Naert, Philippe A. and Alain Bultez (1973), "Logically Consistent Market Share Models," *Journal of Marketing Research*, 10 (August), 334–340.

——— and M. Weverbergh (1981), "On the Prediction Power of Market Share Attraction Models," *Journal of Marketing Research*, 18 (May), 146–153.

Phillips, Lynn W., Dae R. Chang, and Robert D. Buzzell (1983), "Product Quality, Cost Position, and Business Performance: A Test of Some Key Hypotheses," *Journal of Marketing*, 47 (Spring), 26–43.

Polli, Rolando and Victor J. Cook, Jr. (1969), "Validity of the Product Life Cycle," *Journal of Business*, 42 (October), 385–400.

Porter, Michael E. (1980), *Competitive Strategy: Techniques for Analyzing Industries and Competitors*, New York: The Free Press.

Prasad, V. Kanti and L. Winston Ring (1976), "Measuring Sales Effects of Some Marketing Mix Variables and Their Interactions," *Journal of Marketing Research*, 13 (November), 391–396.

Rumelt, Richard P. and Robin C. Wensley (1981), "Market Share and the Rate of Return: Testing the Stochastic Hypothesis," working paper, University of California, Los Angeles.

Schultz, Randall L. (1971), "Market Measurement and Planning with a Simultaneous-Equations Model," *Journal of Marketing Research*, 8 (May), 153–164.

Simmons Market Research Bureau (1981), *Survey of Media & Markets: Malt Beverages & Wine*, New York: Simmons.

Simon, Julian L. (1969), "The Effect of Advertising on Liquor Brand Sales," *Journal of Marketing Research*, 6 (August), 301–313.

Telser, Lester G. (1962), "Advertising and Cigarettes," *The Journal of Political Economy*, 70 (October) 471–499.

Utsey, Marjorie F. and Victor J. Cook (1984), "A Marketing Strategy Paradigm for Case Analysis," in *1984 AMA Educators' Proceedings*, R. Belk et al., eds., Chicago: American Marketing, 96–100.

Webster, Frederick E., Jr., James A. Largay III, and Clyde P. Stickney (1980), "The Impact of Inflation Accounting on Marketing Decisions," *Journal of Marketing*, 44 (Fall), 9–17.

Weiss, Doyle L. (1968), "Determinants of Market Share," *Journal of Marketing Research*, 5 (August), 290–293.

Wildt, Albert R. (1974), "Multifirm Analysis of Competitive Decision Variables," *Journal of Marketing Research*, 11 (February), 50–62.

Wind, Yoram and Vijay Mahajan (1981), "Market Share: Concepts, Findings, and Directions for Future Research," *Review of Marketing*, B. M. Enis and K. J. Roering, eds., Chicago: American Marketing, 31–42.

Wittink, Dick R. (1977), "Exploring Territorial Differences in the Relationship between Marketing Variables," *Journal of Marketing Research*, 14 (May), 145–155.

Woo, Carolyn Y. and Arnold C. Cooper (1982), "The Surprising Case for Low Market Share," *Harvard Business Review*, 60 (November–December), 106–113.

SECTION III

Product Market Strategies

Product & Market Life Cycles

The first article in this section by Professors Rink and Swan reviews the extensive literature on product and market life cycle research. The authors discuss the evidence relating to the validity of product life cycle patterns, the different concepts of "product" used in life cycle research, the forecasting of product life cycle stage transition, the use of the product life cycle in strategic planning, and the gaps in our knowledge of product life cycles. They conclude that the evidence for the existence of the classical bell shaped product life cycle curve is strong. Various concepts of "product" have been used in the literature. Most of the research has concentrated on "product *classes*" and "product *forms*." Product *classes* follow "market" life cycles, while product *forms* follow "product" life cycles.

At every stage in the value chain products are desired only as they relate to an existing system of habitual procedures and users' perceptions about the way things are done. Habits and perceptions are difficult to change. The degree to which a new solution to an existing problem can overcome established habits and change existing perceptions depends on many factors. Among the most important are the *compatibility* of the new solution with the old, the *divisibility* of the trial decision, the ease with which the new solution can be *communicated* to existing users, the *riskiness* of trying the new solution, the *performance* of the new solution relative to the existing one, and its *price*. Professor Wasson outlines how to gain and hold first place in a new market, how strategies differ by stage in the life cycle, the dangers of remaining inactive in a mature market and when to get out of declining markets.

Product and market life cycle theories have largely ignored the effects of competition on the adoption and diffusion of a new technology. Professors Robertson and Gatignon attempt to correct this shortcoming by presenting twelve propositions on how technology diffusion is influenced by competition. They argue that the existing theory of the product life cycle predicts adoption principally as a consequence of the characteristics of the innovation itself and of the adopting organization, as outlined in the previous paragraph. The authors argue that the characteristics of the *competitive* environments in both supplying industry and adopting industry are necessary to explain and predict the adoption process.

Market Segmentation

Increasingly, management is coming to recognize that significantly different segments exist in almost every market, consumer or industrial, product or service, domestic and foreign. While road blocks remain in the way of adopting market segmentation strategies, the success of those companies practicing segmentation continues to build support for this key strategic marketing concept. Resistance to the idea of market segmentation is best reflected in a famous statement attributed to Henry Ford: You

can have any color Ford you want, so long as it's black! Even today, many senior managers argue that market segmentation is uneconomic, or less profitable, than mass production. What they fail to see is the process by which market segmentation leads to a more focused, differentiated solution to a customer's problems. It is perceived as having a higher value in use and therefore generates a higher selling price with a larger margin. This is the fundamental process by which market segmentation produces more satisfied customers and more profitable companies.

Professor Haley reviews 20 years in the practice of segmentation at the *consumer* level. He describes and compares the four basic dimensions of segmentation in consumer markets: geographic, demographic, behavioral, and psychographic. In the next selection, Professors Shapiro and Bonoma pose a "nested" approach to *industrial* market segmentation. The three principle nests of segmentation variables are those relating to the demographics and organizational characteristics of the customer, the situational factors surrounding purchase frequency and use, and the personal characteristics of the various lines of buying influence. The authors thus propose a solution to the segmentation problem based upon a hierarchical approach.

Product Positioning

To succeed in an intensely competitive environment a company must create a "position" in the customer's mind that takes into account not only its own characteristics but also those of its competitors. This simple concept, described by Jack Trout and Al Ries in their classic article, has revolutionized strategic marketing. Product "positioning" is how the product is perceived in a customer's mind. This encompasses all elements of the marketing mix. Product positioning incorporates the performance of the product, the equity in the brand name, quality of its distribution channels, and price, all relative to designated competitors. The article concludes with a discussion of how to position a product. The next paper, by Professors Aaker and Shansby, describes how more sophisticated analyses of positioning alternatives can be undertaken. Each of the steps in product positioning can productively use research techniques to provide needed information. The authors provide several examples on how these more sophisticated techniques can assist in the positioning decision. In a more lighthearted vein, and at the same time establishing the intellectual heritage of the concept, Goscinny and Uderzo describe the development of a positioning strategy in ancient Rome.

While strategies can be characterized generically as "low cost" and "high perceived value," these two characterizations actually represent the end points on a continuum of strategic positionings. Professors Fulmer and Goodwin explain why most firms find themselves caught in the middle between low cost and high differentiation. They argue that it is not only possible, but essential to be both a cost leader and highly differentiated competitor. Yet, since only one company can be the lowest cost supplier, all other firms in the market must find other ways to differentiate their products. The authors explain and illustrate how this is done in the airline industry with the concept of customer bonding.

The last two papers in this section address the critical element of price positioning. The first article by Professor Monroe reviews how buyers' subjective perceptions of price influence their behavior. Recent research indicates there is no simple explanation of how price effects buyers' choice behavior. The author marshals evidence from a number of studies of "price and quality" in an attempt to shake the belief that the inverse price-demand relationship is one of the most substantiated findings in economics. Next, Professor Nagle reviews the economic foundations for pricing. The author discusses the economics of information, spatial competition, and segmented pricing, in the hope increasing understanding of the economic environment in which pricing decisions are made. ■

14

Product Life Cycle Research: A Literature Review

David R. Rink & John E. Swan

What can be said about the PLC based on empirical studies?
What has been the scope of PLC studies?
How much confidence can we have in conclusions about the PLC?

The purposes of this paper are threefold: to review the scope of product life cycle (PLC) research; to pinpoint areas requiring further investigation; and to provide guidelines for future researchers. Because of the paucity of empirical evidence, only tentative conclusions are advanced. For example, the most common PLC pattern is the classical, bell-shaped curve, but it is not the sole shape. The application of various forecasting techniques across the PLC have met with merely moderate success. Very little research has been conducted either on how different characteristics of the firm influence the PLC or on the actual use of various PLC-strategy theories by business planners. Finally, investigators have focused almost exclusively on validating the existence of the PLC concept among nondurable consumer goods. Industrial items, as well as major product changes, have been nearly ignored. The main conclusion is that additional research–more diversified and extensive in nature–is needed on many PLC topics.

SINCE THE INTRODUCTION of the idea of a product life cycle (PLC) almost 30 years ago [27, 28], a great deal has been written on the subject and several empirical studies have appeared. Numerous managerial-oriented articles and books have discussed the PLC. Yet the question remains: What is the scope of empirical evidence relevant to the PLC?

David Rink is a President of Rink & Associates, Genoa, Illinois. John E. Swan is a Professor of Marketing at the University of Alabama–Birmingham.

The amount of empirical research in the PLC field is both meager and concentrated. Researchers have focused almost exclusively on validating the existence of the PLC concept. Nondurable consumer goods have represented the primary products studied.

The Product Life Cycle Concept

The PLC represents the unit sales curve for some product, extending from the time it is first placed on the market until it is removed [10, p. 50]. In portraying "the evolution of product attributes and market characteristics through time, (the PLC concept can be) . . . used prescriptively in the selection of marketing actions and planning" [58, p. 67].

Schematically, the PLC may be approximated by a bell-shaped curve (type I, Figure 1) that is divided into several stages [62]. Although the number of phases suggested in the PLC literature varies between four and six, a four-stage cycle —introduction, growth, maturity, and decline—is adopted.

The theoretical rationale behind the PLC concept emanates from the theory of diffusion and adoption of innovations [61]. That is, unit sales are low in introduction, because few consumers are aware of the new good (or service). With consumer recognition and acceptance, unit sales begin to increase at an increasing rate. This signals the start of the growth stage. However, the rate of growth in unit sales will subside as more competitors enter the industry and the market becomes smaller. Eventually, unit sales reach a plateau, and the product is in the maturity stage. Most of the mass

Figure 1
Types of product life cycle patterns

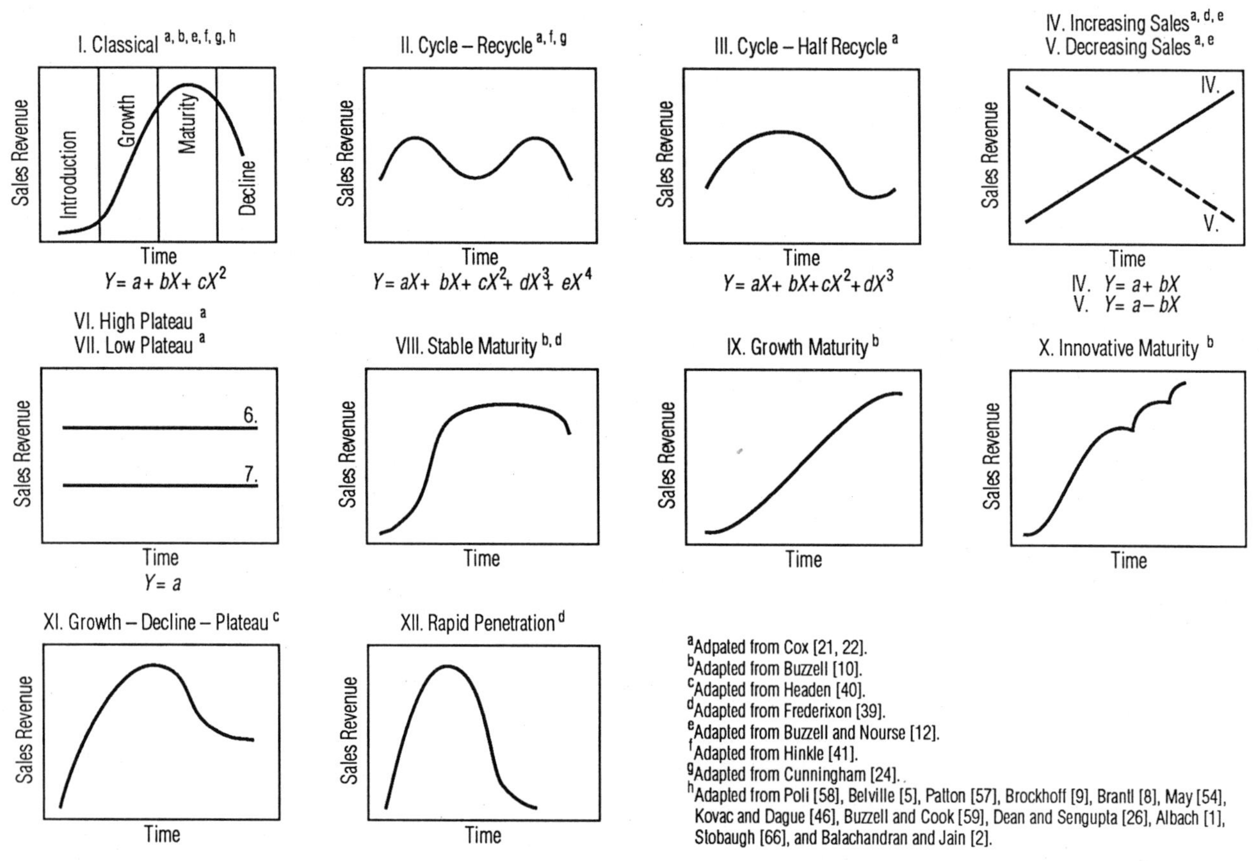

The Product Life Cycle Concept

The PLC represents the unit sales curve for some product, extending from the time it is first placed on the market until it is removed [10, p. 50]. In portraying "the evolution of product attributes and market characteristics through time, (the PLC concept can be) . . . used prescriptively in the selection of marketing actions and planning" [58, p. 67].

Schematically, the PLC may be approximated by a bell-shaped curve (type I, Figure 1) that is divided into several stages [62]. Although the number of phases suggested in the PLC literature varies between four and six, a four-stage cycle —introduction, growth, maturity, and decline—is adopted.

The theoretical rationale behind the PLC concept emanates from the theory of diffusion and adoption of innovations [61]. That is, unit sales are low in introduction, because few consumers are aware of the new good (or service). With consumer recognition and acceptance, unit sales begin to increase at an increasing rate. This signals the start of the growth stage. However, the rate of growth in unit sales will subside as more competitors enter the industry and the market becomes smaller. Eventually, unit sales reach a plateau, and the product is in the maturity stage. Most of the mass market has already purchased the item. As consumers increasingly forsake the product for its newer counterparts, unit sales will decline rapidly. Removal from the market is imminent.

The PLC theory *per se* is directly analogous to other concepts that typify a more or less predictable pattern across time. Such notions represent a summary of a number of forces that determine some outcome of interest. As an example, a seasonal sales pattern for a product may be determined by a large number of factors, including changes in temperature across the seasons, social customs, and conventions, demand stimulation by business firms, and so on. The concept of seasonal sales has been very useful because of the fundamental fact that many products do have sales that vary by season and such variation is predictable enough to be useful for planning purposes. What can be said about the PLC based on empirical studies? What has been the scope of PLC studies? How much confidence can we have in conclusions about the PLC based on the number of studies that are relevant to a specific question about the PLC?

Purpose

The major purpose is to review research on the PLC in order to see what conclusions can be drawn as answers to the following fundamental questions and to assess the weight of evidence that is pertinent to each question:

1. Do recognizable PLC patterns across time in fact occur, and on what sample of industries and products is our knowledge of the PLC based?
2. Can PLC stages be forecasted?
3. Do we know how economic conditions or characteristics of the firm may affect the PLC?
4. To what extent is the PLC used in strategy planning?
5. What are the gaps in our knowledge of the PLC that future research could concentrate on?

A second purpose is to stimulate more extensive and diverse research. This will be accomplished by first, reviewing the scope of PLC studies that have been conducted; second, highlighting areas requiring empirical investigation; and third, providing guidelines for subsequent researchers.

Evidence Relevant to Validating PLC Patterns

Types of PLC Patterns

The classical PLC shape (type 1, Figure 1) has been only one of 12 types of PLC patterns discovered by investigators. Research on the different patterns shown in Figure 1 has been quite uneven.

Some 15 different studies of consumer nondurables and durables, as well as four studies of industrial goods, provide quite a bit of evidence that some products have validated the classical PLC curve (Figure 1). On the other hand, the cycle-recycle pattern has been found in four studies, including drugs [21], food products, household products [41], and industrial fluid measuring devices [24]. An increasing sales pattern was uncovered in three studies [12, 21, 39]. Although two studies support the decreasing sales pattern [12, 21], two other studies found a stable maturity pattern [10, 40]. The remaining PLC types of cycle-half-recycle, growth maturity, innovative maturity, high and low plateau, growth-decline plateau, and rapid penetration are the result of a single study. In summary, with the exception of the classical pattern, more research is needed to substantiate the remaining PLC patterns.

Reasons for Shape of Product Life Cycle Curve

While the studies previously mentioned have documented the general shape of the PLC curve, only a few researchers have extended their analysis to empirically ascertain why the curve assumes this shape. Although Belville concentrated on the initial PLC stages of color televisions, he found that seven factors were significant in triggering the take-off point: price; volume of network color programming; public exposure to color; obsolescence of black-and-white sets; color quality; clarity of black-and-white pictures; and attitude of major set makers [5, p. 82]. Using unit sales data from 11 different automobile models, Brockhoff found that the PLC curve depended both upon time and sales of closely related products manufactured by the firm [9]. Other researchers and writers cite the common reasons of changing market and economic conditions, as well as reactions to competitors, as major factors determining the shape of the PLC curve [31, 43]. To date, however, these have not been empirically confirmed. Additionally, research should be conducted to ascertain whether management can influence these factors that affect the shape of the PLC. If so, what is the extent to which management can alter these factors, and, hence, influence the form of the curve?

Table 1
Industries and Products Included in PLC Studies

Industry (Number of Studies)	Product Category Researchers(s) and Number of Products/Brands
Consumer durable goods (9)	Major appliances: Polli [58] 22; Buzzell and Cook [11] 50[a]
	Color television: Belville [5] 1
	Black and white television: Patton [57] NA
	Refrigerators: Cunningham [24] NA
	Minor appliances: Polli [58] 28; Buzzell and Cook [11] 50[a]
	Automobiles: Brockhoff [9] 11; Brantl [8] 3; May [54] 1
	Automobile tires: Kovac and Dague [46] 1
Consumer nondurable goods (12)	Drugs: Cox [21, 22] 258
	Food: Hinkle [41] 275[b]; Polli [58] 56; Buzzell and Cook [11] 49; Cunningham [24] NA; Polli and Cook [59] 56; Dean and Sengupta [26] NA; Buzzell [10] 9; Buzzell and Nourse [12] 100; Headen [40] NA; Albach [1] 2
	Household products/supplies: Hinkle [41] 275[b]; Polli [58] 45
	Nonfood grocery items: Buzzell and Cook [11] 93
	Health and beauty aids: Hinkle [41] 275[b]; Polli [58] 40; Polli and Cook [59] 51; Cunningham [24]
	Cigarettes: May [54] 4; Polli and Cook [59] 33
Industrial durable goods (2)	General engineering and fluid measuring devices: Cunningham [24] NA
	Automobile components: Cunningham [24] NA
	Established durable: Balachandran and Jain [2] NA
Industrial non-durable goods (2)	Petro-chemicals: Stobaugh [66] 9
	Chemicals: Frederixon [39] 27

[a]Total only; unable to segregate by major versus minor household appliances.

[b]Total only; unable to segregate by food products, household products/supplies, and health and beauty aids.

NA = Not available in published research report.

The Scope of Industries and Products Included in PLC Studies

As shown in Table 1, 12 different studies of consumer nondurable goods have been the major focus of PLC research, followed by nine studies of consumer durable items. Only four studies of industrial goods were discovered by the authors.[1] The most obvious gap in knowledge of the PLC, therefore, involves industrial goods. As to why academic researchers have been loathe to relate the PLC concept to industrial goods, two explanations may be offered. First, with industrial goods, "the time span tends to be extended and the market more conservative and slower to respond due to the historical inertia" [24, p. 34]. Second, since most industries lack records of product introduction, the development of PLC models requires

Figure 2
Classification of consumer products by purchase frequency, price, distribution, and supply.

			Distribution			
		Price Level	Intensive		Limited	
			Supply Variations			
Purchase Frequency	High	Low	1	2	3	4
		High	5	6	7	8
	Low	Low	9	10	11	12
		High	13	14	15	16

> . . . a compilation of new product introductions. The difficulty of preparing such a compilation is perhaps the most serious obstacle to the widespread development of product life cycles for a variety of industries and products [22, p. 376].

Frequency of studies by type of customer—consumer versus industrial—can be misleading. Scrutinizing the type of goods utilized in consumer studies, not only do nondurable items outdistance durable ones by almost a 2:1 margin, but food products were overwhelmingly preferred (Table 1). Also, previous PLC researchers focused primarily upon those consumer products that were frequently purchased, low-priced, widely distributed, and not subject to wide variations on the supply side [58, p. 219]. The reasons investigators preferred nondurable consumer items were

> . . . durables sales data, regardless of adjustment procedures, do not distinguish between adoption and replacement and therefore do not accurately measure the level of market acceptance. In addition, durable sales are heavily influenced by availability of materials (as during war years), income level changes, and consumer expectations. . . . These problems are not severe in nondurables [11, pp. 29,35].

One investigator censured early PLC writers for generalizing "from a small and often biased sample of experiences" [58, p. 42]. This criticism is still appropriate as well as justified from the content and focus of relatively recent research. This conclusion can be substantiated by examining all possible combinations of four variables for consumer products, which were outlined by Polli [58, p. 39]: purchase frequency; price level; degree of distribution; and supply variations (Figure 2). Of the resulting 16 cells, researchers have concentrated almost exclusively on the first cell.

Before the PLC notion can become a theory in the strict scientific sense, extensive empirical observations and descriptions are mandatory. For consumer goods, this can be accomplished by conducting research in each of the remaining 15 cells of Figure 2. The next step would entail replication of these empirical findings.

With industrial goods, the situation is slightly different. Not enough empirical studies have been performed for a theory to be developed. Hence, more industrial situations and products must be examined in order to establish that the PLC theory is applicable. Once this task is completed and a proposition developed, then researchers can attempt to fill the literature gaps by following a scheme similar to Figure 2, but for industrial goods. Replication would then follow.

Different Product Concepts Analyzed in PLC Research

Here the basic question is: To what extent have PLC studies covered different concepts of a new product and different levels of product aggregation?

Level of Product Aggregation

Typically, there are three levels of product aggregation—class, form, and brand. Product class represents items that are substitutes for the same want (e.g., cigarettes, cigars, and pipes). Product form is a finer classification of a product class (e.g., king-sized cigarettes, regulars, menthol cigarettes, etc.). Brand, on the other hand, is unique (e.g., Camels, Kools, etc.).

A major problem with previous, and sometimes current, PLC studies has been: What level of product aggregation was used? It is vital that these levels be differentiated because the PLC notion has a different degree of applicability in these three cases. That is, product classes possess the longest sales curves. Product forms probably exhibit the standard PLC histories. Product brands have very erratic sales trends [45, p. 431].

Most writers have accepted the idea that product forms are the most appropriate level of product aggregation to utilize in PLC research. However, this point requires more investigation as only one study has addressed this question. Based upon the sales histories of nonfood grocery product forms, Polli found no substantive evidence concerning the level of product aggregation that should be adopted by researchers interested in products other than nonfood grocery items [58, pp. 232–233]. Hence, more PLC research is needed utilizing various consumer and industrial goods to determine which product aggregation level should be adopted.

Definition of New Product

A difficulty in PLC studies has been: What is a new product? Does a variation in an established product represent a new product or part of the mother product? For example, should color television sets be considered as a separate product with their own PLC curve or as a part of black-and-white television's unit sales curve? Far from being resolved, this issue continues to plague PLC researchers. One author lamented that this question involves the "most complex element to untangle in understanding the life-cycle concept" [57, pp. 68–69].

A possible solution to the definitional quagmire surrounding the question, "What is a new product?" is to segregate new products into several degrees of newness. According to one writer, this can be accomplished, because "there appear to be a few universally recognized characteristics distinguishing the new product from an improved variation of an old one" [57, p. 69]. Continuing, this writer presented a four-way classification of new products: the unquestionably new product; the partially new product; the major product change; and the minor product change. This delineation, and others like it [12, p. 22], can be instrumental in alleviating the difficulty inherent with determining whether a new product is simply a variation of an old one or is a completely new item.

By integrating some of the previously mentioned variables, such as degree of perishability, customer type, degree of newness, and level of product aggregation, areas for future research can be easily identified. By taking all reasonable combinations of these four variables, the result is a possible 48-cell classification (Figure 3).

The major focus of consumer goods research (durable and nondurable) has been on minor product change-form with some emphasis on minor product change-class and brand. What little research has been directed at both major product change and partially new product has concentrated primarily on class and form. Brand has been almost totally ignored in this case. Other combinations suggested by Figure 3 represent potential areas for additional or new research.

In the industrial goods area (durable and nondurable), most of the studies have focused on minor product change-class and form. To the best of the authors' knowledge, no empirical research has been performed on the other cells of this group. Hence, these cells signify relatively untapped areas for future examination.

Figure 3

Classification of goods by newness, customer, product aggregation, and perishability.

			Level of Product Aggregation			Degree of Newness[a]			
		Degree of Perishability	Class	Form	Brand	UNP	PNP	MCP	MIPC
Type of Customer	Consumer	Nondurable	1	2	3				
		Durable	4	5	6				
	Industrial	Nondurable	7	8	9				
		Durable	10	11	12				

[a] Columns are coded as follows: UNP = unquestionably new product; PNP = partially new product; MCP = major product change; MICP = minor product change.

Levels of Measurement

In the material previously reviewed and summarized in Figures 2 and 3, some potentially continuous variables, such as price level, have been treated as ordinal or nominal variables. This was done to simplify the material and present a clear overview of some of the types of products and markets that have been the focus of PLC research. However, a basic question that should be addressed is: What level of measurement would be appropriate for such variables? This would depend upon the analytical use of such variables in PLC research. The variables may be used either to explain phenomena of interest concerning the PLC or to specify that part of the real world that a particular PLC model is applicable to. As explanatory variables, it would generally be best to retain continuous variables as continuous variables because a wider range of more powerful quantitative tools are available for continuous, interval level variables than are applicable to nominal or ordinal measures. As an example, if a researcher wished to test the idea that the lower the price of a new product, the shorter the introduction and growth stages of the PLC, then price measured as a continuous variable would be appropriate.

The second problem concerns specifying the limits of the application of PLC models. As previously noted, it has been felt that the classical PLC does apply to frequently purchased consumer nondurables. If the objective of a research study was to see if the classical curve could be generalized to infrequently purchased consumer nondurables, then only an ordinal measure of frequency of purchase would be necessary so that two classes of goods—frequently and infrequently purchased—could be contrasted. An initial study should probably contrast very frequently with very infrequently purchased products. Unfortunately, current knowledge of the PLC does not provide precise guidance for cutoff points to determine what is frequent compared to infrequent purchase. This could be an area for future research.

Research on PLC Stages

Forecasting Stage Transition

The main application suggested for the PLC has been to plan changes in marketing strategy as the product moves from stage to stage. It follows that the PLC would be more useful in strategy planning if one could more accurately forecast the time when a product changed PLC phases. To what extent can stages be predicted?

Two of the early researchers used initial data points in the PLC to predict the entire curve or next stage. Utilizing semilog paper to plot annual color set sales and number of color television-equipped households, as well as difference analysis relative to color set saturation, Belville identified the take-off point in color television sales, or the transition from introduction to growth stage [5, pp. 26–29]. Polli and Cook examined the percentage change in a product's real sales from year t to year $t + 1$. Plotting these changes as a normal distribution with mean zero, they determined that if a product had a percentage change less than $\frac{1}{2}\sigma$, it was in the decline phase. A product with the percentage change exceeding $\frac{1}{2}\sigma$, was in the growth stage. In the range $\pm\frac{1}{2}\sigma$, the product was considered to be stable [59, pp. 390–391].

Other researchers have developed new product models that forecast the growth and maturity phases of a new item on the basis of either test market data [3, 4, 23, 36, 42, 47, 53, 68] or pretest research [17]. However, these models are unable to accurately predict the second half of the PLC curve. (This is similar to the problem encountered by various growth curves, e.g., Gompertz and logistics, except that they cannot estimate beyond the sales plateau.) For example, if one of the more accepted new product models [4] were permitted to forecast the remainder of the sales trend, it would predict "a very short maturity phase going into decline much faster than does the actual PLC" [20, p. 374].

In a different direction, researchers have discovered various leading indicators of the timing of the maturity phase, such as declining proportion of new triers versus replacement sales, declining profits, overcapacity in industry, appearance of new replacement products, decline in elasticity of advertising coupled with increasing price elasticity, present users' consumption rate, and style changes [70]. By incorporating these indicators into either technological forecasts, similar product analyses, or epidemological models, a sales forecast for the maturity stage may be derived [4, 16]. In addition to its ex post facto nature, an obvious problem with this technique is that the initial PLC stages are ignored.

Another group of researchers has prescribed a different set of forecasting techniques for each PLC stage, because management must make different decisions at each phase, and "they require different kinds of information as a base" [15, pp. 51–52]. These recommendations, however, are grounded on limited empirical evidence, in particular, two products of Corning Glass Works—glass components for color TV tubes and cookware. But, the major difficulty with this approach is that the user must know the PLC stage the product is in before he can adopt the corresponding set of forecasting devices. Hence, the original problem of forecasting phase transition is encountered.

The forecasting aspect of the PLC concept requires estimation of two items: magnitude of the unit sales increase and length of the cycle. The new product models resolve half of this dilemma by predicting the magnitude and timing of the growth and maturity phases using data from the introduction stage. The problem, therefore, is

> . . . reduced to one of predicting the length of the maturity phase and the rate of decline of the decay phase resulting in a prediction for the entire PLC from the early data points [20, p. 3 74].

This latter problem has been attacked by two researchers, who developed a computer program (LIFER) that uses early data points—known or estimated—to forecast the remainder of the PLC. Assuming that the PLC model "is a continuous real valued function of continuous time, the boundaries of the . . . (various) phases can be determined using techniques of elementary differential calculus" [20, p. 375]. The result is a multiplicative model of the following form

$$Y(t) = C_1 t^{C_2} \exp(C_3 t + C_4 t^2) e(t) t^{C_2} \geq 0$$

where

$Y(t)$ = recorded sales during period $(t-1, t)$,

$e(t)$ = multiplicative random component for period t,

C_1, C_2, C_3, C_4 are parameters to be estimated from available sales data.

Although this model includes "no exogenous variables and a limited number of parameters," it was tested using annual sales data for cigarettes, automobiles, various types of appliances, beer, wine, and ethical drugs and found to possess "the requisite flexibility to fit most (PLC) situations, in particular those involving extended decline phases, as well as a recycle" [20, pp. 374 and 377].

The subsequent step for investigators is to complicate the LIFER model by adding exogenous variables and more parameters. As one researcher stated

> stage identification is difficult because the sales curve is not a function of time alone. External environmental factors and controllable marketing instruments determine the shape of the sales response curve [55, p. 476].

Also, more diverse and varied products should be used in testing the universality of the LIFER model. Another researchable avenue is to examine the possibility of applying the recently acclaimed Box-Jenkins approach to PLC analysis.

Length and Sequence of Product Life Cycle Stages

Do PLCs follow the proposed sequence of four phases—introduction, growth, maturity, and decline? Also, what is the length of each phase? Only a few researchers have empirically examined these two issues. Cox, for example, discovered that the length of the phases for a typical ethical drug was 1 month, 6 months, 15 months, and over 22 months for the introduction, growth, maturity, and decline stages, respectively [22]. Another investigator examined the stability of the PLC phases, as well as the proportion of time various consumer nondurables spent in each stage [58, p. 67]. Dean, the purported Father of the PLC Theory [5, pp. 84–85], maintains that the length of the PLC phases is a function of the rate of technical change, rate of market acceptance, and ease of competitive entry [27, pp. 45–46]. Information concerning these two variables, especially length of PLC stages for a typical product in some industry, would assist managers in more effective management of a product's life cycle. Researchers, therefore, should focus their empirical endeavors on the length and sequence of PLC phases for numerous products and industries.

Economic Conditions

Because the PLC concept was born in the early 1950s, it is basically a theory that describes the unit sales trend for some product during either normal economic conditions or a boom period. Consequently, the PLC notion cannot (nor does it) reflect some product's unit sales history during nonnormal economic circumstances, such as recession or depression.

Economic events of the mid-1970s, however, have substantially increased the need for relating the PLC to an economic downturn. One group of writers have provided a general conceptualization of the impact of a nonnormal domestic economy upon products in various stages of the PLC. In the introduction stage, the product will probably be killed. A product in the growth stage, on the other hand, stands the best chance of resisting

> . . . the adverse effect of a significant downturn in the general economy. . . . It is possible, with proper modifications, for market expansion to continue during this period [65, p. 229].

These modifications include adjusting product form, reducing price, and increasing promotional expenditures. This strategy was employed by electric refrigerator manufacturers during the depression of the 1930s and explains why their sales continued to increase relative to the sales of other appliances [7, p. 277]. Products in the maturity stage will "tend to rise and fall with changes in the general level of business activity because of the postponable nature of such products" [65, p. 229]. Smallwood observed this phenomenon among annual factory shipments of two big-ticket consumer durables, e.g., color televisions and portable dishwashers, during the minirecessions of 1966–67 and 1969–70 [63, p. 32]. Finally, a quicker exit from the market is generally expected for products in the decline phase [65, p. 229].

Future researchers must empirically examine the feasibility of this conceptualization. Completion of this task will stimulate additional research along these lines. The end result will be several PLC theories capable of handling all possible economic conditions.

Is the Concept of PLC Stages Hindering PLC Theory Development?

The concept of PLC stages may be hindering PLC research by diverting attention from other issues concerning product life cycles.[2] Are PLC stages worth the effort that they have received? The authors feel that PLC stages are quite worthwhile, because managerial use of the PLC concept readily flows from the stage notion. Without stages, the PLC concept would be rather difficult to apply to marketing problems. Ideas about stages are somewhat arbitrary, and work is needed to determine the value of different stage concepts for different managerial or conceptual problems. As an example, the decline stage is a critical stage for product abandonment decisions. In fact, for planning purposes, it may be fruitful to subdivide the decline stage into more detailed categories. To illustrate this point, suppose it was found that when half of the brands at the start of the decline stage have exited the market, price declines tend to stabilize and the market moves toward oligopoly. Some firms may find it very useful to try and predict the price stability stage, since the squeeze on profit margins may be less and staying in the market increases in value when that stage is reached.

The stage concept, when understood as a way to organize knowledge and observations about the PLC and to help forecast future developments, is very helpful. Armchair arguments about the exact number or sequence of stages, without an explicit consideration of how the resulting classification will be used, are not likely to be fruitful.

The Firm and the PLC

The size of the firm and the product lines marketed by the firm could influence the PLC. However, little research has been done on either of these issues.

Type of Firm

The magnitude of resources available to a large firm relative to its smaller counterpart would seem to infer two differently shaped PLC curves—even if their products were basically the same. Ambiguity concerning the size of firms examined precludes testing this and related hypotheses.

Likewise, none of the empirical studies distinguished between one-product and multiproduct firms. Allocation of scarce resources among several products may reduce the multiproduct firm's effectiveness in the market, as measured by unit sales, compared to the one-product firm, which can concentrate its efforts on one item. Again, this point has not been elaborated upon in past research.

Product Lines

When discussing product lines, marketing authors are quick to warn managers to be cognizant of the interactions and interrelationships between various products of a line. The axiom is: The sum of the individual products of a product line equal more than the product line itself. If this is true, then would not the PLC curves of products in a line be affected in some way as a result of these interrelationships? Excluding Brockhoff [9], researchers have not addressed themselves to this point.

A critical problem for a multiproduct firm is to determine how its limited resources will be allocated among various products in an optimum fashion. Numerous models have been developed for handling this question. One academician posited that the PLC concept could serve as "a superior basis for optimizing the allocation of the firm's resources" [22].

In managing its product line, the diversified firm will be confronted with multiple PLC curves [63]. To be successful, the firm must maintain a balance among its products in terms of their corresponding life-cycle positions, because such variables as risk and investment requirements vary across the PLC [65, pp. 240–241]. Although Smallwood and Marvin [52] were among the first researchers to conceptualize a balanced product portfolio, no one has empirically examined whether firms do indeed maintain such balanced portfolios. Such investigations would seem to be requisite for product development and planning purposes, formulation of marketing strategy, market segmentation, and eventual product-market positioning and realignment. Moreover, these studies should be segregated according to industry and product types.

Use of the PLC in Strategy Planning

Several academicians have either hypothesized which variable(s) of the marketing mix is (are) most relevant or asserted the nature of the marketing mix to be employed by PLC phase [10, 18, 19, 27, 28, 34, 35, 45, pp. 434–437, 659–660, 48, 49, pp. 183–188, 50, pp. 345–348, 527–528, 670–672, 55, pp. 87–89, 57, 62, 64, pp. 166–182, 67, 69, pp. 247–248]. Other writers have also theorized the application of the PLC concept to their functional areas of interest in terms of strategy formulation, such as finance [37], purchasing [6], logistics [25, pp. 222–225], and sales management [30].

As observed by Wind and Claycamp, however,

> these recommendations have usually been vague, nonoperational, not empirically supported, and conceptually questionable, since they imply that strategies can be developed with little concern for the product's profitability and market share position.[3] . . . Traditional (PLC) analysis . . . ignores the competitive setting of the product, the relevant profit considerations, and the fact that product sales are a function of the marketing effort of the firm and other environmental forces [71, pp. 2 and 8].[4]

Excluding one researcher's study, no one has investigated empirically whether practitioners actually utilize academicians' PLC-strategy theories. The apparent underlying explanation for this complacency is that most academicians accept the PLC concept as a useful model for planning appropriate strategies. The empirical validity of the PLC theory is simply asserted [51, p. 39]. Interviewing industrial purchasing executives, however, Rink found that most were intuitively using Berenson's PLC-purchasing strategy (PS) model in formulating their firm's purchasing strategy across the PLC [60]. But this is an empirical test of only one of the PLC-strategy theories. Others beg examination. Such studies will determine which strategy models are appropriate for the practitioner to consider, as well as when and in what situations. Modifications may be required in some of these basic theories.[5]

Although Mickwitz [55, pp. 87–89] posited that the demand elasticities of the marketing mix variables change over the PLC, the literature provides almost no empirical evidence to substantiate this theory. Reportedly, one packaged goods company measured the advertising elasticities for a wide range of its products at their various PLC phases. The firm found that advertising elasticity tended to decrease as the product progressed through its PLC [44].

In examining the domestic sales and advertising for a household cleanser, Parsons found empirical support for Mickwitz's proposition, at least in the case of advertising. He recommended

> Future research should be directed toward confirming this exploratory find. In addition, marketing mix models should be examined to determine whether there are differential rates of change among the various elasticities. Finally, but most importantly, the elasticities should be expressed as functions of external environmental variables, and controllable marketing instruments instead of explicit functions of time alone [56, p. 480].

Major Research Needs Involving the PLC

In critically appraising various facets of PLC research, numerous avenues for future study have been highlighted. Although these fertile areas have been discussed and some of the major points summarized, integrating the research possibilities into one table may be useful (see Table 2). This may underscore the need for a multidimensional approach to conceptualizing future PLC research.

For ease of reference, the 23 variables have been segregated into three groups: variables internal to the firm; variables external to the firm but internal to the industry; and macroenvironmental variables.

The 23 variables comprising Table 2 are not intended to be an exhaustive enumeration. At best, this table represents the starting point for further conceptualization. Some variables, for example, industry structure and industry type, may be too similar to segregate. In another case, product type, most researchers agree that commodity products do not exhibit the general PLC shape. Perhaps this should be examined more thoroughly. Finally, concerning market reach, an often-used strategy of multinational firms involves transferring a product that has transpired its PLC among highly industrialized countries to markets frequented by less industrialized countries. This permits the firm to reinitiate the PLC of its product, but with substantial cost economies via the experience curve phenomenon.

Additional work is needed in developing, refining, and crystallizing this list of 23 variables. However, the multidimensional approach epitomized in Table 2 will enrich, as well as stimulate, more extensive and diverse empirical PLC research as investigators examine feasible combinations of these variables.

Conclusions and Summary

Some tentative conclusions can be advanced on the basis of the empirical studies reviewed here. Unfortunately, there is little evidence on which to base most of the following conclusions, so the need for additional research is the main conclusion of this report.

PLC Curves

Evidence for the existence of the classical bell-shaped PLC curve is strong, as a number of studies have found such a pattern. At least three studies have found other curves, includ-

Table 2
Multidimensional Approach for Conceptualizing Future Product Life Cycle Research

Variables Internal to the Firm			
Type of customer		Price level	
Consumer	Industrial	High	Low
Degree of perishability		Medium	
Durable	Nondurable	Degree of distribution	
Degree of tangibility		Intensive	Limited
Good	Service	Extensive	
Degree of newness		Number of product lines	
Unquestionably new	Major change	One	
Partially new	Established	Two or more	
Type of firm, such as		Related	Unrelated
Manufacturer	Retailer	Product type	
Wholesaler		Commodity	Noncommodity
Firm size in terms of assets, sales, etc.		Market reach	
Large	Small	Local	International
Medium		Regional	
Function, such as		Degree of promotion	
Marketing	Logistics	High	Low
Finance	Etc.	Medium	
Purchasing		Length and sequence of PLC stages	
Level of aggregation		Market share	
Class	Brand	Small	Dominant
Form		Average	
Variables External to Firm but Internal to Industry			
Industry type, such as		State of industry technology	
Automobile	Home construction	Volatile, ever-changing	
Electrical appliance	Electronic components	Changes periodically	
Etc.		Stable	
Supply variations		Purchase Frequency	
High	Low	High	
Average		Medium	
Industry (or market) structure		Low	
Pure competition			
Oligopoly			
Monopoly			
Monopolistic competitiopn			
Macroenvironmental Variables			
Domestic economy		International economy (optional)	
Boom		Boom	
Bust, e.g., recession, inflation, shortages, depression, etc.		Bust	

ing cycle-recycle, stable maturity, decreasing, and increasing patterns. Some half-dozen other life-cycle patterns have been found, but by only one or two studies. The weight of evidence suggests that the most common curve is the classical, but it is not the only PLC. Only two studies have been conducted that sought to test factors that may cause PLC patterns.

Industries/Products Analyzed

Most of the research on the PLC has been based on either consumer nondurables (12 studies) or consumer durables (nine studies). Only four studies have covered industrial goods. Thus, the confidence that we may have in generalizing about the PLC across types of goods is at least fair within consumer nondurables, but meager for industrial items. Furthermore, with consumer products, researchers have focused on items that are frequently purchased, low-priced, widely distributed, and not subject to wide variations on the supply side. Hence, our ability to generalize the PLC across consumer goods is also limited.

Product Concepts Investigated

A number of combinations can be formed in terms of levels of product aggregation and degree of product newness, specifically class (e.g., tobacco smoking products), form (e.g., cigarettes), brand (e.g., Camels), unquestionably new product (e.g., black-and-white television when it was introduced), partially new product, major product change (e.g., small, portable black-and-white television sets), and minor product change. However, researchers have concentrated mainly on minor product changes for product classes and forms. Brands have been largely ignored.

Forecasting PLC Stages

Some success has been claimed for methods designed to forecast the transition from one PLC stage to another. But these methods typically use data from a current stage to forecast the timing of the next stage. Thus, accurate long-range forecasting is not likely. Little is known about the length and sequence of PLC stages.

The Impact of Economic Conditions on the PLC

Very limited evidence suggests that the usual PLC concept applies to periods of either economic stability or growth. How recessions may influence the PLC is questionable.

Characteristics of the Firm and the PLC

Almost no research has been reported on how different characteristics of the firm may influence the PLC.

Use of the PLC in Business Planning

While much has been written on how the PLC could be used in business planning, the use of the PLC by business planners has only been investigated by one study.

References

1. These numbers result from counting each researcher's study only once under each of the three categories. On the other hand, if counting were with replacement, the corresponding numbers would be 20, 11, and 5 studies for consumer nondurable goods, consumer durable items, and industrial goods, respectively.
2. The authors are grateful to a *JBR* reviewer for suggesting this point.
3. Other interesting theoretical articles and rejoiners that focus on PLC and market share are reviewed in Catry, et al. [13, 14] and Fildes, et al. [33].
4. Other writers concur with the point that PLC is a dependent variable determined by marketing actions rather than an independent variable to which firms adapt their marketing programs [29, p. 1–5, 31, pp. 3–4, 32, p. 48, 33, p. 59].
5. On the basis of discussions with 45 purchasing executives, Fox and Rink [38] expanded Berenson's PLC-PS model [6] to include almost 100 purchasing strategies and tactics.

Bibliography

1. Albach, H., *Zur Theorie des wachsenden Unternehmens, Schriften des Vereins für Socialpolitik, 34NS*, Duncker and Humblot, Berlin, 1965.
2. Balachandran, V., and Jain, Subbash, "A Predictive Model for Monitoring Product Life Cycle," in *Relevance in Marketing/Marketing in Motion*, Fred Allvine, ed., American Marketing Association, Chicago, 1972.
3. Barclay, William, "A Probability Model for Early Prediction of New Product Market Success, *Journal of Marketing* 27 (January, 1963): 63–68.
4. Bass, Frank, "A New Product Growth Model for Consumer Durables," *Management Science* 15 (January, 1969): 215–27.
5. Belville, Hugh Jr., "The Product Life Cycle Theory Applied to Color Television," masters thesis, New York University, New York City, 1966.
6. Berenson, Conrad, "The Purchasing Executive's Adaptation to the Product Life Cycle," *Journal of Purchasing* 3 (May, 1967): 52–68.
7. Borden, Neil, *Advertising in Our Economy*, Richard D. Irwin, Homewood, Ill., 1945.
8. Brantl, C., "American Motors Corporation: An Empirical Study of the Firm," Ph.D. dissertation, Fordham University, New York City, 1963.
9. Brockhoff, Klaus, "A Test for the Product Life Cycle," *Econometrica* 35 (July–October, 1967): 472–484.
10. Buzzell, Robert, "Competitive Behavior and Product Life Cycles," in *New Ideas for Successful Marketing*, John Wright and Jac Goldstucker, eds., American Marketing Association, Chicago, 1966.
11. Buzzell, Robert, and Cook, Victor, *Product Life Cycles*, Marketing Science Institute, Cambridge, 1969.
12. Buzzell, Robert, and Nourse, Robert, *Product Innovation in Food Processing: 1954–1964*, Division of Research, Harvard Business School, Boston, 1967.
13. Catry, Bernard, and Chevalier, Michel, "Market Share Strategy and the Product Life Cycle," *Journal of Marketing* 38 (October, 1974): 29–34.
14. Catry, Bernard, and Chevalier, Michel, "Market Share Strategy: The Concept and the Evidence," *Journal of Marketing* 39 (October, 1975): 59–60.
15. Chambers, John, Mullick, Satinder, and Smith, Donald, "How to Choose the Right Forecasting Technique," *Harvard Business Review* 49 (July–August, 1971): 45–74.
16. Chambers, John, Mullick, Satinder, and Smith, Donald, *An Executive's Guide to Forecasting*, John Wiley and Sons, Inc., New York, 1974.
17. Claycamp, Henry, and Liddy, Lucien, "Prediction of New Product Performance: An Analytical Approach," *Journal of Marketing Resources* 6 (November, 1969): 414–420.
18. Clifford, Jr., Donald, "Leverage in the Product Life Cycle," *Dun's Review of Modern Industry* 85 (May, 1965): 62–70.
19. Clifford, Jr., Donald, "Managing the Product Life Cycle," *Management Review* 54 (June, 1965): 34–38.
20. Cooke, Ernest, and Edmondson, Ben, "Computer Aided Product Investment Decisions," in *Increasing Marketing Productivity and Conceptual and Methodological Foundations of Marketing,* Thomas Greer, ed., American Marketing Association, Chicago, 1973.
21. Cox, Jr., William, "Product Life Cycles and Promotional Strategy in the Ethical Drug Industry," Ph.D. dissertation, University of Michigan, 1963.
22. Cox, Jr., William, "Product Life Cycles as Marketing Models," *Journal of Business* 40 (October, 1967): 375–384.
23. Crawford, C. Merle, "The Trajectory Theory of Goal Setting for New Products," *Journal of Marketing Resources* 3 (May, 1966): 117–126.
24. Cunningham, M. T., "The Application of Product Life Cycles to Corporate Strategy: Some Research Findings," *British Journal of Marketing* (Spring, 1969): 32–44.
25. Davis, Grant, and Brown, Stephen, *Logistics Management*, D. C. Heath and Company, Lexington, 1974.
26. Dean, B., and Sengupta, S., "On a Method for Determining Corporate Research Development Budgets," in Churchman and Verhulst, eds., *Management Science, Models and Techniques*, 2nd ed., Oxford University Press, London, 1960.
27. Dean, Joel, "Pricing Policies for New Products," *Harvard Business Review* 28 (November–December, 1950): 45–53.
28. Dean, Joel, *Managerial Economics*, Prentice-Hall, Inc., Englewood Cliffs, NJ, 1951.
29. Dhalla, Nariman, and Yuspeh, Sonia, "Forget the Product Life Cycle Concept!" *Harvard Business Review* 54 (January-February, 1976): 102–112.
30. Dodge, H. Robert, and Rink, David, "Phasing Sales Strategies and Tactics in Accordance with the Product Life Cycle Dimension Rather Than Calendar Periods," in *Research Frontiers in Marketing: Dialogues and Directions*, Subhash Jain, ed., American Marketing Association, Chicago, 1978.
31. Doyle, Peter, "The Realities of the Product Life Cycle," *Quarterly Review of Marketing* (Summer, 1976): 1–6.
32. Enis, Ben, LaGarce, Raymond, and Prell, Arthur, "Extending the Product Life Cycle," *Business Horizons* 20 (June, 1977): 46–56.
33. Fildes, Robert, and Lofthouse, Stephen, "Market Share Strategy and the Product Life Cycle: A Comment," *Journal of Marketing* 39 (October, 1975): 57–59.
34. Forrester, Jay, "Industrial Dynamics," *Harvard Business Review* 36 (July–August, 1958): 37–66.
35. Forrester, Jay, "Advertising: A Problem in Industrial Dynamics," *Harvard Business Review* 37 (March–April, 1959): 103–11.
36. Fourt, Louis, and Woodlock, Joseph, "Early Prediction of Market Success for New Grocery Products," *Journal of Marketing* 25 (October, 1960): 31–38.
37. Fox, Harold, "Product Life Cycle—An Aid to Financial Administration," *Financial Executive* 41 (April, 1973): 28–34.
38. Fox, Harold, and Rink, David, "Coordination of Purchasing with Sales Trends," *Journal of Purchasing* 13 (Winter, 1977): 10–18.
39. Frederixon, Martin, "An Investigation of the Product Life Cycle Concept and Its Application to New Product Proposal Evaluation within the Chemical Industry," Ph.D. dissertation, Michigan State University, 1969.
40. Headen, Robert, "The Introductory Phases of the Life Cycle for New Grocery Products: Consumer Acceptance and Competitive Behavior," Ph.D. dissertation, Harvard University, Cambridge, 1966.
41. Hinkle, Joel, *Life Cycles*, Nielsen, New York, 1966.
42. King, William, "Early Prediction of New Product Success," *Journal of Advertising Resources* 6 (June, 1966): 8–13.
43. Kotler, Philip, "Phasing Out Weak Products," *Harvard Business Review* 43 (March–April, 1965): 107–118.
44. Kotler, Philip, *Marketing Decision Making: A Model Building Approach,* Holt, Rinehart, and Winston, New York, 1971.

45. Kotler, Philip, *Marketing Management: Analysis, Planning, and Control*, 2nd ed., Prentice-Hall, Englewood Cliffs, N.J., 1972.
46. Kovac, F., and Dague, M., "Forecasting by Product Life Cycle Analysis," *Resources Mananagement* 15 (July, 1972): 66–72.
47. Learner, David, "Profit Maximization Through New Product Marketing Planning and Control," in *Applications of the Sciences in Marketing Management*, Frank Bass, Charles King, and Edgar Pessemier, eds., Wiley, New York, 1968.
48. Levitt, Theodore, "Exploit the Product Life Cycle," *Harvard Business Review* 43 (November–December, 1965): 81–94.
49. Luck, David, and Prell, Arthur, *Market Strategy*, Appleton-Century-Crofts, New York, 1968.
50. McCarthy, E. Jerome, *Basic Marketing: A Managerial Approach*, 4th ed., Richard D.Irwin, Homewood, IL, 1971.
51. Marple, Gary, and Wissman, Harry, eds., *Grocery Manufacturing in the United States*, Praeger, New York, 1968.
52. Marvin, P., "Developing a Balanced Product Portfolio," *Management Review* 48 (April, 1959): 20–26.
53. Massy, William, "Forecasting the Demand for New Convenience Products, *Journal of Marketing Resources* 6 (November, 1969): 405413.
54. May, Charles, "Planning the Marketing Program Throughout the Product Life Cycle," Ph.D. dissertation, Columbia University, New York City, 1961.
55. Mickwitz, Gösta, *Marketing and Competition*, Centraltryckeriet, Helsingfors, 1959.
56. Parsons, Leonard, "The Product Life Cycle and Time-Varying Advertising Elasticities, *Journal of Marketing Resources* 12 (November, 1975): 476–80.
57. Patton, Arch, "Stretch Your Product's Earning Years: Top Management's Stake in the Product Life Cycle," *Management Review* 48 (June, 1959): 9–14, 67–79.
58. Polli, Rolando, *A Test of the Classical Product Life Cycle by Means of Actual Sales Histories*, Ph.D. dissertation, University of Pennsylvania, 1968.
59. Polli, Rolando, and Cook, Victor, "Validity of the Product Life Cycle," *Journal of Business* 42 (October, 1969): 385–400.
60. Rink, David, "The Product Life Cycle in Formulating Purchasing Strategy," *Industrial Marketing Management* 5 (August, 1976): 231–242.
61. Rogers, Everett, *The Diffusion of Innovations*, The Free Press, New York, 1962.
62. Scheuing, Eberhard, "The Product Life Cycle as an Aid in Strategy Decisions," *Management International Review* 9 (1969): 111–124.
63. Smallwood, John, "The Product Life Cycle: A Key to Strategic Marketing Planning," *MSU Business Topics* 21 (Winter, 1973): 29–35.
64. Staudt, Thomas, and Taylor, Donald, *A Managerial Introduction to Marketing*, 2nd ed., Prentice-Hall, Englewood Cliffs, NJ, 1970.
65. Staudt, Thomas, Taylor, Donald, and Bowersox, Donald, *A Managerial Introduction to Marketing*, 3rd ed., Prentice-Hall, Englewood Cliffs, N.J., 1976.
66. Stobaugh, Robert Jr., "The Product Life Cycle, U.S. Exports, and International Investments," Ph.D. dissertation, Harvard Business School, Cambridge, 1968.
67. Thorelli, Hans, "Market Strategy Over the Market Life Cycle," *Bulletin Bureau Market Resources* 26 (September, 1967): 10–22.
68. Urban, Glen, "A New Product Analysis and Decision Model," *Management Science* 14 (April, 1968): 490–517.
69. Wasson, Chester, *Dynamic Competitive Strategy and Product Life Cycles*, revised ed., Challenge Books, St. Charles, 1974.
70. Wilson, Aubrey, "Industrial Marketing Research in Britain," *Journal of Marketing Resources* 6 (February, 1969): 15–28.
71. Wind, Yoram, and Claycamp, Henry, "Planning Product Line Strategy: A Matrix Approach," *Journal of Marketing* 40 (January, 1976): 2–9.

15

The Importance of the Product Life Cycle to the Industrial Marketer

Chester R. Wasson

Different types of industrial product life cycles must be anticipated relative to existing use systems, maintaining a leadership position and strategy changes over time.

BUSINESS LITERATURE has been full of references to "the" product life cycle in recent years, as though there were only one kind of product life cycle, and that the term applied equally to really new products and to minor brand differentiations. Much of this is due to the blinkered eyes of many writers, who are aware of marketing solely in the context of low-priced consumer goods among which the difference is packaging, labeling or mere perception of market position. Differentiation between industrial producers, however, is usually far more substantive, with the result that the marketer must be aware of the real differences in rapidity of market acceptance and of the consequent differences in product life cycles.

Most discussions of the product life cycle deal with heavily advertised consumer goods like beer, breakfast cereals and soap. Far too many confuse brand life cycles (like that for Winston cigarettes) or minor product variants (as for menthol cigarettes or filter tips) with the much more basic product form cycles (like smoking products in general, or for cigarettes as a group). The result is a too simplistic concept of the product life cycle to be of any real planning value for marketing. As a result, many aspects of product acceptance of importance to industrial marketers are overlooked. With few exceptions, discussion has ignored the easily observed wide differences in initial introduction patterns, with the divergences in production planning, financing and planning of marketing strategy that these differences imply. Confusion is added by analyzing what is new entirely in physical terms and judging the degree of revolutionary content in terms of engineering advances rather than that of buyer-perceived performance.

Yet even if we did not have some solid research evidence (which we do), a simple analysis of everyday observation would force us to recognize at least four different kinds of product life cycles, and a number of combinations of these four: slow acceptance cycles, mushrooming acceptance, fashion cycles, and fads. We would quickly realize that the differences are so great that the introductory marketing strategies must also differ in type as well as degree, and perceive that we must find some way to predict probable market acceptance patterns well in advance of market introduction. Fortunately, once we define product offerings in consumer terms, we find a key to such prediction in established knowledge of consumer behavior.

Even with a well-planned launch, a firm can lose its initial advantage if it does not plan to keep ahead of competition and change strategy to parallel changes in consumer habits and perceptions with changes in the phases of the cycle. Pricing and product development strategy can help minimize the intensity of the swarm of competition which will come with accelerating market growth and insure survival of the shakeout which comes with the diminution of the

At the time of this writing Chester R. Wasson was chairman of the Business and Economics program at St. Xavier College, Chicago.

rate of market growth. When the saturation of the mature market is reached, with the resulting stability of competitive positions, the temptation to slack off on the search for product improvements can lose opportunities to start new growth periods by broadening demand, or lead to an earlier than necessary loss of markets to newly developed substitutes. The period of decline always raises the question of when to get out, but the best time for a given firm may even be much earlier.

The Different Types of Industrial Product Life Cycles

The most cursory observation shows that the introductory phase of product life cycles differs radically. Thirty years passed between the initial development of the first man-made fiber—imitation silk, known as rayon today—and the first real spurt in market penetration in the 1920s. By contrast, the first real synthetic fiber, nylon, took off with a bang when it hit the women's hosiery market just before the United States entry into World War II. Likewise, electric typewriters needed over two decades of market development, from initial introduction in 1926, until they began to achieve significant acceptance in the late 1940s, while desktop and hand-held electronic calculators replaced their mechanical predecessors so fast that the makers of the latter lost their market before they could see the threat coming. In the agricultural industry, hybrid corn took more than 10 years to get well established, chlorinated pesticides, starting with DDT, rocketed to heavy use within little more than a year. Monochromatic television had an almost vertical growth, color TV growth scraped bottom for eight very costly years for RCA.

Quite clearly, some ultimately successful product forms require prolonged market development effort and costs before they take off, others attract a mushrooming demand almost from the first. If we take the standard simplistic description of "the" product life cycle as gospel, we will be misled in our plans. That description generally divides the market life cycle into five major phases, as shown in Figure 1:

1. *Introduction, or Market Development*—generally a phase of low growth and deficit investment in sales and promotion.
2. *Rapid Growth*—a period of rapidly accelerating sales, at increasing unit profit.
3. *Decelerating Growth, or Market Turbulence*—unit profits decline and the large number of competitors who have entered during the boom period scramble for a solid niche in the market, with the weakest or least committed shaken out.
4. *Maturity, or Saturation*—a period of relatively stable per capita sales, characterized by a relatively viscous industry structure.
5. *Decline in total market size* as some new substitute proves to do a better job of satisfying customers.

As the exhibit hints, however, some product forms labeled "low learning" do not pass through any prolonged market development phase. Sales rise rapidly almost from the day of introduction, as happened with nylon stockings, electronic calculators and DDT. When this occurs, the introducer must run fast to keep ahead of swarms of competitors slavering over the obvious lush profits (unless a really tight patent bars them). On the other hand, when initial sales are slow, and initial customers must be hunted down, the problem is not competition, but financing the heavy sales and promotional costs, and getting a few select aggressive distributors. As Figure 1 indicates, the fast-start product must be treated from the first with the strategy for the period of rapid growth and this strategy is at odds on almost every point from that for a market development product. Indeed, even the target specifications for the R&D must be different, so as to minimize the learning problem insofar as possible. Since this is so, we need some means of predicting the acceptance climate for any projected product at the concept stage, before any R&D targets are decided upon. We need especially to understand why products which appear to be physically analogous, as do rayon and nylon, electric typewriters and electronic calculators for instance, meet such different market receptions.

Attention to physical similarities leaves us confused. Both rayon and nylon were introduced as continuous fibers, as substitutes for silk. Electric typewriters and desktop calculators both had at least a superficial resemblance to their predecessors, did similar tasks, and were operated in much the same ways. From an engineering point of view, the electric typewriter was a mere evolutionary change, the electronic calculator, a revolutionary one. Both rayon and nylon were, for their days, revolutionary advances, although rayon turned out to be quite similar to a fiber at whose market it was not initially aimed (cotton).

The fog begins to dissipate, however, when we consider these and other seemingly contradictory pairs of introductions from the standpoint of the buyer, when we consider what they promised to do for him and to him. To the potential buyer, any offering of any sort is merely a promise that he can gain fulfillment of a bundle of felt needs—it is merely a set of performance characteristics fitting into some kind of total use-system which is the real source of need satisfaction. Whether the buyer is a housewife purchasing a box of laundry detergent or an industrial organization deciding on a raw material, manufacturing equipment, or an office machine, the proffered item is simply a possible key component of some specific use-system. The purchase decision will be based on how well the satisfaction bundle offered meets a corresponding desire-set, and on what changes must be made in his habits of action and thought involved in the use-system in order to gain the promised performance bundle.

Products as Parts of Use-Systems

Spinners and weavers are not seeking textile fibers. They simply want some way, preferably a familiar one, to produce a finished textile desired by converters and garment makers who buy later on. The latter desire a profitable means of

Figure 1

Dynamic Competitive Strategy and the Market Life Cycle

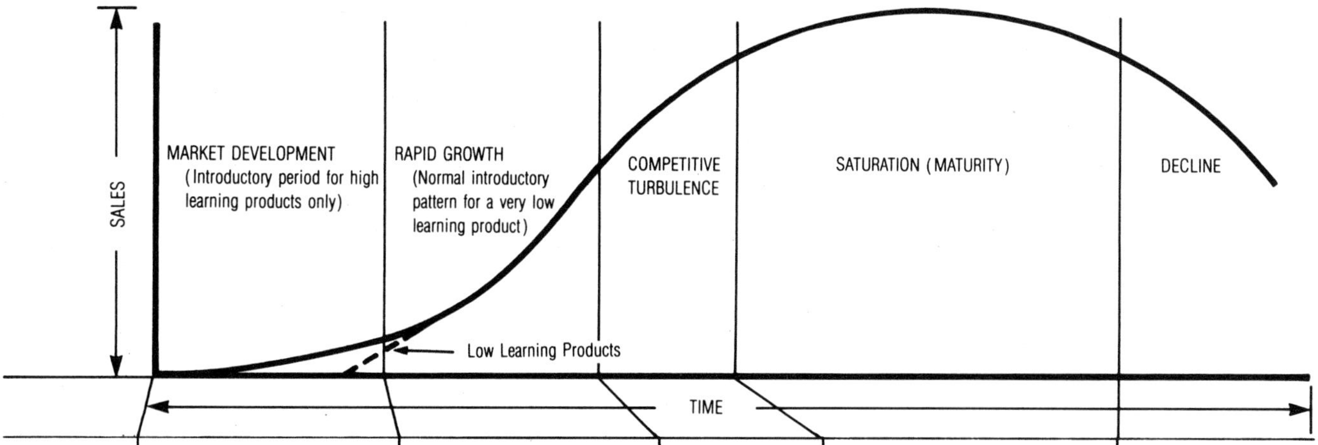

SALES

MARKET DEVELOPMENT (Introductory period for high learning products only)

RAPID GROWTH (Normal introductory pattern for a very low learning product)

COMPETITIVE TURBULENCE

SATURATION (MATURITY)

DECLINE

Low Learning Products

TIME

	MARKET DEVELOPMENT	RAPID GROWTH	COMPETITIVE TURBULENCE	SATURATION (MATURITY)	DECLINE
STRATEGY OBJECTIVE	Minimize learning requirements, locate and remedy offering defects quickly, develop widespread awareness of benefits, and gain trial by early adopters	To establish a strong brand market and distribution niche as quickly as possible	To maintain and strengthen the market niche achieved through dealer and consumer loyalty	To defend brand position against competing brands and product category against other potential products, through constant attention to product improvement opportunities and fresh promotional and distribution approaches	To milk the offering dry of all possible profit
OUTLOOK FOR COMPETITION	None is likely to be attracted in the early, unprofitable stages	Early entrance of numerous aggressive emulators	Price and distribution squeeze on the industry, shaking out the weaker entrants	Competition stabilized, with few or no new entrants and market shares not subject to substantial change in the absence of a substantial perceived improvement in some brand	Similar competition declining and dropping out because of decrease in consumer interest
PRODUCT DESIGN OBJECTIVE	Limited number of models with physical product and offering designs both focused on minimizing learning requirements. Designs cost- and use-engineered to appeal to most receptive segment. Utmost attention to quality control and quick elimination of market-revealed defects in design	Modular design to facilitate flexible addition of variants to appeal to every new segment and new use-system as fast as discovered	Intensified attention to product improvement, tightening up of line to eliminate unnecessary specialties with little market appeal	A constant alert for market pyramiding opportunities through either bold cost- and price-penetration of new markets or major product changes. Introduction of flanker products. Constant attention to possibilities for product improvement and cost cutting. Reexamination of necessity of design compromises	Constant pruning of line to eliminate any items not returning a direct profit
PRICING OBJECTIVE	To impose the minimum of value perception learning and to match the value reference perception of the most receptive segments. High trade discounts and sampling advisable	A price line for every taste, from low-end to premium models Customary trade discounts Aggressive promotional pricing, with prices cut as fast as costs decline due to accumulated production experience Intensification of sampling	Increased attention to market-broadening and promotional pricing opportunities	Defensive pricing to preserve product category franchise. Search for incremental pricing opportunities, including private label contracts, to boost volume and gain an experience advantage	Maintenance of profit level pricing with complete disregard of any effect on market share
PROMOTIONAL GUIDELINES Communications objectives	a) Create widespread awareness and understanding of offering benefits b) Gain trial by early adopters	Create and strengthen brand preference among trade and final users Stimulate general trial	Maintain consumer franchise and strengthen dealer ties	Maintain consumer and trade loyalty, with strong emphasis on dealers and distributors. Promotion of greater use frequency	Phase out, keeping just enough to maintain profitable distribution
Most valuable media mix	In order of value: Publicity Personal sales Mass communications	Mass media Personal sales Sales promotion, including sampling Publicity	Mass media Dealer promotions Personal selling to dealers Sales promotions Publicity	Mass media Dealer-oriented promotions	Cut down all media to the bone – use no sales promotions of any kind
DISTRIBUTION POLICY	Exclusive or selective, with distributor margins high enough to justify heave promotional spending	Intensive and extensive, with dealer margins just high enough to keep them interested. Close attention to rapid resupply of distributor stocks and heavy inventories at all levels	Intensive and extensive, and a strong emphasis on keeping dealer well supplied, but with minimum inventory cost to him	Intensive and extensive, with strong emphasis on keeping dealer well supplied, but at minimum inventory cost to him	Phase out outlets as they become marginal
INTELLIGENCE FOCUS	To identify actual developing use-systems and to uncover any product weakness	Detailed attention to brand position, to gaps in model and market coverage, and to opportunities for market segmentation	Close attention to product improvement needs, to market-broadening chances, and to possible fresh promotion themes	Intensified attention to possible product improvements. Sharp alert for potential new inter-product competition and for signs of beginning product decline	Information helping to identify the point at which the product should be phased out

 Based on Wasson, *Dynamic Competitive Strategy and Product Life Cycles,* Challenge Books, St. Charles, Il. 1974.

producing dresses, shirts, stockings and other garments which are attractive to final customers in terms of their own standards of protection and decoration.

At every stage in the purchase chain, the item purchased produces the result desired only in conjunction with an habitual system of procedures, and usually in the context of an habitual intellectual system of thought about the way things are done. The physical use-systems usually involve other products, often other persons (in industry, nearly always), and always a developed system of habitual skills. Accompanying most such systems are one or more of three systems of intellectual perceptual habits: perceptions of the expected satisfaction sources, perceptions of the social role of the user in relation to the product, and perceptions of the value of a given kind of satisfaction.

Psychological experiments long ago demonstrated what we all know—habit systems take time and energy to develop. The change in any habit sequence is a frustrating, effort-consuming process. Anyone who has ever made even a minor change of switching over from a car with a 3-speed transmission to one with a 4-speed shift can sympathize with the rats in a psychological experiment now 50 years old. They needed more than twice as many trials to learn a simple switch in the location of food in the arms of a T-maze than they needed to learn the original location. The old habit had to be broken before the new one could be perfected.

We should thus expect that introductions which require changes in accepted habits of either use or perceptual habits will be adopted reluctantly. And we would expect to find that products which are accepted with enthusiasm to be those which fit neatly into established systems of use and perception and also promise a substantially better level of performance in some way. Such indeed proves to be a key to understanding the different receptions in the product pairs cited above, and to all other new product experiences the author has been able to analyze.

Consider the cases of rayon and nylon. Rayon was first intended to be a truly man-made silk (the inventor used mulberry leaves as his raw material), and for about 40 years was sold only in continuous filament form, largely for knitted goods. But although labeled initially as artificial silk, it was not really like silk, either to manufacture or use. It felt different to the hand, handled differently in processing and dyeing. It began to build a market only when given its own name, rayon, in the early 1920s, then given the needed heavy promotional backing, with strong technical assistance to processors. The big gains came with a physical change in the product—the introduction of staple (cut) fiber, adaptable to cotton processes. Ironically, it then displaced silk in a major use—women's better dresses. In the Sear's 1929 catalogue for example, all of the better dresses were silk. In the 1939 edition all of them were made of rayon.

Nylon, on the other hand, was not released for sale until processing problems were solved, and then backed up with strong technical assistance and promoted for use in a product making the greatest use of its major tensile strength and wear characteristics—women's hosiery. Since the appearance qualities were at least as good as those of silk stockings, and the durability greater, and since the intervening processors had little trouble adapting, it was an instant smash success (interrupted by the wartime diversion of the fiber to more critical substitute uses in parachutes and other military needs).

The electric typewriter may not, at first glance, seem to pose any major habit change problem. The keyboard was the same, and operated in a similar manner. In fact, however, it required the typist to change the positioning of her hands. Any trained typist had developed the habit of resting her fingers on the middle alphabetical row. With the electric, she had to keep all fingers off all keys until ready to strike. The merest brushing of a key in passing would actuate it. The result was that the best of typists had to go through a substantial period of spoiled copy until she broke her old hand positioning habit—usually an average of two months. Since speed and accuracy were key items in her skill, this was a completely unacceptable price except for the few to whom the small extra uniformity of copy was of very high value. The market share of the electrics was minor until typists began to be taught initially on the electrics, then had problems changing to the heavier feel of typing on the manual machines.

The desktop calculator is a subsidiary tool for most users, and skill and speed in its use not a basic element in the job success. What minor operational differences the electronic versions posed relative to their mechanical predecessors were not significant, and would not disturb well-ingrained habits. Thus, performance-wise, they were simply an improvement in portability and in computational flexibility, even though they were completely revolutionary in terms of the mechanism under the housing. Thus they gained ready acceptance.

Likewise, hybrid corn was really a very minor innovation in terms of the product (dating back, in fact, to the early Indian practice of maintaining several separate strains). But from the farmer's point of view, it changed operation and financing habits drastically. Before, he had simply saved some of the previous crop and used it for the next year's planting. But now he had to dispose of the entire crop and buy new seed at a per-unit cost several times the per bushel price he received for his crop. DDT, on the other hand, was simply another chemical used in much the same way as those he had bought and used before, but more efficient.

Clearly, we must look beyond the physical product itself to make a critical prediction of what a proposed introduction does to user habits if we are to plan a successful introductory market strategy, or even set the correct targets for R&D.

All of the examples used above involved a change in physical procedures, and these can be predicted rather well by the use of simple flow diagrams comparing the step-by-step procedures required in the use-system of the old way of gaining the end desired and the new way required by the proposed introduction. However, products may also involve intellectual habits of valuation of benefits, such as understanding that a more expensive product may be cheaper in use, or accepting a changed role in the production process. Computer typesetting, for example, was certain of a very hostile reception from the lithographers because it downgraded their role in printing. It made original headway best in new enterprises outside union jurisdiction.[1]

Gaining and Holding First Place

As the figure indicates, competition is not the main problem to be met during the introductory phase of a high learning product. The initiator usually has the market to himself, in fact. Whether or not others enter at this point, the crucial problems are appropriate design for initial customer needs, especially reliability and freedom from annoying defects, and education of the potential market.

With low-earning products, vigorous competition must be expected early, and every aspect of planning focussed on keeping well ahead of any newcomers. The first on the market has an advantage in terms of the learning curve, but can easily lose it. Bowmar had the initial advantage in the hand-held electronic computer market, only to lose it through lack of production expertise and economies when aggressive integrated producers came in. IBM was the second maker of computers, not the first, but took over the market because it perceived the need for software libraries and technical assistance as part of the bundle offered. None of the original labels on the automobile market survived the first phase of market growth, and Ford, who introduced the first low-priced utility design lost the market dominance he attained when he refused to follow the emerging market segmentation of the rapid growth phase in the second and third decades, with design variations.

Competitors can enter at any stage except possibly the one that does not matter—the decline phase. They will succeed to the extent that those already established leave open some areas of unfulfilled customer demand. The pattern of demand changes with changes in market maturity, so that every element of strategy must be constantly planned in advance to leave as few openings as possible for competition.

Strategy Must Change with the Cycle

During the rapid growth stage, pricing, product design, and distribution service are all critical. By this time, accumulated production experience will begin to cut unit costs substantially, and burgeoning demand will also cut into per-unit promotional costs and even the necessary distribution margins. Too many firms tend to let price cuts lag decreases in cost during this period, offering a luscious bait that will attract competitors from far and near. If prices are allowed to fall in concert with costs, experience has shown that added competition will be much less strong. Any weakness in distributive availability will cause distributors to encourage the entrance of new suppliers in order to promote their own profits. During this period, also, market demand tends to become differentiated, with both low end and premium segments becoming developed, as well as the need for other kinds of design variations. Even in the absence of a too high profit expectation, some alert enterprisers will find these potential market niches and develop them.

All of these forces tend to create a tendency for the industry as a whole to build capacity which cannot be fully utilized once growth begins to slow down, and some competitors must be shaken out. Those who survive will be those who have developed the strongest relations with final customers and distributors.

By the time the market shakes down into its saturation or maturity stage, the niche of each of the remaining suppliers has become fairly stable. Buyers' perceptions and expectations of each have become fairly well fixed. The core elements of each market segment have found offerings coming very close to their desire-sets and so are neither searching for new suppliers nor paying much attention to promotion of other offerings. Promotion should be primarily aimed at maintaining distribution, at keeping current market segments satisfied, and, of course, attracting the attention of any new buyers coming onto the market. Market entry and market share change become costly simply because customers have no incentive to seek new sources. Nevertheless, market entrance and market share gains, at a profit, are possible to whoever can develop an offering really perceived by buyers as a very substantially greater value to some segment of the market.

If it is to hope for success, any new entry into a saturated market must be perceived by some major market segment as a really substantial improvement in value of some kind over existing offerings; either a substantial gain in the perceived benefit content of the offering as compared to those currently available, a substantial gain in the ratio of those benefits desired to price, or a benefit in terms of purchase ease and availability. Except when the promotion causes buyers to perceive substantial new benefits, added promotional pressure alone is seldom effective.

The most certain route to market entry or market share gains during maturity is that of making a perceived major improvement in the offering. No product is ever likely to do everything the customer desires, at a price he feels worth paying. Furthermore, the market segment attracted by every offering always has fringe buyers who find nothing on the market very close to their desire set. Thus there is nearly always a potential new market niche which can be brought into being by designing an offering that nibbles off the edges of several segments. Changes in consumer desires over time as well as changes in the state of the art open possibilities of winning over large segments. Indeed, the decline of every life cycle is brought about by the revolutionary changes in the state of the art which create better substitute offerings. The corollary of this fact is that R&D focussed on diminution of the natural defects in the offering can raise the barriers to substitute offerings. The steel industry would not have lost as much container business to aluminum, paper and plastics in the 1960s had the industry worked as hard to develop thinner tinplate, before the substitute came in, as they did afterward. Customers would have had less incentive to change their habitual processes. It should be noted that such customer habits give the established source of supply a very substantial protection. Copper cable, for example, had lost only one-third of its utility market by the time aluminum had dropped to less than two-thirds the cost of an equivalent copper capacity cable. But none of the utilities which went through the effort of changing their procedures ever changed back.

Changes in the benefit/cost ratio, provided they are truly perceived as really substantial, can always win substantial market segments. This, after all, is the basic principal behind every merchant's sales promotions. Some of this may be achieved, where production costs permit, by a substantial permanent cut in the price level of a product with an established market position. (But let it be noted that a new entrant, without the established reputation, which offers only a lower price, is very likely to be perceived as simply a lower-end quality.)

Changes in the customers' evaluation of components of the offering, which may come with the maturation of the market itself may open up such opportunities to offer a better benefit/cost ratio for the new desire sets of major market segments in the case of products which needed substantial elements of sales and market services in the introductory stage. Once the consumer is well educated on the product, he may have no further interest in such costly services and be open to a supplier who eliminates them from the offering bundle at an appropriate cost savings.

Such seems to have been the situation when the life cycle of polyethylene resins reached saturation. While the original producers maintained their technical research staffs, and the accompanying costs, sellers whose sales operation consisted of only a price list and a telephone captured a substantial market share at prices below the costs of the product-plus-service package the major producers were still offering. By this time, many buyers no longer had need for new know-how, and many had developed some special technical knowledge they did not care to make available to suppliers who might pass it on to competitors. Such experiences make it obvious that sellers must keep in touch with the changing nature of customer desire-sets at every stage of the cycle, and be prepared to adjust the offering accordingly.

Distribution availability is an important part of the value of any offering, industrial or consumer, but often of more crucial importance to the industrial buyer than to the consumer to whom many nearly identical substitutes are often freely available. A mere advantage in availability may win customers. In the crowded industrial fastener market, one small producer used this means to win a profitable share. His sales force consisted of nothing more than his telephone and a monthly newsletter and price list of readily available items. But in addition, he kept himself available by telephone, day or night, and in the case of emergency, would go immediately to the factory floor, change over machines to any special set-up necessary, and get a critical shipment out by plane the next morning if necessary. He gained a substantial volume from customers of the largest suppliers.

Sometimes the distributor himself can be the critical element of added value needed for market penetration, if he has an established reputation for quality and dependability. This is one reason an established seller of a line of products can often succeed with another item new only to him, and also a reason that the quality of the distributors used can be critical in gaining a strong niche during the growth phase of the market. For instance when a maker of oil seals, with a strong distributive position, decided that the market for 0-rings was becoming attractive, it discovered that an established maker of high quality rings had a weak distributive acceptance, and simply made an agreement to take over the latter's marketing operation instead of going into production. Because of the seal makers' reputation, the first order alone paid for his cataloguing of the item, to the advantage of both firms.

The Dangers of Going to Sleep

The relative stability of the mature market tends to induce a dangerous degree of somnolence on the part of the established firms. There is a dangerous reluctance to "obsolete our own product," with a coincident slackening of attention to possible new improvements in the state of the art which could create new pyramided growth phases by broadening or changing the nature of the demand. Whenever the established firms do this, they leave themselves vulnerable to competition which does not have their commitment to the status quo.

Good examples are the effects of the development of transistors and their more complicated successors on the established makers of electronic appliances, later on the makers of office calculators, and most recently on the watch industry. Bell lab's development of the original transistors was initially ignored by both the major makers of radios and television sets, and even by the military in the United States. The result was the dominance of Japanese firms who had no vested interest in tube electronics. When integrated circuit chips made the compact hand-held calculator possible, the makers of mechanical devices left the R&D and the market to outsiders. At the moment, the major producers of mechanical watches seem to have made the same mistake.

Eventually, of course, the progress of knowledge will lead to some means of obsoleting any product, and decline will set in. At this point, some decision must be made as to when and how to quit.

When to Get Out

Any product whose market is declining is an obvious candidate for elimination. But the exact timing of that exit will depend on the situation of the individual firm, and the market exit may be advisable at some earlier point in the cycle, for some firms. The only general rule is that the firm should withdraw from the market whenever the resources employed would earn a better opportunity profit in some alternate line of activity. For some, this will mean dropping out even before the product is launched on the market, preferably by selling the rights to someone better equipped to develop that market. This is, after all, the choice of most book authors, and it enables them to draw an income before there are any profits, or even when some never come. Even the largest of firms may so choose if the product does not fit their capabilities, they lack the patience to wait out a development period, or lack the aggressive promotional skills to survive the mushrooming growth of the market for a low-learning product. At the other end of the life cycle, there is often room for a well-situated firm to profit from the residual demand from those reluctant to adopt the product's successor. There is still profit to be made by small firms in selling buggies to the Amish, for example.

Whatever the timing decision, the resources devoted to a declining product can and should be minimized. Promotional effort is almost completely ineffective, so marketing costs can be very low. Sometimes, of course, what is obsolete in one market may be what another requires. In the field of processing machinery, batch process equipment which is out-of-date in an advanced country may be best adapted to the needs of one in an earlier stage of technological development.

At every stage in the cycle, market opportunities and profits are functions of consumer habits and needs at that time and in that place. The changes in these which come inexorably with every turn of a calendar page require corresponding changes in market strategy.

Reference

1. For a discussion of methods of predicting the learning requirement, see Wasson, C. R., *Dynamic Competitive Strategy and Product Life Cycles*, pp. 199–207. Challenge Books, St. Charles, IL,1974.

16

Competitive Effects on Technology Diffusion

Thomas S. Robertson & Hubert Gatignon

This article seeks to derive an enriched model for the study of technological diffusion at the organizational level.

This article takes as its central concern the diffusion of high technology innovation among business organizations. A set of propositions is developed that focuses on the competitive factors influencing diffusion. The article suggests how the supply-side competitive environment and the adopter industry competitive environment both affect diffusion of new technologies. The article seeks to extend the current behavioral paradigm for studying innovation diffusion by incorporating competitive factors as explanatory variables.

DIFFUSION RESEARCH within marketing is nested primarily in the behavioral domain. Consumer behavior researchers have adopted the paradigm of Rogers (1983) without much qualification. Research on diffusion has tended to focus at the individual consumer level, and the number of research projects focusing on organizational adoption of innovations is reasonably limited (Baker and Parkinson 1977; Cooper 1979; Czepiel 1976; Robertson and Wind 1980; Webster 1969; Zaltman, Duncan, and Holbek 1973). Similarly, most research has been on reasonably low technology products, with the exception of such work as that of Czepiel (1974), Dickerson and Gentry (1983), Hirschman (1980), and Leonard-Barton (1985).

This article seeks to extend the extant conceptualization for research within marketing on the diffusion of innovations. The objective is to derive an enriched model for the study of *technological diffusion* at the *organizational level*. The theoretical base of the article will be on *competitive behavior* (Weitz 1985), and we will suggest a number of propositions as to how both the supply-side competitive environment and the adopter industry competitive environment affect the diffusion of innovations. Since most of the propositions are derived from other fields of inquiry—particularly economics and organizational behavior—the evidentiary base for consumer behavior is limited.

To the extent that competitive variables have been pursued in diffusion research within marketing, it has been almost exclusively within the *diffusion modeling* domain (Bass 1969; Mahajan and Muller 1979). For example, a number of recent models, which are empirically estimated, have included marketing mix variables, such as advertising, price, and personal selling (Bass 1980; Horsky and Simon 1983; Lilien, Rao, and Kalish 1981; Simon and Sebastian 1982), and have demonstrated the impact of these factors on diffusion rates. In a sense, these are competitive variables since the levels are determined relative to competitive levels, for example, pricing decisions or advertising-to-sales ratios. However, explicit consideration of competitive factors has only been included in analytical diffusion models (Mate 1982; Rao and Bass 1985; Teng and Thompson 1983; Thompson and Teng 1984). Empirical research on diffusion from a behavioral perspective has almost totally ignored competitive factors.

Thomas S. Robertson is a Professor of Marketing and Hubert Gatignon is a Professor of Marketing, The Wharton School, University of Pennsylvania

A Competitive Behavior Paradigm

A diffusion paradigm stressing competitive factors is shown in Figure 1. The most important distinguishing characteristics of this paradigm, versus the Rogers (1983) paradigm, are twofold. First, *the competitive environment of suppliers*

Figure 1
A competitive behavior paradigm for technology diffusion among organizations

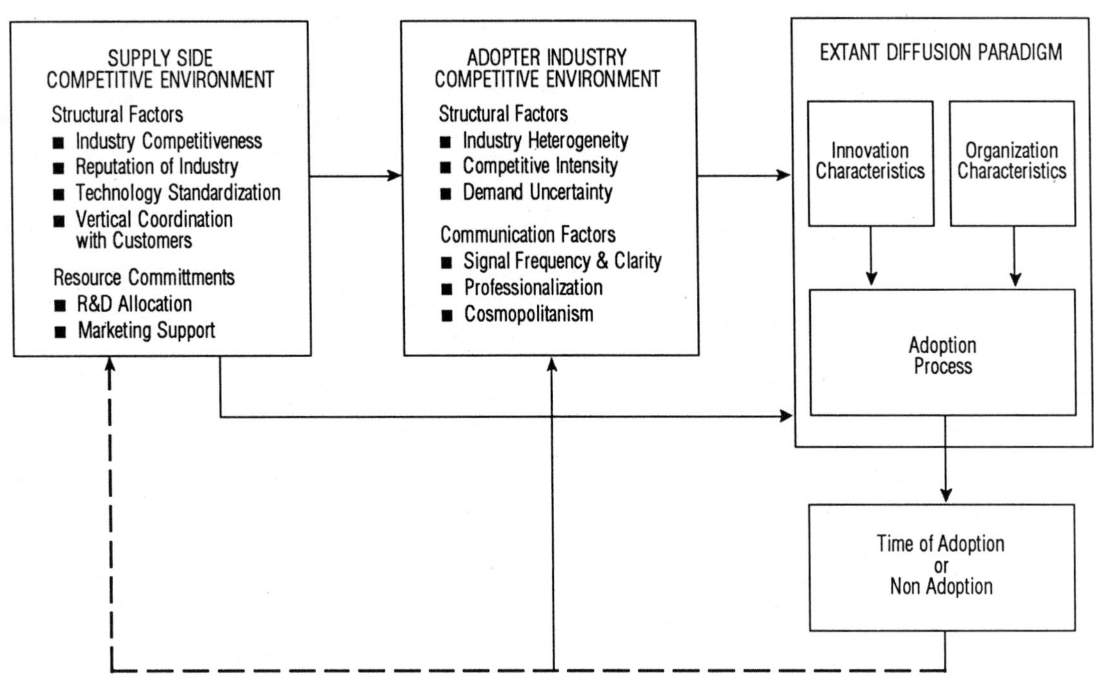

is explicitly linked to the adoption/diffusion process. The structural characteristics of the industry and the resource commitments of supplier firms are shown as determinants of the rate of diffusion. Researchers familiar with diffusion theory within marketing will recognize that supply-side factors have not been pursued in diffusion research. Indeed, to a very large extent most research seems to assume that there is only one firm supplying the innovation—a condition which rarely holds.

Secondly, *the competitive environment among potential adopters* is important in determining receptivity to innovation. Adopter industry variables, such as industry competitiveness, heterogeneity, and return on investment, have been pursued in economics (Mansfield 1968; Stoneman 1981) and organizational behavior research (Kimberly and Evanisko 1981), but the level of conceptualization and research within marketing is meager. This may be due to the belief that competitive variables account for a smaller share of the variance than innovation characteristics and adopter category factors. The lack of research, however, may also be due to a bias among behavioral researchers toward studying only consumer characteristics and not competitive factors.

A description of the enhanced organizational diffusion model is as follows. Diffusion occurs within the boundaries of an industry. The diffusion pattern at the industry level is the outcome of the distribution of individual firm adoption decisions. These individual firm adoption decisions are influenced by the compatibility between the innovation's characteristics and those of the potential adopting unit. Adoption is further influenced and mediated by the supply-side competitive environment and the adopter industry competitive environment.

The objectives now will be to develop a set of propositions for research on organizational diffusion focused on the supply-side and adopter industry variables and to propose some research considerations. First, however, we shall clarify our focus on technological innovations, since this is the thrust of our concern.

Technological Innovations

Many innovations utilize "technology." Our interest, however, is in new products, services, or systems which utilize technology and which are perceived to have significant consequences for existing production or consumption patterns. This type of innovation has often been referred to as a "discontinuous" innovation, that is, an innovation which alters existing patterns of production or consumption or creates new patterns of consumption (Robertson 1971). Examples are microcomputers, electronic mail, or video recording.

The key to defining innovations is the perception of the product among potential adopters. An innovation may be "high technology" from the supplier's vantage point, but if it is not perceived by customers as altering and improving their business functions—that is, a discontinuous innovation —then it is not of interest in the present context. Here, we shall use the term *technological innovations* as synonymous with discontinuous innovations. We are interested in these high technology products which, according to Shanklin and Ryans (1984), have the potential to "create or revolutionize markets and demand" (p. 166).

Technological innovations are generally complex products, possessing attributes with which the potential adopting unit may be unfamiliar. Because of this unfamiliarity, the adopting unit does not have a knowledge structure that can be used to evaluate and make judgments about the product. High technology innovations are typically costly in monetary terms and have high switching costs. The uncertainty about these consequences and about the innovation itself assumes a major importance in the organization's adoption decision process. The severity of the learning requirement for the potential adopting unit makes it difficult to forecast diffusion rates, since it may be necessary to educate potential customers about the new technology before they can evaluate it and render a judgment and a statement of intention to purchase (Wilton and Pessemier 1981).

The concern in the present case is with the adoption of technologies by business firms. These technologies may be designed to provide cost reductions in the production, distribution, or marketing processes. They may also provide a means for producing higher quality or innovative products that afford new benefits for the firm's consumers or allow the firm to reach new market segments. Flexible automation, for example, would seem to have the potential to offer more highly targeted innovations for specific subsegments of the market (Boston Consulting Group 1985).

Because of the emphasis on these technological innovations (process or products), adoption is not the only relevant concern of diffusion research. The *degree of use* of that technology is also an important variable that describes the extent of diffusion of that innovation. Rogers (1985) presents some evidence that a significant number of adopters of a communication technology use the innovation very little. Although throughout the following discussion the focus is on diffusion, we refer to *depth of usage* as well as *time of adoption* in characterizing diffusion.

Supply-Side Factors Affecting Diffusion

The suppliers of a new technology affect the diffusion potential and speed of diffusion based on their actions in determining the characteristics of the innovation and its pricing and in allocating resources to the innovation. This perspective is in many ways contrary to the prevalent focus of marketing research on diffusion of innovations, which has been conducted mainly by consumer behavior researchers utilizing the Rogers (1983) paradigm. Existing research tends to ignore how supply-side competitive actions change the diffusion process.

Diffusion theory is quite incomplete unless it recognizes the proactive nature of these actions. In fact, it is an anomaly that diffusion research in marketing has focused so much on consumer behavior and so little on competitive behavior. For the most part, research takes the innovation as a given and studies the innovation's compatibility with the consumer group leading to an adoption decision. A direct relationship seems to be assumed between customer characteristics and adoption decisions. As a result, the most common form of empirical research has been to study the characteristics of product category innovators.

Recent modeling of the diffusion process has seized the initiative and explicitly considered supply-side factors affecting diffusion levels. In particular, resource allocations to marketing have been modeled in order to forecast the shape of the diffusion process (Bass 1980; Dolan and Jeuland 1981; Horsky and Simon 1983; Robinson and Fornell 1985).

Supply-Side Structural Factors

The structural characteristics of the industry offering the innovation affect the speed of diffusion and the total market potential realized. The competitiveness of the supplier industry, the reputation of supplier firms, the competitive standardization of the technology, and the level of vertical coordination all affect the speed of diffusion. It might also be argued that the organizational culture of the industry and its participant firms affects innovativeness, but given the limited research base (Cherian and Deshpande 1985; Robertson and Wind 1980), this approach will not be developed here.

Competitiveness. Industry competitiveness is generally assessed by the number of competitors, the concentration ratios, and the mobility barriers which competitors are able to erect (Porter 1980). These measures of competitiveness are interrelated and, in turn, affect competitor resource allocations and pricing philosophies (Eliashberg and Chatterjee 1985a; Gatignon 1984). It is our thesis that high levels of supplier competitive intensity lead to more rapid diffusion and the achievement of higher levels of market penetration for the innovation (Brown 1981).

Under high competitive intensity, greater resource allocations and more aggressive pricing policies are likely to materialize, thus encouraging more rapid diffusion. These competitive effects have been reported in the strategic literature (Abell and Hammond 1979). Highly competitive periods correspond to industry "shake-outs;" price wars are likely to occur when sales growth is at a peak. This phenomenon is formalized by Eliashberg and Jeuland (1986), where, through an analytic model, it is shown that prices go down after a new entry, and demand increases as a result of price sensitivity.

At a later stage of the product life cycle, competitive intensity remains high, but producers will be much more focused on secondary demand than on primary demand. Experience curve pricing will drive down industry price levels and bring more customers into the market at a faster pace (Bass 1980). By the same token, however, high competitive intensity is likely to limit the market penetration level for any individual supplier (Karnani 1983).

> *Proposition 1: The greater the competitive intensity of the supplier group, the more rapid the diffusion and the higher the diffusion level.*

Reputation. Supplier reputation may be a somewhat elusive concept. However, particularly when a supplier group is in competition with another supplier group, reputation may be quite important. Given the availability of substitutes, as in paper versus plastic or synthetic versus natural fibers, the reputation of the supplier industry is important. By reputation is meant established relationships and confidence among potential adopters (Berger 1985).

The notion of reputation was developed by Nelson (1970, 1974) as a function of the nature of the product. Nelson makes a distinction between search and experience goods: the quality of search goods can be verified, which is not possible for experience goods. Satterthwaite (1979) reinforces this notion, arguing that even after purchase, quality is difficult to judge. This leads Shapiro (1983) to suggest that sellers might establish reputation upon entry by selling a high quality product, even below cost, and then enjoy the benefits of that reputation.

The thesis is that high reputation supplier groups will achieve faster initial diffusion, although the eventual shape of the diffusion curve and the market potential realized will ultimately depend on the technology and not on supplier reputation. It may also be that for high reputation firms, the source credibility that operates leads to greater source dependence and less operation of interorganizational influence. In particular, borrowing from communications theory, a high reputation supplier will generate a faster penetration rate when there are uncertainties about the new product's performance. Then, the credibility of the supplier mediates uncertainty by potential clients. However, if there is little uncertainty about the performance of the innovation, which would occur mostly for continuous innovations, then reputation might not be a competitive advantage..

Proposition 2: The more favorable the reputation of the supplier group, the more rapid the initial diffusion.

Technology standardization. The speed of diffusion can be enhanced by reasonable standardization of a technology or retarded if competing standards prevail. This is Abernathy and Utterback's (1978) concept of *dominant design.* This factor is particularly important for high technology products, especially those dependent on software and auxiliary components, such as VCRs, computers, and automated tellers (ATMs).

Customer resistance may be a function of the perceived risk of buying a product that may turn out to be the wrong standard. Customer behavior, therefore, suggests that the sooner the industry attains standardization on a dominant design, the more rapid the diffusion process, since customers will be more receptive to the innovation as the perceived risk of buying the wrong standard declines.

There are also positive benefits of standardization, particularly if there is a "network externality" such that a consumer's value for a product increases when other consumers have compatible products—as in telephones or personal computer software (Farrell and Saloner 1985). Rogers (1985) illustrates this thesis with communication technologies. At the extreme, there is no value in being a single adopter, such as with a telephone; the technology is only useful if other adopters exist and if the technologies are standardized. Therefore, technology standardization is a condition for the diffusion of these innovations. In addition, diffusion is a function of the existing mass of current adopters.

Standardization should also have the effect of reducing price levels in the market, thus speeding diffusion. Standardization on a dominant design allows firms industrywide to take advantage of experience curve effects. A standard of technology also reduces product differentiation among suppliers, thus heightening price competition (Farrell and Saloner 1985) and, quite likely, the price levels of replacement parts. The disadvantage of standardization, according to Farrell and Saloner, may be that it can "trap" an industry if it adheres to an absolute or inferior standard when better standards may become available.

Proposition 3: The more standardized the technology, the more rapid the diffusion.

Vertical coordination. In industries where suppliers and customers have a high degree of vertical dependence; such as airframe manufacturers and airlines, there may be a propensity to coordination and interlocking relationship (Palmer 1983; Schoorman, Bazerman, and Atkin 1981). It would be expected that a high degree of vertical coordination is positively associated with more rapid diffusion by increasing the flow of information. This relationship may be demonstrated in the medical equipment and drug industries where interlocks between suppliers and leading edge teaching hospitals advance the acceptance of medical innovations.

Vertical coordination provides access to external informational environments, which are focused and potentially valuable information sources. Such boundary spanning activities (Aiken and Hage 1972) have been found to be positively associated with organizational innovativeness (Kimberly 1978). There is also some preliminary evidence that vertical coordination is more likely to occur under environmental uncertainty. The logic is that as an organization's environment becomes more turbulent, vertical coordination will help an organization 'to gather, analyze, and act on relevant information" (Galaskiewicz 1985, p. 288). However, transaction cost analysis argues that vertical coordination is the appropriate response to uncertainty *only* in the presence of transaction-specific assets to be acquired by the contractual partners (Anderson 1985; Williamson 1979).

A potentially useful extension of the vertical coordination concept is Von Hippel's (1984) notion of "lead users," which he defines as "individuals or firms who have needs which are not now prevalent among users of a given product, but which can be predicted to become general and to constitute a commercially interesting market in the future" (p. 8). These customers, "who face tomorrow's needs today," can be instrumental in identifying new product opportunities, testing new product prototypes, and providing opinion leadership for later adopters. If such lead users can be identified, they can be linked to a manufacturer as an extension of the R&D/marketing process in order to speed technological acceptance and diffusion.

Proposition 4: The greater the vertical coordination between suppliers and customers, the more rapid the diffusion.

Supply-Side Resource Commitments

The allocation of resources which a supplier industry makes to a new technology will have a major bearing on the speed of diffusion. Both resource commitments to (1) ongoing R&D and (2) marketing programs will positively affect diffusion potential.

R&D resource allocation. It has been documented that there is a positive relationship between research and development commitments and the invention/innovation process (Kamien and Schwartz 1982). Greater expenditures in R&D lead to enhanced technologies and, we assume, a more rapid rate of new product introductions by the industry. There is also some evidence that rivalry within an industry stimulates R&D output (Grabowski and Baxter 1973). Existing theory and research tend to suggest that R&D performance is maximized at a degree of industry concentration between pure monopoly and perfect competition (Hambrick and MacMillan 1985; Loury 1979).

Our interest is somewhat different—not in the rate of innovation but in the rate of diffusion. It is our thesis that greater expenditures in R&D by supplier firms will lead to enhanced technologies and a greater range of technological alternatives, which, in turn, will lead to more rapid diffusion and to broader diffusion (Mansfield 1982). McGuinness and Little (1981), for example, have found that intensity of technological effort exerted by an industry is associated with a greater proportion of its output that is exported to other countries, that is, a broader diffusion profile. This is compatible with the Vernon (1971) research stream which indicates that the strength of U.S. exports is in the development of differentiated laborsaving technologies of a price-inelastic nature.

In the domestic market, the enriched technological stream of products offered as a result of high R&D allocations should better meet the range of consumer needs by market segment. This should expand the market potential and lead to more rapid diffusion.

> *Proposition 5: The greater the allocation of R&D resources within an industry, the more rapid the diffusion process for new technologies and the higher the diffusion level.*

Marketing support. Resource allocations to marketing and the particular marketing actions of the supplier group will be pivotal in speeding the diffusion process and affecting the maximum market penetration level. The greater the levels of advertising, personal selling, promotional support, and distribution support, the faster the diffusion process. Recent modeling of the diffusion of innovations has sought to reflect how the actions of the firm marketing the innovation alter the expected shape of the diffusion process (Bass 1980; Dolan and Jeuland 1981; Horsky and Simon 1983; Kalish 1983; Roberts and Urban 1984; Simon and Sebastian 1982).

Allocations of funds to marketing research will be important in providing customer input to help guide R&D and in "positioning" the technology after it is designed to achieve a certain customer perception. Many new technologies, in fact, are customer-initiated, as Von Hippel (1984) has demonstrated. A company's major source of ideas for new product opportunities may be its own customers, and marketing research may be instrumental in providing information in order to positively mediate perceived innovation characteristics.

Marketing expenditures in advertising, personal selling, and other forms of communication are important influences on the speed and pattern of diffusion. Generally, marketing actions are designed to achieve more rapid diffusion acceleration in order to foster a quicker return on investment, to erect barriers to entry, and to establish customer loyalty. Indeed, a few empirical studies, based on models of diffusion and extended to include marketing mix variables, have shown that marketing actions accelerate the diffusion process (Bass 1980; Horsky and Simon 1983; Lilien, Rao, and Kalish 1981; Simon and Sebastian 1982).

Marketing actions also have a major bearing on the organizational characteristics of those firms which will adopt, given explicit allocation of resources by *market segment*. Although it is interesting to study the characteristics of innovators or early adopter firms, it is also worthy of note that these firms may have been targeted by marketing actions and that firms with dissimilar characteristics may have been excluded.

Diffusion research almost totally ignores these intentions and resource allocations of the firms marketing the innovation. Even the research on new product diffusion conducted by marketing and consumer behavior researchers ignores the intentions of supplier firms (Gatignon and Robertson 1985). Thus, research which discovers that innovators are, for example, large firms may only be confirming the market segment selection practice of the marketer.

> *Proposition 6: The greater the allocation of marketing resources, the more rapid the diffusion process and the higher the diffusion level.*

Adopter Industry Factors Affecting Diffusion

The industry within which a potential adopting organization operates affects receptivity to innovation. In some industries there will be competitive pressure to consider new technologies and in others there may be a general lethargy. The willingness to innovate would seem to be a function of two broad sets of variables which we shall consider—structural and communication factors. The structural factors include industry homogeneity, competitive intensity, and demand uncertainty. The communication factors include signal frequency and clarity, level of professionalization, and the cosmopolitanism of the industry.

Adopter Industry Structural Factors

Industry heterogeneity. Speed of diffusion will be maximized at an intermediate level of industry heterogeneity. The transmission of information within a highly homogeneous industry—homophilous communication—is likely to be lower in innovation content than information transmitted within a heterogeneous industry—heterophilous communication. Rogers (1983) notes that "heterophilous communication has a special informational potential, even though it may be realized only rarely" (p. 275).

The value of heterophilous influence was documented in research by Granovetter (1973), who discovered that "weak ties" were important in job searches, mainly because people with homophilous ties were unlikely to know anything more than the information recipients, since their contacts were similar. In the consumer behavior literature, Kaigler-Evans, Leavitt, and Dickey (1977) have used the notion of a "point of optimal heterophily." This is the balance point between personal contact that is so similar as to provide minimum new information versus personal contact that is so dissimilar that communication breaks down. In their research they provide preliminary evidence for the effectiveness of sources who are in this middle range of heterophily.

In drawing a parallel to organizational adoption of technology, it is proposed that intermediate industry heterogeneity is equivalent to the optimal point of heterophily. If the industry is highly homogeneous, informational potential regarding new technologies is reduced. If the industry is highly heterogeneous, communication breaks down due to lack of a common focus.

Proposition 7: Rapidity of technological diffusion will be maximized at an intermediate level of industry heterogeneity.

Competitive intensity. The acceptance of innovation is positively associated with competitive intensity—to a point. Indeed, the relationship between competitive intensity and innovation receptivity is probably curvilinear, much as the relationship between competitive intensity and R&D performance is curvilinear (Loury 1979). Reasonable levels of competitiveness encourage the acceptance of innovation, but beyond some point, the financial resources of the industry are depleted and the acceptance of innovation is stifled. Innovativeness is also stifled under monopolistic conditions whereby the incentive for change is expected to be low, although there is some debate about this in the economics literature (Salter 1960; Swan 1970).

The acceptance of technological innovation by industry participants may be particularly important in building or maintaining barriers to entry. Levin (1978) has shown how innovation preserves cost advantage and maintains market structure: "By financing R&D out of quasi-rents earned on their superior technology, existing firms generate further technical progress which continuously recreates their cost advantage over potential entrants" (p. 347). In fact, Abernathy and Utterback (1978) have suggested that as competition increases, the type of innovations adopted changes from major product innovations to process innovations.

Proposition 8: Rapidity of technological diffusion will be maximized at an intermediate level of competitive intensity.

Demand uncertainty. In industries that are unable to forecast demand accurately, incumbent competitors cannot know the levels of marketing activity and the levels of output necessary to preempt new entrants (Dasgupta and Stiglitz 1980). Consequently, the higher the degree of uncertainty in predicting demand, the more intense competition will be among existing competitors and the more likely firms will be to adopt innovations. This does not hold when competition is stable, as in some regulated industries. In this case, environmental uncertainty decreases the likelihood of adoption of an innovation by an organization behaving rationally (Fidler and Johnson 1984).

This receptivity to innovation is most pronounced if the strategy for preempting new entry requires new technologies for cost reduction or for gaining new market segments. Therefore, the conditions for a positive effect of demand uncertainty on the rate of diffusion of innovations are: when existing competition uses cost as a barrier to entry and there is a potential for price reductions (or for a gain in marketing efficiency); and when the preempting strategy is to fill the gaps in satisfying the heterogeneous needs of the market, given that the new products or new segments require a technological innovation.

Related to demand uncertainty is the inaccuracy of predicting consumer needs (Eliashberg, Tapiero, and Wind 1985). This inaccuracy increases with the heterogeneity in population tastes and with normative changes (Feder and O'Mara 1982; Peterson and Mahajan 1978). Because of the variability in consumer demand, diverse products and services are required to satisfy these segments' needs and, consequently, more innovations are needed which are perceived by consumers as providing important benefits. This was verified empirically by Baldridge and Burnham (1975) in the noncommercial context of innovations adopted by schools.

A similar situation arises when a change in the environment causes changes in consumers' needs, or a technological gap (March and Simon 1958). Thus, the higher the environmental uncertainty, the higher the need for changing technologies and the higher the rate of adoption of innovations (Ettlie 1983). Other researchers have shown that environmental uncertainty stimulates a change in strategy or policy (Eliashberg and Chatterjee 1985b; Hambrick 1981) and, in particular, promotes an aggressive technology policy (Ettlie and Bridges 1982). In turn, aggressive technology policies generate a greater likelihood of adoption of innovations (Ettlie 1983).

Proposition 9: Demand uncertainty is generally positively related to the acceptance of innovations.

Adopter Industry Communication Factors

Signal frequency and clarity. An interesting dimension in analyzing an industry is the amount of signaling which occurs among competitors and the clarity of these signals. Signals may be announced intentions and explanations for such actions as new investments, production processes, pricing systems, or product introductions. In the present case we are interested in the amount of signaling about the adoption of new technologies by member firms and the clarity of these signals. Clarity would be judged by the extent to which a unique cause can be inferred, as well as the past truthfulness of signals from a particular competitor (Heil 1985).

Industries may be characterized as to openness in communication and lack of ambiguity in signaling. Alternatively, industries may be very closed in revealing information, or may send deliberately ambiguous or potentially misleading signals. The communication openness of an industry refers to the amount of potentially useful information that is communicated among competitors. Communication openness can be measured by such variables as the number of trade journals, number of trade associations, attendance at trade association and industry meetings, number of press briefings, informational content of annual reports, and the number of interfirm contacts which occur.

Research by Czepiel (1974) within the steel industry found a high level of communication openness, although we lack comparative research within other industries. According to Czepiel, "While there are available no outside criteria for comparison, . . . industry members have regular opinion/advice relationships with between two and three other firms in the industry . . ." (p. 175). He did find two distinct social networks—a "Big Steel" network and a "Mini-Mill" network. The major source of information about the new technology studied was industry friendship relationships, followed by colleagues and suppliers. Czepiel suggests that the communication openness of the steel industry may be a function of its maturity and commonality of technology and that such openness is less likely in other industries where "production technology may yield significant competitive advantage" (p. 178).

The expectation is that signal frequency and clarity are positively related to the rate of diffusion for new technologies. Communication openness and information sharing are likely to increase the available information about innovations and to ease the adoption decision process. Signal clarity is likely to enhance the information content, such that announcements will be believed by fellow competitors, thus speeding the diffusion process.

Proposition 10: Frequency of signaling and signal clarity are positively related to the speed and level of diffusion.

Professionalization. A key variable in most theories of diffusion and in diffusion models is the amount of social influence transmitted within an industry. Social influence would seem to be increased to the extent that the industry is professionalized, such that a firm's employees identify with their profession as well as with their firm. This would increase the likelihood of accessing extraorganizational information about innovations (Leonard-Barton 1985).

In line with Moch and Morse (1977), it is expected that organizations are more likely to adopt innovations when they have specialist professionals who define the innovation as compatible with their needs and interests. In a similar vein, Robertson and Wind (1983) have argued that professionals are more important than managers (in the hospital domain) in affecting receptivity to innovation. Fennell (1984), however, found that the presence of a professional medical component did not facilitate adoption of employee health programs among private sector firms. Among manufacturing firms (in the shoe industry), Bigoness and Perreault (1981) documented that firms possessing internal technical expertise are more innovative than firms without such expertise. On balance, the evidence supports the proposition that industry professionalization is positively associated with innovation receptivity.

Proposition 11: The greater the professionalization of an industry, the more rapid the diffusion.

Cosmopolitanism. Finally, the greater the cosmopolitanism of an industry, the more rapid the rate of diffusion. This refers to an external (rather than local) orientation. It has generally been found that cosmopolitanism or "external integration" is positively associated with innovativeness. This has been documented in agricultural research (Rogers 1983), consumer research (Gatignon and Robertson 1985), and in organizational behavior research (Kimberly 1978; Ozanne and Churchill 1971; Robertson and Wind 1983). Counte and Kimberly (1974), however, confirm that the role of cosmopolitanism depends on the innovation. In their research on a "locally-based" medical innovation, cosmopolitanism did not separate adopters from nonadopters: "Perhaps this was because receptive individuals perceived possible participation as resulting in status rewards in the local medical community, not in reference to some externally-based group, set, or institution" (p. 196).

Although cosmopolitanism has been studied mainly at the individual or organizational level, we believe that there is value in the notion of industry cosmopolitanism. This could be assessed by level of international sales, number of markets targeted, percentage of employees who have worked in other industries, etc. Just as for the individual organization, industry cosmopolitanism increases access to new information and encourages a more rapid diffusion process. Indeed, Gatignon, Eliashberg, and Robertson (1985) have recently extended the concept to a national level. In seeking to explain diffusion patterns of appliance innovations in a number of European countries, they found that national cosmopolitanism—as measured by levels of international mail, telephone, and travel—was a meaningful explanatory factor.

At an industry level, the value of cosmopolitanism has been studied by Mansfield (1968). He found that the most important source of technology in a number of mature industries was outside rather than within the industry. An industry's integration into external information environments may be an important source of new ideas and complementary technologies.

Proposition 12: The greater the cosmopolitanism of an industry, the more rapid the diffusion.

Future Research

This article has stressed an alternative paradigm for research on diffusion of innovation focused on competitive factors. It has been argued that the prevalent research base has been grounded in behavioral theory and has largely ignored the role of the supplier industry in affecting diffusion rates as well as the competitive environment among potential adopters.

Although this argument could be made for diffusion both at the organizational level and the ultimate consumer level, the focus here has been on organizational adoption of innovations. Similarly, although the argument could hold for both high and low technology products, we have linked our analysis to the realm of high technology, or discontinuous innovations.

A set of propositions has been offered as to how supply-side and adopter industry variables affect diffusion. These propositions have been derived by combining a number of different literature bases in marketing, economics, and organizational behavior. The combination of these vantage points provides a conceptualization for future research probing organizational acceptance of new technologies.

Although some of the propositions suggested have received empirical support in the disciplines from which they are derived, our intent is to provide a conceptual framework that will advance research within the marketing discipline. The framework illustrated in Figure 1 and the propositions to be tested encompass priority areas for systematic investigation. Indeed, many of the propositions have considerable relevance for the practice of new product marketing. An industry's product policy and distribution strategies, for example, should be affected by the relationships suggested as to how diffusion varies according to vertical coordination and technology standardization strategies, as well as how diffusion is affected by marketing resource commitments.

Most marketing research on diffusion theory considers the adoption of a single innovation by multiple adopters—usually individuals but sometimes organizations. Research generally addresses the issue of determining the characteristics of the adopter or the innovation characteristics that affect adoption. When the research objective concerns the properties of the innovation, the research is across products and the adoption unit characteristics are basically ignored. In the study of organizational adoption of innovations, some of our propositions can be researched with the same methodology, that is, a single innovation adopted by multiple organizations or multiple innovations adopted by multiple organizations. However, organizations are nested within industries—a level at which certain propositions in this article are formulated. Therefore, future research must consider another dimension of the unit of analysis—the industry level.

Some propositions can be tested by analyzing the adoption of a single innovation by multiple organizations within an industry. Some require a single innovation adopted by multiple organizations in multiple industries. Other propositions can be tested with a cross section of innovations adopted by multiple organizations within an industry, and others necessitate multiple innovations, multiple organizations, and multiple industries. Clearly, the varying degree of complexity of such tests needs to be considered in the design of a research program. The supply-side propositions require multiple innovations, although some propositions could be studied if multiple firms with various levels of reputation, or various levels of marketing support, for example, offered a similar innovation. On the other hand, the demand-side propositions all require the analysis of adoption by multiple industries.

Although almost all diffusion research has utilized survey methodologies, it would be desirable to extend the research base to experimental approaches. The mechanisms that explain the relationships posited are not easily traceable with surveys, and probing causal processes would be a desirable addition to our knowledge base. A new stream of research might utilize experimental designs in which respondents make adoption decisions facing different competitive environments as described in scenarios (Heil 1985; Robertson and Wind 1980). Although methodological problems arise in this type of experimental setting—particularly concerning external validity—it might be a viable route to test process-based hypotheses.

In conclusion, we have advocated a heightened focus on the diffusion of technological innovations across organizations. Particular stress has been given to how competitive factors affect diffusion patterns, both at the level of the supplier industry and within the potential adopter industry. A set of propositions has been suggested relating a set of variables to expected diffusion patterns. Research has been encouraged at the industry level of analysis as well as at the level of the individual firm . Experimental designs for diffusion research have also been suggested, in addition to the prototypical survey methodologies generally utilized.

Bibliography

Abell, Derek F. and John S. Hammond (1979), *Strategic Market Planning*, Englewood Cliffs, NJ: Prentice-Hall.

Abernathy, William J. and James M. Utterback (1978), "Patterns of Industrial Innovations," *Technology Review*, 80 (June/July), 41–47.

Aiken M. and Jerald Hage (1972), "Organizational Permeabiiity, Boundary Spanners and Organizational Structure," paper presented at the 67th Annual Meeting of the American Sociological Association, New Orleans.

Anderson, Erin (1985), "The Salesperson as Outside Agent or Employee: A Transaction Cost Analysis," *Marketing Science*, 4 (Summer), 234–254.

Baker, Michael J. and Stephen T. Parkinson (1977), "Information Source Preference in the Industrial Adoption Decision," in *Proceedings of the American Marketing Association*, Barnett A. Greenberg and Danny N. Bellenger, eds., Chicago: American Marketing Association, 258–261.

Baldridge, J. Victor and Robert A. Burnham (1975), "Organizational Innovation: Individual, Organizational, and Environmental Impacts," *Administrative Science Quarterly*, 20 (June), 165–176.

Bass, Frank M. (1969), "A New Product Growth Model for Consumer Durables," *Management Science*, 15 (no. 5), 215–227.

——— (1980), "The Relationship Between Diffusion Curves, Experience Curves, and Demand Elasticities for Consumer Durable Technological Innovations," *Journal of Business*, 53 (July), 551–557.

Berger, Lawrence (1985), "Word-of-Mouth Reputation in Auto Insurance Markets," Ph.D. dissertation, University of Pennsylvania.

Bigoness, William J. and William D. Perreault, Jr. (1981), "A Conceptual Paradigm and Approach for the Study of Innovators," *Academy of Management Journal*, 24 (March), 68–82.

Boston Consulting Group (1985), "Perspectives: Flexible Automation," unpublished working paper.

Brown, Lawrence A. (1981), *Innovation Diffusion: A New Perspective*, New York: Methuen.

Cherian, Joseph and Rohit Deshpandé (1985), "The Impact of Organizational Culture on the Adoption of Industrial Innovations," working paper, Department of Marketing, University of Texas, Austin.

Cooper, Robert G. (1979), "The Dimensions of Industrial New Product Success and Failure," *Journal of Marketing*, 43 (Summer), 93–103.

Counte, Michael A. and John R. Kimberly (1974), "Organizational Innovation in a Professionally Dominated System: Responses of Physicians to a New Program in Medical Education," *Journal of Health and Social Behavior*, 15 (September), 188–99.

Czepiel, John A. (1974), "Word-of-Mouth Processes in the Diffusion of a Major Technological Innovation," *Journal of Marketing Research*, 11 (May), 172–80.

——— (1976), "Decision Group and Firm Characteristics in an Industrial Adoption Decision," in *Marketing: 1776–1976 and Beyond*, Kenneth L. Bernhardt, ed., Chicago: American Marketing Association, 340–43.

Dasgupta, P. and J. Stiglitz (1980), "Uncertainty, Industry Structure, and the Speed of R&D," *The Bell Journal of Economics*, 11 (Spring), 1–28.

Dickerson, Mary Dee and James W. Gentry (1983), "Characteristics of Adopters and Non-Adopters of Home Computers," *Journal of Consumer Research*, 10 (September), 225–35.

Dolan, Robert J. and Abel P. Jeuland (1981), "Experience Curves and Dynamic Demand Models: Implications for Optimal Pricing Strategies," *Journal of Marketing*, 45 (Winter), 52–62.

Eliashberg, Jehoshua and Abel P. Jeuland (1986), "The Impact of Competitive Entry in a Developing Market upon Dynamic Pricing Strategies," *Marketing Science*, in press.

——— and Rabikar Chatterjee (1985a), "Analytical Models of Competition with Implications for Marketing: Issues, Findings, and Outlook," *Journal of Marketing Research*, 22 (August), 283–96.

——— and ——— (1985b), "Stochastic Issues in Modeling the Innovation Diffusion Process," in *Innovation Diffusion Models of New Product Acceptance*, V. Mahajan and Y. Wind, eds., Cambridge, MA: Ballinger.

———, Charles C. Tapiero, and Yoram Wind (1985), "New Products Diffusion Models with Stochastic Parameters," working paper, University of Pennsylvania.

Ettlie, John E. (1983), "Organizational Policy and Innovation among Suppliers to the Food Processing Sector," *Academy of Management Journal*, 26 (no. 1), 27–44.

——— and W. P. Bridges (1982), "Environmental Uncertainty and Organizational Technology Policy," *IEEE Transactions on Engineering Management*, EM-29, 2–10.

Farrell, Joseph and Garth Saloner (1985), "Standardization, Compatibility, and Innovations," *Rand Journal of Economics*, 16 (Spring), 70–83.

Feder, Gershon and Gerald T. O'Mara (1982), "On Information and Innovation Diffusion: A Bayesian Approach," *American Agricultural Economics Association Proceedings* (February), 145–47.

Fennell, Mary L. (1984), "Synergy, Influence, and Information in the Adoption of Administrative Innovations," *Academy of Management Journal*, 27 (March), 113–29.

Fidler, Lori A. and J. David Johnson (1984), "Communication and Innovation Implementation," *Academy of Management Journal*, 9 (no. 4), 704–11.

Galaskiewicz, Joseph (1985), "Interorganizational Relations," in *Annual Review of Sociology*, Ralph H. Turner and James F. Short, Jr., eds., Palo Alto, CA: Annual Reviews, Inc., 281–304.

Gatignon, Hubert (1984), "Competition as a Moderator of the Effect of Advertising on Sales," *Journal of Marketing Research*, 21 (4), 387–98.

———, Jehoshua Eliashberg, and Thomas S. Robertson (1985), "Determinants of Diffusion Patterns: A Cross-Country Analysis," working paper, The Wharton School, University of Pennsylvania.

——— and Thomas S. Robertson (1985), "A Propositional Inventory for New Diffusion Research," *Journal of Consumer Research*, 11 (March), 849–67.

Grabowski, H. G. and N. D. Baxter (1973), "Rivalry in Industrial Research and Development," *Journal of Industrial Economics*, 21 (July), 209–35.

Granovetter, Mark S. (1973), "The Strength of Weak Ties," *American Journal of Sociology*, 78 (no. 6), 1360–80.

Hambrick, Donald C. (1981), "Specialization of Environmental Scanning Activities among Upper Level Managers," *Journal of Management Studies*, 18 July), 299–320.

——— and Ian C. MacMillan (1985), "Efficiency of Product R&D in Business Units: The Role of Strategic Context," *Academy of Management Journal*, 28 (September), 527–47.

Heil, Oliver (1985), "Signaling in Competitive Marketing Environments," working paper, The Wharton School, University of Pennsylvania.

Hirschman, Elizabeth C. (1980), "Innovativeness, Novelty Seeking, and Consumer Creativity," *Journal of Consumer Research*, 7 (December), 289–95.

Horsky, Dan and Leonard S. Simon (1983), "Advertising and the Diffusion of New Products," *Marketing Science*, 2 (Winter), 1–17.

Kaigler-Evans, Karen, Clark Leavitt, and Lois Dickey (1977), "Source Similarity and Fashion Newness as Determinants of Consumer Innovation," in *Advances in Consumer Research*, Vol. 5, H. Keith Hunt, ed., Ann Arbor: Association for Consumer Research, 738–42.

Kalish, Shlomo (1983), "Monopolistic Pricing with Dynamic Demand and Production Cost," *Marketing Science*, 2 (no. 2), 135–59.

Kamien, Morton I. and Nancy L. Schwartz (1982), *Marketing Structure and Innovation*, Cambridge: Cambridge University Press.

Kamani, Aneel (1983), "Minimum Market Share," *Marketing Science*, 2 (no. 1), 75–93.

Kimberly, John R. (1978), "Hospital Adoption of Innovation: The Role of Integration into External Informational Environments," *Journal of Health & Social Behavior*, 19 (December), 361–73.

——— and Michael J. Evanisko (1981), "Organizational Innovation: The Influence of Individual, Organizational, and Contextual

Factors on Hospital Adoption of Technological and Administrative Innovations," *Academy of Management Journal*, 24 (December), 689–713.

Leonard-Barton, Dorothy (1985), "Experts as Negative Opinion Leaders in the Diffusion of a Technological Innovation," *Journal of Consumer Research*, 11 (March), 914–26.

Levin, Richard C. (1978), "Technical Change, Barriers to Entry, and Market Structure," *Economica*, 45 (November), 347–361.

Lilien, Gary L., Ambar G. Rao, and Shlomo Kalish (1981), "Bayesian Estimation and Control of Detailing Effort in a Repeat Purchase Diffusion Environment," *Management Science*, 27 (May), 493–506.

Loury, Glenn C. (1979), "Market Structure and Innovation," *Quarterly Journal of Economics*, 33 (August), 395–410.

Mahajan, Vijay and Eitan Muller (1979), "Innovation Diffusion and New Product Growth Models in Marketing," *Journal of Marketing*, 43 (Fall), 55–68.

Mansfield, Edwin (1968), *Industrial Research and Technological Innovation*, New York: Norton.

——— (1982), *Technology Transfer, Productivity, and Economic Policy*, New York: Norton.

March, James G. and Herbert A. Simon (1958), *Organizations*, New York: Wiley.

Mate, Karol V. (1982), "Optimal Advertising Strategies of Competing Firms Marketing New Products," working paper, Washington University, St. Louis.

McGuinness, Norman W. and Blair Little (1981), "The Influence of Product Characteristics on the Export Performance of New Industrial Products," *Journal of Marketing*, 45 (Spring), 110–12.

Moch, M. K. and E. V. Morse (1977), "Size, Centralization, and Organizational Adoption of Innovations," *American Sociological Review*, 42 (October), 716–25.

Nelson, Philip (1970), "Information and Consumer Behavior," *Journal of Political Economy*, 78 (March–April), 311–25.

——— (1974), "Advertising as Information," *Journal of Political Economy*, 82 (July–August), 729–54.

Ozanne, Urban B. and Gilbert A. Churchill, Jr. (1971) "Five Dimensions of the Industrial Adoption Process," *Journal of Marketing Research*, 8 (August), 322–28.

Palmer, Donald (1983), "Broken Ties: Interlocking Directorates and Intercorporate Coordination," *Administrative Science Quarterly*, 28 (March), 40–55.

Peterson, Robert A. and Vijay Mahajan (1978), "Multi-Product Growth Models," in *Research in Marketing*, J. Sheth, ed., Greenwich, CT: JAI Press, 201–231.

Porter, Michael E. (1980), *Competitive Strategy*, New York: The Free Press.

Rao, Ram C. and Frank M. Bass (1985), "Competition, Strategy, and Price Dynamics: A Theoretical and Empirical Investigation," *Journal of Marketing Research*, 22 (August), 283–96.

Roberts, John H. and Glen L. Urban (1984), "New Consumer Durable Brand Choice: Modeling Multiattribute Utility, Risk, and Belief Dynamics," working paper, University of New South Wales.

Robertson, Thomas S. (1971), *Innovative Behavior and Communication*, New York: Holt.

——— and Yoram Wind (1980), "Organizational Psychographics and Innovativeness," *Journal of Consumer Research*, 7 (June), 24–31.

——— and ——— (1983), "Organizational Cosmopolitanism and Innovativeness," *Academy of Management Journal*, 26 (June), 332–38.

Robinson, William T. and Claes Fornell (1985), "Sources of Market Pioneer Advantages in Consumer Goods Industries," *Journal of Marketing Research*, 22 (August), 305–17.

Rogers, Everett M. (1983), *Diffusion of Innovations*, 3rd ed., New York: The Free Press.

——— (1985), "Interdependencies among Users of a New Communication Technology," paper presented at the Association for Consumer Research Conference, Las Vegas (October).

Salter, W. E. G. (1960), *Productivity and Technical Change*, Cambridge: Cambridge University Press.

Satterthwaite, M. (1979), "Consumer Information: Equilibrium Industry Price and the Number of Sellers," *Bell Journal of Economics*, 10 (Autumn), 483–502.

Schoorman, F. David, Max H. Bazerman, and Robert S. Atkin (1981), "Interlocking Directorates: A Strategy for Reducing Environmental Uncertainty," *Academy of Management Review*, 6 (no. 2), 243–51.

Shanklin, William L. and John K. Ryans, Jr. (1984), "Organizing for High-Tech Marketing," *Harvard Business Review*, 84 (November–December), 164–71.

Shapiro, C. (1983), "Premiums for High Quality Products as Returns to Reputation," *Quarterly Journal of Economics*, 97 (no. 4), 659–79.

Simon, Hermann and Karl-Heinz Sebastian (1982), "Diffusion and Advertising: The German Telephone Campaign," working paper no. 0.9, Marketing Science Group of Germany.

Stoneman, P. (1981), "Intra-Firm Diffusion, Bayesian Learning, and Profitability," *The Economic Journal*, 91 (June), 375–388.

Swan, Peter L. (1970), "Market Structure and Technological Progress: The Influence of Monopoly on Product Innovation," *Quarterly Journal of Economics*, 84 (no. 4), 627–38.

Teng, Jinn-Tsair and Gerald L. Thompson (1983), "Oligopoly Models for Optimal Advertising When Production Costs Obey a Learning Curve," *Management Science*, 29 (September), 1087–1101.

Thompson, Gerald L. and Jinn-Tsair Teng (1984), "Optimal Pricing and Advertising Policies for New Product Oligopoly Models," *Marketing Science*, 3 (Spring), 148–68.

Vernon, Raymond (1971), *Sovereignty at Bay*, New York: Basic Books.

Von Hippel, Eric (1984), "Novel Product Concepts from Lead Users: Segmenting Users by Experience," working paper no. 84-109, Marketing Science Institute, Cambridge, MA.

Webster, Frederick E., Jr. (1969), "New Product Adoption in Industrial Markets: A Framework for Analysis," *Journal of Marketing*, 33 (July), 35–39.

Weitz, Barton A. (1985), "Introduction to Special Issue on Competition in Marketing," *Journal of Marketing Research*, 22 (August), 228–36.

Williamson, Oliver E. (1979), "Transaction-Cost Economics: The Governance of Contractual Relations," *Journal of Law and Economics*, 22 (October), 233–62.

Wilton, Peter C. and Edgar A. Pessemier (1981), "Forecasting the Ultimate Acceptance of an Innovation: The Effects of Information," *Journal of Consumer Research*, 8 (September), 162–71.

Zaltman, Gerald, Robert Duncan, and Jonny Holbek (1973), *Innovations and Organizations*, New York: Wiley.

17

Benefit Segmentation —20 Years Later

Russell I. Haley

Benefit segmentation is still being used successfully more than twenty years after its introduction. It works well in advertising planning situations in which cognitive benefits are considered to be the most important types of benefits.

During the more than twenty years since its inception the technique of Benefit Segmentation has become a familiar method of analyzing markets to discover segmentation opportunities. Almost every major marketer of consumer goods and services has attempted to use this method one or more times. However, the degree of success which has attended its use has varied. In this article its originator, Dr. Russell I. Haley, examines the reasons for this variation, offers guidelines for proper use, and suggests directions for further improvements in the method.

RECENT MARKETING TEXTBOOKS define the marketing concept in the following terms: "The marketing concept holds that the key to achieving organizational goals consists in determining the needs and wants of target markets and delivering the desired satisfactions more effectively and efficiently than competitors."[7]

More specifically the marketing concept is thought to involve:

- Focusing on consumer needs.
- Integrating all activities of the organization to satisfy these needs, including production.
- Achieving long-run profits through satisfaction of consumer needs.[6]

Dr. Haley is a Professor Emeritus, University of New Hampshire. Previously he was vice president at D'Arcy and Grey Advertising Agencies and is a recent inductee into the AMA Attitude Research Hall of Fame.

Implicit in these definitions is the fact that long-run profits require consideration of consumer welfare and that consumer needs are not homogeneous. It is increasingly recognized that significant segments exist in almost every market, because different consumers have different needs and wants—they seek different benefits.

There remains considerable confusion over differences between the strategies of market segmentation and product differentiation.[9] *Market segmentation* is customer oriented. It attempts to identify *customer* subgroups of the market as they *currently exist*. The presumption is that once such segments have been identified and understood, it is possible to focus marketing activities on them in such a way as to achieve relatively deep penetration of segments and, at the same time, to make it uneconomic and otherwise difficult for competitors to mount effective counterattacks.

Product differentiation, on the other hand, is product oriented. It concerns the identification of subgroups of competing *products*. Once this has been accomplished, attempts can be made to favorably differentiate the brand of interest from its principal competitors. The presumption is that some *restructuring* of the market is possible—that an unspecified consumer target will perceive the product, in its new and differentiated position, to be superior to alternative choices and therefore will try it.

The two concepts are related but they are not interchangeable. Product clusters are not necessarily centered on benefit delivery combinations and it is occasionally possible for a consumer need group to exist without having its needs well met by any product cluster. Product differentiation, because it does involve some restructuring of the market, seems particularly well suited to new product work. New products, provided they are genuinely new, can and often do cause major changes in the size and nature of existing need groups in a market. Thus the current market structure as defined by need groups may have limited value to a new product group. For example, in the analgesic market the segment concerned about the sensitivity of their stomachs to aspirin was so small as to be virtually nonexistent. With the broad-scale availability of Tylenol and similar products, however, the aforementioned segment (now that a solution was at hand for the problem they didn't know they had) rapidly became a dominant market segment.

Thus the problem of developing effective and differentiating communications for existing brands appears to be an extremely useful tool. Although a few communications campaigns have been known to restructure the need groups of the markets in which they were launched, it is rare for them to do so. More frequently, and in the absence of new products, the underlying need-structure of the market continues for years with no more than minor modifications. However, it does have a strong bearing on the effectiveness of campaigns and, in particular, on the nature of the people whose behavior is affected. Thus to an advertiser or to an advertising agency, a full appreciation of the potential value of market segmentation is critical.

When the concept of Benefit Segmentation was originated,[4] the primary concern was how market segmentation related to target selection. It was hoped that it would be possible to identify subgroups of the population who might be especially responsive to a particular advertising theme. It was soon discovered that, because of the selective processes involved in attention to advertising, the choice of a different benefit or combination of benefits as the focal point of an advertising campaign meant, automatically, the choice of a different market target as well. Marketing judgment was employed liberally in choosing between alternative Benefit Segments. However, the segments that were uncovered were plausible and they provided useful focal points for the advertising that was done. That was state-of-the-art twenty years ago.

Approximately ten years ago an experiment was conducted for *Time* Magazine[5] which showed, to no one's surprise, that knowing people's interest in alternative benefits was very helpful in predicting the attention to copy that is developed around those benefits. This had always seemed a reasonable assumption but hard evidence had been scarce. It has since been provided from other sources as well.

It was found, for example, that air travelers who indicate that they were more interested in "fun while flying" than in "travel planning help" were more apt to attend advertising focused on that theme. Conversely, people more interested in travel planning were more attentive to advertising featuring *that* theme. This relationship held despite the fact that both segments were exposed to both themes. Similarly, when audiences were exposed to the two corporate themes of "ecology concern" and "concern for employees," the segment more interested in the former theme was more likely to attend it and vice versa. Thus the premise that people are more likely to attend commercials that center on benefits of interest to them was substantiated. Similarly, interest in the potential of Benefit Segmentation was reinforced.

Table 1
Segmentation Orientations

Geographic Demographic Behavioral ▪ Volume of use ▪ Brand loyalty ▪ Use occasions or situations	Psychographic ▪ Lifestyles ▪ Benefits sought/problems solved ▪ Values ▪ Category beliefs or perceptions ▪ Brand predispositions

Segmentation Alternatives

Benefit Segmentation is, of course, only one of many ways of segmenting markets. The principal methods are summarized in Table 1.

The word "Psychographics" is used in the broad sense in which it was intended when it was first introduced, despite some misconceptions about its origin.[3] The word first appeared in print in the November 1965 issue of *Grey Matter*, a promotional newsletter issued by Grey Advertising. It came out of a discussion between several research and creative executives who were reviewing the results of the latest "attitude segmentation" study, as it was called in that era. The creative people were showing considerable enthusiasm for the kinds of targets to which the research was pointing. One went so far as to say that this was the first research he had ever seen that really gave creative guidance. Looking at the full-blown segment descriptions, descriptions covering behavior, demographics, benefits sought, and lifestyles, he said, "Boy, this stuff goes way beyond standard demographics. Why, you're showing us people's psychologies! These are psychographics." The word was immediately recognized as an appropriate label and shortly thereafter was featured in *Grey Matter*. The mailing list for this newsletter included almost every package good manufacturer and, of course, all of the major mass media as well. So literally, the word traveled fast.

A few clarifications of the terminology in Table 1 are in order. For example, it is recognized that both "brand loyalty" and "use situations." can be defined attitudinally as well as behaviorally. Similarly, "solving problems" can be considered a somewhat different orientation from "delivering benefits"; however, the author prefers to consider them to be directly related even though they do require slightly different treatment in the measurement process. From an analytic standpoint they can be handled in much the same way.

The term "values" is used in the sense in which it is used in the measures of instrumental and terminal values.[8] In some markets, such as the market for financial services, values such as "life of comfort" and "true friendship" have proven to be potent segmentation factors.

The term "beliefs" refers to consumers' perceptions of truth in the category of interest. They are more product specific than the more general lifestyle measures. The latter cut across product categories. Beliefs usually apply directly to a particular category (although inferences about attitudes toward other categories can sometimes be drawn from them).

They are usually measured by scaling the extent to which people agree or disagree with statements like "all brands are the same." People who strongly endorse this statement, for example, can be expected to be much more sensitive to price appeals than people who strongly reject it. However, people who see all brands the same in one product category do not necessarily feel the same way about another product category. Their view depends, among other things, on the extent of their involvement in the product category.

Belief measures have probably not received the attention that they deserve in the professional literature. Yet there are numerous examples of their importance. For example, in the deodorant category there are people who believe that their deodorant loses its effectiveness if they use the same brand over and over. In the adhesive bandage category there is a sharp difference of beliefs about whether it is better to keep a cut covered or to let the air get at it. In food there is a surprising array of beliefs as to what constitutes a healthy diet. In situations such as these the actual facts are less important than the beliefs themselves. It is the beliefs that determine behavior and that dictate the kinds of advertising messages that will be accepted.

Finally, the term "brand predispositions" refers to the practice of developing brand maps, locating consumers on them on the basis of their feelings about the brands involved, and then clustering respondents occupying similar positions. The resultant clusters can, of course, be viewed as segments.

Comparisons of Segmentation Alternatives

Once the major alternative types of market segmentation have been established, the next logical question would seem to be "Which of these approaches is generally the best basis for segmenting markets?" Surprisingly little work seems to have been done in this area. What has been done suggests that "It all depends." Certainly the most popular approach these days seems to be lifestyles. This is at least partly attributable to the increased use of lifestyle tracking services such as VALS/SRI and the Yankelovich "Monitor," as well as to the inclusion of lifestyle measures in commonly used media databanks. Also anyone who has used them knows how excited the creative people in advertising agencies can become over lifestyle segments. On a subjective basis some concern has been expressed over which particular lifestyles and which particular lifestyle segments ought to be utilized. ABC, for example, in search of lifestyle segments that would be useful in evaluating television programs, decided to reject existing systems and develop one of their own.[11] The problem of choosing between specific lifestyle systems is beyond the scope of this paper, however. We are concerned here only with the choice among types of segmentation.

The issue of the best type extends beyond popularity and subjective choice and implies some sort of data—ideally, comparative data. Those are scarce for lifestyles, and what there is isn't too encouraging for lifestyle enthusiasts. A recent paper[13] showed just how big the gap can be between trends in lifestyles and in the consumption of products seemingly related to those lifestyles. The author found, for instance, that while increasing numbers of consumers were agreeing with a lifestyle statement to the effect that it is important to be attractive to the opposite sex, hair color use was declining. Also, while more and more people have been agreeing with the idea that meal preparation should take as little time as possible, use of frozen vegetables and frozen dinners has been declining.

Tony Adams[1] offered some equally impressive evidence of the kinds of problems associated with the use of lifestyle measures.

Finally, Bill Wilkie and Joel Cohen, in a review of what they called the various "streams of thought in segmentation research," written in 1977 for the Marketing Science Institute,[12] concluded that lifestyle measures were most useful for "media selection and scheduling." This fact, perhaps, accounts for their presence in media service databanks. They also concluded that Benefit Segmentation is most useful for brand positioning strategy. That too seems to be an appropriate conclusion.

An author's confession may be in order. During the first ten years of Benefit Segmentation studies his logic was strictly inductive. Because benefit orientation seemed most likely to produce meaningful segments, it was always recommended over alternative possibilities. Then one day a client issued a challenge to define "meaningfulness." Accordingly, an objective test was devised for measuring how well alternative segmentation schemes performed. Meaningfulness, to brand managers, seemed to involve sharp differences between segments on criteria such as volume of consumption, brand image, and type usage (in markets with type as well as brand differences). Consequently, alternative methods of segmentation were compared in terms of how well they discriminated on key measures. While discrimination may have some faults as a measure of segmentation performance, it does have a degree of face validity. Certainly, if a segmentation approach shows *no* difference on these measures, it is justifiably suspect.

In the first study to be analyzed in this fashion three separate segmentation systems were developed—one based on benefits, one based on beliefs and one based on personality and lifestyles. Each orientation was compared to see which discriminated best on the aforementioned criteria. Moreover, this type of test has now been replicated 36 times. Table 2 shows the scoreboard for winning orientations.

It is apparent that benefits do, as a rule of thumb, discriminate best. However, beliefs do almost as good a job. Lifestyles are a distant third.

Table 2

Benefits	19
Beliefs	15
Personality and lifestyles	3
Total number of studies analyzed	37

As might be anticipated, the categories in which lifestyles do best are those in which people express who they are by the brands they choose. The three winning instances in the above table include liquor, cigarettes, and clothing. In general the results of these comparisons agree with the view of others.[11] The more proximate measures—benefits and beliefs—do a better job of predicting specific purchase choices.

It should be quickly added that the most advisable procedure is not to prejudge but rather to include several universes of content that appear to be good segmentation candidates, to try them, and to choose the one that seems to do the best job in the specific situation at hand.

Before we leave the subject of methodology, it should be strongly emphasized that successful Benefit Segmentation studies cannot be produced automatically. As pointed out in a recent issue of the *Journal of Advertising Research*,[12] there has been a great deal of dissatisfaction with what is labeled the "generic segmentation study." This is a segmentation study done mechanically, following specific steps by rote, under the assumption that clear-cut and insightful segments will somehow magically pop out of the welter of statistical output generated. Most frequently this does not happen. However, the article does say that "Segmentation research does work and can be immensely valuable." What then are the conditions that separate a successful study from one that is a waste of time and money? While there are no hard and fast rules, among the hallmarks of successful studies are:

- Clearly defined objectives, usually focusing on the development of communications strategies rather than on new products.
- Careful organization, usually involving a project team consisting of people from the creative, research, and account management areas,
- A substantial amount of up-front work, reviewing past advertising, past research, and significant market facts and trends.
- A three-phase research design, the second phase of which is the development of *sensitive* and *reliable* attitude measures.
- A thorough examination of alternative modes of segmentation.
- Plans for follow-through activities. At a minimum these should include copy testing in the target segment and tracking studies to obtain feedback on the marketing actions to be taken as a result of the research findings.

Benefit Segmentation in Planning and Executing an Advertising Campaign

The advertising process, if carried out thoroughly and systematically, involves the following seven steps:

1. Setting the advertising goals
2. Specifying the model of how the advertising is expected to accomplish its objectives.
3. Determining the communications strategy
4. Developing the advertising copy
5. Testing the copy
6. Selecting and scheduling media
7. Tracking campaign results

With respect to goal setting, the DAGMAR book by Russell Colley[2] is still a useful reference for it reminds us once again that sales per se are not an appropriate goal for advertising because of the impact of other parts of the market mix, and, of course, competitive activity. Step 2, the specification of how advertising is expected to achieve its objectives, has been widely ignored in the advertising planning process. Perhaps this is so because it is assumed that professionals are in general agreement as to how advertising works. Nothing could be further from the truth. There are at least *five* implicit models of the advertising process in common use.

The first of these can be summed up in the assertion that "We can convince people that our brand is superior." This seems to be the dominant theory of how advertising can influence sales. It involves direct persuasion. Sometimes the persuasion is logical, such as in the case of a product demonstration or in comparative advertising. Sometimes it is indirect—through spokespersons, experts, superiority cues, or simply by citing popularity among people in general. Sometimes it is through preemption, through seizing upon a benefit and repeatedly associating the brand with it. Superiority for a specific occasion is a subset of this model. However it is accomplished, the main thrust of this model is the provision of *cognitive* benefits.

The second school holds that "We can create a more attractive product image for our brand." It differs from the first school primarily in terms of its noncognitive emphasis. Product performance is translated into hedonistic and sensory benefits. The product looks wonderful, feels wonderful, smells wonderful, sounds wonderful, or tastes wonderful—sometimes all five. Other imagery characteristics that may be stressed under this model include newness, modernity, and feelings that the product is fun to buy, to own, or to use. The main thrust of this model is providing *sensory* benefits.

The third school is concerned with perceptions about the users of the brands or products being advertised. Its point of view is that "We can create a more attractive *user* image for our brand." In dealing with user imagery, it provides support for people's self-concepts, allowing them to reinforce their views of themselves or express their personalities to others. The "Charlie" fragrance of Revlon became the category leader through effective use of advertising of this type. The main thrust of this model is to provide *emotional* benefits.

The underlying theory for the fourth model is the concept of the evoked set—the idea that most people have sets of brands, all of which are acceptable given appropriate pricing and availability. Their concept is simply that "We can make our brand more salient" and therefore more likely to be purchased. It holds that, in situations in which brands are reasonably interchangeable from a functional basis, many people simply buy the first acceptable brand that comes to mind at the point of sale. This model does not concern benefits directly, unless the benefit of minimizing the amount of mental effort required by the consumer is considered. Indirectly, however, benefits may have been involved in the classification of brands as acceptable or unacceptable. Advertising for Parkay Margarine and Meow Mix are prototypical for this approach.

The fifth model is newer and perhaps a little more subtle than the others. It calls for approval of the advertising of the brand in question and affiliation with the brand. An attempt is made to make people affiliate with the brand by engaging their emotions in some manner and "forging an emotional link with the consumer." This can be done through situations involving children or animals; situations demonstrating love, affection, or male/female interplay, and through use of cartoon characters, sex, and/or humor. The long-running Miller Lite Campaign, the AT&T Reach Out and Touch Someone campaign, the James Garner and Mariette Hartley series for Polaroid, the recent French's Mustard "You are my sunshine" commercial, and the Coca-Cola Mean Joe Greene commercial all fall under this model type. The goal here is to get people to say to themselves: "I sort of like those guys. They have the right kinds of attitudes toward themselves and their product, the right kinds of values; they make sense." However it is accomplished, the main thrust is to provide *affiliation* benefits—to allow consumers, through their purchases, to vote for the good guys, the brands that engender warm and positive feelings.

An Evaluation of the Utility of Benefit Segmentation

In addition to setting goals and specifying the way in which advertising is expected to work so as to move the brand of interest toward them, it is important that marketers make the communications strategy clear to all members of the brand's marketing team. By now the nature of communications strategies is clear. They require the answers to three basic questions.

1. How is the market best defined?
2. Which market segment represents the most responsive market target?
3. Around what buying incentive should our communications efforts be centered?

The answer to the first question requires the identification of the brands or products with which the brand is competing and, in particular, those from which it can most logically expect to attract sales. The answer to the second involves the evaluation of alternative segmentation systems, the choice of the one that appears most promising, and the selection of one segment as the primary target. The final question involves an analysis of the competitive leverage and supportability of various claims. Benefit Segmentation methodology was developed with the objective of providing answers to those three questions.

How good a job does Benefit Segmentation do in answering them? The evaluation seems to depend both upon which of the five models of advertising you select and on how you go about developing your advertising copy.

If you are operating under Model 1 and attempting to deliver cognitive benefits, the Benefit Segmentation approach works very well indeed. In fact, a good case can be made for the contention that it works better than any alternative approach. To date the author has been involved in 116 Benefit Segmentation studies and two more are in progress. In recent years such studies have been uniformly judged "successful" by one important group of evaluators—study sponsors. While such judgments are subjective, they are nonetheless heartening. Therefore Benefit Segmentation is considered a useful approach when Model 1 is the operating model.

Benefit Segmentation also appears to work reasonably well with Model 4, the brand salience model. Emphasizing cognitive benefits is one effective way of moving a brand into evoked sets.

However, when Models 2, 3, or 5 are assumed—the models dealing with sensory, emotional, or affiliative benefits—the Benefit Segmentation approach is far less successful. Earlier in this article an experiment was mentioned in which an attempt was made to predict people's attention to advertising on the basis of their expressed interest in the benefits on which the advertising was focused. This experiment worked well for cognitive benefits. However, when attempts were made to replicate it with emotional benefits, it was found to work considerably less well. The reasons were not hard to find. The success of advertising aimed at delivering sensory, emotional, or affiliative benefits depends not upon the underlying incentive but upon its *execution*. The traditional Benefit Segmentation research approach, with benefits expressed as phrases on little white cards, or with self-administered questionnaires packed with items to be rated on importance or desirability, is of limited value in predicting how people are likely to respond to finished advertising. In support of this point Dr. Roy Stout of Coca-Cola, a prominent user of Models 2, 3, and 5, has reported that his advertising effectiveness model, a sophisticated model which takes into consideration the effects of both advertising copy and media weight on sales, will not predict sales performance accurately unless copy test scores from *finished* advertising are incorporated into his prediction equations.

Two implications can be drawn from this conclusion. The first is methodological. It has to do with the stimuli that are used by market researchers in the course of segmentation research, or "strategic research," as it is more frequently termed these days. Unless sensory, emotional, and affiliative benefits are to be largely excluded from consideration, it is necessary to use actual advertising executions as the stimuli rather than little white cards or self-administered questionnaires.

The more important implication is that, if we are to make significant progress in preevaluating the probable effects of different types of advertising copy, we are going to have to make a considerable investment in learning how to measure the nonverbal aspects of advertising copy as well as its cognitive effects. We are going to have to make a thorough study of how advertising works at this nonverbal level.

There is no lack of evidence to support the hypothesis that nonverbal effects are important. In fact they may well be more important than the verbal and cognitive effects with which we have traditionally dealt in our advertising planning and copy testing activities. However, the nonverbal areas through which commercials affect us have not even been systematically enumerated. It is small wonder that we have no ready-made instruments to measure such effects.

Lest it be said that this article simply points to a frequently recognized problem without offering improved ways of dealing with it, work is currently under way at the University of New Hampshire to identify the key nonverbal areas involved in television commercials and to develop efficient ways of measuring them. Because this work has been going on for less than six months as of this writing, there is little to report as yet. However, among the areas under investigation are the following:

- *Music*. It seems obvious that music is one key nonverbal factor. If the visual shows a child running across a field, one musical background may suggest he is happily going home from school to a loving family whereas another may imply that he is running because he is being chased by something frightening.
- *Setting*. Indoor, outdoor, city, and country settings all project different feelings. If clouds are introduced into the scene of the child running across the field, the implication may be that he is running to avoid getting caught in the rain.
- *Paralanguage*. This concerns the way people use their voices and the timbre of those voices. Rising inflections and falling inflections can evoke very different reactions, as can rapid and slow speech patterns.
- *Glance*. This concerns the way people use their eyes. It has been found, for example, that people who like each other make frequent eye contact when they are across the room from each other but that there is little eye contact when they are close to each other.
- *Semiotics*. This involves the use of signs, symbols, and artifacts. Objects such as flags, chess sets, grand pianos, and footballs have meanings that extend far beyond the literal definitions of the objects.
- *Proxemics*. How close people stand to each other and the positions they occupy relative to each other are significant. Who is standing and who is sitting?
- *Body language*. A best-selling book was devoted to this topic not long ago.
- *Facial cues*. This concerns how people use their smile, frown, and facial muscles.
- *Dress*. How people are dressed says a great deal about who they are. The old saying that "Clothes make the man" is no less true today and it applies to both men and women.
- *Sound effects*. This concerns both the types of sounds employed and their intended effects. Sound can be used to attract attention, to emphasize humor, to generate suspense, and for a great number of additional purposes. For example, one major School of Communications found a strong association between the sound of breaking glass and violence.

Thus far seventeen such areas have been designated for study and additional ones are under consideration. The investigation concerns how they relate to each other and how they relate to more traditional measures such as related recall, attitude shift, and changes in brand salience. The results of these investigations will be published as soon as they justify publication.

In summary, Benefit Segmentation is still being used successfully more than twenty years after its introduction. It works well in advertising planning situations in which cognitive benefits are considered to be the most important types of benefits. However, if it, or any approach, is to be extended to situations involving sensory, emotional, and affiliative benefits, both new research methods and new measurement tools are needed. Nonverbal communication is clearly the frontier in communications research today. Unless progress is made on that front, we are unlikely to be able to make further significant improvements in strategic research.

References

1. A. J. Adams, "Why Lifestyle Research Rarely Works." 13th Annual Attitude Research Conference, American Marketing Association, Chicago, IL, February 1982.
2. Russell H. Colley, DAGMAR, Association of National Advertisers, 1961.
3. Emanual Denby, "Psychographics and from Whence It Came," in *Life Style and Psychographics*. Chicago: American Marketing Association, Chicago, IL, 1974.
4. "Experimental Research on Attitudes Toward Shampoos" Private Research Report, February 1961. See also *Journal of Marketing*, 32, No. 3 (July 1968), pp. 30–35, Russell I. Haley.
5. "Predicting Attention" Unpublished paper, October 1974, Russell I. Haley.
6. Thomas C. Kinnear and Kenneth L. Bernhardt, *Principles of Marketing* (Chicago: Scott, Foresman and Company, 1983), p. 16.
7. Philip Kotler, *Principles of Marketing* (Englewood Cliffs, NJ.: Prentice-Hall, Inc., 1983), p. 17.
8. Milton Rokeach, *Beliefs, Attitudes and Values* (San Francisco: Jossey-Bass, Inc., 1968).

9. Wendell R. Smith, "Product Differentiation, and Market Segmentation as Alternative Product Strategies," *Journal of Marketing*, 21 (July 1956), pp. 3–8.
10. E. M. Tauber, "Stamp Out the Generic Segmentation Study" Editorial in *Journal of Advertising Research*, 23, No. 2 (April/May 1983), p. 7.
11. William Wells, "Do Trends in Attitudes Predict Trends in Behavior?" Advertising Research Workshop, Association of National Advertisers, New York, December 1981.
12. William L. Wilkie and Joel B. Cohen, "An Overview of Market Segmentation: Behavioral Concepts and Research Approaches." MSI Working Paper, June 1977.
13. Alan Wurtzel, "People and Programs: The Application of Segmentation Techniques in Television Research." 29th Annual Conference, American Marketing Association, New York, 1983.

18

How to Segment Industrial Markets

Benson P. Shapiro & Thomas V. Bonoma

With a nested approach, managers can determine the best segmentation method

Industrial marketers can hardly be blamed for feeling that segmentation is very difficult for them. Not only has little been written on the subject as it affects industrial markets, but such analysis is also more complex than for consumer markets. The problem is to identify the best variables for segmenting industrial markets. The authors present here a "nested" approach to industrial market segmentation. Separated according to the amount of investigation required to identify and evaluate different criteria, the layers are arranged to begin with demographics as the area easiest to assess. Then come increasingly complex criteria, including company variables, situational factors, and personal characteristics. The authors warn, however, that a nested approach cannot be applied in cook-book fashion but rather must be adapted to individual situations and circumstances.

As DIFFICULT as segmenting consumer markets is, it is much simpler and easier than segmenting industrial markets. Often the same industrial products have multiple applications; likewise, several different products can be used in the same application. Customers differ greatly and it is hard to discern which differences are important and which are trivial for developing a marketing strategy.

Little research has been done on industrial market segmentation. None of the ten articles in the *Journal of Marketing Research*'s special August 1978 section, "Market Segmentation Research," for instance, deals with industrial market segmentation in more than a passing manner. Our research indicates that most industrial marketers use segmentation as a way to explain results rather than as a way to plan.

In fact, industrial segmentation can assist companies in several areas:

☐ *Analysis of the market*. Better understanding of the total marketplace, including how and why customers buy.

☐ *Selection of key markets*. Rational choice of market segments that best fit the company's capabilities.

☐ *Management of marketing*. The development of strategies, plans, and programs to profitably meet the needs of different market segments and to give the company a distinct competitive advantage.

In this article we integrate and build on previous schemes for segmenting industrial markets and offer a new approach that enables not only the simple grouping of customers and prospects, but also more complex grouping of purchase situations, events, and personalities. It thus serves as an important new analytical tool.

Consider the dilemma of one skilled and able industrial marketer who observed recently:

> I can't see any basis on which to segment my market. We have 15% of the market for our type of plastics fabrication equipment. There are 11 competitors who serve a large and diverse set of customers, but there is no unifying theme to our customer set or to anyone else's.

His frustration is understandable, but he should not give up, for at least he knows that 15% of the market purchases one product and that knowledge, in itself, is a basis for

Benson P. Shapiro is Professor of Business Administration and Senior Associate Dean, Harvard University. Thomas V. Bonoma is Professor of Business Administration at Harvard University.

segmentation. Segments exist, even when the only apparent basis for differentiation is brand choice.

At other times, a marketer may be baffled by a profusion of segmentation criteria. Customer groups and even individual customers within these groups may differ in demographics (including industry and company size), operating differences (production technology is an example), purchasing organization, "culture," and personal characteristics. Usually, a marketer can group customers, prospects, and purchase situations in different ways depending on the variables used to segment the market. The problem is to identify relevant segmentation bases.

We have identified five general segmentation criteria, which we have arranged as a *nested* hierarchy—like a set of boxes that fit one into the other or a set of wooden Russian dolls. Moving from the outer nest toward the inner, these criteria are: demographics, operating variables, customer purchasing approaches, situational factors, and personal characteristics of the buyers.

Exhibit I shows how the criteria relate to one another as nests. The segmentation criteria of the largest, outermost nest are demographics—general, easily observable characteristics about industries and companies; those of the smallest, inmost nest are personal characteristics—specific, subtle, hard-to-assess traits. The marketer moves from the more general, easily observable segmentation characteristics to the more specific, subtle ones. This approach will become clearer as we explain each criterion.

We should note at this point that it may not be necessary or even desirable for every industrial marketer to use every stage of the nested approach for every product. Although it is possible to skip irrelevant criteria, it is important that the marketer completely understand the approach before deciding on omissions and shortcuts.

Exhibit I
Nested approach

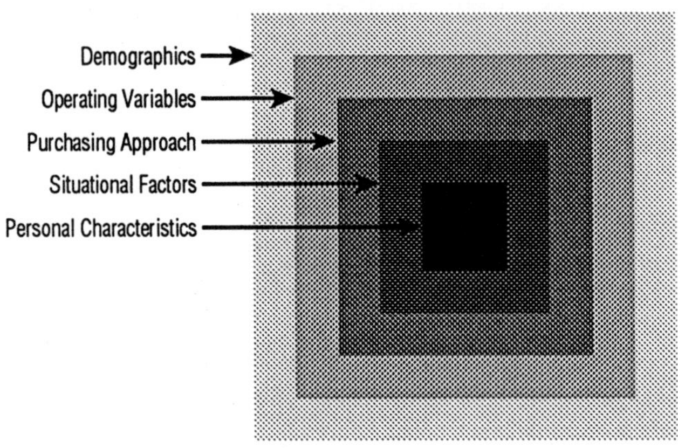

Demographics

We begin with the outermost nest, which contains the most general segmentation criteria, demographics. These variables give a broad description of the company and relate to general customer needs and usage patterns. They can be determined without visiting the customer and include industry and company size, and customer location.

The Industry

Knowledge of the industry affords a broad understanding of customer needs and perceptions of purchase situations. Some companies, such as those selling paper, office equipment, business-oriented computers, and financial services, market to a wide range of industries. For these, industry is an important basis for market segmentation. Hospitals, for example, share some computer needs and yet differ markedly as a customer group from retail stores.

Marketers may wish to subdivide individual industries. For example, although financial services are in a sense a single industry, commercial banks, insurance companies, stockbrokerage houses, and savings and loan associations all differ dramatically. Their differences in terms of product and service needs, such as specialized peripherals and terminals, data handling, and software requirements make a more detailed segmentation scheme necessary to sell computers to the financial services market.

Company Size

The fact that large companies justify and require specialized programs affects market segmentation. It may be, for example, that a small supplier of industrial chemicals, after segmenting its prospective customers on the basis of company size, will choose not to approach large companies whose volume requirements exceed its own production capacity.

Customer Location

The third demographic factor, location, is an important variable in decisions related to deployment and organization of sales staff. A manufacturer of heavy-duty pumps for the petrochemical industry, for example, would want to provide good coverage in the Gulf Coast, where customers are concentrated, while putting little effort into New England. Customer location is especially important when proximity is a requirement for doing business, as in marketing products of low value-per-unit-weight or volume (corrugated boxes or prestressed concrete), or in situations where personal service is essential, as in job shop printing.

As noted, a marketer can determine all of these demographic variables easily. Industry-oriented and general directories are useful in developing lists of customers in terms of industry, size, and location. Government statistics, reports by market research companies, and industry and trade association publications provide a great deal of demographic data.

Many companies base their industrial marketing segmentation approach on demographic data alone. But while demographics are useful and easily obtained, they do not exhaust the possibilities of segmentation. They are often only a beginning.

Operating Variables

The second segmentation nest contains a variety of segmentation criteria called "operating variables." Most of these enable more precise identification of existing and potential customers within demographic categories, Operating variables are generally stable and include technology, user-nonuser status (by product and brand), and customer capabilities (operating, technical, and financial).

Company Technology

A company's technology, involving either its manufacturing process or its product, goes a long way toward determining its buying needs. Soda ash, for example, can be produced by two methods that require different capital equipment and supplies. The production of Japanese color televisions is highly automated and uses a few, large integrated circuits. In the United States, on the other hand, color TV production once involved many discrete components, manual assembly, and fine tuning. In Europe, production techniques made use of a hybrid of integrated circuits and discrete components. The technology used affects companies' requirements for test gear, tooling, and components and thus, a marketer's most appropriate marketing approach.

Product and Brand-Use Status

One of the easiest ways, and in some situations the only obvious way, to segment a market is by product and brand use. Users of a particular product or brand generally have some characteristics in common; at the very least, they have a common experience with a product or brand.

Manufacturers who replace metal gears with nylon gears in capital equipment probably share perceptions of risk, manufacturing process or cost structure, or marketing strategy. They probably have experienced similar sales presentations. Having used nylon gears, they share common experiences including, perhaps, similar changes in manufacturing approaches.

One supplier of nylon gears might argue that companies that have already committed themselves to replace metal gears with nylon gears are better customer prospects than those that have not yet done so, since it is usually easier to generate demand for a new brand than for a new product. But another supplier might reason that manufacturers that have not yet shifted to nylon are better prospects because they have not experienced its benefits and have not developed a working relationship with a supplier. A third marketer might choose to approach both users and nonusers with different strategies.

Current customers are a different segment from prospective customers using a similar product purchased elsewhere. Current customers are familiar with a company's product and service and company managers know something about customer needs and purchasing approaches. Some companies' marketing approaches focus on increasing sales volume from existing customers, via either customer growth or gaining a larger share of the customer's business, rather than on additional sales volume from new customers. In these cases, industrial sales managers often follow a two-step process: first, they seek to gain an initial order on trial and then, to increase the share of the customer's purchases. Banks are often more committed to raising the share of major customers' business than to generating new accounts.

Sometimes it is useful to segment customers not only on the basis of whether they buy from the company or from its competitors, but also, in the latter case, on the identity of competitors. This information can be useful in several ways. Sellers may find it easier to lure customers from competitors that are weak in certain respects. When Bethlehem Steel opened its state-of-the-art Burns Harbor plant in the Chicago area, for example, it went after the customers of one local competitor known to offer poor quality

Customer Capabilities

Marketers might find companies with known operating, technical, or financial strengths and weaknesses to be an attractive market. For example, a company operating with tight materials inventories would greatly appreciate a supplier with a reliable delivery record. And customers unable to perform quality-control tests on incoming materials might be willing to pay for supplier quality checks. Some raw materials suppliers might choose to develop a thriving business among less sophisticated companies, for which lower-than-usual average discounts well compensate added services.

Technically weak customers in the chemical industry have traditionally depended on suppliers for formulation assistance and technical support. Some suppliers have been astute in identifying customers needing such support and in providing it in a highly effective manner.

Technical strength can also differentiate customers. Digital Equipment Corporation for many years specialized in selling its minicomputers to customers able to develop their own software, and Prime Computer sells computer systems to business users who do not need the intensive support and "hand holding" offered by IBM and other manufacturers. Both companies use segmentation for market selection.

Many operating variables are easily researched. In a quick drive around a soda ash plant, for example, a vendor might be able to identify the type of technology being used. Data on financial strength is at least partially available from credit-rating services. Customer personnel may provide other data, such as the name of current suppliers; "reverse engineering" (tearing down or disassembly) of a product may yield information on the type and even the producers of components, as may merely noting the names on delivery trucks entering the prospect's premises.

Purchasing Approaches

One of the most neglected but valuable methods of segmenting an industrial market involves consumers' purchasing approaches and company philosophy The factors in this middle segmentation nest include the formal organization of the purchasing function, the power structure, the nature of buyer-seller relationships, the general purchasing policies, and the purchasing criteria.

Purchasing Function Organization

The organization of the purchasing function to some extent determines the size and operation of a company's purchasing unit. A centralized approach may merge individual purchasing units into a single group, and vendors with decentralized manufacturing operations may find it difficult to meet centralized buying patterns.[1] To meet these differing needs, some suppliers handle sales to centralized purchasers through so-called national account programs, and those to companies with a decentralized approach through field-oriented sales forces.

Power Structures

These also vary widely among customers. The impact of influential organizational units varies and often affects purchasing approaches. The powerful financial analysis units at General Motors and Ford may, for example, have made those companies unusually price-oriented in their purchasing decisions. A company may have a powerful engineering department, for instance, that strongly influences purchases; a supplier with strong technical skills would suit such a customer. A vendor might find it useful to adapt its marketing program to customer strengths, using one approach for customers with strong engineering operations and another for customers lacking these.

Buyer-Seller Relationships

A supplier probably has stronger ties with some customers than others. The link may be clearly stated. A lawyer, commercial banker, or investment banker, for example, might define as an unattractive market segment all companies having as a board member the representative of a competitor.

General Purchasing Policies

A financially strong company that offers a lease program might want to identify prospective customers who prefer to lease capital equipment or who have meticulous asset management. When AT&T could lease but not sell equipment, this was an important segmentation criterion for it. Customers may prefer to do business with long-established companies or with small independent companies, or may have particularly potent affirmative action purchasing programs (minority-owned businesses were attracted by Polaroid's widely publicized social conscience program, for example). Or they may prefer to buy systems rather than individual components.

A prospective customer's approach to the purchasing process is important. Some purchasers require an agreement based on supplier cost, particularly the auto companies, the U.S. government, and the three large general merchandise chains, Sears Roebuck, Montgomery Ward, and J. C. Penney. Other purchasers negotiate from a market-based price and some use bids. Bidding is an important method for obtaining government and quasi-government business; but because it emphasizes price, bidding tends to favor suppliers that, perhaps because of a cost advantage, prefer to compete on price. Some vendors might view purchasers that choose suppliers via bidding as desirable, while others might avoid them.

Purchasing Criteria

The power structure, the nature of buyer-seller relationships, and general purchasing policies all affect purchasing criteria. Benefit segmentation in the consumer goods market is the process of segmenting a market in terms of the reasons why customers buy. It is, in fact, the most insightful form of consumer goods segmentation because it deals directly with customer needs. In the industrial market, consideration of the criteria used to make purchases and the application for these purchases, which we consider later, approximate the benefit segmentation approach.

Situational Factors

Up to this point we have focused on the grouping of customer companies. Now we consider the role of the purchase situation, even single-line entries on the order form.

Situational factors resemble operating variables but are temporary and require a more detailed knowledge of the customer. They include the urgency of order fulfillment, product application, and the size of order.

Urgency of Order Fulfillment

It is worthwhile to differentiate between products to be used in routine replacement or for building a new plant and emergency replacement of existing parts. Some companies have found a degree of urgency useful for market selection and for developing a focused marketing-manufacturing approach leading to a "hot-order shop"—a factory that can supply small, urgent orders quickly.

A supplier of large-size, heavy-duty stainless steel pipe fittings, for example, defined its primary market as fast-order replacements. A chemical plant or paper mill needing to replace a fitting quickly is often willing to pay a premium price for a vendor's application engineering, for flexible manufacturing capacity, and for installation skills that would be unnecessary in the procurement of routine replacement parts.

Product Application

The requirements for a 5-horsepower motor used in intermittent service in a refinery will differ from those of a 5-horsepower motor in continuous use. Requirements for an intermittent-service motor would vary depending on whether its reliability was critical to the operation or safety of the refinery. Product application can have a major impact on the purchase process, purchase criteria, and thus on the choice of vendor.

Size of Order

Market selection can be based at the level of individual line entries on the order form. A company with highly automated equipment might segment the market so that it can concentrate only on items with large unit volumes. A nonautomated company, on the other hand, might want only small quantity, short-run items. Ideally, these vendors would like the order split up into long-run and short-run items. In many industries, such as paper and pipe fittings, distributors break up orders in this way.

Marketers can differentiate individual orders in terms of product uses as well as users. The distinction is important as users may seek different suppliers for the same product under different circumstances. The pipe-fittings manufacturer that focused on urgent orders is a good example of a marketing approach based on these differences.

Situational factors can greatly affect purchasing approaches. General Motors, for example, makes a distinction between product purchases—that is, raw materials or components for a product being produced—and nonproduct purchases. Urgency of order fulfillment is so powerful that it can change both the purchase process and the criteria used. An urgent replacement is generally purchased on the basis of availability, not price.

The interaction between situational factors and purchasing approaches is an example of the permeability of segmentation nests. Factors in one nest affect those in other nests. Industry criteria, for instance, an outer-nest demographic description, influence but do not determine application, a middle-nest situational criterion. The nests are a useful mental construct but not a clean framework of independent units because in the complex reality of industrial markets, criteria are interrelated.

The nesting approach cannot be applied in a cookbook fashion but requires, instead, careful, intelligent judgment.

Buyers' Personal Characteristics

People, not companies, make purchase decisions, although the organizational framework in which they work and company policies and needs may constrain their choices. Marketers for industrial goods, like those for consumer products, can segment markets according to the individuals involved in a purchase in terms of buyer-seller similarity, buyer motivation, individual perceptions, and risk-management strategies.

Some buyers are risk averse, others risk receptive. The level of risk a buyer is willing to assume is related to other personality variables such as personal style, intolerance for ambiguity, and self-confidence. The amount of attention a purchasing agent will pay to cost factors depends not only on the degree of uncertainty about the consequences of the decision but also on whether credit or blame for these will accrue to him or her. Buyers who are risk averse are not good prospects for new products and concepts. Risk-averse buyers also tend to avoid untested vendors.

Some buyers are meticulous in their approach to buying—they shop around, look at a number of vendors, and then split their order to assure delivery. Others rely on old friends and past relationships, and seldom make vendor comparisons.[2] Companies can segment a market in terms of these preferences.

Data on personal characteristics are expensive and difficult to gather. It is often worthwhile to develop good, formal, sales information systems to ensure that salespeople transmit the data they gather to the marketing department for use in developing segmented marketing strategies. One chemical company attributes part of its sales success to its sales information system's routine collection of data on buyers. Such data-gathering efforts are most justified in the case of customers with large sales potential.

Reassembling the Nest

Marketers are interested in purchase decisions that depend on company variables, situational factors, and the personal characteristics of the buyers. The three outer nests, as Exhibit II shows, cover company variables, the fourth inner-middle nest, situational factors, and the inmost nest, personal characteristics.

As we move from the outer to the inner nests, the segmentation criteria change in terms of visibility, permanence, and intimacy The data in the outer nests are generally highly

Exhibit II
Classification of nests

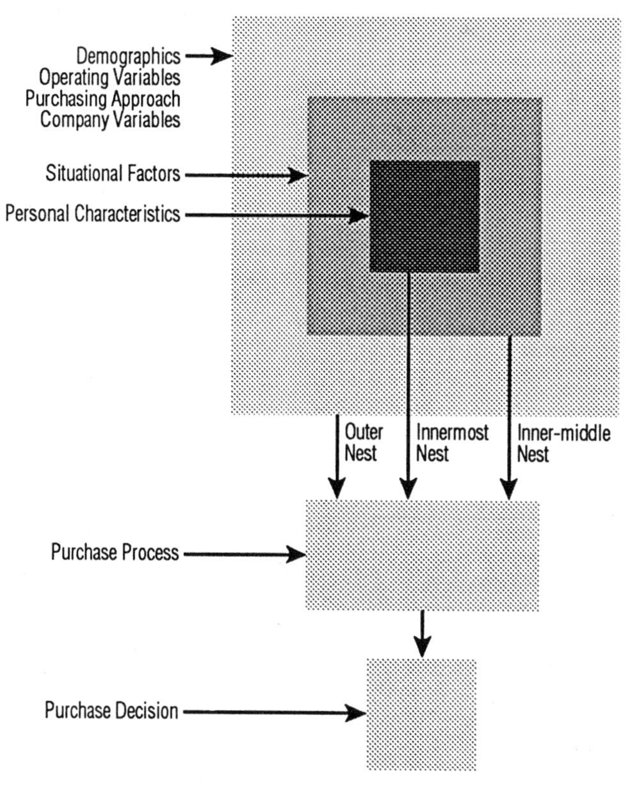

visible, even to outsiders, are more or less permanent, and require little intimate knowledge of customers. But situational factors and personal characteristics are less visible, are more transient, and require extensive vendor research.

An industrial marketing executive can choose from a wide range of segmentation approaches other than the nested approach and, in fact, the myriad of possibilities often has one of the four following outcomes:

☐ *No segmentation.* "The problem is too large to approach."

☐ *After-the-fact segmentation.* "Our market research shows that we have captured a high share of the distribution segment and low shares of the others; thus we must be doing something right for customers in high-share segments."

☐ *Superficial segmentation.* "While we know all banks are different, it's easier to organize marketing plans around banks because we can identify them and tell the salespeople whom to call on." This dangerous outcome gives a false sense of security.

☐ *Obtuse, convoluted, and disorganized segmentation.* "We have a 300-page report on market segmentation and customer buying patterns, but there is just too much data in there. So we have decided to focus on insurance companies and hospitals to avoid another two-day market planning meeting."

Our approach using a hierarchical structure is easy to use. Marketers can, in most cases, work systematically from the outer nests to the inner nests. They can run through the whole set of criteria and identify important factors that otherwise might be neglected. And they can balance between reliance on the easily acquired data of the outer nests and the detailed analyses of the inner nests.

We suggest that a marketer begin at the outside nest and work inward because data are more available and definitions clearer in the outer nests. On the other hand, the situational and personal variables of the inner nests are often the most useful. In our experience, managers most frequently neglect situational criteria. In situations where knowledge and analysis exist, a marketer might decide to begin at a middle nest and work inward or, less probably, outward.

After several attempts at working completely through the process, companies will discover which segmentation criteria are likely to yield greater benefits than others and which cannot be considered carefully without better data. A warning is necessary, however. A company should not decide that an approach is *not* useful because data are lacking. The segmentation process requires that assessments of analytic promise and data availability be made independently. The two steps should not be confused. When the necessary data are gathered, managers can weigh segmentation approaches.

A fine line exists between minimizing the cost and difficulty of segmentation by staying in the outer nests on the one hand and gaining the useful data of the inner nests at appreciable direct and indirect cost on the other The outer-nest criteria are generally inadequate when used by themselves in all but the most simple or homogeneous markets because they ignore buying differences among customers. Overemphasis on the inner-nest factors, however, can be too expensive and time-consuming for small markets. We suggest achieving a sense of balance between the simplicity and low cost of the outer nests and the richness and expense of the inner ones by making the choices explicit and the process clear and disciplined.

References

1. See E. Raymond Corey, "Should Companies Centralize Procurement?" *Harvard Business Review,* November–December, 1978, p. 102.
2. For further discussion of these, see Thomas V. Bonoma, "Major Sales: Who *Really* Does the Buying?" *Harvard Business Review,* May–June, 1982, p. 111, and Benson P. Shapiro and Ronald Posner, "Making the Major Sale," *Harvard Business Review,* March–April, 1976, p. 68.

This article is based on the authors' book, published in 1983, *Segmenting the Industrial Market* (Lexington Books). The research for this project was supported by the Marketing Science Institute and the Associates of the Harvard Business School.

19

The Positioning Era Cometh

Jack Trout & Al Ries

The changes that have come about in advertising strategies as a result of "the positioning era," how it came to be and what it means to us now are examined in this three-part article.

In the '50s, hard sell ads predominated.

In the '60s, creativity came into vogue.

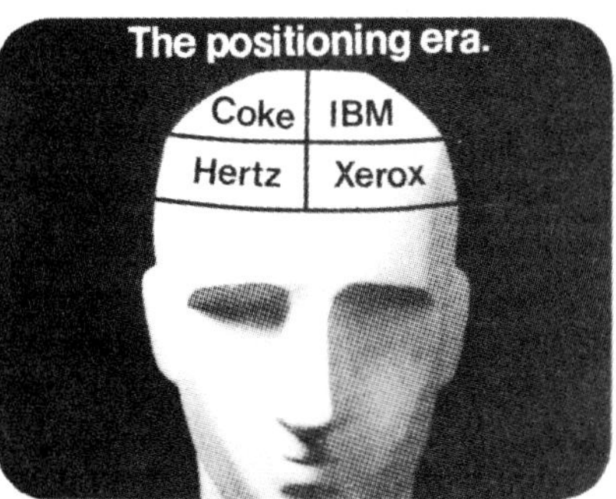

In the '70s, strategy will be king.

TODAY IT HAS BECOME OBVIOUS that advertising is entering a new era. An era where creativity is no longer the key to success.

The fun and games of the '60s have given way to the harsh realities of the '70s. Today's marketplace is no longer responsive to the kind of advertising that worked in the past. There are just too many products, too many companies, too much marketing "noise."

To succeed in our over-communicated society, a company must create a "position" in the prospect's mind. A position that takes into consideration not only its own strength and weaknesses, but those of its competitors as well.

Advertising is entering an era where strategy is king.

Al Ries is Chairman and Jack Trout is President of Trout & Ries, Inc.

A Tale of Two Ads

If you had to pick an official date to mark the end of the last advertising era and the start of the new one, your choice would have to be Wednesday, April 7, 1971. In the *New York Times* that day was a full-page ad that seemed to generate very little excitement in the advertising community.

But then, an abrupt change in the direction of an industry isn't always accompanied by the blowing of bugles. You sometimes need the vantage point of history to realize what has happened.

The ad that appeared that spring morning in 1971 was written by David Ogilvy. And it's no coincidence that the architect of one era called the tune for the next.

In the ad, the articulate Mr. Ogilvy outlined his 38 points for creating "advertising that sells."

In first place on his list was a point Mr. Ogilvy called "the most important decision." Then he went on to say, "The results of your campaign depend less on how we write your advertising than on how your product is positioned."

Blow the bugles, the positioning era has begun.

Five days later, in the *New York Times* and in *Advertising Age*, another ad appeared that confirmed the fact that the advertising industry was indeed changing direction. Placed by Rosenfeld, Sirowitz & Lawson, the ad listed the agency's four guiding principles.

In first place was, you guessed it. According to Ron Rosenfeld, Len Sirowitz and Tom Lawson, "Accurate positioning is the most important step in effective selling."

Suddenly the word and concept was in everybody's ads and on everybody's lips. Hardly an issue of *Advertising Age* passes without some reference to "positioning."

You Can't Beat 'em Head-On

In spite of Madison Ave.'s current love affair with positioning, the concept had a more humble beginning.

In 1969, one of us (Jack Trout) wrote an article entitled "Positioning is a game people play in today's me-too marketplace," which appeared in the June, 1969, issue of *Industrial Marketing*. The article made predictions and named names, all based on the "rules" of a game called positioning.

One prediction, in particular, turned out to be strikingly accurate. As far as RCA and computers were concerned, "a company has no hope to make progress head-on against the position that IBM has established."

The operative word, of course, is "head-on." And while it's possible to compete successfully with a market leader (the article suggested several approaches), the rules of positioning say it can't be done "head-on."

Three years ago this raised a few eyebrows. Who were we to say that powerful, multi-billion-dollar companies couldn't find happiness in the computer business if they so desired?

Desire, alas, was not enough. Not only RCA, but also General Electric bit the IBM dust.

With two major computer manufacturers folding one right after another, the urge to say, "I told you so," was irresistible.

Last November, a follow-up article, "Positioning revisited: Why didn't GE and RCA listen?" appeared in the same publication.

We're an Over-Communicated Society

As GE and RCA found out, advertising doesn't work anymore. At least, not like it used to. One reason may be the noise level in the communications jungle.

The per-capita consumption of advertising in the U.S. is approaching $100 a year. And while no one doubts the advertiser's financial ability to dish it out, there's some question about the consumer's mental ability to take it all in.

Each day, thousands of messages compete for a share of the prospect's mind. And, make no mistake about it, the mind of the battleground. Between six inches of grey matter is where the advertising war takes place. And the battle is rough, with no holds barred and no quarter given.

The new ball game can prove unsettling to companies that grew up in an era where any regular advertising was likely to bring success. This is why you see a mature, sophisticated company like Bristol-Myers run through millions of dollars trying to launch me-too products against strongly dug-in competition. (If you haven't noticed, Fact, Vote and Resolve are no longer with us.)

To understand why some companies have trouble playing in today's positioning game, it might be helpful to take a look at recent communications history.

'50s Were the Product Era

Back in the '50s, advertising was in the "product" era. In a lot of ways, these were the good old days when the "better mousetrap" and some money to promote it were all you needed.

It was a time when advertising people focused their attention on product features and customer benefits. They looked for, as Rosser Reeves called it, the "Unique Selling Proposition."

But in the late '50s, technology started to rear its ugly head. It became more and more difficult to establish the "USP."

The end of the product era came with an avalanche of "me-too" products that descended on the market. Your "better mousetrap" was quickly followed by two more just like it. Both claiming to be better than the first one.

The competition was fierce and not always totally honest. It got so bad that one product manager was overheard to say, "Wouldn't you know it. Last year we had nothing to say, so we put 'new and improved' on the package. This year the research people came up with a real improvement, and we don't know what to say."

In '60s, 'Image' Was King

The next phase was the image era. In the '60s, successful companies found their reputation or "image" was more important in selling a product than any specific product feature.

The architect of the image era was David Ogilvy. As he said in his famous speech on the subject, "Every advertisement is a long-term investment in the image of a brand." And he proved the validity of his ideas with programs for Hathaway shirts, Rolls-Royce, Schweppes and others.

But just as the "me-too" products killed the product era, the "me-too" companies killed the image era. As every company tried to establish a reputation for itself, the noise level became so high that relatively few companies succeeded. And most of the ones that made it, did it primarily with spectacular technical achievements, not spectacular advertising.

But while it lasted, the exciting, go-go years of the middle '60s were like a marketing orgy.

At the party, it was "everyone into the pool." Little thought was given to failure. With the magic of money and enough bright people, a company felt that any marketing program would succeed.

The wreckage is still washing up on the beach. Du Pont's Corfam, Gablinger's beer, Handy Andy all-purpose cleaner, *Look* magazine.

The world will never be the same again and neither will the advertising business. Today we are entering an era that recognizes both the importance of the product and the importance of the company image, but more than anything else stresses the need to create a "position" in the prospect's mind.

Positioning Era Dawns

The great copywriters of yesterday, who have gone to that big agency in the sky, would die all over again if they saw some of the campaigns currently running (successful campaigns, we might add).

Take beer advertising. In the past, a beer copywriter looked closely at the product to find his copy platform. And he found "real-draft" Piels, and "cold-brewed" Ballantine. Back a little farther he discovered the "land of the sky blue waters" and "just a kiss of the hops."

In the positioning era, however, effective beer advertising is taking a different tack. "First class is Michelob" positioned the brand as the first American-made premium beer. "The one beer to have when you're having more than one" positioned Schaefer as the brand for the heavy beer drinker.

But there's an imported beer whose positioning strategy is so crystal clear that those old-time beer copywriters probably wouldn't even accept it as advertising.

"You've tasted the German beer that's the most popular in America. Now taste the German beer that's the most popular in Germany." This is how Beck's beer is effectively positioning itself against Lowenbrau.

Then there's Seven-Up's "Un-Cola" campaign.

And *Sports Illustrated*'s "Third Newsweekly" program.

All of these positioning campaigns have a number of things in common. They don't emphasize product features, customer benefits or the company's image. Yet, they are all highly successful.

Old Word Gets New Meaning

Like any new concept, positioning isn't new. At least not in the literal sense. What is new is the broader meaning now being given to the word.

Yesterday, positioning was used in a narrow sense to mean what the advertiser did to his product. Today, positioning is used in a broader sense to mean what the advertising does for the product in the prospect's mind. In other words, a successful advertiser today uses advertising to position his product, not to communicate its advantages or features.

Positioning has its roots in the packaged goods field where the concept was called "product positioning." It literally meant the product's form, package size, and price as compared to competition.

Procter & Gamble carried the idea one step forward by developing a master copy platform that related each of their competing brands. For example: Tide makes clothes "white." Cheer makes them "whiter than white." And Bold makes them "bright."

Although the advertising for each Procter & Gamble brand might vary from year to year, it never departed from its pre-assigned role or "position" in the master plan.

The big breakthrough came when people started thinking of positioning not as something the client does before the advertising is prepared, but as the very objective of the advertising itself. External, rather than internal positioning.

A classic example of looking through the wrong end of the telescope was Ford's introduction of the Edsel. In the ensuing laughter that followed, most people missed the point. In essence, the Ford people got switched around. The Edsel was a beautiful case of internal positioning to fill a hole between Ford and Mercury on the one hand, and Lincoln on the other. Good strategy inside the building. Bad strategy outside where there was simply no position for this car in a category already cluttered with heavily-chromed, medium-priced cars.

If the Edsel had been tagged a "high performance" car and presented in a sleek two-door, bucket-seat form and given a name to match, no one would have laughed. It could have occupied a position that no one else owned and the ending of the story might have been different.

Remember the Mind Is a Memory Bank

To better understand what an advertiser is up against, it may be helpful to take a closer look at the objective of all advertising programs—the human mind.

Like a memory bank, the mind has a slot or "position" for each bit of information it has chosen to retain. In operation, the mind is a lot like a computer.

But there is one important difference. A computer has to accept what is put into it. The mind does not. In fact, it's quite the opposite.

The mind, as a defense mechanism against the volume of today's communications, screens and rejects much of the information offered it. In general, the mind accepts only that new information which matches its prior knowledge or experience. It filters out everything else.

For example, when a viewer sees a television commercial that says, "NCR means computers," he doesn't accept it. IBM means computers. NCR means National Cash Register.

The computer "position" in the minds of most people is filled by a company called the International Business Machines Corp. For a competitive computer manufacturer to obtain a favorable position in the prospect's mind, he must somehow relate his company to IBM's position.

Yet, too many companies embark on marketing and advertising programs as if the competitor's position did not exist. They advertise their products in a vacuum and are disappointed when their messages fail to get through.

Seven Brands Are Mind's Limit

The mind, as a container for ideas, is totally unsuited to the job at hand.

There are more than 500,000 trademarks registered with the U.S. Patent Office. In addition, untold thousands of unregistered trademarks are in use throughout the country.

During the course of a single year, the average mind is exposed to more than half a million advertising messages.

The target of all this communications ammunition has a reading vocabulary of no more than 25,000 to 50,000 words, and a speaking vocabulary of one-fifth as much.

Another limitation: The average human mind, according to Harvard psychologist George A. Miller, cannot deal with more than seven units at a time. (The eighth company in a given field is out of luck.)

Ask someone to name all the brands he or she remembers in a given product category. Rarely will anyone name more than seven. And that's for a high-interest category. For low-interest products, the average consumer can usually name no more than one or two brands.

Yet in category after category, the number of individual brands multiply like rabbits. In 1964, there were seven soft drinks advertised on network television. Today there are 22.

To cope with complexity, people have learned to reduce everything to its utmost simplicity.

When asked to describe an offspring's intellectual progress, a person doesn't usually quote vocabulary statistics, reading comprehension, mathematical ability, etc. "He's in seventh grade" is a typical reply.

This "ranking" of people, objects, and brands is not only a convenient method of organizing things, but also an absolute necessity if a person is to keep from being overwhelmed by the complexities of life.

You see ranking concepts at work among movies, restaurants, business, and military organizations. (Some day someone might even come up with a rating system for politicians.)

Mind Puts Products on Ladders

To cope with advertising's complexity, people have learned to rank products and brands in the mind. Perhaps this can best be visualized by imagining a series of ladders in the mind. On each step is a brand name. And each different ladder represents a different product category.

Some ladders have many steps. (Seven is many.) Others have few, if any.

For an advertiser to increase his brand preference, he must move up the ladder. This can be difficult if the brands above have a strong foothold and no leverage or positioning strategy is applied against them.

For an advertiser to introduce a new product category, he must carry in a new ladder. This, too, is difficult, especially if the new category is not positioned against an old one. The mind has no room for the new and different unless it's related to the old.

That's why if you have a truly new product, it's often better to tell the prospect what the product is *not*, rather than what it is.

The first automobile, for example, was called a "horseless" carriage, a name which allowed the public to position the concept against the existing mode of transportation.

Words like "offtrack" betting, "lead-free" gasoline and "tubeless" tire are all examples of how new concepts can best be positioned against the old.

Names that do not contain an element of positioning usually die out. The "Astrojet" name dreamed up by American Airlines is an example of a glamorous, but unsuccessful name, because it lacks a positioning idea.

Leading Brand Has Big Edge

The weather forecast for the old, traditional ways of advertising is gloomy at best. And nowhere was this more clearly demonstrated than in the recent Atlanta study conducted by Daniel Starch & Staff.

According to Starch, about 25% of those noting a television commercial attributed it to the competition. With virtually no exceptions, high scoring commercials were the brand leaders in their category.

The also-rans didn't fare nearly as well. A David Janssen Excedrin commercial was associated with Anacin twice as often as Excedrin. A Pristeen commercial helped F.D.S., the brand leader, more than it did Pristeen.

This shattering turn of events is certainly "positioning" at work in our over-communicated society. It appears that unless an advertisement is based on a unique idea or position, the message is often put in the mental slot reserved for the leader in the product category.

Clutter is surely part of the reason for the rise of "misidentification." But another, even more important factor is that times have changed. Today, you cannot advertise your product in splendid isolation. Unless your advertising positions your product in relationship to its competition, your advertising is doomed to failure.

Creativity No Longer Enough

In the positioning era, "strategy" is king. It made little difference how clever the ads of RCA, General Electric, and Bristol-Myers were. Or how well the layout, copy, and typography were executed. Their strategy of attacking the leaders head-on was wrong.

In this context, it's illuminating to take a look at some recent examples of rampant creativity. The Lone Ranger and REA Express, Joe Namath and Ovaltine, Ann Miller and Great American soups. Even though these programs are highly creative, their chances for success are limited because each of them lacks a strong positioning idea.

Even creativity in the form of a slogan no longer serves much of a purpose if it doesn't position the product.

"If you got it, flaunt it" and "We must be doing something right" achieved enormous popularity without doing much for Braniff and Rheingold. And we predict that "Try it, you'll like it" won't do much for Alka-Seltzer.

Positioning Cuts Through Chaos in Marketplace

As far as advertising is concerned, the good old days are gone forever.

As the president of a large consumer products company said recently, "Count on your fingers the number of successful new national brands introduced in the last two years. You won't get to your pinky."

Not that a lot of companies haven't tried. Every supermarket is filled with shelf after shelf of "half successful" brands. The manufacturers of these me-too products cling to the hope that they can develop a brilliant advertising campaign which will lift their offspring into the winner's circle.

Meanwhile, they hang in there with coupons, deals, point of purchase displays. But profits are hard to come by and that "brilliant" advertising campaign, even if it comes, doesn't ever seem to turn the brand around.

No wonder management people turn skeptical when the subject of advertising comes up. And instead of looking for new ways to put the power of advertising to work, management invents schemes for reducing the cost of what they are currently doing. Witness the rise of the house agency, the media buying service, the barter deal.

Ads Don't Work Like They Used To

The chaos in the marketplace is a reflection of the fact that advertising just doesn't work like it used to. But old traditional ways of doing things die hard. "There's no reason that advertising can't do the job," say the defenders of the status quo, "as long as the product is good, the plan is sound, and the commercials are creative." But they overlook one big, loud reason. The marketplace itself. The noise level today is far too high. Not only the volume of advertising, but also the volume of products and brands.

To cope with this assault on his or her mind, the average consumer has run out of brain power and mental ability. And with a rising standard of living the average consumer is less and less interested in making the "best" choice. For many of today's more affluent customers, a "satisfactory" brand is good enough.

Advertising prepared in the old, traditional ways has no hope of being successful in today's chaotic marketplace. In the past, advertising was prepared in isolation. That is, you studied the product and its features and then you prepared advertising which communicated to your customers and prospects the benefits of those features. It didn't make much difference whether the competition offered those features or not. In the traditional approach, you ignored competition and made every claim seem like a preemptive claim. Mentioning a competitive product, for example, was considered not only bad taste, but poor strategy as well.

In the positioning era, however, the rules are reversed. To establish a position, you must often not only name competitive names, but also ignore most of the old advertising rules as well. In category after category, the prospect already knows the benefits of using the product. To climb on his product ladder, you must relate your brand to the brands already there.

Avis Took 'Against' Position

In today's marketplace, the competitor's image is just as important as your own. Sometimes more important. An early

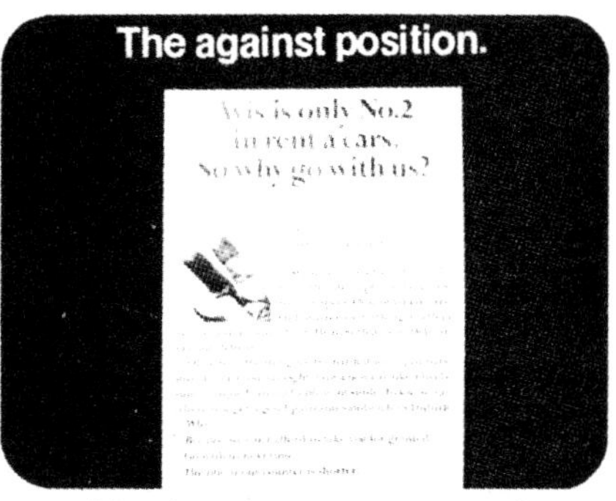

Avis exploited the love for the underdog.

Volkswagen accepted an unwanted position.

Seven-Up became a cola alternative.

'Sports Illustrated' moved into new league.

Eastern is saddled with regional name.

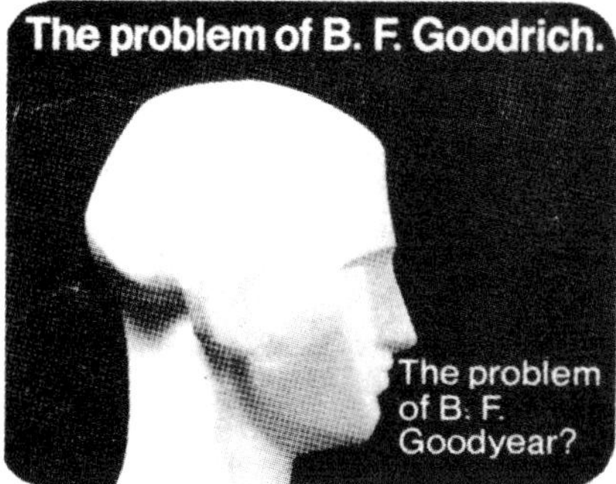

Goodrich is stuck with confusing name.

success in the positioning era was the famous Avis campaign.

The Avis campaign will go down in marketing history as a classic example of establishing the "against" position. In the case of Avis, this was a position against the leader.

"Avis is only No. 2 in rent-a-cars, so why go with us? We try harder."

For 13 straight years, Avis lost money. Then they admitted they were No. 2 and have made money every year since. Avis was able to make substantial gains because they recognized the position of Hertz and didn't try to attack them head-on.

VW Made 'Ugly' Position Work

A company can sometimes be successful by accepting a position that no one else wants. For example, virtually all automobile manufacturers want the public to think they make cars that are good looking. As a result, Volkswagen was able to establish a unique position for themselves. By default.

The strength of this position, of course, is that it communicates the idea of reliability in a powerful way. "The 1970 VW will stay ugly longer" was a powerful statement because it is psychologically sound. When an advertiser admits a negative, the reader is inclined to give them the positive.

A similar principle is involved in Smucker's jams and jellies. "With a name like Smucker's," says the advertising, "you know it's got to be good."

Battle of the Colas

The advantage of owning a position can be seen most clearly in the soft drink field. Three major cola brands compete in what is really not a contest. For every ten bottles of Coke, only four bottles of Pepsi and one bottle of Royal Crown are consumed.

While there may be room in the market for a No. 2 cola, the position of Royal Crown is weak. In 1970, for example, Coca-Cola's sales increase over the previous year (168,000,000 cases) was more than Royal Crown's entire volume (156,000,000 cases).

Obviously, Coke has a strong grip on the cola position. And there's not much room left for the other brands. But, strange as it might seem, there might be a spot for a reverse kind of product. One of the most interesting positioning ideas is the one currently being used by Seven-Up. It's the "Un-Cola" and it seems silly until you take a closer look.

"Wet and Wild" was a good campaign in the image era. But the "Un-Cola" is a great program in the positioning era. Sales jumped something like 10% the first year the product was positioned against the cola field. And the increases have continued.

The brilliance of this idea can only be appreciated when you comprehend the intense share of mind enjoyed by the cola category. Two out of three soft drinks consumed in the U.S. are cola drinks.

By linking the product to what's already in the mind of the prospect, the Un-Cola position establishes Seven-Up as an alternative to a cola drink.

A somewhat similar positioning program is working in the media field. This is the "third newsweekly" concept being used by *Sports Illustrated* to get into the mind of the media buyer.

It obviously is an immensely successful program. But what may not be so obvious is why it works. The "third newsweekly" certainly doesn't describe *Sports Illustrated*. (As the Un-Cola doesn't describe Seven-Up.)

What it does do, however, is to relate the magazine to a media category that is uppermost in the prospect's mind (as the Un-Cola relates to the soft drink category that is uppermost in the mind).

Both the Seven-Up and the *Sports Illustrated* programs are dramatic reminders that positioning is not something you do with the product. Positioning is something you do with the mind. That is, you position the product in the mind of the prospect.

You Can Reposition Competitor

In order to position your own brand, it's sometimes necessary to reposition the competitor.

In the case of Beck's beer, the repositioning is done at the expense of Lowenbrau: "You've tasted the German beer that's the most popular in America. Now taste the German beer that's the most popular in Germany."

This strategy works because the prospect had assumed something about Lowenbrau that wasn't true.

The current program for Raphael aperitif wine also illustrates this point. The ads show a bottle of "made in France" Raphael and a bottle of "made in U.S.A." Dubonnet. "For $1.00 a bottle less," says the headline, "you can enjoy the imported one." The shock, of course, is to find that Dubonnet is a product of the U.S.

Plight of Airline X

In the positioning era, the name of a company or product is becoming more and more important. The name is the hook that allows the mind to hang the brand on its product ladder. Given a poor name, even the best brand in the world won't be able to hang on.

Take the airline industry. The big four domestic carriers are United, American, TWA, and an airline we'll call Airline X.

Like all airlines, Airline X has had its ups and downs. Unfortunately, there have been more downs than ups. But unlike some of its more complacent competitors, Airline X has tried. A number of years ago, it brought in big league marketing people and pushed in the throttle.

Airline X was among the first to "paint the planes," "improve the food," and "dress up the stewardesses" in an effort to improve its reputation. And Airline X hasn't been bashful when it comes to spending money. Year after year, it has one of the biggest advertising budgets in the industry. Even though it advertises itself as "the second largest passenger carrier of all the airlines in the free world," you may not have guessed that Airline X is Eastern. Right up there spending with the worldwide names.

For all that money, what do you think of Eastern? Where do you think they fly? Up and down the East Coast, to Boston, Washington, Miami, right? Well, Eastern also goes to St. Louis, New Orleans, Atlanta, San Francisco, Acapulco. But Eastern has a regional name and their competitors have broader names which tell the prospect they fly everywhere.

Look at the problem from just one of Eastern's cities, Indianapolis. From Indianapolis, Eastern flies *north* to Chicago, Milwaukee, and Minneapolis. And *south* to Birmingham and Mobile. They just don't happen to fly *east*.

And then there is the lush San Juan run which Eastern has been serving for more than 25 years. Eastern used to get the lion's share of this market. Then early last year American Airlines took over Trans Caribbean. So today, who is number one to the San Juan sun? Why American, of course.

No matter how hard you try, you can't hang "The Wings of Man" on a regional name. When the prospect is given a choice, he or she is going to prefer the national airline, not the regional one.

B. F. Goodrich Has Identity Crisis

What does a company do when its name (Goodrich) is similar to the name of a much larger company in the same field (Goodyear)?

Goodrich has problems. They could reinvent the wheel and Goodyear would get most of the credit.

If you watched the Super Bowl last January, you saw both Goodrich and Goodyear advertise their "American-made radial-ply tires." But which company do you think got their money's worth at $200,000 a pop?

We haven't seen the research, but our bet would be on Goodyear, the company that owns the tire position.

Beware of the No-Name Trap

But even bad names like Eastern and Goodrich are better than no name at all. In *Fortune*'s list of 500 largest industrials, there are now 16 corporate nonentities. That is, 16 major American companies have legally changed their names to meaningless initials.

How many of these companies can you recognize: ACF, AMF, AMP, ATO, CPC, ESB, FMC, GAF, NVF, NL, PPG, RCA, SCM, TRW, USM, and VF?

These are not tiny companies either. The smallest of them, AMP, has more than 10,000 employees and sales of over $225,000,000 a year.

What companies like ACF, AMF, AMP and the others fail to realize is that their initials have to stand for something. A prospect must know your name first before he or she can remember your initials.

GE stands for General Electric, IBM stands for International Business Machines. And everyone knows it. But how many people knew that ACF stood for American Car & Foundry?

Furthermore, now that ACF has legally changed its name to initials, there's presumably no way to even expose the prospect to the original name.

An exception seems to be RCA. After all, everyone knows that RCA stands for, or rather used to stand for, Radio Corp. of America.

That may be true today. But what about tomorrow? What will people think 20 years from now when they see those strange initials. Roman Catholic Archdiocese?

And take Corn Products Co. Presumably it changed its name to CPC International because it makes products out of lots of things besides corn, but you can't remember "CPC" without bringing Corn Products Co. to mind. The tragedy is, CPC made the change to "escape" the past. Yet the exact opposite occurred.

Line Extension Can Be Trap, Too

Names are tricky. Consider the Protein 21/29 shampoo, hair spray, conditioner, concentrate mess.

Back in 1970, the Mennen Co. introduced a combination shampoo conditioner called "Protein 21." By moving rapidly with a $6,000,000 introductory campaign (followed by a $9,000,000 program the next year), Mennen rapidly carved out a 13% share of the $300,000,000 shampoo market.

Then Mennen hit the line extension lure. In rapid succession, the company introduced Protein 21 hair spray, Protein 29 hair spray (for men), Protein 21 conditioner (in two formulas), Protein 21 concentrate. To add to the confusion, the original Protein 21 was available in three different formulas (for dry, oily, and regular hair).

Can you imagine how confused the prospect must be trying to figure out what to put on his or her head? No wonder Protein 21's share of the shampoo market has fallen from 13% to 11%. And the decline is bound to continue.

Free Ride Can Be Costly

Another similar marketing pitfall recently befell, of all companies, Miles Laboratories.

You can see how it happens. A bunch of the boys are sitting around a conference table trying to name a new cold remedy.

"I have it," says Harry. "Let's call it Alka-Seltzer Plus. That way we can take advantage of the $20,000,000 we're already spending to promote the Alka-Seltzer name."

"Good thinking, Harry," and another money-saving idea is instantly accepted.

But lo and behold, instead of eating into the Dristan and Contac market, the new product turns around and eats into the Alka-Seltzer market.

And you know Miles must be worried. In every TV commercial, the "Alka-Seltzer" gets smaller and smaller and the "Plus" gets bigger and bigger.

Related to the free-ride trap, but not exactly the same, is another common error judgment called the "well-known name" trap.

Both General Electric and RCA thought they could take their strong positions against IBM in computers. But just because a company is well-known in one field doesn't mean it can transfer that recognition to another.

In other words, your brand can be on top of one ladder and nowhere on another. And the further apart the products are conceptually, the greater the difficulty of making the jump.

In the past when there were fewer companies and fewer products, a well-known name was a much greater asset than it is today. Because of the noise level, a "well-known" company has tremendous difficulty trying to establish a position in a different field than the one in which it built its reputation.

You Can't Appeal to Everyone

A human emotion called "greed" often leads an advertiser into another error. American Motors' introduction of the Hornet is one of the best examples of the "everybody" trap.

You might remember the ads, "The little rich car. American Motors Hornet: $1,994 to $3,589."

A product that tries to appeal to everyone winds up appealing to no one. People who want to spend $3,500 for a car don't buy the Hornet because they don't want their friends to think they're driving a $1,900 car. People who want to spend $1,900 for a car don't buy the Hornet because they don't want a car with $1,600 worth of accessories taken off of it.

Avoid the F.W.M.T.S. Trap

If the current Avis advertising is any indication, the company has "forgotten what made them successful."

The original campaign not only related No. 2 Avis to No. 1 Hertz, but also exploited the love that people have for the underdog. The new campaign (Avis is going to be No. 1) not only is conventional "brag and boast" advertising, but also dares the prospect to make the prediction not come true.

Our prediction: Avis ain't going to be No. 1. Further prediction: Avis will lose ground to Hertz and National.

Another company that seems to have fallen into the forgotten what made them successful trap is Volkswagen.

"Think small" was perhaps the most famous advertisement of the '60s. Yet last year VW ran an ad that said, "Volkswagen introduces a new kind of Volkswagen. Big."

O.K., Volkswagen, should we think small or should we think big?

Confusion is the enemy of successful positioning. Prediction: Rapid erosion of the Beetle's position in the U.S. market.

How to Position Your Product

The world seems to be turning faster. Years ago, a successful product might live 50 years or more before fading away. Today, a product's life cycle is much shorter. Sometimes it can be measured in months instead of years. New products, new services, new markets, even new media are constantly being born. They grow up into adulthood and then slide into oblivion. And a new cycle starts again.

Yesterday, beer and hard liquor were campus favorites. Today, it's wine. Yesterday, the well-groomed man had his hair cut every week. Today, it's every month or two. Yesterday, the way to reach the masses was the mass magazines. Today, it's network TV. Tomorrow, it could be cable.

The only permanent thing in life today is change. And the successful companies of tomorrow will be those companies that have learned to cope with it.

The acceleration of "change" creates enormous pressures on companies to think in terms of tactics rather than strategy. As one respected advertising man commented, "The day seems to be past when long-range strategy can be a winning technique." But is change the way to keep pace with change? The exact opposite appears to be true.

The landscape is littered with the debris of projects that companies rushed into in attempting to "keep pace." Singer trying to move into the boom in home appliances. RCA moving into the boom in computers. General Foods moving into the boom in fast-food outlets. Not to mention the hundreds of companies that threw away their corporate identities to chase the passing fad to initials.

While the programs of those who kept at what they did best and held their ground have been immensely successful. Maytag selling their reliable appliances. Walt Disney selling his world of fantasy and fun. Avon calling.

And take margarine. Thirty years ago the first successful margarine brands positioned themselves against butter. "Tastes like the high-priced spread," said a typical ad.

And what works today? Why the same strategy. "It isn't nice to fool Mother nature," says the Chiffon commercial, and sales go up 25%. Chiffon is once again the best selling brand of soft margarine.

Long-Range Thinking Important

Change is a wave on the ocean of time. Short-term, the waves cause agitation and confusion, but long-term the underlying currents are much more significant.

To cope with change, it's important to take a long-range point of view. To determine your basic business. Positioning is a concept that is cumulative. Something that takes advantage of advertising's long-range nature.

In the '70s, a company must think even more strategically than it did before. Changing the direction of a large company is like trying to turn an aircraft carrier. It takes a

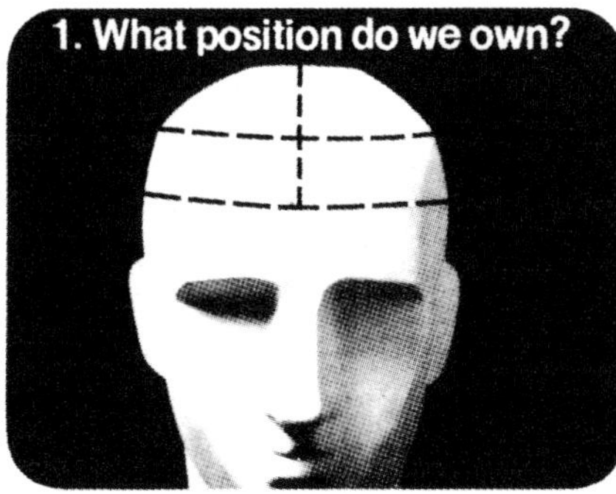

FIND THE ANSWER
in the marketplace.

SELECT A POSITION
that won't become obsolete.

AVOID A CONFRONTATION
with marketing leaders.

SPEND ENOUGH
to accomplish the objective.

EXPECT INTERNAL PRESSURES
for change.

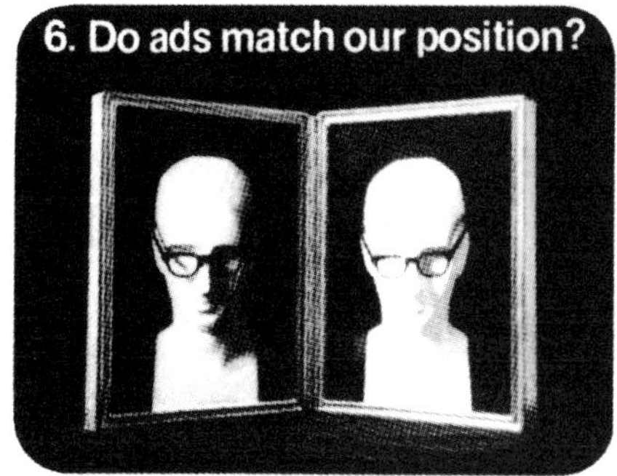

DON'T LET CREATIVITY
get in the way.

mile before anything happens. And if it was a wrong turn, getting back on course takes even longer.

To play the game successfully, you must make decisions on what your company will be doing not next month or next year, but in five years, ten years. In other words, instead of turning the wheel to meet each fresh wave, a company must point itself in the right direction.

You must have vision. There's no sense building a position based on a technology that's too narrow. Or a product that's becoming obsolete. Remember the famous *Harvard Business Review* article entitled "Marketing Myopia?" It still applies.

If a company has positioned itself in the right direction, it will be able to ride the currents of change, ready to take advantage of those opportunities that are right for it. But when an opportunity arrives, a company must be ready to move quickly.

Because of the enormous advantages that accrue to being the leader, most companies are not interested in learning how to *compete* with the leader. They want to be the leader. They want to be Hertz rather than Avis. *Time* rather than *Newsweek*. General Electric rather than Westinghouse,

Historically, however, product leadership is usually the result of an accident, rather than a preconceived plan.

The xerography process, for example, was offered to 32 different companies (including IBM and Kodak) before it wound up at the old Haloid Co. Renamed Haloid Xerox and then finally Xerox, the company has since dominated the copier market. Xerox now owns the copier position.

Were IBM and Kodak stupid to turn down xerography? Of course not. These companies reject thousands of ideas every year.

Perhaps a better description of the situation at the time was that Haloid, a small manufacturer of photographic supplies, was desperate, and the others weren't. As a result, it took a chance that more prudent companies couldn't be expected to take.

When you trace the history of how leadership positions were established, from Hershey in chocolate to Hertz in rent-a-cars, the common thread is not marketing skill or even product innovation. The common thread is seizing the initiative before the competitor has a chance to get established. In someone's oldtime military terms, the marketing leader "got there firstest with the mostest." The leader usually poured in the marketing money while the situation was still fluid.

IBM, for example, didn't invent the computer. Sperry Rand did. But IBM owns the computer position because they built their computer fortress before competition arrived.

And the position that Hershey established in chocolate was so strong they didn't need to advertise at all, a luxury that competitors like Nestle couldn't afford.

You can see that establishing a leadership position depends not only on luck and timing, but also upon a willingness to "pour it on" when others stand back and wait.

Yet all too often, the product leader makes the fatal mistake of attributing its success to marketing skill. As a result, it thinks it can transfer that skill to other products and other marketing situations.

Witness, for example, the sorry record of Xerox in computers. In May of 1969, Xerox exchanged nearly 10,000,000 shares of stock (worth nearly a billion dollars) for Scientific Data Systems Inc. Since the acquisition, the company (renamed Xerox Data Systems) has *lost* millions of dollars, and without Xerox's support would have probably gone bankrupt.

And the mecca of marketing knowledge, International Business Machines Corp., hasn't done much better. So far, the IBM plain-paper copier hasn't made much of a dent in Xerox's business. Touché.

The rules of positioning hold for all types of products. In the packaged goods area, for example, Bristol-Myers tried to take on Crest toothpaste with Fact (killed after $5,000,000 was spent on promotion). Then they tried to go after Alka-Seltzer with Resolve (killed after $11,000,000 was spent). And according to a headline in the Feb. 7 issue of *Advertising Age*, "Bristol-Myers will test Dissolve aspirin in an attempt to unseat Bayer."

The suicidal bent of companies that go head-on against established competition is hard to understand. They know the score, yet they forge ahead anyway. In the marketing war, a "charge of the light brigade" happens every day. With same predictable result.

One Strategy for Leader

Successful marketing strategy usually consists of keeping your eyes open to possibilities and then striking before the product ladder is firmly fixed.

As a matter of fact, the marketing leader is usually the one who moves the ladder into the mind with his or her brand nailed to the one and only rung. Once there, what can a company do to keep its top-dog position?

There are two basic strategies that should be used hand in hand. They seem contradictory, but aren't. One is to ignore competition, and the other is to cover all bets.

As long as a company owns the position, there's no point in running ads that scream, "We're No. 1." Much better is to enhance the product category in the prospect's mind. Notice the current IBM campaign that ignores competition and sells the value of computers. All computers, not just the company's types.

Although the leader's advertising should ignore the competition, the leader shouldn't. The second rule is to cover all bets.

This means a leader should swallow his or her pride and adopt every new product development as soon as it shows signs of promise. Too often, however, the leader pooh-poohs the development, and doesn't wake up until it's too late.

Another Strategy for Non-Leaders

Most companies are in the No. 2, 3, 4 or even worse category. What then?

Hope springs eternal in the human breast. Nine times out of ten, the also-ran sets out to attack the leader, a la RCA's assault on IBM. Result: Disaster.

Simply stated, the first rule of positioning is this: You can't compete head-on against a company that has a strong, established position. You can go around, under or over, but never head-to-head. The leader owns the high ground. The No. 1 position in the prospect's mind. The top rung of the product ladder.

The classic example of No. 2 strategy is Avis. But many marketing people misread the Avis story. They assume the company was successful because it tried harder.

Not at all. Avis was successful because it related itself to the position of Hertz. Avis preempted the No. 2 position. (If trying harder were the secret of success, Harold Stassen would be president.)

Most marketplaces have room for a strong No. 2 company provided they position themselves clearly as an alternative to the leader. In the computer field, for example, Honeywell has used this strategy successfully.

"The other computer company vs. Mr. Big," says a typical Honeywell ad. Honeywell is doing what none of the other computer companies seems to be willing to do. Admit that IBM is, in fact, the leader in the computer business. Maybe that's why Honeywell and Mr. Big are the only large companies reported to be making money on computers.

Some 'Strong' Positions Aren't

Yet there are positions that can be taken. These are the positions that look strong, but in reality are weak.

Take the position of Scott in paper products. Scott has about 40% of the $1.2 billion market for towels, napkins, toilet tissues, and other consumer paper products. But Scott, like Mennen with Protein 21, fell into the line-extension trap.

ScotTowels, ScotTissue, Scotties, Scottkins, even BabyScott. All of these names undermined the Scott foundation. The more products hung on the Scott name, the less meaning the name had to the average consumer.

When Procter & Gamble attacked with Mr. Whipple and his tissue-squeezers, it was no contest. Charmin is now the No. 1 brand in the toilet-tissue market.

In Scott's case, a large "share of market" didn't mean they owned the position. More important is a large "share of mind." The housewife could write "Charmin, Kleenex, Bounty, and Pampers" on her shopping list and know exactly what products she was going to get. "Scott" on a shopping list has no meaning. The actual brand names aren't much help either. Which brand, for example, is engineered for the nose, Scotties or ScotTissue?

In positioning terms, the name "Scott" exists in limbo. It isn't firmly ensconced on any product ladder.

Eliminate Egos From Decision Making

To repeat, the name is the hook that hangs the brand on the product ladder in the prospect's mind. In the positioning era, the brand name to give a product is probably a company's single, most important marketing decision.

To be successful in the positioning era, advertising and marketing people must be brutally frank. They must try to eliminate all ego from the decision making process. It only clouds the issue.

One of the most critical aspects of "positioning" is being able to evaluate objectively products and how they are viewed by customers and prospects.

As a rule, when it comes to building strong programs, trust no one, especially managers who are all wrapped up in their products. The closer people get to products, the more they defend old decisions or old promises.

Successful companies get their information from the marketplace. That's the place where the program has to succeed, not in the product manager's office.

A company that keeps its eye on Tom, Dick, and Harry is going to miss Pierre, Hans, and Yoshio.

Marketing is rapidly becoming a worldwide ball game. A company that owns a position in one country now finds that it can use that position to wedge its way into another.

IBM has 62% of the German computer market. Is this fact surprising? It shouldn't be. IBM earns more than 50% of its profits outside the U.S.

As companies start to operate on a worldwide basis, they often discover they have name problems.

A typical example is U.S. Rubber, a worldwide company that marketed many products not made of rubber. Changing the name to Uniroyal created a new corporate identity that could be used worldwide.

Creativity Takes Back Seat

In the '70s, creativity will have to take a back seat to strategy.

Advertising Age itself reflects this fact. Today you find fewer stories about individual campaigns and more stories about what's happening in an entire industry. Creativity alone isn't a worth while objective in an era where a company can spend millions of dollars on great advertising and still fail miserably in the marketplace.

Consider what Harry McMahan calls the "Curse of Clio." In the past, the American Festival has made special awards to "Hall of Fame Classics." Of the 41 agencies that won these Clio awards, 31 have lost some or all of these particular accounts.

But the cult of creativity dies hard. One agency president said recently, "Oh, we do positioning all the time. But after we develop the position, we turn it over to the creative department." And too often, of course, the creativity does nothing but obscure the positioning.

In the positioning era, the key to success is to run the naked positioning statement, unadorned by so-called creativity.

Ask Yourself These Questions

If these examples have moved you to want to apply positioning thinking to your own company's situation, here are some questions to ask yourself:

1. *What position, if any, do we already own in the prospect's mind?*

Get the answer to this question from the marketplace, not the marketing manager. If this requires a few dollars for research, so be it. Spend the money. It's better to know exactly what you're up against now than to discover it later when nothing can be done about it.

2. *What position do we want to own?*

Here is where you bring out your crystal ball and try to figure out the best position to own from a long-term point of view.

3. *What companies must be outgunned if we are to establish that position?*

If your proposed position calls for a head-to-head approach against a marketing leader, forget it. It's better to go around an obstacle rather than over it. Back up. Try to select a position that no one else has a firm grip on.

4. *Do we have enough marketing money to occupy and hold the position?*

A big obstacle to successful positioning is attempting to achieve the impossible. It takes money to build a share of mind. It takes money to establish a position. It takes money to hold a position once you've established it.

The noise level today is fierce. There are just too many "me-too" companies vying for the mind of the prospect. Getting noticed is getting tougher.

5. *Do we have the guts to stick with one consistent positioning concept?*

With the noise level out there, a company has to be bold enough and consistent enough to cut through.

The first step in a positioning program normally entails running fewer programs, but stronger ones. This sounds simple, but actually runs counter to what usually happens as corporations get larger. They normally run more programs, but weaker ones. It's this fragmentation that can make many large advertising budgets just about invisible in today's media storm.

6. *Does our creative approach match our positioning strategy?*

Creative people often resist positioning thinking because they believe it restricts their creativity. And it does. But creativity isn't the objective in the '70s. Even "communications" itself isn't the objective.

The name of the marketing game in the '70s is "positioning." And only the better players will survive.

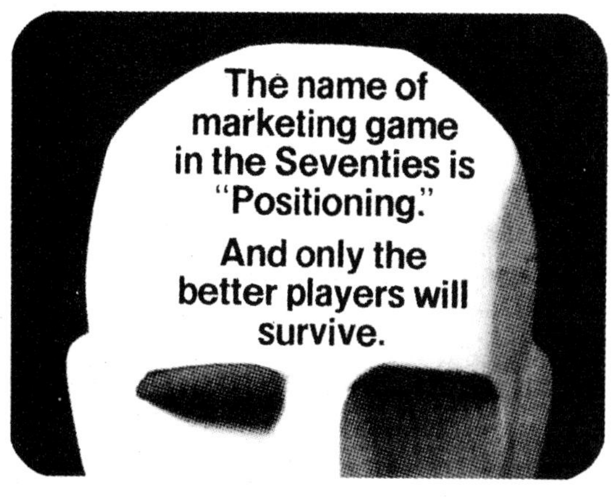

20

Positioning Your Product

David A. Aaker

Sophisticated analysis of all the positioning alternatives can, and should, be done.

HOW SHOULD A NEW BRAND be positioned? Can a problem brand be revived by a repositioning strategy? Most marketing managers have addressed these and other positioning questions; however, "positioning" means different things to different people. To some, it means the segmentation decision. To others it is an image question. To still others it means selecting which product features to emphasize. Few managers consider all of these alternatives. Further, the positioning decision is often made ad hoc, and is based upon flashes of insight, even though systematic, research-based approaches to the positioning decision are now available. An understanding of these approaches should lead to more sophisticated analysis in which positioning alternatives are more fully identified and evaluated.

A product or organization has many associations which combine to form a total impression. The positioning decision often means selecting those associations which are to be built upon and emphasized and those associations which are to be removed or de-emphasized. The term "position" differs from the older term "image" in that it implies a frame of reference, the reference point usually being the competition. Thus, when the Bank of California positions itself as being small and friendly, it is explicitly, or perhaps implicitly, positioning itself with respect to Bank of America.

The positioning decision is often the crucial strategic decision for a company or brand because the position can be central to customers' perception and choice decisions.

David A. Aaker is the J. Gary Shansby Professor of Marketing Strategy at the University of California at Berkeley.

Further, since all elements of the marketing program can potentially affect the position, it is usually necessary to use a positioning strategy as a focus for the development of the marketing program. A clear positioning strategy can insure that the elements of the marketing program are consistent and supportive.

What alternative positioning strategies are available? How can positioning strategies be identified and selected? each of these questions will be addressed in turn.

Positioning Strategies

A first step in understanding the scope of positioning alternatives is to consider some of the ways that a positioning strategy can be conceived and implemented. In the following, six approaches to positioning strategy will be illustrated and discussed: positioning by (1) attribute, (2) price-quality, (3) use or applications, (4) product-user, (5) the product-class, and (6) the competitor.

Positioning by Attribute

Probably the most frequently used positioning strategy is associating a product with an attribute, a product feature, or customer benefit. Consider imported automobiles. Datsun and Toyota have emphasized economy and reliability. Volkswagen has used a "value for the money" association. Volvo has stressed durability, showing commercials of "crash tests" and citing statistics on the long average life of their cars. Fiat, in contrast, has made a distinct effort to position itself as a European car with "European craftsmanship." BMW has emphasized handling and engineering efficiency, using the tag line, "the ultimate driving machine" and showing BMWs demonstrating their performance capabilities at a race track.

A new product can upon occasion be positioned with respect to an attribute that competitors have ignored. Paper towels had emphasized absorbency until Viva stressed durability, using demonstrations supporting the claim that Viva "keeps on working."

Sometimes a product will attempt to position itself along two or more attributes simultaneously. In the toothpaste market, Crest became a dominant brand by positioning itself as a cavity fighter, a position supported by a medical group endorsement. However, Aim achieved a 10 percent market share by positioning along two attributes, good taste and cavity prevention. More recently, Aqua-fresh has been introduced by Beecham as a gel paste that offers both cavity-fighting and breath-freshening benefits.

It is always tempting to try to position along several attributes. However, positioning strategies that involve too many attributes can be most difficult to implement. The result can often be a fuzzy, confused image.

Positioning by Price/Quality

The price/quality attribute dimension is so useful and pervasive that it is appropriate to consider it separately. In many product categories, some brands offer more in terms of service, features, or performance and a higher price serves to signal this higher quality to the customer. Conversely, other brands emphasize price and value.

In general merchandise stores, for example, the department stores are at the top end of the price/quality scale. Neiman-Marcus, Bloomingdale's, and Saks Fifth Avenue are near the top, followed by Macy's, Robinson's, Bullock's, Rich's, Filene's, Dayton's, Hudson's, and so on. Stores such as Sears, Montgomery Ward, and J. C. Penney are positioned below the department stores but above the discount stores like K-Mart. Sears' efforts to create a more upbeat fashion image was thought to have hurt their "value" position and caused some share declines.[1] Sears' recent five-year plan details a firm return to a positioning as a family, middle-class store offering top value. Sears is just one company that has faced the very tricky positioning task of retaining the image of low price and upgrading their quality image. There is always the risk that the quality message will blunt the basic "low-price," "value" position.

Positioning with Respect to Use or Application

Another positioning strategy is associating the product with a use or application. Campbell's Soup for many years was positioned for use at lunch time and advertised extensively over noontime radio. The telephone company more recently has associated long distance calling with communicating with loved ones in their "reach out and touch someone" campaign. Industrial products often rely upon application associations.

Products can, of course, have multiple positioning strategies, although increasing the number involves obvious difficulties and risks. Often a positioning-by-use strategy represents a second or third position designed to expand the market. Thus, Gatorade, introduced as a summer beverage for athletes who need to replace body fluids, has attempted to develop a winter positioning strategy as the beverage to drink when the doctor recommends drinking plenty of fluids. Similarly, Quaker Oats has attempted to position a breakfast food product as a natural whole-grain ingredient for recipes. Arm & Hammer baking soda has successfully positioned their product as an odor-destroying agent in refrigerators.

Positioning by the Product User

Another positioning approach is associating a product with a user or a class of users. Thus, many cosmetic companies have used a model or personality, such as Brut's Joe Namath, to position their product. Revlon's Charlie cosmetic line has been positioned by associating it with a specific life-style profile. Johnson & Johnson saw market share move from 3 percent to 14 percent when they repositioned their shampoo from a product used for babies to one used by people who wash their hair frequently and therefore need a mild shampoo.

In 1970, Miller High Life was the "champagne of bottled beers," was purchased by the upper class, and had an image of being a woman's beer. Phillip Morris repositioned it as a beer for the heavy beer drinking, blue-collar working man. Miller's Lite beer, introduced in 1975, used convincing beer-drinking personalities to position itself as a beer for the heavy beer drinker who dislikes that filled-up feeling. In contrast, earlier efforts to introduce low-calorie beers positioned with respect to the low-calorie attribute were dismal failures. One even claimed its beer had fewer calories than skim milk, and another featured a trim personality. Miller's positioning strategies are in part why its market share has grown from 3.4 percent in 1970 to 24.5 percent in 1979.[2]

Positioning with Respect to a Product Class

Some critical positioning decisions involve product-class associations. For example, Maxim freeze-dried coffee needed to position itself with respect to regular and instant coffee. Some margarines position themselves with respect to butter. Dried milk makers came out with instant breakfast positioned as a breakfast substitute and a virtually identical product positioned as a dietary meal substitute. The hand soap "Caress" by Lever Brothers positioned itself as a bath oil product rather than a soap.

The soft drink 7-Up was for a long time positioned as a beverage with a "fresh clean taste" that was "thirst-quenching." However, research discovered that most people regarded 7-Up as a mix rather than a soft drink. The successful "un-cola" campaign was then developed to position 7-Up as a soft drink, with a better taste than the "colas."

Positioning with Respect to a Competitor

In most positioning strategies, an explicit or implicit frame of reference is the competition. There are two reasons for making the reference competitor(s) the dominant aspect of the positioning strategy. First, a well established competitor's image can be exploited to help communicate another image referenced to it. In giving directions to an address, for example, it's easier to say, it is next to the Bank of America building than it is to detail streets, distances, and turns. Second, sometimes it's not important how good customers think you are; it is just important that they believe you are better (or as good as) a given competitor.

Perhaps the most famous positioning strategy of this type was the Avis "We're number two, so we try harder" campaign. The strategy was to position Avis with Hertz as a major car rental agency and away from National, which at the time was a close third to Avis.

Positioning explicitly with respect to a competitor can be an excellent way to create a position with respect to an attribute, especially the price/quality attribute pair. Thus, products difficult to evaluate, like liquor products, will often be compared with an established competitor to help the positioning task. For example, Sabroso, a coffee liqueur, positioned itself with the established brand, Kahlua, with respect to quality and also with respect to the type of liqueur.

Positioning with respect to a competitor can be aided by comparative advertising, advertising in which a competitor is explicitly named and compared on one or more attributes. Pontiac has used this approach to position some of their cars as being comparable in gas mileage and price to leading import cars. By comparing Pontiac to a competitor that has a well-defined economy image, like a Volkswagen Rabbit, and using factual information such as EPA gas ratings, the communication task becomes easier.

On Determining the Positioning Strategy

What should be our positioning strategy? The identification and selection of a positioning strategy can draw upon a set of concepts and procedures that have been developed and refined over the last few years. The process of developing a positioning strategy involves six steps:

1. Identify the competitors.
2. Determine how the competitors are perceived and evaluated.
3. Determine the competitors' positions.
4. Analyze the customers.
5. Select the position.
6. Monitor the position.

In each of these steps one can employ marketing research techniques to provide needed information. Sometimes the marketing research approach provides a conceptualization that can be helpful even if the research is not conducted. Each of these steps will be discussed in turn.

Identify the Competitors

This first step is not as simple as it might seem. Tab might define its competitors in a number of ways, including:

(a) other diet cola drinks
(b) all cola drinks
(c) all soft drinks
(d) nonalcoholic beverages
(e) all beverages

A Triumph convertible might define its market in several ways:

(a) two-passenger, low-priced, imported, sports car convertibles
(b) two-passenger, low-priced, imported sports cars
(c) two-passenger, low- or medium-priced, imported sports cars
(d) low- or medium-priced sports cars
(e) low- or medium-priced imported cars

In most cases, there will be a primary group of competitors and one or more secondary competitors. Thus, Tab will compete primarily with other diet colas, but other colas and all soft drinks could be important as secondary competitors.

A knowledge of various ways to identify such groupings will be conceptual as well as practical value. One approach is to determine from product buyers which brands they considered. For example, a sample of Triumph convertible buyers could be asked what other cars they considered and perhaps what other showrooms they actually visited. A Tab buyer could be asked what brand would have been purchased had Tab been out of stock. The resulting analysis will identify the primary and secondary groups of competitive products. Instead of customers, retailers or others knowledgeable about customers could provide the information.

Another approach is the development of associations of products with use situations.[3] Twenty or so respondents might be asked to recall the use contexts for Tab. For each use context, such as an afternoon snack, respondents are then asked to identify all appropriate beverages. For each beverage so identified respondents are then asked to identify appropriate use contexts. This process would continue until a large list of use contexts and beverages resulted. Another respondent group would then be asked to make judgments as to how appropriate each beverage would be for each use situation. Groups of beverages could then be clustered based upon their similarity of appropriate use situations. If Tab was regarded as appropriate with snacks, then it would compete primarily with other beverages regarded as appropriate for snack occasions. The same approach would work with an industrial product such as computers, which might be used in several rather distinct applications.

The concepts of alternatives from which customers choose and appropriateness to a context can provide a basis for identifying competitors even when market research is not employed. A management team or a group of experts, such as retailers, could employ one or both of these conceptual bases to identify competitive groupings.

Determine How the Competitors Are Perceived and Evaluated

The challenge is to identify those product associations used by buyers as they perceive and evaluate competitors. The product associations will include product attributes, product user groups, and use contexts. Even simple objects such as beer can evoke a host of physical attributes like container, aftertaste, and price, and relevant associations like "appropriate for use while dining at a good restaurant" or "used by working men." The task is to identify a list of product associations, to remove redundancies from the list, and then to select those that are most useful and relevant in describing brand images.

One research-based approach to product association list generation is to ask respondents to identify the two most similar brands from a set of three competing brands and to describe why those two brands are similar and different from the third. As a variant, respondents could be asked which of two brands is preferred and why. The result will be a rather long list of product associations, perhaps over a hundred. The next step is to remove redundancy from the list using logic and judgment or factor analysis. The final step is to identify the most relevant product associations by determining which is correlated highest with overall brand attitudes or by asking respondents to indicate which are the most important to them.

Determine the Competitors' Positions

The next step is to determine how competitors (including our own entry) are positioned with respect to the relevant product associations and with respect to each other. Although such judgments can be made subjectively, research-based approaches are available. Such research is termed multidimensional scaling because its goal is to scale objects on several dimensions (or product associations). Multidimensional scaling can be based upon either product associations data or similarities data.

Product-association-based multidimensional scaling. The most direct approach is simply to ask a sample of the target segment to scale the various objects on the product association dimensions. For example, the respondent could be asked to express his or her agreement or disagreement on a seven-point scale with statements regarding the Chevette:

With respect to its class, I would consider the Chevette to be:

sporty
roomy
economical
good handling

Alternatively, perceptions of a brand's users or use contexts could be obtained:

I would expect the typical Chevette owner to be:

older
wealthy
independent
intelligent

The Chevette is most appropriate for:

short neighborhood trips
commuting
cross country sightseeing

In generating such measures there are several potential problems and considerations (in addition to generating a relevant product association list) of which one should be aware:

1. *The validity of the task*. Can a respondent actually position cars on a "sporty" dimension? There could be several problems. One, a possible unfamiliarity with one or more of the brands, can be handled by asking the respondent to evaluate only familiar brands. Another is the respondent's ability to understand operationally what "sporty" means or how to evaluate a brand on this dimension.
2. *Differences among respondents*. Subgroups within the population could hold very different perceptions with respect to one or more of the objects. Such diffused images can have important strategic implications. The task of sharpening a diffused image is much different from the task of changing a very tight, established one.
3. *Are the differences between objects significant and meaningful?* If the differences are not statistically significant, then the sample size may be too small to make any managerial judgments. At the same time, a small difference of no practical consequence may be statistically significant if the sample size is large enough.
4. *Which product associations are not only important but also serve to distinguish objects?* Thus, airline safety may be an important attribute, but all airlines may be perceived to be equally safe.

Similarities-based multidimensional scaling. Product-association approaches have several conceptual disadvantages. A complete, valid, and relevant product association list is not easy to generate. Further, an object may be perceived or evaluated as a whole that is not really decomposable in terms of product associations. These disadvantages lead us to the use of non-attribute data—namely, similarity data.

Similarity measures simply reflect the perceived similarity of two objects. For example, respondents may be asked to rate the degree of similarity of assorted object pairs without a product association list which implicitly suggests criteria to be included or excluded. The result, when averaged over all respondents, is a similarity rating for each object pair. A multidimensional scaling program then attempts to locate objects in a two-, three- (or more if necessary) dimensional space termed a perceptual map. The program attempts to construct the perceptual map such that the two objects with the highest similarity are separated by the shortest distance, the object pair with the second highest similarity are separated by the second shortest distance, and so on. A disadvantage of the similarity-based approach is that the interpretation of the dimensions does not have the product associations as a guide.

Analyzing the Customers

A basic understanding of the customer and how the market is segmented will help in selecting a positioning strategy. How is the market segmented? What role does the product class play in the customer's lifestyle? What really motivates the customer? What habits and behavior patterns are relevant?

The segmentation question is, of course, critical. One of the most useful segmentation approaches is benefit segmentation, which focuses upon the benefits or, more generally, the product associations that a segment believes to be important. The identity of important product associations can be done directly by asking customers to rate product associations as to their importance or by asking them to make trade-off judgments between product associations[4] or by asking them to conceptualize and profile "ideal brands." An ideal brand would be a combination of all the customer's preferred product associations. Customers are then grouped into segments defined by product associations considered important by customers. Thus, for toothpaste there could be a decay preventative segment, a fresh breath segment, a price segment, and so on. The segment's relative size and commitment to the product association will be of interest.

It is often useful to go beyond product association lists to get a deeper understanding of consumer perceptions. A good illustration is the development of positioning objectives for Betty Crocker by the Needham, Harper & Steers advertising agency.[5] They conducted research involving more than 3,000 women, and found that Betty Crocker was viewed as a company that is:

- honest and dependable
- friendly and concerned about consumers
- a specialist in baked goods

but

- out of date, old, and traditional
- a manufacturer of "old standby" products
- not particularly contemporary or innovative

The conclusion was that the Betty Crocker image needed to be strengthened and to become more modern and innovative and less old and stodgy.

To improve the Betty Crocker image, it was felt that an understanding was needed of the needs and lifestyle of today's women and how these relate to desserts. Thus, the research study was directed to basic questions about desserts. Why are they served? Who serves them? The answers were illuminating. Dessert users tend to be busy, active mothers who are devoted to their families. The primary reasons for serving dessert tend to be psychological and revolve around the family.

> Dessert is a way to show others you care.
>
> Dessert preparation is viewed as an important duty of a good wife and mother.
>
> Desserts are associated with and help to create happy family moments.

Clearly, family bonds, love, and good times are associated with desserts. As a result, the Betty Crocker positioning objective was to associate Betty Crocker uniquely with the positive aspects of today's families and their feelings about dessert. Contemporary, emotionally involving advertising was used to associate Betty Crocker with desserts that contribute to happy family moments.

Making the Positioning Decision

The four steps or exercises just described should be conducted prior to making the actual positioning decision. The exercises can be done subjectively by the involved managers if necessary, although marketing research, if feasible and justifiable, will be more definitive. However, even with that background, it is still not possible to generate a cookbook solution to the positioning questions. However, some guidelines or checkpoints can be offered.

1. *Positioning usually implies a segmentation commitment.* Positioning usually means that an overt decision is being made to concentrate only on certain segments. Such an approach requires commitment and discipline because it's not easy to turn your back on potential buyers. Yet, the effect of generating a distinct, meaningful position is to focus on the target segments and not be constrained by the reaction of other segments.

Sometimes the creation of a "diffuse image," an image that will mean different things to different people, is a way to attract a variety of diverse segments. Such an approach is risky and difficult to implement and usually would be used only by a large brand. The implementation could involve projecting a range of advantages while avoiding being identified with any one. Alternatively, there could be a conscious effort to avoid associations which create positions. Pictures of bottles of Coca-Cola with the words "It's the real thing" superimposed on them, or Budweiser's claim that "Bud is the king of beers," illustrate such a strategy.

2. *An economic analysis should guide the decision.* The success of any positioning strategy basically depends upon two factors: the potential market size × the penetration probability. Unless both of these factors are favorable, success will be unlikely. One implication of this simple structure is that a positioning strategy should attract a sizable segment. If customers are to be attracted from other brands, those brands should have a worthwhile market share to begin with. If new buyers are to be attracted to the product class, a reasonable assessment should be made of the potential size of that growth area. The penetration probability indicates that there needs to be a competitive weakness to attack or a competitive advantage to exploit to generate a reasonable market penetration probability. Further, the highest payoff will often come from retaining existing customers, so this alternative should also be considered.

3. *If the advertising is working, stick with it.* An advertiser will often get tired of a positioning strategy and the advertising used to implement it and will consider making a change. However, the personality of image of a brand, like that of a person, evolves over many years, and the value of consistency through time cannot be overestimated. Some of the very successful, big-budget campaigns have run for ten, twenty, or even thirty years.

4. *Don't try to be something you are not.* It is tempting but naïve—and usually fatal—to decide on a positioning strategy that exploits a market need or opportunity but assumes that your product is something it is not. Before positioning a product, it is important to conduct blind taste tests or in-home or in-office use tests to make sure that the product can deliver what it promises and that is compatible with a proposed image.

Consider Hamburger Helper, successfully introduced in 1970 as an add-to-meat product that would generate a good-tasting, economical, skillet dinner.[6] In the mid-1970s, sales suffered when homemakers switched to more exotic, expensive foods. An effort to react by repositioning Hamburger Helper as a base for casseroles failed because the product, at least in the consumers' mind, could not deliver. Consumers perceived it as an economical, reliable, convenience food and further felt that they did not need help in making casseroles. In a personality test, where women were asked to describe the product as if it were a person, the most prevalent characteristic ascribed to the product was "helpful." The result was a revised campaign to position the product as being "helpful."

Monitoring the Position

A positioning objective, like any marketing objective, should be measurable. To evaluate the positioning and to generate diagnostic information about future positioning strategies, it is necessary to monitor the position over time. A variety of techniques can be employed to make this measurement. Hamburger Helper used a "personality test," for example. However, usually one of the more structured techniques of multidimensional scaling is applied.

Summary

A variety of positioning strategies is available to the advertiser. An object can be positioned:

1. By attributes—e.g., Crest is a cavity fighter.
2. By price/quality—e.g., Sears is a "value" store.
3. By competitor—e.g., Avis positions itself with Hertz.
4. By application—e.g., Gatorade is for flu attacks.
5. By product user—e.g., Miller is for the blue-collar, heavy beer drinker.
6. By product class—e.g., Carnation Instant Breakfast is a breakfast food.

The selection of a positioning strategy involves identifying competitors, relevant attributes, competitor positions, and market segments. Research based approaches can help in each of these steps by providing conceptualization even if the subjective judgments of managers are used to provide the actual input information to the positioning decision.

References

1. "Sears' New 5-Year Plan: To Serve Middle America," *Advertising Age*, December 4, 1978.
2. "A-B, Miller Brews Continue to Barrel Ahead," *Advertising Age*, August 4, 1980: 4.
3. George S. Day, Alan D. Shocker, and Rajendra K. Srivasta, "Customer-Oriented Approaches to Identify Product Markets," *Journal of Marketing*, Fall 1979: 8–19.
4. Paul E. Green and Yoram Wind, "New Ways to Measure Consumers' Judgments," *Harvard Business Review*, July–August 1975: 107–15.
5. Keith Reinhard, "How We Make Advertising" (presented to the Federal Trade Commission, May 11, 1979): 22–25.
6. Reinhard: 29.

The authors thank John G. Myers for his helpful and stimulating comments.

21

Positioning Strategy in Ancient Rome

Goscinny & Uderzo

To suggest the intellectual heritage of the concept, cartoons depict the development of a positioning strategy in ancient Rome.

THE FOLLOWING PASSAGE WILL BE DIFFICULT FOR THOSE OF YOU UNACQUAINTED WITH THE ANCIENT BUSINESS WORLD TO UNDERSTAND, ESPECIALLY AS, THESE DAYS, SUCH A STATE OF AFFAIRS COULD NEVER EXIST, SINCE NO ONE WOULD DREAM OF TRYING TO SELL SOMETHING UTTERLY USELESS...

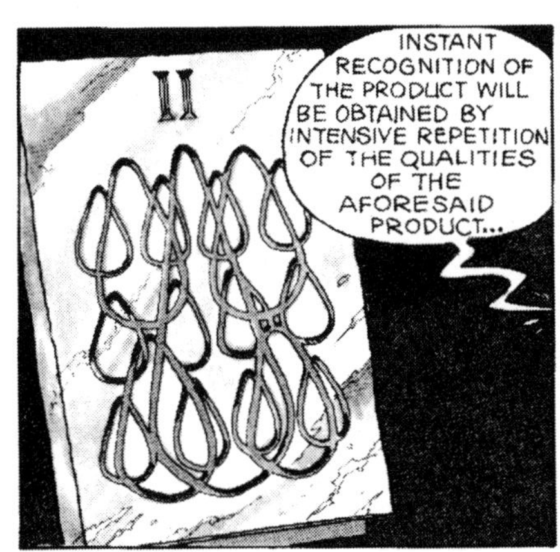
II
INSTANT RECOGNITION OF THE PRODUCT WILL BE OBTAINED BY INTENSIVE REPETITION OF THE QUALITIES OF THE AFORESAID PRODUCT...

III
...WHICH MAY BE DEFINED AS FOLLOWS: A: DURABILITY; B: SOLIDITY; C: OTHER QUALITIES.
A B C

IV
THUS I MAKE NO RASH PROMISES WHEN I SAY THAT WE SHOULD SUCCEED IN OBTAINING POSITIVE RESULTS, SALESWISE, AT NO VERY DISTANT DATE.
DEC.
NOV.
OCT.
SEPT.
SEX.
QVIN.
JVN.
MAI.
APR.
MARS.
FEB.
JAN.

UH?

ME THINK YOU ABLE SELL HEAP BIG HEAP MENHIRS PLENTY QUICK.

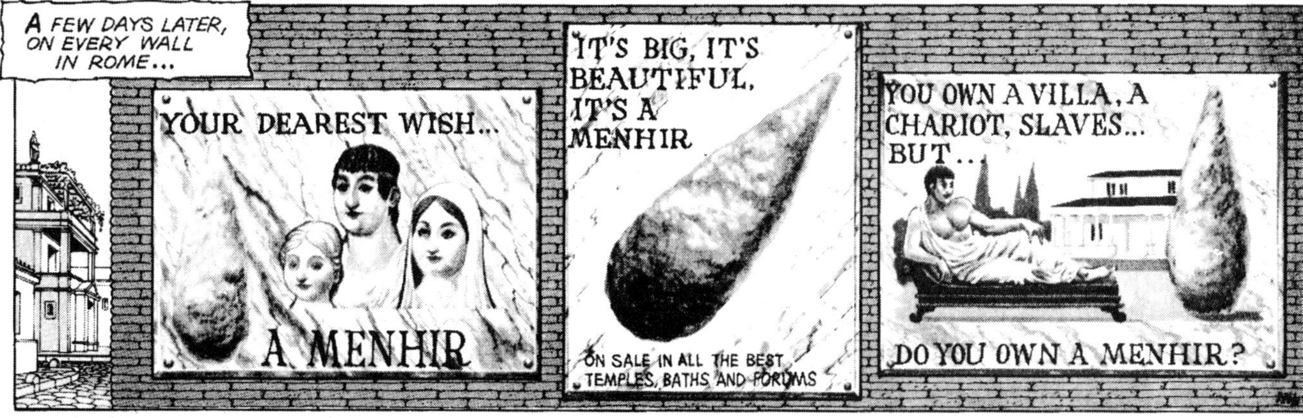
A FEW DAYS LATER, ON EVERY WALL IN ROME...
YOUR DEAREST WISH...
A MENHIR
IT'S BIG, IT'S BEAUTIFUL, IT'S A MENHIR
ON SALE IN ALL THE BEST TEMPLES, BATHS AND FORUMS
YOU OWN A VILLA, A CHARIOT, SLAVES... BUT...
DO YOU OWN A MENHIR?

AND NOW, FOLKS, AS WE WAIT FOR THE NEXT ACT, THERE WILL BE A SHORT INTERLUDE...

IT'S THE RIGHT ONE,
IT'S NOT THE LIGHT ONE,
IT'S A MENHIR...

A MENHIR...

YOU KNOW, INCONGRUOUS AND HIS WIFE NEXT DOOR BOUGHT A MENHIR. THEY'RE VERY PLEASED WITH IT!
A MENHIIIR!

AND THE RESULTS OF THE PUBLICITY CAMPAIGN ARE NOT LONG COMING IN...
IT'S A KNOCKOUT! MENHIRS ARE SELLING LIKE HOT CAKES!

22

Differentiation: Begin with the Consumer

William E. Fulmer & Jack Goodwin

Low-cost leadership is merely one form of differentiation, and since only one firm can provide the lowest cost, other firms must choose other methods. A good place to start is with the customer.

One of the hottest buzzwords in business strategy today is "competitive advantage." Since the concepts of strategy are specific to competitive arenas, those speaking of competitive advantage are reinforcing the idea that strategies are designed to beat competitors. Consequently, managers are constantly searching for terminology, frameworks, and matrices that will help them better understand their companies' strategies as well as those of their competitors.

In the 1960s, the early work of the Boston Consulting Group focused on the importance of a low-cost position. The importance of market share was emphasized, because market share resulted from a firm's ability to move rapidly down the experience curve and thereby achieve the lowest-cost position in its industry.

By the late 1970s, Michael Porter was arguing that in addition to cost leadership, which he defined as a strategy by which the firm chooses to "become the low-cost producer in its industry," there was another "generic" strategy. He used the term "differentiation" to represent efforts by a company to "be unique in its industry along some dimensions that are widely valued by buyers."[1]

Although there are examples of firms successfully employing a highly differentiated strategy seemingly without much regard for cost (Hewlett Packard in calculators, for example), and others that have dominated an industry for some period of time with a virtually undifferentiated product at the lowest possible cost (such as Texas Instruments), these easily perceived extremes are rare in practice.

A problem with the either/or approach is that most of us know firms that seem to fit both categories. For example, it has been our experience that many executives and MBA students, when analyzing the Crown Cork & Seal policy case, have difficulty deciding whether the firm has a low-cost or differentiated strategy. We think the confusion arises partially because Crown Cork & Seal is both a low-cost *and* a differentiated player in the metal-container industry.

Using the either/or approach of cost vs. differentiation provides little help in distinguishing the players in most industries. Most firms cluster toward the middle of the low-cost/high-differentiation spectrum. For example, in the airline industry it has been very difficult to defend either a low-cost strategy (as People Express discovered) or a highly differentiated, unique strategy (as Atlanta Air and Presidential discovered). As a result, most of the major airlines offer a relatively similar product to the customer, both in characteristics and cost. In this middle ground, where most companies in many industries seem to fall, arises the greatest confusion about strategy.

Why Not Be Both

Although Porter suggests that a firm can achieve both differentiation and low cost, his interpreters often seem to treat the two strategies as incompatible. But forcing firms to view the strategic choice as one of either low cost or differentiation significantly restricts management's competitive responses.

William E. Fulmer is a Visiting Professor at Harvard University, Cambridge, Mass. Jack Goodwin is an Associate Professor of Business Administration at the College of William and Mary, Williamsburg, Va.

Figure 1
The differential trade-off

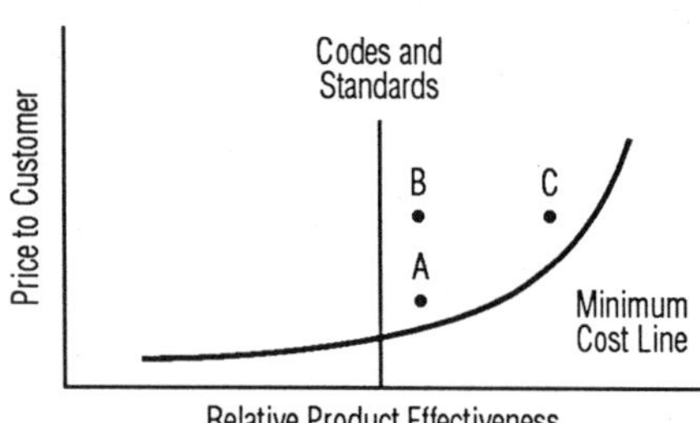

Adapted from John L. Colley, Jr., *Corportate and Divisional Planning: Text and Cases* (Reston, Virginia: Reston Publishing, 1984).

With increased competition in the marketplace from low-cost countries, U.S. firms should look for ways to combine low cost and differentiation.

In reality, most firms' strategies reflect a trade-off between cost and other forms of differentiation. Figure 1 illustrates this behavior (relative product effectiveness is used as a surrogate for differentiation of the product). To achieve a given level of effectiveness, a firm must accept a minimum cost. In addition, consumers, regulatory agencies, and legislatures place minimum requirements on the effectiveness of any product. We usually refer to this as the minimum acceptable level of quality.

Given these restrictions, we would expect firm A to outperform firm B, since A achieves the same level of effectiveness at a lower cost (reflected in the selling price). Firm C, on the other hand, has chosen to differentiate itself (increase its effectiveness). Greater differentiation has been obtained at the expense of cost. The success of this strategy will depend on the consumer's willingness to pay a higher price for C's product to obtain the increased effectiveness. If this increase in effectiveness is perceived by the customer as sufficient to justify the additional cost, then C's strategy will be successful.

Figure 1 suggests that it is impossible to achieve the same level of effectiveness as C at A's cost. In fact, the minimum cost frontier may be much flatter than that illustrated in Figure 1; more differentiation is not necessarily achieved through substantial increases in cost.

Our argument is based in part on experiences of U.S. manufacturers in their struggles with foreign competitors, particularly the Japanese. For years, most American manufacturers seemed to believe that cost and quality were conflicting priorities and that trade-offs between them were unavoidable. Recent experiences have shown this to be false. In fact, current practice indicates that improved quality can decrease, rather than increase, cost. With the advent of robotics, CAD/CAM, flexible manufacturing systems, and other technological advances, combinations of lower costs and higher levels of differentiation seem to be a reasonable expectation. Hall's research on strategy in hostile environments identifies Caterpillar and Philip Morris as companies achieving both low-cost and differentiated positions in their respective industries.[2] Other recent research also suggests that cost leadership and differentiation are independent and that each is a continuum.[3]

It is our contention that it is not only possible but essential to be both low cost and differentiated. In fact, since only one firm can be the true cost leader in a given industry, all other firms, if they are successful, are differentiated in some way. All firms, in essence, follow a differentiated strategy. Only one company can differentiate itself with the lowest cost; the remaining firms in the industry must find other ways to differentiate their products. This, then, is the focus of this article—how can companies differentiate themselves for competitive advantage?

Focus on the Customer

There are some relatively low-cost ways in which firms can differentiate themselves—with benefits that are far greater than the costs incurred. Peter Drucker suggests the place to start—the customer.

> To know what a business is we have to start with its *purpose*. Its purpose must lie outside of the business itself. In fact, it must lie in society since business enterprise is an organ of society. There is only one valid definition of business purpose: to create a *customer.*
>
> What the customer thinks he is buying, what he considers value, is decisive—it determines what a business is, what it produces, and whether it will prosper. And what the customer buys and considers value is never a product. It is always utility, that is, what a product or service does for him. And what is value for the customer is . . . anything but obvious.[4]

One problem with Drucker's statement is the difficulty of defining and measuring value. Value is a personal assessment of worth and therefore is unique to each individual customer. In addition, it is frequently influenced by events or activities beyond the control of the producer. Figure 2 illustrates the critical producer-customer interface that determines value and some of the factors influencing the customer's decision. But we need a better way of understanding and describing this relationship between producer and customer, a link between the customer's personal concept of value and that of the producer.

Figure 2
Producer-customer interface

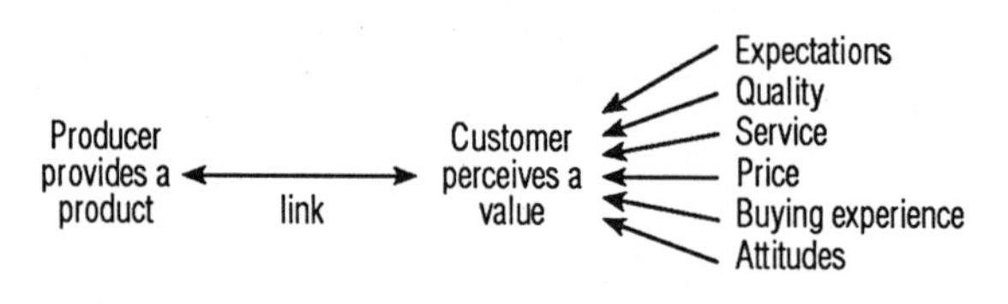

We have found the concept of customer bonding useful in creating value in customers' minds. We define customer bonding as *the process of tying a customer to a particular firm's product or service*. Although it can be done by effective advertising that ties a customer's self-perception to a particular product (Yuppies and BMWs), we believe a more enduring bond, loyalty, is built by good service at the producer-customer interface.

We have used a rough, three-level measure of bonding—high bonding, medium bonding, and low bonding—to study the performance of several businesses within an industry. The U.S. airline industry has been used as an illustration. This industry is a good example of many firms bunched in the middle ground between the extremes of strategic choice. As a result, it is difficult to distinguish among the players in this industry using traditional strategic concepts.

The Airline Industry

The major players in the airline industry all pursue strategies based on structural factors. By routing all flights in a geographic region through a single city, the airline creates a hub-and-spoke configuration. This approach benefits the carrier in several ways. It eliminates thousands of potential routes in the network while still connecting all cities in the region that are served by the carrier. The airline can operate much more efficiently and dominate the geographic region through its ability to provide service to most or all of the airports in that region.

A hub-and-spoke strategy thus contributes to bonding by increasing availability. However, availability falls far short of providing an adequate measure of the strength of the bond between airline and customer. Another measure prominent in recent public discussions is on-time service. Once again, this measure does not seem to capture the essence of our concept. Perhaps the deficiency of these measures is that they ignore the personal touch. They address the *where* and *when* of travel but ignore the *how*. Airlines have used frequent-flyer programs and airport clubs to increase the personal touch, but these perks are utilized by a small percentage of customers. A study that British Airways conducted several years ago illustrates the problem.

In launching a "Customer First" campaign, British Airways (BA) administered a customer questionnaire to find out what factors customers consider most important in traveling by air and how BA compared to its competition. Two of the top four factors, care/concern and problem-solving, were not surprising results. However, BA had never consciously thought about the other two factors considered most important by their customers: spontaneity and recovery—the ability to break out of the routine systems to accommodate a customer's individual needs and the ability to recover after a mistake has been made. Both factors go beyond the mechanics of providing what is expected, the ability to get to your destination on time, and address the more personal issues: What does the airline do for you if there is potential for failure of service in a situation or after a failure of service has occurred?[5]

Table 1

The Number of Complaints to the Department of Transportation from January through September for Each 100,000 Passengers Flown

Airline	Complaints
World Airways*	15.06
People Express	7.76
Pan American	4.50
Trans World	4.21
Continental	3.76
United	2.77
Eastern	2.59
Republic	2.38
American	1.46
Northwest	1.46
USAir	1.45
Western	1.33
Piedmont	1.18
Delta	.57
Southwest	.51

*Stopped operating scheduled flights September 15.

Source: *The Wall Street Journal*, November 10, 1986.

Table 2

How Business Travelers Rated the Airlines

Airline	Rating
Delta	82
American	77
United	76
Northwest Orient	73
Western	72
Piedmont	71
TWA	70
Republic	67
USAir	67
Continental	66
Pan Am	64
Eastern	58
People Express	47

*Calculated from ratings of excellent, good, fair, poor for each airline. Excellent equaled 4 points; poor, 1 point.

Source: *USA Today* survey, reported September 15, 1986, p. 1E.

In an attempt to capture the personal nature of the concept, we used a weighted average of two measures as a proxy for bonding to compare the 13 largest U.S. airlines in late 1986. The measures are the number of complaints to the Department of Transportation from January–September 1986 for each 100,000 passengers flown (Table 1), and *USA Today*'s 1986 survey of business travelers (Table 2). Table 3 combines the rank of each airline on both surveys and uses the combined score as a measure of bonding. This enabled us to split the 13 airlines into three roughly equal categories: high bonding, medium bonding, and low bonding.

Financial results for 1985 (Table 4) show a strong correlation between the level of bonding and financial returns. It is particularly interesting to note that revenue per employee

Table 3
Bonding Measurement for the 13 Largest U.S. Airlines

	Airline	Rank DOT	Rank *USA Today*	Rank Combined Score
High Bonding	Delta	1	1	2
	American	5	2	7
	Western	3	5	8
	Piedmont	2	6	8
Medium Bonding	Northwestern	5	4	9
	United	9	3	12
	USAir	4	8	12
	Republic	7	8	15
Low Bonding	TWA	11	7	18
	Eastern	8	12	20
	Continental	10	10	20
	Pan Am	12	11	23
	People Express	13	13	26

Table 4
Financial Performance of 13 Largest U.S. Airlines by Category

Bonding Rank	Airline	1985 Net Income as a Percentage of* Revenues	Equity	Assets	Revenue per Employee (000)
1	Delta	5.5%	20.2	7.2	120.0
2	American	5.6	15.5	5.4	117.7
3	Western	5.1	27.9	7.1	127.5
3	Piedmont	4.4	13.3	4.5	95.7
Category I Averages		5.2	19.2	6.1	115.2
5	Northwestern	2.8	7.7	3.2	159.6
6	United	(0.8)	(2.7)	(0.6)	84.0
6	USAir	6.6	12.3	6.0	125.9
8	Republic	10.2	88.4	13.8	114.1
Category II Averages		4.7	26.4	5.6	120.9
9	TWA	(5.2)	(35.8)	(7.0)	128.1
10	Eastern	0.1	2.4	0.2	117.2
10	Continental	4.7	75.7	4.7	122.3
12	Pan Am	1.5	11.5	2.1	142.0
13	People Express	(2.8)	(13.1)	(2.6)	130.4
Category III Averages		(0.3)	8.1	(0.5)	128.0

*1985 data were used, since *Fortune's* 1986 data reflected consolidation of several of the firms, making it difficult to use the rankings shown in Tables 1 and 2.

Source: *Fortune*, June 9, 1986, pp. 138–39.

increases as bonding decreases. This may indicate that low-bonding organizations are trading efficiency for good service. If this is true, the other financial measures indicate that the trade-off is not a wise one.

We suspect that a similar relationship holds for traditional manufacturing companies. There is some evidence that American car companies have recognized the problem. It was recently reported in the *Wall Street Journal* that Ford Motor Company, recognizing narrowing price and quality differences between companies, has begun using a buyer-happiness index to award Merkur luxury-import franchises. However, in attempts to learn more about this program, we have been unable to find any Ford field representative who knows of the program's existence. Perhaps this lack of knowledge is symptomatic of the problem addressed here. Recognition of the need for stronger bonds with the customer is often not translated into real programs. (In a similar fashion, General Motors' Buick division is reportedly considering making such indexes a basis for distributing new models.[6])

Management Implications of Bonding

Although our analysis suggests that there are financial implications in the concept of bonding, we believe that the operating and strategic implications are at least as great—if not more important.

Operating Implications

The concept of bonding has significant implications for many operating issues. They involve most of the functional areas of the firm, encompass both human and technical problems, and have external as well as internal orientations. In spite of their diversity, they possess a common thread—a potential for influencing the customer—that relates them to the concept of bonding.

Culture. With the rapid transfer of technology, it is becoming increasingly difficult for companies in most industries to sustain competitive advantages based on superior product or process technology. Increasingly, companies are selling products with low perceived levels of differentiation. The attitude of managers and employees is often the one major distinguishing feature of competing products and companies. IBM, Procter & Gamble, Johnson & Johnson, and other firms have employed their customer-centered cultures with great success for many years.

A newsletter from the PIMS organization on "The Strategic Management of Service Quality" states:

> In his book *A Business and Its Beliefs*, Thomas Watson, Jr., writes, "'IBM means service' states exactly what we stand for. We want to give the best customer service of any company in the world." It was this perspective on the "soft" dimension of customer needs, so logical in hindsight, that was the trigger to IBM's rise to dominance.[7]

It was not only this belief that triggered IBM's success, but also its ability to inspire several hundred thousand employees to live by it. Procter & Gamble has been equally successful in developing a common set of values and beliefs that differentiates it from competitors in a market that is dominated by products we normally would consider commodities. An anecdote from Peters and Austin's *A Passion for Excellence* illustrates the point:

> A Procter & Gamble manufacturing manager remembers a call in the middle of the night. It came from a district sales manager, soon after this fellow (now a fifteen-year vet) had become a manager: "George, you've got a problem with a bar of soap down here." Down here, George explains (in 1983) was three hundred miles

away. "George, think you could get down here by six-thirty this morning?" Our informant adds, "It sounded like something more than an invitation." And finally, he concludes, "After you've finished your first three-hundred-mile ride through the back hills of Tennessee at seventy miles an hour to look at one damned thirty-four cent bar of soap, you understand that the Procter & Gamble Company is very, very serious about product quality. You don't subsequently need a detailed two-hundred-page manual to prove it to you."[8]

Johnson & Johnson's response to both Tylenol scares convinced customers that the company cared about them, and twice Tylenol did the impossible by recovering the lost market share.

Customer involvement. By involving the customer in the delivery of the service, firms have in some instances been able to reduce the cost of delivery while enhancing the quality of the service. We are all familiar with the self-service approach and encounter it daily at fast-food restaurants, salad bars in full-service restaurants, mini-bars in hotels, direct-dial long-distance telephoning, and automatic teller machines (ATMs), to mention only a few examples. For this approach to be successful, the customer must perceive that the value of the service is enhanced in some way by his or her involvement.

The ATM provides an excellent example of the potential of this approach. An ATM gives the customer much greater access to the services of a bank. Access is available on a continual basis, a marked departure from the historical practice of limited banking hours. Thus, the service is significantly enhanced. What is not as apparent is the substantial decrease in the cost of the service to the bank. A bank's three greatest costs, after the cost of money, are bricks and mortar, people, and paper. All of these are largely eliminated with the ATM. It is widely accepted in banking that cost per transaction can be reduced 80 percent or more if a sufficient number of transactions can be moved from tellers to ATMs.

Of course, accessibility is not the only factor the bank's customers consider when selecting how, when, and where they bank. The challenge to the bank, and to other businesses using self-service applications, is to convince customers that the added value of the service offsets the additional cost to them. In addition to accessibility, the value-enhancing factors of increased customer involvement include time savings, confidentiality, accuracy, and quality control.

It is interesting to note that although customer involvement can increase bonding, it can also reduce human interaction. By becoming more "personal," we do not necessarily become more "human." The term "personal" does not refer to the amount of human interaction but to the extent that personal needs of customers are satisfied. The ATM enables a bank to respond to some customer needs more effectively and address a broader range of needs than previously possible.

Decentralization. Because the customer is the key, the organization must be structured to facilitate better service. In most cases, this means a decentralized organization with considerable authority delegated to people close to the customer. You want your people to run the business as if it were their own.

Today's popular business folklore is filled with tales of organizations that have gained tremendous competitive advantage by pushing authority to lower levels. We could name company after company that has successfully employed a decentralized structure. However, no one has better explained why this strategy works than Robert Townsend in his classic *Up the Organization*. In explaining decision making in the organization, Townsend makes the analogy: "The Charge of the Light Brigade was ordered by an officer who wasn't there looking at the territory."[9]

People who interact with the customer, frequently those at the lowest levels in the organization, have the greatest possible visibility. Bill Marriott, Jr., notes, "We receive over a thousand customer forms and letters every day . . . and the most complimentary . . . are those written by guests who are impressed by our people and by some small thing that one of our staff went out of his or her way to do for them." Interaction with the customer gives employees a different perspective. They typically are the first to know when something is wrong, what customers' needs are, and how best to satisfy them. The organization that delegates the authority to act decisively in fulfilling these needs and solving the customers' problems often succeeds; the one that doesn't often fails.

Managing supply and demand. The adept use of capacity is a formidable competitive weapon in any business. Often the proper balance of supply and demand is singled out as a special problem in service organizations. However, in today's world of just-in-time inventories and outsourcing of components, this skill has become equally important in manufacturing. In either type of industry, the ability to meet demand when it occurs with a high-quality product is central to the bonding concept. This is often more difficult than it seems.

Airlines have been particularly active in managing this problem, since additions to their capacity are extremely expensive and come not in single units but usually in blocks of 100 or more seats. In supplying this capacity, airlines are restricted again by their inability to divide capacity into units smaller than the size of their aircraft. A number of practices have been used to deal with the problem. Reservation systems assist in anticipating demand levels and planning for both the appropriate size of aircraft to be assigned to a particular route and the proper number of flights between two cities. Pricing is widely used to encourage customers to fly in periods of low demand rather than in peak-demand periods. By using dynamic yield-management programs, airlines can increase or reduce the number of seats sold for various prices, depending on the level of customer demand at various price points. In addition, a few airlines have shared capacity on a regular basis by leasing aircraft to another airline when the lessor's demand was low and the lessee's demand was high.

Standardization of key operating policies. Although at first glance standardization seems to conflict with decentralization, it is our contention that key operating policies should be standardized so people close to the customers can be free to provide customized service. This is not to say that people interacting with the customer should not be consulted in the establishment of the policies. They are more likely to feel ownership of the policies if they have been involved.

The Marriott Corporation is an oft-cited example of an organization that follows this operating principle very effectively:

> The company became one of the industry's most efficient by applying a tightly centralized system of policies, procedures, and controls to the slightest operational detail. Every job has a manual that breaks down the work into a mind-boggling number of steps. A hotel maid, for instance, has 66 things to do in cleaning up a room . . . ."[10]

Electronic Data Systems Corporation has standardized not only training programs but also purchasing procedures for such ordinary items as raised flooring, air conditioning, power sources, and other routine equipment needed in a reliable computer environment. In addition, all of its regional data centers are as standardized as possible; even capacity level is standardized. As one official says, "If you have something go down and you don't have the specialist at hand to shoot the problem, he can look at the way it's done at another place and duplicate it."

This level of standardization normally has several positive results. Need for supervision is significantly reduced, so the cost of providing good service is lowered. The burden of making many decisions is removed from the person delivering the service, so more time can be devoted to providing the personal touch required for bonding. Finally, organizations that focus on detail to this extent spend little time correcting mistakes and invariably place more emphasis on training for good service.

Substituting information for assets. With the rapid improvements in information technology, some firms have been able to use information in innovative ways to better serve the customer and gain competitive advantage. By substituting more accurate and timely information for inventory and fixed assets, firms have been able to reduce costs and be more responsive to customer needs at the same time.

Italian-based Benetton, the world's largest manufacturer of knitware, has used the rapid collection and communication of information—in conjunction with a highly responsive manufacturing system—to operate its retail stores with substantially less inventory than its competitors. Its stores have no back-room storage. What is on the shelf is the only inventory in the store. By tracking sales very closely and identifying the items in greatest demand, the manufacturing system is able to respond rapidly to replenish the hot sellers. Not only are customers served better, but the critical performance measures of any retail operation, inventory turnover and sales per square foot, are maximized.

Strategic Implications

As pointed out earlier, Michael Porter has identified two generic strategies for successful major players in an industry—low cost and differentiation. We have tried to suggest that those who would view these as either/or options greatly limit their strategic choices.

As we tried to point out with the airline example, there is a basic difficulty in distinguishing among differentiation strategies within many industries, especially those industries in which most of the major firms seem to be offering fairly similar products. We believe the concept of customer bonding provides an extra dimension that makes such distinctions possible. For example, in the early 1980s, although Delta and Eastern airlines had fairly similar route structures, planes, and staff levels, Delta clearly had a closer bond with flyers—an almost family bond. To a lesser degree, American and United had similar routes—but American's innovation and high quality service seemed to suggest a more professional and dependable operation to many travelers.

Clearly, supplying a custom-made or unique product is the ultimate in a differentiated strategy. Custom products have a natural advantage in bonding—attention to personal needs and desires. Nevertheless, some firms that have chosen low-cost strategy, producing even a standard, commodity-type product, have been very successful in bonding. For example, although Kimberly Clark's newsprint division sells a commodity, it provides sufficient personal attention to its regular customers that it is able to avoid many of the price-cutting tactics of its competitors and yet keep its customers coming back, even when newsprint can be purchased at a lower price from a competitor. Crown Cork & Seal, by being close to its customers and providing them with an array of services, is able to maintain relatively high margins and returns in what is largely a commodity business. Thus, bonding can be combined with both low-cost and differentiated strategies.

All successful strategies are differentiation; cost is just one of the factors in which a firm can be different from the competition. If differentiation is considered in this manner, as a series of factors or dimensions in which a company can be better than or outperform the competitors, then only one company can be the best, or the industry leader, in any one dimension. For example, only one airline has the best food; only one has the friendliest employees; and only one is on time most frequently. With automobile manufacturers, only one has the best gas mileage; only one has the best repair service. Bonding occurs when a firm is able to identify and establish a leadership position in one, or more likely several, of these dimensions while meeting the other dimensions at some satisfactory level.

Creating the Bond

Although there are many ways to bond customers to a particular company's products (including effective advertising), and although some practices will be unique in various industries, in general the greater the personal attention to customers, the more enduring the bond. Service to the customer is the key issue. However, service to the customer is not the same as customer service. Service to the customer may mean not only providing special services but also making the product convenient to acquire, easy to use, and reliable over time. At a basic level it means showing a willingness to help customers solve problems and just being concerned or friendly. In the words of Peters and Austin:

> As IBM's Buck Rodgers . . . correctly (unfortunately) observes, "It's a shame, but whenever you get good service, it's an exception, and you're excited about it. It ought to be the other way around." We agree. Common decency, common courtesy toward the customer ("Guest") is indeed the exception. Economists may not buy it as the ultimate barrier to competitor entry or as a crucial form of sustainable strategic advantage, but such disparate actors (and extremely successful competitors) as IBM and McDonald's certainly do.[11]

Yet the *Wall Street Journal* recently reported that despite the furor over the poor quality of service, American companies are spending only $2.58 per employee to improve their dealings with the public—and most of the money goes to train workers to sell more or to calm complaining customers.[12]

Satisfying Expectations

We have found the concept of the psychological contract helpful in understanding how bonding takes place and why it is so important. This concept has traditionally been used to examine the relationship between an employer and its employees. We have applied it to the seller-customer relationship. In this exchange the customer comes to the seller with a set of expectations concerning the transaction. If these expectations are not fulfilled by the seller, the contract is violated and the seller has failed to complete a satisfactory transaction (create a happy customer). Hence, the seller must understand the nature of customers' expectations and how to satisfy them.

Gronroos has suggested that management of this process, in his terminology "service quality," is two-dimensional.[13] Customers are concerned with *what* is exchanged as well as *how* it is exchanged. Gronroos refers to the what of the transaction as the "technical quality dimension" and the how of the transaction as the "functional quality dimension." Sellers must be aware of both dimensions to adequately meet the expectations of their customers. For example, patients are highly unlikely to continue to see a physician if the physician always has dirty hands, even if the physician has outstanding professional qualifications. The technical quality dimension is clearly fulfilled, but the functional dimension is not.

This dichotomy provides a framework for analysis of the expectations of customers. We believe that many firms focus the majority, if not all, of their attention on the technical quality dimension. Executives frequently point out how tremendous improvements in their products have made them as good as or superior to the competition. Furthermore, these improvements can be documented and demonstrated. Nevertheless, the irrational customers fail to recognize the improvements and do not purchase the products. There is no reason to doubt the truth of the executives' statements. What can be questioned is the functional dimension of their service quality. Has enough care and attention been given to the delivery of the product?

Another interesting aspect of the service dilemma revealed in the executives' comments is their reliance on truth and fact. Whether the superiority of the product is real or not is of no consequence. The perception of the customer concerning the product is *the only reality of any significance*. Thus, managers are compelled to take proactive measures that address both dimensions of service quality and perceptions of service to shape and influence expectations. Their success in doing so can be the difference in gaining or losing competitive advantage.

Consequences of Bonding

The TARP (Technical Assistance Research Programs, Inc.) studies cited in Albrecht and Zemke's *Service America* highlight the grave consequences of poor customer bonding through inferior service. The results include:

- For every complaint received, the average business has 26 customers with a problem. Six of these customers have "serious" problems.
- The average customer with a problem tells nine or ten people. Thirteen percent of the problem customers tell more than 20 others.
- Noncomplainers are less likely to do business with the offending firm than complainers.

Perhaps the most disturbing finding in the TARP studies is that customers share so few of their complaints with businesses. Being close to the customer takes on a new meaning in light of these revelations. An active program to respond positively to complaining customers is obviously necessary, but it cannot discern the expectations and perceptions of a firm's customer base.

The positive results of good service and a high level of bonding seem to be as encouraging as the negative results are discouraging. According to Albrecht and Zemke, a loyal customer in the auto industry represents an average revenue of $140,000 over his or her lifetime. A similar figure for supermarkets is estimated to be $22,000 over a five-year period. Hence, the customer's value must be viewed in terms of revenues (and profits) that result over the long term. The value of bonding and the potential rewards would therefore appear to justify dedicating considerable resources to managing the bonding process.

The concept of bonding can help us understand the relationship that businesses have with their customers—obviously a key to their continued success and prosperity. What is needed now is a way to operationalize the concept. To achieve this goal it will be necessary to measure bonding. It is not likely that a universal measure of bonding for all companies or industries will ever be developed. However, a company might be able to establish a reasonably accurate surrogate for the level of bonding by monitoring repeat business. In addition, answers to the following questions, asked of customers on a regular basis, would provide valuable insight to the firm's progress in this area:

- Would you recommend this product to a close friend or relative? Why?
- Would you buy this product again? Why?

Other information relevant to this process and worthy of examination would be what the firm does in situations where mistakes have been made and the customer's expectations have not been met. In the British Airways study cited above, recovery was one of the customers' top concerns. It suggests that the customers don't expect perfection, but they do expect that errors will be corrected. Thus it is necessary to check if errors *are* being corrected, if they are corrected *before* the customer complains, and how much time elapsed before the correction took place.

These suggested measures are tentative at best. When more precise measures are developed, they will be invaluable in assisting managers to gain and maintain competitive advantage through stronger customer bonding.

References

1. Michael Porter, *Competitive Strategy* (New York: The Free Press, 1980). In this article we consider only the generic strategies of low cost and differentiation. Porter's third generic strategy, focus, is not considered, since we are interested in the major players in industries and a focus player pursues only a narrow segment of the market. Furthermore, even focus players pursue either a low-cost or a differentiation strategy, if on a smaller scale.
2. William K. Hall, "Survival Strategies in a Hostile Environment," *Harvard Business Review*, September–October 1980, pp. 75–80.
3. V. Govindarajan and Deven Sharma, "Generic Competitive Strategies: An Empirical Analysis," *1986 Decision Sciences Institute Proceedings*, pp. 1243–1245.
4. Peter F. Drucker, *Management: Tasks, Responsibilities, Practices* (New York: Harper& Row, 1973), p. 61.
5. Karl Albrecht and Ron Zemke, *Service America! Doing Business in the New Economy* (Homewood, Ill.: Dow Jones-Irwin, 1985), pp. 33–34.
6. *The Wall Street Journal*, March 19, 1987, p. 1.
7. Phillip Thompson, Glenn DeSouza, and Bradley T. Gale, "The Strategic Management of Service Quality," *PIMSLETTER*, 33, p. 1.
8. Tom Peters and Nancy Austin, *A Passion for Excellence* (New York: Random House, 1985), pp. 30–35.
9. Robert Townsend, *Up the Organization* (New York: Alfred A. Knopf, 1970), p. 45.
10. Thomas Moore, "Marriott Grabs for More Room," *Fortune*, October 31, 1983, p. 108.
11. Peters and Austin (note 8), p. 44.
12. *The Wall Street Journal*, March 17, 1987, p. 1.
13. Christian Gronroos, *Strategic Management and Marketing in the Service Sector* (Lund, Sweden: Studentlitteratur ab, 1984). Gronroos' research and conclusions were directed at firms in the service sector. Nevertheless, we believe that they are equally applicable in the manufacturing environment because of the mix of tangible and intangible attributes in most products. For additional reading in this area see Theodore Levitt, *The Marketing Imagination* (New York: The Free Press, 1983).

23

Buyers' Subjective Perceptions of Price

Kent B. Monroe

Marketing researchers recently have expended considerable effort to investigate how price influences buyers' decisions yielding a variety of results, some not entirely explainable. This article reviews the relevant research literature, organizes the results, and suggests new research directions.

In recent years there has been a growing awareness of the complex role of price as a determinant of a purchase decision. Recent behavioral research indicates there is no simple explanation of how price influences individual buyers' purchase decisions. In some situations a change in price produces behavioral responses consistent with the assumption of Marshallian demand theory; in other situations these responses are not consistent with this theory. This article reviews the research on individual response to price and organizes the knowledge obtained from these studies.

The response of interest is individual's perception of price. However, price is only one aspect of the product stimulus confronting a buyer; i.e., the buyer responds to brand name, color, package, size, label, as well as price. The organization of these information cues as purchase decision inputs depends on the perceptual process an individual uses to give meaning to the raw material provided by the external world.

Psychological Pricing: Traditional View

Many basic marketing textbooks provide examples indicating greater demand at particular price points, suggesting that demand falls at prices just above and below the critical price points. Depending on the situation, these psychological prices are referred to as customary prices, odd prices, or price lines. Theoretically, this phenomenon indicates that the consumer is perceptually sensitive to certain prices, and departure from these prices in either direction results in a decrease in demand.

Customary pricing excludes all price alternatives except a single price point. The traditional example has been the five-cent candy bar or package of gum. With customary prices, sellers adapt to changes in costs and market conditions by adjusting product size or quality, assuming the buyer would consider paying only one price.

Odd pricing assumes that prices ending with an odd number (e.g., 1, 3, 5, 7, 9), or just under a round number (e.g., 99, 98) increase consumer sensitivity. Evidence justifying such prices has largely been of an anecdotal nature. However, Ginzberg [28] imposed experimental patterns of odd and even prices on selected items in regional editions of a large mail-order catalog. Taking account of all variables influencing demand, he could not discern any generalizable result of the study. More recently, Gabor and Granger [21] concluded that the dominance of pricing below the round figure in some markets may be largely an artifact. That is, if sellers use odd pricing, then some buyers will consider the odd price as the real price and the round figure price as incorrect and respond accordingly. Again, there was no significant evidence supporting the psychological explanation of increased perceptual sensitivity.

Psychological Pricing: A Partial Explanation

Although the research of Ginzberg and Gabor and Granger suggests that buyers tend to expect certain prices after being

Kent B. Monroe is a Professor of Marketing at Virginia Tech.

exposed to them over a period of time, Friedman [19], noting a general consistency in grocery stores' and suppliers' pricing patterns, offers reasons why certain psychological prices may have their roots in tradition:

1. Multiples of 12 are the most popular number of selling units packed in a case accounting for 74.5% of all test items.
2. Prices ending in 9 or 5 account for as much as 80% of retail food prices.
3. There was extensive multiple-unit pricing with the multiples never dividing evenly into the price.

However, using only odd prices in multiple-unit pricing is inconvenient to the buyer intent on comparing prices. As a recent *Progressive Grocer* study showed, if the multiple is too complicated, the buyer will buy only in quantities most easily calculated [30]. This *Progressive Grocer* finding suggests some discriminating process being applied by the buyer, but only if the comparative method used leads to a conclusion vis-à-vis the particular product offer. Otherwise, the buyer apparently withdraws from the complicated pricing situation.

4. Nearly 50% of all special off-price promotions were in multiples of 5, even-number discounts were more predominant, one-cent discounts were not found, with two-cent and nine-cent discounts very rare.

These findings imply the need to reduce price sufficiently to allow the buyer to perceive a price difference compared to the old price. Given earlier findings on odd number pricing and the rule of 9 and 5, the even-number discounts and the rarity of nine-cent discounts are easily understood.

Ad hoc explanations of traditional pricing practices suggesting critical prices or magical numbers have not been supported by the limited research available. Perhaps there are some logical explanations for these pricing practices based on traditional distribution practices. But, retailers have found some pricing practices work better than others, thereby suggesting there are some buyer behavioral phenomena underlying the observed response patterns.

Price-Consciousness

According to economic theory, price is assumed to influence buyer choice because price serves as an indicator of purchase cost. That is, assuming the buyer has perfect information concerning prices and wants satisfaction of comparable product alternatives, he can determine a product mix that maximizes his satisfaction for a given budget constraint. However, the extent that buyers are conscious of the prices they pay influences the way prices are perceived and the role price plays in buyer choice.

Using thhree measures of price-consciousness, Gabor and Granger [20] surveyed 640 housewives to determine their awareness of grocery prices last paid. The first measure was simply the percentage of prices remembered (82%) irrespective of the correctness of the price named. The researchers also discovered that price-consciousness was inversely correlated with social class (income) with the exception of the poor, and that price-consciousness was lower for branded items. Second, 57% of the prices were named correctly, with the same general relationship with social class and branded goods. Finally, for a subsample of 184 incorrectly named prices, 52% of the prices differed from the correct price by not more than 10%.

Progressive Grocer also found that price-consciousness varied over products [31]. For 60 advertised and price-competitive brand items, the percentage of correct prices named varied from 86% for Coca-Cola to 2% for shortening, and for these items 91% and 34% of the named prices were with 5% of the correct prices.

Explicitly, no research evidence has linked price-consciousness with price perception, although these studies did assume that some recollection of the price paid can be taken as evidence of conscious concern for the price of a given item [20, p. 177]. However, Wells and LoSciuto [76], using direct observation, found that concern for price was exhibited by 13%, 17%, and 25% of shoppers purchasing cereal, candy, and detergent respectively.

Similar to Wells, Brown [4, 5] hypothesized that shopping behavior would be a better indicator of the ability to perceive price differences than conscious concern for price. His study was based on market basket price indices for 80 items in 27 supermarkets in 5 cities and personal interviews covering price perceptions of supermarkets, store patronage behavior, and patronage motives.

Analysis of the data revealed that shopping variables (number of stores shopped, concern for price, use of a shopping list) were the best discriminators of perceptual validity, which was measured by comparing shoppers' ordinal rankings of stores' price levels with the stores' market basket price indices. Further, price-consciousness was a better discriminator of perceptual validity than was price level of the store patronized; very price-conscious shoppers were more valid perceivers of price than non-price-conscious shoppers, but for intermediate levels of price-consciousness no generalizations were possible. In contrast to Gabor and Granger, Brown was unable to establish significant relationships between perceptual validity and socioeconomic variables.

Brown's findings partially corroborate Gabor and Granger's assumption of a positive relationship between price-consciousness and price perception. Both Gabor and Granger and the *Progressive Grocer* study found that for some items the brand influence exhibited dominance over price, thereby suggesting (as Wells did) that price is not of sufficient universal importance to be the primary determinant of choice. Evidence of an inverse relationship between socioeconomic standing and price perception validity found in the Gabor and Granger study was not found by Brown. Further complicating this relationship is the emerging tendency to find positive relationship between socioeconomic variables and use of unit price [50]. Who uses price and when is not well documented by research.

The Price-Quality Relationship

Finding some degree of price-consciousness among buyers does not necessarily imply that price is used solely as a measure of purchase cost. As Scitovsky [62] has noted, the buyer generally does not have complete information about the quality of alternative product offerings, yet he forms perceptions from the information available. When price information is available, and when the buyer is uncertain about product quality, it would seem reasonable to use price as a criterion for assessing quality.

The process of converting explicit and subjective information into perceptions is affected by the buyer's dispositions and his prior experience with the product. Another parameter of the perceptual situation is the symbolic value of the product—its capacity to evoke reactions relevant to a state of affairs it represents [7]. As the Bruner studies [6, 7] have shown, symbolic value leads to perceptual accentuation, i.e., subjectively magnified. Thus, the perceived value of a product may produce an accentuation in the assessed quality of the product, either positive or negative, and the direction and magnitude of the accentuation will depend on the particular prices and needs involved. Hence, as a criterion for assessing quality, or value, price may serve either to make the product more or less attractive.

Single-Cue Studies

Originally, price-quality studies considered situations where the only differential information available to respondents was price. Initiating these studies, Leavitt [37] asked 30 Air Force officers and 30 male and female graduate students to choose between two differentially priced, lettered, imaginary brands, for four products (moth flakes, cooking sherry, razor blades, and floor wax) and then indicate the "degree of satisfaction" with their choice. Subjects tended to be less satisfied when choosing lower-priced brands and also tended to choose the higher-priced brand when (1) price was the only differential information; (2) the products were perceived to be heterogeneous in quality; and (3) the price difference was large. Tull, et al. [73] replicated Leavitt's experiment using table salt, aspirin, floor wax, and liquid shampoo and found that the respondents tended to choose the higher-priced brands of products perceived to be heterogeneous.

Distinguishing between the effects of price as an indicator of quality on the perception of product attractiveness or on the perception of purchase offer attractiveness, Ölander [53] experimentally tested the effect of price for household textiles on more than 100 young women's perceptions of product attractiveness. When consequences were related to pairwise choices, similar towels were more often preferred when assigned a high price than when assigned a low price.

McConnell [38, 39, 40, 41] tested the hypothesis that product quality perception is a function of price. Sixty married students in each of 24 trials chose one bottle of an identical beer differing only in brand name and price. Analysis revealed that perceived quality was significantly and positively related to price. In an extensive experiment, Shapiro [64] found that for 600 women (1) price was generally an indicator of quality; (2) price could not overcome product preferences; (30 the use of price to judge quality was a generalized attitude; and (4) price reliance varied over products, but was more significant in situations of high risk, low self-confidence, and absence of other cues. Lambert [35, 36] found that for 200 undergraduates the frequency of choosing high-priced brands was positively correlated with perceived variations in product quality and perceived ability to judge quality. Finally, Newman and Becknell [52] found an apparent positive price-quality relationship for ratings of different models of a durable product.

Multicue Studies

A frequent criticism of the single-cue studies is that when price is the only information available, subjects naturally associate price and quality. Although this criticism applies directly to the Leavitt and Tull studies, the other studies cited included other experimentally controlled information, such as actual product samples or promotional information. Generally, when price was the only differential information, a positive price-quality relationship was observed which was enhanced when the products were perceived to be heterogeneous in quality and when the comparative price differences were accentuated.

To overcome the criticism of the single-cue studies, other price-quality studies have experimentally varied other cues in addition to price. Three experiments specifically tested the single-cue, price-quality relationship as a part of the overall experimental design. Using home economics students, housewives, carpet buyers, and salesmen, Enis and Stafford [16, 17] discovered that perception of the quality of carpeting was directly related to price. Although store information did not significantly affect perception of carpet quality, the interactive effect of price and store information was significant. Jacoby, et al. [32] asked 136 adult male beer drinkers to taste and rate four test beers. By experimentally manipulating price, composition differences, and brand image, it was determined that price, except when considered in isolation, did not have a significant effect on quality perception, whereas brand image did. Gardner [27] also found a brand-quality relationship replacing the price-quality relationship in an experiment testing students' perceptions of toothpaste, men's shirts, and men's suits. Moreover, in an earlier experiment using the same product categories, Gardner [26] could find no significant relationship between perceived quality and frequency of purchase or time spent shopping for the test products.

Although these three studies provide evidence of a positive price-quality relationship, their results do imply that price may not be the dominant cue in quality perception. Unfortunately, this diminished saliency of the price cue has not been a generalized finding in other multicue studies. Andrews and Valenze [3] asked 50 female students to rate the quality of sweaters and shoes. Quality ratings for each product were obtained first for each cue presented separately (price, store name, brand name), then for all 27 variable combinations. The results indicated that the lower the price the greater the influence of brand names, but in combined quality judgments price was clearly the dominant cue.

Rao [59, 60], using 144 graduate students, experimentally tested the role of price in quality perceptions for electric razors and razor blades. Using the multidimensional model of individual differences, he discovered that after accounting for prior product knowledge, personality variables, and brand display, price did not significantly affect perception of product quality. Both prior product knowledge and consumer test information produced significant effects on quality perceptions.

Smith and Broome [67, 68] experimentally tested the effects of price and market standing information on brand preference using 196 student wives and toothpaste, aspirin, green peas, and coffee. Their findings suggest that price and market standing information influence preference of unknown brands, but neither influences preference for known brands. Della Bitta [13] experimentally determined that students used price as an indicator of product attractiveness for table and pocket radios. Moreover, a positive relation between an evaluator's uncertainty about ability to assess product attractiveness and the use of price as an evaluative criterion was discovered.

Finally, using coffee, fabric softener, and spray cologne, Monroe [48] discovered that when housewives had prior differential purchase or use experience, brand attitude overcame the price influence, implying less use of price as a preference decision cue. Departing from previous studies, Monroe disaggregated the data and discovered that when price was the only differential information, the respondents found it very difficult to decide which brand to prefer. In contrast to most previous studies, respondents were permitted to indicate no brand preference for any test situation, and when price was the only differential information, nearly 25% of all responses indicated indifference even when comparative prices were more than 40% apart.

Determining the specific effect price has on buyers' perceptions of quality is complicated by the multitude of research designs and products tested. But throughout the findings surveyed here emerges the suggestion that brand name is important and possibly dominates price for relatively inexpensive grocery products and beverages. For clothing there is an apparent increasing concern with price, although price may not always dominate the influence of brand name. Perhaps one major disadvantage of experimental research in this area is the difficulty of presenting a wide range of prices to obtain individuals' perceptions of product quality. Only Andrews and Valenzi and Monroe offered a systematic range of prices to the experimental respondents. Also, as suggested in the research reported in the section on differential price thresholds, the range of stimuli (prices) presented does affect respondents' perceptions.

Functional Form of the Price-Quality Relationship

As Gardner [27] has suggested, the research evidence precludes any generalization about a price-quality relationship. The single-cue studies unanimously observed a price-quality relationship, but the multicue studies often found little direct price-quality relations. In those studies where brand names were a part of the manipulations, the brand influence seemingly dominated the price influence, a result consistent with the price-consciousness studies.

Apart from the issue of generalizability, some of the studies produced evidence on the functional form of the price-quality relationship. McConnell [38, 39] observed a nonlinear relationship—the \$1.30 and \$1.20 brands of beer were separated by a greater perceptual distance than were the \$1.20 and \$0.99 brands. Also, Rao [59] observed: (1) that the price-quality relationship was not unidirectional and (2) that brand quality was exponentially related to price.

Noting the implied nonlinear or even discontinuous relationships in some of the previous studies, Peterson [58] estimated the price-quality functional form and discovered a parabolic relationship of the form:

$$\bar{Q}_i = a + bX_i - cX_i^2, \tag{1}$$

where $\bar{Q}_i$ is mean quality rating at the ith price level, X_i is the ith price level, $i = 1, 2, \ldots, n$, and a, b, c are parameters. It should also be noted that the general form of the relationship found by Peterson can also be represented by the exponential form suggested by Rao, except that the exponential form will asymptotically approach an upper limit.

Related to the functional form of the price-quality relationship is the implied demand curve resulting from such a relationship. Although none of these studies specifically examined the price-quality demand relationship, the evidence cited infers that, at least over some range of prices, demand is greater for higher prices, and the demand curve has a positive slope. Other than for such unique situations as inferior and "snob-appeal" goods, economists are understandably reluctant to accept such a possibility, since the positively sloping demand curve for a price-quality relationship is an inference without empirical evidence.

Price-Quality Mapping

How people use price to evaluate quality is suggested by a paradigm developed by Emery [14] in which buyers are hypothesized to categorize the product's price, categorize the assessed quality, and then judge whether the assessed quality is equivalent to the expected quality for the categorized price. His model is shown in Figure 1.

Mapping (a) to (b) and (c) to (d) is done simultaneously. Matching (b) and (c) depends on prior purchase experience with the product. If the line linking (b) and (c) has a negative slope, the item will be judged as high-priced relative to assessed quality, while a positive slope would provide a low

Figure 1
Subjective mapping of price and quality

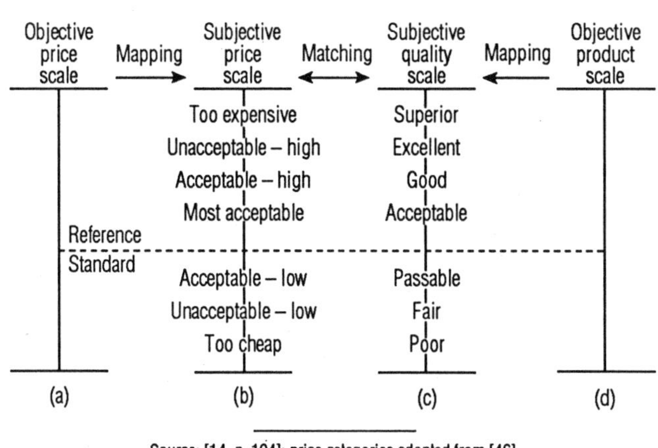

Source: [14, p. 104]; price categories adopted from [46].

price judgment. In either situation, if the value of the slope is perceived to be relatively large, the buyer may refrain from comparing his "standard" price-quality relationship against the one observed.

Absolute Price Thresholds

Research evidence reviewed so far has been directed toward the questions of whether buyers are aware of prices they pay and whether price is used as an indicator of quality without relating price perception to the perceptual process per se. But it is necessary to determine whether certain perceptual phenomena relating sensory processes to physical stimuli are analogous to price perception. In this section and the next, attention is directed to two perceptual phenomena: absolute and differential thresholds.

Every human sensory process has an upper and lower limit of responsiveness to a stimulus—*absolute thresholds* that mark the transition between response and no response. Within the stimulus set in which responsiveness occurs the *differential threshold* is the minimum amount of change in a stimulus necessary to produce "just noticeable difference" or JND. In a pricing situation, we are interested in the buyer's ability to discriminate between various product choices (stimuli). Therefore, two questions arise: (1) Do buyers have upper and lower price limits? and (2) Given differentially priced products, how do buyers discriminate among choices?

Theoretical Framework

The hypothesis that a buyer has lower and upper price limits for a contemplated purchase has foundation in psychophysics, the study of quantitative relationships between physical objects and corresponding psychological events. Originating much of the interest in threshold research was Weber's law which suggests that small, equally perceptible increments in a response correspond to proportional increments in the stimulus:

$$\Delta S/S = K \tag{2}$$

where S is the magnitude of the stimulus, ΔS is the increment in S corresponding to a defined unitary change in response, and K is a constant.

In judging differences between two intensities of a stimulus Weber's law holds only over limited ranges of stimulus intensity. In particular, when stimuli values approach the lower threshold, K may become considerably higher, and it also may increase for high stimuli values. Fechner argued that subjective sensation must be measured indirectly by using differential increments and derived the Weber-Fechner law (see [47] for a complete derivation):

$$R = k \log S + a \tag{3}$$

where R is the magnitude of response, S the magnitude of the stimulus, k a constant of proportionality, and a the constant of integration.

The Weber-Fechner law provides a means of experimentally determining the absolute threshold because a least squares regression relating R to $\log S$ can be fitted from the data. Then the threshold is operationally defined as the stimulus value with a probability of producing a response 50% of the time [12]. The importance of the Weber-Fechner law to pricing is it produces the hypothesis that the relationship between price and an operationally defined response is logarithmic.

Empirical Evidence for Absolute Price Thresholds

The hypothesis of lower and upper price thresholds implies the existence of a range of acceptable prices where some prices greater than $0 are unacceptable because they are considered too low. Stoetzel [70] demonstrated the existence of a range of prices buyers are willing to pay for a radio. Adam [1] then developed a technique for quantifying buyers' attitudes toward price. Interviewing over 6,000 people Adam determined upper and lower price thresholds for nylon stockings, an underwear item, children's shoes, men's dress shirts, a gas lighter, and refrigerators.

Fouilhé [18] extended the work of Stoetzel and Adam to include two household products and package soup and confirmed evidence for a range of acceptable prices. Fouilhé's methodology differed from Stoetzel and Adam in that he actually showed the products to each respondent, including brand name for two of them, and found that the known products had a distinctly narrower acceptable price range.

Gabor and Granger [22, 23] interviewed over 3,000 housewives to determine acceptable price ranges for a carpet, nylon stockings, food, and 2 household products. Gabor and Granger not only confirmed the acceptable price range hypothesis, but also found that the range shifted downward as income fell. Moreover, as income fell, the upper price threshold dropped less than the lower one, implying that low price was a more potent deterrent to the higher-income groups than was high price to lower-income groups.

Investigating social categorization as a function of acceptance and series range, Sherif [65] found price thresholds for a winter coat using 334 high school white and Indian students to be distinctly lower for the Indian students, particularly as the price stimulus set was lengthened to include higher prices. Monroe and Venkatesan [51] adapted psychophysical experimental methodology using college students, and upper and lower price limits were determined for a variety of clothing and personal care items. In a second experiment replicating Sherif's study using high school students, Monroe [46] determined price limits for a sport coat and dress shoes.

Alexis, et al. [2] asked 150 housewives to indicate the perceived importance of specific physical attributes and price for five articles of clothing and concluded that "the consumer goes shopping with a 'target' price in mind around which there is an acceptable deviation" [2, p. 28].

Functional Form of the Buy-Response Function

One implication of the price threshold concept is that the probability distribution a buyer will find an acceptable price is bell-shaped (the buy-response function) [23, 45]. Thus, if a buyer's perception follows the normal law, the cumulative response function is an S-shaped curve. Further, as hypothesized by the Weber-Fechner law, if equal increments in cumulative responses are produced only when price is increased by a constant proportion, the plotting the logarithm of price against cumulative response to show a uniform response increase will produce a symmetrical ogive.

Adam [1] proposed the logarithmic response function by suggesting that the size of the acceptable price range is proportional to the reference price:

$$\Delta P/P = K \tag{4}$$

where ΔP is the acceptable price range, P is the reference price, and K is the constant of proportionality—essentially Weber's law. As indicated earlier, the logarithmic hypothesis is easily derived from this proportional relationship. In addition, Adam tested for a logarithmic relationship and concluded that the psychological scale of prices followed a logarithmic scale. Fouilhé [18] found that the logarithmic scale "appears to be well established, at least within the limits of the prices shown" [18, p. 90], as did Gabor and Granger [23].

Independently of these efforts, Cooper [10, 11] tested the relationship:

$$Q = K \log P \tag{5}$$

where Q is perceived quality, P is price, and K is the constant of proportionality. Testing four products, he found a cumulative S-shaped function (ogive) and concluded, "judgments of value . . . when compared to objective cash scales follow a relatively stable logarithmic form" [10, p. 119]. In addition, he observed that the value of K varies with the magnitude of price, but is constant for a given product. Finally, Monroe [49] also found logarithmic relationships provided good fits in his psychophysical experiments.

Differential Price Threshold

Usually a buyer has several choices for a contemplated purchase whose prices may provide cues that facilitate the discriminating process. However, even if the numerical prices are different, it cannot be assumed that the prices are perceived to be different. Hence, the problem becomes one of determining the effect of perceived price differences on buyer choice; and the major concern is when and under what circumstances are differentially priced but similar products perceived as different offers? Very little research has been reported on differential thresholds in pricing. This lack of research is surprising because of its practical implications for product line and sale pricing. Thus, the research to be reviewed comes primarily from psychological studies, with pricing implications drawn by analogy.

Weber's Law

Weber's law has often been cited as the basis for inferences about perceived price differences [15, 33, 43, 61, 75], but most writers have ignored other important variables affecting perception of price differences and simply assumed K to be constant for an individual over all price comparisons. But just as K varies over different physical stimuli and as stimuli values approach minimal or high intensity, so should K vary over different products (similarly priced) and over divergent price levels.

Uhl [74] postulated that behavioral response to price changes depends on exposure to and perception of a price change and motivation to alter behavior as a result of it. Further, the perception of a retail price change depends on the magnitude of the price change—in (2) the magnitude of ΔS. In the Uhl study, 74% of the experimental price changes were correctly identified, with the 5% deviations correctly identified 64% of the time, and the 15% deviations 84% of the time. Uhl interpreted the data to mean that the larger price changes exceeded the differential price thresholds of greater numbers of respondents.

Uhl also attempted a modified test of Weber's law during the study hypothesizing that, for example, a 15% change in the price of a 15¢ product should be perceived by more consumers than a 15% change for a 55¢ product. However, the respondents perceived the 15% price deviations better on the higher-priced items.

Finally, Uhl indicated that while perception of price changes was independent of their direction, the dominance of reaction thresholds made respondents more sensitive to price increases. Moreover, 26% perceptual errors due to differential price thresholds and directional errors suggested a significant portion of the respondents were perceptually limited in responding to price changes.

Although not directly concerned with measuring price change perception, Pessemier [55, 56] in his market simulation studies also found price sensitivity to be different for price increases as compared to price decreases. And in a later field experiment he observed that a price change for a specific brand had little short-run effect on demand [57].

As (5) indicates, Cooper [10, 11] tested the Weber-Fechner law relating perceived quality to price. In addition to his findings on the shape of the response function, Cooper found that the value of K varied for different products. The immediate implication is that consumers will be more sensitive to price changes for some products, i.e., have lower differential price thresholds. In other words, for some products a price increase or decrease may not be perceived, suggesting these products have a relatively high K value, using (2).

Recently Kamen and Toman [33, 34] criticized the attempt of marketing textbook writers to infer analogically that Weber's law can be applied to a variety of marketing situations. Using a mail survey, they obtained buyer preferences for 36 pairs of gasoline prices and concluded that their data contradicted Weber's law and, therefore, Weber's law had been invalidated. Later, Stapel [69] supported Kamen and Toman and suggested that everybody can notice even a one-cent price difference. However, Monroe [47], and Gabor, Granger, and Sowter [25] have indicated there is ample evidence to support the plausibility of Weber's law applying within a pricing context, particularly when a buyer perceives the entire purchase offer as different. *There is still no valid test of the applicability of Weber's law to pricing.*

Adaptation-Level Theory

Various researchers have suggested that one determinant of price perception is the price "last paid," or the buyers' notion of a "fair price," relative to the present price level, actual or perceived. This price perception hypothesis has theoretical foundation in Helson's adaptation-level theory [29].

Classical psychophysics provided the concept that judgments of stimulus differences are dependent on the magnitude of the standard against which the judgments are made. However, this notion considers the differential threshold to be dependent only on the standard or reference stimulus. Adaptation-level theory provides for a changing zero point from which behavioral responses are made and provides an explicit statement of the frame of reference to which behavior is relative.

According to Helson, an individual's behavioral response to stimuli represents modes of adaptation to environmental and organismic forces. These forces are not random, but rather impinge on organisms already adapted to past stimuli, internal as well as external. The pooled effect of three classes of stimuli—focal, contextual, and organic—determines the adjustment or adaptation level (AL), underlying all forms of behavior. In price perception, focal stimuli are those the individual is directly responding to, and contextual or background stimuli are all other stimuli in the behavioral situation providing the context within which the focal stimuli are operative. Adaptation processes result in behavioral responses that are commonly expressed along a continuum ranging from rejection to acceptance with a neutral zone or point of indifference in the transitional region(s).

Perceptual judgment of a stimulus depends on the relationship between the physical value of that stimulus and the physical value of the current AL. In a pricing context, adaptation-level theory suggests that price perception depends on the actual price and the individual's reference price or AL.

Emery [14] has noted some important implications of adaptation-level theory on price perception:

1. Price perceptions are relative to other prices and to associated use-values.
2. This is a standard price for each discernible quality level for each product category.
3. The standard price serves as an anchor for judgments of other prices.
4. There is a region of indifference about a standard price such that changes in price within this region produce no change in perception.
5. The standard price will be some average of the prices for similar products.
6. Buyers do not judge each price singly, but rather each price is compared with the standard price and the other prices in the price range.
7. The standard price need not correspond with any actual price nor the price of the leading brand.

Evidence of a Standard Price

Although the hypothesis of a standard price serving as an AL for price judgments has not been directly tested, evidence does support the plausibility of this hypothesis. Initially, Scitovsky [62] suggested that buyers consider traditional past prices as a product's fair price. When fair and actual prices differ, the judgment of cheap or expensive may be applied. Similarly, Shapiro [63] suggests that price does not indicate quality without a perceptible difference in price from the fair price. Gabor and Granger [22, 23, 24] indicate a buyer will probably decide to purchase if the product's price falls within an acceptable price range whose limits are related to prevailing market prices and the price of the product normally purchased. Data available to Ölander [53] also suggested that a buyer's price judgment is influenced by his perception of prevailing market prices and his perception of the price most frequently charged. McConnell [38, 40, 41], explaining the nonlinearity of perceptual distance between the high-, middle-, and low-priced brands, found evidence that subjects used the high-priced brand as a frame of reference.

Explaining the respondents' lack of success in identifying the price last paid, Uhl [74] observed that in judging a price change consumers use the range of prices last paid as a reference point. Moreover, consumer perception of price changes was related to the importance of the product in the budget and the frequency of product purchase (contextual variables in the AL paradigm), Kamen and Toman [33] advanced the notion consumers have a fair price for a given item. Respondents in Cooper's research [11] believed the standard price provided above average value; average value was judged for products priced 20–30% below current market prices (standard price). Alexis [2] discovered that the consumer goes shopping with a "target price" in mind around which there is an acceptable deviation. Finally, Peterson [58] found that the perceived quality ratings for some subjects appeared to result from an interaction between price and product frame of reference.

Assimilation-Contrast Effects

Several of the pricing studies cited suggest that the prevailing range of prices affects the standard or reference price. Since the stimulus range is affected by the extreme or end stimuli values, to explore the influence of price range on perception attention could be centered on the end prices. In particular, what happens to perceptions when the end prices are varied? Stimuli values used by individuals to make perceptual judgments (AL, end values) are called anchoring stimuli. When an anchor is introduced at or near the end of the stimulus series, the judgment scale is displaced toward the anchor and the new reference point is assimilated into the series. However, when the end reference point is too remote, displacement is away from the anchor and the end point is perceived as belonging to another scale (category)—the contrast effect [66].

Evidence of assimilation-contrast in a pricing context is meager, but if applicable the implications are profound. First, the high and low prices in a definable product offering may be more noticeable to a buyer and thus influence his perceptions. These end prices [44], along with the standard price, may accentuate the perceived value for a given product (a bargain) or may diminish the perceived value (too expensive), depending where the product's price lies in the price range. In addition, if either or both end prices are outside the acceptable price range, the reference price cues may increase the ambiguity of the price stimuli.

Second, the perception of a sale price may depend on its position in the price range. Positioning it below other offerings may lead to the perception of a bargain (assimilation effect) or to a disbelief that the sale price is a reduction from the advertised original (contrast effect) [42].

A third consideration is the effect of reducing the range of stimuli by shifting one or both end values toward the stimulus center. Available evidence indicates that respondents then have greater difficulty in discriminating among stimuli, and that this increase in ambiguity leads to assimilation [7, 9, 71, 72]. Thus, as the range of alternative prices narrows, buyers may have greater difficulty in discriminating between choices, leading to a judgment of no price differences (assimilation effect); in these cases it can be expected that other cues (e.g., brand name) will dominate the decision process.

Compounding the selection of an appropriate hypothesis is that concomitant with the price series is a value series (perceived quality), and as has already been observed, the price and value series may vary concurrently. Value is not a physical stimulus, although it is an important attribute, and efficient discrimination between stimuli in terms of differences in value usually is more important than discrimination in terms of price. Accentuation of price differences may lead to a greater accentuation of perceived value differences [6. 8, 71, 72]. The resultant purchase response in terms of current phenomenology is not predictable.

Sherif's work [65] is the only research evidence available directly testing the assimilation-contrast hypothesis in a pricing context [62, p. 155]:

> When a (price) range exceeded the latitude of acceptance (range of acceptable prices), higher values were assimilated into acceptable categories; but at the same time, a contrast effect occurred, as revealed in the tendency to lump together highly discrepant values into a broad objectionable category. . . . As a result of the interaction between internal anchor and stimulus range, subjects discriminated most keenly among the acceptable values when they were not faced with numerous objectionable items . . . . The results indicate that the range of stimulus values presented for judgment is an important variable in determining whether effects of internal anchors will be detected at all.

Summary and Conclusions

The purpose of this article has been to organize existing research on buyer's subjective perceptions of price, contrasting existing research knowledge and current pricing practices with the unknown knowledge on buyer's price perceptions, and to shake the belief that the inverse price-demand relationship is "one of the best substantiated findings in economics" [54, p. 26]. Although Palda [54] argues that departures from the inverse price-demand relationship—for example, a positive relationship due to quality connotations—are caused by buyers' perceptual changes, the evidence suggests that the perceptual mechanism need not change to infer a positive price-demand relationship.

Findings on the price-quality relationship are mixed, although there are indications that a positive relationship exists, at least over some range of prices for some product categories. Implications of the price-quality relationship on the shape of the demand curve are inconclusive and must be explored directly through empirical studies. There appears to be a general lack of awareness of prices paid for recent purchases. And when buyers do compare prices, the range of prices offered, the reference price, and the end prices may affect judgment and, therefore, buyers' responses. If the price range and the end prices do affect judgment, the extent that the competitive environment leads to little price variation within alternative purchase choices decreases the likelihood of consumer awareness of prices paid and increases the likelihood that price changes within the narrow price range are not perceived.

Despite the evidence available from specific effect of price on choice studies, the evidence available from the absolute and differential price threshold research suggests we know very little about how price affects a buyer's perceptions of alternative purchase offers, and how these perceptions affect his response. Perception is one intervening variable between a stimulus and a response, and as suggested by adaptation-level theory, the stimulus context is indeed an important variable affecting perception. To direct research only to the focus variable (price) and ignore or assume constant the context variables is indeed a grave error. Because of the seemingly heavy reliance on the inverse price-demand function by price setters, it should be realized that a number of psychological and other contextual factors may lead to a perception of price by the buyer that is different from the perception assumed by the price setter.

References

1. Adam, Daniel. *Les réactions du consummateur devant le prix*, Paris: SEDES, 1958.
2. Alexis, Marcus, George Haines, Jr., and Leonard Simon. "A Study of the Validity of Experimental Approaches to the Collection of Price and Product Preference Data," paper presented at 17th International Meeting of the Institute of Management Sciences, 1970.
3. Andrews, P. R. and E. R. Valenzi. "Combining Price, Brand, and Store Cues to Form an Impression of Product Quality," paper presented at Conference of the American Psychological Association, 1971.
4. Brown, F. E. "Price Perception and Store Patronage," *Proceedings*, Fall Conference, American Marketing Association, 1968, 371–6.
5. ———. "Who Perceives Supermarket Prices Most Validly?" *Journal of Marketing Research*, 8 (February 1971), 110–3.
6. Bruner, Jerome and Cecile Goodman, "Value and Need as Organizing Factors in Perception." *Journal of Abnormal and Social Psychology*, 42 (January 1947), 33–44.
7. Bruner, Jerome and A. Leigh Minturn. "Perceptual Identification and Perceptual Organization," *Journal of General Psychology*, 53 (July 1955), 21–8
8. Bruner, Jerome and Leo Postman. "Symbolic Value as an Organizing Factor in Perception," *Journal of Social Psychology*, 27 (February 1948), 203–8.
9. Campbell, Donald, William Hunt, and Nan Lewis. "The Effects of Assimilation and Contrast in Judgments of Clinical Materials," *American Journal of Psychology*, 70 (September 1957), 347–60.
10. Cooper, Peter. "Subjective Economics: Factors in a Psychology of Spending," in Bernard Taylor and Gordon Wills, eds., *Pricing Strategy*, Princeton, NJ: Brandon/Systems Press, 1970, 112–21.
11. ———. "The Begrudging Index and the Subjective Value of Money," in Bernard Taylor and Gordon Wills, eds., *Pricing Strategy*, Princeton, NJ: Brandon/Systems Press, 1970, 122–31.
12. Corso, John. "A Theoretic-Historical Review of the Threshold Concept," *Psychological Bulletin*, 60 (July 1963), 356–70.
13. Della Bitta, Albert. "An Experimental Examination of Conditions Which May Foster the Use of Price as an Indicator of Relative Product Attractiveness," unpublished doctoral dissertation, University of Massachusetts, 1971.
14. Emery, Fred. "Some Psychological Aspects of Price," in Bernard Taylor and Gordon Wills, eds., *Pricing Strategy*, Princeton, NJ: Brandon/Systems Press, 1970, 98–111.
15. Engel, James, David Kollat, and Roger Blackwell. *Consumer Behavior*. New York: Holt, Rinehart and Winston, 1968
16. Enis, Ben and James Stafford. "Consumers' Perception of Product Quality as a Function of Various Information Inputs," *Proceedings*, Fall Conference, American Marketing Association, 1969, 340–4.
17. ———. "The Price-Quality Relationship: An Extension," *Journal of Marketing Research*, 6 (November 1969), 256–8.
18. Fouilhé, Pierre. "The Subjective Evaluation of Price: Methodological Aspects," in Bernard Taylor and Gordon Wills, eds., *Pricing Strategy*. Princeton, NJ: Brandon/Systems Press, 1970, 89–97.
19. Friedman, Lawrence. "Psychological Pricing in the Food Industry," in Almarin Phillips and Oliver Williamson, eds., *Prices: Issues in Theory, Practice, and Public Policy*. Philadelphia: University of Pennsylvania Press, 1967, 187–201.
20. Gabor, André and Clive Granger. "On the Price Consciousness of Consumers," *Applied Statistics*, 10 (November 1961), 170–88.
21. ———. "Price Sensitivity of the Consumer," *Journal of Advertising Research*, 4 (December 1964), 40–4.
22. ———. "The Pricing of New Products," *Scientific Business*, 3 (August 1965), 141–50.
23. ———. "Price as an Indicator of Quality, Report on an Enquiry," *Economica*, 46 (February 1966), 43–70.
24. ———. "The Attitude of the Consumer to Price," in Bernard Taylor and Gordon Wills, eds., *Pricing Strategy*. Princeton, NJ: Brandon/Systems Press, 1979, 132–51.
25. ———, and Anthony Sowter. "Comments on 'Psychophysics of Prices,'" *Journal of Marketing Research*, 8 (May 1971), 251–2.
26. Gardner, David. "An Experimental Investigation of the Price-Quality Relationship," *Journal of Retailing*, 46 (Fall 1970), 25–41.
27. ———. "Is There a Generalized Price-Quality Relationship?" *Journal of Marketing Research*, 8 (May 1971), 241–3.
28. Ginzberg, Eli. "Customary Prices," *American Economic Review*, 26 (June 1986), 296.
29. Helson, Harry. *Adaptation-Level Theory*. New York: Harper & Row, 1964.
30. "How Multiple-Unit Pricing Helps—and Hurts," *Progressive Grocer*, 50 (June 1971), 52–8.
31. "How Much Do Customers Know About Retail Prices?" *Progressive Grocer*, 43 (February 1964), C104–6.
32. Jacoby, Jacob, Jerry Olson, and Rafael Haddock. "Price, Brand Name, and Product Composition Characteristics as Determinants of Perceived Quality," *Journal of Applied Psychology*, 55 (December 1971), 470–9.
33. Kamen, Joseph and Robert Toman. "Psychophysics of Prices," *Journal of Marketing Research*, 7 (February 1970), 27–35.
34. ———. "'Psychophysics of Prices': A Reaffirmation," *Journal of Marketing Research*, 8 (May 1971), 252–7.
35. Lambert, Zarrel. "Price and Choice Behavior," *Journal of Marketing Research*, 9 (February 1972), 35–40.
36. ———. "Product Perception: An Important Variable in Price Strategy," *Journal of Marketing*, 34 (October 1970), 68–71.
37. Leavitt, Harold. "A Note on Some Experimental Findings About the Meaning of Price," *Journal of Business*, 27 (July 1954), 205–10.
38. McConnell, J. Douglas. "An Experimental Examination of the Price-Quality Relationship," *Journal of Business*, 41 (October 1968), 439–44.

39. ———. "The Development of Brand Loyalty: An Experimental Study," *Journal of Marketing Research*, 5 (February 1968), 13–9.
40. ———. "Effects of Pricing on Perception of Product Quality," *Journal of Applied Psychology*, 52 (August 1968), 313–4.
41. ———. "The Price-Quality Relationship in an Experimental Setting," *Journal of Marketing Research*, 5 (August 1968), 300–3.
42. McDougall, Gordon. "Credibility of Price-offs in Retail Advertising," unpublished doctoral dissertation proposal, University of Western Ontario, 1970.
43. Miller, Richard. "Dr. Weber and the Consumer," *Journal of Marketing*, 26 (January 1962), 57–61.
44. Monroe, Kent. "A Method for Determining Product Line Prices with End-Price Constraints," unpublished doctoral dissertation, University of Illinois, 1968.
45. ———. "The Information Content of Prices: A Preliminary Model for Estimating Buyer Response," *Management Science*, 17 (April 1971), B519–32.
46. ———. "Measuring Price Thresholds by Psychophysics and Latitudes of Acceptance," *Journal of Marketing Research*, 8 (November 1971), 460–4.
47. ———. "'Psychophysics of Prices': A Reappraisal," *Journal of Marketing Research*, 8 (May 1971), 248–50.
48. ———. "The Influence of Price and the Cognitive Dimension on Brand Attitudes and Brand Preferences," paper presented at Attitude Research and Consumer Behavior Workshop, 1970.
49. ———. "Some Findings on Estimating Buyers' Response Functions for Acceptable Price Thresholds," *Proceedings*. Northeast Conference, the American Institute for Decision Sciences, 1972, in press.
50. ——— and Peter LaPlaca. "What Are the Benefits of Unit Pricing?" *Journal of Marketing*, 36 (July 1972), 16–22.
51. Monroe, Kent and M. Venkatesan. "The Concept of Price Limits and Psychophysical Measurement: A Laboratory Experiment," *Proceedings*. Fall Conference, American Marketing Association, 1969, 345–51.
52. Newman, Diane and James Becknell. "The Price-Quality Relationship as a Tool in Consumer Research," *Proceedings*. 78th Annual Conference, American Psychological Association, 1970, 729–30.
53. Ölander, Folke. "The Influence of Price on the Consumer's Evaluation of Products and Purchases," in Bernard Taylor and Gordon Wills, eds., *Pricing Strategy*. Princeton, NJ: Brandon/Systems Press, 1970, 50–69.
54. Palda, Kristian. *Pricing Decisions and Marketing Policy*. Englewood Cliffs, NJ: Prentice-Hall, 1971.
55. Pessemier, Edgar. "An Experimental Method for Estimating Demand," *Journal of Business*, 33 (October 1960), 373–83.
56. ———. *Experimental Methods of Analyzing Demand for Branded Consumer Goods*. Economic and Business Study No. 39, Pullman, WA: Washington State University Press, 1963.
57. ——— and Richard Teach. "Pricing Experiments, Scaling Consumer Preferences, and Predicting Purchase Behavior," *Proceedings*. Fall Conference, American Marketing Association, 1966, 541–57.
58. Peterson, Robert. "The Price-Perceived Quality Relationship: Experimental Evidence," *Journal of Marketing Research*, 7 (November 1970), 525–8.
59. Rao, Vithala. "The Salience of Price in the Perception and Evaluation of Product Quality: A Multidimensional Measurement Model and Experimental Test," unpublished doctoral dissertation, University of Pennsylvania, 1970.
60. ———. "Salience of Price in the Perception of Product Quality: A Multidimensional Measurement Approach," *Proceedings*. Fall Conference, American Marketing Association, 1971, 571–7.
61. Roth, Elmer. "How to Increase Room Revenue," *Hotel Management*, 67 (March 1955), 52ff.
62. Scitovsky, Tibor. "Some Consequences of the Habit of Judging Quality by Price," *Review of Economic Studies*, 12 (1944–45), 100–5.
63. Shapiro, Benson. "The Psychology of Pricing," *Harvard Business Review*, 46 (July–August 1968), 14–8, 20, 22, 24–5, 160.
64. ———. "Price as a Communicator of Quality: An Experiment," unpublished doctoral dissertation, Harvard University, 1970.
65. Sherif, Carolyn. "Social Categorization as a Function of Latitude and Acceptance and Series Range," *Journal of Abnormal and Social Psychology*, 67 (August 1963), 148–56.
66. Sherif, Muzafer and Carl Hovland. "Judgmental Phenomena and Scales of Attitude Measurement: Placement of Items with Individual Choice of Number of Categories," *Journal of Abnormal and Social Psychology*, 48 (January 1953), 135–41.
67. Smith, Edward and Charles Broome. "A Laboratory Experiment for Establishing Indifference Prices Between Brands of Consumer Products," *Proceedings*. Fall Conference, American Marketing Association, 1966, 511–9.
68. ———. "Experimental Determination of the Effect of Price and Market-Standing Information on Consumers' Brand Preferences," *Proceedings*. Fall Conference, American Marketing Association, 1966, 520–31.
69. Stapel, Jan. "'Fair' or 'Psychological' Pricing?" *Journal of Marketing Research*, 9 (February 1972), 109–10.
70. Stoetzel, Jean. "Psychological/Sociological Aspects of Price," in Bernard Taylor and Gordon Wills, eds., *Pricing Strategy*. Princeton, NJ: Brandon/System Press, 1970, 70–4.
71. Tajfel, H. "Value and the Perceptual Judgment of Magnitude," *Psychological Review*, 64 (May 1957), 192–204.
72. ———. "Quantitative Judgment in Social Perception," *British Journal of Psychology*, 50 (February 1959), 16–29.
73. Tull, Donald, R. A. Boring, and M. H. Gonsior. "A Note on the Relationship of Price and Imputed Quality," *Journal of Business*, 37 (April 1964), 186–91.
74. Uhl, Joseph. "Consumer Perception of Retail Food Price Changes," paper presented at First Annual Meeting of the Association for Consumer Research, 1970.
75. Webb, Eugene. "Weber's Law and Consumer Prices," *American Psychologist*, 16 (July 1961), 450.
76. Wells, William and Leonard LoSciuto. "Direct Observation of Purchasing Behavior," *Journal of Marketing Research*, 3 (August 1966), 227–33.

The author gratefully acknowledges the assistance of Kathleen Shea in compiling and abstracting material from the research literature. Financial assistance was provided by the Research Council, University of Massachusetts.

24

Economic Foundations for Pricing

Thomas Nagle

Our goal in this paper will be to review those areas of economics that offer the most promise for practical application to pricing.

Understanding the economic environment in which pricing decisions are made is an important first step toward making them effectively. This paper reviews the theoretical literature in economics that is most helpful in furthering that understanding. It explains the implications for pricing of three general areas of research: the economics of information, the economics of spatial competition, and the economics of segmented pricing. It also reviews a number of papers that deal with specific pricing problems.

PRICING, LIKE MOST BUSINESS DECISIONS, is an art. This is not, however, a justification for basing pricing decisions purely on the "hunch" of a talented manager. Art is beyond neither critical judgment nor scientific analysis. And talent is rarely by itself sufficient for artistic success. An architect's exceptional creativity, for example, could hardly compensate for an ignorance of structural engineering. No less important are the principles of economics to the successful study and practice of the art of pricing.

Yet, if one approaches economics expecting too much, one may well come away with too little. Economic models are not designed to describe realistically the way firms make pricing decisions or the way consumers respond to those decisions.[1] Economic models are abstractions; they hold constant many real variables that are not germane to their theoretical objectives. Consequently, they rarely provide practical algorithms for implementing pricing strategies.[2]

Thomas Nagle is Managing Partner of The Strategic Pricing Group, Boston, Mass.

But marketing academicians and practitioners, whose goal is to help firms make better pricing decisions, can little afford to ignore the interrelationships between price and other marketing variables that economists hold constant. Consequently, they are soon disillusioned if they look to economics for practical solutions to pricing problems.

Still, it would be shortsighted to label the theoretical models of economics irrelevant to practical pricing problems. Economic models may be weak in specific prescriptions for individual action, but they are strong in useful heuristics for understanding the consequences of action. To draw on an earlier analogy, no one rejects structural engineering as irrelevant because it "fails" to show architects how to design buildings. Likewise, the role of economics is not to price products, but to explain the economic principles to which successful pricing strategies will conform. Pricing products—including the development and testing of practical pricing procedures—is appropriately the task of marketing. If, however, economists are doing their job well—that is, if the principles they identify in theory have actual counterparts in reality—the marketer's task should prove less strenuous when he stands on a sound foundation of economic theory.

Economics is not, of course, the only useful foundation for research in marketing. Psychology, sociology, and even biology may also serve the marketer's purpose. Our premise here is simply that research with a theoretical base is more likely to be productive than ad hoc research and that economic theory provides a particularly sound basis for pricing research. Our goal in this paper will be to review those areas of economics that offer the most promise for practical application to pricing. Before proceeding with that review, however, a brief example, illustrating how pricing research can benefit from a foundation in economic theory, seems in order.

Dealing—that is, temporary price cutting—is an important element of pricing strategy for many frequently purchased, packaged goods. Marketers have long wondered whether consumers who responded to such deals were simply a cross-section of regular buyers or were a clearly identifiable segment. If the latter, marketers wanted to know how to identify that segment so as to target dealing where it would be most effective. Numerous statistical studies (e.g., Webster 1965; Montgomery 1971) that approached the problem without a theoretical foundation found little or no correlation between deal proneness and the demographic, socioeconomic, and personality characteristics the authors considered (Frank, Massey, and Wind 1972, p. 124). It appeared that deal proneness was simply randomly distributed among consumers.

That conclusion proved too hasty, however, when Blattberg et al. (1978) took a new look at deal proneness from the perspective of a newly developed branch of economic theory: the economics of the family. Economists in this area (primarily Gary Becker and his students) had characterized the family as a production unit, optimally allocating its resources (money, time, and talents) by making economic trade-offs.[3] Blattberg et al. hypothesized that deal proneness might be explicable as the result of such an optimal allocation. The advantage of this theoretical starting point was that it allowed the authors to select variables that should influence deal proneness and to hypothesize about their expected effect.

If the economics of the family characterized some aspect of purchase decisions among the families in the authors' sample, then families with a lower opportunity cost of buying on deal should have been more deal prone. Consequently, the authors hypothesized that

1. families that own homes and cars should be more deal prone because they generally have more storage space (i.e., lower inventory holding costs) and lower costs of transporting extra purchases of products on deal; and
2. families that have preschool children at home, a working wife, or high incomes should be less deal prone because of the high value of alternative demands on their time.

Without a theoretical foundation, one would not intuitively have suspected (and earlier authors apparently did not suspect) that variables such as auto ownership, home ownership, or preschool children might influence a family's propensity to buy aluminum foil on deal. Yet the authors found that those variables did influence deal proneness for aluminum foil, as well as for waxed paper, headache remedies, liquid detergent, and facial tissue. With economic theory as a guide, they were able to identify a market segment that could not be identified by earlier empirical studies lacking an underlying theoretical structure.

A complete review of all economic theory with potential application to pricing is impossible within the confines of one paper. We will instead review topics in economic theory that (1) offer particularly fertile ground for the future growth of pricing theory and practice, and (2) have not yet been integrated into marketing.[4] Three general areas of economic theory that meet these criteria are the economics of information, the economics of spatial competition, and the economics of segmented pricing. Our discussions of them will necessarily be selective, since entire volumes could be written on each of these subjects. In addition, we will review individual papers that are not part of developing paradigms in economics but that are by themselves noteworthy in pricing research. In all cases, we will focus on the current and potential usefulness of the theories as a foundation for practical application rather than on their technical details.

The Economics of Information

George Stigler's seminal article (1961) precipitated an explosion of theoretical research on the economics of information. In that article, Stigler noted that economists traditionally ignored problems of information and, in doing so, failed to appreciate much that falls within the purview of marketing. Yet, in the years following, the economics profession has more than made up for lost time. Two subsets of that literature are of particular importance to pricing: one dealing with asymmetric information, the other with consumer information acquisition.

Pricing and Asymmetric Information

An exchange involves asymmetric information when one party to the exchange has more information than does the other. For example, a seller may know the quality of the goods he sells, but buyers do not know the quality until after they have purchased the product. If buyers cannot identify a seller's product quality, they must rely on some average quality as a guide to purchase. That leads to a clear problem for products above the average quality, which may be most products in the market. Uninformed buyers will be unwilling to pay an above-average price, forcing sellers of superior quality either to depreciate it, to withdraw from the market, or to accept a price that does not accurately reflect their products' value.

The study of this problem began with a paper by George Akerlof (1970), who cited the used car market as an example. The price that a seller can get for a used car, even one of the current model year, is usually substantially below the new car price adjusted for depreciation. A commonly heard rule of thumb is that a new car loses 10% of its value the moment it leaves the showroom and becomes "used." Akerlof rejected the contention that the price difference reflected simply the pure joy of owning a "new" car. Instead he explained it as a symptom of asymmetric information.

Among new cars, he argued, there are always some "lemons" that prove less reliable than the average car of its brand. For a new car purchase, there is some probability of getting a lemon, but neither the dealer nor the buyer knows whether or not the particular new car being sold will be one. For new cars, therefore, there is no problem of asymmetric information. For used cars, however, the problem is different. The previous owner, who is the seller of the used car, has learned from experience whether or not his car is atypically unreliable.

Those first owners who have lemons—and large repair bills—have an incentive to sell their cars sooner than those who are lucky enough to get more reliable cars. They do not, however, have the incentive to share that information honestly with buyers. Consequently, the used car market has proportionately more lemons than the new car market, though buyers still cannot distinguish them from more reliable cars. Recognizing this asymmetry of information between sellers and themselves, buyers demand a substantial discount on a used car before they are willing to risk getting a lemon. The pricing problem is that sellers who know that their cars are not lemons, and so worth more, are unable to price them accordingly.

Were this just a problem with automobiles, it would be of little interest to marketers. In fact, it is a general marketing problem occurring any time that sellers know more about their products' quality than do buyers, who then use average quality in determining the price they will pay. The problem has never been completely solved by restaurants in locations where there is little repeat business; consequently they rarely offer exceptional quality. The problem is also a common one for innovative manufactured products because, if an early entrant's product is a lemon, it can sour the market for later entrants whom buyers will view more skeptically. But, as Akerlof suggests, branding is a common solution to this problem, since brand names with which buyers have had past experience can signal quality above the average in a product class, enabling a firm to charge an above-average price.[5]

But how much more can a firm charge because its product is branded? Can it get just enough to cover the cost of its higher quality, or can it get a premium? Klein and Leffler (1981) attempt to answer these questions in a way that provides much insight into the relationship between branding and pricing. They show that in product classes characterized by asymmetric information about product quality a seller whose product quality is above average would not have the incentive to maintain it unless his price more than reflected his extra costs. A seller whose price just reflected the extra cost of high quality would have an incentive to reduce his quality (and production costs), thus earning extra profits until buyers learned about the reduction through disappointing purchases. Consequently, the price of a high-quality product "must not only compensate the firm for the increased average production costs incurred when [high quality] is produced, but must also yield a normal rate of return on the forgone gains from exploiting consumers' ignorance" (Klein and Leffler 1981, p. 624).

This analysis has important implications for pricing strategy. It implies that buyers who desire high quality in a market with asymmetric information will be influenced by the familiar "price-quality effect" even for repeat purchases.[6] The reason is that the higher the price, the greater the seller's incentive to establish and maintain high quality. If buyers recognize this effect, price competition should be less effective in markets with asymmetric information. Competitors who claim to offer high quality at lower prices should simply be less credible than those who claim to offer the same quality for a higher price.

Moreover, the Klein-Leffler paper implies that branding will be more valuable, that is, yield a higher price premium, for some products than for others, an important implication for a firm seeking to diversify. According to this theory, consumers should pay more of a premium for a high-quality brand (1) the more they think an opportunistic seller could depreciate quality without prepurchase detection and (2) the fewer the expected number of repeat purchases. Either of these effects raises the gains from cheating relative to those from repeat sales, requiring a high-price premium for quality maintenance.

Finally, the theory's most interesting implication is that, other things such as market size held equal, producing quality is particularly profitable. Marketers have often maintained this proposition on empirical grounds (e.g., Schoeffler, Buzzell, and Heany 1974), but heretofore without a theoretical explanation. The relative profitability of producing high quality may, under certain circumstances, be maintained even after competition has driven profits to their long-run equilibrium level. The reason is that because price cutting is an ineffective way to attract customers, competition necessarily takes the form of investments in "nonsalvageable capital" such as advertising or attractive places of business. If some firms have a cost advantage in making such investments (perhaps because of scale or experience economies), then they can earn profits (or more correctly "rents") that cannot be competed away by the entry of higher cost firms.

The Klein-Leffler paper is just one example of an idea in information theory that Telser (1980) formalized and titled "self-enforcing agreements." No one in the Klein-Leffler model must force the seller to supply the product quality he promises; he does so because, at the price he sets for that quality, it is in his interest to do so. There are numerous other applications of the theory of self-enforcing contracts that either have been, or could be, used to explain and prescribe pricing strategies. In one of the most interesting, Klein, Crawford, and Alchian (1978) use the idea to explain, among other things, why a successful pricing strategy for some products will involve primarily outright sales, while for others it will involve primarily leasing.

In the analysis of oligopolistic price competition, the self-enforcing agreement becomes a self-enforcing threat. Each firm attempts to deter its current or potential competitors from encroaching on its market share by threatening to cut price as low as necessary to maintain its intended sales level.[7] But how can it make such a threat credible? Spence (1977), Salop (1979), and Dixit (1980) argue that irrevocable investment in fixed assets, often at a rate faster than market growth would otherwise justify, can make the threat credible. By creating a cost structure with high sunk costs, the firm increases the losses it would suffer if it failed to attain its expected sales level because of new competition.[8] By boxing itself into one strategic option—to fulfill its threat to defend its market—the firm discourages competitive challenges and precludes the need to make good on the threat.

Pricing and Consumer Information Acquisition

The most fundamental concept in pricing is that of price elasticity, which measures the percentage sales loss (gain) from a certain percentage price increase (decrease). A firm may lose sales because buyers are willing to do without the product at a higher price or because they change suppliers. Since changing suppliers is generally less painful than doing without, buyers' willingness and ability to substitute one brand for another is, for most products, the dominant factor determining a brand's price elasticity.

Prior to their study of information, economists assumed that the importance of interbrand price competition, inducing consumers to substitute one brand for another, depended on the number of brands available and on their similarity. But Philip Nelson (1970) pointed out the error in that reasoning. In a world of imperfect information, what really determines price sensitivity is not the number and similarity of substitutes in the marketplace, but the number and similarity about which a typical consumer is aware.[9] That distinction is important, Nelson argued, because the cost of such information differs predictably depending upon the nature of a product's characteristics. Consequently, one can make a priori predictions, based on an analysis of product attributes, about the importance of price in interbrand competition.

Nelson classified product attributes into two types depending on how buyers learn about them.[10]

Search attributes are those that a buyer can readily evaluate prior to purchase. He may judge them from observation —as he would the style of a dress or the scheduled departure time of an airline—or with the aid of a simple test—as he would the purity of an industrial chemical. He therefore knows what he is buying before he makes a purchase decision.

Experience attributes are those that a buyer can evaluate only after consuming the product. He therefore does not know exactly what he is getting the first time he buys it. After having purchased once, however, he can repeat purchase the product in the future, having a good estimate of its attributes based on knowledge from past experience. The taste of a packaged food, the effectiveness of a dishwashing detergent, or the durability of a paint are examples of experience attributes.

Darby and Karni (1973) quickly followed Nelson's article with one of their own noting a third category:

Credence attributes are those that a buyer cannot confidently evaluate even after one purchase. He therefore must rely heavily on the product's reputation with respect to those attributes, even for repeat purchases. A buyer normally cannot, for example, evaluate a doctor's competence after one visit for the treatment of one complaint. In fact, such an evaluation may require a more controlled experiment and a larger sample than is achievable even over a single patient's lifetime.

The importance of these classifications lies in their relationship to the cost of consumer information acquisition. Information about price itself can be obtained directly for all types of products. But as one moves from the search to the experience and on to the credence category, information about brands' differentiating attributes becomes more costly. The greater the cost of information, the less of it people try to obtain. Consequently, other things equal, consumers should choose to inform themselves about the differentiating characteristics of fewer brands, and inform themselves less completely, in categories with high costs of collecting such information.[11]

The fewer brands about which buyers are informed, according to Nelson, the less price sensitive they will be to the price of any one brand. As a result, the effectiveness of price competition is reduced as is the ability of new competitors to enter the market with a strategy of low, penetration pricing. Nelson formally tested this proposition by classifying goods into search and experience categories and comparing the degree to which output is concentrated in a few competitors. He found markets for experience goods significantly more concentrated than those for search goods. Moreover, casual observation seems to confirm the value of this distinction as an analytical marketing tool. For example, the attributes differentiating brands of airline travel—time of departure, type of planes, airports used—are primarily search attributes and price competition for air travel is intense. Those differentiating brands of dishwashing liquids are primarily experience attributes and price competition is less intense. Those differentiating brands of photographic film are primarily credence attributes (at least for the casual photographer) and price competition in that market is notably ineffective.[12]

The literature on the economics of information is rich in its implications for pricing.[13] Moreover, it complements the work being done by marketers specializing in consumer behavior (e.g., Bettman 1979). In the hands of marketing researchers, the economics of information could aid in explaining even more marketing phenomena.

The Economics of Spatial Competition

In the analysis of product positioning, current research in economics has a structure very similar to that in marketing. Known as the economics of spatial competition, this work analyzes the effect on price competition of a brand's location in physical space. The spatial location of brands serves in economics, as it does in marketing, as a metaphorical representation of product variety in any product attribute that is measurable and, therefore, spatially representable.[14] Models of spatial competition have a long history in economics beginning with Hotelling (1929) and Smithies (1941). Recently, however, the models have developed to a point that they have become useful tools for analyzing realistic positioning strategies and their effect on pricing. They now offer the potential to advance substantially our understanding of the relationship between product variety and interbrand price competition.

Though each author structures his model differently, I will attempt to illustrate the basic principles of spatial competition using one simple model adapted from Hay (1976). Assume that consumer preferences—what marketers call "ideal points"—are uniformly located along a straight line

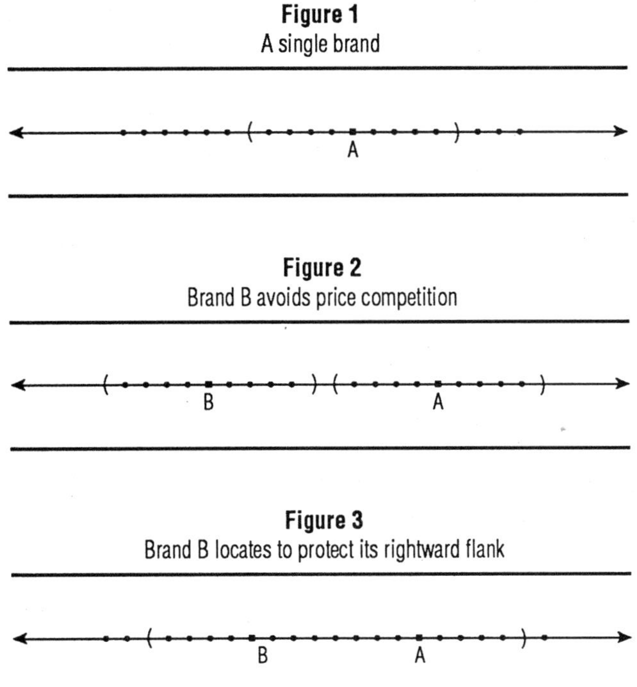

Figure 1
A single brand

Figure 2
Brand B avoids price competition

Figure 3
Brand B locates to protect its rightward flank

measuring some dimension of product variety. An individual consumer's demand depends both on the brand's price and on its closeness to his ideal point. All consumers have the same demand function; they differ only in the location of their ideal points.[15] Figure 1 illustrates the position of the first brand, A, in the market. Brand A's market area, the range of ideal points for which it is close enough to attract some sales, extends five units in each direction. Now, how should firms locate additional brands along this line in order to minimize price competition and, thus, maximize their long-run profitability?[16]

Hay (1976) shows that a new entrant can maximize his prices and profits in the short run by locating so as to avoid any overlaps (and thus any price competition) between his market area and the market area of A (Figure 2).[17] But that is not a good long-run strategy. To maximize long-run profits, B need consider not only potential price competition with A, but also with potential entrants. To maximize long-run profitability, B must locate closer to A, suffering some price competition in the short run but precluding even more intense competition in the long run.

For example, if at current prices a later entrant would need to serve a market area of at least four units (two in each direction), then B could preclude new entry on its right flank by locating less than eight units from A (Figure 3). No entrant would try to squeeze between A and B, because it would achieve only slightly less than its minimum market share (four units) after sharing the market with B on its left flank and A on its right (Figure 3).[18] Both B and A pay a cost for this preemption, a bit more than one unit each on their shared flank, but they insure no further erosion of profitability in the long run. Moreover, if the new entrant anticipated that A and B would cut prices in response to its entry between them, it would anticipate the need to have a market area even longer than four units to survive. In that case, B could leave even more than eight units between itself and A while still precluding new entry between them.

There are also options that A could use to protect itself from B's encroachment. Richard Schmalensee (1978), in an analysis of the breakfast cereal market, showed how brand proliferation could be a profitable entry-deterring strategy when there are shared costs among brands of the same firm. For example, if the producer of A could produce other brands that could be profitable with market areas of only three units (as opposed to four for a new entrant with one brand), he might profitably preempt emerging market opportunities. His lower costs would enable each brand to be profitable while keeping a potential new entrant from finding a viable market for its first brand.[19] Eaton and Lipsey (1979) show that such a preemptive proliferation strategy is profitable even if established firms have no cost advantages when introducing new brands. The reason is that an established firm can reduce the negative effect of its new brands on the sales of its already established brands when selecting prices and locations. Rao and Rutenberg (1980) develop dynamic decision rules for the optimal timing of preemption, given expectations about rivals' actions based on past experiences.

Marketers are already using spatial representations of product positions and have techniques (called multidimensional scaling) for spatially representing actual markets. They use them to find "holes" for new product entries and to evaluate competitive interactions. A useful next step would be to incorporate the strategic principles from the economics of spatial competition into the analysis of product positioning, identifying not only where a firm might introduce a brand to maximize market potential, but also where it might introduce one to minimize potential competition from later entrants.[20]

The Economics of Segmented Pricing

Though the "marketing concept" may be the essence of marketing theory, the guiding principle of marketing practice is "market segmentation." In fact, the process of segmenting buyers by designing marketing strategies more consistent with their diverse preferences is arguably the marketing concept's operational counterpart. In the last decade, marketing academicians have produced an abundance of research on segmenting markets for product and promotional targeting (see Frank et al. 1972; Blattenberg and Sen 1974; Mahajan and Jain 1978) but research on segmenting for pricing has been notably small.[21] Fortunately, market segmentation for pricing has a long history in economic research. Since the economics literature on segmented pricing arose from attempts to explain specific pricing strategies, often to lawyers rather than to other economists, it is also usually accessible and directly applicable.

Segmented pricing is the policy of pricing differently to different groups of buyers. It may involve "price discrimination": the offering of different prices for the same product, usually in the form of discounts to more price-sensitive buyers. More often it involves offering the same prices to all buyers, but with a structure of prices for different points in time, places of purchase, or product types[22] that results in some buyers' paying more relative to marginal cost than do other buyers who are more price sensitive. Airlines, for example, segment buyers by time of flight (weekend and evening versus weekday flights) and by product type (regular tickets allowing flexible scheduling versus discount tickets with scheduling restrictions; first class versus coach seating).

Ralph Cassady (1946*a*, 1964*b*) reviewed and illustrated the basic techniques of segmented pricing in two classic (though much neglected) articles that are as valid today as they were when written.[23] I will not repeat what is said there. Instead, I will review those advances in our understanding of segmented pricing that have occurred since then.

Segmenting by Tie-Ins and Metering

Segmentation by metering or tie-ins is often extremely important for the pricing of assets. The reason is that buyers generally value an asset more the more intensely they use it. The buyer of a photocopying machine who makes 20,000 copies a month will value it more than the buyer who makes just 5,000 copies. And food processors canning fruit year round in California will value canning machines more than will fish packers in Alaska who can salmon only a few months each year. In such cases, tactics that segment buyers by use intensity can substantially improve the effectiveness of a pricing strategy.

Before the Clayton Antitrust Act of 1914, a common method of monitoring use was the tie-in sale. Along with the purchase or lease of a machine, a buyer contractually agreed to purchase a commodity used with the machine exclusively from the seller. Thus, the Heaton Peninsular Company sold its shoemaking machines with the provision that buyers buy only Heaton Peninsular buttons. The A. B. Dick Company sold its mimeograph equipment with the provision the buyers buy paper, stencils, and ink only from the A. B. Dick Company. The Morgan Envelope Company sold its bathroom tissue dispensers with the provision that they forever dispense only Morgan's own brand (see *Morgan Envelope Co. v. Albany Perforated Paper Co.* [1893]; *Heaton Peninsular v. Eureka Specialty Co.* [1896]; *Henry v. A. B. Dick* [1912]). While the courts actually supported tying arrangements in these cases, they completely reversed themselves after 1914, claiming that tying arrangements were an illegal attempt to extend monopoly power from one product to the next. In the words of the Supreme Court "the illegality in tying arrangements is the wielding of monopolistic leverage; a seller exploits his dominant position in one market to expand his empire into the next" (*Times-Picayune Publishing v. United States* [1953]).

Economists were naturally skeptical of this argument because if an individual buyer must pay more for the tied good than he would have to pay elsewhere, that simply reduces the amount that he is willing to pay for the tying asset. Consequently, "extension of monopoly" would make sense only if it enabled the firm actually to increase the monopoly restriction—and thus the equilibrium market price—for the tied good. But, in almost all cases, the tying arrangements give the seller an insignificant amount of the market for the tied good. Consequently, the extension of monopoly argument seems highly implausible.

Economists instead explained tying as an effective device for price discrimination. Bowman (1957) and Burstein (1960*a*, 1960*b*) studied numerous tying cases in detail and found that, in each case, the asset itself was sold for a very low explicit price, close to the incremental cost of production. The tied commodity, however, was sold for a premium price. Thus, the true cost of the asset was its low explicit price plus the sum of the price premiums paid for the tied commodity. Since buyers who used the asset more intensely bought more of the tied commodity, they effectively paid more for the asset. The tied commodity was effectively a device for measuring a buyer's value of the asset and automatically charging for each incremental unit of value received.

Since the passage of the Clayton Act, the courts have refused to allow tying contracts in most cases.[24] In 1917, the Supreme Court refused to enforce a sales contract for a motion picture projector requiring that it be used to show only films produced by or under license from the seller. In 1922, United Shoe Machinery Corporation was ordered to cease the same tying policy that had been approved earlier for Heaton Peninsular. Later, IBM was ordered to stop tying computer punch cards in the leases for its machines (*Motion Picture Patents Co. v. Universal Film Manufacturing Co.* [1917]; *United Shoe Machinery Corp. v. United States* [1922]; *International Business Machines v. United States* [1936]).

Nevertheless, many tying opportunities without contracts still exist. Replacement parts and maintenance service are natural devices for measuring use intensity and for pricing accordingly. So also is food consumed in a theater or amusement park. Razor manufacturers design unique shaving technologies that naturally tie blades to razors. In the 1970s, a lower court did order Kodak to introduce no unique camera designs without first revealing the film's technology to its competitors, but that ruling was overturned on appeal (see *Berky Photo v. Eastman Kodak Co.* [1979]). It seems clear that, even without explicit contracts, the tie-in sale is still an important pricing tactic, and the literature in economics provides unusually explicit direction for its use.

The courts have nevertheless severely limited tying arrangements in precisely the cases where it is most dramatically effective. Their rulings challenge sellers to monitor use without restricting competition. In modern times, that challenge has frequently been met by renting assets rather than selling them outright, with the rental fee determined by a simple metering device. Xerox, for example, traditionally rented its copiers for a fixed fee plus so much per copy made.

As a final note, the tactic of monitoring use intensity is not limited to machines and may not involve an actual physical counting device. Nationally syndicated newspaper columns are sold to local papers at prices based on use intensity. The monitoring device is simply the paper's circulation figures. Film distributors rent movies at prices based on the number of seats in the theater. And franchisors lease their brand names and reputations to franchisees not for a fixed fee but for a percentage of sales. No matter how intangible the asset, monitoring use can be an important part of its pricing.

Segmenting by Product Bundling

Product bundling is perhaps the most widely used tactic to achieve segmented pricing, though its rationale often goes unnoticed. Retailers bundle "free" parking with a purchase in their stores. Grocery stores bundle trading stamps or chances in games with purchase of their groceries. Newspapers with morning and evening editions bundle advertising space in both of them. Restaurants bundle foods into fixed price dinners, generally a cheaper alternative to ordering the same items à la carte. And symphony orchestras bundle diverse concerts into season subscription tickets. These are but a small fraction of the goods sold in bundles, but they illustrate the breadth of the practice, from commodities to services and from necessities to entertainment. The question all these examples raise is "under what conditions does it pay to bundle goods for pricing?"

George Stigler (1963) answered that question in an article explaining the bundling of first-run movies, a practice known as block booking. The movie industry at the time would not rent individual films to theaters, but required they rent a block of films. As an example, Stigler cited the blocking together of *Gone with the Wind* and *Getting Gertie's Garter*. Why, he asked, would it make sense to require a theater to buy both films together? It cannot be that the distributors simply used their good films to force junk films on theaters, since a theater would not pay more for the two films together than the sum of what it would pay for the two separately.

Stigler explained this pricing strategy with the aid of the following illustration. Suppose that the dollar amounts that two theaters A and B would pay for the films is given by the following table:

	Gone with the Wind	*Getting Gertie's Garter*
Theater A	8,000	2,500
Theater B	7,000	3,000

The owners of both theaters would pay substantially more to show *Gone with the Wind* than *Getting Gertie's Garter*. The key to an effective bundling strategy, however, is the reversal in the relative valuations of the two films. *Gone with the Wind* is more valuable to theater A than to theater B, while the reverse is true for *Getting Gertie's Garter*.

To rent the films separately to both theater A and theater B at fixed prices, the movie distributor could have charged no more than $7,000 for *Gone with the Wind* and $2,500 for *Getting Gertie's Garter*, for a total of $9,500 for the pair. But theater A values the pair at $10,500 and theater B at $10,000. Thus by selling the films as a block for $10,000, the distributor can charge $500 more for the pair than if he sold them separately. Why is this segmented pricing? Because each theater pays the difference between the price of the films when sold separately ($9,500) and the price when sold together ($10,000) for different products. Theater A pays the extra $500 for *Gone with the Wind* while theater B pays it for *Getting Gertie's Garter*. Consequently, by charging a single price for an indivisible bundle, the distributor can effectively charge different prices for the components.

Adams and Yellen (1976) explain the conditions for bundling more formally and explicitly. In doing so, they show why products are not generally sold in indivisible bundles only. Most firms follow the tactic of "mixed bundling," whereby the individual products can be bought separately, but at prices exceeding their cost if bought together in the bundle. Mixed bundling is more profitable than indivisible bundling whenever some buyers value one of the items in the bundle very highly but value the other less than it costs to produce. Schmalensee (1982) shows that mixed bundling can be profitable even for a single-product monopolist who buys a competitively produced product from other firms to bundle with his own. Schmalensee (1984) formally derives the explicit conditions that make a bundling strategy profitable.[25]

Focusing on the pure theory and the obvious examples, one could easily underestimate the importance of bundling to pricing strategy. Most bundling opportunities are in fact quite subtle, but the principle of bundling is ubiquitously applied in both consumer and industrial markets. The marketing researcher who understood the principle could no doubt use it to explain many more applications; the marketing practitioner could no doubt find new applications not thought of heretofore.

Economic Analyses of Specific Pricing Problems

In addition to the general areas of economic theory just reviewed, the economics literature of recent years contains a number of more narrowly focused papers analyzing specific pricing problems. These papers offer perspectives that could be immediately applied in marketing theory and practice.

Pricing Through a Distribution Channel

Managing a product through channels of distribution is a problem of growing interest to marketers (Stern and El-Ansary 1977). Part of that problem involves pricing to the channel, a topic that economic theorists have studied with some success.

Machlup and Taber (1960) have shown that when the uniqueness of a manufacturer's product gives a retailer some "monopoly power" over price, the retailer will set his resale price too high and sell too little to maximize the total channel (manufacturer plus retailer) profits. To avoid this problem, they show how the manufacturer can couple his wholesale pricing with maximum resale prices (which may be enforced merely by advertising a suggested retail price), minimum retail sales requirements, or a more complicated two-part pricing strategy.

Telser (1960) explains the conditions that make it profitable for a manufacturer to impose minimum resale prices. Essentially, his argument rests on the need to reward retailers for offering promotional and maintenance services that positively influence a product's demand. Officials in the current Justice Department have recently recognized this argument and are now committed to changing the courts' negative view of resale price maintenance ("Big Shift in Antitrust Policy" 1981).

The most ambitious study of the relationship between pricing and distribution channels is Porter's (1976) *Interbrand Choice, Strategy, and Bilateral Market Power.* Marketers often write about the "bargaining power" of various channel members. Porter seeks to identify the causes and effects of such power, relying not just on traditional economic concepts such as concentration, but also upon applications of the economics or information. In particular, he argues that bargaining power over margins shifts for manufacturers toward retailers the more buyers rely on retailers for the information they need to make interbrand choices. Adopting this same approach, a number of marketing researchers have recently begun to analyze the effect of channel relationships on pricing and have developed suggestions for favorably controlling those relationships (Farris and Albion 1980; McGuire and Staelin 1981; Zusman and Etgar 1981; Jeuland and Shugan 1982). This work is reviewed in part by Rao (1984).

Pricing Unique Durable Goods

Coase (1972) raised the problem of pricing a unique durable good. He noted that a rational buyer would not pay a monopoly price for a good, even though he valued it by more than the price, if he expected the price to come down. Consequently, a "skimming strategy" of progressively lower prices should fail to the extent that buyers recognize the seller's incentive to cut price and expand his market. Stokey (1981) shows, however, that a skimming strategy is theoretically viable, even if buyers have perfectly accurate expectations, to the extent that the adjustment to a new price level takes time. The reason is that the more highly a buyer values the services of the durable good, the higher is his cost of waiting. Thus, the longer the adjustment period that buyers anticipate, the less problematic are their anticipations of future price reductions.[26] Stokey's work also complements the theoretical research on price declines due to the "experience effect" (Robinson and Lakhani 1975; Dolan and Jeuland 1981; Kalish, in press), which is reviewed in Rao (1984).

Pricing for Peak Loads

Pricing strategy frequently must accommodate predictable variations in demand without the luxury of a storable product. In order to accommodate temporary peaks in demand, the firm must build production capacity that is excessive at other times. Economists have analyzed this problem of peak-load pricing in great detail (Houthakker 1951; Steiner 1957; Hirshleifer 1958; Williamson 1966; Symposium on Peak-Load Pricing 1976) and have shown how to allocate capacity costs in order to select profit maximizing prices and sales levels.[27] Unfortunately, because these analyses are almost always in the context of large public enterprises, their broad applicability is generally unappreciated. The principles of peak-load pricing are in fact equally applicable to such private enterprises as hotels, restaurants, health clubs, airlines, theaters, and to some degree most retail establishments. The economic literature in this area is ripe for profitable application.

Pricing by Priority

Harris and Raviv (1981) show that whenever a product is fixed in supply and has demand that potentially exceeds supply, a (monopolistic) seller can increase his profits by "priority pricing." The seller sets a schedule of prices for the product and then serves first those buyers who elect to pay the highest price, second those buyers who elect to pay the next highest price, and so forth until the supply is exhausted. Buyers who elect to pay higher prices increase the probability that they will be able to buy before the product is sold out. The authors' conclusion that this is a superior pricing scheme for products in fixed supply seems consistent with standard practice. They note that priority pricing is used for such obvious cases as antiques and oil leases, as well as for discontinued styles of consumer products that are sold at progressively increasing discounts.

Pricing in Two Parts

Two-part pricing is an important strategy in a large number of industries. Health clubs, amusement parks, auto rental agencies, and the telephone company all charge fixed fees plus variable usage charges for their products.[28] The seller's motivation for two-part pricing is to capture some of the consumer's surplus (excess of value over price for all but the last unit purchased). A number of authors (Hotelling 1938; Gabor 1955; Burstein 1960) analyzed two-part pricing for the case where buyers are homogeneous or where a unique two-part pricing schedule can be implemented for each buyer. They showed that two-part pricing in these cases could capture all consumer surplus for the seller. It was not, however, until Oi (1971) that anyone dealt with the more realistic, and complicated, case of calculating a single two-part schedule for a population with demands of more than one type. Oi showed that with two types of buyers, the optimal variable fee must be higher and the fixed fee lower relative to the case of homogeneous buyers.[29] This substantially reduces the efficiency of two-part pricing, leaving some buyers with much of their surplus. Schmalensee (1982) provides the first completely general analysis of two-part pricing schedules, allowing for buyers with completely heterogeneous demand curves, for income effects (from which previous authors abstracted), and for sales to competitive firms whose derived demands depend on the selling prices of their own goods.

Pricing When Facing a Used Product Market

The effect of a resale market on the prices of new durable goods poses a problem that many durable good manufacturers face. Each unit a manufacturer sells today will add to the used market tomorrow, increasing competition with new units. The manufacturer must decide whether to encourage the used market, as do the automobile companies and some office equipment manufacturers, or to discourage it, as do textbook publishers. The rationale for encouraging the used market is that a high resale value will raise the prices buyers will pay for new goods. The rationale for discouraging the used market is that a smaller used market reduces competition with new product sales. Benjamin and Kormendi (1974) show that either strategy may be profit maximizing depending upon the substitutability of used for new products, the marginal cost of production, and the degree of competition in the industry.

Pricing Superstars

One recent and unique article in the literature of economics is "The Economics of Superstars" by Sherwin Rosen (1981). It has important, intuitively appealing implications for product pricing. The phenomenon that Rosen attempts to explain is the disproportionately high profits that the highest quality products—superstars—can earn in some markets. He cites, for example, the services of outstanding lawyers and physicians, performances by outstanding musicians, and copies of textbooks that are outstanding in their fields as examples of the superstar phenomenon. His explanation rests on the simple observation that, for some products, "quality" is not perfectly additive. No number of concerts by mediocre pianists can effectively substitute for an evening with Horowitz; no number of obtusely written textbooks can effectively substitute for one that makes the subject perfectly clear. This is not true for all products. Larger quantities of a mediocre detergent, for example, can give the same cleaning power as the highest quality brand. Thus, when pricing a high-quality product (or when deciding whether to produce one), an important factor to consider is the ability of more mediocre alternatives to compete with it by substituting quantity for quality.

Conclusion

Understanding the economic environment in which pricing decisions are made is a first step toward making them effectively. While economics traditionally offered a basic understanding of that environment, advances in the last two decades have significantly refined it. Economic theory now has much more to say about the roles of information, competition, and market segmentation in pricing strategy. Economic theorists have also analyzed specific pricing problems and opportunities in ways that shed much light on pricing practice.

Still, economic theory is just that—theory. No economic model captures the full richness of a practical pricing problem or sets out a complete prescription for solving it. Even with an understanding of economic theory, marketers are still left with the problem of how to price products. But they are left also with insights and perspectives that should make solutions more attainable and effective.

References

1. Because of this lack of realism, some marketers approach economics with hostility. They, in effect, judge economics by the standards of good psychology, which it is not. Economic theorists do not claim to describe the processes by which people actually make decisions; they claim rather to explain why certain decisions persist. Economic theory assumes that persistent and widespread behavior, whatever the underlying psychological process leading to it, must somehow be reinforced by success at furthering economic well-being. Such reinforcement encourages people, on average, to act "as if" they understood and responded "rationally" to the economic process that rewards their behavior (Alchian 1950; Friedman 1953).
2. For example, the fundamental economic principle, that current profit is maximized when marginal revenue equals marginal cost is neither a practical nor "optimal" prescription for action when demand is uncertain and when tomorrow's demand, cost, and competition are affected by today's pricing decision (see Alchian 1950; Dean 1951; Robinson and Lakhani 1975; Dolan and Jeuland 1981).
3. See Becker (1981) for a comprehensive statement of this work and for references to earlier contributions. For a critique of this literature that would be of particular interest to marketers applying it to practical problems, see Mack and Leighland (1982).
4. One important topic in economic theory that has been partially integrated into marketing is the hedonic theory (sometimes called the "New Theory") of consumer choice. According to this theory, consumers do not value a good holistically. Instead, they value it as the sum of the values of its individual characteristics. For a review of this literature that emphasizes marketing application, see Ratchford (1975).
5. For an interesting study of the "lemons" problem in the Soviet Union where branding is restricted, see Goldman (1960).
6. Charles Wilson (1980) offers another rationale for a price-quality effect with asymmetric information: that a higher price enables the buyer to draw from a distribution of products with a higher mean quality.
7. Threats are only one way to deter entry. In the section below on spatial competition, we will examine others.
8. See Porter (1980, pp. 335–40) for factors to consider before making such investments in a growing market.
9. Tibor Scitovsky (1950) actually pointed out this effect long before there was "economics of information," but with little effect on economists' thinking about these problems.
10. Actually, Nelson did his early analysis based on search and experience goods rather than attributes. See Nelson (1978, 1980) and Wilde (1980) for reformulations based directly on attributes.
11. The cost of collecting information may, of course, differ across buyers. Assuming such a difference, Salop and Stiglitz (1977) explain the persistence of high- and low-priced stores for the same products. In their model, high-priced stores cater to buyers with a high cost of information collection.

12. One might object that the lack of price competition for photographic film is due to a lack of competitors. But the lack of competitors is a symptom of the information problem, because when new firms have tried to enter by undercutting Kodak's prices, they have failed to attract buyers (see "Kodak Fights Back" 1982).
13. See Wilde (1980) for a review of the development of this literature.
14. In contrast, however, to the multidimensional product maps generated by marketers, economic theorists usually assume that brands vary along a single product dimension (Eaton and Lipsey [1976] is an exception), which they represent spatially as distance along a line (with or without finite length) or around the perimeter of a circle. This simply reflects economists' predilection for tractable models at the expense of descriptive realism. The principles of spatial competition they derive are nonetheless conceptually applicable to the multidimensional case (Baumol 1967; Lancaster 1975). These models have also been used to analyze the positioning of political candidates (see, e.g., Riker and Ordeshook 1973).
15. See Hay (1976) for a more specific and complete listing of assumptions. Eaton and Lipsey (1978) show the implications of changes in the standard assumptions.
16. Eaton and Lipsey (1978) prove formally that some spatial locations can maintain long-run profitability.
17. Assuming that sufficient room exists between A's market area and the end points of the market to enable B to gain an equally large market area without encroaching on A.
18. Of course, a new entrant would never even try to squeeze between competitors unless other more open areas were already filled. In addition, the model assumes that because of sunk capital expenditures, his entry will not prompt A and B to spread out further giving him more room.
19. A new entrant could, of course, enter with multiple brands. Schmalensee argues, however, that the cost of finding multiple attractive entry opportunities all at the same time generates a barrier to entry (1978, pp. 317–18). Schmalensee also argues that brand introduction by established firms may involve less uncertainty than by new entrants, reinforcing the tendency toward brand proliferation (p. 317).
20. Porter (1980, pp. 335–38) has begin to bring preemptive investment to the attention of practitioners.
21. Marketers do universally acknowledge the need for segmented pricing as part of an overall segmented marketing strategy, but research on strategies for price segmentation has not kept pace with that for product and promotional segmentation. Notable exceptions are Frank and Massy (1965), Elrod and Winer (1982), and Narasimhan (1982).
22. Eli Clemens (1951) shows that there is conceptually no difference between the pricing of different products produced with the same resources and the pricing of identical products for different market segments.
23. See also Joan Robinson (1936), for the seminal analysis of price discrimination, and Fritz Machlup (1955). Nagle (1983) discusses the implications of segmented pricing for the marketing practitioner.
24. The exceptions are tying contracts for service on new, highly technical products where it can be proven essential to maintain the product's performance and therefore its reputation. See *United States v. Jerrold Electronics Co.* (1961).
25. An interesting discovery of this paper is that the preference reversal, which Stigler and others have used to demonstrate the value of bundling, is neither strictly necessary nor sufficient.
26. Consequently, a firm attempting skim pricing might rationally commit itself not to cut price for a certain length of time.
27. Essentially, the optimal solution is to allocate that portion of capacity costs to the peak demand periods that is not covered by positive marginal revenues at other times.
28. In fact, the tie-in sale discussed above is, in theory, a two-part pricing strategy for the *services* of the asset.
29. Murphy (1979) presents a more intuitive discussion and relates the two-part pricing to other tactics.

Bibliography

Adams, William James, and Yellen, Janet T. 1976. "Commodity Bundling and the Burden of Monopoly," *Quarterly Journal of Economics*, 40 (May): 475–98.

Akerlof, George. 1970. "The Market for 'Lemons': Quality Uncertainty and the Market Mechanism," *Quarterly Journal of Economics* 84, no. 3 (August): 488–500.

Alchian, Armen A. 1950. "Uncertainty, Evolution, and Economic Theory," *Journal of Political Economy*, 58:211–21. Reprinted 1958 in R. Heflebower and G. Stocking, eds., *A.E.A. Readings in Industrial Organization and Public Policy.* Homewood, IL: Irwin.

Baumol, William J. 1967. "Calculation of Optimal Product and Retailer Characteristics: The Abstract Product Approach," *Journal of Political Economy*, 75 (October): 674–85.

Becker, Gary. 1981. *A Treatise on the Family.* Cambridge, MA: Harvard University Press.

Benjamin, Daniel K., and Kormendi, Roger C. 1974. "The Interrelationship Between Markets for New and Used Durable Goods," *Journal of Law and Economics*, 17 (October): 381–402.

Berky Photo v. Eastman Kodak Co. 603 F.2d 263 (2d Cir. 1979).

Bettman, James R. 1979. *An Information Processing Theory of Consumer Choice*. Reading, MA: Addison-Wesley.

"Big Shift in Antitrust Policy." 1981. *Dun's Review* 111, no. 2 (August): 39–40.

Blattberg, Robert, and Sen, Subrata. 1974. "Market Segmentation Using Models of Multidimensional Purchasing Behavior," *Journal of Marketing*, 38 (October): 17–28.

Blattberg, Robert; Buesing, Thomas; Peacock, Peter; and Sen, Subrata. 1978. "Identifying the Deal-Prone Segment," *Journal of Marketing Research*, 15 (August): 369–77.

Bowman, Ward S. 1957. "Tying Arrangements and the Leverage Problem, *Yale Law Journal*, 67 (November): 19–36.

Burstein, M. L. 1960*a*. "The Economics of Tie-In Sales," *Review of Economics and Statistics*, 27 (February): 68–73.

———. 1960*b*. "A Theory of Full Line Forcing," *Northwestern University Law Review*, 55 (March–April): 62–95.

Cassady, Ralph. 1946*a*. "Some Economic Aspects of Price Discrimination Under Nonperfect Market Conditions," *Journal of Marketing*, 11 (July): 7–20.

———. 1964*b*. "Techniques and Purposes of Price Discrimination," *Journal of Marketing*, 11 (July): 135–50.

Clemens, Eli. 1951. "Price Discrimination and the Multiproduct Firm," *Review of Economic Studies*, 19:1–11. Reprinted 1958 in R. Heflebower and G. Stocking, eds., *A.E.A. Readings in Industrial Organization and Public Policy,* Homewood, IL: Irwin.

Coase, Ronald H. 1972. "Durability and Monopoly," *Journal of Law and Economics*, 15 (April): 143–50.

Darby, Michael R., and Karni, Edi. 1973. "Free Competition and the Optimal Amount of Fraud," *Journal of Law and Economics*, 16 (April): 67–88.

Dean, Joel. 1951. *Managerial Economics*. New York: Prentice-Hall.

Dixit, Avinash D. 1980. "The Role of Investment in Entry-Deterrence," *Economic Journal*, 90 (March): 95–106.

Dolan, Robert, and Jeuland, Abel. 1981. "Experience Curves and Dynamic Demand Models: Implications for Optimal Pricing Strategies," *Journal of Marketing*, 45 (Winter): 52–62.

Eaton, C. Curtis, and Lipsey, Richard G. 1976. "The Non-Uniqueness of Equilibrium in the Löschian Location Model," *American Economic Review*, 66 (March): 71–93.

———. 1978. "Freedom of Entry and the Existence of Pure Profit," *Economic Journal*, 88 (September): 455–69.

———. 1979. "The Theory of Market Pre-emption: The Persistence of Excess Capacity and Monopoly in Growing Spatial Markets," *Economica*, 46 (May): 149–58.

Elrod, Terry, and Winer, Russell S. 1982. "An Empirical Evaluation of Aggregation Approaches for Developing Market Segments," *Journal of Marketing*, 46 (Fall): 65–74.

Farris, Paul W., and Albion, Mark. 1980. "The Impact of Advertising on the Price of Consumer Products," *Journal of Marketing*, 44 (Summer): 17–35.

Frank, Ronald E., and Massy, William. 1965. "Market Segmentation and the Effectiveness of a Brand's Price and Dealing Policies," *Journal of Business*, 38 (April): 186–200.

Frank, Ronald E.; Massy, William; and Wind, Yoram. 1972. *Market Segmentation*. Englewood Cliffs, NJ: Prentice-Hall.

Friedman, Milton. 1953. "The Methodology of Positive Economics," in *Essays in Positive Economics*. Chicago: University of Chicago Press.

Gabor, Andre. 1955. "A Note on Block Tarriffs," *Review of Economic Studies*, 23:32–41.

Goldman, Marshall I. 1960. "Product Differentiation and Advertising: Some Lessons from Soviet Experience," *Journal of Political Economy*, 68 (August): 346–57.

Harris, Milton, and Raviv, Arthur. 1981. "A Theory of Monopoly Pricing Schemes with Demand Uncertainty," *American Economic Review*, 71 (June): 347–65.

Hay, D. A. 1976. "Sequential Entry and Entry-Deterring Strategies in Spatial Competition," *Oxford Economic Papers*, 28 (July): 240–57.

Heaton Peninsular v. Eureka Specialty Co., 77 F.2d 288 (6th Cir. 1896).

Henry v. A. B. Dick, 224 U.S. 1 (1912).

Hirshleifer, Jack. 1958. "Peak Loads and Efficient Pricing: Comment," *Quarterly Journal of Economics*, 72 (August): 451–62.

Hotelling, Harold. 1929. "Stability in Competition," *Economic Journal*, 39:41–57. Reprinted 1952 in George Stigler and Kenneth Boulding, eds., *A.E.A. Readings in Price Theory*. Homewood, IL: Irwin.

———. 1938. "The General Welfare in Relation to Problems of Taxation and of Railway and Utility Rates," *Econometrica*, 6 (July): 242–69. Reprinted 1959 in R. A. Musgrave and C. S. Shoup, eds., *Readings in the Economics of Taxation*. Homewood, IL: Irwin.

Houthakker, Hendrik. 1951. "Electricity Tariffs in Theory and Practice," *Economic Journal*, 61 (March): 1–25.

International Business Machines Corp. v. United States, 298 U.S. 131 (Sup. Ct. 1936).

Jeuland, Abel P., and Shugan, Steven M. 1982. "Managing Channel Profits," working paper. Chicago: University of Chicago, Center for Research in Marketing.

Kalish, Shlomo. In press. "Monopolist Pricing with Dynamic Demand and Production Cost," *Marketing Science*.

Klein, Benjamin; Crawford, Robert G.; and Alchian, Armen A. 1978. "Vertical Integration, Appropriable Rents, and the Competitive Contracting Process," *Journal of Law and Economics*, 21 (October): 297–326.

Klein, Benjamin, and Leffler, Keith B. 1981. "The Role of Market Forces in Assuring Contractual Performance," *Journal of Political Economy*, 89, no. 4 (August): 615–42.

"Kodak Fights Back." 1982. *Business Week*, February 1, pp. 48–54.

Lancaster, Kelvin J. 1975. "Socially Optimal Product Differentiation," *American Economic Review*, 65 (September): 567–85.

McGuire, T. W., and Staelin, Richard. 1981. "An Industry Equilibrium Analysis of Downstream Vertical Integration," working paper. Pittsburgh: Carnegie Mellon University.

Machlup, Fritz. 1955. "Characteristics and Types of Price Discrimination," in *Business Concentration and Public Policy*. Princeton, NJ: Princeton University Press (for National Bureau of Economic Research).

Machlup, Fritz, and Taber, Martha. 1960. "Bilateral Monopoly, Successive Monopoly, and Vertical Integration," *Economica*, 27 (May): 101–19.

Mack, Ruth P., and Leighland, T. James. 1982. "Optimizing in Households: Toward a Behavioral Theory," *American Economic Review*, 72, no. 2 (May): 103–8.

Mahajan, Vijay, and Jain, Arun K. 1978. "An Approach to Normative Segmentation," *Journal of Marketing Research*, 15 (August): 338–45.

Montgomery, David. 1971. "Consumer Characteristics Associated with Dealing: An Empirical Example," *Journal of Marketing*, 8 (February): 118–20.

Morgan Envelope Co. v. Albany Perforated Paper Co., 152 U.S. 425 (1893).

Motion Picture Patents Co. v. Universal Film Mfg. Co., 243 U.S. 502 (1917).

Murphy, Michael M. 1977. "Price Discrimination, Market Separation, and the Multi-Part Tariff," *Economic Enquiry*, 15 (October): 587–99.

Nagle, Thomas T. 1983. "Pricing as Creative Marketing," *Business Horizons*, 26 (July/August): 14–19.

Narasimhan, Chakravarthi. 1982. "Coupons as Price Discrimination Devices—A Theoretical Perspective and Empirical Analysis," working paper. Chicago: University of Chicago, Center for Research in Marketing.

Nelson, Philip. 1970. "Information and Consumer Behavior," *Journal of Political Economy*, 78 (March/April): 311–29.

———. 1978. "Advertising as Information Once More," in D. Tverck, ed., *Issues in Advertising*. Washington, DC: American Enterprise Institute.

———. 1980. "Comments on 'The Economics of Consumer Information Acquisition,'" *Journal of Business*, 53, no. 3 (July): S163–S165.

Oi, Walter Y. 1971. "A Disneyland Dilemma: Two-Part Tariffs for a Mickey Mouse Monopoly," *Quarterly Journal of Economics*, 85 (February): 77–96.

Porter, Michael E. 1976. *Interbrand Choice, Strategy, and Bilateral Market Power*. Cambridge, MA: Harvard University Press.

———. 1980. *Competitive Strategy: Techniques for Analyzing Industries and Competitors*. New York: Free Press.

Rao, Ram C., and Rutenberg, David P. 1979. "Preempting an Alert Rival: Strategic Timing of the First Plant by Analysis of Sophisticated Rivalry," *Bell Journal of Economics*, 10 (Autumn): 412–28.

Rao, Vithala R. 1984. "Pricing Research in Marketing: The State of the Art," in this issue.

Ratchford, Brian T. 1975. "The New Economic Theory of Consumer Behavior: An Interpretive Essay," *Journal of Consumer Research*, 2(September); 65–75.

Riker, William H., and Ordeshook, Peter C. 1973. *An Introduction to Positive Political Theory.* Englewood Cliffs, NJ: Prentice-Hall.

Robinson, Bruce, and Lakhani, Chet. 1975. "Dynamic Price Models for New Product Planning," *Management Science*, 21 (June): 1113–22.

Robinson, Joan. 1936. *The Economics of Imperfect Competition.* London: Macmillan.

Rosen, Sherwin. 1981. "The Economics of Superstars," *American Economic Review*, 71 (December): 845–58.

Salop, Steven C. 1979. "Strategic Entry Deterrence," *American Economic Review*, 69:335–38.

Salop, Steven C., and Stiglitz, Joseph. 1977. "Bargains and Ripoffs: A Model of Monopolistically Competitive Price Dispersion," *Review of Economics and Statistics*, 54 (December): 493–510.

Schoeffler, Sidney; Buzzell, Robert D.; and Heany, D. F. 1974. "Impact of Strategic Planning on Profit Performance," *Harvard Business Review*, 52 (March): 137–45.

Schmalensee, Richard. 1978. "Entry Deterrence in the Ready-to-Eat Breakfast Cereal Industry," *Bell Journal of Economics*, 9 (Autumn): 305–27.

———. 1982. "Commodity Bundling by Single-Product Monopolies," *Journal of Law and Economics*, 25 (April): 67–72.

———. 1984. "Gaussian Demand and Commodity Bundling," in this issue.

Scitovsky, Tibor. 1950. "Ignorance as the Source of Oligopoly Power," *American Economic Review*, 40 (May): 48–53.

Smithies, Arthur. 1941. "Optimal Location in Spatial Competition," *Journal of Political Economy*, 44:423–39. Reprinted 1952 in *A.E.A. Readings in Price Theory.* Homewood, IL: Irwin.

Spence, Michael. 1977. "Entry, Investment, and Oligopolistic Pricing," *Bell Journal of Economics*, 8 (Autumn): 534–44.

Steiner, Peter O. 1957. "Peak Loads and Efficient Pricing," *Quarterly Journal of Economics*, 71 (November): 485–610.

Stern, Louis W., and El-Ansary, Abel I. 1977. *Marketing Channels.* Englewood Cliffs, NJ: Prentice-Hall.

Stigler, George. 1961. "The Economics of Information," *Journal of Political Economy*, 69, no. 3 (June): 213–25.

———. 1963. "United States v. Loew's Inc.: A Note on Block-Booking," *Supreme Court Review*, pp. 152–57.

Stokey, Nancy L. 1981. "Rational Expectations and Durable Goods Pricing," *Bell Journal of Economics*, 12 (Spring): 112–38.

"Symposium on Peak-Load Pricing." 1976. *Bell Journal of Economics*, 7 (Spring): 197–250.

Telser, Lester G. 1960. "Why Should Manufacturers Want Fair Trade? *Journal of Law and Economics*. 3 (October): 86–104.

———. 1980. "A Theory of Self-Enforcing Agreements," *Journal of Business*, 53, no. 1 (January): 27–44.

Times-Picayune Publishing v. United States, 345 U.S. 594, 611 (1953).

United Shoe Machinery Corp. v. United States, 258 U.S. 451 (Sup. Ct. 1922).

United States v. Jerrold Electronics Co., 365 U.S. 567 (1961).

Webster, Frederick E. 1965. "The 'Deal-Prone' Consumer," *Journal of Marketing Research*, 2 (May): 186–89.

Wilde, Louis. 1980. "The Economics of Consumer Information Acquisition," *Journal of Business*, 53, no. 3 (July): S143–S158.

Williamson, Oliver E. 1966. "Peak-Load Pricing and Optimal Capacity Under Indivisibility Constraints," *American Economic Review*, 56 (September): 810–27.

Wilson, Charles. 1980. "The Nature of Equilibrium in Markets with Adverse Selection," *Bell Journal of Economics*, 11 (Spring): 108–30.

Zusman, Pinhas, and Etgar, Michael. 1981. "The Marketing Channel as an Equilibrium Set of Contracts," *Management Science*, (March), pp. 284–302.

The author is indebted for helpful comments to Mark Albion, Terry Elrod, Abel Jeuland, Roger Kormendi, Chakravarthi Narasimhan, Kenneth Novak, Ram Rao, Subrata Sen, and to an anonymous reviewer.

SECTION IV

Product Portfolio Strategies

Product portfolio models have a checkered history in the practice of strategic marketing. In various renditions, product portfolio models have been viewed by some as the guiding light of corporate strategy, and by others as a road block to effective management. The purpose of this section on product portfolio strategies is to provide a balanced perspective on traditional product portfolio models, how they relate to the riskiness of marketing decisions, and where they fit in competitive and corporate strategies.

Traditional Product Portfolio Models

The stage of the product life cycle and competitive market position are two dimensions of the product portfolio that are common to all its renditions. In the first article in this section Professor Day describes how the product portfolio model developed by the Boston Consulting Group works. He also outlines the pitfalls to be found in assumptions behind this model, the objectives of using a product portfolio model, the pitfalls in measures of its principle dimensions, and the conclusions to be drawn from such models. This is followed by an empirical comparison of four standardized portfolio models by Professors Wind, Mahajan, and Swier. The authors describe and compare each of these four versions of the product portfolio both visually and numerically. They classify 15 strategic business units from the PIMS database using each of the different portfolio models. The authors report significant differences in the classification and conclusions to be drawn depending upon which standardized model is used.

In a further application of the Boston Consulting Group's product portfolio model, Professor Larréché demonstrates how portfolio analysis can reveal significant strategic problems and opportunities when applied at the international level. In the process of developing this application the author demonstrates the need for detailed, market-by-market application of the concept to specific competitive situations.

Risk in Marketing Decisions

One of the underlying motivations for product portfolio models is to assess the riskiness of one market as compared with another. Implicit in the concept of a "cash cow" is the notion of not only higher cashflows, but also less risk. A company with a dominant position in a stable market is less likely to be the target of an aggressive

competitor. Two papers in this section deal more formally with the concept of marketing, or specific risk. Professors Aaker and Jacobson investigate the role of risk in explaining differences in profitability. The authors apply the Capital Asset Pricing Model (CAPM) to the PIMS database. They evaluate the role and significance of both systematic and unsystematic risk in the determination of ROI. They find that unsystematic, or specific risk has a highly significant effect on rate of return.

In their attempt to assess specific marketing risk, Professors Cook and Page identify the elements of a marketing strategy which make it more or less risky. Following the implications of product portfolio models, the authors take "primary demand risk" and "market share" as the two principle sources of risk in strategic marketing. They propose a model of marketing risk in which the sources of risk are influenced by management decisions to enter or exit specific market segments and by management's decisions to build, hold or harvest market share. The model of marketing risk is applied to results from several *Markstrat* simulations.

Competitive & Corporate Strategy

As Professor Porter says in the final paper in this section, competitive strategy concerns the search for competitive advantage in each of the individual markets in which the company competes. *Corporate* strategy, on the other hand, concerns very different questions. These are questions concerning which businesses the corporation should be in and how the central office should manage the array of businesses. The author identifies four general approaches to corporate strategy. These include portfolio, restructuring, skills transferring, and sharing of activities. Professor Porter concludes that in highly developed economies portfolio management is no way to conduct corporate strategy.

The development of an effective corporate strategy requires an action program that recognizes the value added by the corporation to the collection of its businesses. ■

25

Diagnosing the Product Portfolio

George S. Day

How to use scarce cash and managerial resources for maximum long-run gains.

THE PRODUCT PORTFOLIO APPROACH to marketing strategy formulation has gained wide acceptance among managers of diversified companies. They are first attracted by the intuitively appealing concept that long-run corporate performance is more than the sum of the contributions of individual profit centers or product strategies. Secondly a product portfolio analysis suggests specific marketing strategies to achieve a balanced mix of products that will produce the maximum long-run effects from scarce cash and managerial resources. Lastly the concept employs a simple matrix representation which is easy to communicate and comprehend. Thus it is a useful tool in a headquarters campaign to demonstrate that the strategic issues facing the firm justify more centralized control over the planning and resource allocation process.

With the growing acceptance of the basic approach has come an increasing sensitivity to the limitations of the present methods of portraying the product portfolio, and a recognition that the approach is not equally useful in all corporate circumstances. Indeed, the implications can sometimes be grossly misleading. Inappropriate and misleading applications will result when:

- The basic *assumptions* (especially those concerned with the value of market share dominance and the product life cycle) are violated.
- The *measurements* are wrong, or
- The *strategies* are not feasible.

George S. Day is Magna International Professor of Business Strategy, University of Toronto.

This article identifies the critical assumptions and the measurement and application issues that may distort the strategic insights. A series of questions are posed that will aid planners and decision-makers to better understand this aid to strategic thinking, and thereby make better decisions.

What Is the Product Portfolio?

Common to all portrayals of the product portfolio is the recognition that the competitive value of market share depends on the structure of competition and the stage of the product life cycle. Two examples of this approach have recently appeared in this journal.[1] However, the earliest, and most widely implemented is the cash quadrant or share/growth matrix developed by the Boston Consulting Group.[2] Each product is classified jointly by rate of present or forecast *market growth* (a proxy for stage in the product life cycle) and a measure of *market share dominance*.

The arguments for the use of market share are familiar and well documented.[3] Their basis is the cumulation of evidence that market share is strongly and positively correlated with product profitability. This theme is varied somewhat in the BCG approach by the emphasis on relative share —measured by the ratio of the company's share of the market to the share of the largest competitor. This is reasonable since the strategic implications of a 20% share are quite different if the largest competitor's is 40% or if it is 5%. Profitability will also vary, since according to the experience curve concept the largest competitor will be the most profitable at the prevailing price level.[4]

The product life cycle is employed because it highlights the desirability of a variety of products or services with different present and prospective growth rates. More important, the concept has some direct implications for the cost of gaining and/or holding market share:

Exhibit 1
The Cash Quandrant Approach to Describing the Product Portfolio*

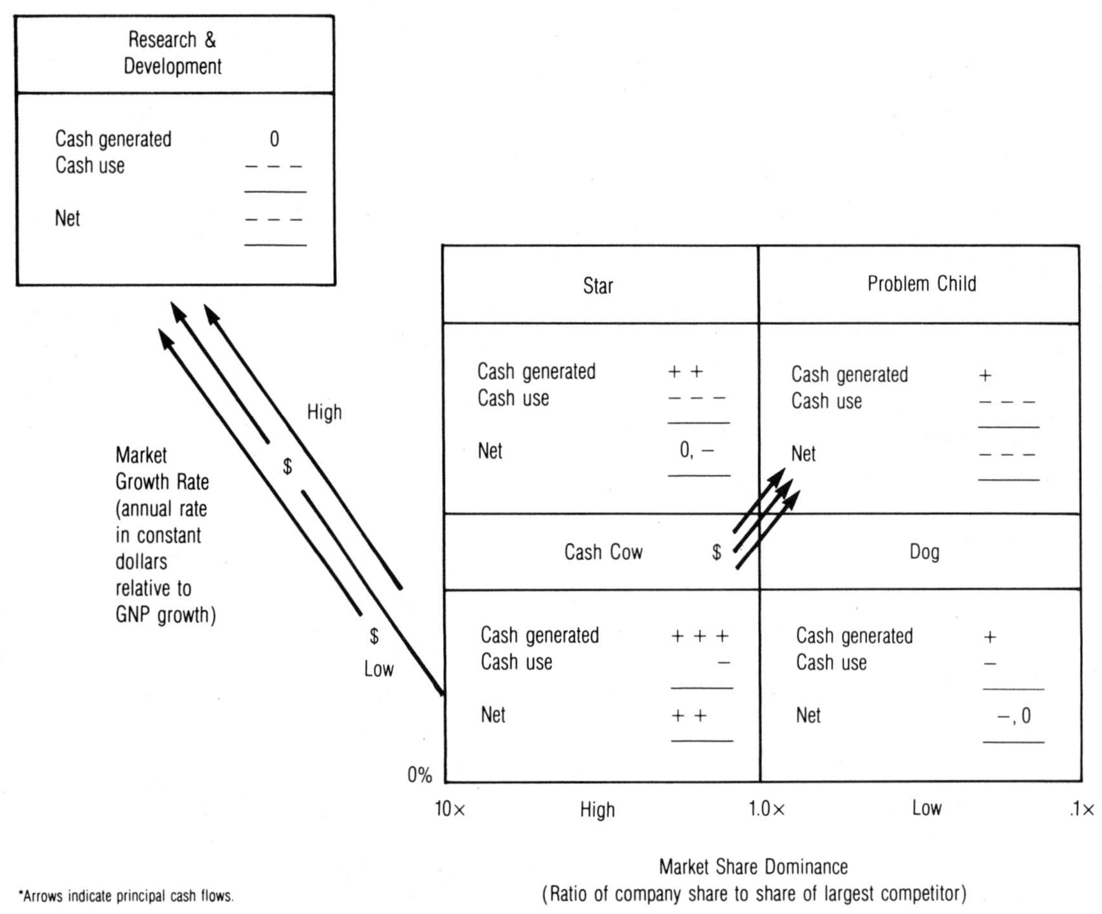

*Arrows indicate principal cash flows.

- During the *rapid growth stage*, purchase patterns and distribution channels are fluid. Market shares can be increased at "relatively" low cost by capturing a disproportionate share of incremental sales (especially where these sales come from new users of applications rather than heavier usage by existing users).
- By contrast, the key-note during the *maturity stage* swings to stability and inertia in distribution and purchasing relationships. A substantial growth in share by one competitor will come at the expense of another competitor's capacity utilization, and will be resisted vigorously. As a result, gains in share are both time-consuming and costly (unless accompanied by a breakthrough in product value or performance that cannot be easily matched by competition).

Product Portfolio Strategies

When the share and growth rate of each of the products sold by a firm are jointly considered, a new basis for strategy evaluation emerges. While there are many possible combinations, an arbitrary classification of products into four share/growth categories (as shown in Exhibit 1) is sufficient to illustrate the strategy implications.

Low Growth/Dominant Share (Cash Cows)

These profitable products usually generate more cash than is required to maintain share. All strategies should be directed toward maintaining market dominance—including investments in technological leadership. Pricing decisions should be made cautiously with an eye to maintaining price leadership. Pressure to over-invest through product proliferation and market expansion should be resisted unless prospects for expanding primary demand are unusually attractive. Instead, excess cash should be used to support research activities and growth areas elsewhere in the company.

High Growth/Dominant Share (Stars)

Products that are market leaders, but also growing fast, will have substantial reported profits but need a lot of cash to finance the rate of growth. The appropriate strategies are designed primarily to protect the existing share level by reinvesting earnings in the form of price reductions, product improvement, better market coverage, production efficiency increases, etc. Particular attention must be given to obtaining a large share of the new users or new applications that are the source of growth in the market.

Low Growth/Subordinate Share (Dogs)

Since there usually can be only one market leader and because most markets are mature, the greatest number of products fall in this category. Such products are usually at a cost disadvantage and have few opportunities for growth at a reasonable cost. Their markets are not growing, so there is little new business to compete for, and market share gains will be resisted strenuously by the dominant competition.

The slower the growth (present or prospective) and the smaller the relative share, the greater the need for positive action. The possibilities include:

1. Focusing on a specialized segment of the market that can be dominated, and protected from competitive inroads.
2. Harvesting, which is a conscious cutback of all support costs to some minimum level which will maximize the cash flow over a foreseeable lifetime—which is usually short.
3. Divestment, usually involving a sale as a going concern.
4. Abandonment or deletion from the product line.

High Growth/Subordinate Share (Problem Children)

The combination of rapid growth and poor profit margins creates an enormous demand for cash. If the cash is not forthcoming, the product will become a "Dog" as growth inevitably slows. The basic strategy options are fairly clear-cut; either invest heavily to get a disproportionate share of the new sales or buy existing shares by acquiring competitors and thus move the product toward the "Star" category or get out of the business using some of the methods just described.

Consideration also should be given to a market segmentation strategy, but only if a defensible niche can be identified and resources are available to gain dominance. This strategy is even more attractive if the segment can provide an entree and experience base from which to push for dominance of the whole market.

Overall Strategy

The long-run health of the corporation depends on having some products that *generate* cash (and provide acceptable reported profits), and others that *use* cash to support growth. Among the indicators of overall health are the size and vulnerability of the "Cash Cows" (and the prospects for the "Stars," if any), and the number of "Problem Children" and "Dogs." Particular attention must be paid to those products with large cash appetites. Unless the company has abundant cash flow, it cannot afford to sponsor many such products at one time. If resources (including debt capacity) are spread too thin, the company simply will wind up with too many marginal products and suffer a reduced capacity to finance promising new product entries or acquisitions in the future.

The share/growth matrix displayed in Exhibit 2 shows how one company (actually a composite of a number of

Exhibit 2
Balancing the product portfolio

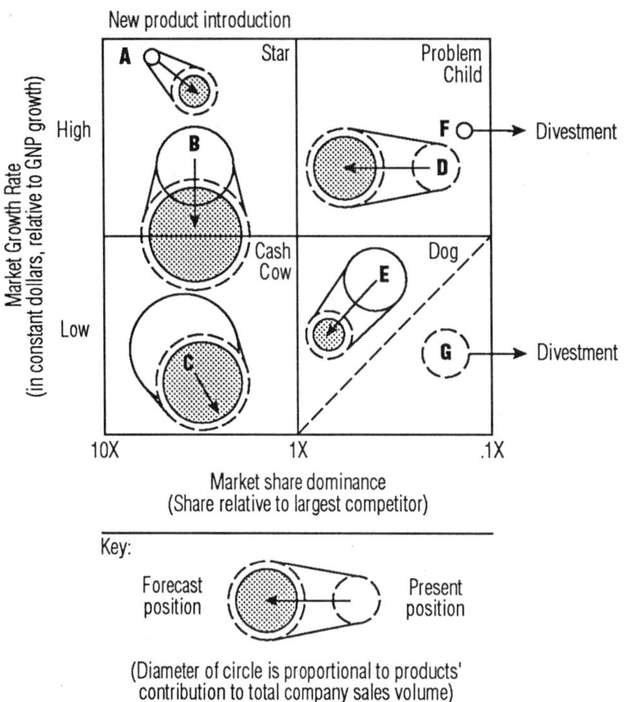

situations) might follow the strategic implications of the product portfolio to achieve a better balance of sources and uses of cash. The *present* position of each product is defined by the relative share and market growth rate during a representative time *period*. Since business results normally fluctuate, it is important to use a time period that is not distorted by rare events. The *future* position may be either (a) a momentum forecast of the results of continuing the present strategy, or (b) a forecast of the consequences of a change in strategy. It is desirable to do both, and compare the results. The specific display of Exhibit 2 is a summary of the following strategic decisions.

- Aggressively *support* the newly introduced product A, to ensure dominance (but anticipate share declines due to new competitive entries).
- Continue present strategies of products B and C to ensure *maintenance* of market share.
- Gain share of market for product D by investing in *acquisitions*.
- Narrow and modify the range of models of product E to *focus* on one segment.
- *Divest* products F and G.

Pitfalls in the Assumptions

The starting point in the decision to follow the implications of a product portfolio analysis is to ask whether the underlying assumptions make sense. The most fundamental assumptions relate to the role of market share in the businesses being portrayed in the portfolio. Even if the answers here are affirmative one may choose to not follow the implications if other objectives than balancing cash flows take priority, or there are barriers to implementing the indicated strategies.

What Is the Role of Market Share?

All the competitors are assumed to have the same overhead structures and experience curves, with their position on the experience curve corresponding to their market share position. Hence market share dominance is a proxy for the *relative* profit performance (e.g., GM vs. Chrysler). Other factors beyond market share may be influential in dictating *absolute, profit performance (e.g., calculators versus cosmetics).*

The influence of market share is most apparent with high value-added products, where there are significant barriers to entry and the competition consists of a few, large, diversified corporations with the attendant large overheads (e.g., plastics, major appliances, automobiles, and semiconductors). But even in these industrial environments there are distortions under conditions such as:

- One competitor has a significant technological advantage which can be protected and used to establish a steeper cost reduction/experience curve.
- The principal component of the product is produced by a supplier who has an inherent cost advantage because of an integrated process. Thus Dupont was at a cost disadvantage with Cyclohexane vis-à-vis the oil companies because the manufacture of the product was so highly integrated with the operations of an oil refinery.[5]
- Competitors can economically gain large amounts of experience through acquisitions or licensing, or shift to a lower (but parallel) cost curve by resorting to off-shore production or component sourcing.
- Profitability is highly sensitive to the rate of capacity utilization, regardless of size of plant.

There are many situations where the positive profitability and share relationship becomes very tenuous, and perhaps unattainable. A recent illustration is the building industry where large corporations—CNA with Larwin and ITT with Levitt—have suffered because of their inability to adequately offset their high overhead charges with a corresponding reduction in total costs.[6] Similar problems are also encountered in the service sector, and contribute to the many reasons why services which are highly labor-intensive and involve personal relationships must be approached with extreme caution in a product portfolio analysis.[7]

There is specific evidence from the Profit Impact of Market Strategies (PIMS) study[8] that the value of market share is not as significant for consumer goods as for industrial products. The reasons are not well understood, but probably reflect differences in buying behavior, the importance of product differentiation and the tendency for proliferation of marginally different brands in these categories. The strategy of protecting a market position by introducing line extensions, flankers, and spin-offs from a successful core brand means that product class boundaries are very unclear. Hence shares are harder to estimate. The individual brand in a category like deodorants or powdered drinks may not be the proper basis for evaluation. A related consequence is that joint costing problems multiply. For example, Unilever in the U.K. has 20 detergent brands all sharing production facilities and marketing resources to some degree.

When Do Market Shares Stabilize?

The operating assumption is that shares tend toward stability during the maturity stage, as the dominant competitors concentrate on defending their existing position. An important corollary is that gains in share are easier and cheaper to achieve during the growth stage.

There is scattered empirical evidence, including the results of the PIMS project, which supports these assumptions. Several qualifications must be made before the implications can be pursued in depth:

- While market share *gains* may be costly, it is possible to mismanage a dominant position. The examples of A&P in food retailing, and British Leyland in the U.K. automobile market provide new benchmarks on the extent to which strong positions can erode unless vigorously defended.
- When the two largest competitors are of roughly equal size, the share positions may continue to be fluid until one is finally dominant.
- There are certain product categories, frequently high technology oriented, where a dominant full line/full service competitor is vulnerable if there are customer segments which do not require all the services, technical assistance, etc., that are provided. As markets mature this "sophisticated" segment usually grows. Thus, Digital Equipment Corp. has prospered in competition with IBM by simply selling basic hardware and depending on others to do the applications programming.[9] By contrast, IBM provides, for a price, a great deal of service backup and software for customers who are not self-sufficient. The dilemma for the dominant producer lies in the difficulty of serving both segments simultaneously.[10]

What Is the Objective of a Product Portfolio Strategy?

The strategies emerging from a product portfolio analysis emphasize the balance of cash flows, by ensuring that there are products that use cash to sustain growth and others that supply cash.

Yet corporate objectives have many more dimensions that require consideration. This point was recognized by Seymour Tilles in one of the earliest discussions of the portfolio approach.[11] It is worth repeating to avoid a possible myopic focus on cash flow considerations. Tilles' point was that an investor pursues a balanced combination of risk, income, and growth when acquiring a portfolio of securities. He further argued that "the same basic concepts apply equally well to product planning." The problem with concentrating on cash flow to maximize income and growth is that strategies to balance risks are not explicitly considered.

What must be avoided is excessive exposure to a specific threat from one of the following areas of vulnerability:

- The economy (e.g., business downturns).
- Social, political, environmental pressures.
- Supply continuity.
- Technological change.
- Unions and related human factors.

It also follows that a firm should direct its new product search activities into several different opportunity areas, to avoid intensifying the degree of vulnerability. Thus, many companies in the power equipment market, such as Brown Boveri, are in a quandary over whether to meet the enormous resource demands of the nuclear power equipment market, because of the degree of vulnerability of this business compared to other possibilities such as household appliances.

The desire to reduce vulnerability is a possible reason for keeping, or even acquiring, a "Dog." Thus, firms may integrate backward to assure supply of highly leveraged materials.[12] If a "Dog" has a high percentage of captive business, it may not even belong as a separate entity in a portfolio analysis.

A similar argument could be used for products which have been acquired for intelligence reasons. For example, a large Italian knitwear manufacturer owns a high-fashion dress company selling only to boutiques to help follow and interpret fashion trends. Similarly, because of the complex nature of the distribution of lumber products, some suppliers have acquired lumber retailers to help learn about patterns of demand and changing end-user requirements. In both these cases the products/businesses were acquired for reasons outside the logic of the product portfolio, and should properly be excluded from the analysis.

Can the Strategies Be Implemented?

Not only does a product portfolio analysis provide insights into the long-run health of a company; it also implies the basic strategies that will strengthen the portfolio. Unfortunately, there are many situations where the risks of failure of these strategies are unacceptably high. Several of these risks were identified in a recent analysis of the dangers in the pursuit of market share.[13]

One danger is that the company's financial resources will not be adequate. The resulting problems are enormously compounded should the company find itself in a vulnerable financial position if the fight were stopped short for some reason. The fundamental question underlying such dangers is the likelihood that competitors will pursue the same strategy, because they follow the same logic in identifying and pursuing opportunities. As a result, there is a growing premium on the understanding of competitive responses, and especially the degree to which they will be discouraged by aggressive action.

An increasingly important question is whether government regulations will permit the corporation to follow the strategy it has chosen. Antitrust regulations—especially in the U.S.—now virtually preclude acquisitions undertaken by large companies in related areas. Thus the effort by ITT to acquire a "Cash Cow" in Hartford Fire and Indemnity Insurance was nearly aborted by a consent decree, and other moves by ITT into Avis, Canteen Corp., and Levitt have been divested by court order at enormous cost. Recent governmental actions—notably the *ReaLemon* case—may even make it desirable for companies with very large absolute market share to consider reducing that share.[14]

There is less recognition as yet that government involvement can cut both ways; making it difficult to get in *or out of* a business. Thus, because of national security considerations large defense contractors would have a difficult time exiting from the aerospace or defense businesses. The problems are most acute in countries like Britain and Italy where intervention policies include price controls, regional development directives and employment maintenance which may prevent the replacement of out-moded plants. Unions in these two countries are sometimes so dedicated to protecting the employment status quo that a manager may not even move employees from one product line to another without risking strike activity.

The last implementation question concerns the viability of a niche strategy, which appears at the outset to be an attractive way of coping with both "Dogs" and "Problem Children." The fundamental problem, of course, is whether a product or market niche can be isolated and protected against competitive inroads. But even if this can be achieved in the long-run, the strategy may not be attractive. The difficulties are most often encountered when a full or extensive product line is needed to support sales, service and distribution facilities. One specialized product may simply not generate sufficient volume and gross margin to cover the minimum costs of participation in the market. This is very clearly an issue in the construction equipment business because of the importance of assured service.

Pitfalls in the Measures

The "Achilles' Heel" of a product portfolio analysis is the units of measure; for if the share of market and growth estimates are dubious, so are the interpretations. Skeptics recognize this quickly, and can rapidly confuse the analysis by attacking the meaningfulness and accuracy of these measures and offering alternative definitions. With the present state of the measurements there is often no adequate defense.

What Share of What Market?

This is not one, but several questions. Each is controversial because they influence the bases for resource allocation and evaluation within the firm:

- Should the definition of the product-market be broad (reflecting the generic need) or narrow?

- How much market segmentation?
- Should the focus be on the total product-market or a portion served by the company?
- Which level of geography: local versus national versus regio-centric markets?

The answers to these questions are complicated by the lack of defensible procedures for identifying product-market boundaries. For example, four-digit SIC categories are convenient and geographically available but may have little relevance to consumer perceptions of substitutability which will influence the long-run performance of the product. Furthermore, there is the pace of product development activity which is dedicated to combining, extending, or otherwise obscuring the boundaries.

Breadth of Product-Market Definition? This is a pivotal question. Consider the following extremes in definitions:

- Intermediate builder chemicals for the detergent industry *or* Sodium Tri-polyphosphate.
- Time/information display devices *or* medium-priced digital-display alarm clocks.
- Main meal accompaniments *or* jellied cranberry.

Narrow definitions satisfy the short-run, tactical concerns of sales and product managers. Broader views, reflecting longer-run, strategic planning concerns, invariably reveal a larger market to account for (a) sales to untapped but potential markets, (b) changes in technology, price relationships, and supply which broaden the array of potential substitute products, and (c) the time required by present and prospective buyers to react to these changes.

Extent of Segmentation? In other words, when does it become meaningful to divide the total market into subgroups for the purpose of estimating shares? In the tire industry it is evident that the OEM and replacement markets are so dissimilar in behavior as to dictate totally different marketing mixes. But how much further should segmentation be pushed? The fact that a company has a large share of the high-income buyers of replacement tires is probably not strategically relevant.

In general the degree of segmentation for a portfolio analysis should be limited to grouping those buyers that share situational or behavioral characteristics that are strategically relevant. This means that different marketing mixes must be used to serve the segments that have been identified, which will be reflected in different cost and price structures. Other manifestations of a strategically important segment boundary would be a discontinuity in growth rates, share patterns, distribution patterns and so forth when going from one segment to another.

These judgments are particularly hard to make for geographic boundaries. For example, what is meaningful for a manufacturer of industrial equipment facing dominant local competition in each of the national markets in the European Economic Community? Because the company is in each market, it has a 5% share of the total EEC market, while the largest regional competitor has 9%. In this case the choice of a regional rather than national market definition was dictated by the *trend* to similarity of product requirements throughout the EEC and the consequent feasibility of a single manufacturing facility to serve several countries.

The tendency for trade barriers to decline for countries within significant economic groupings will increasingly dictate regio-centric rather than nationally oriented boundaries. This, of course, will not happen where transportation costs or government efforts to protect sensitive industry categories (such as electric power generation equipment), by requiring local vendors, creates other kinds of barriers.

Market Served Versus Total Market?

Firms may elect to serve only just a part of the available market; such as retailers with central buying offices or utilities of a certain size. The share of the market served is an appropriate basis for tactical decisions. This share estimate may also be relevant for strategic decisions, especially if the market served corresponds to a distinct segment boundary. There is a risk that focusing only on the market served may mean overlooking a significant opportunity or competitive threat emerging from the unserved portion of the market. For example, a company serving the blank cassette tape market only through specialty audio outlets is vulnerable if buyers perceive that similar quality cassettes can be bought in general merchandise and discount outlets.

Another facet of the served market issue is the treatment of customers who have integrated backward and now satisfy their own needs from their own resources. Whether or not the captive volume is included in the estimate of total market size depends on how readily this captive volume can be displaced by outside suppliers. Recent analysis suggests that captive production—or in-feeding—is "remarkably resilient to attack by outside suppliers."[15]

What Can Be Done?

The value of a strategically relevant product-market definition lies in "stretching" the company's perceptions appropriately—far enough so that significant threats and opportunities are not missed, but not so far as to dissipate information gathering and analysis efforts on "long shots." This is a difficult balance to achieve, given the myriads of possibilities. The best procedure for coping is to employ several alternative definitions, varying specificity of product and market segments. There will inevitably be both points of contradiction and consistency in the insights gained from portfolios constructed at one level versus another. The process of resolution can be very revealing, both in terms of understanding the competitive position and suggesting strategy alternatives.[16]

Market Growth Rate

The product life cycle is justifiably regarded as one of the most difficult marketing concepts to measure—or forecast.

There is a strong tendency in a portfolio analysis to judge that a product is maturing when there is a forecast of a decline in growth rate below some specified cut-off. One difficulty is that the same cut-off level does not apply equally to all products or economic climates. As slow growth or level GNP becomes the reality, high absolute growth rates become harder to achieve for all products, mature or otherwise. Products with lengthy introductory periods, facing substantial barriers to adoption, may never exhibit high growth rates, but may have an extended maturity stage. Other products may exhibit precisely the opposite life cycle pattern.

The focus in the product portfolio analysis should be on the long-run growth rate forecast. This becomes especially important with products which are sensitive to the business cycle, such as machine tools, or have potential substitutes with fluctuating prices. Thus the future growth of engineered plastics is entwined with the price of zinc, aluminum, copper and steel; the sales of powdered breakfast beverages depends on the relative price of frozen orange juice concentrate.

These two examples also illustrate the problem of the self-fulfilling prophecy. A premature classification as a mature product may lead to the reduction of marketing resources to the level necessary to defend the share in order to maximize net cash flow. But if the product class sales are sensitive to market development activity (as in the case of engineered plastics) or advertising expenditures (as is the case with powdered breakfast drinks) and these budgets are reduced by the dominant firms then, indeed, the product growth rate will slow down.

The growth rate is strongly influenced by the choice of product-market boundaries. A broad product type (cigarettes) will usually have a longer maturity stage than a more specific product form (plain filter cigarettes). In theory, the growth of the individual brand is irrelevant. Yet, it cannot be ignored that the attractiveness of a growth market, however defined, will be diminished by the entry of new competitors with the typical depressing effect on the sales, prices and profits of the established firms. The extent of the reappraisal of the market will depend on the number, resources, and commitment of the new entrants. Are they likely to become what is known in the audio electronics industry as "rabbits," which come racing into the market, litter it up, and die off quickly?

Pitfalls from Unanticipated Consequences

Managers are very effective at tailoring their behavior to the evaluation system, *as they perceive it*. Whenever market share is used to evaluate performance, there is a tendency for managers to manipulate the product-market boundaries to show a static or increasing share. The greater the degree of ambiguity or compromise in the definition of the boundaries the more tempting these adjustments become. The risk is that the resulting narrow view of the market may mean overlooking threats from substitutes or the opportunities within emerging market segments.

These problems are compounded when share dominance is also perceived to be an important determinant of the allocation of resources and top management interest. The manager who doesn't like the implications of being associated with a "Dog," may try to redefine the market so he can point to a larger market share or a higher than average growth rate. Regardless of his success with the attempted redefinition, his awareness of how the business is regarded in the overall portfolio will ultimately affect his morale. Then his energies may turn to seeking a transfer or looking for another job, and perhaps another prophecy has been fulfilled.

The forecast of market growth rate is also likely to be manipulated, especially if the preferred route to advancement and needed additional resources is perceived to depend on association with a product that is classified as "Star." This may lead to wishful thinking about the future growth prospects of the product. Unfortunately the quality of the review procedures in most planning processes is not robust enough to challenge such distortions. Further dysfunctional consequences will result if ambitious managers of "Cash Cows" actually attempt to expand their products through unnecessary product proliferation and market segmentation without regard to the impact on profits.

The potential for dysfunctional consequences does not mean that profit center managers and their employees should not be aware of the basis for resource allocation decisions within the firm. A strong argument can be made to the effect that it is worse for managers to observe those decisions and suspect the worst. What will surely create problems is to have an inappropriate reward system. A formula-based system, relying on achievement of a target for return on investment or an index of profit measures, that does not recognize the differences in potential among businesses, will lead to short-run actions that conflict with the basic strategies that should be pursued.

Alternative Views of the Portfolio

This analysis of the share/growth matrix portrayal of the product portfolio supports Bowman's contention that much of what now exists in the field of corporate or marketing strategy can be thought of as contingency theories. "The ideas, recommendations, or generalizations are rather dependent (contingent) for their truth and their relevance on the specific situational factors."[17] This means that in any specific analysis of the product portfolio there may be a number of factors beyond share and market growth with a much greater bearing on the attractiveness of a product-market or business; including:

- The contribution rate.
- Barriers to entry.
- Cyclicality of sales.
- The rate of capacity utilization.
- Sensitivity of sales to change in prices, promotional activities, service levels, etc.
- The extent of "captive" business.
- The nature of technology (maturity, volatility, and complexity).

- Availability of production and process opportunities.
- Social, legal, governmental, and union pressures and opportunities.

Since these factors are situational, each company (or division) must develop its own ranking of their importance in determining attractiveness.[18] In practice these factors tend to be qualitatively combined into overall judgments of the attractiveness of the industry or market, and the company's position in that market. The resulting matrix for displaying the positions of each product is called a "nine-block" diagram or decision matrix.[19]

Although the implications of this version of the product portfolio are not as clear-cut, it does overcome many of the shortcomings of the share/growth matrix approach. Indeed the two approaches will likely yield different insights. But as the main purpose of the product portfolio analysis is to help guide—but not substitute for—strategic thinking, the process of reconciliation is useful in itself. Thus it is desirable to employ both approaches and compare results.

Summary

The product portfolio concept provides a useful synthesis of the analyses and judgments during the preliminary steps of the planning process, and is a provocative source of strategy alternatives. If nothing else, it demonstrates the fallacy of treating all businesses or profit centers as alike, and all capital investment decisions as independent and additive events.

There are a number of pitfalls to be avoided to ensure the implications are not misleading. This is especially true for the cash quadrant or share/growth matrix approach to portraying the portfolio. In many situations the basic assumptions are not satisfied. Further complications stem from uncertainties in the definitions of product-markets and the extent and timing of competitive actions. One final pitfall is the unanticipated consequences of adopting a portfolio approach. These may or may not be undesirable depending on whether they are recognized at the outset.

Despite the potential pitfalls it is important to not lose sight of the concept; that is, to base strategies on the perception of a company as an interdependent group of products and services, each playing a distinctive and supportive role.

References

1. Bernard Catry and Michel Chevalier, "Market Share Strategy and the Product Life Cycle," *Journal of Marketing*, Vol. 38 No. 4 (October 1974), pp. 29–34; and Yoram Wind and Henry J. Claycamp, "Planning Product Line Strategy: A Matrix Approach," *Journal of Marketing*, Vol. 40 No. 1 (January 1976), pp. 2–9.
2. Described in the following pamphlets in the *Perspectives* series, authored by Bruce D. Henderson, "The Product Portfolio" (1970), "Cash Traps" (1972) and "The Experience Curve Reviewed: The Growth-Share Matrix or the Product Portfolio." (Boston Consulting Group, 1973). By 1972 the approach had been employed in more than 100 companies. See "Mead's Technique to Sort Out the Losers," *Business Week* (March 11, 1972), pp. 124–30.
3. Sidney Schoeffler, Robert D. Buzzell and Donald F. Heany, "Impact of Strategic Planning on Profit Performance," *Harvard Business Review*, Vol. 52 (March–April 1974), pp. 137–45; and Robert D. Buzzell, Bradley T. Gale and Ralph G. M. Sultan, "Market Share—A Key to Profitability," *Harvard Business Review*, Vol. 53 (January–February 1975), pp. 97–106.
4. Boston Consulting Group, *Perspectives on Experience* (Boston: 1968 and 1970), and "Selling Business a Theory of Economics," *Business Week*, September 8, 1974, pp. 43–44.
5. Robert B. Stobaugh and Philip L. Towsend, "Price Forecasting and Strategic Planning: The Case of Petrochemicals," *Journal of Marketing Research*, Vol. XII (February 1975), pp. 19–29.
6. Carol J. Loomis, "The Further Misadventures of Harold Geneen," *Fortune*, June 1975.
7. There is incomplete but provocative evidence of significant share-profit relationships in the markets for auto rental, consumer finance, and retail securities brokerage.
8. Same as reference 3 above.
9. "A Minicomputer Tempest," *Business Week*, January 27, 1975, pp. 79–80.
10. Some argue that the dilemma is very general, confronting all pioneering companies in mature markets. See Seymour Tilles, "Segmentation and Strategy," *Perspectives* (Boston: Boston Consulting Group, 1974).
11. Seymour Tilles, "Strategies for Allocating Funds," *Harvard Business Review*, Vol. 44 January–February 1966), pp. 72–80.
12. This argument is compelling when $20,000 of Styrene Monomer can affect the production of $10,000,000 worth of formed polyester fiberglass parts.
13. William E. Fruhan, "Pyrrhic Victories in Fights for Market Share," *Harvard Business Review*, Vol. 50 (September–October 1972), pp. 100–107.
14. See Paul N. Bloom and Philip Kotler, "Strategies for High Market-Share Companies," *Harvard Business Review*, Vol. 53 (November–December 1975), pp. 63–72.
15. Aubrey Wilson and Bryan Atkin, "Exorcising the Ghosts in Marketing," *Harvard Business Review*, Vol. 54 (September–October 1976), pp. 117–27. See also, Ralph D. Kerkendall, "Customers as Competitors," *Perspectives* (Boston: Boston Consulting Group, 1975).
16. George S. Day and Allan D. Shocker, *Identifying Competitive Product-Market Boundaries: Strategic and Analytical Issues* (Boston: Marketing Science Institute, 1976).
17. Edward H. Bowman, "Epistemology, Corporate Strategy, and Academe," *Sloan Management Review* (Winter 1974), pp. 35–50.
18. The choice of factors and assessment of ranks is an important aspect of the design of a planning system. These issues are described in Peter Lorange, "Divisional Planning: Setting Effective Direction," *Sloan Management Review* (Fall 1975), pp. 77–91.
19. William E. Rothschild, *Putting It All Together: A Guide to Strategic Thinking* (New York: AMACOM, 1976).

26

An Empirical Comparison of Standardized Portfolio Models

Yoram Wind, Vijay Mahajan & Donald J. Swire

Standardized portfolio models have been widely accepted, despite obvious limitations. Dominance of standardized portfolio models is likely to continue. The critical question is which of the various standardized models management should select.

Given the popularity and diversity of the various standardized portfolio models, a critical management question is which of the various standardized portfolio models to select. Using PIMS data for 15 businesses (SBUs) of a Fortune 500 firm, this paper compares the positionings of these businesses on a number of standardized portfolio models. Managerial implications of these results are discussed.

INCREASED COMPLEXITY of the business environment and the multiproduct, multimarket and multinational nature of an increasing number of firms have led management to consider explicitly the need to plan how, when and where to add new products or services, delete any of the existing ones or modify any of them. It has become imperative for companies, big or small, to plan their product offerings and assess the compatibility of the strategy for each individual product with the needs, resources and objectives of the organization. Should we be in this business? What are the company's core products and businesses? How can we win and hold a position of leadership in the marketplace? What new businesses should we be entering? These are the questions imbedded in the product-market planning of many organizations.

In seeking answers to probing questions of product-market planning, many firms view product mix decisions as portfolio decisions. Management's role is thus to determine the products (or businesses) that will comprise the portfolio and to allocate resources among them.[1]

To assist management in determining the desired product (or business) portfolio and allocating resources to different products (or businesses), a number of product portfolio models have been proposed and implemented over the last several years. Examples of these models include the standardized portfolio models (such as the models developed by the Boston Consulting Group, McKinsey, Shell International and A. D. Little) and the customized portfolio models.[2] The standardized portfolio models have been accepted widely, despite some of their obvious limitations and their focus on product/business classification rather than the selection of an optimal portfolio (Day 1977, Larréché and Srinivasan 1981, Wensley 1981). Furthermore, given that the conceptually more attractive customized models are more difficult to implement and require greater top management involvement, dominance of standardized portfolio models is likely to continue. This raises the critical question of which of the various standardized portfolio models management should select.

If the various models yield the same results (in terms of the classification of the businesses and the strategic guidelines for each business), the question is not as critical and the models can be viewed as interchangeable. If on the other hand the same set of products or businesses is classified differently depending on the model used or the specific measures used within a given portfolio model, then the selection of a model becomes critical.

Yoram Wind is Professor of Marketing at The Wharton School, University of Pennsylvania. Vijay Mahajan is Herman W. Lay Professor of Marketing, Cox School of Business, Southern Methodist University. Donald J. Swire is Director of Corporate Planning Programs, Strategic Planning Institute.

FIGURE 1
Outline of Comparisons

I. Within Model Comparisons

A. Different definitions of the dimensions in the Growth-Share Matrix

Market Share Definitions[a] \ Market Growth Definitions[b]	1 Real Market Growth	2 Market Growth	3 Forecast Real Market Growth	4 Forecast Real Short- and Long-Term Market Growth
1. Share of served market	1	2	3	4
2. Share vs. 3 leaders	5	6	7	8
3. Share vs. leader	9	10	11	12
4. Share index (normalized "share of served market" + normalized share vs. 3 leaders')	13	14	15	16

B. Rules for dividing the dimension into "low" and "high" categories
1. Internal rule (sample mean)
2. External rule (mean of all PIMS businesses)

C. Weights of variables in the Shell International Type Matrix
1. Weighted (according to the PIMS PAR ROI model)
2. Unweighted

II. Across Model Comparisons

A. A typical growth share matrix (cell 9 above)

B. A shell International type matrix

C. PAR based indices of business position vs. industry attractiveness (McKinsey/GE Type Matrix)

D. A. D. Little type matrix

[a]Definitions of Market Share
1. Your sales/total sales to served market.
2. Your sales/total sales of Big-3 competitors.
3. Your sales/sales of largest competitor.
4. Normalized market share plus normalized relative market share vs. 3 leaders.

[b]Definitions of Market Growth
1. Average annual growth of served market, 1976–79, adjusted for selling prices.
2. Average annual growth of served market, 1976–79, in current dollars.
3. Company's own forecast of average annual real market growth over next 4 years.
4. Average of company's forecasts for next 4 years and 6 years after that (i.e., approximately a 10-year average growth outlook).

The importance of the measurement aspect of portfolio models is quite evident from the diversity of dimensions and their definitions used in the various approaches. It is quite surprising, however, that most of the portfolio literature has focused on the selling of specific approaches and discussions of the strategic implications of a "dog" or a "cash cow," for example, rather than on the fundamental measurement and validation issues involved.

This paper compares empirically a number of standardized portfolio models. Using the PIMS data[3] for the 15 SBUs of a Fortune 500 firm, the classification of these businesses based on a number of portfolio models are compared. The analyses include both within model comparisons (i.e., comparison of the results obtained from different operational definitions, of the dimensions, rules for dividing each into low and high, and the weights of the dimensions of a given model) and across models (i.e., comparison of the results of classifying the selected businesses based on different portfolio models).

The data used for analyses are briefly discussed next, followed by the actual results. The final section of the paper focuses on some managerial implications.

The Approach

This study is based on data for 15 SBUs of a large Fortune 500 multinational industrial firm. The SBUs included a number of industrial components and commodity type businesses.

A subset of the PIMS data for these SBUs for the period 1976–79 was utilized to construct 16 portfolio matrices corresponding to different definitions of the portfolio dimensions (4 definitions of share and 4 of growth for the BCG type growth/share matrix approach), two rules for dividing the dimensions of growth and share into "low" and "high," two different weighting schemes of the portfolio dimensions (equal weighting of the components constituting the dimensions of the two-array Shell International type matrix vs. empirically derived weighting based on the regression coefficients of these factors in the PIMS Limited Information PAR ROI Model)[4] and different portfolio models (the growth/share matrix vs. the Shell International type matrix vs. par based indices of business position and industry attractiveness vs. an A. D. Little type model).[5] The specific comparisons are summarized in Figure 1.

All the portfolio analyses are based on served market data as defined in the PIMS data. Table 1 provides the mean and standard deviations of the 15 SBUs on the share and growth measures. The relative market share (SBU share/leader) of these businesses ranged from 14.6 to 400 and the real market growth from −4.7% to 24.3%. In addition, 13 out of the 15 SBUs have been identified as mature SBUs by the management (see Figure 2, an A. D. Little type matrix).

Within Model Comparisons

Sixteen Growth-Share Matrices

The first set of within model comparisons involved the analysis of the impact of different definitions of the two portfolio dimensions. As discussed above and summarized in the upper

Table 1
Mean, Standard Deviation and Range of the 15 Businesses on Each of the 4 Share and 4 Growth Dimensions

	Mean	Standard Deviation	Range Min	Range Max
Share Definitions				
Share of served market	30.7	15.71	9.4	68.0
Share vs. 3 leaders	115.3	114.5	11.9	480.9
Share vs. leader	166.6	96.8	14.6	400.0
Share index	1.23	2.2	−1.5	6.9
Growth Definitions				
Real market growth	6.5	6.5	−4.7	24.3
Market growth	13.6	7.4	−4.7	27.4
Forecast real market growth	5.4	2.3	2.4	9.3
Forecast short- and long-term real market growth	5.2	2.0	2.4	9.0

Figure 2
A comparison of four standardized portfolio models

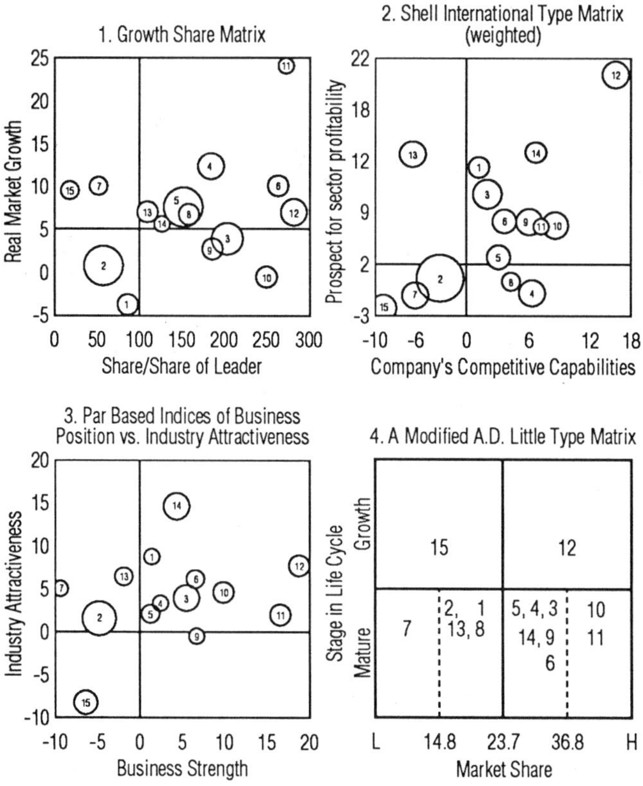

panel of Figure 1, four definitions of share and four definitions of growth were explored. The first question such multiple definitions raise is, 'What is the correlation among these definitions?" If all these measures are highly correlated, obviously portfolio models based on these definitions would not be very different. The average rank order correlation (of the 15 businesses) among the four share definitions is very high—0.92 with a very small standard deviation of 0.04. The average rank order correlation among the four growth definitions is considerably lower—0.34 with a very high standard deviation of 0.40 and with one out of the six correlations being negative. The rank correlations for the specific definitions are summarized in Table 2.

Given that the correlations among the various definitions of growth were not very high, a comparison of the 16 models —all possible combinations of the various definitions—is a meaningful next step. The portfolios based on the 16 models were developed. In order to separate each of the 16 matrices into four quadrants and to classify each of the 15 businesses into one of the resulting four categories (low share/low growth, low share/high growth, high share/low growth and high share/high growth), the mean values of the four share measures and two of the growth measures (real market growth and market growth) based on 2000 businesses in the PIMS data base were used as the cut-off points.[6] For the remaining two growth measures (forecast real market growth and forecast short- and long-term real market growth), the mean values of the sample (see Table 1) were used to separate the quadrants since these values are not available for the PIMS 2000 businesses. The resulting classification is summarized in Table 3. This exhibit is based on the examination of the 16 matrices such as the one presented for illustrative purposes in the upper left comer of Figure 2.

An examination of Table 3 suggests that only three out of the 15 businesses (businesses 2, 11 and 12) are consistently classified in the same category regardless of which model is used. It is further interesting to note that these three cases are classified into the two extreme categories of low share/low growth (category 1) and high share/high growth (category 4). The other 12 businesses can be classified in two or more categories depending on the specific definitions used.

The specific pattern of classification includes (1 = low share/low growth, 2 = low share/high growth, 3 = high share/low growth, and 4 = high share/high growth):

- Eight businesses (3, 4, 5, 6, 7, 9, 10 and 15) were classified in two different categories, depending upon the specific measures used, i.e.

Businesses	*Categories*
7, 15	1, 2
3, 4, 5, 6, 9, 10	3, 4

- Four businesses (1, 8, 13 and 14) were classified in all four categories.
- The number of businesses classified as low share businesses (by the four share definitions) ranged from 4 to 6, while the number of growth businesses (across the four growth measures) ranged from 5 to 9. This latter difference is primarily due to the change from forecasted growth (definitions 3 and 4) to historical growth (definitions 1 and 2).

These results clearly suggest that classification of SBUs in the various portfolio categories are affected by the operational definitions of the variables.

Classifying the Dimensions into "Low" and "High" Categories

The previous analysis of the 16 growth share matrices was based on classification of the businesses into one of the four

Table 2
Rank Order Correlations (of the 15 businesses) Among the Various Definitions of Share and Growth

	1	2	3	4
Correlations Among the Share Definitions				
1. Share of served market	1.00	.85	.91	.92
2. Share vs. 3 leaders		1.00	.93	.97
3. Share vs. leader			1.00	.94
4. Share index				1.00
Correlations Among the Growth Definitions				
1. Real market growth	1.00	.77	.13	.11
2. Market growth		1.00	.01	−.08
3. Forecast real market growth			1.00	.93
5. Forecast short- and long-term real market growth				1.00

Table 3

Classification of the 15 Businesses into 4 Share/Growth Categories Based on the 16 Share/Growth Matrices

The 16 Share/Growth Matrices		Classification of the 15 Businesses*														
		1	2	3	4	5	6	7	8	9	10	11	12	13	14	15
Share of Served Market	1. Real mkt growth (rmg)	2	1	3	4	4	4	2	2	3	3	4	4	2	3	2
	2. Market growth	1	1	4	4	4	4	2	2	4	3	4	4	2	3	1
	3. Forecast rmg	1	1	3	3	3	3	1	1	3	4	4	4	2	4	2
	4. Forecast short- and long-term rmg	1	1	3	3	3	3	1	2	3	4	4	4	1	4	2
Share vs. 3 Leaders	5. rmg	4	1	3	4	4	4	2	4	3	3	4	4	2	1	2
	6. Market growth	3	1	4	4	4	4	2	4	4	3	4	4	2	1	1
	7. Forecast rmg	3	1	3	3	3	3	1	3	3	4	4	4	2	2	2
	8. Forecast short- and long-term rmg	3	1	3	3	3	3	1	4	3	4	4	4	1	2	2
Share vs. Leader	9. rmg	4	1	3	4	4	4	2	4	3	3	4	4	4	1	2
	10. Market growth	3	1	4	4	4	4	2	4	4	3	4	4	4	1	1
	11. Forecast rmg	3	1	3	3	3	3	1	3	3	4	4	4	4	2	2
	12. Forecast short- and long-term rmg	3	1	3	3	3	3	1	4	3	4	4	4	3	2	2
Share Index	13. rmg	4	1	3	4	4	4	2	4	3	3	4	4	2	1	2
	14. Market growth	3	1	4	4	4	4	2	4	4	3	4	4	2	1	1
	15. Forecast rmg	3	1	3	3	3	3	1	3	3	4	4	4	2	2	2
	16. Forecast short- and long-term rmg	3	1	3	3	3	3	1	4	3	4	4	4	1	2	2

Consistent Classification:	3 businesses:	2, 11, 12
Inconsistent Classification:	12 businesses	
1 2 – –	2 businesses:	7, 15
– – 3 4	6 businesses:	3, 4, 5, 6, 9, 10
1 2 3 4	4 businesses:	1, 8, 13, 14

*Key: 1. low share/low growth 2. low share/high growth 3. high share/low growth 4. high share/high growth

categories (of "dogs," "stars," etc.) based on a predominantly external rule (the value for all businesses in the PIMS data base) for dividing the dimensions into low and high categories. An interesting question is whether the resulting classification would be consistent with that derived if an internal criterion (sample mean) is to be used. To answer this question, a comparison was made between the two resulting classification schemes.[7]

The results of this analysis are presented in Table 4. An examination of this exhibit suggests that 9 out of the 15 businesses were classified in the same way by the two approaches, while 6 were misclassified. Since the definition of the cut-off points was biased toward greater agreement (both measures used the sample means for the two forecasted growth measures), the incongruent results are especially alarming, suggesting the need for a careful and conceptually justified determination of the desired cut-off rule.

Weighted and Unweighted Models

The third within model comparison was conducted for the Shell International Type Matrix. The model was formulated with equally weighted dimensions and empirically derived weights. The latter were based on the regression coefficients of the PIMS Limited Information PAR ROI model.[8]

The Shell International Matrix uses two composite dimensions—"Prospects for Sector Profitability" and "Company's Competitive Capabilities." The factors that comprised the dimensions were used by Shell International as the basis for one of their portfolio analyses. These factors are:

Prospects for Sector Profitability

- Industry Growth
- Share of 4 largest firms
- % of Customers = 50% of Sales
- Investment/Sales
- Fixed Capital Intensity
- Vertical Integration
- Value Added per Employee
- Capacity Utilization

Company's Competitive Capabilities

- Market Share
- Relative Market Share
- Relative Quality
- Relative Price
- R&D/Sales
- Marketing/Sales

In assessing the similarity between the two portfolio analyses, the rank order correlations between the positions of the 15 SBUs on each of the 2 dimensions were calculated. In addition, in order to classify the SBUs in various categories, the two matrices were divided into four quadrants by standardizing the values of the SBUs on the two dimensions.[9] (Note that the cut-off points for both dimensions are

Table 4
A Comparison of "External" and "Internal" Cut-Off Points of the Growth and Share Dimensions*

Business I.D. Number	Internal Cut-Off Point (sample mean)	External Cut-Off Point (mostly mean of PIMS businesses)
Consistent Classification		
2	1	1
11	4	4
12	4	4
Inconsistent Classification		
1	1	1, 2, 3, 4
3	1, 3	3, 4
4	3, 4	3, 4
5	1, 2	3, 4
6	3, 4	3, 4
7	1, 2	1, 2
8	1, 2, 3, 4	1, 2, 3, 4
9	1, 2, 3, 4	3, 4
10	3, 4	3, 4
13	1, 2	1, 2, 3, 4
14	1, 2	1, 2, 3, 4
15	1, 2	1, 2

*Key:
1. low share/low growth
2. low share/high growth
3. high share/low growth
4. high share/high growth

zero.) The weighted portfolio matrix is depicted in the upper right panel of Figure 2.

An examination of the resulting two portfolios revealed a number of significant differences in the evaluation of the 15 businesses. The rank correlation between the position of the 15 businesses on each of the 2 dimensions is relatively low: 0.17 for the prospect for sector profitability and 0.43 for the company's competitive capabilities. The rank of each business on the weighted and unweighted factors and the rank difference between the two is presented in Table 5. An examination of the table reveals a substantial range of absolute rank differences with only 2 matched ranks (businesses 6 and 12) on prospects for sector profitability and 4 matched ranks (businesses 1, 2, 5 and 15) on the company's competitive capabilities dimension.

Comparing the classification of the 15 businesses into the 4 categories of low-low (1), low-high (2), high-low (3), and high-high (4) results in the following classifications:

Business	*Weighted*	*Unweighted*
1	4	2
2	1	2
3	4	4
4	3	4
5	4	3
6	4	4
7	1	1
8	3	3
9	4	4
10	4	4
11	4	4
12	4	4
13	2	2
14	4	3
15	1	2

Examination of these results suggest that about half of the businesses were classified in the same way using a weighted and unweighted approach. Yet, seven of the 15 businesses were classified differently depending on whether a weighted or unweighted model was used.

Across Model Comparisons

Ideally the comparison among portfolio models would have included a comparison of the position of the 15 businesses

Table 5
A Comparison of the Shell InternationalType Matrix with Weighted and Unweighted Factors: Rank Order of the 15 Businesses on the 2 Dimensions

Prospect for Sector Profitability				Company's Competitive Capabilities			
Business Unit	Rank of Weighted Factor	Rank of Unweighted Factor	Absolute Rank Difference	Business Unit	Rank on Weighted Factor	Rank on Unweighted Factor	Absolute Rank Difference
1	4	11	7	1	11	11	0
2	11	8	3	2	12	12	0
3	5	10	5	3	10	7	3
4	13	7	6	4	2	1	2
5	10	12	2	5	8	8	0
6	9	9	0	6	7	5	2
7	14	15	1	7	14	13	1
8	12	14	2	8	6	3	3
9	7	5	2	9	5	9	4
10	8	4	4	10	3	2	1
11	6	2	4	11	4	10	6
12	1	1	0	12	1	4	3
13	3	6	3	13	13	14	1
14	2	13	11	14	9	6	3
15	15	3	12	15	15	15	0

on the BCG, Shell International, McKinsey and A. D. Little standardized models. Since we did not have the data and weights to replicate these models, the analysis was confined to a set of similar (but not identical) models. The compared models, as depicted in Figure 2, are:

1. *Growth Share Matrix*

Given that the growth share matrix can result in different business classifications depending on the specific measures used, the matrix used for comparison with the other 3 models is one similar to the BCG type model—share of the business vs. its leading competitor and real market growth (cell 9 in Figure 1).

2. *A Shell International Type Matrix*

As discussed earlier, we constructed a matrix similar to the one used by Shell International. This matrix focuses on "Prospects for Sector Profitability and Company's Competitive Capabilities." The dimensions were defined using eight and six variables from the PIMS data base respectively. When the variables are empirically weighted based on the regression coefficients of the PIMS PAR ROI model, this Shell International Model is the closest we could come to the actual model used by Shell, and it offers a close approximation for this type of model.

3. *Par Based Indices of Business Position vs. Industry Attractiveness*

This model is patterned after the McKinsey/GE type model using PAR ROI factors. The factors considered in the PIMS PAR model have each been identified as belonging to market position or industry attractiveness dimensions:

Market Position

- Market Share Index
  - Market Share
  - Relative Market Share
- Relative Product Quality
- Relative Price
- Relative Direct Cost
- Patents re. Process or Products
- Relative Range of Customer Sizes
- Labor Productivity
- Relative Employee Compensation
- Shared Production Facilities

Industry Attractiveness

- Real Market Growth, Long Run
- Unionization (%)
- New Products (% of Sales)
- Research & Development/Sales
- Selling-Price Growth Rate
- Marketing/Sales
- Purchase Amount by Immed. Cust.
- Percent of All End User's Purchases
- No. Customers = 50% of Sales
- Products Produced to Order?
- Industry Concentration
- Investment Intensity Index
  - Investment/Sales
  - Investment/Value Added
- Capacity Utilization
- Gross Book Value of Plant and Equipment/Investment
- Vertical Integration
- Investment per Employee
- Accounting Convention
- Receivables/Investment
- Raw Materials and Work-in-Process/Value Added

The impact of the factors within each dimension (the product of the term and its coefficient) were summed and reported as an index. Separate indices were developed for each of the two dimensions. To facilitate a comparison to the other models the values of the businesses on the two dimensions were standardized and zero was used as the cut-off value for the four quadrants.

4. *An A. D. Little Type Model*

An A. D. Little type portfolio matrix was developed using the two dimensions of stage in business life cycle and market position. The market position was measured by market share, and in order to classify the SBUs in various cells, this dimension was initially divided into 5 parts by using the 1/5 cut-off points from the PIMS data base. The classification of the 15 businesses on the four levels of business life cycle was done by management. Since management used only two stages (mature and growth) to characterize the life cycle of the 15 businesses, the ADL matrix was collapsed into a 2 × 2 matrix corresponding to low and high share and mature vs. growth businesses. This matrix is presented in the lower right panel of Figure 2.

The Comparison

The 15 businesses were classified according to these four models and the results are depicted in Figure 2. An examination of these matrices suggests considerable differences in the classification of the 15 businesses.

Common to these four models is the reliance on two dimensions representing business strength and industry attractiveness. The first examination of these models was therefore a comparison of the rank order correlation of the 15 businesses on the corresponding dimensions of three of these models. (The A. D. Little model was not included in this analysis since the businesses were assigned judgmentally by management and no continuous scale was available for the life cycle dimension.) The results of this analysis are summarized in Table 6. They suggest very low correlations among the various measures of business strength, ranging from 0.13 to 0.25. The range of correlations for the industry attractiveness dimension is from −0.88 to 0.36 with positive correlation only between prospect for sector profitability and industry attractiveness par based index.

The primary test of the degree of similarity or difference among the four portfolio models is an examination of the

Table 6

Rank Correlation (of the 15 Businesses) Among the 3 Portfolio Models

	1	2	3
Business Strength Dimensions			
1. Share in the share/growth matrix	1.00	.25	.13
2. Company's competitive capabilities		1.00	.24
3. Business position par based index			1.00
Industry attractiveness Dimensions			
1. Real growth in share/growth matrix	1.00	−.88	−.76
2. Prospect for sector profitability		1.00	.36
3. Industry attractiveness par based index			1.00

resulting classification of the 15 businesses into one of four categories: low/low, low/high, high/low and high/high.[10]

The resulting classification is presented in Table 7. An examination of this exhibit suggests that only one business (12) falling into the high/high category was consistently classified in the same category by the four models. The remaining 14 businesses were classified into the following patterns:

Patterns	*Number of Businesses*	*Businesses*
(3) high/low, (4) high/high	7	3, 4, 5, 6, 9, 10, 11
(1) low/low, (2) low/high	3	2, 7, 15
(1) low/low, (3) high/low, (4) high/high	2	8, 14
(1) low/low, (2) low/high, (4) high/high	1	13
(1) low/low, (4) high/high	1	1

Note that three out of the 14 businesses were classified into three different categories depending on the specific model used.

Conclusions

The preceding analysis suggests that when using standardized portfolio models, the classification of any business into a specific portfolio position such as low share and low growth (dog) or a high share and high growth (star) category depends on four specific factors:

- the operational definition of the dimensions used,
- the rule used to divide a dimension into low and high categories,
- the weighting of the variables constituting the composite dimensions, if composite dimensions ire used, and
- the specific portfolio model used.

These findings strongly suggest that a minor change in definition, the rule for determining the cut-off points on the various dimensions, weights of dimensions or the model used could result in a different classification of the businesses involved (and hence in the strategic guidelines for these businesses).[11] In the specific case examined here only one business (12) was consistently classified as a star, or high/high in all matrices regardless of the definitions of the dimension, the cut-off points, weights or underlying models. The classification of the other 14 businesses was quite sensitive to the specific definitions, cut-off points, weights or models used. Hence, any strategic generalizations concerning them is suspect and at best unstable.

It should be acknowledged, however, that the various portfolio models tend to emphasize different portfolio objectives (e.g., management of cash flows in the case of the BCG approach and return on investment in the case of the McKinsey/GE business assessment array) and offer different levels of flexibility to conduct portfolio analysis. Hence, the selection of the appropriate portfolio model would clearly depend upon the portfolio objective of the organization.

Given our results and the proliferation of portfolio models, it might be desirable to avoid using a single portfolio model and instead to integrate the various models to take advantage of their unique capabilities. Such hybrid models would allow management to test the sensitivity of the portfolio classification of businesses to various portfolio objectives, definition of variables and weights (used to develop composite dimensions). Such an approach could reduce the risk involved in employing a single standardized portfolio model as a basis for portfolio analysis and strategy. An integrated approach combining stochastic dominance rules (Mahajan, Wind and Bradford 1982) and a McKinsey/GE portfolio model have already been tested and implemented (Mahajan

Table 7

A Comparison of the Classification of the 15 Businesses Based on the 4 Portfolio Approaches*

	Classification of the 15 Businesses														
Portfolio Models	1	2	3	4	5	6	7	8	9	10	11	12	13	14	15
Growth/share	4	1	3	4	4	4	2	4	3	3	4	4	4	1	2
Pseudo Shell International	4	1	4	3	4	4	1	3	4	4	4	4	2	4	1
Par based indices of business position and attractiveness	4	2	4	4	4	4	2	1	3	4	3	4	2	4	1
A. D. Little	1	1	3	3	3	3	1	1	3	3	3	4	1	3	2

*Key	Business Position	Industry Attractiveness
1.	low	low
2.	low	high
3.	high	low
4.	high	high

and Wind 1983). This application clearly demonstrates the additional insight from an integrated multi-model approach.

Given the sensitivity of an SBU's portfolio position to the operational definition of the dimensions, cut-off points, weighting scheme and the specific model used, the risk is high when employing a single standardized portfolio model as a basis for portfolio analysis and strategy. It further suggests the need to test the sensitivity of the portfolio classification of businesses to various definitions, cut-off rules, weights and models. Carefully examine the pattern of classification of businesses into the various categories and consider the use of multiple models, rather than reliance on a single portfolio model. Following these recommendations would increase the value of portfolio analysis as a sound basis for corporate strategy and may help avoid the current situation (revealed in our analysis) that the same business, depending on which model is used, can be classified as a dog, star, cash cow or problem child.

References

1. Portfolio analysis can be conducted at every level of operations: a portfolio of SBUs at the corporate level, a portfolio of product lines at the SBU level or portfolio of products at the product group level.
2. For an overview and comparison of the standardized and customized portfolio models, see Wind and Mahajan (1981a), Wind (1982).
3. For a brief discussion of the PIMS program, data base and the actual questions, see Abell and Hammond (1979). For a brief critical review of the PIMS philosophy, models, data and results, see Wind and Mahajan (1981b).
4. For a brief description of the PAR ROI model, see Abell and Hammond (1979).
5. In any application of the Shell International and business position/industry attractiveness portfolio models, the weights for the various variables should be determined by management. Since this information was not available to us, any defensible differential weighting scheme could have been used to illustrate the scope of the measurement issues involved. The empirically derived weights in the PIMS PAR ROI model were used purely because of convenience. It is not our intention to endorse the use of such weights as standardized weights for the application of these models.
6. The separation of the matrices into four quadrants should be based on some independent external criteria. In the absence of such criteria, the mean values based on the PIMS data base are used. These values are: share/served market = 23.4; share vs. 3 leaders = 61.85; share/ leader = 100; share index = 0.0; real market growth = 4.11%; and market growth = 11.4%.
7. One should note, however, that as discussed earlier, the "external" classification is not purely external since it includes the internal values for the two forecasted growth measures.
8. These coefficients are proprietary to the member companies of the Strategic Planning Institute and are not reported here.
9. The Shell International Matrix typically contains nine cells. The four-cell approach was used to facilitate the comparison across models in the next section.
10. A statistical test of the degree of similarity/differences between the resulting portfolios would have been desirable. No such test is available yet, but work is underway to develop such a test.
11. Further studies should be undertaken to assess whether the results can be replicated in other companies and to explore the impact of other measurement divisions such as other operational definitions; other cut-off rules, taking into consideration the distribution of the businesses on the selected dimension (note that the current use of a mean ignores the question of whether the results are driven by small (less than 10) variations); other weighting schemes of the variables constituting each driven and different weights for the two divisions (most portfolio models assume equal weight for the two divisions); and other portfolio models such as risk-return based models.

Bibliography

Abell, Derek F. and John S. Hammond (1979), *Strategic Market Planning*, Englewood Cliffs, NJ: Prentice-Hall, Inc.

Day, George S. (1977), "Diagnosing the Product Portfolio," *Journal of Marketing*, 41 (April), 29–38.

Larréché, Jean-Claude and V. Srinivasan (1981), "STRATPORT: A Decision Support System for Strategic Planning," *Journal of Marketing*, 45 (Fall), 39–52.

Mahajan, Vijay and Yoram Wind (1983), "Integrating Financial Portfolio Analysis with Product Portfolio Models," in *Strategic Marketing and Management*, David Gardner and Howard Thomas, eds., New York: John Wiley.

———, ——— and John W. Bradford (1982), "Stochastic Dominance Rules for Product Portfolio Models," *Management Science: Special Studies in Marketing Planning Models*, Andy Zoltners, ed., New York: North-Holland Publishing Company.

Wensley, Robin (1981), "Strategic Marketing: Betas, Boxes or Basics," *Journal of Marketing*, 45 (Summer), 173–182.

Wind, Yoram (1982), *Product Policy: Concepts, Methods and Strategy*, Reading, MA: Addison-Wesley.

——— and Vijay Mahajan (1981a), "Designing Product and Business Portfolios," *Harvard Business Review*, 59 (January–February), 155–65.

——— and ——— (1981b), "Market Share: Concepts, Findings and Directions for Future Research," in *Review of Marketing 1981*, B. Enis and K. Roering, eds., Chicago, IL: American Marketing Association.

The authors would like to acknowledge the financial support of the Center for Marketing Strategy Research of The Wharton School and the helpful comments of an anonymous *JM* reviewer.

27

The International Product-Market Portfolio

Jean-Claude Larréché

This paper examines the potential application to international markets of the product portfolio approach developed by the Boston Consulting Group (BCG). Special attention is given to the limitations of product-market portfolio analysis in the international context.

IN RECENT YEARS, a number of product portfolio models have been proposed to guide the formulation of marketing strategies. The Boston Consulting Group (BCG) approach to product portfolio analysis is certainly the best known of these models. It has already gained wide acceptance among managers as well as academicians, and has been discussed extensively in the literature [2, 5, 8]. Although previous writings have suggested that the BCG approach may be used for the formulation of international marketing strategies, the implications of this particular type of application have not been explicitly considered. The purpose of this paper is to investigate the potential of the product portfolio approach in the formulation of international marketing strategies. In particular, a critical evaluation is made of the additional problems introduced by the consideration of an international as opposed to a domestic environment in the application of the product portfolio approach.

Application of the Product Portfolio to International Markets

The BCG Product Portfolio

The BCG product portfolio analysis centers on two determinants of marketing strategy, market dominance and stage of product life cycle, operationally defined for measurement purposes as relative market share (unit sales of the product divided by units sales of the major competitor) and market growth. Each product in the portfolio is represented on a relative market share-market growth matrix by a circle, the diameter of which is proportional to the sales volume of the product. This matrix gives a convenient and explicit visual representation of the relative contribution of each product to the sales volume, growth, and competitive posture of the firm.

According to their positioning on the relative market share-market growth matrix, products are classified into four categories: "problem children" (low relative market share/high market growth); "stars" (high relative market share/high market growth); "cash cows" (high relative market share/low market growth); and "dogs" (low relative market share/low market growth). Research results on the relationship between market share and profitability, as well as expected competitive behavior over the product life cycle are then used to infer cash inflows and outflows for each of these product categories. "Cash cows" are expected to be cash generators and "problem children" to be cash users, while "stars" and "dogs" should generally break even. To survive in the long-term, the firm needs a balanced portfolio where "cash cows" generate sufficient funds to support "problem children" and "stars," which will eventually become "cash cows" themselves at a later point in time. In this perspective, the objective of the firm's master marketing strategy will result in the allocation of resources among the various entries of the product portfolio, and in the establishment of guidelines for specific product strategies such as: holding (for "cash cows" and "stars"), building (for selected "problem children"), harvesting, divestment, or abandonment (for other "problem children" and "dogs").

Jean-Claude Larréché is a Professor of Marketing at INSEAD, Fontainebleau, France.

Figure 1
Example of the International Product-Market Portfolio

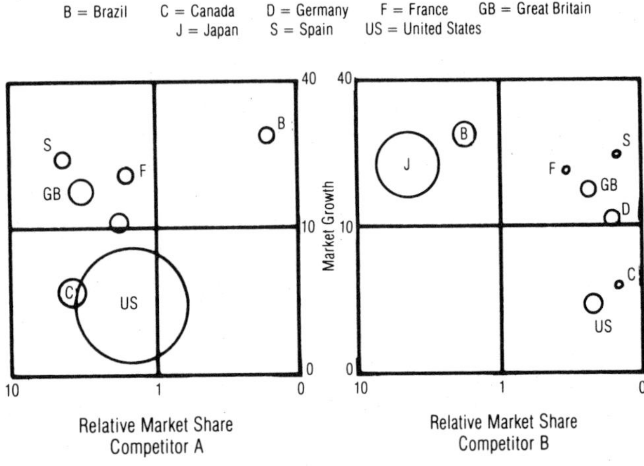

Application to International Markets

Although the expressions "product portfolio" and "business portfolio" are generally used to describe this BCG approach, they are unfortunately misleading. Indeed, the structure of the relative market share-market growth matrix requires that the entries be defined not only in terms of products but also of markets. The definition of these entries is a major difficulty in the practical application of the portfolio and may lead to erroneous conclusions. For instance, a product could be globally evaluated as being a "dog," while it may have the position of a "star" in a developing segment of the market. The portfolio entries should then be defined as product-market domains and the BCG approach should more appropriately be termed the product-market portfolio.

There is obviously no clear-cut solution to the selection of a disaggregation level in the definition of portfolio entries. Splitting a product into several product-market entries may clarify some strategic issues and isolate varying growth rates, competitive structures, and emerging trends in different segments. These entries will no longer be independent as they rely on common technology, production, and hence experience effects. This is certainly one of the reasons why portfolio entries in a domestic context have traditionally been defined in terms of products or businesses rather than product-markets.

On the other hand, in international applications of the product portfolio, significant differences between countries in terms of market growth and market structures will generally lead to the consideration of multiple market entries for a given product. To illustrate the particularities inherent in the application of the product-market portfolio in an international as opposed to a domestic environment, we will concentrate here on the case of a given product with markets in different countries.

Figure 1 represents the product-market portfolio of two competitors, A and B, marketing the same product (or product line) in several countries. Competitor A is a market leader in most countries it operates in. Its largest sales volume comes from the United States, a mature market, where it only has a small market share advantage compared to its closest competitor. Its market dominance is stronger in Canada, also a mature market, and in European countries which are still at a high growth stage. In Brazil, however, the firm has not succeeded in gaining a substantial market share. In terms of the product-market portfolio, the firm has two "cash cows" (U.S. and Canada), four "stars" (Germany, Great Britain, France, Spain) and one "problem child" (Brazil). It should certainly consider diverting some of its revenues from North America to sustain its share of the European countries, to invest heavily in Brazil and possibly in new markets to provide for future growth. A closer look at the product-market portfolio of competitors will, however, provide a more threatening picture of the situation. The total unit sales volume of competitor B is smaller than that of competitor A. Its weak position in the North American and European markets does not represent an immediate danger, but it clearly dominates two fast-growing and potentially large markets. It is thus conceivable that competitor B will eventually generate total unit sales exceeding those of competitor A, and will be able to benefit from lower costs through greater experience effects. This cost advantage may place competitor B in a position to gain shares in mature markets (U.S. and Canada) which may have previously appeared safe from any major competitive disturbance. If competitor A does not take any drastic remedial action, a probable picture of the situation five years hence is represented in Figure 2.

This example is indeed representative of the evolution of international competition, in several industries as varied as ball bearings, color TV, shipbuilding, or motorcycles [13, 15]. If competitor A does not perform a product-market portfolio analysis, or limits the analysis to its domestic environment, it will consider its product as a "cash cow" which can easily be protected because of the dominant situation and the cost advantages that it enjoys on the home market.

Figure 2
Example of the International Product-Market Portfolio Five-Year Predictions

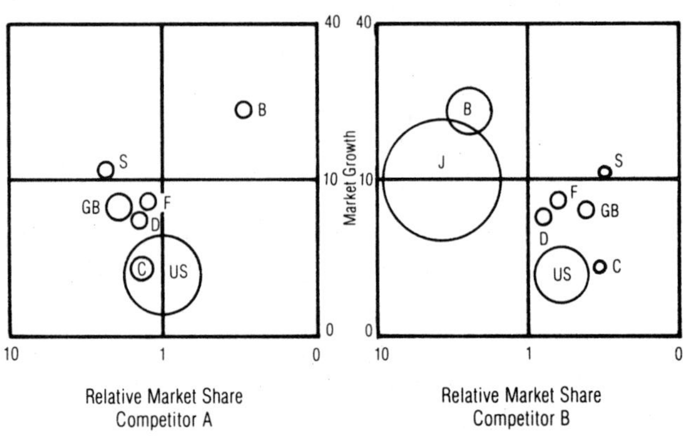

As a matter of fact, the same conclusions will be reached if the analysis is performed globally for the world market, because of the disproportionate importance of the U.S. market at this point in time. Only a detailed product-market portfolio analysis with international markets as entries will give a correct picture of the competitive situation. As illustrated above, the procedure should consider three successive steps:

1. an analysis of the firm's current international product-market portfolio,
2. an analysis of the main competitors' current international product-market portfolios,
3. a projection of the firm's and competitors' future international product-market portfolios.

Such applications of the international product-market portfolio may be particularly helpful for the formulation of a marketing strategy and the allocation of marketing resources across international markets. In the above example, a possible course of action would be to capitalize on the resources and cost advantages stemming from the U.S. market to build market share in Japan, Brazil, and possibly other high growth markets. This would ensure future international growth, but would also protect the "cash cow" position in the North American market by keeping a long-term cost advantage compared to competitor B.

Benefits from Applications of the International Product-Market Portfolio

More generally, there are four main advantages which may be derived from international product-market portfolio analysis:

1. *A global view of the international competitive structure.* The international product-market portfolio analysis provides a clear picture of the current competitive situation and of its evolution in the future. Competitive positions which are thought to be dominant and secure when the analysis is limited to a single country (or a restricted group of countries representing, for instance, the market "served" by a firm) may in fact appear to be threatened in the long term when considering the growth and structure of other international markets.
2. *A guide for the formulation of a global international marketing strategy.* By considering international markets as basic investment units, generators or users of cash, the international product-market portfolio approach places the emphasis on the strategic issue of allocating scarce resources between these investment units in order to attain a stable long-term growth in sales and profits. It provides a framework for analyzing the long-term market opportunities, competitive threats, and the flow of resources which have to be considered in the formulation of this global marketing strategy. It thus centers on the longer term and more strategic aspects which have traditionally been neglected in conceptual or empirical research in international marketing. For instance, the issue of standardization-vs-adaptation of marketing policies [3, 10, 17] or the analysis of differences between international markets [6, 12] have been more concerned with the formulation of the marketing mix in different countries. In addition, the international product-market portfolio analysis provides an opportunity to build on other research areas such as those concerning the clustering of world markets [9, 16] or the international product life cycle [13, 20].
3. *A guide for the formulation of marketing objectives for specific international markets.* Without prejudging the respective values of centralized and decentralized organizations in international marketing, imposed or self-assigned marketing objectives for specific international markets may be dysfunctional if the role of each market within the global marketing strategy is not well understood [14]. In some fast growing markets, management may limit expansion because of limited cash resources or in order to show profits which are more in line with company "norms." In other countries the high levels of cash generated by a mature product may be spent on extensive promotional or product differentiation programs to try and generate some growth. Elsewhere, management may try to keep a small market share product alive in a mature market through expensive price cutting.

   The product-market portfolio analysis helps to determine the primary role of each specific market in the international context. This role may, for instance, be to generate cash, to provide growth, to contribute to production volume, or to block the expansion of competition. Once this role has been defined, objectives can be determined for each specific market to ensure that country marketing strategies are consistent with the global marketing strategy.
4. *A convenient visual communication goal.* There is no doubt that part of the success of the BCG portfolio approach among practitioners and academicians is due to the convenient graphical representation that it provides. The relative market share-market growth matrix allows the integration of a substantial amount of information in a concise, visual way and this advantage is obviously also valid for international applications.

Limitations of the International Product-Market Portfolio

In an excellent article, George Day [5] has investigated the main limitations of the product-market portfolio approach, including: the problem of defining products and markets, and consequently measuring market growth and market share; the use of market share dominance as a proxy for relative profit performance; the assumption that shares tend to stabilize during the maturity stage; the emphasis placed on cash flows; and finally, the problem of implementing strategies derived from the analysis.

Obviously, most of these limitations are equally valid here, but we will primarily discuss the problems more specifically associated with the application of the product-market portfolio to international markets, in terms of four main assumptions underlying this approach:

- the expected patterns of competitive behavior
- the relationship between market share and profitability
- the independence of product-market portfolio entries
- the consideration of cash flow generation as the ultimate marketing objective.

International Competitive Behavior

This product-market portfolio approach relies to a large extent on expected patterns of competitive behavior over the product life-cycle. It basically assumes that market share gains are easier to realize in the growth stage than in the maturity stage. This is reinforced by the consideration of experience effects which should give a cost advantage to the market leader in the maturity stage. Heavy marketing investments should thus be expected in the growth stage, while in the maturity stage neither the market leader nor its competitors would benefit from aggressive action which would primarily lower the profit volume.

This pattern of competitive behavior is based on the following three assumptions:

1. Cost differences between competitors come uniquely from differences in experience.
2. Differences in experience effects between competitors in a given product-market entry depend uniquely on their respective cumulative production in this entry, and can hence be inferred from their relative market shares.
3. The management teams of competing firms share common social and financial responsibilities which impose some boundaries on the realm of acceptable managerial practices.

In the international context, these assumptions lose much of the validity that they may have in a closed economy. Differences in wages, sources of supplies, inflation, exchange rates, tariffs, transport, and government subsidies may have a considerable effect on competitive cost advantages. The relative market share of competitors in a given country may be affected by sales volume in other international markets. Finally, a firm may often encounter competitors in world markets who do not obey the same managerial principles as it does. This firm may be used to dealing, in its domestic market, with competitors who have, for instance, similar pressures for profits from their shareholders, similar requirements on capital structure imposed by financial institutions, and similar flexibility to dispose of the labor force in hard times. In addition, because of the educational system, historical practices, and managerial mobility, these national competitors may have similar philosophies. On the other hand, the firm's competitors in international markets may have shareholders who favor capital gains and long-term returns over short-term dividends; they may obtain a higher capital leverage from their bankers; they may have stronger pressures to keep their labor force and hence to maintain production volume, even if this is to the detriment of profits; they may be less concerned with profits than with national prestige or the collection of foreign currencies; finally, their management may come from different educational, managerial, and cultural traditions. The successive domination of some European markets by American firms, then of some Western markets by Japanese firms can, indeed, partly be attributed to a misunderstanding by local manufacturers of the competitive behavior of the new entrants.

Market Share and Profitability in International Markets

The BCG product portfolio approach assumes that market dominance, as measured by relative market share, is associated with high profitability. When considering a specific product, this assumption is supported by the existence of experience effects which have been found to reduce total unit production costs by 20 to 30 percent every time cumulative production is doubled, in various industries [7]. A strong relationship between market share and return on investment has also been found across a wide range of consumer and industrial goods in the PIMS project [4]. This evidence indicates that (a) for a given product, competitors with high market shares should have a higher profitability than competitors with low market shares, and (b) a given firm is expected to have a higher profitability on products which have a high market share than for products which have a low market share. This double association between market share and profitability, across products and across competing firms, is one of the main elements to guide the allocation of resources in the product portfolio approach.

There is, however, no empirical evidence yet of an association between market share and profitability across international markets. Obviously, some of the traditional arguments such as market power and economies of scale in marketing operations may still be valid in the international context. However, there may also be a number of reasons why a firm may experience a lower level of profitability in a country where it has a higher market share than in other international markets. Differences in cost arising from disparities in wages, sources of supplies, inflation, exchange rates, tariffs, transport, and government subsidies have already been mentioned. Discrepancies in the efficiency of elements of the marketing system, such as distribution channels or advertising media, may also have an impact on profitability. Because of cultural or income differences, the same product may be addressed to different consumer segments in different countries. Finally, the same product may command different price levels in different countries. Even within the EEC, despite the abolition of tariff barriers, Andrienssens has observed price differences close to 100 percent for some consumer goods such as vacuum cleaners and basic food products [1].

Interdependence of International Markets

The product-market portfolio assumes independence of the entries considered, the only link between these entries being their generation and use of a common resource: cash. In particular, there should not be any cost nor demand cross-elasticities between product-market entries. In this way, the decision concerning a single entry, such as the divestment of a "dog," should have no impact on the competitive situation of other entries.

For the international product-market portfolio, this assumption will generally not be tenable, as the entries represent the position of the same product in different world markets. On the cost side, the sales in one market may affect the situation in other international markets, inasmuch as they contribute to total production volume, and hence to experience effects. Depending on the importance of experience effects, transport costs, production adaptations, and restrictions to competition, the degree of cost interdependence may vary considerably. This raises the basic issue of the relative importance to be given to market shares in individual international markets and to world market share. While the product-market portfolio places the emphasis on the market share of specific entries, world market share is certainly a major determinant of international marketing strategy for some products, such as in the case of the motorcycle industry [18]. The trends towards freer international trade and more efficient freight transport play in favor of an increasing interdependence of international markets and a greater importance of world market share.

There are additional reasons on the demand side for interdependence of international markets. Consumer migrations and overlapping of advertising media between countries certainly place constraints on the flexibility that one may have in the implementation of different marketing strategies in different world markets [1]. In addition, disparities in the pricing policy for the same product in various countries may result in the creation by distribution of an uncontrolled secondary trade between these countries. A cursory analysis of the international product-market portfolio could thus lead to marketing strategies in specific world markets which are not implementable or dysfunctional from a global perspective.

Marketing Objectives in International Markets

Present or future generation of cash is considered as the ultimate marketing objective of individual entries in the product-market portfolio. There are, however, other objectives which may be pursued in allocating marketing resources in various international markets. One objective may be the gathering of strategic information about the evolution of consumer needs, competitive moves, or technological developments in leading markets. In an analysis of companies in five industries, Leroy [11] has demonstrated that different product innovations occur in different countries, and that there are clear advantages for a firm to be present in these markets, as in the case of Gillette for disposable lighters. In the car industry, experience in front-wheel drive technology was gained in Europe by Ford and Chrysler before being exploited in the U.S. market.

Another objective in entering a market may be to prevent competition from gaining cost advantages because of unchallenged world expansion, and thus indirectly to protect other international markets. Finally, the development of a good relationship with local government may be a primary marketing objective. It may lead to some specific actions such as keeping a product which does not meet the firm's profitability norms, product adaptations, local production facilities, or exports to a country which was not considered in the international marketing strategy of the firm, as in the case of Ford which accepted to deliver cars from Argentina to Cuba, following a desideratum expressed by the Argentinean government. In all these instances, it is clear that the consideration of a wide range of objectives results in different marketing strategies to those which would have been generated by an analysis of the international product-market portfolio.

Conclusion

The product portfolio approach developed by the BCG provides a new tool for the analysis of international marketing strategies. This approach has a number of advantages, the main one being an integrative representation of the current and projected international competitive posture of the firm. There are also a number of limitations to the application of this approach: international competitive behavior does not always follow the same rules as in the firm's domestic market; the relationship between market share and profitability may be blurred by a number of factors in an international environment; the international markets considered as entries in the portfolio are frequently not independent; finally, marketing strategies in international markets should often consider other objectives than short-term or long-term generation of cash.

These limitations do not affect the usefulness of the international product-market approach as a tool for analysis. Indeed, this approach will generally single out issues which may otherwise have gone unnoticed. The main danger of these limitations is that conclusions may be drawn too hastily in the formulation of marketing strategies. In particular, the implicit association is made in the BCG product portfolio approach between the classification of products as "dogs," "problem children," "stars," and "cash cows," and desirable strategies such as "liquidation," "disinvestment," "investment," "maintenance," and "milking," which may lead to erroneous, undesirable, or unrealistic actions.

As adapted now from the BCG developments, the international product-market portfolio is of greatest value as a tool for analysis. In this domain, it may even present greater potential for analytical developments than applications of the product portfolio to domestic markets, as it can build on other concepts which have been well documented, such as the international product life cycle or the clustering of world markets. It should not, however, be used for the design of international marketing strategies without considering other international factors.

References

1. Andrienssens, J. E., "Les Conséquences de l'intégration économique européenne pour le marketing des Entreprises," *Revue Francaise du Marketing*, 47, (2ème trimestre, 1973), pp. 81–114.
2. Boyd Jr., H. W. and Larréché, J. C., "The Foundations of Marketing Strategy," in G. Zaltman and T. V. Bonoma, eds., *Review of Marketing 1978*, (Chicago: American Marketing Association, 1978), pp. 41–72.
3. Buzzell, R. D.,"Can You Standardize Multinational Marketing?" *Harvard Business Review*, 46:6 (November–December 1968). pp. 102–113.
4. ———, Gale, B. T., and Sultan, R. G. M., "Market Share—A Key to Profitability," *Harvard Business Review*, 53 (January–February 1975), pp. 97–106.
5. Day, G. S.,"Diagnosing the Product Portfolio," *Journal of Marketing*, 41:2 (April 1977), pp. 29–38.
6. Douglas, S. P. and Wind, Y., "Environmental Factors and Marketing Practices," *European Journal of Marketing*, 7:3 (1973), pp. 155–165.
7. Hedley, B., "A Fundamental Approach to Strategy Development," *Long Range Planning*, 9:6 (December 1976), pp. 2–11.
8. ———. "Strategy and the Business Portfolio," *Long Range Planning*, 10:1 (February 1977), pp. 9–15.
9. Jaffe, E. D., *Grouping: A Strategy for International Marketing* (New York: American Management Association, 1974).
10. Keegan, W. G., "Multinational Product Planning: Strategic Alternatives," *Journal of Marketing*, 33:1 (January 1969), pp. 58–62.
11. Leroy, G., *Multinational Product Strategy* (New York: Praeger, 1976).
12. Moyer, R., "International Market Analysis," *Journal of Marketing Research*, 5:4 (November 1968), pp. 353–360.
13. Rapp, W. V., "Strategy Formulation and International Competition," *Columbia Journal of World Business*, 8 (Summer 1973), pp. 98–112.
14. Robbins, S. M. and Stobaugh, R. B., "The Bent Measuring Stick for Foreign Subsidiaries," *Harvard Business Review*, 51:5 (September–October 1973), pp. 80–88.
15. Rose, S., "The Secret of Japan's Export Prowess," *Fortune* (January 30, 1978), pp. 56–63.
16. Sethi, S., "Comparative Cluster Analysis for World Markets," *Journal of Marketing Research*, 8:3 (August 1971), pp. 348–354.
17. Sorenson, R. Z. and Wiechman, U. G., "How Multinationals View Marketing Standardization," *Harvard Business Review*, 53:3 (1975), 38ff.
18. "Strategy Alternatives for the British Motorcycle Industry," a report prepared for the Secretary of State for Industry by the Boston Consulting Group Limited (London: HMSO, 1975).
19. de la Torre, J., "Product Life Cycle as a Determinant of Global Marketing Strategies," in T. V. Greer, ed., *1973 Combined Proceedings* (Chicago: American Marketing Association), pp. 76–82.
20. Wells, Jr., L. T., "A Product Life Cycle for International Trade," *Journal of Marketing*, 32:3 (July 1968), pp. 1–6.

28

The Role of Risk in Explaining Differences in Profitability

David A. Aaker & Robert Jacobson

This study examined the role of risk in explaining cross-sectional differences in the profitability of business units.

Applying suggestions of financial theory, we disaggregated risk into two components—systematic and unsystematic—that are thought to have different effects on return. Drawing on the PIMS data base, we found each component of risk to have a substantial, significant, and different impact on return on investment (ROI). The research and strategy implications of the roles of risk are discussed.

THE TWO KEY FACTORS in any investment decision are return and risk. Under the assumption that investors are risk-averse and seek to minimize the risk for any level of expected return, intuition suggests that additional return must compensate investors for assuming additional risk. Scholars in finance and other disciplines have devoted a great deal of work to refining and formalizing this intuition.

This same logic applies in the context of strategy, as Wensley (1981), Bettis and Mahajan (1985), and others have observed. A strategic investment decision should explicitly consider risk—decision makers should demand a higher return for an investment involving high risk. Yet, in typical practice, strategic investment decisions are adjusted for risk ad hoc, if at all. Firms typically set relatively high hurdle rates in making go/no go investment decisions and apply these rates to all investments, regardless of their riskiness (Hayes & Gavin, 1982). Further, historical evaluation of existing strategies, whether it concerns evaluating present management or attempting to place values on businesses to be divested or acquired, focuses almost exclusively on return and rarely attempts to quantify risk,

These failures to account for risk adequately will unquestionably lead to inappropriate decisions. All else being equal, if firms judge business performance only in terms of return, regardless of risk, they will place more resources than warranted in risky strategies, forgo profitable opportunities, and apply misguided performance evaluations. Further, if researchers do not control for risk in studies assessing the effects of strategic factors on profitability, they will obtain biased estimates of the effects on return of those strategic factors correlated with risk.

Although a number of data bases have been specifically constructed to analyze the determinants of the profitability of business units, empirical work investigating differences in profitability has all but ignored the possible role of risk. The numerous studies that use the Profit Impact of Market Strategies (PIMS) data base of the Strategic Planning Institute have focused on factors such as market share, product quality, and marketing efforts as determinants of profitability, to the exclusion of risk (Branch, 1980; Schoeffler, Buzzell, & Heany, 1974). Similarly, the many studies using the Line of Business data base of the Federal Trade Commission have neglected risk, focusing instead on market structure variables (Ravenscraft, 1983; Schmalensee, 1985). Both sets of studies implicitly assume that risk is not an important determinant of profitability or that strategic and public policy decision making can largely ignore it.

The few empirical studies that have looked at the association between return and risk in firms, as measured by

David A. Aaker is the J. Gary Shansby Professor of Marketing Strategy at the University of California at Berkeley. Robert Jacobson is an Associate Professor of Marketing at the University of Washington.

standard deviation or variance in accounting ROI, have produced inconsistent conclusions. Cardozo and Smith (1983) found a positive correlation of .67 between annual ROI and the standard deviation in accounting ROI. Fisher and Hall (1969) also found a positive and significant, though small, association. Others (Bettis & Mahajan, 1985; Stigler, 1963) found no statistically significant association. Shepherd (1972) reported a negative, though insignificant, association, and Bowman (1980) found a significant negative association between risk and return.

A major limitation in all these studies is their use of variation in ROI as the measure of risk, a practice that ignores financial theory. The Capital Asset Pricing Model (CAPM) (Lintner, 1965; Sharpe, 1964) separates risk into two components: (1) systematic risk, that part of variation in return caused by economy-wide disturbances affecting all investments, and (2) unsystematic risk, variation in return not associated with economy-wide conditions. According to the CAPM, these two different types of risk have different effects on return, and investors receive compensation only for systematic risk because they can eliminate unsystematic risk simply by holding diversified portfolios.

Many research efforts assessing the influence of risk on return have based their analyses on the CAPM financial theory, but they have not made this fundamental and crucial distinction between systematic and unsystematic risk. By using a measure of total risk, investigators are likely to misinterpret both empirically and conceptually the role of risk in influencing return.

This study attempted to assess the importance of risk in explaining differences in profitability between strategic business units. We partitioned risk into the two components hypothesized by the CAPM to have different effects on return. Using the PIMS data base, we found systematic and unsystematic risk to have substantial, significant, and different effects on the profitability of firms.

Systematic Versus Unsystematic Risk

The Capital Asset Pricing Model

The CAPM postulates that only systematic risk, that variation in an investment's return associated with the economy-wide or market return,[1] is relevant. This model depicts the expected return on an investment as equal to the rate of return on a risk-free asset plus a factor, beta, reflecting the systematic risk of the investment, times the expected value of the difference between the market-return and the risk-free return:

$$E(R_{jt}) = R_{ft} + \beta_j \times E(R_{mt} - R_{ft}), \qquad (1)$$

where R_{jt} = return on asset j at time t, R_{ft} = return on a risk-free asset at time t, R_{mt} = return on a market portfolio at time t, and β_j = a factor reflecting the association of the return on asset j with the market return.

Hundreds of studies using stock market data have assessed the validity of the CAPM by testing its implications. Two primary implications of the model are that (1) a positive linear relationship exists between return and systematic risk, as measured by beta, with a slope equal to average risk premium and a zero intercept, and (2) no association exists between return and unsystematic risk. The consensus from these studies is that the CAPM adequately, although imperfectly, describes the association between risk and return.[2]

Unsystematic Risk in a Strategic Context

The CAPM's logic directly applies to the evaluation of a business or project (Van Horne, 1980). The appropriate discount rate to use in discounted present-value analysis depends on a project's systematic risk (beta) and is independent of its unsystematic risk. When differences in profitability are evaluated, businesses with high betas will need to compensate for additional risk by showing higher average rates of return, as indicated by Equation 1, than businesses with low betas.

The CAPM implies that unsystematic risk should not influence managers' decisions. However, some of this theory's assumptions and conditions, although perhaps valid in the context of the stock market, may be inappropriate in a strategic context. It is useful to examine these assumptions and rationales as to why unsystematic risk should not influence strategic decisions.

One assumption that may be inappropriate to strategy is that investors are price takers (Devinney, Stewart, & Shocker, 1985) who can invest as much or as little as they like and receive comparable returns. However, there are usually strategically optimal levels of investment, and using portfolio diversification as the criterion for setting a level of investment is usually not feasible.

Another assumption of the CAPM is that insolvency or bankruptcy cost nothing and that a business can sell its assets at their economic value. However, if an SBU fails, it may have to sell assets at distress prices far below their market value because of legal fees, expensive delays, costly service obligations, or a premature collapse of sales. Thus, investors may need additional return to compensate for costs associated with business failure if they are to assume unsystematic risk.

One of modern financial theory's most important implications for managers—who are assumed to act as agents for shareholders—is that diversification, or the reduction of unsystematic risk, should not in itself be a goal of management. It is easier and less costly for an investor to diversify by buying a portfolio of stocks than for a firm to diversify by buying a portfolio of companies. Diversification strategies undertaken by management only benefit investors to the extent that these strategies have synergistic value.

However, there are incentives for managers to reduce unsystematic risk by diversification or other strategic choices. Bonuses, and perhaps even job security, may depend on avoiding some consequences of unsystematic risk. It is reasonable to assume that managers are risk-averse individuals who invest significant human capital in specific businesses; thus, they are concerned about the total variability in the value of their SBUs, including that portion of variance that investors of capital can eliminate by holding diversified portfolios of investments.

Some talented managers may avoid firms where unsystematic risk, and thereby career risk, is high. To the extent that reduction of unsystematic risk may increase the quality of management, it may be an appropriate consideration for investors.

It might be argued that managers receive incentives, such as golden parachutes, that eliminate some of the adverse consequences of unsystematic risk and encourage them to act as agents for shareholders. However, such devices typically affect only a few very top executives, and in many cases managers have deemed them inadequate compensation. In addition, the recent high level of merger and antimerger activity suggests that managers have not put agency theory completely into practice. A second option, which 3M and some other firms employ as a matter of policy, is to tolerate failure associated with unsystematic risk by guaranteeing that the failure of an enterprise need not adversely affect careers. The most common policy, however, places the burden of unsystematic risk on managers. Thus, they should be expected to consider unsystematic risk important and may take actions that create an association between unsystematic risk and return.

Hackett (1985) commented that it is unrealistic to assume that managers are merely agents for shareholders. Instead, managers attempt to reconcile the interests of all stakeholders —labor, suppliers, customers, and communities in which their businesses operate, including those furnishing economic resources. Like managers, these stakeholders have limited ability to compensate for unsystematic risk through diversification, and protecting them provides an additional incentive for managers to avoid consequences of unsystematic risk. Doing so is likely to create a positive association between unsystematic risk and return.

Modeling the Role of Risk in Strategic Contexts

The notion of risk aversion implies that a positive association will exist between risk and return. According to the CAPM, the different elements of risk—systematic and unsystematic —have different influences on return, and only systematic risk influences return on stocks. However, in the context of strategic decision making, it is consistent with this model to expect unsystematic risk to also affect return. These considerations give rise to two central null hypotheses concerning the effects of risk on the profitability of businesses:

Hypothesis 1: Systematic risk does not influence return.

Hypothesis 2: Unsystematic risk does not influence return.

Designers of models of SBUs' profitability that do not incorporate measures of risk assume implicitly that both of these hypotheses are appropriate. Strict adherence to the CAPM requires rejection of Hypothesis 1 and acceptance of Hypothesis 2. Advocates of models with measures of total risk assume that both hypotheses can be rejected and that the effects of systematic and unsystematic risk on return do not differ. Our discussion of risk in strategic contexts also suggests that both hypotheses can be rejected. However, we expect systematic risk to have the greater impact on return, because firms can to some extent eliminate the effects of unsystematic risk through diversification and various compensations for managers.

The literature has paid increased attention to the applicability —or lack of applicability—of financial theory to strategy (Bettis, 1983), but no one appears to have tested the analysis we propose in a strategic context at either a corporate or SBU level. Certainly, a great many conceptual and empirical problems exist in applying financial theory to SBUs. However, the payoff of modeling the role of different types of risk in influencing return is high. Such modeling can provide insights and guidance to managers and strategic theorists who would like to introduce risk into the assessment of business performance more formally. Further, to the extent that risk is important in explaining return, including it in profitability models reduces the likelihood of omitted variable bias affecting the estimated effects of other variables thought to influence return.

Methods

Source of Data

For a vast number of strategic decisions, analysis based on the aggregate of business units composing a corporation is highly inappropriate. Differences in such central factors as product offerings, competitive environments, and managerial expertise make for a heterogeneity among business units within firms that more often than not mandates separate decision making and analysis for each SBU. The motivation behind both the PIMS data base of the Strategic Planning Institute and the Line of Business data base of the Federal Trade Commission was the realization that corporate data were too highly aggregated to offer the necessary basis for analysis of SBUs.

Of the two, the PIMS data base offers the better opportunity to look at the trade-offs between risk and return at the SBU level because it contains time series information for a longer period than the Line of Business data base covers.[3] Reports of over 2,000 SBUs that are components of the more than 200 participating corporations are the basis of the PIMS data. The PIMS project defines an SBU as a business unit within a firm selling a distinct set of products to an identifiable set of customers in competition with a well-defined set of competitors (Strategic Planning Institute, 1980). Businesses use a standardized form to report information on their strategies and market environments, as well as items from annual balance sheets and income statements. Because the data are kept confidential and participants use the data base, they are motivated to be accurate and conscientious when supplying information. Established SBUs from large firms are overrepresented; very few small firms and new businesses participate in the project. All businesses in the PIMS data base having 5 to 13 annual data points were included in this study; after applying this criterion, 1,376 businesses remained for study.

Estimating the Systematic Risk of SBUs

Stock price data. In order to test risk's influence on return, we required an estimate of beta for each business. Estimates of beta based on stock price data, reflecting the variation between a stock's return and the return to the market as a whole, are widely available, However, corporations typically include many different business units and divisions, perhaps operating in drastically different environments. It would be extravagant to assume that firms have homogeneous risk and to use their stock price betas as estimates of risk for individual business units. Also, data on stock prices may not be pertinent in strategic decisions. The concept of efficient markets implies that stock prices will react only to unanticipated shocks, as prices will already reflect the influence of anticipated events. Conditions influencing firms' rates of return thus may not constantly influence stock return, although in the long run profitability and stock return should be associated.

One approach to obtaining an estimate of an SBU's beta that would reflect its systematic risk better than its firm's stock price does would be to average the stock price betas of firms engaged in a similar line of business. Another would be to simply make a judgment as to the business' correlation with the economy-wide return. Both methods can be criticized, especially in an empirical context, as having a large potential for error and subjectivity.

Accounting data. Alternatively, accounting data can provide an estimate of beta for an individual SBU. Using accounting ROI as the relevant measure of return, an accounting beta can be calculated by comparing a business unit's ROI with the economy-wide ROI. Although it seems the most objective and reliable option, this approach also has potentially serious problems.

Despite its widespread use in practice, scholars have extensively criticized ROI as being a totally inadequate indicator of rate of return (Fisher & McGowan, 1983; Harcourt, 1965; Solomon, 1971). ROI does not properly relate a stream of profits to the investment that produced it. Its earnings numerator is a consequence of investment decisions made in the past, but its assets denominator can be expected not only to have influenced past and current earnings, but also to influence future earnings. Because ROI provides an inaccurate mapping, critics have said it is so seriously flawed as to bear little, if any, resemblance to the underlying concept of internal or economic rate of return (Fisher & McGowan, 1983). This possible invalidity would adversely influence an empirical investigation of the association between risk and return that used accounting ROI both as a dependent variable and as the basis for estimating beta.

Two factors suggest that there might, however, be some validity in the use of accounting ROI to assess risk's role. First, using data from the University of Chicago's Center for Research in Security Prices and from Standard and Poor's COMPUSTAT® for 241 firms over the period 1963–82, Jacobson (1987) found a significant association between annual accounting ROI and a well-accepted measure of economic return, stock return. Although the relatively small correlation of 0.14 indicated that the market also uses much other information, it does seem to use information concerning profitability that ROI to some extent depicts. Surprisingly, given the conceptual problems with ROI as a measure, Jacobson could not reject the hypothesis that there is a unit correspondence between ROI and stock return.[4] Cross-sectional analysis also yielded this association. Thus, ROI does contain information that is associated with differences in profitability between firms. Second, a number of studies have found a correlation between stock price beta and accounting beta (Beaver & Manegold, 1975). Although the extent of the association seems to depend on the accounting measure used as an indicator of return and the time period under study (Hill & Stone, 1980), almost all studies have tended to find a positive association.

The fact that associations seem to exist between ROI and stock return and between accounting and stock price beta suggested to us that by using accounting data we might obtain insights into the trade-off between risk and return at the SBU level, However, several empirical considerations made it unlikely that we would find the associations the CAPM implies, or even those found in tests of the CAPM based on stock price data.

Empirical limitations. The notion that risk is an exogenous factor influencing return may be especially inappropriate in a strategic context (Bettis, 1982). Risk, which is likely to be influenced by strategic management decisions—as is return—should be considered an endogenous variable in a larger system of equations. For example, a firm's promotional expenditures might reduce its beta by stimulating sales and ROI in periods of weak demand, Further, ROI may in turn influence promotional expenditures, thus creating a simultaneity between return and beta that, uncaptured in a least-squares regression, would bias results. However, the systematic risk of a business to a large extent depends on the nature of the business itself. The ability of management to influence beta and any resulting potential for simultaneity bias may well be small.

The measurement error in accounting ROI as an indicator of economic return will lead to a downward bias in estimates of beta's effects on ROI. Measurement error in the dependent variable, ROI, will still allow for an unbiased coefficient estimate of such effects, although variance in the coefficient estimate will increase. However, measurement error in accounting beta, the independent variable, will produce a coefficient estimate of systematic risk that is biased toward zero.

In this study, measurement error in estimates of beta may arise from two main sources. First, the beta measures

Table 1
Descriptive Statistics for Return and Risk

Variables	All Businesses	Consumer Goods Businesses	Capital Goods Businesses	Materials, Components, and Supply Businesses
ROI				
Means	17.50	14.94	15.10	19.59
Standard deviations	31.00	30.26	30.54	31.36
Correlations with systematic risk	.20	.21	.18	.21
Correlations with unsystematic risk	.12	.13	.00	.22
Systematic risk (β)				
Means	0.93	0.90	1.08	0.88
Standard deviations	2.08	2.13	1.96	2.10
Correlations with unsystematic risk	.01	.14	.01	.00
Unsystematic risk (σ)				
Means	15.39	12.83	18.60	15.41
Standard deviations	15.41	10.48	23.86	12.95
Numbers of observations	5,455	1,394	1,099	2,962

are estimated rather than known with certainty. The standard error of each beta estimate indicates the extent of this potential for error. Second, we calculated betas from accounting ROI, which is far from a perfect measure of economic return. No study has determined the possible extent of this measurement error, but it is likely to be large. We hope, of course, that the bias created by the measurement error does not generate so much distortion as to rule out insights into the trade-off between risk and return, Using a large amount of data, as we do, can dissipate some of the problems of measurement error.

Estimating Beta and Unsystematic Risk

An initial step in determining the association of risk and return is to estimate both systematic risk and unsystematic risk for businesses in the data base. We used Equation 2, an operational definition of the CAPM expressed in terms of risk premium, to estimate beta for each SBU:[5]

$$(ROI_{jt} - R_{Ft}) = \alpha_j + \beta_j \times (R_{mt} - R_{Ft}) + \epsilon_{jt}, \quad (2)$$

where ROI_{jt} = return on investment of business j in year t, R_{Ft} = long-term bond rate of U.S. government securities for year t,[6] R_{mt} = average *ROI* of all PIMS business units for year t, and α_j and β_j = coefficients to be estimated. This equation also provides an estimate of the unsystematic risk of an SBU—the standard error of the residual ϵ_{jt} denoted as σ_j.

Statistical Procedures

Least-squares estimation of Equation 2 will, under the usual assumptions, produce the best unbiased linear estimates of beta. Using empirical Bayes procedures will, however, provide beta estimates with a lower mean square error than those obtained through least-squares estimation, These procedures, described in the Appendix, were especially suitable for this research, which entailed relatively few time series observations and much cross-sectional information. They permit adjustment of raw beta estimates, an adjustment that will be greater if a beta estimate has an unusually large difference from the average and/or if the estimate has an unusually large variance. In our context, outliers and large variance estimates were common because of the relatively short time series. We expected substantial improvement in the accuracy of the beta estimate through use of those empirical Bayes procedures.

Results

Influences of Risk on Return

Table 1 presents the means, standard deviations, and interseries correlations of: *ROI*, measured as the deviation of *ROI* from the long-term U.S. government bond rate; systematic risk, measured by beta; and unsystematic risk, measured by the standard error of unsystematic return (σ_j, the standard error of the residual of Equation 2). Table 1 gives statistics for the entire group of businesses and for three subgroups:[7] (1) consumer goods businesses, (2) capital goods businesses, and (3) materials, components, and supply businesses.

Table 2 presents the results of a regression of annual *ROI* on systematic risk and unsystematic risk, which indicate that for the entire group of businesses, both components of risk are significantly associated with *ROI*. The coefficients 2.86 and .22 indicate that a premium is attached to the assumption of both types of risk. As we anticipated, a nonnested hypothesis test (Hotelling, 1940) indicated that systematic risk has significantly more power in explaining *ROI* than does unsystematic risk. The correlation of beta with *ROI* (r = .20) is significantly stronger (p = .001) than the correlation of unsystematic risk with *ROI* (r = .12).

The association of systematic risk with *ROI* is significant (p = .001) and extremely similar in magnitude for each of

Table 2
Results of Regression of *ROI* on Components of Risk[a]

Coefficient Estimates	All Businesses	Consumer Goods Businesses	Capital Goods Businesses	Materials, Components, and Supply Businesses
Intercepts	11.52**	8.62**	12.52**	9.17**
	(.60)	(1.26)	(1.23)	(.88)
Systematic risk (β_j)	2.86**	2.82**	2.86**	2.92**
	(.20)	(.37)	(.47)	(.26)
Unsystematic risk (σ_j)	.22**	.29*	−.03	.51**
	(.03)	(.08)	(.04)	(.04)
R^2	.05	.06	.03	.09
Degrees of freedom	5,452	1,391	1,096	2,959

[a]Standard errors are in parentheses.
*$p < .05$
**$p < .01$

the subgroups. The association of unsystematic risk with return is less uniform across the business groupings. It is positive and significant for consumer goods businesses and for businesses producing components, materials, and supplies, but small and insignificant for capital goods businesses.

However, the regression results shown in Table 2 must be interpreted cautiously. The model does not include a number of other factors that have been theorized and shown empirically to be correlated with return. Studies of the association between risk and return using stock price data have not usually taken the absence of these factors into consideration, as current stock prices are thought to incorporate all available pertinent information. Since the return to a firm is not similarly inclusive, correlations between some of these omitted factors and the risk terms could cause bias and inconsistency in coefficient estimates of the risk terms' effects on *ROI*. A number of studies (e.g., Bettis, 1982; Subrahmanyam & Thomadakis, 1980) have suggested that both systematic and unsystematic risk may be correlated with strategic factors that also influence ROI. Lessening the possibility of omitted variable bias required formulating a model depicting the principal determinants of return.

Other Factors Influencing Profitability

The PIMS data base includes a host of potentially relevant variables that investigators have used in efforts to develop models to explain cross-sectional differences in ROI (Abell & Hammond, 1979; Branch, 1980; Gale, Heany, & Swire, 1977). We selected 13 variables that previous researchers have regarded as the most important determinants of profitability.[8] They include market share; level of vertical integration; marketing intensity; capacity utilization; relative price; relative cost; relative quality; relative newness of products; market growth; relative expenditures for sales force, advertising, and promotions; and relative image of products.

Market share may affect profitability because firms with high market shares can employ economies of scale and scope, or market power. Vertical integration is important in that it allows firms the option of not sacrificing high margins to other members of the vertical system. The less a firm's excess or underutilized capacity, the higher its return. The ability to charge a high price may represent a firm's success in differentiating its product from the competition, and thus it may be associated with high return. A low relative cost position allows for higher return because a firm need not pass all of its cost savings along to customers as low prices. High product quality is theorized to lead to high return, since customers may be willing to pay a premium for high quality. Introducing new products indicates an SBU's ability to innovate, which should be a differentiating factor allowing for high return. With higher market growth, price competition decreases, and return increases. A good image results in a halo effect allowing a firm to charge a high price. Finally, the effects on return of such marketing variables as marketing intensity and expenditures for sales force, advertising, and promotions are not clear. However, studies have shown that these variables tend to be negatively associated with return, possibly because firms overspend on marketing.

In assessing the effects of risk on return, it is important to control for factors influencing profitability that, if omitted, could bias the estimates of risk. Studies (Freeman, Ohlson, & Penman, 1982; Jacobson & Aaker, 1985) have found that lagged values of accounting return have the largest amount of explanatory power in predicting current accounting return. Lagged *ROI* is able to capture a number of firm-specific factors that influence current *ROI*—even factors such as management quality and luck, which may be difficult, if not impossible, to measure. Cross-sectional studies often do not include lagged dependent variables as explanatory factors, although they are rather common in time series studies.[9] Their inclusion in the model should add considerably to its explanatory power and act as an excellent control to reduce omitted variable bias. In fact, *ROI* lagged for one year explains more of the variation in *ROI* than the estimate generated by the PIMS equation for *ROI* using 28 variables.

The likely collinearity between lagged *ROI*—or any of the other variables in the model—and the risk measures will not cause inconsistent estimates of the effects of risk on return. Possible collinearity tends to increase the standard errors of coefficients, but it still allows for obtaining consistent estimates of the coefficients and standard errors in a model. This increase in standard errors is not an especially serious problem in our analysis; the large number of pooled time series, cross-sectional observations available in the PIMS data base should alleviate the consequences of even extreme multicollinearity.

Estimated Influences of Risk

Modeling the effects on *ROI* of (1) *ROI* lagged one and two years, (2) the 13 variables theorized to influence *ROI*, and (3) the measures of systematic and unsystematic risk should reduce omitted variable bias. Coefficient estimates better depicting the trade-off between risk and return should be possible. Table 3 presents the results of estimating this model for the 1,376 businesses in the PIMS data base and for each of the business groupings. The coefficients for β_j, the measure of systematic risk, were significantly positive for all businesses and for each of the three business groupings. In terms of explanatory power, beta is one of the most important factors influencing *ROI*. Thus, the CAPM risk measure does contribute to the ROI model. The effects of beta shown in Table 3 (1.72 for all businesses) are smaller than those shown in Table 2, which is consistent with the judgment that the inclusion of the other factors in Table 3 removed omitted variable bias. This estimated effect of beta on *ROI* is about one-eighth of the value of the average risk premium for the period that the CAPM would postulate under the conditions of stock market investment. This smaller than postulated value is an expected consequence of the measurement error present in the beta estimate.

Given the small number of observations used in estimating accounting beta—from 5 to 13 annual observations—the accuracy of the beta estimate is suspect. As measurement

Table 3
Association of Risk with *ROI* Controlling for Other Influences[a]

Coefficient Estimates	All Businesses	Consumer Goods Businesses	Capital Goods Businesses	Materials, Components, and Supply Businesses
Iintercepts	−24.39**	−18.31**	−9.31	−34.77
	(3.06)	(6.55)	(8.86)	(3.93)
ROI lagged one year	.62**	.68**	.53**	.60**
	(.01)	(.03)	(.03)	(.02)
ROI lagged two years	.05**	.12**	−.05	.08**
	(.01)	(.02)	(.02)	(.02)
Market share	.07**	1.10**	−.06	.07**
	(.02)	(.03)	(.04)	(.02)
Vertical integration	24.66**	20.72**	33.23**	24.80**
	(1.78)	(3.19)	(4.99)	(2.35)
Marketing intensity	−33.46**	−17.76**	−89.95**	−9.98
	(4.05)	(5.82)	(8.96)	(7.96)
Capacity utilization	.16**	.15**	.16**	.21**
	(.01)	(.02)	(.03)	(.02)
Relative price	.09**	.07	.09	.10*
	(.03)	(.05)	(.08)	(.04)
Relative cost	−.09**	−.08	−.24	−.07
	(.03)	(.06)	(.07)	(.04)
Relative quality	.04**	−.01	.06*	.04**
	(.01)	(.02)	(.03)	(.01)
Relative newness of products	.01	−.02	.01	−.02
	(.02)	(.04)	(.05)	(.04)
Market growth	.05*	.01	.09	.03
	(.02)	(.05)	(.05)	(.04)
Relative sales force expenditures	−.02	−.33	−.04	.53
	(.29)	(.48)	(.68)	(.41)
Relative advertising expenditures	−.14	−.72	.05	−.60
	(.30)	(.44)	(.73)	(.47)
Relative promotional expenditures	−.24	−.73	.55	−.20
	(.34)	(.50)	(.84)	(.51)
Relative product image	.33	.58	.87	.30
	(.35)	(.60)	(.90)	(.46)
Systematic risk (β_j)	1.72**	1.25**	1.97**	1.93**
	(.13)	(.21)	(.34)	(.18)
Unsystematic risk (σ_j)	.16**	.18**	.07*	.25**
	(.02)	(.04)	(.03)	(.03)
R^2	.62	.73	.53	.62
Degrees of freedom	5,437	1,376	1,081	2,944

[a]Standard errors are in parentheses.
*$p < .05$
**$p < .01$

error in an independent variable leads to downward bias, the finding of a highly significant association indicates the power of the CAPM in depicting the association between return and risk. The measurement error will lead to an estimate of the effect of accounting beta on ROI that understates the underlying effect. In the bivariate regression case, this understatement is a factor of $1 + (\sigma_\eta^2/\sigma_\beta^2)$ where σ_η^2 is the variance of the measurement error η, and σ_β^2 is the variance of the accounting beta.

Using this formula, and estimates of σ_η^2 and σ_β^2 based on calculations of the variance of empirical Bayes estimates suggested by Morris (1983), and the output of the empirical Bayes estimation procedure described in the Appendix, we could obtain a crude indication of the effect of the measurement error. We estimate the downward bias resulting from this measurement error to be substantial—on the order of 60 percent, which suggests that a more accurate estimate of the effect of beta on *ROI* in Table 3 would be 2.9 rather than the reported 1.72. Even this estimate should be taken as a lower bound, because other measurement error resulting from the use of accounting data can be expected to produce additional downward bias.

Unsystematic risk also had a significant influence on *ROI* for the entire group of businesses and for each of the subgroupings. This significant effect, which is inconsistent with the CAPM's predictions in the context of the stock market, might be an outgrowth of empirical limitations, or it might reflect conditions in strategic context differing from those postulated by the CAPM. Since the consequences of some kinds of unsystematic risk may greatly influence a business and its managers, an association between unsystematic risk and return seems theoretically reasonable.

Despite all the caveats, the findings suggest the extent of the association between risk and return. As financial theory suggests, there is an association between systematic risk and return, measured by accounting beta and accounting return, respectively, across each of the business subgroupings. The effects of beta are highly significant and, even without attempting to adjust for the bias from measurement error, among the most important explanatory factors of *ROI*. For the entire group of businesses, beta's standardized regression coefficient of .12 is lower in magnitude only than those of *ROI* lagged one year and vertical integration, which had standardized regression coefficients of .63 and .13, respectively.[10] Factors such as capacity utilization, market share, and market growth, which have received a great deal more attention in the literature investigating strategy, had smaller effects as evidenced by their standardized regression coefficients of .09, .04, and .007, respectively.

Unsystematic risk was also found to have a highly significant effect on return. Managers' careers may well depend on consequences related to this type of risk. In the absence of any premium, strong incentives exist for managers to emphasize businesses with low unsystematic and systematic risk. However, as the coefficient of .16 for the entire group of businesses indicates, there is a premium attached to unsystematic risk.[11] Although somewhat small in magnitude, unsystematic risk's standardized regression coefficient of .08 was among the largest observed. The fact that the effects of unsystematic risk are smaller than those of systematic risk is consistent with the notion that even managers can sometimes do away with some of the adverse consequences of unsystematic risk through diversification.

To provide another perspective on the effects of the risk terms on ROI, we obtained an average value and a value below which 95 percent of the SBUs would fall for both components of risk. Multiplying these values times the regression coefficients yields a measure of their effects on *ROI*. Thus, the contribution of systematic risk is 1.6 percent (160 basis points) for the average firm and 7.1 percent for a business that is in the 95th percentile with respect to systematic risk. Similarly, unsystematic risk contributes 2.5 percent for the average business and 6.1 percent for a business in the 95th percentile. Clearly, these numbers are substantial enough to affect choices of strategies.

The factors that cause return are for the most part unquantified in our model and, for that matter, in other models of ROI, Lagged *ROI* has far and away the most power in explaining current return. The factors that lagged ROI hypothetically represents—luck, shocks, and quality of management—remain unquantified. It is also possible that *ROI* may be reflecting some elements of risk not captured by the empirical risk measures used in the analysis. Since our estimated risk measures may not fully capture the underlying risk of a business, other measures may serve as proxies for this unmeasured risk. Future research directed at isolating the causes of the predictive power of lagged *ROI* would be useful in providing both a better understanding of profitability and the influence of risk.

Implications

Any and every type of analysis or decision based on profitability should control for different levels of risk; all else being equal, an analysis that does not gives incentives to engage in inappropriately risky ventures. We have suggested how different types of risk can be quantified and introduced into strategic decision making. The role of risk in explaining differences in profitability has implications for both researchers and managers.

Researchers cannot ignore the role of risk in influencing return in profitability models; rather, they can expect both systematic and unsystematic risk to have substantial effects—relative to other key strategy variables like vertical integration, market share, and product quality—in explaining ROI. Profitability models need to depict the role of risk, not only to explain return better, but also to avoid effects of omitted variable bias on the coefficients of other influences on profitability. The extent of such bias will depend on the association of the risk measures with these other strategic factors. Research assessing the influence of strategic factors on risk is clearly needed to provide insights into the risk characteristics of strategies theorized to influence return.

A number of studies have looked at the association of total risk and return in order to assess whether synergistic effects exist between firms' business units. It is important to recognize that financial theory posits that diversification can be expected to reduce total risk by reducing unsystematic risk. Reduction of total risk is thus not evidence of synergy. Diversification designed to reduce unsystematic risk is likely to be of little value and may actually diminish a corporation's value if investors can reduce unsystematic risk more efficiently in another way. The appropriate test of synergy involves assessing whether the trade-off between return and risk is better for a corporation as a whole than its separate components indicate.

One of the most important managerial implications of the role of risk pertains to assessing the performance of different business units. A high return may merely reflect the high risk of an SBU, rather than superior performance of a business area or of management. Businesses with high risk should be required to have higher average rates of return than businesses with low risk.

Strategic choices may affect risk as well as return. For example, managers can use promotional expenditures to affect the systematic risk of their businesses. Using a fixed percent-of-sales decision rule to set promotional budgets—which implies cutting back promotional expenditures in bad times and increasing them in good times—will exacerbate systematic fluctuations. Firms following this practice will have higher systematic risk, and we must question if this high systematic risk is compensated by higher return.

Managers need estimates of systematic and unsystematic risk to make the types of adjustments we suggest. They can obtain these estimates by taking the stock price betas of firms in similar industries as guides and estimating SBU betas subjectively, or by estimating Equation 2. In fact, a manager is likely to get better estimates than those obtained in our analysis by using quarterly or monthly data, instead of the annual data available to us, because the greater frequency allows for more observations and the selection of a time period more characteristic of the current risk conditions facing a business.

The exact trade-off between risk and return is subject to question and further study. The CAPM dictates that the relevant measure for the evaluation of the profitability of a business or project is return adjusted to reflect the systematic risk (beta) of a business and the economy-wide return. However, this measure may not be appropriate in a strategic context. The results presented in Table 3 suggest that a one-unit increase in systematic risk is associated with a 1.72 percent increase in return (172 basis points), and a one-unit increase in unsystematic risk tends to be associated with a 0.16 increase in return. This might serve as a starting point for adjusting return so that it is appropriate compensation for the different types of risk.

However, the extent of these average risk premiums requires further research and thought. As was discussed, empirical limitations in these estimates make them lower bound estimates. In addition, it is unclear if businesses should be compensated for additional unsystematic risk. Attaching a risk premium to unsystematic risk may not be in the best interests of stockholders; an association may suggest that shareholders need to take actions that better insure management is acting in their best interests. Or perhaps the trade-off between unsystematic risk and return is an unavoidable consequence of the impossibility of providing management compensation agreements insuring that managers will act strictly as agents for shareholders. Allowing this premium may be the best way to protect all stakeholders. Corporate policy might well establish risk premiums for both systematic and unsystematic risk in order to evaluate businesses' profitability. Future research determining the appropriate risk/return trade-offs in strategic contexts should be directed both at current and ideal policies. Research in this area should consider financial theory, as well as its lack of direct applicability in the strategy context.

References

1. The market return is conceptually the return on all investments, but is typically represented in empirical research by the Standard and Poor's *Index* of common stocks.
2. For a different view, see Roll (1977).
3. However, even the PIMS data base has a relatively short span of time series data for the calculation of beta estimates. It contains annual information on SBUs for all or parts of the period 1970–83. For our analysis, we estimated betas for firms having from 5 to 13 annual observations; stock return betas are typically estimated on the basis of data of greater frequency or from longer periods.
4. The hypothesis of ROI being an unbiased estimate of stock return—the joint hypothesis of zero intercept and unit slope—could be rejected on the basis of a significant intercept. Given the likely existence of positive present value of growth opportunities, ROI should understate stock return.
5. Although this is the most frequently used formulation for obtaining an estimate of accounting beta, others have been recommended. Calculating accounting beta in terms of cash flows or growth rates of ROI are two commonly advocated alternatives. Analysis based on alternative beta measures is a possible direction for future research.
6. This estimate of the risk-free return, obtained from the *Business Conditions Digest* (U.S. Department of Commerce, 1985), was used to approximate the maturity of a business unit. The return is, in fact, only risk-free if hold to maturity.
7. We calculated ROI as the difference from the risk-free rate so as to better induce stationarity in the series and thus justify the pooling of the time series and cróss-sectional data. As the Stein estimator takes a weighted, rather than simple, average of the least squares estimates of beta, the mean value of the empirical Bayes estimate of beta is not 1.00.
8. For a discussion of the theoretical and empirical justification of the variables used in the model, see Klein and Leffler (1981), Phillips, Chang, and Buzzell (1983), Porter (1980), and Schoeffler and colleagues (1974).
9. The use of lagged values as surrogates for other factors is, in fact, the basis for the Box and Jenkins (1980) approach to time series analysis.
10. We do not use the more common term for standardized regression coefficient—beta weight—for obvious reasons,
11. The different components of this unsystematic risk measure will have different associations with ROI. For instance, unsystematic risk contains variation resulting from managerial actions as well as variation resulting from external shocks. Unlike uncontrollable unsystematic risk, the variation in ROI driven by marketing programs—controllable unsystematic risk—may not be undesirable, because it may actually represent a high level of control over the environment. To obtain estimates of the associations of controllable and uncontrollable unsystematic risk, we separated unsystematic return into the part influenced by strategic factors and the part not influenced by these factors. The standard errors of these estimates were taken as indicators of controllable and uncontrollable unsystematic risk, respectively. We then reestimated the Table 3 model with unsystematic risk replaced with these two components. As anticipated, uncontrollable unsystematic risk had a positive (0.21) and significant effect. Consistent with the idea that controllable unsystematic risk is actually desirable, it had a significant negative (−1.14) effect. For further details and a discussion of this analysis see Aaker and Jacobson (1988).

Bibliography

Aaker, D. A., and Jacobson, R. 1988. "The Risk of Marketing: The Roles of Systematic, Uncontrollable and Controllable Unsystematic, and Downside Risk," in R. Bettis, ed., *Strategy and Risk*. Forthcoming, Greenwich, CT.: JAI Press.

Abell, D. F., and Hammond, J. S. 1979. *Strategic Market Planning*. Englewood Cliffs, NJ: Prentice-Hall.

Beaver, W., and Manegold, J. 1975. "The Association Between Market-Determined and Accounting-Determined Measures of Systematic Risk: Some Further Evidence, *Journal of Financial and Quantitative Analysis*, 10: 231–284.

Bettis, R. A. 1982. "Risk Considerations in Modeling Corporate Strategy," *Academy of Management Proceedings*: 654–682.

Bettis, R. A. 1983. "Modern Financial Theory, Corporate Strategy, and Public Policy," *Academy of Management Review*, 8: 406–415.

Bettis, R. A., and Mahajan, V. 1985. "Risk/Return Performance of Diversified Firms," *Management Science*, 31: 785–799.

Bowman, E. H. 1980. "A Risk/Return Paradox for Strategic Management," *Sloan Management Review*, 21 (3): 17–31.

Box, G. E. P., and Jenkins, G. M. 1980. *Time Series Analysis, Forecasting, and Control*, 2nd ed., San Francisco: Holden-Day.

Branch, B. 1980. "The Laws of the Marketplace and ROI Dynamics," *Financial Management*, 9(2): 58–65.

Cardozo, R. N., and Smith D. K., Jr. 1983. "Applying Financial Portfolio Theory to Product Portfolio Decisions: An Empirical Study." *Journal of Marketing*, 47(2): 110–119.

Devinney, T. M., Stewart, D. W., and Shocker, A. D. 1985. "A Note on Product Portfolio Theory: A Rejoinder to Cardozo and Smith," *Journal of Marketing*, 49(4): 107–112.

Efron, B., and Morris, C. 1973. Stein's Estimation Rule and Its Competitors—An Empirical Bayes Approach," *Journal of the American Statistical Association*, 68: 117–130.

———. 1975. "Data Analysis Using Stein's Estimator and Its Generalizations," *Journal of the American Statistical Association*, 70: 311–319.

Fay, R. E. Ill, and Herriot, R.A. 1979. "Estimation of Income for Small Places: An Application of James-Stein Procedures to Census Data," *Journal of the American Statistical Association*, 74: 269–277.

Fisher, F., and Hall, G. 1969. "Risk and Corporate Rates of Return," *Quarterly Journal of Economics*, 83: 79–82.

Fisher, F. M., and McGowan, J.J. 1983. On the Misuses of Accounting Rates of Return to Infer Monopoly Profits," *American Economic Review*, 73: 66–80.

Freeman, R. N., Ohlson, J. A., and Penman, S. H. 1982. "Book Rate-of-Return and Prediction of Earnings Changes: An Empirical Investigation," *Journal of Accounting Research*, 20: 639–653.

Gale, B. T., Heany, D. F., and Swire, D. S. 1977. *The Par ROI Report: Explanation and Commentary on Report*. Cambridge, MA: Strategic Planning Institute,

Hackett, J. T. 1985. "Concepts and Practice of Agency Theory with the Corporation," in E. I. Altman and M. G. Subrahmanyam, eds., *Recent Advances in Corporate Finance*: 163–172. Homewood, IL: Richard D. Irwin.

Harcourt, G. C. 1965. "The Accountant in a Golden Age," *Oxford Economic Papers*, 17: 66–80.

Hayes, R. H., and Gavin, D. A. 1982. "Managing as if Tomorrow Mattered," *Harvard Business Review*, 60(3): 70–79.

Hill, N. C., and Stone, B. K. 1980. "Accounting Betas, Systematic Operating Risk, and Financial Leverage: A Risk-Composition Approach to the Determination of Systematic Risk," *Journal of Financial and Quantitative Analysis*, 15: 595–638.

Hotelling, H. 1940. "The Selection of Variables for Use in Prediction with Some Comments on the General Problem of Nuisance Parameters," *Annals of Mathematical Statistics*, 11: 271–283.

Jacobson R. 1987. "The Validity of ROI as a Measure of Business Performance," *American Economic Review*, in press.

Jacobson, R., and Aaker, D.A. 1985. "Is Market Share All That It's Cracked Up To Be?" *Journal of Marketing*, 49(4): 11–22.

Klein, B., and Leffler, K. 1981. "The Role of Market Forces in Assuring Contractual Performance," *Journal of Political Economy*, 89: 615–641.

Lintner, J. 1965. "The Valuation of Risk Assets and the Selection of Risky Investments in Stock Portfolios and Capital Budgets," *Review of Economics and Statistics*, 47: 13–37.

Morris, C. N. 1983. "Pragmatic Empirical Bayes Inference: Theory and Applications," *Journal of the American Statistical Association*, 78: 45–57.

Phillips, L. W., Chang, D. R., and Buzzell, R. D. 1983. "Product Quality, Cost Position, and Business Performance: A Test of Some Key Hypotheses," *Journal of Marketing*, 47(2): 26–43.

Porter, M. 1980. *Competitive Strategy*. New York: Free Press.

Ravenscraft, D.J. 1983. "Structure-Profit Relationship at the Line of Business and Industry Level," *Review of Economics and Statistics*, 65: 22–31.

Robbins, H. E. 1955. "An Empirical Bayes Approach to Statistics," in J. Neyman, ed., *Proceedings of the Third Berkeley Symposium on Mathematical Statistics and Probability*, 157–163. Berkeley: University of California Press.

Roll, R. 1977. "A Critique of the Asset Pricing Theory's Tests," *Journal of Financial Economics*, 4: 129–176.

Schamalensee, R. 1985. "Do Markets Differ Much?" *American Economic Review*, 75: 341–351.

Schoeffler, S., Buzzell, R. D., and Heany, D. F. 1974. "Impact of Strategic Planning on Profit Performance, *Harvard Business Review*, 52(2): 137–145.

Sharpe, W.F. 1964. "Capital Asset Prices: A Theory of Market Equilibrium Under Conditions of Risk," *Journal of Finance*, 19: 425–442.

Shephard, W. 1972. "The Elements of Market Structure," *Review of Economics and Statistics*, 54: 25–38.

Solomon, E. 1971. "Return on Investment: The Relation of Book-Yield to True Yield," in J. L. Livingstone and T. J. Bruns, eds., *Income Theory and Rate of Return*, 105–117. Columbus: Ohio State University.

Stein, C. 1955. "Inadmissibility of the Usual Estimator for the Mean of a Multivariate Normal Distribution," in J. Neyman, ed., *Proceedings of the Third Berkeley Symposium on Mathematical Statistics and Probability*, 197–206. Berkeley: University of California Press.

Stigler, G. 1963. *Capital and Rates of Return in Manufacturing*, Princeton, NJ: Princeton University Press.

Strategic Planning Institute. 1980. *PIMS Program*, Cambridge, MA.

Subrahmanyam, M.G., and Thomadakis, S.B. 1980. "Systematic Risk and the Theory of the Firm," *Quarterly Journal of Economics*, 94: 437–451.

U.S. Department of Commerce. 1985. *Business Conditions Digest*, 25(9): 98.

Van Horne, J. C. 1980. *Financial Management and Policy*, 5th ed., Englewood Cliffs, NJ: Prentice-Hall.

Wensley R. 1981. "Strategic Marketing: Betas, Boxes, or Basics," *Journal of Marketing*, 45(3): 173–182.

Appendix

Empirical Bayes Estimates of Beta

Stein (1955) showed that it is possible to uniformly improve maximum likelihood estimates (MLEs). His process decreases total square error in estimates of several parameters from independently normal observations; the estimates of individual values of beta for each of a large cross section of SBUs that we required are an example. In effect, Stein estimators take a weighted average of the MLE and a fixed point estimate, usually the average value of an entire sample of MLEs. Stein estimators are often called "shrinkage estimators," as they operate by shrinking each parameter estimate towards a fixed point. Any specific Stein estimate cannot be expected to outperform any specific maximum likelihood estimate, but the set of Stein estimates should outperform the set of maximum likelihood estimates.

A number of studies have extended and generalized Stein's results (e.g., Efron and Morris, 1973, 1975). The most relevant extension for this study would appear to be use of a Stein estimator allowing the variances for the estimates of beta for the different business units to be unequal. Assuming that

$$\beta_i \mid \boldsymbol{\beta}_i \sim N(\boldsymbol{\beta}_i, \boldsymbol{D}_i) \qquad i = 1, \ldots k,$$

and

$$\boldsymbol{\beta}_i \sim N(\boldsymbol{\beta}, \boldsymbol{A}) \qquad i = 1, \ldots k,$$

a Stein estimator of the underlying beta of a particular business unit ($\hat{\beta}_i^*$) can be defined to be

$$\hat{\beta}_i^* = \bar{\boldsymbol{\beta}} + c(\hat{\beta}_i - \bar{\boldsymbol{\beta}}),$$

where $\hat{\beta}_i$ is the least-squares estimate of β_i, $\bar{\boldsymbol{\beta}}$ is an estimate of $\boldsymbol{\beta}$, and $c = 1 - [\hat{D}_i/(\hat{A} + \hat{D}_i)]$, with $\hat{D}_i$ being the least-squares estimate of the variance of β_i for an individual business unit, and $\hat{A}$ being an estimate of the variance of $\boldsymbol{\beta}_i$ about the mean value $\boldsymbol{\beta}$.

The Stein estimate is composed of the maximum likelihood estimator and the mean of an entire sample of MLEs. The value c has the effect of shrinking the estimator to the sample estimate of the mean of beta. The shrinkage is greatest as c approaches 0 and least as c approaches 1. By allowing for different variances, $\boldsymbol{D_i}$, the procedure shrinks the estimate closer to the mean the larger the variance of the estimate, and it allows for less shrinkage for estimates with smaller variances.

The estimates of $\hat{\beta}_i$ and $\hat{D}_i$ can be obtained from least-squares regressions of Equation 2. We obtained the estimates of $\bar{\boldsymbol{\beta}}$, which is the weighted sample mean, and $\hat{A}$, an estimate of the unknown total variance A, via the iterative procedure described in Fay and Herriot (1979).

Although Stein's results were written as a statistical paradox, they have a straightforward, empirical Bayes interpretation. Robbins (1955) showed that it is possible to achieve the same minimum risk associated with Bayes's rule without knowledge of a prior distribution, as long as the number of means being estimated is very large. Because we estimated beta for some 1,300 SBUs, with limited time series data for each, we expected substantial improvement through use of Stein estimates. However, given the small amount of time series data, we could not test for the extent of the improvement, but instead had to rely on findings reached by other studies (Efron and Morris, 1973).

The authors would like to thank the Strategic Planning Institute for providing access to the data used in this study.

29

Assessing Marketing Risk

Victor J. Cook, Jr. & John R. Page

The risk-return characteristics of financial and marketing decisions are fundamentally different. Theoretically, marketing managers have some control over these characteristics, while financial managers do not. The *Markstrat* environment offers a useful context in which to explore the effects of portfolio and investment decisions on marketing risk.

A model for assessing the risks specific to a marketing strategy is developed and applied to data generated by executive decisions made in the *Markstrat* environment. The specific risks of a marketing strategy are those associated with changes in primary demand and market share. The riskiness and profitability of different strategies are assessed statistically. Primary-demand risk and return on investments are found to be positively correlated. More volatile, risky, market segments yield higher average returns. The strong temptation to harvest market share is isolated in the positive correlation between harvesting risk and rate of return. The pressure not to build long-term positions is found in the high negative correlation between building risk and return on investments. Overall, the model successfully explains risk-taking behavior in the *Markstrat* environment, and offers theoretical direction for future research in the real world.

MANAGERS DO NOT HAVE useful tools for assessing the risks specific to a marketing strategy. Specific risk in marketing strategy traditionally has been quantified in three ways. First, risk has been defined as the standard error of market-response parameter estimates [13, 22, 27]. While this approach provides measures of "parametric risk" in marketing, most managers operate in a world of unknown parameter errors. A second measure of specific risk in marketing strategy is found in the "strengths and weaknesses" of standardized product portfolio models [18, 10, 26]. While this approach provides measures of "strategic risk" in marketing, the results are so subjective that the true riskiness of a project is hidden by interpretive judgments. A third approach to specific risk is the direct adaptation to marketing of financial portfolio models [1, 3, 9, 11, 12, 14, 15, 19, 25]. While this approach provides an objective measure of "systematic risk," management cannot diversify away the residual risks specific to a marketing strategy.

Victor J. Cook, Jr. is Professor of Marketing Strategy and John R. Page is Associate Professor at the A. B. Freeman School of Business, Tulane University.

Financial and Marketing Risk

Product markets differ from financial markets in significant ways. In product markets, managers have some control over the risk-return characteristics of their marketing investments. Product managers, for example, set the market prices of their products, while financial managers must take market prices as given. Product managers also influence a project's rate of return by their use of resources. The total level of marketing investment as well as its distribution among the firm's capacities to produce, promote, and distribute, influence the risk-return characteristics of its product portfolio. A product manager's rate of return is also affected by competitive investments. The return to financial portfolios is not, in principle, affected either by the level of investment, its distribution among markets, or by the characteristics of competitive portfolios.

Marketing management is charged with allocating resources in such a way as to yield the maximum long-run net present value to shareholders [21] within the context of risky product-market investments. From this perspective, a marketing strategy is the manner in which company resources

Table 1
Measures of Marketing Risk

Sources of Risk	Measures of Risk
1. Primary-demand risk:	
Segment-size weight	$\omega = Q_i \div Q$
Product-life-cycle stage	$\sigma\{\Delta Q_i \div Q_i\}$
2. Market-share risk:	
Building	$\sqrt{\Sigma\,(x_b - m)^2(s_b)}$
Harvesting	$\sqrt{\Sigma\,(x_h - m)^2(s_h)}$
Balancing	$(x_h - x_b)$

ω = weight.
Q = segment demand in units.
i = segment index; 1, 2, . . . , 10.
σ = standard deviation of percent change.
Δ = year-to-year change in segment demand.
x = company share of marketing capacity.
m = company share of unit segment demand.
s = budget share of company investments.
b = investments that build share; $x > m$.
h = investments that harvest share; $x < m$.

are put at risk in the search for differential advantage [5]. Being unable to diversify away the risks arising from the creation of differential advantages, management must understand and measure these risks in order that resource commitments are made that maximize the net present value of each project. To achieve this goal, a cost of capital adjusted for specific risk is necessary, yet the sources of these marketing risks have been neither formally identified nor objectively measured.

This article identifies two sources of marketing risk and applies component measures of each. In the next section, definitions, measures, and assumptions are proposed. This is followed by development of a model of marketing risk. An application of this model to data generated by executive decisions in the *Markstrat* environment [16, 17] is presented and the results are discussed. The article concludes with implications and directions for further research.

Definitions, Measures, and Assumptions

Two general sources of marketing risk and their corresponding component measures are presented in Table 1. The sources of marketing risk are changes in primary demand and market share. Primary-demand risk derives from the size of market segments in a firm's product portfolio and the life-cycle stage of each segment. Market-share risk arises from building, harvesting, and balancing decisions. These decisions are a product of management's search for differential advantage, the firm's strategic objectives, and budget allocations among the factors of marketing. Each of these components of marketing risk can be identified and measured objectively.

Primary-Demand Risk

Selection of target markets is the first critical decision affecting the riskiness of a marketing strategy. To the extent a product portfolio addresses market segments accounting for a large proportion of total market demand and is subject to significant rates of change in primary demand, it should be considered risky. To the extent served market segments are small, with stable demand, a marketing strategy should be considered low risk.

The size of a market segment incorporates the idea that a large market is inherently riskier than a smaller one. This fact is implicit in the concept of a market-niche strategy. In formulating a measure of primary-demand risk, segment size serves as a scaling factor to weight the relative importance of one segment compared with another. The weight is defined in Table 1 as the ratio of segment primary demand to total industry demand.

The product-life-cycle stage affects the level of primary-demand risk by the degree to which a market segment is found attractive to competitors and introduces volatility into demand expectations. A market in the growth stage of its life cycle is riskier than one in maturity because it attracts competition. A mature market segment is less risky than a declining one because of less uncertainty about future demand. The greater the variation in rates of change in demand for products in the company's portfolio, the greater the risk.

Variations in segment demand are measured by the percent change in unit consumption. In a test of the validity of the product life cycle [20], this measure was found to be normally distributed with an expected value of zero and a standard deviation of 14% in a sample of 140 categories of nondurable consumer products. In *Markstrat*, primary-demand risk is measured in Table 1 as the segment-size weighted standard deviation of percent change in unit sales among products in the firm's portfolio.

Market-Share Risk

Market-share risk is introduced in three ways. First, risk is introduced in the firm's search for competitive or differential advantages. Second, risk may be increased as a result of the firm's strategic objectives. Third, the balancing of resources among the factors of marketing strategy influence risk.

The search for differential advantage is a major force in the creation of marketing risk. If segment demand in each year of the planning horizon is Q_{it}, and future market-share expectations are μ_{it}, then future unit volume is $v_{it} = \mu_{it} Q_{it}$. Market-share expectations depend on a firm's prices and marketing capacity. A *Markstrat* firm's capacity to produce, promote, and distribute its products is built with fixed marketing investments [6, 7, 8, 24]. Designate the total fixed costs of a firm's marketing strategy as the sum of expenditures "e_j" assignable to a number of different marketing factors, where "j" is an index of factors. In *Markstrat*, factor costs are the same for all firms.

If a firm's total expenditure on a marketing strategy aggregated over segments and factors is "e," the budget share of total expenditures on each marketing factor is $s_{jt} = e_{jt} \div e_t$. The market's total expenditure on each factor by all competitors is E_{jt}. The ratio $x_{jt} = e_{jt} \div E_{jt}$ is one firm's share of competitive capacity on any given marketing factor. A firm's current share of a market segment is $m_{it} = q_{it} \div Q_{it}$. Differential advantages exist whenever $x_{jt} > m_t$. Disadvantages exist whenever $x_{jt} < m$, [4, 7]. The market-share attraction model [2] is implicit in this formulation of differential advantage.

Strategic Objectives. Market-share risks arise from the increasing variation in cost and revenue estimates associated with strategic moves that place the firm farther and farther from its current market share m_{it}, to a future market-share μ_{it} position that is either greater or less than current share. A building strategy causes current market share and future share of marketing capacity to diverge. Expected unit volumes differ ever more significantly, and thus variances in estimates of expected costs and revenues increase. At the same time, the asset base is built up gradually reducing returns on the current position. A harvesting strategy leads to the risk of opportunity losses associated with moves that weaken the firm's future market position. The risks of harvesting are the most insidious of all. The asset base gradually is reduced leading to higher short-run returns. In the short run, there is a positive effect on the financial statements and the potential long-term negative effects are not revealed in the accounts. A holding strategy that sets current share of market and future share of marketing capacity equal minimizes the risks introduced by strategic objectives.

Balancing Resources. Variability in resource allocations among the factors of marketing strategy introduces further risk. Under the assumption of equal linear–additive response and equal factor costs, allocation risk is minimized when each capacity share equals market share. It may be possible, however, to achieve target share of market by investing more heavily in one factor to compensate for a weakness in another. Figure 1 illustrates this trade-off. The curved schedule T represents the various allocations that, ceteribus paribus, would achieve target market share. This schedule is a "contour of equilibrium market share [14]." It is nonlinear if the firm cannot eliminate its investment in one factor by increasing investments in another. The straight lines c_1 and c_2 correspond to different factor-cost schedules. If factor costs are equal, schedule c_1 implies the minimum cost-investment decision is at points x_4 and x_5. Generally, the balancing component of marketing risk is minimized if $x_{1t} = x_{2t} \ldots x_{jt} = m_t$. Schedule c_2 applies if the factor cost of advertising is twice that of salesforce. The minimum cost investment then shifts to x'_4 and x'_5. The minimum risk investment, however, remains at $x_4 = x_5$.

Assumptions

For simplicity, and because it fits the *Markstrat* world reasonably well, it is assumed (1) that the long-run average $x_{jt} = \mu_{jt}$, (2) primary-demand elasticities with respect to marketing capacity and segment price are constant, (3) market-share elasticities are constant and equal among all brands, (4) the factor costs c_{jt} of all marketing investments are equal among competitors and linear over the decision range, (5) the total revenue function is linear over the decision interval, (6) price is a dimension of perceived product performance, and (7) all firms face a market-response function that may be taken to be linear-additive [5, 23].

Figure 1
Balancing the factors of marketing

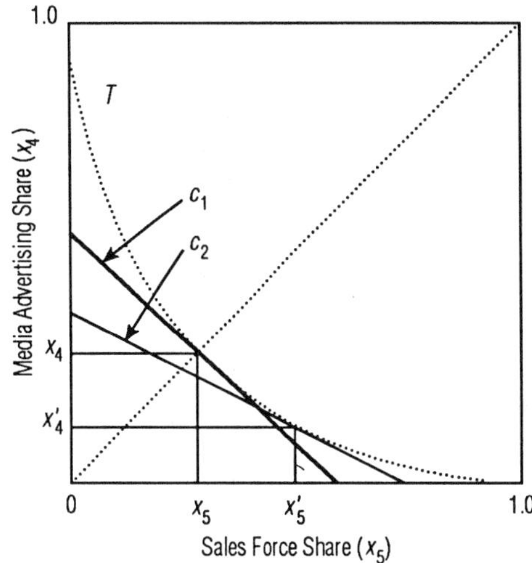

A Model of Marketing Risk

A model for assessing marketing risk is presented in Figure 2. The selection of which market segments to enter defines the level of primary-demand risk in each time period. Primary-demand is labeled μ in Figure 2. This represents the base rate of risk exposure elected by management in selection of the target markets in its product portfolio.

Changes in market share induced by management decisions to increase or decrease the level of resource commitments among marketing factors lead to additional risks. Deviations on either side of the firm's current market-share

Figure 2
A model of marketing risk

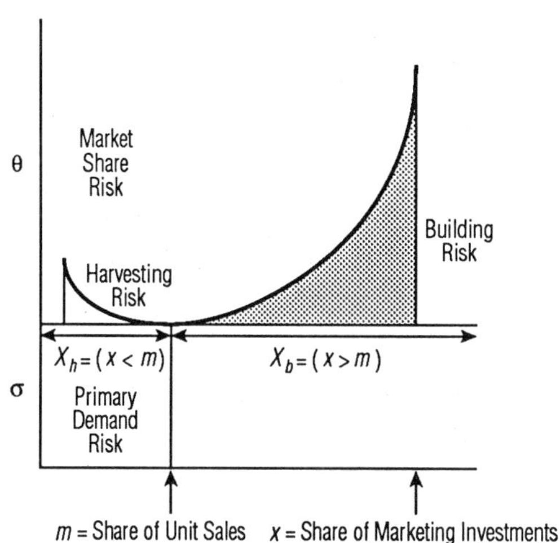

position introduce greater uncertainty with respect to both consumer response (variance in revenues) and fixed costs of marketing capacity (variance in costs). The budget weighted root mean square of positive differences between current market share and expected share of marketing investments captures the effect of risk induced by a "building" strategy. The budget weighted root mean square of negative differences between market share and share of marketing investments measures the effect of risk induced by a "harvest" strategy. The sum of these differentials measures market-share risk. This risk component is labeled Θ in Figure 2. Theta may be interpreted as a strategic orientation coefficient (SOC). The SOC's indicate the direction and degree of "tilt" away from a balanced, low-risk, share-holding strategy.

Application and Results

The data used in the following analysis were produced in an eight-year play of the *Markstrat* game by 25 senior marketing executives of a multibillion dollar international corporation [7, 23].

Application

The mean rate of change in segment demand during this eight-year play of the game was +20.1%, with a standard deviation of 28.6%. Both the mean and standard deviation in growth rates were significantly higher than the average of real-world experience [20].

The management of *Markstrat* firms, like their real-world counterparts, pursued the growth segments over the course of the game, dropping the declining markets as they appeared. Primary-demand risk ranged from a low of .002 (Firm 4, period 2), to a high of 1.34 (Firm 4, period 4). Management of Firm 4 shifted its portfolio from one that was literally equivalent with the market, to one that was 1.34 sigmas above the mean risk of competitive portfolios. Its segment-weighted rate of portfolio growth moved from approximately 20% to over 58% in three years. Growth of this magnitude is difficult to manage in any environment.

Different segment-entry-time combinations are also important to a firm's portfolio. For example, firms that had a portfolio entry in segment 5 during periods 5 through 8 were in markets that accounted for 21% of cumulative eight-year primary demand, but represented only 10% (4/40) of the entry opportunities in the eight years of play.

Market share is compared with each firm's share of marketing capacity on seven marketing investment variables in the panels of Figure 3. In each panel, marketing capacity is expressed as a proportion of cumulative *Markstrat* industry totals. A firm's share of unit sales (m) to the left side of each panel represents its true "weighted average market share [6, 7, 8]." The marketing capacity variables (x) appear from left to right across each panel. Share of unit production is identified as x_1, share of ending inventory is x_2, share of research-and-development expenditures is x_3, share of media advertising is x_4, salesforce share is x_5, marketing-research share is x_6, and share of (inverted) volume-weighted

Figure 3
Market share and share of marketing capacity

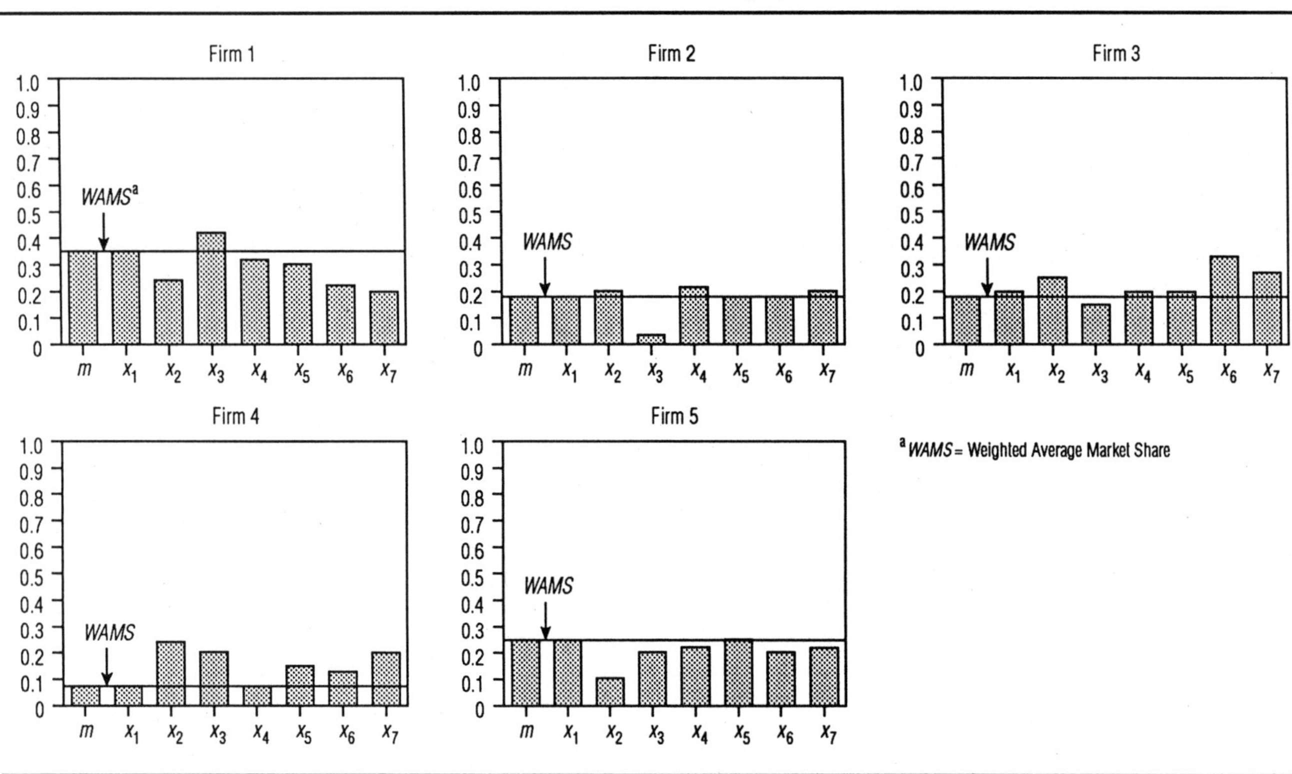

Figure 4
Primary demand risk and rate of return

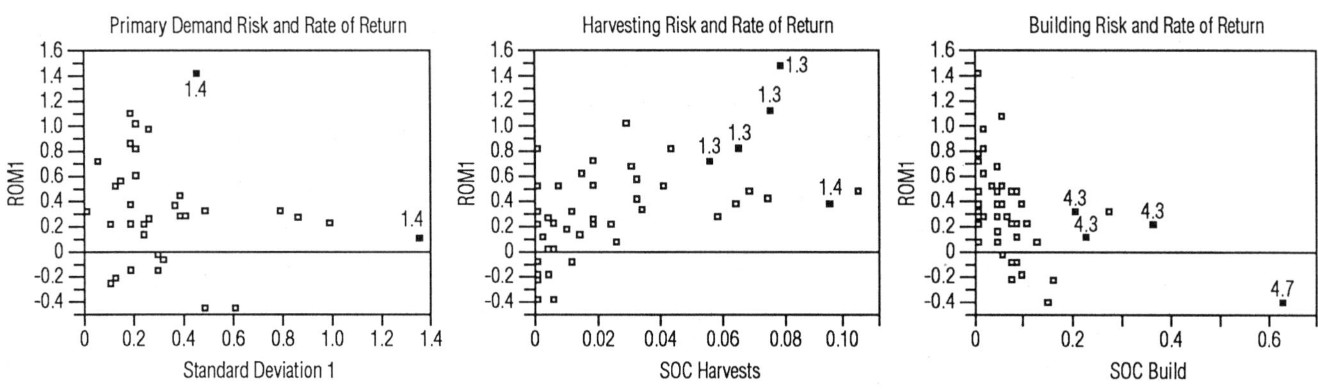

interpoint distances between each brand in the firm's portfolio and all segment ideal points is x_7. The comparison of actual market share with the shares of each marketing investment is emphasized by the horizontal line in Figure 3.

From these data, it is clear that Firm 1 followed a harvesting strategy over the eight years of play on all variables except research and development. The risky effects of this strategy appear in panel 2 of Figure 4. The strategic orientation coefficients (SOC) for Firm 1 tilted to the high side of the harvesting risk scale. For example, the highest rates of return on marketing investment as well as one of the largest harvest SOC's was due to Firm 1, in period 4 (labeled 1,4 in panel 2 of Figure 4). In five of eight decisions, Firm 1 management exhibited very risky harvest coefficients.

The success of the risky strategy adopted by Firm 1 turned on the time pattern of a *single* R&D investment and of segment-entry decision. In period 3, management invested in 37.2% of the industry's R&D, while its market share was 23.7%. The outcome of its R&D effort was a brand that was introduced dead center on the ideal point of segment 4. The same year (period 4), that segment grew by 85% in volume, followed by a 50% increase the next period. On two counts, the management of Firm 1 was making a risky play—market-share harvesting in a rapidly growing market. In that year, the growth in segment 4 demand was 2.28 sigmas beyond the average for the game. Overall share of market for Firm 1 increased to 35.0% in period 4, and further to 44.0% in period 5 as a direct consequence of this one significant decision. The company continued its harvest throughout the next three years, ending the game with 34.4% share of market in period 8, and an industry-leading return on marketing investments.

Firm 4, on the other hand, followed an equally risky build strategy throughout the eight years of play. Four of the eight strategies adopted by Firm 4 management exhibited the highest strategic orientation coefficients of share building found in the game. The most significant share building SOC was observed for Firm 4 in period 7 (identified as 4,7 in panel 3, Figure 4). Its rate of return on marketing investments in that period was −42%. The depressing effects on ROMI of an unsuccessful build orientation is clear. Firm 4 management also shouldered a double-barreled risk by taking an even heavier position than Firm 1 in the same market segment in period 4, with near zero rate of return (indicated as 4,4 in panel 1, Figure 4). This turned out not to be a wise move for Firm 4, because of the success of Firm I in the same segment and time period.

To illustrate the variability in marketing risks to which firms were exposed in one key period, primary-demand and market-share risks for each firm in period 4 are presented in Table 2. The components of market-share risk are also identified for each firm. Firms 1 and 4 took the highest marketing risk positions at 0.57 and 1.58, respectively. While Firm 4 had three times the exposure of Firm 1, the sources of risk were also very different. Firm 4 was totally committed to a growth portfolio. Its primary-demand risk was 1.34, which demanded a heavy commitment to share building. With an SOC for its build strategy at 0.23, Firm 4 was over twice as risky as its nearest competitor.

Statistical Results

The formulations of marketing risk presented here give direction to marketing scientists in their search for understanding, and to management in its attempts to achieve maximum return at minimum risk.

Primary-demand risk measured with *Markstrat* data fits the model reasonably well. The simple correlation coeffi-

Table 2
Marketing Risks in a Single Period

Firm	Primary-Demand Risk	+	Harvesting Risk	+	Building Risk	=	Marketing Risk
1	0.47		0.08		0.02		0.57
2	0.21		0.00		0.09		0.30
3	0.34		0.04		0.06		0.44
4	1.34		0.01		0.23		1.58
5	0.39		0.03		0.03		0.45

cient between primary-demand risk and return on marketing investments is +0.36. As risk increases, so does rate of return, but there is a high variance in this result.

Market-share risk associated with harvesting objectives is positively correlated (+0.58) with return on marketing investment. The risks of a building strategy are negatively correlated (−0.45) with return on marketing investments. The temptation for firms in the *Markstrat* world to harvest is evident. The pressure not to build market share is equally clear *if* the criterion is return on investment.

Implications and Future Research

The risk-return characteristics of financial and marketing decisions are fundamentally different. Theoretically, marketing managers have some control over these characteristics, while financial managers do not. The control exercised by marketing management centers around decisions of (1) which *segments*to include in the portfolio and (2) the level and timing of *investments*in marketing capacity. The *Markstrat* environment offers a particularly useful context in which to explore the effects of portfolio and investment decisions on marketing risk, because it offers comprehensive, error-free measurements of competitive activity.

Since management has some control over exposure to marketing risks and can influence the observed rate of return on investments, the links between the two must be isolated explicitly. This article attempted to isolate such explicit links. Two major sources of marketing risk are changes in primary demand and market share. The model presented here appears to explain risk-taking behavior in the *Markstrat* environment, and offers theoretical direction to future research.

Research on objective, variance-based measures of marketing risk is only beginning. The next steps should include formal testing of hypotheses with larger samples and applications to real-world data. What may be gained from future research on measures of marketing risk is the possibility of explaining the residual contribution of primary-demand risk and market-share risk to a product portfolio's overall risk-return characteristics. In turn, this will help management better control the impact of marketing decisions on the risk-return characteristics of product-market investments.

The authors thank Tracey Post for her assistance in development and analysis of the data base used in this study, and the A. B. Freeman School of Business for financial support.

References

1. Aaker, David A., and Jacobson, Robert, "The Role of Risk in Strategic Decision Making: The Asset Risk Pricing Model," ORSA/TIMS Marketing Science Conference, Vanderbilt University, Session SA2-B, March 1985.
2. Bell, David K., Kenney, Ralph L., and Little, John D. C., "A Market Share Theorem," *Journal of Marketing Resources*, 12 (May 1975): 136–141.
3. Cardozo, Richard N., and Smith, David K., Jr., "Applying Financial Portfolio Theory to Product Portfolio Decisions: An Empirical Study," *Journal of Marketing*, 47 (Spring 1983): 110–119.
4. Cook, Victor J., Jr., "Marketing Strategy and Differential Advantage," *Journal of Marketing*, 47 (Spring 1983): 68–75.
5. ———, "Understanding Marketing Strategy and Differential Advantage," *Journal of Marketing*, 49 (Spring 1985): 137–142.
6. ———, "The Net Present Value of Market Share," *Journal of Marketing*, 49 (Summer 1985): 49–63.
7. ———, and Strong, Edward C., "Strategic Concepts in MARKSTRAT," working paper 85-1445-07, A. B. Freeman School of Business, Tulane University, November 1985.
8. ———, and Nolan, Johannah J., "Strategic Planning Tutorials for the MARKSTRAT Environment: SONITE ONE and TWO," working paper 86-1445-05, A. B. Freeman School of Business, Tulane University, July 1986,
9. Corstjens, M., and Weinstein, D., in *Marketing Planning Models,* A. A. Zoltners, ed., Amsterdam, North-Holland Publishing Company, 1982, p. 141.
10. Day, George S., *Strategic Market Planning:The Pursuit of Competitive Advantage*, West Publishing Co., St. Paul, MN, 1984.
11. Devinney, Timothy M., and Stewart, David W., "A Generalized Investment Portfolio Model," working paper #83-127, Owen Graduate School of Management, Vanderbilt University, December 1984.
12. ———, ———, and Shocker, Allan D., "A Note on the Application of Portfolio 'Theory': A Comment on Cardozo and Smith," 49 (Fall 1985): *Journal of Marketing*, 113–115.
13. Hertz, David D., "Risk Analysis in Capital Investment," *Harvard Business Review,* 42 (January–February 1964): 95–106.
14. Karnani, Aneel, "Equilibrium Market Share—A Measure of Competitive Strength," *Strategic Management Journal*, 3 (January–March 1982): 43–51.
15. ———, "Impact of Strategic Marketing Decisions on Systematic Risk," ORSA/TIMS Marketing Science Conference, Vanderbilt University, Session SA-2B, March 1985.
16. Larréché, Jean-Claude, and Gatignon, Hubert, *Markstrat: A Marketing Strategy Game*, The Scientific Press, Palo Alto, CA, 1977.
17. ——— and ———, *Markstrat: A Marketing Strategy Game* (*Teaching Notes*), The Scientific Press, Palo Alto, CA, 1977.
18. ———, and Srinivasan, V., "STRATPORT: A Model for the Evaluation and Formulation of Business Portfolio Strategies," *Management Science*, 28 (September 1982): 979–1001.
19. Mahajan, Vijay, Wind, Yoram, and Bradford, John, "Stochastic Dominance Rules for Product Portfolio Analysis," in *TIMS Studies in the Management Sciences: Marketing Planning Models*, A. A. Zoltners, ed., North-Holland, Amsterdam, 1982, p. 161.
20. Polli, Rolando, and Cook, Victor J., "Validity of the Product Life Cycle," *Journal of Business*, 42 (October 1969): 385–400.
21. Rappaport, Alfred, "Selecting Strategies that Create Shareholder Value," *Harvard Business Review,* 59 (May–June 1981): 139–149.
22. Urban, Glen L.,and Hauser, John R., *Design and Marketing of New Products*, Prentice-Hall, Englewood Cliffs, NJ, 1980, p. 618.

23. Utsey, Marjorie F., "A Study of the Achievement of Profit Potential in a Simulated Environment," unpublished Ph.D. dissertation, Tulane University, New Orleans, LA., 1985.
24. ———, and Cook, Victor J., Jr., "A Marketing Strategy Paradigm for Case Analysis," in *AMA Educator's Proceedings*, Russell W. Belk, et al., eds., American Marketing Association, Chicago, 1984, pp. 96–100.
25. Wind, Yoram, and Mahajan, Vijay, "Designing Product and Business Portfolios," *Harvard Business Review*, 59 (January–February 1981): 155–165.
26. ———, ———, and Swire, Donald J., "An Empirical Comparison of Standardized Portfolio Models," *Journal of Marketing*, 47 (Spring 1983): 89–99.
27. ———, and Eliashberg, Jehoshua, "The Measurement and Management of Marketing Risk in New Product Growth Markets," ORSA/TIMS Marketing Science Conference, Vanderbilt University, Session SA-2B, 1985.

30

From Competitive Advantage to Corporate Strategy

Michael E. Porter

The need to rethink corporate strategy could hardly be more urgent. To survive, companies must understand what good corporate strategy is.

Corporate strategy, the overall plan for a diversified company, is both the darling and the stepchild of contemporary management practice—the darling because CEOs have been obsessed with diversification since the early 1960s, the stepchild because almost no consensus exists about what corporate strategy is, much less about how a company should formulate it.

A DIVERSIFIED COMPANY has two levels of strategy: business unit (or competitive) strategy and corporate (or companywide) strategy. Competitive strategy concerns how to create competitive advantage in each of the businesses in which a company competes. Corporate strategy concerns two different questions: what businesses the corporation should be in and how the corporate office should manage the array of business units.

Corporate strategy is what makes the corporate whole add up to more than the sum of its business unit parts.

The track record of corporate strategies has been dismal. I studied the diversification records of 33 large, prestigious U.S. companies over the 1950–1986 period and found that most of them had divested many more acquisitions than they had kept. The corporate strategies of most companies have dissipated instead of created shareholder value.

The need to rethink corporate strategy could hardly be more urgent. By taking over companies and breaking them up, corporate raiders thrive on failed corporate strategy. Fueled by junk bond financing and growing acceptability, raiders can expose any company to takeover, no matter how large or blue chip,

Recognizing past diversification mistakes, some companies have initiated large-scale restructuring programs. Others have done nothing at all. Whatever the response, the strategic questions persist. Those who have restructured must decide what to do next to avoid repeating the past; those who have done nothing must awake to their vulnerability. To survive, companies must understand what good corporate strategy is.

A Sober Picture

While there is disquiet about the success of corporate strategies, none of the available evidence satisfactorily indicates the success or failure of corporate strategy. Most studies have approached the question by measuring the stock market valuation of mergers, captured in the movement of the stock prices of acquiring companies immediately before and after mergers are announced.

These studies show that the market values mergers as neutral or slightly negative, hardly cause for serious concern.[1] Yet the short-term market reaction is a highly imperfect measure of the long-term success of diversification, and no self-respecting executive would judge a corporate strategy this way.

Michael E. Porter is professor of business administration at the Harvard Business School and author of *Competitive Advantage* (Free Press, 1985) and *Competitive Strategy (Free Press*, 1980).

Exhibit I
Diversification Profiles of 33 Leading U.S. Companies

Company	Number Total Entries	All Entries into New Industries	Percent Acquisitions	Percent Joint Ventures	Percent Start-Ups	Entries into New Industries That Represented Entirely New Fields	Percent Acquisitions	Percent Joint Ventures	Percent Start-Ups
ALCO Standard	221	165	99%	0%	1%	56	100%	0%	0%
Allied Corp.	77	49	67	10	22	17	65	6	29
Beatrice	382	204	97	1	2	61	97	0	3
Borden	170	96	77	4	19	32	75	3	22
CBS	148	81	67	16	17	28	65	21	14
Continental Group	75	47	77	6	17	19	79	11	11
Cummins Engine	30	24	54	17	29	13	46	23	31
Du Pont	80	39	33	16	51	19	37	0	63
Exxon	79	56	34	5	61	17	29	6	65
General Electric	160	108	47	20	33	29	48	14	38
General Foods	92	53	91	4	6	22	86	5	9
General Mills	110	102	84	7	9	27	74	7	19
W. R. Grace	275	202	83	7	10	66	74	5	21
Gulf & Western	178	140	91	4	6	48	88	2	10
IBM	46	38	18	18	63	16	19	0	81
IC Industries	67	41	85	3	12	17	88	6	6
ITT	246	178	89	2	9	50	92	0	8
Johnson & Johnson	88	77	77	0	23	18	56	0	44
Mobil	41	32	53	16	31	15	60	7	33
Procter & Gamble	28	23	61	0	39	14	79	0	21
Raytheon	70	58	86	9	5	16	81	19	6
RCA	53	46	35	15	50	19	37	21	42
Rockwell	101	75	73	24	3	27	74	22	4
Sara Lee	197	141	96	1	4	41	95	2	2
Scovill	52	36	97	0	3	12	92	0	8
Signal	53	45	67	4	29	20	75	0	25
Tenneco	85	62	81	6	13	26	73	8	19
3M	144	125	54	2	45	34	71	3	56
TRW	119	82	77	10	13	28	64	11	25
United Technologies	62	49	57	18	24	17	23	17	39
Westinghouse	129	73	63	11	26	36	61	3	36
Wickes	71	47	83	0	17	22	68	0	32
Xerox	59	50	66	6	28	18	50	11	39
Total	3,788	2,644				906			
Average	114.8	80.1	70.3%	7.9%	21.8%	27.4	67.9%	7.0%	25.9%

Note: Beatrice, Continental Group, General Foods, RCA, Scovill, and Signal were taken over as the study was being completed. Their data cover the period up through takeover but not subsequent divestments.

Studying the diversification programs of a company over a long period of time is a much more telling way to determine whether a corporate strategy has succeeded or failed. My study of 33 companies, many of which have reputations for good management, is a unique look at the track record of major corporations. (For an explanation of the research, see the insert "Where the Data Come From.") Each company entered an average of 80 new industries and 27 new fields. Just over 70% of the new entries were acquisitions, 22% were start-ups, and 8% were joint ventures. IBM, Exxon, Du Pont, and 3M, for example, focused on start-ups, while ALCO Standard, Beatrice, and Sara Lee diversified almost solely through acquisitions (Exhibit I has a complete rundown).

My data paint a sobering picture of the success ratio of these moves (see Exhibit II). I found that on average corporations divested more than half their acquisitions in new industries and more than 60% of their acquisitions in entirely new fields. Fourteen companies left more than 70% of all the acquisitions they had made in new fields. The track record in unrelated acquisitions is even worse—the average divestment rate is a startling 74% (see Exhibit III). Even a highly respected company like General Electric divested a very high percentage of its acquisitions, particularly those in new fields: Companies near the top of the list in Exhibit II achieved a remarkably low rate of divestment. Some bear witness to the success of well-thought-out corporate strategies.

Exhibit II
Acquisition Track Records of Leading U.S. Diversifiers Ranked by Percent Divested

Company	All Acquisitions in New Industries	Percent Made by 1980 and Then Divested	Percent Made by 1975 and Then Divested	Acquisitions in New Industries That Represented Entirely New Fields	Percent Made by 1980 and Then Divested	Percent Made by 1975 and Then Divested
Johnson & Johnson	59	17%	12%	10	33%	14%
Procter & Gamble	14	17	17	11	17	17
Raytheon	50	17	26	13	25	33
United Technologies	28	25	13	10	17	0
3M	67	26	27	24	42	45
TRW	63	27	31	18	40	38
IBM	7	33	0*	3	33	0*
Du Pont	13	38	43	7	60	75
Mobil	17	38	57	9	50	50
Borden	74	39	40	24	45	50
IC Industries	35	42	50	15	46	44
Tenneco	50	43	47	19	27	33
Beatrice	198	46	45	59	52	51
ITT	159	52	52	46	61	61
Rockwell	55	56	57	20	71	71
Allied Corp.	33	57	45	11	40	80
Exxon	19	62	20*	5	80	50*
Sara Lee	135	62	65	39	80	76
General Foods	48	63	62	19	93	93
Scovill	35	64	77	11	64	70
Signal	30	65	63	15	70	67
ALCO Standard	164	65	70	56	72	76
W. R. Grace	167	65	70	49	71	70
General Electric	51	65	78	14	100	100
Wickes	38	67	72	15	73	70
Westinghouse	46	68	69	22	61	59
Xerox	33	71	79	9	100	100
Continental Group	36	71	72	15	60	60
General Mills	86	75	73	20	65	60
Gulf & Western	127	79	78	42	75	72
Cummins Engine	13	80	80	6	83	83
RCA	16	80	92	7	86	100
CBS	54	87	89	18	88	88
Total	2,021			661		
Average per Company†	61.2	53.4%	56.5%	20.0	60.0%	61.5%

*Companies with three or fewer acquisitions by the cutoff year.

†Companies with three or fewer acquisitions by the cutoff year are excluded from the average to minimize statistical distortions.

Note: Beatrice, Continental Group, General Foods, RCA, Scovill, and Signal were taken over as the study was being completed. Their data cover the period up through takeover but not subsequent divestments.

Others, however, enjoy a lower rate simply because they have not faced up to their problem units and divested them.

I calculated total shareholder returns (stock price appreciation plus dividends) over the period of the study for each company so that I could compare them with its divestment rate. While companies near the top of the list have above-average shareholder returns, returns are not a reliable measure of diversification success. Shareholder return often depends heavily on the inherent attractiveness of companies' base extremely profitable base businesses that subsidized poor diversification track records.

I would like to make one comment on the use of shareholder value to judge performance. Linking shareholder value quantitatively to diversification performance only works if you compare the shareholder value that is with the shareholder value that might have been without diversification. Because such a comparison is virtually impossible to make, my own measure of diversification success—the number of units retained by the company—seems to be as good an indicator as any of the contribution of diversification to corporate performance.

My data give a stark indication of the failure of corporate strategies.[2] Of the 33 companies, 6 had been taken over as my study was being completed (see the note on Exhibit II). Only the lawyers, investment bankers, and original sellers have prospered in most of these acquisitions, not the shareholders.

Exhibit III
Diversification Performance in Joint Ventures, Start-Ups, and Unrelated Acquisitions
(Companies in same order as in Exhibit II)

Company	Joint Ventures as a Percent of New Entries	Percent Made by 1980 and Then Divested	Percent Made by 1975 and Then Divested	Start-Ups as a Percent of New Entries	Percent Made by 1980 and Then Divested	Percent Made by 1975 and Then Divested	Unrelated Acquisitions as a Percent of Total Acquisitions	Percent Made by 1980 and Then Divested	Percent Made by 1975 and Then Divested
Johnson & Johnson	0%	†	†	23%	14%	20%	0%	†	†
Procter & Gamble	0	†	†	39	0	0	9	†	†
Raytheon	9	60%	60%	5	50	50	46	40%	40%
United Technologies	18	50	50	24	11	20	40	0*	0*
3M	2	100*	100*	45	2	3	33	75	86
TRW	10	20	25	13	63	71	39	71	71
IBM	18	100*	†	63	20	22	33	100*	100*
Du Pont	16	100*	†	51	61	61	43	0*	0*
Mobil	16	33	33	31	50	56	67	60	100
Borden	4	33	33	19	17	13	21	80	80
IC Industries	3	100*	100*	13	80	30	33	50	50
Tenneco	6	67	67	13	67	80	42	33	40
Beatrice	1	†	†	2	0	0	63	59	53
ITT	2	0*	†	8	38	57	61	67	64
Rockwell	24	38	42	3	0	0	35	100	100
Allied Corp.	10	100	75	22	38	29	45	50	0
Exxon	5	0	0	61	27	19	100	80	50*
Sara Lee	1	†	†	4	75	100*	41	73	73
General Foods	4	†	†	6	67	50	42	86	83
Scovill	0	†	†	3	100	100*	45	80	100
Signal	4	†	†	29	20	11	67	50	50
ALCO Standard	0	†	†	1	†	†	63	79	81
W. R. Grace	7	33	38	10	71	71	39	65	65
General Electric	20	20	33	33	33	44	36	100	100
Wickes	0	†	†	17	63	57	60	80	75
Westinghouse	11	0*	0*	26	44	44	36	57	67
Xerox	6	100*	100*	28	50	56	22	100	100
Continental Group	6	67	67	17	14	0	40	83	100
General Mills	7	71	71	9	89	80	65	77	67
Gulf & Western	4	75	50	6	100	100	74	77	74
Cummins Engine	17	50	50	29	0	0	67	100	100
RCA	15	67	67	50	99	55	36	100	100
CBS	16	71	71	17	86	80	39	100	100
Average per company‡	7.9%	50.3%	48.9%	21.8%	44.0%	40.9%	46.1%	74.0%	74.4%

*Companies with two or fewer entries.
†No entries in this category.
‡Average excludes companies with two or fewer entries to minimize statistical distortions.
Note: Beatrice, Continental Group, General Foods, RCA, Scovill, and Signal were taken over as the study was being completed. Their data cover the period up through takeover but not subsequent divestments.

Premises of Corporate Strategy

Any successful corporate strategy builds on a number of premises. These are facts of life about diversification. They cannot be altered, and when ignored, they explain in part why so many corporate strategies fail.

Competition occurs at the business unit level. Diversified companies do not compete; only their business units do. Unless a corporate strategy places primary attention on nurturing the success of each unit, the strategy will fail, no matter how elegantly constructed. Successful corporate strategy must grow out of and reinforce competitive strategy.

Diversification inevitably adds costs and constraints to business units. Obvious costs such as the corporate overhead allocated to a unit may not be as important or subtle as the hidden costs and constraints. A business unit must explain its decisions to top management, spend time complying with planning and other corporate systems, live with parent company guidelines and personnel policies, and forgo the opportunity to motivate employees with direct equity ownership. These costs and constraints can be reduced but not entirely eliminated.

Shareholders can readily diversify themselves. Shareholders can diversify their own portfolios of stocks by selecting

Where the Data Come From

We studied the 1950–1986 diversification histories of 33 large diversified U.S. companies. They were chosen at random from many broad sectors of the economy.

To eliminate distortions caused by World War II, we chose 1950 as the base year and then identified each business the company was in. We tracked every acquisition, joint venture, and start-up made over this period —3,788 in all. We classified each as an entry into an entirely new sector or field (financial services, for example), a new industry within a field the company was already in (insurance, for example), or a geographic extension of an existing product or service. We also classified each new field as related or unrelated to existing units. Then we tracked whether and when each entry was divested or shut down and the number of years each remained part of the corporation.

Our sources included annual reports, 10K forms, the F&S Index, and Moody's, supplemented by our judgment and general knowledge of the industries involved. In a few cases, we asked the companies specific questions.

It is difficult to determine the success of an entry without knowing the full purchase or start-up price, the profit history, the amount and timing of ongoing investments made in the unit, whether any write-offs or write-downs were taken, and the selling price and terms of sale. Instead, we employed a relatively simple way to gauge success: *whether the entry was divested or shut down.* The underlying assumption is that a company will generally not divest or close down a successful business except in a comparatively few special cases. Companies divested many of the entries in our sample within five years, a reflection of disappointment with performance. Of the comparatively few divestments where the company disclosed a loss or a gain, the divestment resulted in a reported loss in more than half the cases.

The data in Exhibit I cover the entire 1950–1986 period. However, the divestment ratios in Exhibit II and Exhibit III do not compare entries and divestments over the entire period because doing so would overstate the success of diversification. Companies usually do not shut down or divest new entries immediately but hold them for some time to give them an opportunity to succeed. Our data show that the average holding period is five to slightly more than ten years, though many divestments occur within five years. To accurately gauge the success of diversification, we calculated the percentage of entries made by 1975 and by 1980 that were divested or closed down as of January 1987. If we had included more recent entries, we would have biased upward our assessment of how successful these entries had been.

As compiled, these data probably understate the rate of failure. Companies tend to announce acquisitions and other forms of new entry with a flourish but divestments and shutdowns with a whimper, if at all. We have done our best to root out every such transaction, but we have undoubtedly missed some. There may also be new entries that we did not uncover, but our best impression is that the number is not large.

---

those that best match their preferences and risk profiles.[3] Shareholders can often diversify more cheaply than a corporation because they can buy shares at the market price and avoid hefty acquisition premiums.

These premises mean that corporate strategy cannot succeed unless it truly adds value—to business units by providing tangible benefits that offset the inherent costs of lost independence and to shareholders by diversifying in a way they could not replicate.

Passing the Essential Tests

To understand how to formulate corporate strategy, it is necessary to specify the conditions under which diversification will truly create shareholder value. These conditions can be summarized in three essential tests:

1. *The attractiveness test.* The industries chosen for diversification must be structurally attractive or capable of being made attractive.
2. *The cost-of-entry test.* The cost of entry must not capitalize all the future profits.
3. *The better-off test.* Either the new unit must gain competitive advantage from its link with the corporation or vice versa.

Of course, most companies will make certain that their proposed strategies pass some of these tests. But my study clearly shows that when companies ignored one or two of them, the strategic results were disastrous.

How Attractive Is the Industry?

In the long run, the rate of return available from competing in an industry is a function of its underlying structure, which I have described in another HBR article.[4] An attractive industry with a high average return on investment will be difficult to enter because entry barriers are high, suppliers and buyers have only modest bargaining power, substitute products or services are few, and the rivalry among competitors is stable. An unattractive industry like steel will have structural flaws, including a plethora of substitute materials, powerful and price-sensitive buyers, and excessive rivalry caused by high fixed costs and a large group of competitors, many of whom are state supported.

Diversification cannot create shareholder value unless new industries have favorable structures that support returns exceeding the cost of capital. If the industry doesn't have such returns, the company must be able to restructure the industry or gain a sustainable competitive advantage that leads to returns well above the industry average. An industry need not be attractive before diversification. In fact, a company might benefit from entering before the industry shows its full potential. The diversification can then transform the industry's structure.

In my research, I often found companies had suspended the attractiveness test because they had a vague belief that the industry "fit" very closely with their own businesses. In the hope that the corporate "comfort" they felt would lead to a happy outcome, the companies ignored fundamentally poor industry structures. Unless the close fit allows substantial competitive advantage, however, such comfort will turn into pain when diversification results in poor returns. Royal Dutch Shell and other leading oil companies have had this unhappy experience in a number of chemicals businesses, where poor industry structures overcame the benefits of vertical integration and skills in process technology.

Another common reason for ignoring the attractiveness test is a low entry cost. Sometimes the buyer has an inside track or the owner is anxious to sell. Even if the price is actually low, however, a one-shot gain will not offset a perpetually poor business. Almost always, the company finds it must reinvest in the newly acquired unit, if only to replace fixed assets and fund working capital.

Diversifying companies are also prone to use rapid growth or other simple indicators as a proxy for a target industry's attractiveness. Many that rushed into fast-growing industries (personal computers, video games, and robotics, for example) were burned because they mistook early growth for long-term profit potential. Industries are profitable not because they are sexy or high tech; they are profitable only if their structures are attractive.

What Is the Cost of Entry?

Diversification cannot build shareholder value if the cost of entry into a new business eats up its expected returns. Strong market forces, however, are working to do just that. A company can enter new industries by acquisition or start-up. Acquisitions expose it to an increasingly efficient merger market. An acquirer beats the market if it pays a price not fully reflecting the prospects of the new unit. Yet multiple bidders are commonplace, information flows rapidly, and investment bankers and other intermediaries work aggressively to make the market as efficient as possible. In recent years, new financial instruments such as junk bonds have brought new buyers into the market and made even large companies vulnerable to takeover. Acquisition premiums are high and reflect the acquired company's future prospects —sometimes too well. Philip Morris paid more than four times book value for Seven-Up Company, for example. Simple arithmetic meant that profits had to more than quadruple to sustain the preacquisition ROI. Since there proved to be little Philip Morris could add in marketing prowess to the sophisticated marketing wars in the soft-drink industry, the result was the unsatisfactory financial performance of Seven-Up and ultimately the decision to divest.

In a start-up, the company must overcome entry barriers. It's a real catch-22 situation, however, since attractive industries are attractive because their entry barriers are high. Bearing the full cost of the entry barriers might well dissipate any potential profits. Otherwise, other entrants to the industry would have already eroded its profitability.

In the excitement of finding an appealing new business, companies sometimes forget to apply the cost-of-entry test. The more attractive a new industry, the more expensive it is to get into.

Will the Business Be Better Off?

A corporation must bring some significant competitive advantage to the new unit, or the new unit must offer potential for significant advantage to the corporation. Sometimes, the benefits to the new unit accrue only once, near the time of entry, when the parent instigates a major overhaul of its strategy or installs a first-rate management team. Other diversification yields ongoing competitive advantage if the new unit can market its product, through the well-developed distribution system of its sister units, for instance. This is one of the important underpinnings of the merger of Baxter Travenol and American Hospital Supply

When the benefit to the new unit comes only once, the parent company has no rationale for holding the new unit in its portfolio over the long term. Once the results of the one-time improvement are clear, the diversified company no longer adds value to offset the inevitable costs imposed on the unit. It is best to sell the unit and free up corporate resources.

The better-off test does not imply that diversifying corporate risk creates shareholder value in and of itself. Doing something for shareholders that they can do themselves is not a basis for corporate strategy. (Only in the case of a privately held company, in which the company's and the shareholder's risk are the same, is diversification to reduce risk valuable for its own sake.) Diversification of risk should only be a by-product of corporate strategy, not a prime motivator.

Executives ignore the better-off test most of all or deal with it through arm waving or trumped-up logic rather than hard strategic analysis. One reason is that they confuse company size with shareholder value. In the drive to run a bigger company, they lose sight of their real job. They may justify the suspension of the better-off test by pointing to the way they manage diversity. By cutting corporate staff to the bone and giving business units nearly complete autonomy, they believe they avoid the pitfalls. Such thinking misses the whole point of diversification, which is to create shareholder value rather than to avoid destroying it.

Concepts of Corporate Strategy

The three tests for successful diversification set the standards that any corporate strategy must meet; meeting them is so difficult that most diversification fails. Many companies lack a clear concept of corporate strategy to guide their diversification or pursue a concept that does not address the tests. Others fail because they implement a strategy poorly.

My study has helped me identify four concepts of corporate strategy that have been put into practice—portfolio management, restructuring, transferring skills, and sharing activities. While the concepts are not always mutually exclusive, each rests on a different mechanism by which the corporation creates shareholder value and each requires the diversified company to manage and organize itself in a different way. The first two require no connections among business units; the second two depend on them. (See Exhibit IV.) While all four concepts of strategy have succeeded under the right circumstances, today some make more sense than others. Ignoring any of the concepts is perhaps the quickest road to failure.

Portfolio Management

The concept of corporate strategy most in use is portfolio management, which is based primarily on diversification through acquisition. The corporation acquires sound, attrac-

Exhibit IV
Concepts of Corporate Strategy

	Portfolio Management	Restructuring	Transferring Skills	Sharing Activities
Strategic Prerequisites	Superior insight into identifying and acquiring undervalued companies Willingness to sell off losers quickly or to opportunistically divest good performers when buyers are willing to pay large premiums Broad guidelines for and constraints on the types of units in the portfolio so that senior management can play the review role effectively A private company or undeveloped capital markets Ability to shift away from portfolio management as the capital markets get more efficient or the company gets unwieldy	Superior insight into identifying restructuring opportunities Willingness and capability to intervene to transform acquired units Broad similarities among the units in the portfolio Willingness to cut losses by selling off units where restructuring proves unfeasible Willingness to sell units when restructuring is complete, the results are clear, and market conditions are favorable	Proprietary skills in activities important to competitive advantage in target industries Ability to accomplish the transfer of skills among units on an ongoing basis Acquisitions of beachhead positions in new industries as a base	Activities in existing units that can be shared with new business units to gain competitive advantage Benefits of sharing that outweigh the costs Both start-ups and acquisitions as entry vehicles Ability to overcome organizational resistance to business unit collaboration
Organizational Prerequisites	Autonomous business units A very small, low-cost, corporate staff Incentives based largely on business unit results	Autonomous business units A corporate organization with the talent and resources to oversee the turnarounds and strategic repositionings of acquired units Incentives based largely on acquired units' results	Largely automous but collaborative business units High-level corporate staff members who see their role primarily as integrators Cross-business-unit committees, task forces, and other forums to serve as focal points for capturing and transferring skills Objectives of line managers that include skills transfer Incentives based in part on corporate results	Strategic business units that are encouraged to share activities An active strategic planning role at group, sector, and corporate levels High-level corporate staff members who see their roles primarily as integrators Incentives based heavily on group and corporate results
Common Pitfalls	Pursuing portfolio management in in countries with efficient capital marketing and a developed pool of professional management talent Ignoring the fact that industry structure is not attractive	Mistaking rapid growth or a "hot" industry as sufficient evidence of a restructuring opportunity Lacking the resolve or resources to take on troubled situations and to intervene in management Ignoring the fact that industry structure is not attractive Paying lip service to restructuring but actually practicing passive portfolio management	Mistaking similarity or comfort with new businesses as sufficient basis for diversification Providing no practical ways for skills transfer to occur Ignoring the fact that industry structure is not attractive	Sharing for its own sake rather than because it leads to competitive advantage Assuming sharing will occur naturally without senior management playing an active role Ignoring the fact that industry structure is not attractive

tive companies with competent managers who agree to stay on. While acquired units do not have to be in the same industries as existing units, the best portfolio managers generally limit their range of businesses in some way, in part to limit the specific expertise needed by top management.

The acquired units are autonomous, and the teams that run them are compensated according to unit results. The corporation supplies capital and works with each to infuse it with professional management techniques. At the same time, top management provides objective and dispassionate review of business unit results. Portfolio managers categorize units by potential and regularly transfer resources from units that generate cash to those with high potential and cash needs.

In a portfolio strategy, the corporation seeks to create shareholder value in a number of ways. It uses its expertise and analytical resources to spot attractive acquisition candidates that the individual shareholder could not. The company provides capital on favorable terms that reflect corporate-wide fund-raising ability. It introduces professional management skills and discipline. Finally, it provides high-quality review and coaching, unencumbered by conventional wisdom or emotional attachments to the business.

The logic of the portfolio management concept rests on a number of vital assumptions. If a company's diversification plan is to meet the attractiveness and cost-of-entry tests, it must find good but undervalued companies. Acquired companies must be truly undervalued because the parent does little for the new unit once it is acquired. To meet the better-off test, the benefits the corporation provides must yield a significant competitive advantage to acquired units. The style of operating through highly autonomous business units must both develop sound business strategies and motivate managers.

In most countries, the days when portfolio management was a valid concept of corporate strategy are past. In the face of increasingly well-developed capital markets, attractive companies with good managements show up on everyone's computer screen and attract top dollar in terms of acquisition premium. Simply contributing capital isn't contributing much. A sound strategy can easily be funded; small to medium-size companies don't need a munificent parent.

Other benefits have also eroded. Large companies no longer corner the market for professional management skills; in fact, more and more observers believe managers cannot necessarily run anything in the absence of industry-specific knowledge and experience. Another supposed advantage of the portfolio management concept—dispassionate review—rests on similarly shaky ground since the added value of review alone is questionable in a portfolio of sound companies.

The benefit of giving business units complete autonomy is also questionable. Increasingly, a company's business units are interrelated, drawn together by new technology, broadening distribution channels, and changing regulations. Setting strategies of units independently may well undermine unit performance. The companies in my sample that have succeeded in diversification have recognized the value of interrelationships and understood that a strong sense of corporate identity is as important as slavish adherence to parochial business unit financial results.

But it is the sheer complexity of the management task that has ultimately defeated even the best portfolio managers. As the size of the company grows, portfolio managers need to find more and more deals just to maintain growth. Supervising dozens or even hundreds of disparate units and under chain-letter pressures to add more, management begins to make mistakes. At the same time, the inevitable costs of being part of a diversified company take their toll and unit performance slides while the whole company's ROI turns downward. Eventually, a new management team is installed that initiates wholesale divestments and pares down the company to its core businesses. The experiences of Gulf & Western, Consolidated Foods (now Sara Lee), and ITT are just a few comparatively recent examples. Reflecting these realities, the U.S. capital markets today reward companies that follow the portfolio management model with a "conglomerate discount"; they value the whole less than the sum of the parts.

In developing countries, where large companies are few, capital markets are undeveloped, and professional management is scarce, portfolio management still works. But it is no longer a valid model for corporate strategy in advanced economies. Nevertheless, the technique is in the limelight today in the United Kingdom, where it is supported so far by a newly energized stock market eager for excitement. But this enthusiasm will wane—as well it should. Portfolio management is no way to conduct corporate strategy.

Restructuring

Unlike its passive role as a portfolio manager, when it serves as banker and reviewer, a company that bases its strategy on restructuring becomes an active restructurer of business units. The new businesses are not necessarily related to existing units. All that is necessary is unrealized potential.

The restructuring strategy seeks out undeveloped, sick, or threatened organizations or industries on the threshold of significant change. The parent intervenes, frequently changing the unit management team, shifting strategy, or infusing the company with new technology. Then it may make follow-up acquisitions to build a critical mass and sell off unneeded or unconnected parts and thereby reduce the effective acquisition cost. The result is a strengthened company or a transformed industry. As a coda, the parent sells off the stronger

An Uncanny British Restructurer

Hanson Trust, on its way to becoming Britain's largest company, is one of several skillful followers of the restructuring concept. A conglomerate with units in many industries, Hanson might seem on the surface a portfolio manager. In fact, Hanson and one or two other conglomerates have a much more effective corporate strategy. Hanson has acquired companies such as London Brick, Ever Ready Batteries, and SCM, which the city of London rather disdainfully calls "low tech."

Although a mature company suffering from low growth, the typical Hanson target is not just in any industry; it has an attractive structure. Its customer and supplier power is low and rivalry with competitors moderate. The target is a market leader, rich in assets but formerly poor in management. Hanson pays little of the present value of future cash flow out in an acquisition premium and reduces purchase price even further by aggressively selling off businesses that it cannot improve. In this way, it recoups just over a third of the cost of a typical acquisition during the first six months of ownership. Imperial Group's plush properties in London lasted barely two months under Hanson ownership, while Hanson's recent sale of Courage Breweries to Elders recouped £1.4 billion of the original £2.1 billion acquisition price of Imperial Group.

Like the best restructurers, Hanson approaches each unit with a modus operandi that it has perfected through repetition.

Hanson emphasizes low costs and tight financial controls. It has cut an average of 25% of labor costs out of acquired companies, slashed fixed overheads, and tightened capital expenditures. To reinforce its strategy of keeping costs low, Hanson carves out detailed one-year financial budgets with divisional managers and (through generous use of performance-related bonuses and share option schemes) gives them incentive to deliver the goods,

It's too early to tell whether Hanson will adhere to the last tenet of restructuring—selling turned-around units once the results are clear. If it succumbs to the allure of bigness, Hanson may take the course of the failed U.S. conglomerates.

unit once results are clear because the parent is no longer adding value and top management decides that its attention should be directed elsewhere. (See the insert "An Uncanny British Restructurer" for an example of restructuring.)

When well implemented, the restructuring concept is sound, for it passes the three tests of successful diversification. The restructurer meets the cost-of-entry test through the types of company it acquires. It limits acquisition premiums by buying companies with problems and lackluster images or by buying into industries with as yet unforeseen potential. Intervention by the corporation clearly meets the better-off test. Provided that the target industries are structurally attractive, the restructuring model can create enormous shareholder value. Some restructuring companies are Loew's, BTR, and General Cinema. Ironically, many of today's restructurers are profiting from yesterday's portfolio management strategies.

To work, the restructuring strategy requires a corporate management team with the insight to spot undervalued companies or positions in industries ripe for transformation. The same insight is necessary to actually turn the units around even though they are in new and unfamiliar businesses.

These requirements expose the restructurer to considerable risk and usually limit the time in which the company can succeed at the strategy. The most skillful proponents understand this problem, recognize their mistakes, and move decisively to dispose of them. The best companies realize they are not just acquiring companies but restructuring an industry. Unless they can integrate the acquisitions to create a whole new strategic position, they are just portfolio managers in disguise. Another important difficulty surfaces if so many other companies join the action that they deplete the pool of suitable candidates and bid their prices up.

Perhaps the greatest pitfall, however, is that companies find it very hard to dispose of business units once they are restructured and performing well. Human nature fights economic rationale. Size supplants shareholder value as the corporate goal. The company does not sell a unit even though the company no longer adds value to the unit. While the transformed units would be better off in another company that had related businesses, the restructuring company instead retains them. Gradually, it becomes a portfolio manager. The parent company's ROI declines as the need for reinvestment in the units and normal business risks eventually offset restructuring's one-shot gain. The perceived need to keep growing intensifies the pace of acquisition; errors result and standards fall. The restructuring company turns into a conglomerate with returns that only equal the average of all industries at best.

Transferring Skills

The purpose of the first two concepts of corporate strategy is to create value through a company's relationship with each autonomous unit. The corporation's role is to be a selector, a banker, and an intervenor.

The last two concepts exploit the interrelationships between businesses. In articulating them, however, one comes face-to-face with the often ill-defined concept of synergy. If you believe the text of the countless corporate annual reports, just about anything is related to just about anything else! But imagined synergy is much more common than real synergy. GM's purchase of Hughes Aircraft simply because cars were going electronic and Hughes was an electronics concern demonstrates the folly of paper synergy. Such corporate relatedness is an ex post facto rationalization of a diversification undertaken for other reasons.

Even synergy that is clearly defined often fails to materialize. Instead of cooperating, business units often compete. A company that can define the synergies it is pursuing still faces significant organizational impediments in achieving them.

But the need to capture the benefits of relationships between businesses has never been more important. Technological and competitive developments already link many businesses and are creating new possibilities for competitive advantage. In such sectors as financial services, computing, office equipment, entertainment, and health care, interrelationships among previously distinct businesses are perhaps the central concern of strategy.

To understand the role of relatedness in corporate strategy, we must give new meaning to this often ill-defined idea. I have identified a good way to start—the value chain.[5] Every business unit is a collection of discrete activities ranging from sales to accounting that allow it to compete. I call them value activities. It is at this level, not in the company as a whole, that the unit achieves competitive advantage.

I group these activities in nine categories. *Primary* activities create the product or service, deliver and market it, and provide after-sale support. The categories of primary activities are inbound logistics, operations, outbound logistics, marketing and sales, and service. *Support* activities provide the input and infrastructure that allow the primary activities to take place. The categories are company infrastructure, human resource management, technology development, and procurement.

The value chain defines the two types of interrelationships that may create synergy The first is a company's ability to transfer skills or expertise among similar value chains. The second is the ability to share activities. Two business units, for example, can share the same sales force or logistics network.

The value chain helps expose the last two (and most important) concepts of corporate strategy. The transfer of skills among business units in the diversified company is the basis for one concept. While each business unit has a separate value chain, knowledge about how to perform activities is transferred among the units. For example, a toiletries business unit, expert in the marketing of convenience products, transmits ideas on new positioning concepts, promotional techniques, and packaging possibilities to a newly acquired unit that sells cough syrup. Newly entered industries can benefit from the expertise of existing units and vice versa.

These opportunities arise when business units have similar buyers or channels, similar value activities like government relations or procurement, similarities in the broad configuration of the value chain (for example, managing a multisite service organization), or the same strategic concept (for example, low cost). Even though the units operate separately, such similarities allow the sharing of knowledge.

Of course, some similarities are common; one can imagine them at some level between almost any pair of businesses. Countless companies have fallen into the trap of diversifying too readily because of similarities; mere similarity is not enough.

Transferring skills leads to competitive advantage only if the similarities among businesses meet three conditions:

1. The activities involved in the businesses are similar enough that sharing expertise is meaningful. Broad similarities (marketing intensiveness, for example, or a common core process technology such as bending metal) are not a sufficient basis for diversification. The resulting ability to transfer skills is likely to have little impact on competitive advantage.
2. The transfer of skills involves activities important to competitive advantage. Transferring skills in peripheral activities such as government relations or real estate in consumer goods units may be beneficial but is not a basis for diversification.
3. The skills transferred represent a significant source of competitive advantage for the receiving unit. The expertise or skills to be transferred are both advanced and proprietary enough to be beyond the capabilities of competitors.

The transfer of skills is an active process that significantly changes the strategy or operations of the receiving unit. The prospect for change must be specific and identifiable. Almost guaranteeing that no shareholder value will be created, too many companies are satisfied with vague prospects or faint hopes that skills will transfer. The transfer of skills does not happen by accident or by osmosis. The company will have to reassign critical personnel, even on a permanent basis, and the participation and support of high-level management in skills transfer is essential. Many companies have been defeated at skills transfer because they have not provided their business units with any incentives to participate.

Transferring skills meets the tests of diversification if the company truly mobilizes proprietary expertise across units. This makes certain the company can offset the acquisition premium or lower the cost of overcoming entry barriers.

The industries the company chooses for diversification must pass the attractiveness test. Even a close fit that reflects opportunities to transfer skills may not overcome poor industry structure. Opportunities to transfer skills, however, may help the company transform the structures of newly entered industries and send them in favorable directions.

The transfer of skills can be one-time or ongoing. If the company exhausts opportunities to infuse new expertise into a unit after the initial post-acquisition period, the unit should ultimately be sold. The corporation is no longer creating shareholder value. Few companies have grasped this point, however, and many gradually suffer mediocre returns. Yet a company diversified into well-chosen businesses can transfer skills eventually in many directions. If corporate management conceives of its role in this way and creates appropriate organizational mechanisms to facilitate cross-unit interchange, the opportunities to share expertise will be meaningful.

By using both acquisitions and internal development, companies can build a transfer-of-skills strategy. The presence of a strong base of skills sometimes creates the possibility for internal entry instead of the acquisition of a going concern. Successful diversifiers that employ the concept of skills transfer may, however, often acquire a company in the target industry as a beachhead and then build on it with their internal expertise. By doing so, they can reduce some of the risks of internal entry and speed up the process. Two companies that have diversified using the transfer-of-skills concept are 3M and Pepsico.

Sharing Activities

The fourth concept of corporate strategy is based on sharing activities in the value chains among business units. Procter & Gamble, for example, employs a common physical distribution system and sales force in both paper towels and disposable diapers. McKesson, a leading distribution company, will handle such diverse lines as pharmaceuticals and liquor through superwarehouses.

The ability to share activities is a potent basis for corporate strategy because sharing often enhances competitive advantage by lowering cost or raising differentiation. But not all sharing leads to competitive advantage, and companies can encounter deep organizational resistance to even beneficial sharing possibilities. These hard truths have led many companies to reject synergy prematurely and retreat to the false simplicity of portfolio management.

A cost-benefit analysis of prospective sharing opportunities can determine whether synergy is possible. Sharing can lower costs if it achieves economies of scale, boosts the efficiency of utilization, or helps a company move more rapidly down the learning curve. The costs of General Electric's advertising, sales, and after-sales service activities in major appliances are low because they are spread over a wide range of appliance products. Sharing can also enhance the potential for differentiation. A shared order-processing system, for instance, may allow new features and services that a buyer will value. Sharing can also reduce the cost of differentiation. A shared service network, for example, may make more advanced, remote servicing technology economically feasible. Often, sharing will allow an activity to be wholly reconfigured in ways that can dramatically raise competitive advantage.

Sharing must involve activities that are significant to competitive advantage, not just any activity. P&G's distribution system is such an instance in the diaper and paper towel business, where products are bulky and costly to ship. Conversely, diversification based on the opportunities to share only corporate overhead is rarely, if ever, appropriate.

Sharing activities inevitably involves costs that the benefits must outweigh. One cost is the greater coordination required to manage a shared activity. More important is the need to compromise the design or performance of an activity so that it can be shared. A salesperson handling the products of two business units, for example, must operate in a way that is usually not what either unit would choose were it independent. And if compromise greatly erodes the unit's effectiveness, then sharing may reduce rather than enhance competitive advantage.

Many companies have only superficially identified their potential for sharing. Companies also merge activities without consideration of whether they are sensitive to economies of scale. When they are not, the coordination costs kill the benefits. Companies compound such errors by not identifying costs of sharing in advance, when steps can be taken to minimize them. Costs of compromise can frequently be mitigated by redesigning the activity for sharing. The shared salesperson, for example, can be provided with a remote computer terminal to boost productivity and provide more customer information. Jamming business units together without such thinking exacerbates the costs of sharing.

Despite such pitfalls, opportunities to gain advantage from sharing activities have proliferated because of momentous developments in technology, deregulation, and competition. The infusion of electronics and information systems into many industries creates new opportunities to link businesses. The corporate strategy of sharing can involve both acquisition and internal development. Internal development is often possible because the corporation can bring to bear clear resources in launching a new unit. Start-ups are less difficult to integrate than acquisitions. Companies using the shared-activities concept can also make acquisitions as beachhead landings into a new industry and then integrate the units through sharing with other units. Prime examples of companies that have diversified via using shared activities include P&G, Du Pont, and IBM. The fields into which each has diversified are a cluster of tightly related units. Marriott illustrates both successes and failures in sharing activities over time. (See the insert "Adding Value with Hospitality.")

Following the shared-activities model requires an organizational context in which business unit collaboration is encouraged and reinforced. Highly autonomous business units are inimical to such collaboration. The company must put into place a variety of what I call horizontal mechanisms—a strong sense of corporate identity, a clear corporate mission statement that emphasizes the importance of integrating business unit strategies, an incentive system that rewards more than just business unit results, cross business-unit task forces, and other methods of integrating.

A corporate strategy based on shared activities clearly meets the better-off test because business units gain ongoing tangible advantages from others within the corporation. It also meets the cost-of-entry test by reducing the expense of surmounting the barriers to internal entry. Other bids for acquisitions that do not share opportunities will have lower reservation prices. Even widespread opportunities for sharing activities do not allow a company to suspend the attractiveness test, however. Many diversifiers have made the critical mistake of equating the close fit of a target industry with attractive diversification. Target industries must pass the strict requirement test of having an attractive structure as well as a close fit in opportunities if diversification is to ultimately succeed.

Choosing a Corporate Strategy

Each concept of corporate strategy allows the diversified company to create shareholder value in a different way. Companies can succeed with any of the concepts if they clearly define the corporation's role and objectives, have the skills necessary for meeting the concept's prerequisites, organize themselves to manage diversity in a way that fits the strategy, and find themselves in an appropriate capital market environment. The caveat is that portfolio management is only sensible in limited circumstances.

Adding Value with Hospitality

Marriott began in the restaurant business in Washington, D.C. Because its customers often ordered takeouts on the way to the national airport, Marriott eventually entered airline catering. From there, it jumped into food service management for institutions. Marriott then began broadening its base of family restaurants and entered the hotel industry More recently, it has moved into restaurants, snack bars, and merchandise shops in airport terminals and into gourmet restaurants. In addition, Marriott has branched out from its hotel business into cruise ships, theme parks, wholesale travel agencies, budget motels, and retirement centers.

Marriott's diversification has exploited well-developed skills in food service and hospitality. Marriott's kitchens prepare food according to more than 6,000 standardized recipe cards; hotel procedures are also standardized and painstakingly documented in elaborate manuals. Marriott shares a number of important activities across units. A shared procurement and distribution system for food serves all Marriott units through nine regional procurement centers. As a result, Marriott earns 50% higher margins on food service than any other hotel company. Marriott also has a fully integrated real estate unit that brings corporatewide power to bear on site acquisitions as well as on the designing and building of all Marriott locations.

Marriott's diversification strategy balances acquisitions and start-ups. Start-ups or small acquisitions are used for initial entry, depending on how close the opportunities for sharing are. To expand its geographic base, Marriott acquires companies and then disposes of the parts that do not fit.

Apart from this success, it is important to note that Marriott has divested 36% of both its acquisitions and its start-ups. While this is an above-average record, Marriott's mistakes are quite illuminating. Marriott has largely failed in diversifying into gourmet restaurants, theme parks, cruise ships, and wholesale travel agencies. In the first three businesses, Marriott discovered it could not transfer skills despite apparent similarities. Standardized menus did not work well in gourmet restaurants. Running cruise ships and theme parks was based more on entertainment and pizzazz than the carefully disciplined management of hotels and mid-price restaurants. The wholesale travel agencies were ill fated from the start because Marriott had to compete with an important customer for its hotels and had no proprietary skills or opportunities to share with which to add value.

A company's choice of corporate strategy is partly a legacy of its past. If its business units are in unattractive industries, the company must start from scratch. If the company has few truly proprietary skills or activities it can share in related diversification, then its initial diversification must rely on other concepts. Yet corporate strategy should not be a once-and-for-all choice but a vision that can evolve. A company should choose its long-term preferred concept and then proceed pragmatically toward it from its initial starting point.

Both the strategic logic and the experience of the companies I studied over the last decade suggest that a company will create shareholder value through diversification to a greater and greater extent as its strategy moves from portfolio management toward sharing activities. Because they do not rely on superior insight or other questionable assumptions about the company's capabilities, sharing activities and transferring skills offer the best avenues for value creation.

Each concept of corporate strategy is not mutually exclusive of those that come before, a potent advantage of the third and fourth concepts. A company can employ a restructuring strategy at the same time it transfers skills or shares activities. A strategy based on shared activities becomes more powerful if business units can also exchange skills. As the Marriott case illustrates, a company can often pursue the two strategies together and even incorporate some of the principles of restructuring with them. When it chooses industries in which to transfer skills or share activities, the company can also investigate the possibility of transforming the industry structure. When a company bases its strategy on interrelationships, it has a broader basis on which to create shareholder value than if it rests its entire strategy on transforming companies in unfamiliar industries.

My study supports the soundness of basing a corporate strategy on the transfer of skills or shared activities. The data on the sample companies' diversification programs illustrate some important characteristics of successful diversifiers. They have made a disproportionately low percentage of unrelated acquisitions, *unrelated* being defined as having no clear opportunity to transfer skills or share important activities (see Exhibit III). Even successful diversifiers such as 3M, IBM, and TRW have terrible records when they have strayed into unrelated acquisitions. Successful acquirers diversify into fields, each of which is related to many others. Procter & Gamble and IBM, for example, operate in 18 and 19 interrelated fields respectively and so enjoy numerous opportunities to transfer skills and share activities.

Companies with the best acquisition records tend to make heavier-than-average use of start-ups and joint ventures. Most companies shy away from modes of entry besides acquisition. My results cast doubt on the conventional wisdom regarding start-ups. Exhibit III demonstrates that while joint ventures are about as risky as acquisitions, start-ups are not. Moreover, successful companies often have very good records with start-up units, as 3M, P&G, Johnson & Johnson, IBM, and United Technologies illustrate. When a company has the internal strength to start up a unit, it can be safer and less costly to launch a company than to rely solely on an acquisition and then have to deal with the problem of integration. Japanese diversification histories support the soundness of start-up as an entry alternative.

My data also illustrate that none of the concepts of corporate strategy works when industry structure is poor or implementation is bad, no matter how related the industries are. Xerox acquired companies in related industries, but the businesses had poor structures and its skills were insufficient to provide enough competitive advantage to offset implementation problems.

An Action Program

To translate the principles of corporate strategy into successful diversification, a company must first take an objective look at its existing businesses and the value added by the corporation. Only through such an assessment can an understanding of good corporate strategy grow. That understanding should guide future diversification as well as the development of skills and activities with which to select further new businesses. The following action program provides a concrete approach to conducting such a review. A company can choose a corporate strategy by:

1. *Identifying the interrelationships among already existing business units.*

A company should begin to develop a corporate strategy by identifying all the opportunities it has to share activities or transfer skills in its existing portfolio of business units. The company will not only find ways to enhance the competitive advantage of existing units but also come upon several possible diversification avenues. The lack of meaningful interrelationships in the portfolio is an equally important finding, suggesting the need to justify the value added by the corporation or, alternately, a fundamental restructuring.

2. *Selecting the core businesses that will be the foundation of the corporate strategy.*

Successful diversification starts with an understanding of the core businesses that will serve as the basis for corporate strategy. Core businesses are those that are in an attractive industry, have the potential to achieve sustainable competitive advantage, have important interrelationships with other business units, and provide skills or activities that represent a base from which to diversify

The company must first make certain its core businesses are on sound footing by upgrading management, internationalizing strategy, or improving technology. My study shows that geographic extensions of existing units, whether by acquisition, joint venture, or start-up, had a substantially lower divestment rate than diversification.

The company must then patiently dispose of the units that are not core businesses. Selling them will free resources that could be better deployed elsewhere. In some cases disposal implies immediate liquidation, while in others the company should dress up the units and wait for a propitious market or a particularly eager buyer.

3. *Creating horizontal organizational mechanisms to facilitate interrelationships among the core businesses and lay the groundwork for future related diversification.*

Top management can facilitate interrelationships by emphasizing cross-unit collaboration, grouping units organizationally and modifying incentives, and taking steps to build a strong sense of corporate identity

4. *Pursuing diversification opportunities that allow shared activities.*

This concept of corporate strategy is the most compelling, provided a company's strategy passes all three tests. A company should inventory activities in existing business units that represent the strongest foundation for sharing, such as strong distribution channels or world-class technical facilities. These will in turn lead to potential new business areas. A company can use acquisitions as a beachhead or employ start-ups to exploit internal capabilities and minimize integrating problems.

5. *Pursuing diversification through the transfer of skills if opportunities for sharing activities are limited or exhausted.*

Companies can pursue this strategy through acquisition, although they may be able to use start-ups if their existing units have important skills they can readily transfer.

Such diversification is often riskier because of the tough conditions necessary for it to work. Given the uncertainties, a company should avoid diversifying on the basis of skills transfer alone. Rather it should also be viewed as a stepping-stone to subsequent diversification using shared activities. New industries should be chosen that will lead naturally to other businesses. The goal is to build a cluster of related and mutually reinforcing business units. The strategy's logic implies that the company should not set the rate of return standards for the initial foray into a new sector too high.

6. *Pursuing a strategy of restructuring if this fits the skills of management or no good opportunities exist for forging corporate interrelationships.*

When a company uncovers undermanaged companies and can deploy adequate management talent and resources to the acquired units, then it can use a restructuring strategy. The more developed the capital markets and the more active the market for companies, the more restructuring will require a patient search for that special opportunity rather than a headlong race to acquire as many bad apples as possible. Restructuring can be a permanent strategy, as it is with Loew's, or a way to build a group of businesses that supports a shift to another corporate strategy.

7. *Paying dividends so that the shareholders can be the portfolio managers.*

Paying dividends is better than destroying shareholder value through diversification based on shaky underpinnings. Tax considerations, which some companies cite to avoid dividends, are hardly legitimate reason to diversify if a company cannot demonstrate the capacity to do it profitably.

Creating a Corporate Theme

Defining a corporate theme is a good way to ensure that the corporation will create shareholder value. Having the right theme helps unite the efforts of business units and reinforces the ways they interrelate as well as guides the choice of new businesses to enter. NEC Corporation, with its "C&C" theme, provides a good example. NEC integrates its computer, semiconductor, telecommunications, and consumer electronics businesses by merging computers and communication.

It is all too easy to create a shallow corporate theme. CBS wanted to be an "entertainment company," for example, and built a group of businesses related to leisure time. It entered such industries as toys, crafts, musical instruments, sports teams, and hi-fi retailing. While this corporate theme sounded good, close listening revealed its hollow ring. None of these businesses had any significant opportunity to share activities or transfer skills among themselves or with CBS's traditional broadcasting and record businesses. They were all sold, often at significant losses, except for a few of CBS's publishing-related units. Saddled with the worst acquisition record in my study, CBS has eroded the shareholder value created through its strong performance in broadcasting and records.

Moving from competitive strategy to corporate strategy is the business equivalent of passing through the Bermuda Triangle. The failure of corporate strategy reflects the fact that most diversified companies have failed to think in terms of how they really add value. A corporate strategy that truly enhances the competitive advantage of each business unit is the best defense against the corporate raider. With a sharper focus on the tests of diversification and the explicit choice of a clear concept of corporate strategy, companies' diversification track records from now on can look a lot different.

Author's note: The research for this article was done with the able assistance of my research associate Cheng G. Ong. Malcolm S. Salter, Andrall E. Pearson, A. Michael Kechner, and the Monitor Company also provided helpful comments.

References

1. The studies also show that sellers of companies capture a large fraction of the gains from merger. See Michael C. Jensen and Richard S. Ruback, "The Market for Corporate Control: The Scientific Evidence," *Journal of Financial Economics*, April 1983, p. 5, and Michael C. Jensen, "Takeovers: Folklore and Science," *Harvard Business Review*, November–December 1984, p. 109.
2. Some recent evidence also supports the conclusion that acquired companies often suffer eroding performance after acquisition. See Frederick M. Scherer, "Mergers, Sell-Offs and

Managerial Behavior," in *The Economics of Strategic Planning*, ed. Lacy Glenn Thomas (Lexington, MA: Lexington Books, 1986), p. 143, and David A. Ravenscraft and Frederick M. Scherer, "Mergers and Managerial Performance," paper presented at the Conference on Takeovers and Contests for Corporate Control, Columbia Law School, 1985.

3. This observation has been made by a number of authors. See, for example, Malcolm S. Salter and Wolf A. Weinhold, *Diversification Through Acquisition* (New York: Free Press, 1979).
4. See Michael E. Porter, "How Competitive Forces Shape Strategy," *Harvard Business Review*, March–April 1979, p. 86.
5. ———, *Competitive Advantage* (New York: Free Press, 1985).

SECTION V

The Strategic Marketing Spirit

Strategic marketing is a high stakes game, shrouded in uncertainty, played in a combative field where mastery of the numbers is often more important than even creativity or ambition. This section attempts to portray the various dimensions of the strategic marketing spirit.

Managing by the Numbers

An executive who can't manage to achieve his business objective is no manager at all, argues Harold Geneen, former Chairman of ITT. To meet your goals consistently, you have to know the business. And to know the business, you have to know the numbers—cold. The "numbers" include the whole range of costs of a division's operation that effect its market position. These cover design and engineering, supplies, labor, plants, advertising, sales, and distribution expenses, to name a few. The numbers also include anticipated income from sales, based on market share projections and back orders. A solid understanding of these numbers is an important part of the strategic marketing spirit. The strategic marketing manager does not "run it up the flagpole to see who salutes." Instead he or she carefully evaluates the numbers relating to the company, the customer, and the competition to identify strategic opportunities and threats.

Marketing Is War

Another dimension of the strategic marketing spirit is the need for a company to become actively competitor oriented. In the military, the numbers are so important that most armies have an intelligence branch devoted to collecting information about the enemy. The reason is, argue Al Ries and Jack Trout, that no other principle of warfare is as fundamental as the principle of force. The big fish eat the small fish. The big company beats the small company. Of course, there is a future for small companies, but their managers need to think like field commanders. They must keep in mind the first principle of warfare, the principle of force. Napoleon is quoted saying "the art of war with a numerically inferior army consists in always having larger forces than the enemy at the point which is to be attacked or defended." The authors introduce the mathematics of the defensive fire fight and explain how the principle of force operates. They conclude with a discussion of the critical importance of segmentation as a way of redefining the battlefield.

Henderson on Strategy

The strategic marketing spirit has been heavily influenced by Professor Henderson, formerly Chairman of the Boston Consulting Groups. In this selection from his book we discover the complex relationship between pricing strategy, inflation, fixed and variable costs, production capacity, and market share. We are also treated to Professor Henderson's own rendition of the BCG Growth/Share Matrix. The author effectively translates the principles of marketing warfare in the previous article, into modern competitive marketing terminology.

Marketing Strategy & Differential Advantage

The strategic marketing spirit exemplified by managing with the numbers and understanding the principle force is the philosophical foundation on which Professor Cook's article is based. The basic question of the paper is "on what product, promotion, place, and price strategy does market share depend?" The author introduces the concept of strategic marketing ambition, calibrates that concept and describes a strategic marketing paradigm where investments are linked to market share through a strategic marketing cost function. These concepts and measures are illustrated in a comparison of United States and foreign automobile marketers.

The paper by Chattopadhyay, Nedungadi, and Chakravarti takes serious issue with many of the concepts and measures presented in the previous paper on marketing strategy and differential advantage. However, in the process of criticizing the concepts of strategic ambition, differential advantage, and the analysis of competition for the U.S. auto market, the authors do more to *explain* and *extend* the strategic marketing paradigm than to discredit it. Of particular importance in this regard, is the authors' discussion of the underlying response function and their formulation of the strategic marketing paradigm in the context of the market share attraction model. The important issues raised and the expectations for share of market based upon shares of strategic marketing investments in the automobile industry, represent clearly the role of management judgment and experience as part of the strategic marketing spirit.

First Mover Advantages

One of the riskiest and potentially most profitable strategic marketing moves is to be the first player in a newly defined game. Professors Lieberman and Montgomery review this important decision in terms both of its advantages and disadvantages. They developed the bases of first mover advantages arising from technological leadership, preemption of resource assets, and buyer switching costs. The authors then document the disadvantages of being the first player or pioneering firm in a new market arising from free-rider effects, technological and market uncertainties, shifts in technology and customer needs, and the incumbent inertia of taking the initial position. The authors argue that whatever the extra profits earned by first movers, they are fundamentally attributable to the company's proficiency and good luck, rather than "pioneering" per se. Even after success or failure, disentangling the contribution of exceptional foresight or skill from that of mere luck is not an easy task. And failure among first movers is a common occurrence in practice. ■

31

The Case for Managing by the Numbers

Harold S. Geneen

An executive who can't manage to achieve his business objectives is no manager at all, argues the former chairman of ITT. To meet your goals consistently, you have to know the business. And to know the business, you have to know the numbers—cold.

MANAGEMENT must manage! Management MUST manage! Management must MANAGE! It is a very simple credo, probably the closest thing to the secret of success in business. The strange thing is that everybody knows it, but somehow managers forget it all the time.

To want to achieve certain year-end results is not enough. Managing means that once you set your business plan and budget for the year, you *must* achieve the sales, the market share, and the earnings to which you committed yourself. If you don't manage to achieve those results, you're not a manager.

Managers in all too many American companies do not achieve the desired results because nobody makes them do it. Explanations and rationalizations are all too readily accepted. You get what you expect to get. Seldom, if ever, do you get more.

A manager must set standards for production, sales, market share, earnings, whatever, and anything short of those standards should be unacceptable to him. Recently I met a man who operates the jewelry concession in a number of department stores. He told me: "I don't think I'm doing my job unless I get 4% of the store's traffic." "How do you know it's 4% you need?" I asked. "I don't," he replied, "it just works out that way." "Why not 5%?" I asked. "No just 4%," he insisted, explaining that 4% was more than any other counter in the department store got. Without sophisticated controls, this man had set his own standards. He couldn't sleep if he did not get that 4%. He would feel guilty if he did not get it. He would work through the night, he would do anything he had to, but he would get that 4%. I don't know precisely what he did to achieve the 4%, and perhaps 5% or even 8% would have been possible, but it makes little difference: he was managing.

The efficacy of management is quantifiable. It can be measured by the profit and loss statement. In an established company, you can measure performance by the quarter. I used to tell my management team at ITT that making the first quarter's quotas was the most important challenge of the year. If you don't make your budget quota that first quarter, then you probably won't be able to catch up in subsequent quarters. Worrying about the quarterly numbers is not short-term management: careful study of them will alert you to potential long-term problems in time to take appropriate action.

What do you do if your company or your division or your department has not made its quota for the quarter? First of all you locate the problem. Then you find the cause. Then you fix it. That is why we had the controllers of every ITT company sending us in headquarters the figures of their companies every week. Less than satisfactory results showed up in those reports very clearly. That's why our line managers "red-flagged" their major problems for immediate

In 17 years as chief executive of ITT, Harold Geneen became widely known as the hardest of hard-nosed executives. *Fortune*'s coverage of ITT during the Geneen years found fault with his management more than once but never underestimated the man or the power of his ideas.

attention. That's why we held monthly managers' meetings. We wanted to pinpoint the causes of the problems and find the best possible solutions as quickly as possible.

Management must manage became our credo at ITT. It meant that we would do everything we had to that was honest and legal to bring in the results we desired. If one solution to a problem did not work, we tried another. And another. Our red-flag items remained on the first page of each division's monthly report, updated for changes, every single month until they were solved. A red-flag item was like a thorn in an ITT manager's side. He had to solve it. He could not merely walk into one of our meetings and announce that he still had the problem, that nothing had changed. He had to tell me and our headquarters management team and his peers what he was doing and what he proposed to do about that problem. If he was stumped, we would send him help. Together we would manage.

But we *would* manage. I brought this point home at a general managers' meeting early in my reign at ITT when the man in charge of our Latin America operations reported that he had failed to sell our newest, multimillion-dollar telephone switching system to the government of Brazil. I probed for quite a while into the efforts that had been made. He told me of all the avenues he had explored.

"Who makes the final decision there on whether or not they buy our system?" I asked.

"President Kubitchek."

"Did you see him?"

"No."

"Why not?"

"Because ——— really makes the decision and he recommends the decision and the president follows his advice," he explained, adding, "Besides, I don't think I can get in to see Kubitchek."

"Well, why don't you try? You have everything to gain and nothing to lose."

The following month he returned with a sheepish grin on his face to announce that he had seen the president of Brazil and had sold the ITT system. The men in the room applauded him.

At a succession of general managers' meetings in Europe we were all stumped over a serious problem of inventory control. Our European inventory of supplies, which usually ran between two and three billion dollars, had risen some $500 million above desired levels, and we were paying interest every month on those idle supplies. Task force after task force had investigated, and month after month those inventories seemed to be rising. Finally, at one meeting, one manager suggested that he had solved his own inventory problem by placing a man at the receiving dock of each of his factories with instructions to turn back any supplies that were not ordered or needed. It was such a simple solution. And it worked. We put a staff man at the receiving dock of every one of our factories to check supplies being unloaded, often in advance of our orders.

At ITT we used everything available to us to get results. We used everything we had learned at school, everything we had learned from our own experience in business, everything we could learn from one another. We used our intuition. We used our brains. And we always used the numbers.

No business could run without them. Numbers serve as a thermometer that measures the health and well-being of the enterprise. They serve as the first line of communication to inform management what is going on. The more precise the numbers are, the more they are based upon unshakable facts, the clearer the line of communication.

When a manager makes up a budget for the coming year, he is putting down on paper a series of expectations, expressed in numbers. They include the whole gamut of costs of his division's product—design, engineering, supplies, labor, plants, marketing, sales, distribution—and also anticipated income from sales, based on market share projections and back orders. These figures had better not be pulled out of the air. They must be based on the best facts available. When all the figures are pulled together for one company or one division, you have its budget. At ITT we had 250 of these profit centers. Their annual budgets, when lined up side by side, occupied 30-odd feet of shelf space.

For numbers to tell their whole story, they have to be compared to other numbers. As the budget year proceeds, the numbers reflecting actual operations pour into headquarters. Actual costs, sales profit margins, and earnings can be compared to the budget forecasts. Does one set of numbers match the other? Is the actuality above or below the company's expectations? If it is either, what are you going to do about it?

Any significant variation is a signal for action. The sooner you see the numbers, the sooner you can take action if needed. If one of your products is selling above expectations, you may want to increase production immediately. If, as happens more often, one or more of your products is not selling as well as expected, then you may have to find some way to get those sales up or begin to reduce the costs and expenses involved, and the sooner the better. However—and this is most important—the numbers themselves will not tell you what to do. The key issue in business is to find out what is happening behind those numbers.

Once you start digging into the areas that the numbers represent, then you get into the guts of your business. If sales are off, is it because of the design of your product? Its cost? Marketing? Distribution?

When you find the source of the problem, you insist that management must manage to solve that problem. You don't want them to manage the numbers—pushing sales or receivables from one quarter to another. That is like treating the thermometer instead of the patient.

The difference between well-managed companies and not-so-well managed companies is the degree of attention they pay to numbers, the temperature chart of their business. How often are the numbers reported up the chain of command? How accurate are those numbers? How much variation is tolerated between budget forecasts and actual results? How deep does management dig for its answers?

At ITT we took our numbers very seriously indeed. Our budget planning, which began as early as February and March and continued through the year, was negotiated very carefully. The final budget was considered a solid commitment for performance expected the following year. Our monthly managers' meetings focused on the variations, if any, between budget forecasts and the results for that given month.

We wanted no surprises. As soon as we discovered something amiss, or going amiss, we threw every means and every effort into solving our problems. As a result, we felt that we were in control. The unexpected shocks and surprises that accost everyone in life became manageable for us.

Numbers can be accurate or not so accurate, precise or rounded off, detailed or averaged and vague. Their quality, as reported, usually depends upon the chief executive of the company and what he expects from the men reporting to him. If he does not give much personal attention to the detailed figures beyond ascertaining the earnings per share, no one else in his company is going to worry about them. They will round off their figures, averaging the odd numbers, perhaps shaving off a few points from the costs, adding something to boost profit margins. As the practice spreads from division to division, the accumulation of inexact, fuzzy, and then plain incorrect figures can cause havoc with managerial decisions.

If an executive begins to look closely at all the figures that come in from the divisions of his company and insists that they be timely, accurate, and detailed, things will happen in that company that change it ever so imperceptibly into a well-managed enterprise. He will have to keep at it constantly, or else things will begin to slip again. Managing a company is like writing in the snow: you have to go over and over the same words as the snow falls if you want your writing to remain legible. The reward, however, is that you get better and better at it as you repeat the same process.

Sometimes, however, outside events beyond the control of any individual company overtake even the early warning system that good numbers provide. A sudden rise in the cost of energy, a significant international event, a plunge into recession of a whole national economy can make a shambles of the best-laid plans.

Consider, for example, one company with $40 million in annual sales, reaping a handsome profit. It expands to $60 million in annual sales, earning even more money. It builds its sales volume to $80 million a year, and profits rise proportionally. Then the economy slumps, customers suddenly stop buying, annual sales slide back down to the old level of $40 million a year. But now the company is losing money on that volume. What happened? What can you do about it?

At ITT, when outside events overtook us and there was nothing else we could do, we restructured the business so that it could cope with its new environment. We went over every relevant figure of every operation and scaled the business back down to the size it was when it was making money on annual sales of $40 million. It is simply amazing how many expenses once deemed necessary become luxuries when your company is operating at a loss.

At the same time, we made it a practice that while restructuring we put on a tremendous effort to try to increase sales a little bit, even 5% or 10%. We cut the company back to the $40-million structure and then tried to do $42 million or $44 million in business. We called it our one-two punch.

There is a price to pay for all this analysis, of course: paying attention to the numbers is a dull, tiresome routine—it's drudgery. The more you want to know about your business, the more numbers there will be. They cannot be skimmed. They must be read, understood, and compared to other sets of numbers that you have read that day, that week, or earlier that year. And you have to do it alone, all by yourself, even when you know that it would be far more stimulating to be doing almost anything else.

If you are running a well-managed company, most of the numbers will be those you expect. That makes them even more mundane and dull. But you cannot skip over them; you dare not allow your concentration to flag. Those numbers are your controls, and you read them until your mind reels or until you come upon one number or set of numbers that stand out from all the rest, demanding your attention, and getting it.

What you are seeking is *comprehension* of the numbers: what they mean. That will come only with constant exposure, constant repetition, retention of what you read in the past, and a familiarity with the actual activities that the numbers represent. You cannot speed up the process. Comprehension seeps into your brain by a process of osmosis and gradually you find yourself at ease with numbers and what they really represent.

The truth is that the drudgery of the numbers will make you free. The confidence that you are in control, that you are aware of the significant variations from the expected, gives you the freedom to do things that you would have been unable to do otherwise. You can build a new plant, or finance risk-laden research, or go out and buy a company, and you can do it with assurance because you are able to sit down and figure out what that new venture will do to the balance sheet. You will be able, in short, to manage.

32

Marketing Is War

Al Ries & Jack Trout

War belongs to the province of business competition, which is also a conflict of human interests and activities.
Karl von Clausewitz

THE BEST BOOK ON MARKETING was not written by a Harvard professor. Nor by an alumnus of General Motors, General Electric, or even Procter & Gamble.

We think the best book on marketing was written by a retired Prussian general, Karl von Clausewitz. Entitled *On War*, the 1832 book outlines the strategic principles behind all successful wars.

Clausewitz was the great philosopher of war. His ideas and concepts have lasted more than 150 years. Today, *On War* is widely quoted at places like West Point, Sandhurst, and St. Cyr.

War has changed dramatically since *On War* was first published. The tank, the airplane, the machine gun, and a host of new weapons have been introduced. Yet the ideas of Clausewitz are still as relevant today as they were in the nineteenth century.

Weapons may change, but warfare itself, as Clausewitz was first to recognize, is based on two immutable characteristics: strategy and tactics. His clear exposition of the strategic principles of war are likely to guide military commanders well into the twenty-first century.

Marketing Needs a New Philosophy

The classic definition of marketing leads one to believe that marketing has to do with satisfying consumer needs and wants.

Al Ries is Chairman and Jack Trout is President of Trout & Ries, Inc.

Marketing is "human activity directed at satisfying needs and wants through exchange processes," says Philip Kotler of Northwestern University.

Marketing is "the performance of business activities that direct the flow of goods and services from producer to consumer," says the American Marketing Association.

Marketing is "the performance of those activities which seek to accomplish an organization's objectives by anticipating customer or client needs and directing a flow of need-satisfying goods and services from producer to customer or client," says E. Jerome McCarthy of Michigan State University.

Perhaps the most complete explanation of the "needs and wants" theory is the definition provided by John A. Howard of Columbia University in 1973. Marketing, says Mr. Howard, is the process of: "(1) identifying customer needs, (2) conceptualizing those needs in terms of an organization's capacity to produce, (3) communicating that conceptualization to the appropriate laws of power in the organization, (4) conceptualizing the consequent output in terms of the customer needs earlier identified, and (5) communicating that conceptualization to the customer."

Are those the five steps on the road to marketing success today? Would identifying, conceptualizing, and communicating help American Motors compete successfully with General Motors, Ford, and Chrysler? Let alone Toyota, Datsun, Honda, and the rest of the imports?

Let's say American Motors develops a product strategy based on identifying customer needs. The result would be a line of products identical to those of General Motors, which spends millions of dollars researching the same marketplace to identify those same customer needs.

Is this what marketing is all about? The victory belongs to the side that does a better job of marketing research?

Clearly something is wrong. When American Motors ignores customer needs, the company is much more successful. The Jeep, a product borrowed from the military, is a winner. American Motors passenger cars are losers.

No focus group is likely to have conjured up the Jeep. Nor is identifying customer needs likely to help an also-ran compete with a leader.

Becoming Customer-Oriented

Marketing people traditionally have been customer-oriented. Over and over again they have warned management to be customer- rather than production-oriented.

Ever since World War II, King Customer has reigned supreme in the world of marketing.

But it's beginning to look like King Customer is dead. And like marketing people have been selling a corpse to top management.

Companies who have dutifully followed the directions of their marketing experts have seen millions of dollars disappear in valiant but disastrous customer-oriented efforts.

To see how we got into this predicament, you have to go back to the twenties when business was production-oriented. This was the heyday of Henry "You Can Have Any Color You Want As Long As It's Black" Ford.

In the production era, business discovered advertising. "Mass advertising creates mass demand which makes mass production possible," said the advertising experts.

In the aftermath of World War II, the leading companies became customer-oriented. The marketing expert was in charge and the prime minister was marketing research.

But today every company is customer-oriented. Knowing what the customer wants isn't too helpful if a dozen other companies are already serving the same customer's wants. American Motors's problem is not the customer. American Motors's problem is General Motors, Ford, Chrysler, and the imports.

Becoming Competitor-Oriented

To be successful today, a company must become competitor-oriented. It must look for weak points in the positions of its competitors and then launch marketing attacks against those weak points. Many recent marketing success stories illustrate this.

For example, while others were losing millions in the computer business, Digital Equipment Corporation was making millions by exploiting IBM's weakness in small computers.

Similarly, Savin established a successful beachhead in small, inexpensive copiers, a weak point in the Xerox lineup.

And Pepsi took advantage of its sweeter taste to challenge Coke in the hotly contested cola market. At the same time, Burger King was making progress against McDonald's with its "broiling, not frying" attack.

There are those who would say that a well-thought-out marketing plan always includes a section on the competition. Indeed it does. Usually toward the back of the plan in a section entitled "Competitive Evaluation." The major part of the plan usually spells out the marketplace, its various segments, and a myriad of customer research statistics carefully gleaned from endless focus groups, test panels and concept and market tests.

The Marketing Plan of the Future

In the marketing plan of the future, many more pages will be dedicated to the competition. This plan will carefully dissect each participant in the marketplace. It will develop a list of competitive weaknesses and strengths as well as a plan of action to either exploit or defend against them.

There might even come a day when this plan will contain a dossier on each of the competitors' key marketing people which will include their favorite tactics and style of operation (not unlike the documents the Germans kept on Allied commanders in World War II).

What does all this portend for marketing people of the future?

It means they have to be prepared to wage marketing warfare. More and more, successful marketing campaigns will have to be planned like military campaigns.

Strategic planning will become more and more important. Companies will have to learn how to *attack* and to *flank* their competition, how to *defend* their positions, and how and when to wage *guerrilla* warfare. They will need better intelligence on how to anticipate competitive moves.

On the personal level, successful marketing people will have to exhibit many of the same virtues that make a great military general—courage, loyalty, and perseverance.

Maybe Clausewitz Is Right

Maybe marketing is war, where the competition is the enemy and the objective is to win the battle.

Is this quibbling over details? Not really. Compare the game of football with the profession of marketing.

The football team that scores the most points wins the game. The marketing team that makes the most sales wins the marketing game. So far they're equivalent.

But try to play football the way you would play a marketing game.

Let's insert a marketing manager into a football game and watch him or her identify the goal line as the place to score points, that is, make sales. Then watch as the marketing manager lines up the team and heads straight for the goal line with the ball.

You don't have to be a sports expert to know that the direct approach in football leads to certain disaster.

In football, you win by outwitting, outflanking, outplaying the other team. The points on the scoreboard are only a reflection of your ability to do these things.

In war, you win by outwitting, outflanking, and overpowering the enemy. The territory you take is only a reflection of your ability to do these things.

Why should marketing be any different?

Why do the hundreds of definitions of the marketing concept almost never mention the word *competition?* Or suggest the essential nature of the conflict?

The true nature of marketing today involves the conflict between corporations, not the satisfying of human needs and wants.

If human needs and wants get satisfied in the process of business competition, then it is in the public interest to let the competition continue. But let us not forget the essential nature of what marketing is all about.

In Defense of Marketing Warfare

You might object to the direct application of military principles to marketing. War is horrible enough in wartime, people have told us, without extending it to peacetime.

And anyone who is opposed to the free enterprise system would probably also object to having the participants in the system practice the principles of marketing warfare. So be it.

Even people who defend the free enterprise system might think that marketing warfare is going too far. If you are one of those people, we would urge you to consider the results of the warfare analogy rather than the analogy itself.

A study of American business history of the past decade or so suggests that many of the appalling financial losses registered by companies like RCA, Xerox, Western Union, and others might have been avoided by the application of the principles of war. The study of warfare is not just a study of how to win. Equally as important is how not to lose.

The American economy has more to fear from unlimited and senseless corporate aggression than it has from the skilled competition of marketing gladiators in the art of war.

Free enterprise is marketing warfare. If you want to play in the free enterprise game, it seems to make sense to learn the principles first.

The Principle of Force

The greatest possible number of troops should be brought into action at the decisive point.

KARL VON CLAUSEWITZ

How many times have you heard company people say it's easier to get to the top than to stay there?

Forget it. That's a myth created by people who are more interested in the study of sociology than they are in recognizing the realities of business competition.

It's far easier to stay on top than to get there. The leader, the king of the hill, can take advantage of the principle of force.

No other principle of warfare is as fundamental as the principle of force. The law of the jungle. The big fish eat the small fish. The big company beats the small company.

The Mathematics of a Firefight

When you examine the mathematics of a firefight, it's easy to see why the big company usually wins. Let's say that the Red squad with nine soldiers meets a Blue squad with six. Red has a 50 percent numerical superiority over the Blue. 9 versus 6. Or it could be 90 versus 60 or 9000 versus 6000. It makes no difference what the numbers are, the principle is the same.

Let's also say that, on the average, one out of every three shots will inflict a casualty.

After the first volley, the situation will have changed drastically. Instead of a 9 to 6 advantage, Red would have a 7 to 3 advantage. From a 50 percent superiority in force to a more than 100 percent superiority.

The same deadly multiplication effect continues with the passage of time.

After the second volley, the score would be 6 to 1 in favor of Red.

After the third volley, Blue would be wiped out completely.

Notice how the casualties were divided between the two sides. The superior force (Red) suffered only half the casualties of the inferior force (Blue).

This result may be just the opposite of what you have been led to believe by all those Hollywood movies—the handful of marines decimating a company of Japanese before the marines are finally overrun.

In real life it's different. What happens when a Volkswagen Beetle hits a GMC bus in a head-on collision? You wind up with a few scratches on the bumper of the bus and a very thin German pancake. (The bigger you are, the harder they fall.)

The two vehicles have exchanged momentum. It's a basic law of physics. The larger, heavier vehicle sustains less damage than the smaller, lighter force.

There's no secret to why the Allies won World War II in Europe. Where the Germans had two soldiers, we had four. Where they had four, we had eight. The skill and experience of an enemy who had practically invented modern warfare and the leadership of men like Rommel and Von Rundstedt could not change the mathematics of the battleground.

In the military, the numbers are so important that most armies have an intelligence branch known as the order of battle. It informs commanders of the size, location, and nature of the opposing force. (The case of General William C. Westmoreland against CBS was based on whether order of battle documents in the Vietnam War were falsified or not.)

The Mathematics of a Marketing Melee

When two companies go head to head, the same principle applies. God smiles on the larger sales force.

Given a virgin territory, the company with the larger sales force is likely to wind up with the larger share of the market.

Once the market is divided up, the company with the larger share is likely to continue to take business away from the smaller company.

The bigger company can afford a bigger advertising budget, a bigger research department, more sales outlets, etc. No wonder the rich get richer and the poor get poorer.

Is there no future for the small competitor? Of course there is, which is one reason why this book was written. (General Motors, General Electric, and IBM don't need to study Clausewitz to be successful.)

But smaller companies with smaller market shares do need to think like field commanders. They must keep in mind the first principle of warfare, the principle of force, be it military or marketing. "The art of war with a numerically inferior army," said Napoleon, "consists in always having larger forces than the enemy at the point which is to be attacked or defended."

Custer could have become one of our nation's most famous heroes if he could have gotten the Sioux to attack over the hill one at a time.

Military generals know the importance of the principle of force. That's why they spend so much time studying the order of battle of an opposing force. For purposes of morale, however, a general tries to fire up his troops by telling them what good soldiers they are and what great equipment they have.

"Now we have the finest food, equipment, the best spirit and the best men in the world," said George C. Scott in his role as General George S. Patton, Jr. "You know, by god, I actually pity those poor bastards we're going up against."

Many marketing generals do the same thing and fall victim to their own rhetoric. In particular they talk themselves into the "better people" or the "better product" fallacies.

The "Better People" Fallacy

It's easy enough to convince your own staff that better people will prevail, even against the odds. It's what they want to hear. And surely in a marketing war quality is a factor as well as quantity.

It is, but superiority of force is such an overwhelming advantage that it overcomes most quality differences.

We have no doubt that the poorest team in the National Football League could consistently beat the best team in the NFL if it could field 12 men against the opposition's 11.

In business, where the teams are much larger, your ability to amass a quality difference is much more difficult.

The clear-thinking marketing manager won't confuse the pep talk at a sales rally with the reality of the marketing arena. A good general never makes military strategy based on having better personnel. Nor should a marketing general. ("Our army," said Wellington, "is composed of the scum of the earth, the mere scum of the earth.")

Obviously you'd be in deep trouble inside your company if you used Wellington's words to describe your own army. Tell your people how terrific they are, but don't plan on winning the battle with superior personnel.

Count on winning the battle with a superior strategy.

Yet many companies cling deeply to the better people strategy. They're convinced they can recruit and hire substantially better people than the competition can, and that their better training programs can help them keep their "people" edge.

Any student of statistics would laugh at this belief. Sure, it's possible to put together a small cadre of superior people. But the larger the company, the more likely the average employee will be average.

And when it comes to the megacompanies, the possibility of assembling an intellectually superior team becomes statistically almost zero.

At last count, IBM had 369,545 employees, a number which is growing rapidly. On a one-to-one basis, there may be more white shirts at IBM but not more gray matter.

IBM is winning the computer war the Eisenhower way. Where the competition has 2, IBM has 4. Where the competition has 4, IBM has 8.

The "Better Product" Fallacy

Another fallacy ingrained in the minds of most marketing managers is the belief that the better product will win the marketing battle.

Behind the thinking of many marketing managers is the thought that "truth will out."

In other words, if you have the "facts" on your side, it's only necessary to find a good advertising agency who can communicate those facts to the prospect and a good sales force who can close the sale.

We call this approach "inside-out thinking"—that somehow the advertising agency or the sales force can take the truth, as the company knows it, and use this truth to clear up the misconceptions that reside inside the mind of the prospect.

Don't be fooled. Misconceptions cannot easily be changed by an advertising or sales effort.

What is truth? Inside every human being is a little black box. When a human being is exposed to your advertising or sales claim, that person looks inside the box and says "That's right" or "That's wrong."

The single most wasteful thing you can do in marketing today is to try to change a human mind. Once a mind is made up, it's almost impossible to change.

What is truth? Truth is the perception that's inside the mind of the prospect. It may not be your truth, but it's the only truth you can work with. You have to accept that truth and then deal with it.

"If You're So Smart, How Come You're Not Rich?"

Even if you succeed in convincing the prospect that you have a better product, the prospect soon has second thoughts. "Hey, if your computer is better than IBM's, how come you're not the leader, like IBM is?"

Even if you get a few black boxes to go along with you, the owners of those black boxes soon let the unsold majority sway their judgment.

If you're so smart, how come you're not rich? That's a tough question to answer. In a marketing war you can't win just by being right.

There's the illusion, of course, that over the long run, the better product will win. But history, military and marketing, is written by the winners, not the losers.

Might is right. Winners always have the better product, and they're always available to say so.

The Superiority of the Defense

The defensive form of war is in itself stronger than the offense.

KARL VON CLAUSEWITZ

The second principle of Clausewitz is the superiority of the defense.

No military commander would seek out combat with the odds stacked against him. The rule of thumb is that an attacking force, to be successful, should have a superiority of at least 3 to 1 at the point of attack.

Yet how many marketing generals are all too willing to start an offensive war with totally insufficient force? Like Cardigan at Balaclava and Lee at Gettysburg, many marketing generals launch offensive attacks with advertising and marketing dollars that are insufficient by a factor of 2 to 1, 3 to 1, even 10 to 1. With the same predictable results.

The Mathematics of a Defensive Firefight

In an open field a firefight between two squads is rapidly decided in favor of the larger unit.

But what happens when one of the two squads is on defense? How does this change the mathematics of the situation?

Let's say a Red commander with a force of 9 soldiers meets a Blue commander with only 6 (a 50 percent superiority of force). But on this occasion the Blue force is on defense, say, in a trench or foxhole.

For a Blue soldier, the odds are still the same, 1 out of 3 shots, that he will hit one of the Red attackers.

What changes are the odds that a Red soldier will be able to hit one of the Blue forces, which now has the security of a defensive position? Instead of 1 out of 3, let's say the odds increase to 1 out of 9 shots.

(This corresponds to the difficulty of making "conquest" sales—that is, taking business away from an established competitor is usually much more difficult than getting business from a previously uncommitted prospect.)

After the first volley, the Red force still outnumbers the Blue, but by a margin of only 7 to 5. After the second volley, the margin is further reduced to 5 to 4. After the third volley the forces are the same, 4 to 4.

Red started the attack with a 50 percent superiority of force, but it's now even. At this point, the Red commander would presumably call off the attack since he no longer has superiority of numbers.

The Fruit of Victory

Throughout military history, defense has proved to be the stronger form of warfare. In the Korean War, America won in the South on defense and lost in the North on offense.

England lost in the Colonies on offense and won at Waterloo on defense.

Offense gets the glamour, but defense wins football games, as any NFL coach will hasten to tell you.

Why fight an offensive war at all if defense is so attractive? The paradox is the fruit of victory. If you can win a marketing battle and become the leading brand in a given category, you can enjoy that victory for a long time. Simply because you can now play defense, the stronger form of warfare.

A survey of 25 leading brands from the year 1923 proves this point. Sixty years later, 20 of those brands were still in first place. Four were in second place and one was in fifth place.

In six decades, only 5 out of 25 brands lost their leadership position. It's difficult to dethrone a king.

Ivory in soap, Campbell in soup, Coca-Cola in soft drinks. These represent strong marketing positions which can be taken only at great expense and with great skill and energy.

Don't Be a Hero

The biggest mistake marketing people make is failing to appreciate the strength of a defensive position.

The glamour of offensive war and the thrill of victory makes the average marketing manager eager to pick up a lance and go charging off at the nearest entrenched competitor.

Nothing in marketing is so pathetic as the charge of the light brigade. RCA and GE against IBM in computers. Exxon and Lanier against IBM in office automation. Western Union against everybody in electronic mail.

"Heroism" is a disease among too many marketing people eager to do or die for their company. If you approach the subject of marketing warfare looking for ways to cover yourself with marketing glory, you're reading the wrong book.

"Now I want you to remember that no bastard ever won a war by dying for his country," said George C. Scott in his Patton role. "He won it by making the other poor dumb bastard die for his country."

There are no heroes at IBM. No medals of honor awarded posthumously. Winners may be hard to admire, but as most losers will tell you, love is no consolation for having lost.

Friction Favors the Defense

One of the reasons the defensive form of warfare is so strong is the difficulty of launching a surprise attack.

"In theory," says Clausewitz, "surprise promises a great deal. In practice, it generally strikes fast by the friction of the whole machine."

In theory, the 1916 battle of the Somme was going to be a surprise attack. But after moving a million men into position and waiting a week for the artillery to do its job, the Allies were left with little surprise.

The larger the operation, the less the surprise. A small company might be able to surprise a big company with a new product. But Ford is unlikely to pull any fast ones on General Motors. The friction of the whole machine gets in the way.

When you look at case histories of leaders who were taken by surprise, you usually find they had ample warning. Leaders get overrun when they ignore those warnings or pooh-pooh the efforts of the competition.

In *Mein Kampf*, a book that sold some 10 million copies, Hitler told England and France exactly what he intended to do. A decade later he did it.

An Attack Takes Time

An attacker in a military campaign not only tends to sacrifice surprise but also wastes time in bringing the forces into action. Because of logistics problems, it can be days or weeks before the full force of an attack is felt by a defender —time that can be enormously useful to the defense.

On D day, only 156,115 troops were put ashore on the Normandy beaches in spite of a massive effort. Because of transportation and supply problems, it took several months to build up Allied strength to the millions of troops necessary to ensure success.

In a marketing attack, transportation is usually not a problem. A company can deliver products to thousands of outlets in days.

The bottleneck is communication. Getting a marketing message across to millions of customers can take months or years. There is often plenty of time for the defender to blunt the attacker's sales message by undercutting it in one form or another.

But to take advantage of time, the defender has to remain alert to potential threats from any direction.

The New Era of Competition

Some statesmen and generals try to avoid
the decisive battle. History has destroyed this illusion.
KARL VON CLAUSEWITZ

The most bloodthirsty language in the newspapers today is not found in the international pages. It's found on the business pages.

"We'll murder them."

"It's kill or be killed."

"This is a life-or-death struggle."

No, these are not the words of a leftist guerrilla or a right-wing dictator. These are typical quotes from three business leaders discussing forthcoming marketing campaigns.

The language of marketing has been borrowed from the military. We *launch* a marketing *campaign*. Hopefully, a *breakthrough* campaign.

We *promote* people to higher *positions*. In *divisions, companies, units*. We *report gains* and *losses*. Sometimes we *issue uniforms*.

From time to time we go into the *field* to *inspect* those uniforms and *review* the progress of the *troops*. We have even been known to *pull rank*.

Up till now, it's only the language that has been borrowed from the military, not the strategic thinking behind the language.

Marketing warfare is an attempt to apply military thinking to marketing problems.

Marketing, as a scientific discipline, is less than 100 years old. Marketing is long on "seat of the pants" thinking and short on theory. Military theory can help bridge the gap.

The Headline Wars

If you've been reading *Business Week, Forbes*, or *Fortune*, you've probably had your fill of military language. The *beer war*, the *cola war*, and the *hamburger war* are recent examples of journalistic militarism.

But underneath the headlines, the writers totally ignore the most elementary military principles.

"New Xerox push in the office," said a recent headline in *The New York Times*. "Seeks lead in automation," said the subhead.

If Denmark invaded West Germany, a country 12 times its size, the press would express shock and incredulity.

Lead in automation? Xerox, a company with less than $2 billion in annual sales of office automation products, going up against IBM, a company with more than $40 billion?

There are many more examples of the semantic smoke without the strategic fire.

"National Semiconductor is crossing the Rubicon," said President Charles E. Sporck in the headline of an advertisement announcing the company's line of micro- and minicomputers.

When Julius Caesar crossed the real Rubicon in 49 B.C., he did so with a full legion of men (with two more in reserve). So awesome was Caesar's strength that his opponent, Pompey, promptly decided to evacuate Italy.

Where are Sporck's legions? Will IBM give up so quickly? You don't have to be a military genius to know that this semi-invasion won't be very successful.

Predictions or Propaganda?

When Coca-Cola announced its new, sweeter formula, it also confidently predicted a 1 percent gain in market share over each of the next 3 years. Was this a prediction or just propaganda? If it was meant to be propaganda, it missed the mark. No military commander in his right mind gives a timetable for victory.

"I shall return," said Douglas MacArthur when he left the Philippines in March 1942. If he had added "by the end of the year," his reputation would have been seriously dampened by the time he waded ashore in 1944. Unkept promises undermine morale. Marketing promises should be as vague as political ones. Otherwise, they will erode the effectiveness of your forces.

When Hitler promised to take Stalingrad and failed, he lost more than his military reputation. He also lost his "master of propaganda" image.

The Reality of Marketing Conflict

Rhetoric aside, it's clear that marketing is entering a new era, an era that will make the sixties and seventies look like a Sunday school picnic. Competition is getting brutal. The name of the game has become "taking business away from somebody else."

As companies experiment with different ways to increase sales, they are turning more and more to warfare strategies in general.

But aggressiveness alone is not the mark of a good military strategy. Especially aggressiveness as represented by the "more" school of management. More products, more sales people, more advertising, more hard work.

Especially more hard work. Somehow we feel better about success if we have to work hard to achieve it. So we schedule more meetings, more reports, more memos, more management reviews.

Yet military history teaches the reverse. A single-minded commitment to winning the battle on effort alone usually dissolves into defeat. From the trenches of World War I to the streets of Stalingrad in World War II, the military commander that lets his armies get bogged down in a hand-to-hand slugging match is usually defeated.

The dogged determination of Xerox to make it in the office automation market is not a sign of future success. It's a mark of futility.

Much better are quick, lightninglike strokes that depend more on timing than muscle. (What the Germans call *blitzkreig*.) Not that muscle, or the principle of force, is not important. Far from it. But unless an attack is properly planned, you throw away your advantage if you let the battle degenerate into a war of attrition.

Whenever you hear your commander say "We have to redouble our efforts," you know you're listening to a loser talk. The lights don't need to burn late in places like Armonk. IBM wins by thinking smarter, not longer.

The Nature of the Battleground

It is from the character of our adversary's position that we can draw conclusions as to his designs and will therefore act accordingly.

KARL VON CLAUSEWITZ

In a military battle the terrain is so important that a battle is invariably named after its geographic location.

The Plain of Marathon, the river Metaurus, the village of Waterloo, a town named Gettysburg, a hill named Bunker, a mountain called Cassino.

In a marketing battle, the terrain is important too. But the question is "Where." Where is the terrain? Where are marketing battles being fought?

A Mean and Ugly Place

In this book you'll read about the value of holding the marketing "high ground" and the need to avoid a "well-entrenched" competitor. Where is the high ground? Where are the trenches?

If you want to go out and do battle with your competitors, it's helpful to know where to go.

Marketing battles are not fought in the customer's office or in the supermarkets or the drugstores of America. Those are only distribution points for the merchandise whose brand selection is decided elsewhere.

Marketing battles are not fought in places like Dallas, Detroit, or Denver. At least not in the physical sense of a city or a region.

Marketing battles are fought in a mean and ugly place. A place that's dark and damp with much unexplored territory and deep pitfalls to trap the unwary.

Marketing battles are fought inside the mind. Inside your own mind and inside the mind of your prospects, every day of the week.

The mind is the battleground. A terrain that is tricky and difficult to understand.

The entire battleground is just 6 inches wide. This is where the marketing war takes place. You try to outmaneuver and outfight your competitors on a mental mountain about the size of a cantaloupe.

A marketing war is a totally intellectual war with a battleground that no one has ever seen. It can only be imagined in the mind, which makes marketing warfare one of the most difficult disciplines to learn.

Mapping the Mind

A good general carefully studies the terrain before the battle. Every hill, every mountain, every river is analyzed for its defensive or offensive possibilities.

A good general also studies the enemy's position. Hopefully, the exact location and strength of each unit is plotted on a map and studied before the battle begins. The best surprise is no surprise. What a commander hopes to avoid at all costs is a surprise attack from an unexpected direction.

In a marketing war, reconnaissance is extraordinarily difficult. How do you see inside a human mind to find out what the terrain looks like and what strong points the enemy holds?

One way to reconnoiter the human mind is to use marketing research. But not in the traditional way of asking customers what they want to buy. That's yesterday's approach.

What you're trying to find out is what positions are held by what companies. Who owns the high ground?

Done correctly, you can contour the mind of the average prospect to produce a map that is just as useful to a marketing general as the Michelin maps that Patton carried across Europe.

Mapping the mental battleground can give you an enormous advantage. Most of your competitors won't even know where the battle is being fought. They will be preoccupied with their own camp: their own products, their own sales force, their own plans.

Mountains in the Mind

Any attempt to describe a human mind in physical terms is bound to be symbolic. Yet there are certain symbols used in both military and marketing operations that seem to be especially appropriate.

In a military war, hills or mountains are usually considered strong positions, especially useful for defense. In a marketing war, management people often refer to strong positions as "high ground." So it seems appropriate to use the mountain as a key concept in marketing warfare.

But in warfare, a mountain can be either occupied or unoccupied. Tissue mountain, for example, is occupied by the brand Kleenex. Ketchup mountain is owned by Heinz. Computer mountain by IBM.

Some mountains are being strongly contested. Cola mountain is partially occupied by Coca-Cola, but is under heavy attack by Pepsi-Cola.

When a customer uses a brand name in place of a generic, you know the mountain in their mind is strongly held. When someone points to a box of Scott tissues and says, "Hand me a Kleenex," you know who owns the tissue mountain in that person's mind.

Segmentation Is Tearing Up the Terrain

Who owns the automobile mountain in the United States? Many years ago Ford did. But Ford got torn apart by the segmentation strategy of General Motors.

So today Chevrolet, Pontiac, Oldsmobile, and Buick each own different segments of the automotive mountain, with perhaps Cadillac in the strongest position as the owner of the high-priced luxury segment. (Today people will use the name Cadillac as a synonym for a high-quality product. "It's the Cadillac of television sets.") As a result of its five strong independent positions, General Motors owns the dominant share of the U.S. automotive market.

Monolithic mountains are being fought over and cut up into segments, each owned by a different warlord. This long-term trend is likely to continue well into the twenty-first century.

The original owner has a choice: extend or contract. Faced with an enemy that attempts to segment the market, a company can extend its forces to try to control the entire territory, or shrink them to protect home base.

The owner's instincts are usually wrong. Greed encourages a brand leader to extend its forces to try to control all segments. Too often everything is lost in an effort to protect a small portion of the mountain. As Frederick the Great once said, "He who attempts to defend everywhere defends nothing."

Is there no defense against a competitor who attempts to segment your mountain? Fortunately for the big companies of this world, there is.

33

On Corporate Strategy

Bruce D. Henderson

Only a diversified company with a balanced portfolio can use its strengths to truly capitalize on its growth opportunities.

Price Strategy with Inflation

EXPERIENCE CURVE THEORY says that about 3 percent steady annual growth on trend in physical volume is required to reduce costs enough to offset 1 percent of annual inflation. Only products with growth rates more than three times inflation can expect to hold a constant price in current dollars without producing a shakeout.

There are some general pricing rules. Price parallel to experience curve costs if market shares are to be kept constant. Raise prices faster than experience curve costs to cause the smallest producers to grow fastest. Lower prices faster than experience curve costs to shakeout all except a few competitors. These relationships are not affected by inflation. However, inflation has the effect of an automatic price cut if you do not raise dollar prices.

Significant inflation cannot be offset by growth except in a few fast-growth products. Therefore, constant prices in current dollars means an automatic competitive shakeout for most products. Even maintaining margins in slow-growth products requires upward price leadership by some competitor. Failure to raise prices during inflation is, in fact, a price war of attrition.

The effects of price changes are unequal. Small-share competitors are characteristically high-cost producers. Failure to increase prices is very punishing to them. Failure to

There are some general pricing rules. Price parallel to experience curve costs if market shares are to be kept constant. Raise prices faster than experience curve costs to cause the smallest producers to grow fastest. Lower prices faster than experience curve costs to shakeout all except a few competitors. These relationships are not affected by inflation. However, inflation has the effect of an automatic price cut if you do not raise dollar prices.

Significant inflation cannot be offset by growth except in a few fast-growth products. Therefore, constant prices in current dollars means an automatic competitive shakeout for most products. Even maintaining margins in slow-growth products requires upward price leadership by some competitor. Failure to raise prices during inflation is, in fact, a price war of attrition.

The effects of price changes are unequal. Small-share competitors are characteristically high-cost producers. Failure to increase prices is very punishing to them. Failure to
increase prices during inflation naturally tends to concentrate market share in the already leading producer.

However, if one competitor increases prices and no others follow suit, the competitor holding prices constant will tend to gain share rapidly—often fast enough to offset the lower price. If the price differential is allowed to continue for an extended period, the growth in volume will lead eventually to an improvement in relative cost for the competitor gaining share. This can actually more than offset the price decrease on trend if capacity is added fast enough to keep lead time short.

It is ironic that public policy calls for holding prices steady during inflation. The result must inevitably be the squeezing out of the higher cost and smaller competitors. The same action in the absence of inflation would be viewed as extremely aggressive.

The corporate strategist must first decide whether market share is worth buying before he can evaluate pricing strategy. Inflation does offer the leading producer a chance to

Bruce D. Henderson is Professor of Management at Owen Graduate School of Management, Vanderbilt University.

lower real prices methodically and slowly squeeze out higher cost competition. This can be done by just holding prices constant.

This is no small opportunity. True prices can be steadily reduced this way. In a noninflationary environment, the same result would require a series of highly visible steps that would provoke very strong reaction from competitors and perhaps from antitrust administrators.

Experience curves and inflation work in opposite directions. In the absence of inflation, the leading producer tends to hold prices up in the face of declining costs until his loss of market share becomes unbearable. His very size provides the opportunity to maintain a price umbrella. With inflation every producer is automatically the price leader on the down side until he takes specific action to raise prices.

Passive price behavior by the leading producer means that without inflation he keeps prices too high for his own good in fast-growth situations. He loses share steadily and prices eventually decline anyhow.

Passive price behavior by the leading producer in modest and slow-growth industries during inflation means that the price is steadily lowered below the level of competitors' costs. Competitors cannot raise prices to offset inflation unless the leading producer follows suit.

Inflation changes the direction in which active price decisions must be made. However, inflation does not change the fact that there is an equilibrium price at which market share will stay constant. Either higher or lower levels will cause share to shift. Inflation makes the equilibrium price a moving target with an upward bias.

Prices Must Exceed Inflation

Prices must go up faster than inflation. Return on assets must increase faster than inflation. Failure leads first to change in financial policies, then to elimination of the higher cost competitors, and finally to shortage.

Inflation is financial growth. It is not enough for prices to increase parallel to inflation. They must go up enough to provide financing for the increased valuation of assets, as well as cover increased costs.

A company faced with a 10-percent increase in inflation rate must increase its rate of growth in assets an added 10-percent annually. That requires an additional 10-percent net return on the assets used. This is true even if there is no change in physical volume growth.

Inflation financing can come from reduced dividends, increased debt, or increased profit margin. Suppose percentage profit margin does not increase. Debt financing becomes far more difficult with inflation. Interest rates rise with inflation and rise even more if monetary restraint is used. High interest makes larger margins of profit necessary for a given amount of debt to support itself.

Reduction in dividends without faster physical growth is merely proof of financial starvation.

The marginal company is the first to feel inflation. Its past survival against lower cost competitors depended on those competitors' self-restraint, in the form of dividend payout instead of growth, of low debt instead of lower prices.

Thus, inflation turns the low-cost competitor into a marginal competitor if profit margins are not raised. It turns the high-cost competitor into a shrinking competitor if the profit margins are held down.

Truly marginal competitors rarely pay a dividend. They have little unused debt capacity. They can grow as fast as their competitors only by paying lower dividends and issuing a larger proportion of debt. Deny them this, and they must fall behind because of financial starvation.

Higher inflation may well be with us for a long time. If you are an investor, beware of the high Beta shares,which have a lower ROA than the industry leader. Invest in industry leaders even if profits are down, particularly if they are gaining market share. Subtract inflation from current return on net work (after taxes) to find the real performance index.

If you are the manager of a low margin company, get your long-term credit lined up—fast. If you are the manager of an industry leader, now is the time to choose your future. You can hold your historic percentage profit margin, use your debt capacity to maintain adequate capacity, and shake off much of your competition. If you prefer more short-term profit at the expense of future profits and market share, then raise prices now faster than inflation. This will protect your competitors, as well as cause public censure for inflationary pricing.

Of course, if you hold traditional profit margins, you will tend to become a monopolist and that will bring public censure, too. Take your choice. An increase in inflation will force you to choose.

A period of high inflation is a period in which each company must choose its future. It is a time of truth in strategy decision.

Price Policy

Price increases are instant additions to profit margin. Price decreases are instant decreases in margin for everyone. That is the immediate effect. The longer term effect is quite different.

Prices which increase profit margin invite entry of new competitors, expansion of capacity, and price competition. Prices which narrow profit margin discourage investment and lead to fewer competitors.

Since all competitors do not have the same costs, the changes in margin do not have the same influence on investment decision. Low margins go with low share of market. Therefore, low share causes increased sensitivity to price level.

Since the high share competitor usually has the lowest costs, he has an option. He can either maintain share and margin, or increase margin but lose share. This is not an obvious or easy choice. It depends on such factors as industry growth rate, alternative investment opportunities, and relative market shares. It is actually a choice available *only* to the high share low-cost producer. His return is greater; his margin is greater. His range of options is greater than all others. The low share competitor cannot hold a price umbrella. He loses share too fast if he tries.

Prices should parallel costs when market shares are stable. This seems to be an observable fact which is generally true. Market shares are usually unstable under all other conditions. Characteristically, costs follow a pattern described by the experience curve. Typically, costs in constant monetary units go down between 20 and 30 percent when accumulated experience doubles.

Experience curve costs are expressed in *constant* monetary units—that is, after adjusting for inflation. Therefore, constant margins may mean either rising or falling prices in *current* monetary units. As a rule of thumb, real costs decline about 1 percent for each 3 percent of annual growth in physical volume. That is why almost all current prices must rise. Inflation offsets cost declines in all except the most rapidly growing products.

Virtually all products and services follow a characteristic set of price patterns based on these relationships. Consequently, it is possible to predict price behavior, net of inflation, by identifying the current phase of the pattern. Conversely, it is possible to predict shifts in market share by identification of the price pattern.

The managerial economic issue remains the same: which is more valuable—higher profit margin now or higher market share in the future? This is an investment decision.

The Pricing Paradox

The profit equation has three variables—price, volume, and cost. Of these, price is the most common candidate for manipulation since nothing else need change to produce profits for all competitors, provided they all change prices together. That togetherness is what gives birth to dreams of "industry statesmanship" as a means of achieving better profits through higher prices.

In fact, both volume and cost are easier to change than industry price levels. Efforts to change prices can cause them to ebb and flow like the tide, with equal net effect on mean sea level. Above-normal prices inevitably attract additional capacity until prices become depressed. Depressed prices inhibit capacity replacement or additions until prices rise. This is a corollary of the economic truism that competition will force prices down to approach costs, or it will cause costs to rise to approach prices.

The consequences of a price advance are predictable. At best, other producers will follow the leader and there will be a substantial price rise. But this in turn sets up a ready-made umbrella for the new capacity of these other competitors, which *must* force their way into the market to fill their added capacity.

The usual result is an artificial list price which hides real price cuts at the expense of the market leader. Because of the price leader's price rise, its profit erosion is obscured temporarily until it is decided at some later date that the company must retain its share of market. In the meantime, it has subsidized the invasion of its market share by competitors and justified their investment in more capacity.

In the short term, the others may not follow this price leadership. Consequently, the leader must not only retract the price increase, but also suffer some market volume loss.

Over the longer term, the consequences are quite different. The share of the market is determined by what company has the capacity and can use it fully. In the long term, the maintenance or addition of capacity is nearly always a function of past profits and their effect on profit expectations in the future.

Over the long term, profit and profit expectations are based upon anticipated relative costs and operating rates. As a consequence, short-term higher prices for the industry tend to encourage capacity additions and provide the cash flow to justify that expansion.

This is simply classic economics, but the strategic implications are not immediately obvious:

> *If you have the lowest cost at nominal capacity,* then it is to your advantage to keep prices down sufficiently at all times to dissuade competition from making additional capacity investments, unless, of course, you can raise prices and still stay at nominal capacity.
>
> Also, it is to your advantage to invest in added capacity as long as you can do so and maintain your cost advantage. This requires that the added capacity be operated at a load factor high enough to provide cost levels no higher than competitors' average cost. In fact, in an active technology you must make capacity additions to maintain a cost advantage.
>
> *If your fixed costs are higher but your operating costs are lower than those of competitors,* then you are more sensitive to changes in operating rate. It is to your advantage to accept any kind of short-term price depression which provides a high operating rate. Only under these conditions can you maintain a relative cost advantage. For the same reason, you can accept a lower price level without out-of-pocket loss than your competitors can. This situation is usually true of the new facility.

If your company is the low-cost producer with the newest facilities, then any price which is required to operate your facility at nominal capacity is not only justified, but is a prerequisite for maintaining your relative cost advantage. Any higher price is relatively disadvantageous. Conversely, high-cost producers must keep prices high or obtain a higher operating rate.

Competitive strategy comes into play in the effort to induce competitors to accept practices which shift *relative* costs. The corporate strategist with the new low-cost facility must persuade competitors that he can and will depress prices indefinitely—until prices are below their cost, if need be—to the point that the new facility is operating at average industry capacity. In fact, he has the power to do this. He benefits most, however, if he does not need to depress prices to fill his new capacity.

The strategist who has higher cost facilities but is in possession of the market must convince competitors that high prices for the industry are to everyone's advantage. In this way, he can offset his relative cost disadvantage. He may also find it necessary to convince competitors that it will be too costly to wrest his existing market share by price action. If he can induce competitors to use a nonprice means of competing, then their added costs may defer for a long time their realization of the inherent advantage of newer and more efficient capacity.

In the short term, the really critical elements of strategy are those which induce a competitor, for whatever reason, to accept a lower operating rate. This imposes a relative cost handicap which has no offsetting virtues.

In the long term, the critical elements are those which determine the willingness of competitors to make further capital investment in capacity. Any uncertainty, risk, or competitive policy which can delay this kind of decision produces a higher profit level on average for those already in production.

Viewed in this light:

Short-term price increases tend to depress industry profits in the long-term by accelerating the introduction of new capacity and depressing market demand.

Short-term price increases favor the high-cost producer relatively more than the low-cost producer.

The lower cost producer has everything to gain and little to lose by depressing prices until the company is operating at nominal capacity.

The perfect strategy for the low-cost producer is one which persuades others to permit him to obtain maximum use f capacity with minimum price depression—at the others' expense in terms of operating rate and profit.

The perfect strategy for the high-cost producer is one which persuades others that market shares cannot be shifted except over long periods of time, and, therefore, that the highest practical industry prices are to everyone's advantage.

Paradoxically, it is often the strongest and lowest cost producer which leads the way in establishing higher prices, even though the company itself may be operating below optimum capacity. When this happens, it must be considered a strategic victory for the higher cost producer in the market.

If all of this seems obvious, it is difficult to explain the concern of businessmen, security analysts, and others with industry price levels. It would appear that the factor of vital concern should be relative costs—or, rather, relative profit margins. The focus on short-term profits, which are often transient, frequently influences long-term performance in the opposite way from that desired.

Pattern for Success

Successful companies make almost all of their profit from products in which they dominate the relevant market. Usually their market share for these products exceeds the combined share of the next two competitors. This seems to be true no matter how large or small the company, and in spite of U.S. antitrust philosophy.

But this characteristic pattern for success is not always obvious. Identical products do not necessarily serve identical markets, and different markets may have quite different distribution methods and costs. However, when products and markets are properly defined, it becomes apparent that there are only a few significant competitors in any given market for a given product.

The most profitable producers are those which dominate the market segments they serve. Conversely, when a company does not clearly dominate a product market segment, its profit margin is distinctly inferior to that of the producer that does dominate.

This pattern should surprise no one. Pareto's Law states that most of the volume should be concentrated in a few producers. Experience curve theory shows that the producer with the largest market share should have the lowest cost. It follows that the products with the largest volume and lowest costs should provide most of the profit.

If profit margin is a function of market share, then market share becomes very valuable. Investment in market share is worthwhile when the market is growing rapidly and the value of market share is being rapidly multiplied.

The most rewarding way to obtain market share is to acquire it early. This requires early recognition of the large-growth product, as well as early commitment to the investment required to obtain and hold the dominant share during the growth period. The return on such an investment can be very high indeed when the product becomes mature. The earlier the investment is made, the higher the return for leadership will be. This is why R&D can pay off so handsomely, even with the uncertainty and long delay before there is a return.

Company success requires a series of products. Products must eventually mature. When they do, they provide the cash flow for investment in a new series of high-potential, high growth products. Thus, mature products fund investment in market share of growth products until they, too, become mature and the cycle can be repeated.

This seems to be the pattern successful companies follow. The implications are far-reaching. Those who understand the underlying logic, and can control their investments accordingly, have the opportunity to achieve and sustain high levels of growth and profitability. Those who do not understand the full consequences of this pattern will constantly exchange long-term success for short-term improvements in current performance.

Capacity

The timing of capacity additions determines both market share and profitability. Lack of capacity at peak demand inevitably means loss of market share to those companies which do have capacity. Excess capacity means added cost with no benefit.

Capacity must be added before it is needed. Adding capacity requires time: to plan, to build, and to debug. For this reason, capacity additions must always be started well before capacity is needed.

Capacity is the determinant of market share. Inadequate capacity means long lead times at best, and perhaps sales lost forever. Differences in lead time are a compelling motive for changing suppliers. The resulting change in market share is often permanent. The size of the backlog is a measure of the probable loss in market share.

Shift of market share is the basis for a shift in relative cost. Therefore, a loss of market share can be and often is a permanent loss of future profit margin, even though output continues to grow and existing capacity is normally utilized.

A competitor in a growth business will automatically lose market share if capacity additions are delayed until existing capacity is fully required. Any industry growth while your own company's capacity is fixed and fully used is by definition a proportionate loss of your share.

However, market share is always lost to a competitor. His capacity had to be in existence for you to lose share to him. Therefore, his decisions on timing of capacity additions determine his delivery capability versus your own. Delivery capability is far more often a determinant of market share shift than price competition itself.

The surest way to gain market share, other things being relatively normal, is to persuade your competitor *not* to invest in added capacity at the same time that you do so. But since your ability to inhibit competitive investment must be indirect by nature, then the real battle is in the mind of your competitor. Your initiative in adding capacity affects your competitor's subsequent decision. Capacity, once created, is irreversible in cost commitment.

The competitor who adds capacity first may not make a profit, but the competitor who lags the leader cannot win, whether or not he eventually adds capacity. Price competition is thus a psychological weapon that affects investment choices, not a means of attacking or taking business away from competitors.

Know your competitor's investment decision rules and patterns. Manage your competitor's investment decisions by your own initiative in adding capacity before it is needed.

The Market Share Paradox

Market share is very valuable. It leads to lower relative cost and, therefore, higher profits. Unfortunately, most efforts to improve market share depress profits, at least in the short term.

There are two principal reasons for a shift in market share between competitors. The more common is lack of capacity. The other reason is a willingness to lose share to maintain price.

Lack of capacity is a common problem, because it is expensive to maintain unused capacity for very long. Even in the face of projected *industry* growth, it is not surprising that not all *individual* producers feel they can justify the incremental investment in added capacity. On the other hand, nothing is more obvious than the fact that capacity limits market share. If the market grows and capacity does not, then the company which has the capacity takes the growth, and increases its share of the market—at your expense.

The decision to add capacity is a fateful one. Add too soon, and extra costs are incurred with no benefits. Add too late, and market share is lost. Added capacity means more than bricks and machines. It also means capable personnel in the proper proportions in the proper places. Because the lead time required is long, the decision must anticipate the need.

The competitive implications are made more complex by the cost differentials among competitors. Simple arithmetic shows that the high-cost producer must add capacity in direct proportion to the low-cost firm, if relative market shares are to remain constant. But the high-cost producer's return on the capacity investment is lower than that of the more efficient firm, because of the difference in profit margins.

The market share paradox is that if the low-cost firm would accept the high-cost producer's return on assets, the low-cost firm would preempt all market growth. The resulting increase in the latter's accumulated experience would further improve its costs and thereafter steadily increase the cost *differential* between the competitors.

> *In short, if the same investment criteria were used by all firms, then the low-cost firm would always expand capacity first and other firms never would.*

However, all firms do *not* use the same investment criteria. The fact that market share is stable proves this. However, this also means that shares are unstable if there is vigorous competition.

The low-cost producer can only take market share if he is willing to sacrifice near-term profit. The high-cost producer can obtain a significant return only because he is allowed to do so in order to maintain current prices.

The tradeoff is inviting. Since the low-cost firm typically has the largest market share, higher expectations for return often lead it to sacrifice share to maintain near-term margins. The loss of a modest amount of the market may seem far less costly in the short-term than meeting a price concession of a minor competitor, or spreading the price reduction necessary to fill proposed new capacity over the firm's entire sales volume.

Unfortunately, the tradeoff is cumulative. More and more share must be given up over time to maintain price. Costs are a function of market share because of the experience effect. Lost market share leads to loss of cost advantage. Eventually, there is no way to maintain profitability.

The rate of growth is the critical variable in resolving the market share paradox and the tradeoff between share and near-term profits.

> Without growth, it is virtually impossible to shift market share. Competitors can neither justify adding capacity, nor afford to lose share at the price of idle capacity. Under such constraints, since prices will tend to be very stable, the appropriate strategy is to maximize profits within existing market shares.
>
> With little growth, a higher near-term profit may be worth considerably more than continued modest profit. The only competitors which should hold share into the no-growth period are those with enough share—and the resulting cost position—to anticipate satisfactory profits.
>
> With rapid growth, market share is both very valuable and very easy to lose. On the one hand, any improvement in share will be compounded by growth of the market itself, and then again by improved margins as cost improvement accrues from increased volume and, hence, experience. On the other hand, growth means that capacity must be added rapidly, in advance of the growth, or share will be lost automatically; to gain share, capacity addition must be based on preempting the growth component.

Any shift in market share should be regarded as either investment or disinvestment. The rate of return can and should be evaluated just as it would be in any other business situation.

Change in market share should be an investment decision.

Industrial Pricing Policy and Market Share

Price policy is usually established at the highest management levels in a company. Yet there are few management decisions that are more subject to intuition and more clearly the product of corporate mythology.

There is a reason for this. All price decisions are based on assumptions about what a competitor will do under certain hypothetical circumstances. There is no way to know that for sure—hence, the characteristic reliance on intuition.

Yet there *is* a logic to competitive behavior. In addition, there is abundant evidence that industrial prices follow certain kinds of patterns that are stable over long periods of time, regardless of what competitors try to do. If there is a logic and a rationale for this pattern, then there is a basis for analysis and predictions of the consequences of changing a given price. What follows is an example of that kind of analysis.

We start with the assumption that prices are set on the basis of constrainsts determined by competition. Assume also that each competitor will be unable or unwilling to sell below cost for any protracted period of time. This leads to the obvious conclusion that most of the competitors in any given product market area will be operating at a high percentage of their capacity. In other words, only a modest proportion of their organization and facilities are not being put to use. In a growing economy this means that each producer must periodically add to its capacity or it will lose market share.

This decision to add to capacity is a fateful one. Additional funds are being committed to the business. The risk and exposure are compounded. But competitive position will be affected adversely if the capacity is not added.

If we assume that all producers do not have the same costs, why is it that the most profitable producer does not add capacity first and preempt all of the growth? The question can be stated another way: what is it that keeps investment decisions in step with each other and, therefore, keeps market shares constant? We do assume that all producers have the same equivalent price level, whether or not they have the same cost levels.

If prices are the same but costs are different, each producer must have a different return on new capacity investment. But why will one demand more return before investing than others? Is there some reason to assume that each producer cannot change its share of the market if it adds capacity first?

The answer is that there is no reason why not, if the producer then has capacity and its competitors do not. The answer is the opposite, however, if all competitors have adequate capacity at all times. How, indeed, would share change if all suppliers were equal?

Consider the hypothesis that market share almost never changes hands between two competent competitors unless one has inadequate capacity while the other does not.

It is a generally accepted fact that competitors will meet price competition at once and meet nonprice competition as soon as they realize that they are being hurt. If this is true, then there is no way for market share to change except by mistake or because of lack of capacity. This leads to the conclusion that the real role of price level is to determine which product is willing to add capacity first, and when its competitors will be willing to follow.

This view of the competitive world casts the low-cost producer in the role of the giant with the whip hand. It casts the high-cost producer in the role of the challenger whose decisions to invest and take risks in the face of the giant's cost advantage will determine the price level. Two different scenarios in the competitive drama are possible.

In the first scenario, the giant with the lower cost is faced with large reductions in price and, therefore, in profit, in order to prevent the smaller and higher cost producer from adding capacity. The smaller producer does in fact add the capacity. However, to do so requires a price differential, or its equivalent in added cost for added services, to attract the added volume. The larger and more efficient competitor permits the price differential or equivalent to exist rather than take the substantial loss in near-term profit that would be necessary to prevent the shift. However, the added capacity and growth of the high-cost producer leads to an improvement in the relative cost positions. Thus, the entire process is repeated until the former small, high-cost producer becomes the dominant, large, low-cost producer.

In this scenario there is no shortage of capacity, but the low-cost producer prefers immediate payout to future market share and profitability.

The second scenario unfolds if the low-cost producer adds capacity as necessary in order to maintain market share and then does whatever is necessary to fill this capacity and maintain market share. If this is strictly adhered to, the high-cost producer still sets the actual level of prices. There is no way that the high-cost producer can buy market share because the low-cost producer will not let that happen. If the high-cost producer does not add any capacity, there will be a shortage as the industry grows. The leader has only provided added capacity in proportion to its own share. The shortage raises prices. When the return becomes attractive enough, then the high-cost producer does indeed add more capacity and relieve the shortage, thus setting the price level.

This series of events is highly stable. The profit margin required for the high-cost producer to be induced to invest determines the price level for the industry and the rate of return for all competitors. The actual profit margin of the high-cost producer usually turns out to be just enough to finance the growth in capacity required to hold position, but not enough to permit any significant amount of capital to be taken out as dividends to the owners of the business.

There is a third possible scenario. Suppose that the high- and low-cost producers are willing to accept the same return on investment. The relationship between competitors becomes increasingly unstable. As the market grows, the low-cost producer will preempt all the growth because it will be the only competitor that adds capacity as the need grows. However, its costs will go down with its rapidly accumulating market share and experience. A peculiar thing happens. Over time both the market share and the profit margin of the low-cost producer widen, even though prices are still so low that the other producers cannot justify adding any capacity.

Several factors make this last scenario, as a strategy, rather unusual in practice:

> Accounting conventions tend to overstate the costs compared to the trend line average during the early phases of a new capacity addition. This inhibits investment until the need and the opportunity become obvious to all, including the higher cost producers.
>
> Business conventions have established return on assets as the goal, instead of return on equity or growth in the business. This tends to bias investment decisions toward maintenance of the status quo, rather than aggressive pursuit of position in the future.
>
> Management accountability of the publicly held, professionally managed company puts rather heavy emphasis on reported earnings in the present, rather than on the present value of future earnings that may be the actual result. The "bird-in-the-hand-is-worth-two-in-the-bush" concept naturally tends to dominate.

The interesting aspect, however, is that under certain circumstances the willingness to add capacity and depress prices can lead to very handsome returns on investment, particularly in fast-growing product areas. Whether this occurs depends upon the investment policies of competitors, not upon their price policies.

> *Price policies, it appears, are in fact a product of investment policies. Conversely, it appears that true consequence of price changes is to affect the investment decisions of competitors.*
>
> *Price changes do affect short-term profitability of all competitors equally as a percentage of sales. But in the long run, it appears that only the investment return standards determine prices or profits. The strategist who is willing to invest when others are not sets the price level for everyone by virtue of that investment.*

New Product Pricing

The prospects of an exciting new product are often destroyed by a conventional introductory pricing strategy. Early market domination is much more valuable than most companies realize, and internal compromises on initial pricing tactics are frequently disastrous to long-term profitability.

The basic objective in pricing a new product should be to prevent competitors from gaining experience and market share before the new product has achieved major volume. If this is done, it is possible to achieve a cost advantage over competitors which cannot ever profitably be overcome by normal performance on the part of competitors.

Unit costs are necessarily very high in the early stages of any product. In many cases, a product may not find a market if it has to be sold at its initial cost in competition with existing alternative products. However, if prices are set at a level which will move the product, then costs come down with experience. This means, of course, that operations are conducted at a loss until costs decline below that initial price.

Ignoring competition, there is an optimum initial price which may well be below initial cost. It must be low enough to find a market. If the market is at all price sensitive, there are some major advantages to forcing the development of the market as rapidly as is practical, and thus compressing the time required to get volume up and costs down. Assume, however, that the market growth rate is unaffected by the price policy of individual competitors. Market elasticity simply exaggerates the results of pricing actions, since lowering prices usually increases the total market, as well as participation in market growth.

In the absence of competition, there would be every reason to set prices as high as possible and lower them only when volume times margin would be increased by lowering price. This approach is often adopted, even though it can be a serious mistake if potentially strong competition exists. Indeed, in a competitive market, and assuming that a new product has substantial potential for future volume, the competitive cost differential in the future should be of greater concern than current profitability.

The lower the initial price set by the first producer, the more rapidly that company builds up volume and a differential cost advantage over succeeding competitors, and the faster the market develops. In a sense, this is a purchase of time advantage. However, the lower the initial price, the greater the investment required before the progressive reduction of cost will result in a profit. This means that, once again, the comparative investment resources of the competitors involved can become a significant, or even the critical, determinant of competitive survival.

It is even conceivable that the financial resources required to follow this type of initial pricing strategy may exceed those available to the firm. This apparently happened with the supersonic transport. Even when one firm can supply the financial resources required, the sum required may be so large that failure in the strategy would bankrupt the firm.

In addition to financial resources, another limit on extremely low initial prices is that set by the potential return on investment. Assuming that the price, once set, will not be raised but will be maintained until costs fall below it, the lower the price, the longer the time that any return is deferred and the larger the investment. When future cost differentials are discounted to present value, there is an obvious limit.

However, under ordinary circumstances the future growth of the market is uncertain. Consequently, initial prices tend to be set on initial costs in the absence of clear competitive threats. As volume builds up and costs decline, this normally produces visible profitability, which, in turn, induces new competitors to enter the field. The market leader now has the classic problem of choosing between current profitability and market share.

It should also be pointed out that, characteristically, it is impractical to attempt to take physical volume away from a competitor. The critical stake is ordinarily the share of the growth of the market. Once the product matures enough so that its annual growth in volume ceases, then all of the preceding discussion is essentially academic.

Pricing of a new product is of critical importance because it determines the participation possible in that product's future growth. For the product with a real future, this is obviously far more important than near-term profitability.

Most businessmen are intuitively aware of the tradeoffs which must be made when a new product is introduced. Miscalculations result from the uncertainties involved and the difficulty of justifying short-term losses in return for future market position. Fortunately, with the discovery of cost-experience relationships, it is now possible to deal quantitatively with the principal tradeoffs. Cost is related in constant terms to cumulative volume and that, in turn, is related to market share. Understanding these relationships has enabled businessmen to focus on the major issues in new product introduction and to set appropriate price levels with greater confidence than in the past.

The Product Portfolio

To be successful, a company should have a portfolio of products with different growth rates and different market shares. The portfolio composition is a function of the balance between cash flows. High-growth products require cash inputs to grow. Low-growth products should generate excess cash. Both kinds are needed simultaneously.

Four rules determine the cash flow of a product:

Margins and cash generated are a function of market share. High margins and high market share go together. This is a matter of common observation, explained by the experience curve effect.

Growth requires cash input to finance added assets. The added cash required to hold share is a function of growth rates.

High market share must be earned or bought. Buying market share requires additional investment.

No product market can grow indefinitely. The payoff from growth must come when the growth slows, or it will not come at all. The payoff is cash that cannot be reinvested in that product.

Products with high market share and slow growth are "cash cows." Characteristically, they generate large amounts of cash, in excess of the reinvestment required to maintain share. This excess need not, and should not, be reinvested in those products. In fact, if the rate of return exceeds the growth rate, the cash *cannot* be reinvested indefinitely, except by depressing returns.

Products with low market share and slow growth are "dogs." They may show an accounting profit, but the profit must be reinvested to maintain share, leaving no cash throw-off. The product is essentially worthless, except in liquidation.

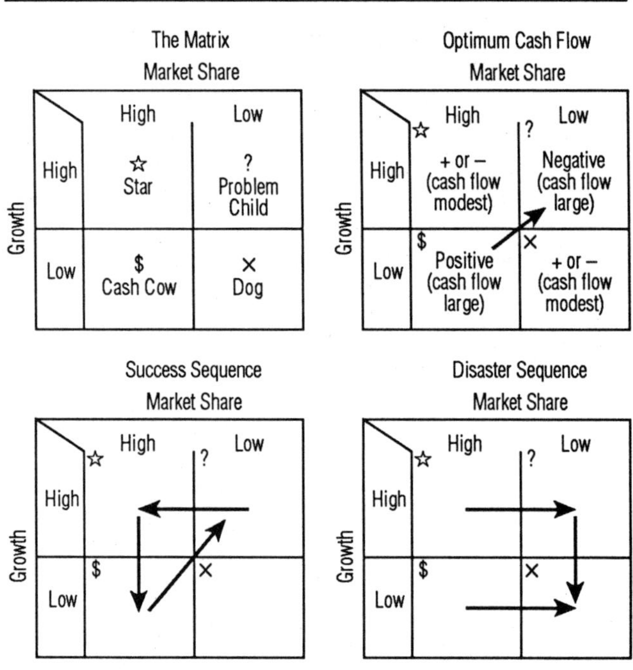

All products eventually become either a "cash cow" or a "dog." The value of a product is completely dependent upon obtaining a leading share of its market before the growth slows.

Low market share, high-growth products are the "problem children." They almost always require far more cash than they can generate. If cash is not supplied, they fall behind and die. Even when the cash is supplied, if they only hold their share, they are still dogs when the growth stops. The "problem children" require large added cash investment for market share to be purchased. The low market share, high-growth product is a liability unless it becomes a leader. It requires very large cash inputs that it cannot generate itself.

The high share, high growth product is the "star." It nearly always shows reported profits, but it may or may not generate all of its own cash. If it stays a leader, however, it will become a large cash generator when growth slows and its reinvestment requirements diminish. The star eventually becomes the cash cow—providing high volume, high margin, high stability, security—and cash throw-off for reinvestment elsewhere.

The payoff for leadership is very high indeed, if it is achieved early and maintained until growth slows. Investment in market share during the growth phase can be very attractive—if you have the cash. Growth in market is compounded by growth in share. Increases in share increase the margin. Higher margin permits higher leverage with equal safety. The resulting profitability permits higher payment of earnings after financing normal growth. The return on investment is enormous.

The need for a portfolio of businesses becomes obvious. Every company needs products in which to invest cash. Every company needs products that generate cash. And every product should eventually be a cash generator; otherwise, it is worthless.

Only a diversified company with a balanced portfolio can use its strengths to truly capitalize on its growth opportunities. The balanced portfolio has:

> "stars," whose high share and high growth assure the future; "cash cows," that supply funds for that future growth; and "problem children," to be converted into "stars" with the added funds.

"Dogs" are not necessary. They are evidence of failure either to obtain a leadership position during the growth phase, or to get out and cut the losses.

Note

1. The public interest *requires* the concentration of production and distribution in the minimum practical number of competitors. This is necessary to achieve the lowest consumer prices and the highest national productivity.

   Characteristically, if the size of the smallest effective competitor's market share is doubled, the price to the user should be expected to approach a level about 25 percent lower than it could have been otherwise. This can occur without affecting the profit margin of that producer.

   The public is served best by concentration of marketing and distribution in a few producers for any given product, whether the companies involved are large or small. Unfortunately, it requires a diversified company to provide the capital necessary to develop and market a rapidly growing product at the rate which is optimum for both the company and the product users. Consequently, the most desirable situation from the users' point of view would be vigorous competition among a few large-scale, diversified companies that rapidly dominate the markets for their products.

34

Marketing Strategy & Differential Advantage

Victor J. Cook, Jr.

Differential advantages and disadvantages are implicit in the marketing strategies of every firm. The concept of strategic ambition, calibrated from military conventions and correlated with the classical mix, produce a unique marketing-oriented paradigm of strategic options.

Extending portfolio analysis and PIMS studies to include military concepts of strategic force produces a new paradigm of marketing strategies. The author introduces and calibrates the concept of strategic marketing ambition, relates this concept to the marketing mix, and then derives a theoretical function linking strategic ambitions and investments with market share. An operational measure of differential marketing advantage is introduced, and the methods of analysis are applied in an illustration of competitive investments, marketing strategy and differential advantage.

STRIVING TO ACHIEVE differential advantages in product, promotion, place and price, firms risk their futures on a set of contemporary marketing strategies. Three major research directions emerged in the 1970s to address these problems. Henderson's (1979) strategic matrix, the Buzzell, Gale and Sultan (1975) studies of the PIMS data, and Kotler and Singh's (1981) reports on marketing warfare have had a profound effect on strategic decision making. This paper builds on the foundation of these classic works in an effort to extend and sharpen the tools of strategic marketing analysis.

Victor J. Cook, Jr., is Professor of Marketing Strategy at the A. B. Freeman School of Business, Tulane University.

Marketing and Business Strategy

Henderson designed portfolio analysis for use in the development of business strategies. Marketing was not the focus of his strategic matrix. Rather, his interests lay in strategic business unit (SBU) and divisional resource allocations. Product portfolio analysis does not address the marketing problems of differential advantage in promotion, place and price precisely because these are functional, not divisional issues.

In a comprehensive evaluation of the variety of strategic models available in marketing, Wensley (1981) concluded:

> In undertaking strategic *marketing* analysis of any particular investment option it is important to avoid the use of classificatory systems that deflect the analysis from why there is a potential for *significant competitive* advantage (p. 181, italics added).

The conceptual framework developed in this paper leads the manager and the scholar to focus on the issues of why a "significant competitive" or differential advantage exists in a given product or service market. The inputs of portfolio analysis (share of market and growth rate in primary demand) are the outputs of marketing strategy. On what product, promotion, place and price strategies does share of market depend? That is the central question of this paper. The decision to brighten a star, milk a cow or kill a dog are larger than product strategy issues. Divisional resource allocations like these should be linked more directly to the other functional elements of the marketing mix. What seems needed is an extension of this divisional matrix into a completely marketing-oriented strategic paradigm.

PIMS and Marketing Costs

In one of the most influential reports on the PIMS data, Buzzell, Gale and Sultan (1975) caution "neither PIMS nor any other empirical research can lead to a 'formula' for strategic choices" (p. 106). Following this conclusion, propositions in this paper are built not on empirical evidence but on theoretical foundations. This theoretical approach leads to new questions about the behavior of marketing costs.

Most recently Buzzell (1981, p. 48) concluded "the PIMS data show that costs are inversely related to relative market share." The concept of marketing strategy presented here adds a new dimension to the complex relationship between the costs of achieving a given share of market and the size of that share. A new perspective is also provided on the costs of maintaining market share, compared to the profit impact of harvesting market share.

Marketing and Military Strategy

Concepts from military strategy were introduced into the marketing literature by Trout and Ries (1978) and Kotler and Singh (1981). The contribution of these concepts has been to focus management attention more directly on the impact of competitive resource deployment in calculating the effect of a firm's marketing strategy. The operational measure of differential advantage proposed here builds upon the tie between marketing strategy and competitors' behavior.

Objectives

The objectives of this paper are to (1) introduce and calibrate the concept of strategic marketing ambition, (2) relate this concept to the marketing mix as a new paradigm of marketing strategy, (3) derive a theoretical function linking strategic ambition with market share, (4) illustrate the methods of analysis with the case of USAUTO vs. FORNAUTO, and (5) introduce an operational measure of differential marketing advantage.

The Concept of Strategic Marketing Ambition

In a competitive market, as on a military field, a strategy can be defined with reference to the behavior of rivals. In marketing, the behavior of interest is competitive deployment of marketing resources. Defining ambition is the first step in understanding strategy. One firm has ambitions with respect to a targeted share of market, which require the deployment of its strategic resources in direct competition with the commitments of designated competitors. Conceptually the total commitment of marketing resources among all competitors vying for a share of the market is defined by the identity:

$$E = e + e^* \qquad (1)$$

Total marketing investments (E) are the sum of one firm's expenditures (e) and the expenditures of competitors (e^*).

On what does the value of e depend? Often the answer is that it depends on historical spending levels or industry norms. If an organization was spending \$100,000 and suddenly increased expenditures to \$500,000, one is tempted to conclude the firm is following an "attack" marketing strategy. There is, however, insufficient evidence for this conclusion. It is first necessary to know what are the commitments or expenditures of competitors. If the value of competitive expenditures is \$10,000,000, the aggressive nature of even a five-fold increase in spending becomes uncertain. A more revealing answer is that a strategic expenditure depends on the ambitions of the firm. This leads to the conclusion that a strategy implies a formal relationship between the ambitions of an organization and the expenditures of competitors:

$$e = ye^* \qquad (2)$$

A strategic expenditure is the (arithmetic) product of a competitor's ambitions and the expenditures of rivals. The value of the strategic multiply y denotes a firm's ambition. In the example cited above, the organization's five-fold increase in spending is significant, yet it nevertheless reflects a limited strategic ambition. Before the spending increase the firm's strategic multiple is exactly 0.01 times competitive expenditures. After the increase, its strategic multiple is 0.05. With respect to the commitments of rivals, each of these may be viewed as retreat, or niching, strategies.

Strategic ambitions are usually given categorical labels, as if ambition were a discrete variable. Thus, reference is often made to a firm's intention to "dominate" on media spending, to "match" its competitors' commitments in distribution, or to "flank" the superior product performance of a rival.

A Calibration of Strategic Marketing Ambition

Military conventions offer an important point of reference in calibrating the concept of strategic ambition:

> The "principle of force" says that the side with the greater manpower (resources) will win the engagement. This is modified if the defender has greater firing efficiency or a terrain advantage. The military rule of thumb is that for a frontal attack to be successful against a well-entrenched opponent or one controlling the "high ground," the attacking forces must deploy a 3:1 advantage in combat firepower (Kotler and Singh 1981, p. 34).

A "3 to 1 advantage" establishes the first point of reference in the calibration of strategic ambition. A "dominate strategy" consists of the ambition to achieve a strategic multiple of three times competitors' expenditures by deploying resources at the level $e = 3e^*$. The expenditure level implied

Table 1
A Calibration of Strategic Marketing Ambition

Ambition	Calibration (y)
Dominate	y = 3.00
	y = 2.00
Attack	y = 1.50
Match	y = 1.00
Flank	y = 0.33
Retreat	y = 0.05

by such ambition depends on competitive behavior, not on the firm's historical spending rate.

Dominate is the most ambitious strategy short of monopoly. At the other extreme, a retreat strategy invests at the rate implied by a strategic multiple approaching zero. In the mid-range of ambition, a match strategy is, by definition, investing at a rate that matches, or equals competitive resource deployments. The strategic multiple is therefore equal to 1.0 with a match strategy.

These three points of reference assign specific meaning to the military labels frequently used to identify different strategic ambitions. The result is presented in Table 1. The calibration of a flank strategy at a multiple of 0.33 is formal recognition of the most cost efficient level of ambition. The strategic multiple symbolizing attack set at 1.5 is arbitrary, though it must be calibrated somewhere between an ambition to match and to dominate. Implicit in Table 1 is the strategy of disengagement or rout, with $y = 0.00$.

One should not conclude that retreat is equivalent to a harvest strategy. It all depends on where the firm starts from. A strategic multiple of 0.05 may represent either a retreat or a harvest strategy, depending on whether the organization has already amassed sufficient market strength to harvest from prior investments, and whether harvesting is logistically feasible.

A Strategic Marketing Paradigm

Convention has long identified the four basic components of the marketing mix as conceptually related to product, promotion, place and price (Culliton 1948). It is thus natural to correlate strategic ambitions with the components of the marketing mix. The result, presented in Table 2, is a categorical specification of 20 exclusive and exhaustive strategic marketing options. In this way explicit meaning is given the term marketing strategy. A marketing strategy is any feasible combination of four decisions relating strategic ambition to components of the marketing mix. A feasible combination is any set of four mnemonic descriptors from Table 2. Note, it is not feasible simultaneously to dominate and retreat on the same mix variable in the same competitive field and time interval. The strategic marketing paradigm gives rise to a large number of (categorical) combinations applicable to as many different instances of marketing strategy.

Marketing Mix Investment Measures

If marketing expenditures represent true investment options, further inquiry must be made into the nature of these investments. What are the marketing investment options in product, promotion, place and price, and how are they measured? The payoff, the net present value of market share, is the output of a set of marketing strategies. It is important to be more specific about the nature of the inputs. The variables and their measures differ from market to market, yet a common core of marketing investment variables and measures can be identified. A partial list of the variables where significant differential advantages may be found in the marketing mix is presented in Table 3.

Strategic Marketing Descriptors

Very specific and comprehensive statements about the marketing strategy of a firm may be made by combining the strategic descriptors presented in Table 2 with the list of variables in Table 3. For example, in short form one marketing strategy may be described efficiently as:

$$[D1.4, D2.1, D3.1, A4.2] \qquad (3)$$

The expression in equation (3) specifies the following marketing strategy: In product, the firm is dominating all rivals by offering a product line equal to three times the combined product offerings of these competitors. The short form identifier of this strategy is [D1.4], or "dominate on product assortments." Such a strategy assumes the production capacity and plant inventories necessary to support this product ambition. In promotion, the firm is similarly dominating the media investments of competitors, as signified by the notation [D2.1]. Probably such a dominant strategy in media is coupled with similar strengths in positioning, message impact and media production values. Further, this firm's ambitions with respect to place investments are equally impressive. The descriptor [D3.1] signifies an ambition to dominate rivals on number of retail outlets. No doubt a dominate strategy in retail outlets is combined with a similar position with respect to salespersons, field inventories and selling space. Finally,

Table 2
A Strategic Marketing Paradigm

Ambition	Marketing Mix Component: Product	Promotion	Place	Price
Dominate	D1	D2	D3	D4
Attack	A1	A2	A3	A4
Match	M1	M2	M3	M4
Flank	F1	F2	F3	F4
Retreat	R1	R2	R3	R4

Table 3
Marketing Mix Variables and Measures

1.0 Product Investment Variables (Measures)
- 1.1 Research and development (money/employees)
- 1.2 Patents (number issued and pending)
- 1.3 Production capacity (value/employees/units)
- [1.4] *Assortment* (number offered)
- 1.5 Plant inventories (value/units)
- 1.6 Product performance (technical/perceptual)
- 1.7 Trademarks (value/number of brands)
- 1.8 Warranties (value/terms)

2.0 Promotional Investment Variables (Measures)
- [2.1] *Media* (money/number of messages)
- 2.2 Salespersons (money/number/calls)
- 2.3 Promotion (money/number)
- 2.4 Publicity (number of messages)
- 2.5 Positioning (metric distance)
- 2.6 Message (impact)
- 2.7 Production (value)

3.0 Place Investment Variables (Measures)
- [3.1] *Retail Outlets* (number)
- 3.2 Retail salespersons (number)
- 3.3 Field inventories (value/units)
- 3.4 Selling space (square feet)
- 3.5 Shelf space (linear feet/facings)
- 3.6 Hours of business
- 3.7 Special measures (e.g., flights per city pair)
- 3.8 Trade support (dollar margins × volume)

4.0 Price Investment Variables (Measures)
- 4.1 Primary demand elasticity
- [4.2] *Price Relative* $(1 - P/P^*)$
- 4.3 Rebates/discounts (money)
- 4.4 Trade margins (percent)
- 4.5 Terms of sale (time/interest)
- 4.6 Refund policy (recovery value)
- 4.7 Transaction cost (money)

the firm is attacking with its retail price strategy, [A4.2]. This signifies retail prices below those of rivals and probably is associated with more favorable trade margins, discounts, terms and transaction costs. The bracket notation used to identify strategic variables in Table 3 provides a rich assortment of strategic options as well as an efficient convention for discussion of marketing strategies.

The Strategic Marketing Cost Function

Discussions of marketing strategy often lead one to think in terms of discrete strategic options. In fact, ambitions are continuous. The calibration of strategic marketing ambitions presented in Table 1 gives rise to a continuous measure of strategic marketing costs. This measure has sufficient general utility in strategic planning to serve as a link between marketing strategy and the mix.

A marketing strategy consists of ambitions calculated to achieve specific shares of deployments in product, promotion, place and price. Identify these shares of marketing investments by the vector x' and recognize that it has at least four dimensions in marketing strategy corresponding to each mix component. Thus, x' fully describes each of four or more investment decisions. The share of strategic investments implied by a firm's marketing ambition is calculated from the expression:

$$x' = y'/(1 + y') \tag{4}$$

The relationship between ambition and share of investments defined in equation (4) is visualized easily in the case of a match strategy. If the firm's ambition is to match rivals on a given mix variable, the implication is that it will deploy its resources at a rate equal to 1.0 times competitors' investments and achieve a share of investments equal to 50%. In a similar fashion the share of investment implied by any strategic product, promotion or place ambition may be calculated from equation (4). The competitive price ambitions of a firm require the special expression in Table 3 (measure 4.2). Figure 1 presents the strategic multiples and their implicit shares of marketing investment for all feasible levels of ambition short of outright monopoly.

For planning purposes it is often convenient to express the strategic marketing expenditures implied by a firm's ambition in terms of its targeted share of competitive investments:

$$e' = [x'/(1 - x')]e'^* \tag{5}$$

It is apparent from Figure 1 that a firm faces sharply increasing marketing costs as its ambitions grow. A retreat strategy, the nicher's haven, implies a share of investments nearly equal to its strategic multiple, a 1 to 1 ratio of ambition (and therefore marketing cost) to share of investments. Moving from a retreat to a match strategy requires exactly a twenty-fold increase in an organization's strategic multiple, while it achieves just under a ten-fold increase in its share of investments, a 2 to 1 ratio. Moving from a match to a leader's dominate strategy demands a three-fold increase in expenditures, while it yields only a 50% increase in investment share, a 6 to 1 ratio of marketing costs to share of effort.

Figure 1
The strategic marketing cost function

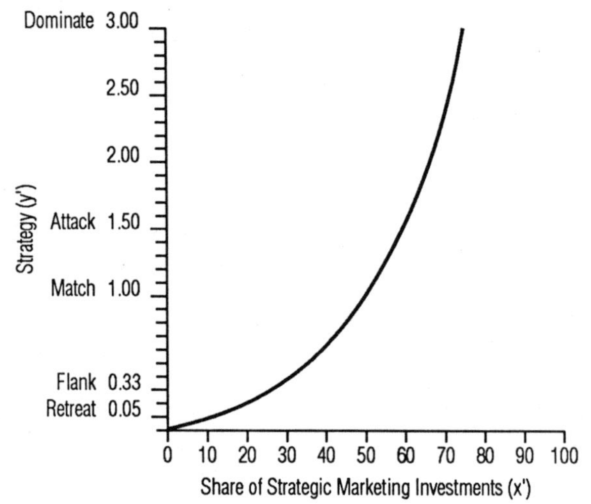

Incremental costs per share of investment increase even more dramatically with strategic marketing ambition.

Equations (4) and (5) are two forms of the same generalized marketing cost function relating strategic ambition, costs and share of marketing investment to competitive commitments.

Profit Impact and Marketing Costs

It has become widely accepted in recent years that marketing costs behave in the same way as do direct and total costs: they decrease significantly as proportion of total revenue with increases in share of market. This belief remains clouded by inconclusive evidence (Buzzell, Gale and Sultan 1975, p. 99). Empirical findings are inconclusive because of the complexity of the problem. Short-term harvesting decisions by market leaders as well as the unbridled ambitions of nichers can easily cloud the empirical results found in accounting statements.

An early study by the Marketing Science Institute presented evidence of the profit impact of private brand policies among over 100 companies in many lines of trade (Cook and Schutte 1967). A strong positive relationship was found to exist between marketing costs (both total and as a percent of sales) and share of market. MSI's private brand study also confirmed the PIMS results reported by Buzzell and others. As share of market increases, pretax earnings tend to rise along with margins, while the total cost ratio declines.

The classical expectation is that higher levels of performance earn higher operating margins and require at the same time investment of a larger proportion of revenues in marketing support services. Marketing costs are an enduring investment in the goodwill of a consumer franchise. One of the realities of a competitive market is that the leaders offer more quality per dollar of consumer expenditure (Ferguson 1982, p. 104) and achieve higher shares of market because of their proportionately higher levels of marketing investment. This conclusion does not deny that scale economies reduce the per unit costs of marketing warfare.

In light of the theoretical demonstration that marketing costs increase with market share, the classical expectation in support of this view and the confounding effects of strategic decisions on accounting reports, further research on this complex issue is warranted. To illustrate these methods of analysis, consider competitive investments, marketing strategy and differential advantage in the following case.

The Case of USAUTO vs. FORNAUTO

If ambition is the first step in understanding strategy, differential advantage is the last step to success. Few examples serve to make this point more effectively than the U.S. automobile industry. In the 1975 model year the marketing strategy of USAUTO was nothing if not ambitious. Evidence of this strategy is presented in Table 4. Henderson's strategic paradigm recognizes the ratio of 1975 secondary demand between USAUTO and FORNAUTO (7.33/1.39 from column one, Table 4) as equivalent to a market share multiple of 5.3 times. USAUTO dominates the terrain. The computed values of y show USAUTO dominated on every element of the mix but price, where it adopted a retreat strategy.

Table 4
Consumer Demand and Strategic Resource Deployments: USAUTO vs. FORNAUTO, 1975

	Quantity	Product	Promotion	Place	Price
USAUTO	7.33 mil	357	$270.0 mil	23,800	$3,838
FORNAUTO	1.39 mil	121	$123.2 mil	6,200	$4,208
Totals	8,72 mil	478	$393.2 mil	30,000	—
(y)	5.3	3.0	2.2	3.8	0.912

Sources: Star et al. (1977), *Leading National Advertisers* (1974), *NADA* (1981). Mix entries are strategic commitments for USAUTO (e'), (e'^*), and Total market (E').

Competitive Mix Investments

In product investments, USAUTO offered 357 distinct models compared with FORNAUTO's more limited line of 121 models. This represents a strategic multiple of 3.0 in favor of USAUTO. Its product strategy is identified in Table 3 as [D1.4]. Similarly, Table 4 shows USAUTO deployed its investments in national media promotion at a rate of $270.0 million to FORNAUTO's $123.2 million, posting a strategic multiple of 2.2 times its foreign rivals, designated [D2.1]. USAUTO's highest levels of ambition were achieved through its franchise dealer network. With 23,800 dealers to FORNAUTO's 6,200 franchises, USAUTO maintains a strategic multiple equal to 3.8 times, indicated with the notation [D3.1]. Finally, USAUTO even offers a small price advantage. The weighted median (MSRP) price of USAUTO's products was $3,838 to a median weighted price for FORNAUTO's products of $4,208 [A4.2]. If the "principle of force" alone applied, USAUTO was the clear winner in its 1975 model year deployment of strategic resources. Apparently, something is missing from this analysis of strategic resource deployment.

Competitive Marketing Strategy

These strategic investments in product, promotion, place and price are converted to their corresponding shares of marketing investments for USAUTO vs. FORNAUTO in Table 5. In 1975 USAUTO held 84.0% of unit sales, relin-

Table 5
Share of Market and Shares of Strategic Marketing Investments: USAUTO vs. FORNAUTO, 1975

	Market Share	Product	Promotion	Place	Price*
USAUTO	84.0%	74.7%	68.7%	79.3%	92.8
FORNAUTO	16.0	25.3	31.3	20.7	6.4
Totals	100.0%	100.0%	100.0%	100%	—

*Relative price differences are calculated from the expression $m_1 + (1 - P/P^*)$.

quishing 16.0% to its foreign rivals. Table 5 leads to the question, "How can USAUTO maintain 84.0% of unit sales with only 74.7% of product investments and 68.7% of national media investments?" The answer is that it maintained 79.3% of strategic place investments and a 8.8% price advantage.

Share of units sold is one of three measures of market share. To distinguish among these, designate share of units sold as m_1, share of buyers as m_2 and share of money sales as m_3. Shares of units sold are the "spoils" of marketing warfare. To the extent this share is supported with comparable resource deployments on conventional mix investments, it will be maintained, other things equal. Share of units sold is the balancing mechanism, the center of gravity, of a free, competitive market. This center or balance point shifts in response to the lead of a firm's shares of strategic investments in product, promotion, place and price.

When a firm or group of competitors maintains a share of strategic marketing investments below its share of market quantity, m_1 will be "pulled down" in search of a new balance in consumer preferences. On the other hand, when a firm's share of strategic investments is greater than its share of units sold, m_1 will be "pulled up" to a new and higher balance, again reflecting consumer preferences. The tendency persists regardless of the response function one assumes to equate share of market with share of strategic investments. These arguments are simply a restatement of the fundamental law of market share determination (Kotler 1980, p. 218).

This analysis also provides a more complete understanding of a harvest strategy. An organization is harvesting whenever its share of investments is less than its share of unit sales. No matter what its intentions may have been, USAUTO was harvesting on its product, promotion and place investments in the model year 1975.

A Measure of Differential Advantage

Differential marketing advantages are the keys to success. If x' is the firm's share of strategic investments and m_1 is its share of market quantity, the differential advantages are calculated by subtraction:

$$da = x' - m_1 \tag{6}$$

The shares of strategic marketing investments from Table 5 are expressed as their corresponding differential marketing advantages in Table 6. In the model year 1975 USAUTO posted an average 9.8 point competitive *disadvantage* in product, promotion and place investments. With an unsustainable price advantage, USAUTO was poised on the brink of at least a nine point loss in share of market as early as the 1975 model year. The response function is obviously exponential. In the last ten-day reporting period of 1981, FORNAUTO had achieved nearly a 36% share of market. No doubt the underlying investment strategies of these two world class rivals have been transformed as well.

Table 6
Differential Advantages USAUTO vs. FORNAUTO, 1965*

	Product	Promotion	Place	Price
USAUTO	−9.3	−15.3	−4.7	+8.8
FORNAUTO	+9.3	+15.3	+4.7	−9.6

*Note the signs of the price variable are naturally reversed in computing its differential.

Case Discussion

Quite likely a balanced strategy is less risky than an unbalanced one. The variance in x' about m_1 suggests a useful measure of strategic marketing risk. Couple this with the notion that harvesting implies a negative marketing differential, and it is clear how easily a harvest strategy from a dominant position can lead to losses in share of market. Since 1975 USAUTO has been harvesting the goodwill of its dominant consumer franchise. How long can one harvest from a position of strength? It all depends on the "length of the planting cycle," which is to say, the consumer's average time between purchase occasions.

The long run in marketing should be defined in this instance as the time it takes for the last regular buyer to make his/her first repurchase decision. In automobiles this is about seven years. By 1982 most U.S. new car buyers have made at least one repurchase. A repurchase occasion provides the consumer with the ultimate weapon, the opportunity to switch.

The length of the purchase cycle is an important consideration in assessing the long-term impact of a given strategic marketing differential. The nature of the market is another. Some markets are essentially product markets; among these are legal services. The act of consumption is intensely private. Neither promotion nor availability will alter our preferences for attorneys. In these and similar markets, greater weight must be assigned the impact of product investments. Other markets are more heavily influenced by place investments. Most consumers will not walk a mile for either a Camel or a Coke. Some markets are promotion oriented, like cosmetics and music. Others are cleared more directly by price. Gasoline is one of these.

Consumer preferences for automobiles would seem to be about evenly divided among product, promotion, place and price utilities. The legacy of following a harvest strategy on three of four mix variables in a market where the long run is counted in years is now apparent to USAUTO. The problems of shrinking primary demand which aggravated USAUTO's decline in share of market are skillfully told by Tucker (1980).

Conclusions

The concept of strategic ambition was calibrated from military conventions and correlated with the classical mix to produce a unique marketing oriented paradigm of strategic options. With a list of specific mix investment variables and reasonable measures of these supply side factors, comprehensive analyses may be made of a firm's marketing strategy and costs. An operational measure of marketing differentials was introduced and the methods of analysis were illustrated with the case of USAUTO vs. FORNAUTO over the industry's most recent purchase cycle. The predicted decline in USAUTO's share of market was fully realized by the 1980 model year.

Differential advantages and disadvantages are implicit in the marketing strategies of every firm. There is a persistent tendency for long run share of market to follow the differentials associated with strategic commitments. Whether or not market share responds precisely in the way suggested by the analysis of USAUTO depends primarily on the distribution of consumer utilities among the four mix components.

Measures of these underlying relationships may be disturbed by a variety of factors. Chief among these are market definition and structure. If the market is defined too broadly, competitive substitution effects no longer apply. Define the market too narrowly and the result is omission of important competitors. With regard to market structure, the strategic options of a dominant firm vastly outnumber those of a nicher. Competitive response and accounting practice may also confound the conclusions of strategic analysis. The marketing ambitions of a firm may not be realized if rivals are determined to block a strategic move, while accounting records may conceal the harvesting strategies of a dominant rival. Finally, changes in primary demand may so effect profit impact that strategic ambitions are never realized. The principles presented in this paper are sufficiently robust to permit their successful application in a market where the rivals are aggregates of international manufacturers, each with significantly different marketing strategies spanning nearly a decade in time.

Scholars can add to our understanding of marketing behavior with further research on these methods of analysis. Application of the strategic paradigm to a variety of other industries and testing the calibrations of marketing ambition should provide new insights about the nature of supply side marketing decisions. Specification of econometric models to include marketing differentials on each of the mix components may enrich their face validity as well as improve their reliability. The properties of the strategic marketing cost function suggest the need for future research on the costs of achieving, compared with maintaining, a given share of market. Measures of the risks of a marketing strategy should be explored in terms of the variance of investment shares about market share. Management in other industries should calculate coldly the differential advantages implicit in their own product, promotion, place and price strategies.

The author wishes to thank Art Beard, Bob Rothberg, Ed Strong and Marjorie Utsey for their helpful reviews of earlier drafts of this paper. Special thanks are due Bill Mindak and several *Journal of Marketing* reviewers whose insight and direction were invaluable in the revisions.

Bibliography

Buzzell, Robert (1981), "Are There 'Natural' Market Structures?" *Journal of Marketing*, 45 (Winter), 42–51.

———, Bradley T. Gale and Ralph G. M. Sultan (1975), "Market Share—A Key to Profitability," *Harvard Business Review*, 53 (January–February), 97–106.

Cook, Victor J. and Thomas F. Schutte (1967), *Brand Policy Determination*, Boston: Allyn and Bacon, Inc.

Culliton, James W. (1948), *The Management of Marketing Costs*, Boston: Harvard University Division of Research, Graduate School of Business Administration.

Ferguson, James M. (1982), "Comments on 'The Impact of Advertising on the Price of Consumer Products,'" *Journal of Marketing*, 46 (Winter), 102–105.

Henderson, Bruce D. (1979), *Henderson on Corporate Strategy*, Cambridge: Abt Books.

Kotler, Philip (1980), *Marketing Management, Analysis, Planning and Control*, 4th ed., Englewood Cliffs, NJ: Prentice-Hall Inc.

——— and Ravi Singh (1981), "Marketing Warfare—1980's," *The Journal of Business Strategy*, 3 (Winter), 30–41.

Leading National Advertisers (1974), *Ad $ Summary*, Norwalk, CT: Leading National Advertisers.

National Automobile Dealers Association (1981), *NADA Data for 1981*, McLean, VA: National Automobile Dealers Assn., Research Division.

Star, Steven H., Gary J. Davis, Christopher H. Lovelock and Benson P. Shapiro (1977), *Problems in Marketing*, 5th ed., New York: McGraw-Hill Inc.

Trout, Jack and Al Ries (1978), "Recycling Battles: Study the Classics to Avoid Checkmate in Business War," *Marketing Times*, 25 (May/June), 17–20.

Tucker, William (1980), "The Wreck of the Auto Industry," *Harper's* (November), 37–50.

Wensley, Robin (1981), "Strategic Marketing: Betas, Boxes or Basics," *Journal of Marketing*, 45 (Summer), 173–182.

35

"Marketing Strategy & Differential Advantage": A Comment

Amitava Chattopadhyay, Prakash Nedungadi, & Dipankar Chakravarti

This article suggests a need to focus not only on the relationship between market shares and mix investment shares but also on the level of industry sales response to aggregate competitive spending levels.

This article critiques the "new paradigm of marketing strategies" proposed by Cook (*Journal of Marketing*, Spring 1983). It is shown that his formulation of the strategic marketing ambition and differential advantage concepts does not provide general or actionable links between a firm's market performance goals and its marketing mix decisions. The consequent limitations of Cook's framework are discussed, and alternative formulations that may overcome these limitations are suggested.

THE DIALECTICS of marketing strategy formulation would benefit greatly from the development of a direct and actionable link between a firm's market performance goals and its marketing mix expenditure decisions. Cook (1983) made an interesting and thought-provoking attempt to address this important and difficult problem in his paper entitled "Marketing Strategy and Differential Advantage." He introduced and calibrated a concept he termed "strategic marketing ambition," developed an operational measure of "differential marketing advantage," and derived a "theoretical function relating strategic marketing ambition with market share." He also related these concepts to the marketing mix and provided an illustrative analysis which interpreted the competitive dynamics of the automobile industry over its most recent purchase cycle.

Amitava Chattopadhyay is an Assistant Professor at McGill University; Prakash Nedungadi is an Assistant Professor at the University of Toronto; and Dipankar Chakravarti is Professor and Head of Department of Marketing, Karl Eller Graduate School of Management, University of Arizona.

Since Cook addressed a major marketing management issue and claimed to have developed "a new paradigm of marketing strategies," the ideas presented in his paper deserve to be closely examined and extended, if possible. We undertake a critical examination of Cook's conceptual framework and his method of operationalization and analysis. First, we discuss Cook's development of the strategic marketing ambition and differential advantage concepts, and show that key conceptual problems and restrictive assumptions limit the value of his framework for competitive marketing strategy formulation. Next, we show that the interpretive logic of Cook's analysis of the automobile industry tends to break down when one examines the competitive dynamics at the level of individual firms in that marketplace. Finally, we point out that Cook's attempt to relate his concepts to the marketing mix in fact stops short of a specific link between a firm's market performance goals and its marketing mix decisions. Together these assessments suggest that several of Cook's key assertions are open to serious question and that his conceptual framework is perhaps richer in rhetoric than in substance. In conclusion, this article discusses some key considerations in developing an analytical framework linking a firm's competitive market performance goals and its marketing mix decisions.

Conceptual Aspects of Cook's Framework

Cook claimed to have calibrated the concept of strategic marketing ambition, to have provided an operational measure of differential marketing advantage, and to have derived a theoretical function linking strategic ambitions and investments with market share. These claims are examined sequentially in this section.

Strategic Marketing Ambition

Cook devoted considerable space to developing the relationship between a firm's spending level and its strategic ambition. He first noted (equation 1, p. 69) that total marketing investments are the sum of the target firm's expenditures and the expenditures of its competitors. Thereafter (equation 2, p. 69), he denoted the target firm's ambition by the strategic multiple, y, which is essentially the ratio between the target firm's desired expenditures and the expenditures of its rivals. Cook calibrated strategic marketing ambition by assigning labels to specific values of this ratio (e. g., 3 = Dominate, 1.5 = Attack, 1 = Match, etc.).

The relevance of the military analogies serving as the bases for these labels may be questioned. One may argue that empirical efforts in the substantive marketing arena may enable a more meaningful calibration of strategic marketing ambition. However, Cook's development of this concept may be criticized on at least two other counts. First, in developing this concept, Cook ignored the fact that differences in competitive structure within an industry may impact upon the competitive stance implied by particular strategic investment share levels. For example, in Cook's framework, a target firm with 5% share of strategic investments would have a strategic multiple, y, of .05/.95 = .053 and would be designated as being in *retreat*. Such a label may be appropriate if the firm was competing against one other firm holding 95% share of strategic investments. However, if the firm was one of twenty firms, with approximately equal investment shares, the retreat label may be quite inappropriate even though the value of the strategic multiple is the same as in the previous instance. In fact, a consistent application of Cook's framework would view every firm in this industry as in retreat. Clearly, this would not be very meaningful.

Second, a target firm's choice of a strategic ambition level would presumably involve consideration of the effects of the implied marketing costs on a measure of market performance, say, market share. Cook seems to imply that the exponentially increasing nature of the "strategic marketing cost function" (Figure 1, p. 72) constitutes a "theoretical demonstration that marketing costs increase with market share." However, Cook's definition and calibration of strategic marketing ambition is along an *expenditure continuum* (equation 2, p. 69). Also, equation 4 (p. 71) and equation 5 (p. 72) are alternative restatements of the equivalence between a firm's strategic multiple, y, and its share, x, of strategic investments. None of these equations link strategic marketing ambition to any index of market performance. Consequently, it should be recognized that the strategic marketing cost function in Figure 1 merely maps the transformation of a ratio to a percentage. Thus, when a firm decides to *dominate* in Cook's framework, by definition it chooses to outspend its competitors by a ratio of 3:1. The fact that this decision translates to a 75% share of strategic investments is a matter of simple arithmetic rather than a theoretical demonstration of any relationship between marketing cost and market share.

In summary, Cook's strategic marketing ambition concept is merely a ratio specifying how much the target firm chooses to spend vis-à-vis its competitors. Since this choice is not conditioned upon a consideration of the effects of these expenditures on market performance, the concept in and of itself does not provide a meaningful basis for strategy formulation. Moreover, as discussed earlier, the construct could be of limited meaning if industry structure is ignored in operationalization.

Differential Advantage

It is commonly accepted that strategic marketing mix investment decisions need to be formulated with specific market performance objectives in mind (Kotler 1980). One such market performance measure may be the target firm's share of units sold (m_1, in Cook's terminology). The firm's decision on the appropriate share of strategic marketing mix investments, x^*, to achieve a desired market share, m_1^*, has to be based on knowledge of the response function relating m_1 and x.

Cook's market response function. Although Cook did not explicitly postulate a response function linking m_1 and x, his discussion of differential advantage clarified his implicit assumptions. He stated that if a given market share, m_1, "is supported with comparable resource deployments on conventional mix elements, it will be maintained, other things equal" (p. 73). The term *comparable resource deployments* takes on a specific meaning when Cook elaborated (p. 73):

> When a firm or group of competitors maintains a share of strategic investments below its share of market quantity, m_1 will be "pulled down" in search of a new balance in consumer preferences. On the other hand, when the firm's share of strategic investments is greater than its share of units sold, m_1 will be "pulled up" to a new and higher balance, again reflecting consumer preferences.

Thus, it is clear that Cook assumed that the stable equilibrium status of the market response function is $m_1 = x$. In other words, at equilibrium, m_1 and x are linearly related with zero intercept and slope = 1. If this were indeed the case, the pattern of adjustments Cook predicted would hold unequivocally. The existence of a positive or negative differential advantage (i.e., a situation where $m_1 \neq x$) would represent a market in disequilibrium. Hence, market forces would adjust m_1 as Cook predicted and would restore the market to equilibrium, perhaps over a time period corre-

Figure 1
Alternative Plots of the Equilibrium Response Function (3)

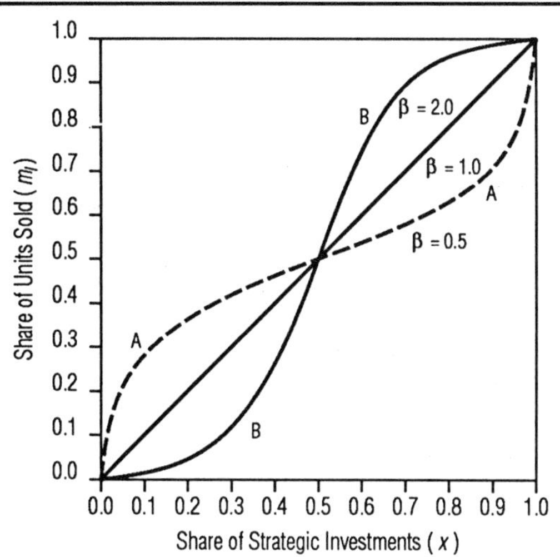

sponding to the product's purchase cycle. In fact, this process could be modeled with a response function such as:

$$m_{1_{i,t}} = (\alpha)m_{1_{i,t-1}} + (1 - \alpha)(x_{i,t}) \qquad (1)$$

where $m_{1_{i,t}}$ and $x_{i,t}$ represent firm i's share of units sold and share of strategic investments respectively in period t. The parameter α, $(0 \leq \alpha \leq 1)$, would determine the rate of convergence of the process. A system of such equations, one for each competing firm, would represent the competitive dynamics of the marketplace in a logically consistent manner (McGuire and Weiss 1976, Naert and Bultez 1973, Naert and Weverbergh 1981). Under this model, if each firm maintained a constant share of strategic investments, i.e., $x_{i,t} = x_i$, it may be verified that $m_{1_i} = x_i$ at equilibrium.

More general market response formulations. Cook therefore seems to have made a very specific assumption about the relationship between market share and share of strategic investments. It is, however, clearly possible to postulate alternative systems of nonlinear equations that will represent this relationship more generally while satisfying the logical consistency requirements of market share models.

For example, consider a market consisting of n firms where the competitive dynamics are summarized by a system of equations such that the ith firm's market response is given by:

$$m_{1_{i,t}} = (\alpha)m_{1_{i,t-1}} + (1 - \alpha)\left\{x_{i,t}^{\beta}\Big/\sum_i x_{i,t}^{\beta}\right\} \qquad (2)$$

with α, $m_{1_{i,t}}$, and $x_{i,t}$ defined as in (1) and β being a parameter related to investment share elasticity.[1] It may be verified that the equilibrium status of this response function is given by:

$$m_{1_{i,t}} = x_i^{\beta}\Big/\sum_i x_i^{\beta} \qquad (3)$$

Figure 1 shows this equilibrium response function for a two-firm market. For $\beta > 1$, the curve takes the general form BB which is shown plotted for $\beta = 2$. Here market share responds slowly until a threshold level of investment is reached. After this, incremental investment share commitments produce rapid market share gains. However, beyond a certain level of strategic investment share, the marginal market share response declines. Such a pattern of market share response is consistent with the economic and behavioral assumptions of the theory underlying many advertising response models in the literature (Kotler 1980, Little 1979).

For $0 < \beta < 1$, the curve takes the general form labeled AA (plotted for $\beta = 0.5$ in Figure 1). This form, although less common, may be observed in industries with low entry costs such that smaller firms entering the market could acquire shares higher than the equivalent investment share. One may speculate that the market for long-distance telephone services may show such patterns of share response. New entrants such as MCI and SPRINT could capitalize on AT&T's installed network infrastructure and could gain market share beyond their investment share levels. Note Cook's equilibrium response function is a special case $(\beta = 1)$ of the above model.

This nonlinear response formulation (equations 2 and 3) is consistent with the market share theorems presented by Kotler (1980, pp. 218–219) and by Bell, Keeney, and Little (1975). When developing the assumptions required to postulate a linear normalized market share model, these authors describe a construct called *attraction* which is permitted to be a nonlinear function of a firm's mix investments. Thus, if firm i's attraction score, a_i, is related to its investment share by the function $a_i = x_i^{\beta}$, equation (3) satisfies all the required assumptions of a linear normalized attraction model. While in this formulation an individual firm's attraction score is dependent upon the investment decisions of its competitors, this is permissible under the Bell, Keeney, and Little attraction framework. Perhaps more importantly, such a dependence may be a fact of life in a competitive marketplace.

Does the response function matter? The preceding discussion has shown that nonlinear equilibrium response functions such as (3) are theoretically plausible representations of the relationship between share of market and share of marketing investments. There is also considerable empirical support for such formulations (Kotler 1980, Little 1981, Naert and Weverbergh 1981).

Cook asserted that his predicted pattern of m_1 adjustments would persist "regardless of the response function one assumes to equate share of market with share of strategic investments" (Cook 1983, p. 73). The generality of this assertion is highly questionable, since his prediction was based on a specific assumption about the nature of the response function. The following discussion shows that unless one knows β (and thus the level of equilibrium market share for a given share of strategic investments), it is not possible to make unequivocal predictions about the nature of adjustment in m_1 associated with a specific value of Cook's differential advantage measure $(x - m_1)$. In many instances, the direction of the adjustment may be exactly the reverse of that predicted by Cook.

For example, consider a two-firm market with an equilibrium response function as in (3) with $\beta = 2$ and the configuration of market shares and investment shares given below:

	Firm 1	*Firm 2*
Current market share (m_1)	0.65	0.35
Current investment share (x)	0.60	0.40
Differential advantage ($x - m_1$)	−0.05	0.05

According to Cook's model, since firm 1 has a negative differential advantage score, it would lose market share, and firm 2 would gain share, since it has a positive differential advantage. However, the specified response function predicts equilibrium market shares of 0.692 and 0.308 for investment shares of 0.60 (firm 1) and 0.40 (firm 2) respectively. Hence, if the firms maintained their investment shares, firm 1 would gain 4.2 market share points and firm 2 would lose a corresponding amount. These adjustments are in precisely opposite directions to those predicted by Cook's framework.

Competitive dependencies. Given the nonlinear function (3), a firm's equilibrium market share will change in general if competing firms adjust their share of investments even if these adjustments do not affect the target firm's investment share. For example, in a three-firm market where investment shares are 0.2, 0.3, and 0.5, the equilibrium market shares predicted by (3) with $\beta = 2$ will be 0.105, 0.237, and 0.658 respectively. If the investment shares now change to, say, 0.2, 0.4, and 0.4 respectively, the new equilibrium market share will be 0.111, 0.444, and 0.444 respectively. Thus, a shift in the investment shares of the latter two firms affects the market share of the first firm, even though its investment share remains unchanged. This implies that a target firm's market performance would be influenced not only by its own investment share decision (i.e., its strategic ambition), but also by the distribution of the residual investment share between its competitors.

Problems with dichotomous analyses. If market response is nonlinear, a related feature becomes important in markets that have more than two competing firms. The estimate of the equilibrium market share associated with a given investment share of a target firm will be biased in general if an analyst treats the market dichotomously (i.e., the target firm versus its aggregated competitors). For example, it was shown above that in a three-firm market with investment shares distributed as .2, .3, and .5, the equilibrium market share of the first firm (predicted by (3) with $\beta = 2$) would be 0.105. However, if the competitors' investment shares are aggregated (0.8) and a dichotomous analysis is conducted, the first firm's equilibrium market share is estimated as 0.059. Thus, in this particular instance, there is a fairly serious downward bias produced by the dichotomous analysis.

The preceding discussion suggests that there is considerable theoretical and empirical basis to expect that the response function equating share of market with share of marketing investments may be nonlinear. If this is indeed the case, use of Cook's differential advantage concept to predict market share dynamics may produce entirely misleading results. Further, in the absence of specific knowledge about the response function operant in the market, no clear relationship may be formulated between a firm's strategic ambition (or equivalently, its investment share decision) and its equilibrium market performance. To complicate matters further, a dichotomous analysis of the competitive dynamics in markets with more than two firms will yield biased equilibrium market share predictions if the market response function is nonlinear.

In summary, this section has identified several major conceptual limitations of Cook's framework. The strategic marketing ambition concept (a) was not calibrated using a credible empirical basis in marketing, (b) ignored the vital issue of industry structure, and (c) did not provide a link between implied marketing costs and any index of market performance. The concept of differential advantage (a) was shown to be based on extremely restrictive assumptions regarding the nature of market response, and (b) made specific predictions about the direction of market share adjustments in response to strategic investment share movements which are violated under more general market response formulations. These limitations may significantly detract from the value of Cook's framework in marketing strategy formulation.

Empirical Aspects of Cook's Framework

The preceding discussion raised several questions about Cook's development of the strategic marketing ambition and differential advantage concepts. This section focuses on Cook's analysis of the competitive dynamics in the automobile industry. The robustness of his interpretive logic is tested by examining whether his framework provides a consistent explanation of the market share movements of *individual* auto manufacturers as a function of their strategic marketing investments.

Cook's Analysis

The author conducted a dichotomous examination of the patterns of consumer, demand and strategic resource deployments of U.S. and foreign automakers for the 1975 model year. Based on data reproduced in Tables 1 and 2, Cook found that U.S. auto manufacturers (USAUTO) held 84% of unit sales, as against 74.7% of product investments (number of distinct models), 68.7% of national media investments, 79.3% of strategic place investments (number of franchised dealers), and an 8.8% relative price advantage. He next computed differential advantage scores from these figures and showed (Table 3) that USAUTO had negative differential advantage scores of −9.3, −15.3, and −4.7 in product, promotion, and place investments respectively, comprising an average "9.8 points competitive disadvantage" in these elements of the marketing mix. He then concluded that given this competitive disadvantage, the 8.8% relative price

Table 1
Consumer Demand and Strat egic Resource Deployments in the Auto Industry 1975*

	Quantity (Units)	Product (Number of Models)	Promotion (National Media Investments)	Place (Number of Dealers)	Price
GM	3.65 Mil	164	$110.7 Mil	10,990	$3870
Ford	2.17 Mil	80	98.5 Mil	6,275	$4186
Chrysler	1.18 Mil	93	50.1 Mil	4,810	$3660
AMC	0.33 Mil	20	10.7 Mil	1,725	$3062
USAUTO (total)	7.33 Mil	357	270.0 Mil	23,800	$3838
FORNAUTO	1.39 Mil	121	123.2 Mil	6,200	$4208
Grand Total	8.72 Mil	478	$393.2 Mil	30,000	—

*Sources: Leading National Advertisers (1974), National Automobile Dealers Association (1981), Star et al. (1977), *Ward's Automotive Yearbook* (1975).

advantage was "unsustainable" and that these data signalled the precipitous drop in USAUTO's market share that was observed through 1981. Since the drop was larger than the computed average competitive disadvantage, he speculated that the response function was "obviously exponential" (p. 74).

A Critique of Cook's Analysis

Cook's interpretive logic may be questioned on several grounds. For instance, it is not clear that in 1975 it would have been possible to label the 8.8% price advantage as a priori "unsustainable" on the bases of just these data and without additional significant insights into the automobile industry. In fact, had the market shares moved in the other direction, one could reasonably conclude that the price advantage was "unassailable" and compensated for the relative disadvantages in the other mix investments.

This indeterminacy of Cook's framework becomes more evident if one studies the competitive dynamics of the automobile industry at the level of individual competitors. Tables 1 and 2 show the market share and strategic investment data for 1975 at the level of individual competitors. Table 3 presents the differential advantage scores computed from these figures.

Table 2
Share of Market and Shares of Strategic Marketing Investments in the Auto Industry, 1975

	Market Share (m_1)	Product	Promotion	Place	Price*
GM	41.8%	34.3%	28.2%	36.6%	42.9%
Ford	24.9%	16.7%	25.1%	20.9%	15.3%
Chrysler	13.5%	19.5%	12.7%	16.0%	20.7%
AMC	3.8%	4.2%	2.7%	5.8%	26.5%
USAUTO (total)	84.0%	74.7%	68.7%	79.3%	92.8%
FORNAUTO	16.0%	25.3%	31.3%	20.7%	6.4%
Grand Total	100.0%	100.0%	100.0%	100.0%	

*Relative price differences are calculated from the expression $m_1 + (1 - p/p^*)(p^*)$ has been calculated as a weighted average price of the rest of the industry, excluding the specific firm under consideration.

Table 3
Differential Advantages for Individual Manufacturers 1975*

	Product	Promotion	Place	Price
GM	−7.5	−13.6	−5.2	+1.1
Ford	−8.2	+0.2	−4.0	−9.6
Chrysler	+6.0	−0.8	+2.5	+7.2
AMC	+0.4	−1.1	+2.0	+22.7
USAUTO	−9.3	−15.3	−4.7	+8.8
FORNAUTO	+9.3	+15.3	+4.7	−9.6

*Differential advantages are computed following Cook (1983) from the data in Table 2.

Relative to the average USAUTO figures, General Motors had approximately comparable differential disadvantages in product, promotion, and place investments and, in fact, had a smaller relative price advantage. According to Cook's framework, GM should have lost market share over the period considered. Yet, as a comparison of 1975 and 1981 market shares shows (Table 4), GM was the only U.S. automaker that gained market share. Chrysler held differential advantages in its product and place investments, had approximate parity in its promotional investments, and also held a strong relative price advantage. Yet, this company lost share in the period under consideration, and its overall financial performance by 1981 was a much publicized disaster. One could perhaps argue that these "differential advantages" were portents of Chrysler's post-1981 resurgence, but this would probably be far-fetched. Also note that since AMC held differential advantages in product, place, and price and had only a small differential disadvantage in promotional investments, Cook's framework would have probably predicted a rosy future for this company. Yet Table 4 shows that AMC lost market share and, as is well-known, had to merge with a foreign manufacturer to survive. Thus, of the four U.S. auto manufacturers, only Ford's market share performance was approximately consistent with the predictions of Cook's framework.

In his analysis Cook was clearly inferring causation from correlational data. However, even the correlations on which

Table 4
Market Share Movements for Individual Manufacturers 1975–81*

	1975	1981	Difference 1981–1975
GM	41.8	44.5	+2.7
Ford	24.9	16.3	−8.6
Chrysler	13.5	8.7	−4.8
AMC	3.8	1.6	−2.2
USAUTO	84.0	71.1	−12.9
FORNAUTO	16.0	28.9	+12.9

*Source: *Automotive News* (1982).

his interpretation was based are weak when examined at the level of individual firms. For instance, the correlations between the market share changes in Table 4 and the differential advantage scores in Table 3 (based on the five observations) are 0.54, 0.49, and 0.45 for the product, promotion, and place mix elements, and −0.27 for relative price. None of these correlations are statistically significant.

Several conceptual problems with Cook's framework may have contributed to this indeterminacy. First, as was shown earlier, if market response is nonlinear and its parameters are unknown, the direction of market share adjustments cannot be predicted unequivocally based on only the differential advantage scores. Second, the timeframe of the analysis may have been inappropriate, and no account was taken of changes in the firms' competitive strategies in the intervening five years. Finally, Cook used only one particular index of investment for each of the mix elements (e.g., number of models for product). The share movements may have been driven by other variables, such as product performance and positioning, that were ignored in his analysis. Regardless of the reason(s) that may have contributed to the indeterminacies in this specific instance, it is clear that Cook's approach cannot be easily applied to assess prospects for an individual firm.

In summary, Cook's illustrative analysis probably raises more questions about the value of his framework than it provides answers about the competitive dynamics of the automobile industry. Perhaps a simpler explanation for the shifts in shares lies in the fact that in the period under study, foreign manufacturers were typically offering small fuel-efficient cars, whereas USAUTO's subcompact line was thin and below par on critical factors such as fuel efficiency. Given rising fuel costs, U.S. consumers switched to smaller subcompact cars, a segment which imports had traditionally dominated (Star et al. 1977). Interestingly, even as early as 1970, USAUTO had started gaining share in this segment (Star et al. 1977). However, these gains did not compensate for the decline in the demand for larger sized cars where USAUTO had traditionally generated most of its sales. Cook's framework had little insight to offer regarding this dynamic of shifting segment sizes.

Cook's Strategic Marketing Paradigm

Cook's "strategic marketing paradigm" (Table 2, p. 70) attempted to relate strategic ambitions to the components of the marketing mix and defined "20 exclusive and exhaustive strategic marketing options." He also provided a partial list of marketing mix variables and measures (Table 3, p. 71). Marketing strategy was defined as "any feasible combination of four decisions relating strategic ambitions to components of the marketing mix" (p. 70).

The possibility that a firm may take differentially aggressive investment positions on the various mix elements is interesting. However, as was pointed out earlier, the term *strategic ambition* in Cook's framework pertained only to positions that a firm might take on a competitive expenditure continuum. The *strategic marketing descriptors* that Cook provided were essentially mnemonics for a firm's investment decisions. Again, the link between these descriptors and market performance was not explicitly developed. While the concept of differential advantage might have provided such a link, the previously discussed weaknesses severely limit its use in this regard. Thus, as presented, Cook's strategic marketing paradigm merely elaborated on a firm's investment options. While any of these options may be "feasible" for a given firm, Cook provided no normative framework for evaluating the alternative investment decisions in market performance terms.

Dealing with Individual Mix Components

Equations 2 and 3 have treated x as a measure of aggregate share of strategic mix investments. It is necessary, however, that a response function linking market share to marketing mix investment shares should explicitly consider the individual mix elements in its formulation. Broadly speaking, the four Ps define the elements to be considered. However, even under each of these broad categories, there are multiple arenas in which a firm may wish to commit its marketing resources. The issue then is how each of these individual investments are to be weighted to arrive at a measure of overall strategic marketing investment share. The following formulation generalizes the market response function (3) to allow consideration of a firm's investment in each of a set of j marketing mix elements:

$$m_{1_{i,t}} = (\alpha)m_{1_{i,t-1}} + (1-\alpha)\left\{\sum_j \gamma_j x_{ij,t}^{\beta_j} \Big/ \sum_i \sum_j \gamma_j x_{ij}^{\beta_j}\right\} \quad (4)$$

The equilibrium response function corresponding to (4) is:

$$m_{1_i} = \sum_j \gamma_j x_{ij}^{\beta_j} \Big/ \sum_i \sum_j \gamma_j x_{ij}^{\beta_j} \quad (5)$$

It may be seen that the jth component of the marketing mix receives a weightage γ_j, ($\sum_j \gamma_j = 1$), in the computation of firm i's attraction score, $a_i = \sum_j \gamma_j x_{ij}^{\beta_j}$. While other representations, such as multiplicative formulations (Nakanishi and Cooper 1974, Naert and Weverbergh 1981), may also be tenable, it may be seen that in his discussion of the automobile industry, Cook weighted each mix component equally, i.e., $\gamma_j = 1/j$, and also assumed that $\beta_j = 1$ for all j. Clearly, equation 5 is a more general formulation than the one that Cook assumed.

Finally, it must be noted that the riskiness of a particular configuration of strategic mix expenditures (Cook 1983, p. 75) has more to do with the variability associated with market response for that mix expenditure configuration than with the variance of investment shares around m_1, i.e., $E_j(x_j - m_1)^2$. Thus, from a traditional standpoint, the riskiness of a strategy would be related to the uncertainty associated with the parameters γ_j and β_j. Whether more risk is associated with an unbalanced versus a balanced strategy is therefore an empirical question. The answer depends upon the precision with which the response function parameters are known in a particular instance.

Conclusion

While Cook addresses a very important question, the conceptual weaknesses of his framework severely limit its value for marketing strategy formulation. The key problem stems from his inability to relate his concept of strategic marketing ambition defined in expenditure terms to an index of market performance.

Clearly, the thrust of Cook's work is the development of a general marketing mix decision framework which focuses on long-term competitive market performance. At a descriptive level, such a framework needs adequate general theoretical specifications of market response to marketing mix investments. This article has argued that Cook's framework needs more work in this key regard; it has also provided some alternative specifications that may be more viable candidates for general market response descriptions than Cook's implicit special cases. It is also equally important to develop procedures to estimate the parameters of the market response function for the specific marketing situation to which the model is applied. Both econometric and judgmental methods remain available for this purpose. While each of these approaches has its own pitfalls and limitations (Chakravarti, Mitchell, and Staelin 1981; Little 1970, 1975; Little and Lodish 1981), these traditional procedures may be expected to provide better and more meaningful parameterization than calibrations based on analogies to warfare theory.

As Cook pointed out, considerations related to the length of the purchase cycle in the product category and the stage of the product life cycle, among other factors, may be used to condition judgments regarding response function structure and parameter values or to interpret the results of data-based econometric procedures. Appropriate market definition will continue to be an important issue for decision makers in this domain. However, despite these difficulties, a response function that explicitly or implicitly links marketing investment decisions to market performance outcomes must provide the basis on which normative evaluations of alternative strategies must be founded.

In a competitive marketplace, the market performance outcomes of a firm's strategic marketing expenditure ambitions will depend on the resilience of competitors and the likelihood that one or more competitors will retaliate against a change in the target firm's marketing strategy. In mature markets where primary demand is limited, attempts to neutralize competitors' differential advantages could result in vicious cycles of competitive spending and a scenario of chaos, much as a warfare model would predict. On the other hand, in new growing markets such increases in levels of competitive spending may stimulate primary demand, leaving all competing firms better off without drastic alterations in market shares. This suggests a need to focus not only on the relationship between market shares and mix investment shares but also on the level of industry sales response to aggregate competitive spending levels.

Only a careful competitive analysis may reveal to a firm what competitive scenario is likely to obtain. While one notes the danger of endorsing specific analytical frameworks as precursors to success in the marketplace, Porter's (1980) framework for competitive analysis could provide the marketing manager with a set of criteria against which the competitive characteristics of the environment may be assessed prior to strategy formulation. Clearly, the terrain is complex and many simplifying assumptions will need to be made in specific applications. However, the assumptions should not be so simplistic as to lose the essence of the analytical task. The credibility of Cook's framework suffers from such critical oversimplifications. Nevertheless, the ideas presented in his paper are interesting and address an extremely important marketing management topic. It is hoped that the critique provided here will stimulate further research on marketing strategy formulation approaches based on theoretically meaningful and empirically well-calibrated market response descriptions.

Note

1. In this formulation, β cannot be directly interpreted as the traditional investment share elasticity exponent. However, it can be shown that β is indeed a function of investment share elasticity.

References

Automotive News (1982), "Market Data Book Issue," (April 28).

Bell, David E., Ralph L. Keeney, and John D. C. Little (1975), "A Market Share Theorem," *Journal of Marketing Research*, 12 (May), 136–141.

Chakravarti, Dipankar, Andrew Mitchell, and Richard Staelin (1981), "Judgment Based Marketing Decision Models: Problems and Possible Solutions," *Journal of Marketing*, 45 (Fall), 13–23.

Cook, Victor J., Jr. (1983), "Marketing Strategy and Differential Advantage," *Journal of Marketing*, 47 (Spring), 68–75.

Kotler, Philip (1980), *Marketing Management: Analysis, Planning, and Control*, 4th ed., Englewood Cliffs, NJ: Prentice-Hall.

Leading National Advertisers (1974), *Ad $ Summary*, Norwalk, CT: LNA.

Little, John D. C. (1970), "Models and Managers: The Concept of a Decision Calculus," *Management Science*, 16 (April), B466–B485.

——— (1975), "BRANDAID: A Marketing Mix Model, Part 1, Structure, and Part 2, Implementation," *Operations Research*, 23 (July–August), 628–673.

——— (1979), "Aggregate Advertising Models: The State of the Art," *Operations Research*, 27 (July–August), 629–667.

——— and Leonard M. Lodish (1981), "Commentary on 'Judgment Based Marketing Decision Models,'" *Journal of Marketing*, 45 (Fall), 24–29.

McGuire, Timothy W. and Doyle L. Weiss (1976), "Logically Consistent Market Share Models II," *Journal of Marketing Research*, 13 (August), 296–302.

Naert, Philippe and Alain Bultez (1973), "Logically Consistent Market Share Models," *Journal of Marketing Research*, 10 (August), 334–340.

——— and M. Weverbergh (1981), "On the Prediction Power of Market Share Attraction Models," *Journal of Marketing Research*, 18 (May), 146–153.

Nakanishi, Masao and Lee G. Cooper (1974), "Parameter Estimation for a Multiplicative Competitive Interaction Model–Least Squares Approach," *Journal of Marketing Research*, 11 (August), 303–311.

National Automobile Dealers Association (1981), *NADA Data for 1981*, McLean, VA: NADA, Research Division.

Porter, Michael E. (1980), *Competitive Strategy*, New York: Free Press.

Star, Steven H., Nancy J. Davis, Christopher H. Lovelock, and Benson P. Shapiro (1977), *Problems in Marketing*, 5th ed., New York: McGraw-Hill.

Ward's Automotive Yearbook (1975), Detroit, MI: Ward's Communication, Inc.

36

First-Mover Advantages

Marvin B. Lieberman & David B. Montgomery

Mechanisms that promote first-mover advantages include proprietary learning effects, patents, preemption of input factors and locations, and development of buyer switching costs.

This article surveys the theoretical and empirical literature on mechanisms that confer advantages and disadvantages on first-mover firms. Major conceptual issues are addressed, and recommendations are given for future research. Managerial implications are also discussed.

WHAT, EXACTLY, are first-mover advantages? Under what conditions do they arise, and by what specific mechanisms? Do first-movers make above-average profits? And when is it in a firm's interest to pursue first-mover opportunities, as opposed to allowing rivals to make the pioneering investments?

In this paper we examine these and other related questions. We categorize mechanisms that confer advantages and disadvantages on first-mover firms, and critically assess the relevant theoretical and empirical literature. The recent burgeoning of theoretical work in industrial economics provides a rich set of models that help make understanding of first-mover advantages more precise. There is also a growing body of empirical literature on order-of-entry effects. Our aim is to begin to provide a more detailed mapping of mechanisms and outcomes, to serve as a guide for future research.

We define first-mover advantages in terms of the ability of pioneering firms to earn positive economic profits (i.e. profits in excess of the cost of capital). First-mover advantages arise endogenously within a multi-stage process, as illustrated in Figure 1. In the first stage some asymmetry is generated, enabling one particular firm to gain a head start over rivals. This first-mover opportunity may occur because the firm possesses some unique resources or foresight, or simply because of luck. Once this asymmetry is generated a variety of mechanisms may enable the firm to exploit its position; these mechanisms enhance the magnitude or durability (or both) of first-mover profits.

Our discussion is organized as follows. We first consider theoretical models and empirical evidence on three general

Martin Lieberman is Assistant Professor at Stanford University. David Montgomery is the Robert A. Magowan Professor of Marketing at Stanford University.

Figure 1
Endogenous generation of first-mover advantages

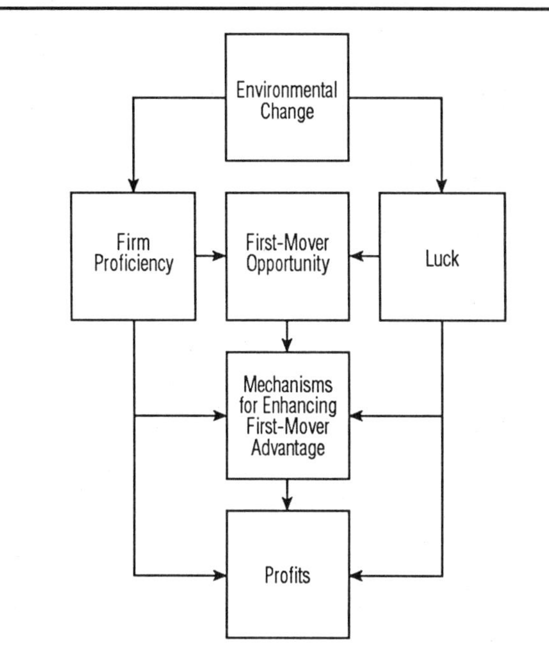

categories in which first-mover advantage can be attained: leadership in product and process technology, preemption of assets, and development of buyer switching costs. We then examine potential *disadvantages* of first-mover firms (or conversely, relative advantages enjoyed by late-mover rivals). These include free-rider problems and a tendency toward inertia or sluggish response by established incumbents. The next section addresses a series of basic conceptual issues. These include the endogenous nature of first-mover opportunities, and various definitional and measurement questions. We conclude with an assessment of opportunities for additional research and a discussion of managerial implications.

Mechanisms Leading to First-Mover Advantages

First-mover advantages arise from three primary sources: (1) technological leadership, (2) preemption of assets, and (3) buyer switching costs. Within each category there are a number of specific mechanisms.[1] In this section we survey existing theoretical and empirical literature on these three general categories of first-mover advantages.

The theoretical models surveyed in this section assume the existence of some initial asymmetry among competitors that can be exploited by the first-mover firm. This initial asymmetry is critical; without it, first-mover advantages do not arise. Ways in which this asymmetry may come about are considered later in the paper.

Technological Leadership

First-movers can gain advantage through sustainable leadership in technology. Two basic mechanisms are considered in the literature: (1) advantages derived from the 'learning' or 'experience' curve, where costs fall with cumulative output, and (2) success in patent or R&D races, where advances in product or process technology are a function of R&D expenditures.

Learning Curve. In the standard learning-curve model, unit production costs fall with cumulative output. This generates a sustainable cost advantage for the early entrant if learning can be kept proprietary and the firm can maintain leadership in market share. This argument was popularized by the Boston Consulting Group during tile 1970s and has had a considerable influence on the strategic management field.

In a seminal theoretical paper, Spence (1981) demonstrated that when learning can be kept proprietary, the learning curve can generate substantial barriers to entry. Fewer than a handful of firms may be able to compete profitably.[2] Despite high seller concentration, incentives for vigorous competition remain. Firms that do enter may initially sell below cost in an effort to accumulate greater experience, and thereby gain a long-term cost advantage. Such competition sharply reduces profits.

Empirical evidence of learning-based preemption is given by Ghemawat (1984) in the case of DuPont's development of an innovative process for titanium dioxide, and by Porter (1981), who discusses Procter and Gamble's sustained advantage in disposable diapers in the U.S. Similarly, Shaw and Shaw (1984) argue that late entrants into European synthetic fiber markets failed to gain significant market shares or low cost positions, and many ultimately exited. Learning-based advantages are also evident in the case of Lincoln Electric Company (Fast, 1975); the firm's early market entry with superior patented products, coupled with a managerial system promoting continued cost reduction in an evolutionary technological environment, has enabled the company to maintain high profitability for decades.

Inter-firm diffusion of technology, which diminishes first-mover advantages derived from the learning curve, is emphasized in theoretical papers by Ghemawat and Spence (1985) and Lieberman (1987c). It is now generally recognized that diffusion occurs rapidly in most industries, and learning-based advantages are less widespread than was commonly believed in the 1970s. Mechanisms for diffusion include workforce mobility, research publication, informal technical communication, 'reverse engineering,' plant tours, etc. For a sample of firms in ten industries, Mansfield (1985) found that process technology leaks more slowly than product technology, but competitors typically gain access to detailed information on both products and processes within a year of development. Lieberman (1982, 1987b) shows that diffusion of process technology enabled late entry into a sample of 40 chemical product industries, despite strong learning curve effects at the industry level.

R&D and Patents. When technological advantage is largely a function of R&D expenditures, pioneers can gain advantage if technology can be patented or maintained as trade secrets. This has been formalized in the theoretical economics literature in the form of R&D or patent-races where advantages are often enjoyed by the first-mover firm. Gilbert and Newbery (1982) were the first to develop a model of preemptive patenting, in which a firm with an early head-start in research exploits its lead to deter rivals from entering the patent-race. Subsequent papers by Reinganum (1983), Fudenberg *et al*. (1983) and others show that successful preemption by the leader depends on assumptions regarding the stochastic nature of the R&D process and on the inability of followers to 'leapfrog' ahead of the incumbent. One general defect of the patent-race literature is the assumption that all returns go exclusively to the winner of the race.

As an empirical matter, such patent-races seem to be important in only a few industries, such as pharmaceuticals. In most industries, patents confer only weak protection, are easy to 'invent around,' or have transitory value given the pace of technological change. For a sample of 48 patented product innovations in pharmaceuticals, chemicals and electrical products, Mansfield *et al*. (1981) found that, on average, imitators could duplicate patented innovations for about 65 percent of the innovators cost; imitation was fairly rapid, with 60 percent of the patented innovations limited within 4 years. Imitation appears relatively more costly in the pharmaceutical industry, where imitators must go through the same regulatory approval procedures as the innovating firm. Levin *et al.* (1984) found wide inter-industry variation in the cost and time required for imitation. They also found inter-industry differences in appropriability mechanisms, with lead-time and learning curve advantages relatively important in many industries, and patents important in few. In a study using the PIMS data base, Robinson (1988) found that pioneer firms benefit from patents or trade secrets to a significantly greater extent than followers (29 percent vs. 13 percent). However, he also found that patents accounted for only a small proportion of the perceived quality advantages enjoyed by pioneers.

Several case studies have examined the role of patents in sustaining first-mover advantages. Bresnahan (1985) discusses Xerox's use of patents as an entry barrier. In addition to key patents on the basic Xerography process, Xerox patented a thicket of alternative technologies which defended the firm from entry until challengers used anti-trust actions to force compulsory licensing. Bright (1949) argues that GE's long-term dominance of the electric lamp industry was initially derived from control of the basic Edison patent, and later maintained through the accumulation of hundreds of minor patents on the lamp and associated equipment.

R&D and innovation need not be limited to physical hardware; firms also make improvements in managerial systems and may invent new organizational forms. Organizational innovation is often slow to diffuse, and hence may convey a more durable first-mover advantage than product or process innovation (Teece, 1980). Chandler (1977) describes managerial innovations that enabled producers to exploit newly available scale economies in manufacturing and distribution in the late nineteenth century. Many of these firms —e.g., American Tobacco, Campbell Soup, Quaker Oats, Procter and Gamble—still retain dominant positions in their industries.

Preemption of Scarce Assets

The first-mover firm may be able to gain advantage by preempting rivals in the acquisition of scarce assets. Here, the first-mover gains advantage by controlling assets that already exist, rather than those created by the firm through development of new technology. Such assets may be physical resources or other process inputs. Alternatively, the assets may relate to positioning in 'space,' including geographic space, product space, shelf space, etc.

Preemption of Input Factors. If the first-mover firm has superior information, it may be able to purchase assets at market prices below those that will prevail later in the evolution of the market. Such assets include natural resource deposits and prime retailing or manufacturing locations. Here, the returns garnered by the first-mover are pure economic rents.' A first-mover with superior information can (in principle) collect all such rents earned on nonmobile assets such as resource deposits and real estate. The firm may also be able to appropriate some of the rents that accrue to potentially mobile assets such as employees, suppliers and distributors. The firm can collect such rents if these factors are bound to the firm by switching costs, so that their mobility is restricted.

One empirical study of first-mover advantages in controlling natural resources is Main (1955). Main argues that the concentration of high-grade nickel deposits in a single geographic area made it possible for the first company in the area to secure rights to virtually the entire supply, and thus dominate world production for decades.

Preemption of Locations in Geographic and Product Characteristics Space. First-movers may also be able to deter entry through strategies of spatial preemption. In many markets there is 'room' for only a limited number of profitable firms; the first-mover can often select the most attractive niches and may be able to take strategic actions that limit the amount of space available for subsequent entrants. Preemptable 'space' can be interpreted broadly to include not only geographic space, but also shelf space and 'product characteristics space' (i.e. niches for product differentiation).

The theory of spatial preemption is developed in papers by Prescott and Visscher (1977), Schmalensee (1978), Rao and Rutenberg (1979) and Eaton and Lipsey (1979, 1981). The basic argument is that the first-mover can establish positions in geographic or product space such that latecomers find it unprofitable to occupy the interstices. If the market is growing, new niches are filled by incumbents before new entry becomes profitable.[5] Entry is repelled through the threat of price warfare, which is more intense when firms are positioned more closely. Incumbent commitment is provided through sunk investment costs.[6]

Empirical evidence suggests that successful preemption through geographic space packing is rare. In their study of the cement industry, Johnson and Parkman (1983) found no evidence of successful geographic preemption even though structural characteristics of the industry suggest that such strategies would be likely. In a study of local newspaper markets, Glazer (1985) found no difference in survival rates between first- and second-mover firms. One explanation for these findings is that all firms in cement and newspaper markets have similar technologies and entry opportunities, so preemptive competition for preferred sites drives profits to zero. In other words, there were no initial asymmetries in timing or information to be exploited.

One counter-example illustrating effective geographic preemption is a case study of the Wal-Mart discount retailing firm (Ghemawat, 1986b). Wal-Mart targeted small southern towns located in contiguous regions that competitors initially found unprofitable to service. By coupling spatial preemption at the retail level with an extremely efficient distribution network, the firm has been able to defend its position and earn sustained high profits.

Schmalensee's (1978) model of product space preemption was developed in the context of a lawsuit brought by the Federal Trade Commission against the three major U.S. breakfast cereal companies. The FTC alleged that these firms had sustained their high profit rates through a strategy of tacit collusion in preempting supermarket shelf space and product differentiation niches. Although the lawsuit was dismissed, the cereal firms have continued to sustain exceptionally high profit rates.[7]

Robinson and Fornell (1985) found that new consumer product pioneers initially held product quality superiority over imitators and subsequently developed advantages in the form of a broader product line. Thus, there is evidence that pioneers try to reinforce their early lead by filling product differentiation niches.

Preemptive Investment in Plant and Equipment. Another way in which an established first-mover can deter entry is through preemptive investment in plant and equipment. Here, the enlarged capacity of the incumbent serves as a commitment to maintain greater output following entry, with price cuts threatened to make entrants unprofitable. In these models the incumbent may successfully deter new entry, as in Spence (1977), Dixit (1980), Gilbert and Harris (1981) and Eaton and Ware (1987). Alternatively, preemptive investment by the pioneer may simply deter the growth of smaller entrants, as in Spence (1979) and Fudenberg and Tirole (1983).

These investment tactics do not seem to be particularly important in practice. Gilbert (1986) argues that most industries lack the cost structure required for preemptive investment to prove effective. Lieberman (1987a) shows that preemptive investment by incumbents was seldom successful in deterring entry into chemical product industries. One exception was magnesium, where Dow Chemical maintained a near-monopoly position for several decades, based largely on investments (threatened or actual) in plant capacity (Lieberman, 1983).

The role of scale economies is intentionally deemphasized in the above-mentioned models of preemptive investment.[8] When scale economies are large, first-mover advantages are typically enhanced, with the limiting case being that of natural monopoly. However, outside of public utilities, scale economies approaching the natural monopoly level are seldom observed in U.S. manufacturing industries.[9] In a theoretical treatment, Schmalensee (1981) shows that in most realistic industry settings, scale economies provide only minor entry barriers and hence potential for enhanced profits.

Switching Costs and Buyer Choice Under Uncertainty

Switching Costs. First-mover advantages may also arise from buyer switching costs. With switching costs, late entrants must invest extra resources to attract customers away from the first-mover firm. Several types of switching costs can arise. First, switching costs can stem from initial transactions costs or investments that the buyer makes in adapting to the seller's product. These include the time and resources spent in qualifying a new supplier, the cost of ancillary products such as software for a new computer, and the time, disruption, and financial burdens of training employees. A second category of switching costs arises due to supplier-specific learning by the buyer. Over time, the buyer adapts to characteristics of the product and its supplier and thus finds it costly to change over to another brand (Wernerfelt, 1985). For example, nurses become accustomed to the intravenous solution delivery systems of a given supplier and are reluctant to switch (Porter, 1980). A third type of switching cost is contractural switching cost that may be intentionally created by the seller. Airline frequent-flyer programs fit in this category (Klemperer, 1986).

Theoretical models of market equilibrium with buyer switching costs include Klemperer (1986) and Wernerfelt (1986, 1988). Switching costs typically enhance the value of market share obtained early in the evolution of a new market. Thus they provide a rationale for pursuit of market share. However, first-movers with large market shares do not necessarily earn high profits; early competition for share can dissipate profits; and under some conditions the inertia of an incumbent with a large customer base can make the firm vulnerable to late entrants, who prove to be relatively more profitable (Klemperer, 1986).

Buyer Choice Under Uncertainty. A related theoretical literature (e.g. Schmalensee, 1982) deals with the imperfect information of buyers regarding product quality. In such a context, buyers may rationally stick with the first brand they encounter that performs the job satisfactorily. Brand loyalty of this sort may be particularly strong for low-cost 'convenience goods' where the benefits of finding a superior brand are seldom great enough to justify the additional search costs that must be incurred (Porter, 1976). In such an environment, early-mover firms may be able to establish a reputation for quality that can be transferred to additional products through umbrella branding and other tactics (Wernerfelt, 1987).

Similar arguments derived from the psychology literature suggest that the first product introduced received disproportionate attention in the consumer's mind. Late entrants must have a truly superior product, or else advertise more frequently (or more creatively) than the incumbent in order to be noticed by the consumer. In a laboratory study using consumer products, Carpenter and Nakamoto (1986) found that the order-of-entry influences the formation of consumer preferences. If the pioneer is able to achieve significant consumer trial, it can define the attributes that are perceived as important within a product category. Pioneers such as Coca-Cola and Kleenex have become prototypical, occupying a unique position in the consumer's mind. Their large market shares tend to persist because perceptions and preferences, once formed, are difficult to alter.

More traditional marketing studies confirm the existence of such perceptual effects. In a study of two types of prescription pharmaceuticals—oral diuretics and antianginals—

Bond and Lean (1977) found that physicians ignored 'me-too' products, even if offered at lower prices and with substantial marketing support.[10] Montgomery (1975) found that a product's newness was one of the two key variables necessary to gain acceptance onto supermarket shelves.

These imperfect information effects should be greater for individual consumers than corporate buyers, since the latter's larger purchase volume justifies greater investment in information acquisition activities.[11] Using the PIMS data base, Robinson (1988) and Robinson and Fornell (1985) found that pioneers had larger market shares than followers in both consumer and industrial markets, but the effect was much greater for consumer goods—order of entry explained 18 percent of the variance in market share in consumer goods markets, but only 8 percent in industrial markets. For a sample of 129 consumer packaged goods, Urban *et al.* (1986) found a strong inverse relation between order-of-entry and market share.

Brand positions remain remarkably durable in many consumer markets. Ries and Trout (1986) noted that of 25 leading brands in 1923, 20 were still in first place some 60 years later. Davidson (1976) found that two-thirds of the pioneers in 18 United Kingdom grocery product categories developed since 1945 retained their market leadership through the mid-1970s.

First-Mover Disadvantages

The mechanisms that benefit the first-mover may be counterbalanced by various disadvantages. These first-mover disadvantages are, in effect, advantages enjoyed by late-mover firms. Late-movers may benefit from: (1) the ability to 'free-ride' on first-mover investments, (2) resolution of technological and market uncertainty, (3) technological discontinuities that provide 'gateways' for new entry, and (4) various types of 'incumbent inertia' that make it difficult for the incumbent to adapt to environmental change. These phenomena can reduce, or even completely negate, the net advantage of the incumbent derived from mechanisms considered previously.

Free-Rider Effects

Late-movers may be able to 'free-ride' on a pioneering firm's investments in a number of areas including R&D, buyer education, and infrastructure development. As mentioned previously, imitation costs are lower than innovation costs in most industries. However, innovators enjoy an initial period of monopoly that is not available to imitator firms. The ability of follower firms to free-ride reduces the magnitude and durability of the pioneer's profits, and hence its incentive to make early investments.

The theoretical literature has focused largely on the implications of free-rider effects in the form of information spillovers in R&D (Spence, 1984; Baldwin and Childs, 1969), and learning-based productivity improvement (Ghemawat and Spence, 1985; Lieberman, 1987c). As mentioned previously, empirical studies document a high rate of inter-firm diffusion of technology in most industries.

Guasch and Weiss (1980) assess free-rider effects operating in the labor market. They give a theoretical argument that late-mover firms may be able to exploit employee screening performed by early entrants, and thus acquire skilled labor at lower cost. This is in addition to the fact that early entrants may invest in employee training, with benefits enjoyed by later entrants who may be able to hire away the trained personnel.

Teece (1986a,b) argues that the magnitude of free-rider effects depends in part on ownership of assets that are complementary or 'co-specialized' with the underlying innovation. For example, EMI developed the first CT scanner but lost in the marketplace because the firm lacked a technology infrastructure and marketing base in the medical field. Pilkington, by comparison, was able to profit handsomely from its pioneering float glass process due to its assets and experience in the glass industry. In other instances late-mover firms have been successful largely because they were able to exploit existing assets in areas such as marketing, distribution, and customer reputation—e.g. IBM in personal computers and Matsushita in VCRs (Schnaars, 1986).

Resolution of Technological or Market Uncertainty

Late-movers can gain an edge through resolution of market or technological uncertainty.[12] Wernerfelt and Karnani (1987) consider the effects of uncertainty on the desirability of early versus late market entry. Entry in an uncertain market obviously involves a high degree of risk. They argue that early entry is more attractive when the firm can influence the way that uncertainty is resolved. For example, the firm may be able to set industry standards in its favor. Firm size may also be important—large firms may be better equipped to wait for resolution of uncertainty, or to hedge by maintaining a more flexible investment portfolio.

In many new product markets, uncertainty is resolved through the emergence of a 'dominant design.' The Model T Ford and the DC-3 are examples of dominant designs in the automotive and aircraft industries. After emergence of such a design, competition often shifts to price, thereby conveying greater advantage over firms possessing skills in low-cost manufacturing (Teece, 1986b).

Shifts in Technology or Customer Needs

Schumpeter (1961) conceived of technological progress as a process of 'creative destruction' in which existing products are superseded by the innovations of new firms. New entrants exploit technological discontinuities to displace existing incumbents. Empirical studies which consider these technological discontinuities or 'gateways' for new entry include Yip (1982) and Bevan (1974). Foster (1986) gives practical advice on how such discontinuities can be exploited by entrants, who might be defined as 'first-movers' into the next technological phase. Scherer (1980) provides a list of innovative entrants who revolutionized existing industries with new products and processes. He also cites numerous examples of dominant incumbents that proved slow innovators but aggressive followers.

Since the replacement technology often appears while the old technology is still growing, it may be difficult for an incumbent to perceive the threat and take adequate preventative steps. Cooper and Schendel (1976) provide several examples, such as the failure of steam locomotive manufacturers to respond to the invention of diesel. Foster (1986) cites American Viscose's failure to recognize the potential of polyester as a replacement for rayon, and Transitron's inattention to silicon as a substitute for germanium in semiconductor fabrication. This perceptual failure is closely related to 'incumbent inertia' considered below.

Customer needs are also dynamic, creating opportunities for later entrants unless the first-mover is alert and able to respond. Docutel, as the pioneer, supplied virtually all of the automatic teller machine market up to late 1974. Over the next 4 years its market share declined to less than 10 percent under the onslaught of Honeywell, IBM and Burroughs, all of whom offered computer systems to meet the emerging need for electronic funds transfer (Abell, 1978).

Incumbent Inertia

Vulnerability of the first-mover is often enhanced by 'incumbent inertia.' Such inertia can have several root causes: (1) the firm may be locked-in to a specific set of fixed assets, (2) the firm may be reluctant to cannibalize existing product lines, or (3) the firm may become organizationally inflexible. These factors inhibit the ability of the firm to respond to environmental change or competitive threats.

Incumbent inertia is often a rational, profit-maximizing response, even though it may lead to organizational decline. For example, Tang (1988) presents a model that rationalizes the decisions of most U.S. steel producers to continue investing in open-hearth furnace technology even after it had become clear that basic oxygen furnaces were superior. A firm with heavy sunk costs in fixed plant or marketing channels that ultimately prove sub-optimal may find it rational to 'harvest' these investments rather than attempt to transform itself radically.[13] MacMillan (1983) suggests that in the rapidly changing environment of health care, old health care systems may currently be harvesting from their initial investments in locations and personnel. The appropriate choice between adaptation and harvesting depends on how costly it is to convert the firm's existing assets to alternative uses. And, as we discuss below, organizational inertia has often led firms to continue investing in their existing asset base well beyond the point where such investments are economically justified.

Much of the literature on cannibalization-avoidance refers to R&D. Arrow (1962) was the first to lay out the theoretical argument that an incumbent monopolist is less likely to innovate than a new entrant, since innovation destroys rents on the firm's existing products. More recent theoretical studies along these lines include Reinganum (1983) and Ghemawat (1986a). Bresnahan (1985) argues that Xerox exhibited such behavior following the expiration of its patent-enforced monopoly—Xerox lagged in certain types of innovations and was sluggish to cut prices on account of its large fleet of rental machines in the field. Brock (1975) and Ghemawat (1986a) make similar arguments regarding the innovative responses of IBM in computers and AT&T in PBX's. However, Conner (1988) shows that under a broad range of conditions the incumbent's optimal strategy is to develop an improved product but delay market introduction until challenged by the appearance of a rival product.

From an organizational theory perspective, Hannan and Freeman (1984) outline factors that limit adaptive response by incumbents. These include the development of organizational routines and standards, internal political dynamics and the development of stable exchange relations with other organizations.[14]

While Hannan and Freeman argue that organizational inertia is often a positive outcome of selection processes, numerous dysfunctional examples of such inertia can be cited. Abernathy and Wayne (1974) assess Henry Ford's decision to persist in production of the Model T, long after changes in the competitive environment had made it clear that new products were required. Bevan (1974) cites organizational blinders as a key factor contributing to the decline of the major potato chip producer in the U.K. Historically, the vast majority of chips were consumed by men in pubs. It took the incumbent five years to realize that the challenger had invented a whole new market segment—supermarket sales to women and children. Similarly, Jacobson and Hillkirk (1986) discuss Xerox's inability to perceive the growing threat of Japanese competition in the 1970s. Cooper and Schendel (1976) note that even when an incumbent makes a commitment to change, organizational factors often sabotage the effort; in their sample, 15 incumbents made major commitments to the new technologies but only two of them ultimately proved successful.

General Conceptual Issues

Endogeneity of First-Mover Opportunities

A given firm cannot simply choose whether or not to pioneer; pioneering opportunities arise endogenously, through the process illustrated in Figure 1. A firm gains first-mover opportunities through some combination of proficiency and luck. Various types of proficiency may be involved, including technological foresight, perceptive market research, or skillful product or process development. For example, Procter and Gamble's initial lead in disposable diapers can be attributed to most of these proficiency factors.

In addition to generating first-mover opportunities, proficiency and luck also influence the firm's success in exploiting the specific mechanisms discussed earlier. In the case of disposable diapers, Procter and Gamble's initial lead was enhanced by its skill in maintaining a proprietary learning curve in manufacturing, and in preempting supermarket shelf space.

Proficiency and luck also affect profits in ways that are unrelated to first-mover advantages. For instance, some component of Procter and Gamble's disposable diaper profits can be traced to the firm's economies of shared distribution channels and general manufacturing proficiency. The recent increase in the U.S. birth rate has augmented industry profits, representing the direct effect of luck.

In the endogenous process illustrated in Figure 1, profits earned by first-movers are fundamentally attributable to proficiency and luck, rather than 'pioneering' *per se*. But as a practical matter, it is often exceedingly difficult to distinguish between proficiency and luck, particularly at the stage where first-mover opportunities are generated. Entrepreneurs often perceive 'great opportunities,' many of which ultimately prove disappointing. Investors face the problem of distinguishing between 'true' and 'false' entrepreneurial vision. Even after success or failure is observed, disentangling the contribution of exceptional foresight or skill from that of mere luck is no easier.[15] We leave this difficult problem to venture capitalists, and extremely ambitious empirical researchers.

Nevertheless, in a purely conceptual way one can usefully distinguish between these two sources. Profits linked to first-mover opportunities arising from exceptional skill or foresight can be viewed as returns to superior entrepreneurship. Figure 1 shows that skill can also affect profits more directly, as in situations where the firm possesses know-how that enables it to manufacture products at lower costs than its competitors. These returns may not always be visible as company profits, as they may be captured, in part, by the employees responsible for their generation.

Similarly, luck can affect profits directly (e.g. a factory damaged by fire) and indirectly by influencing the quality of first-mover opportunities available to the firm.[16] This effect of luck on first-mover opportunities has important implications for empirical research, since it leads to sample selection biases that have sometimes been overlooked.

Sample Selection Bias

When first-mover opportunities are generated by processes of chance, firms that draw less attractive opportunities may choose not to enter, or they may exit quickly and thus not be observed. Pioneers that survive this screening process would be expected to earn above-average returns.[17]

The role of luck is illustrated by the following simple example. Assume that a given firm (having no exceptional proficiency in research) faces an opportunity to engage in risky R&D on a pioneering new product, with a 50 percent probability of technical success. Expected profits are the average of two components: a gain of $\pi + \epsilon$ if the research succeeds, versus a loss of π if the project fails. The firm enters the market only if the project proves technically successful. Significant profits will thus be observed contingent on entry, even though expected profits ($\epsilon/2$) may be barely sufficient for the firm to be induced to undertake the project. With free entry, competition among R&D-performing firms should drive these expected profits to near zero.

Thus, first-mover advantages may enable successful pioneers to earn high returns even though an unbiased sample earns zero economic profits. One extension is that as the 'riskiness' of R&D increases, the average profit rate observed for successful firms increases as well.[18]

Failure is a common occurrence in practice. For example, Mansfield (1968) found that more than one-fourth of corporate R&D projects fail to achieve their technical objectives. Davidson (1976) observed that about 70 percent of test market brands are not expanded nationally and hence can be considered failures. In an empirical study that considered the endogenous nature of first-mover opportunities, Boulding and Moore (1987) found that pioneering firms were marginally unprofitable on average.

The fact that luck- or skill-based asymmetries are required to generate above-normal profits is confirmed by the results of theoretical models where such initial asymmetries are absent, e.g. Glazer (1985), Fudenberg and Tirole (1985), and Gilbert and Harris (1984). Firms in these models face an investment timing decision—e.g., when to enter an emerging market that is initially too small to support even a single entrant. If all firms have identical information and investment opportunities, the initial entrant fails to earn excess returns; competition for the first-mover position drives the associated profits to zero. Preemptive investment occurs at the earliest point in time that the initial entrant can earn a nonnegative present value of profits.

Definitional and Measurement Issues

What Constitutes a 'First-Mover'? Perhaps the most fundamental problem with the concept of 'first-mover' is that of definition. If a firm enters an established market, but exploits some technological discontinuity or appeals to new demand segment, should it be classified as a first-mover? In general, how large a discontinuity from existing practice is required to cross the threshold for definition as a pioneer?

We offer no good answers to these questions; available data and expedience have been the criteria used in most empirical studies. Clearly, adopting a loose definition causes a large fraction of entrants to be classified as pioneers.[19] In the PIMS data, for example, more than half of all business units are 'pioneers,' including multiple competitors within the same market segment (Buzzell and Gale, 1987).

There is also the question of whether the criterion for first-movership is actual market entry, or the initiation of preliminary work such as R&D. The standard definition is based on market entry, which we agree is the appropriate criterion.

Assuming some reasonable definition of what constitutes a pioneer, for empirical work there remains the problem of distinguishing among later entrants. Such entrants can be classified by (1) their numerical order in the sequence of entry, (2) elapsed time since entry of the pioneer, or (3) general categories such as early follower, late follower, differentiated follower, 'me-too' follower, etc. These categories are not, in general, consistent or comparable across markets. For example, a firm that is third in the order of entry is likely to have been an early follower in a market with 20 firms, but a late follower in a market with four.

Alternative Measures of 'First-Mover Advantage': Profits vs. Market Share vs. Probability of Survival. Earlier we argued that economic profits are the appropriate measure of first-mover advantage. Profit maximization is the sole objective of stockholders in all modern theories of the firm. First-mover advantages exist when the pioneering firm earns positive present value of profits as the consequence of its early entry (i.e. positive profits net of those attributable to more general types of firm proficiency).

A serious problem confronting those engaged in empirical work is the fact that disaggregate profit data are seldom obtainable.[20] Hence, market shares and rates of company survival are typically used as surrogate measures. Market share and survival have both been shown to be correlated with profits and thus have some validity as proxies. But the correlation of these measures with profits is not always strong and causality is often ambiguous. For example, managers can often increase share at the expense of profits, e.g. by drastically cutting price, or increasing promotional activity. Moreover, measures of market share can vary greatly depending on whether markets have been broadly or narrowly defined.

Market share and survival also have some spurious correlations with first-movership and are thus inherently biased. Consider, as a stylized example, a market with two identical firms, A and B, that grow at identical rates, say 20 percent per year. Assume that both firms earn zero economic profits. A enters 1 year ahead of B, making A the 'first-mover.' In this case firm A will always maintain a market share 20 percent greater than B, even though by our definition there are no 'first-mover advantages.' While this example is extreme, our point is that early entrants have natural advantages in market share that do not necessarily translate into higher profits.

Survival rates suffer from similar biases. For example, first-movers may be intrinsically 'stronger' or more proficient than later entrants. Consider first-mover advantages generated through firm proficiency, as illustrated in Figure 1. First-movers may exhibit higher survival rates, but it may be exceedingly difficult to ascertain whether this stems from pioneering, *per se*, or whether it reflects some more basic characteristic of the firm.

Magnitude and Duration of First-Mover Advantages. The term 'first-mover advantage' suggests that the pioneer remains more profitable than later entrants, but careful reflection reveals that this need not be the case. Pioneering firms can enjoy significant first-mover advantages but be less profitable than later entrants when viewed over an extended period.

Consider, for example, a pioneer with patent protection, whose economic profits fall to near-zero after the patent expiration date. This pioneer has clearly gained a first-mover advantage, even though after expiration of the patent the pioneer may be less profitable and hold a smaller market share than other firms. Indeed, many pioneers exploit their initial advantages, then exit or sell out to others.[21]

Note that this raises the possibility that there may be both first-mover and late-mover advantages in a given market. For example, the pioneering firm described above may earn high initial profits based on its patent, but ultimately be overshadowed by a larger firm with unique marketing skills that yield above-average returns. In this case, first-mover advantages accrue to the pioneer, and late-mover advantages to the marketing firm. Whether the first-mover or late-mover has greater relative advantage depends on the point in time that the market is observed.

Moreover, for any given firm, the question of whether early or late entry is more advantageous depends on the firm's particular characteristics. In the above example, if one firm has unique R&D capabilities while the other has strong marketing skills, it is in the interest of the first firm to pioneer and the second firm to enter at a later date. Both may earn significant profits entering in this sequence, but neither would gain if the (attempted) order of entry were reversed.

Issues for Future Research

Given the problems discussed in the previous section, is 'first-mover advantage' a useful research concept? Clearly, it does provide a unifying framework for a broad class of phenomena. But as a focus for empirical research, the concept of first-mover advantage may be too general and definitionally elusive to be useful. In recent years a number of cross-section empirical studies have attempted to detect and categorize a wide range of 'pioneering advantages.' While these studies provide useful groundwork, we feel that future empirical research needs to be more precise in elucidating specific first-mover mechanisms. Theoretical work in the area has often suffered from the opposite problem: models have been designed to articulate one piece of the first-mover puzzle but have failed to embed it within a suitably endogenous system.

Below, we develop these points further and offer some specific suggestions for future research. We propose several directions that we regard as interesting, even though we doubt that all our suggestions are truly feasible.

Theoretical and Conceptual Issues

In this survey we have stressed the endogenous nature of first-mover advantages. Most theoretical studies have begun by assuming some initial asymmetry, thereby sidestepping the endogeneity issue. The fundamental (and in our view most interesting) question of how first-mover opportunities arise and are pursued by specific firms remains almost completely unexplored. An important theoretical challenge is to flesh out this dynamic process, and distinguish the impact of firm proficiency from that of luck.

A related need is for more theoretical work linking individual firm characteristics to optimal timing strategy. For example, what types of firms are best suited to pioneer, and what types are best suited to follow? Models from the economics literature typically make only the most rudimentary distinctions among firms—indeed, firms are usually assumed identical along all dimensions except timing and size. The strategic management field has traditionally emphasized a wider set of inter-firm differences. The implications of these differences in the context of mechanisms for first-mover advantage needs to be explored in greater depth. Work by Teece (1986a,b) and Wernerfelt and Karnani (1987) provides a useful start, but many opportunities remain.

Despite its deficiencies, theoretical work on first-mover *advantages* remains far ahead of our understanding of mechanisms that assist late-movers. There has, for example, been little conceptual work on resolution of technological and market uncertainty, even though this is often the major factor affecting the timing of entry in practice. Similarly, incumbent inertia is one area where our understanding remains weak. For example, we have few frameworks (with the exception of population ecology, and the model by Tang, 1988) that enable us to determine when inertia is desirable, and when it is dysfunctional (Lambkin, 1988).

Empirical Issues

In our view, an important priority for empirical research is to focus more precisely on the evaluation of specific first-mover mechanisms, rather than on general investigations of the merits of pioneer versus follower strategies. Researchers should aim to test specific models and carefully distinguish among mechanisms. For example, additional empirical research is needed on the topic of switching costs, where first-mover advantages seem to be significant. Here it may be possible to distinguish empirically between risk-based models (such as Schmalensee, 1982) and those based on psychological framing effects (e.g. Carpenter and Nakamoto, 1986). The initial efforts of Carpenter and Nakamoto suggest that experimental methods may prove fruitful for disentangling the fundamentals of such first-mover mechanisms.

New data are required in order to broaden and deepen understanding of first-mover advantages and disadvantages and the mechanisms that generate them. Researchers need to wean themselves from convenient but much-used data bases (e.g. PIMS). Wherever possible, data should be collected on non-survivors, as well as surviving firms, to alleviate the censored sample problem. More difficult to obtain, but even more important, would be appropriate measures of profit, in order to reduce the dependence of empirical knowledge on market share effects.

The endogeneity issue has been ignored in most empirical studies as well as in theoretical work. Recent research by Boulding and Moore (1987) suggests some possible empirical approaches. Models with endogenous structure are necessary for exploring the linkage between firm characteristics, first-mover opportunities, and performance. Potentially, such research might be able to disentangle the relative importance of proficiency versus luck in generating first-mover advantage.

While we are skeptical about the value of more broad-brush empirical efforts, we do think there are a number of interesting but unanswered questions regarding the relative importance of first-mover advantages. Such assessments might be made across several dimensions. First, it would be interesting to assess the magnitude of first-mover advantages relative to profits derived from more general forms of firm proficiency, such as superior manufacturing or marketing skills. How much of the inter-firm variance in profit rates can be attributed to first-mover effects, as opposed to more general proficiency differentials? And to what extent should managerial effort be allocated toward searching out preemption opportunities, as opposed to building more general organizational capabilities? We are intrigued with the possibility of obtaining some rough quantitative evidence on this score, despite the obvious difficulties.

Similar comparisons might be made among specific first-mover mechanisms and the industries in which they operate. It would be useful to know which of the various mechanisms are most important in practice, and in what industries they operate most strongly. Some empirical first-mover studies (e.g. Robinson, 1988 and Robinson and Fornell,1985) have highlighted inter-industry differences; their results suggest that first-mover effects are more powerful in consumer-goods industries than in producer-goods. It would be interesting to extend such comparisons to service industries where casual observation suggests that imitation occurs rapidly. Still, this producer/consumer/service industry trichotomy is rudimentary; a more precise mapping between industry characteristics and first-mover mechanisms would be useful.

Another set of comparisons relates to the duration of first-mover advantages. Under what conditions are they ephemeral versus long-lived? How does this vary by mechanisms and by industry? And what steps can management take to enhance sustainability? The existing empirical literature provides some evidence on these issues, but our knowledge is still quite limited.

Implications for Managers

Although our focus has been primarily on research issues, we conclude with a brief discussion of managerial implications.

One of the first lessons of the first-mover literature is that pioneering carries both advantages and disadvantages. The net impact may well be negative, as illustrated by the demise of Bomar and Osborne, pioneers in electronic calculators and portable computers respectively. In a cross-sectional study, Boulding and Moore (1987) found pioneering to be marginally unprofitable on average. On the other hand, numerous studies have found enduring market share advantages for surviving pioneers (Bond and Lean, 1977; Carpenter and Nakamoto, 1986; Urban *et al.* 1986; Robinson,

1988; Robinson and Fornell, 1985). Thus, pioneering may prove advantageous to some firms in some circumstances, but it is not necessarily a superior strategy for all entrants.

In order for a firm to become a first-mover or pioneer, a feasible opportunity must present itself. The occurrence of such an opportunity depends on the firm's own foresight, skill and luck, and that of competitors. These factors are interdependent—or as MacMillan (1983) has put it, 'Good generals make their luck by shaping the odds in their favor.' The likelihood of being a first-mover may be enhanced, often substantially, by managements' actions, but opportunities for first-movership are by no means controlled by the firm alone.

Firms must decide whether to invest resources in search of first-mover opportunities. Moreover, when a specific first-mover opportunity arises, managers must decide whether and how to exploit it. Sony, for example, aggressively pursues first-mover advantages from new product innovation. Its rival, Matsushita (whose nickname in Japanese, *maneshita denki* translates as 'electronics that have been copied'), generally lets Sony and others innovate; Matsushita then takes a position based on its manufacturing and marketing capabilities. Matsushita invests in R&D to be ready to enter the market when it begins rapid growth, but the firm will not launch new products until others have proven the market. Choice between these two alternative approaches depends on the firm's specific characteristics and skills. Firms whose entrepreneurial vision and new-product R&D are excellent will tend to find first-movership attractive, whereas firms having relative skill bases in manufacturing and marketing may not. Then too, firms having a strategy of first-movership may often be forced to follow in related product areas in order to provide a more complete product line.

Managers who have chosen to emphasize pioneering must address a number of issues. First, how can the pioneer protect itself from imitation, to prevent later entrants from free-riding' on the pioneer's efforts? Patents are one obvious way to achieve this; designs that are deliberately difficult to reverse engineer are another. Pioneers can sometimes preempt key resources, such as the most desirable retailing locations or distribution networks. If the product is one where consumer switching costs will be important, it may be essential that the pioneer induce trial by the majority of potential customers before rivals have an opportunity to do so.

First-movers must also guard against incumbent inertia, which may result from complacency, arrogance, or inattention to shifts in technology or customer needs. Changes in the environment can give potential competitors a window of opportunity. Pioneers may want to consider broadening the product line, thereby thickening their relationship with customers and blocking opportunities for competitors to enter.

First-movers must recognize that initial success does not automatically confer a franchise for permanent competitive advantage. Rather, first-mover advantages must be sustained by careful nurturing. Even companies with long-established leadership positions, based in part on pioneering, can dissipate their advantages. In the late 1970s, for example, Kleenex tissues, which had established the industry standard, lost significant market share (Carpenter, 1988). Subsequent research indicated that consumers' preferences had shifted to competing brands that were perceived as being softer. This preference shift was the result of Kleenex's production economy choices that had gradually increased the level of recycled wood pulp in the tissues. Once Kleenex restored and enhanced the level of softness, it regained and even surpassed its previous market share (*Wall Street Journal*, 1987).

Alert pioneers take proactive steps to protect their pioneering advantages. Pioneers need to increase capacity sufficiently, especially in high-growth markets, to avoid being overtaken by aggressive followers. Tohatsu, the leading Japanese motorcycle producer in the late 1950s, failed to do so and was overtaken by Honda (Abegglen and Stalk, 1985). Continual product innovation is another key to retaining competitive advantage. Caterpillar, by neglecting to re-engineer their low-end models in the early 1970s, gave John Deere an opportunity to enter the over-100 horsepower bulldozer market using an innovative transmission as a differentiating feature (HBS, 1977). Finally, quality and breadth of product line may also be used to sustain pioneer advantage. Robinson (1988) found that pioneer quality advantages tend to diminish over time, but product line breadth advantages are more sustainable. In general, pioneers that build adequate capacity, innovate to meet changing technologies and customer requirements, and fill up available market niches, are formidable opponents and exceedingly difficult to overcome.

For firms with a follower strategy (whether by design or inevitable) the major issue is whether to attack the pioneer directly, or seek a less confrontational, differentiated position. If the pioneer is small, lacks resources, or has not yet achieved much market penetration or recognition, he may be vulnerable to aggressive attack by a follower. Urban *et al.* (1986) found that followers in consumer packaged goods were able to overcome the pioneer's market share advantage by substantially out-spending the pioneer on advertising. However, a number of studies have found that 'me-too' strategies tend to be unsuccessful (Bond and Lean, 1977; Montgomery, 1975; Davidson, 1976; Carpenter and Nakamoto, 1986). Even substantial price cuts may fail to wrest significant market share (Bond and Lean, 1977; Carpenter and Nakamoto, 1986). In general, 'me-too' strategies seem to be effective only when the innovator has not done its marketing properly or intensely enough.[22]

Followers may find it preferable to avoid direct confrontation with a strong pioneer, at least initially. Golden Wonder developed a totally new market segment and distribution channel in the U.K. potato chip market, thereby distinguishing itself from the dominant incumbent (Bevan, 1974). Urban *et al.* (1986) found that superior positioning of a follower brand with respect to consumer needs was the single most important predictor of a follower's share relative to a first-mover. Foster (1986) cites numerous examples of followers that were able to successfully differentiate themselves by exploiting technological discontinuities. Once the follower has gained a strong foothold, direct challenge of the pioneer often becomes feasible.

Summary

This article has surveyed theoretical and empirical research on mechanisms that confer advantages and disadvantages on first-mover firms. Mechanisms that promote first-mover advantages include proprietary learning effects, patents, preemption of input factors and locations, and development of buyer switching costs. Conversely, first-mover disadvantages may result from free-rider problems, delayed resolution of uncertainty, shifts in technology or customer needs, and various types of organizational inertia.

We have discussed key conceptual issues and research priorities. Future research should consider the endogenous nature of first-mover opportunities and the potential for sample selection bias. Greater emphasis should be given in empirical analysis to economic profits as a criterion. Perhaps most important, basic questions still need to be addressed on how 'first-movers' are defined and identified in practice.

Finally, managers must decide whether a strong emphasis on pioneering is appropriate, given their firm's resource base. In specific situations where skill and good fortune have generated a first-mover opportunity, managers must decide whether the firm should pursue it, and if so, how best to enhance its value. And managers of follower firms must determine whether and how the first-mover advantages of the pioneer can be subverted.

ACKNOWLEDGEMENTS

We thank Piet Vanden Abeele, Rajiv Lal, Mark Satterthwaite and Birger Wernerfelt for helpful discussions on earlier drafts. The Strategic Management Program at Stanford Business School provided financial support.

Notes

1. Rumelt (1987) refers to these as 'isolating mechanisms,' since they protect 'entrepreneurial rents' from imitative competition.
2. In a related setting where learning depends on accumulated investment rather than output, Gilbert and Harris (1981) show that a first-mover will preempt in the construction of new plants over multiple generations.
3. The basic argument is standard economic analysis, and can be traced back to Ricardo's analysis of rents captured by landowners (first-movers) in the market for wheat in nineteenth-century England.
4. Note that, with complete markets, a first-mover with superior information need not actually own or control such assets to capture economic rents. Hirshleifer (1971) argues that if futures markets exist, the firm can simply assume forward market position that exploit its superior information.
5. Incumbents fill these niches in order to sustain monopoly profits at nearby locations; these profits may be dissipated if new entry occurs.
6. Judd (1985) argues that sunk costs are not sufficient; exit costs are required as well.
7. Of course, these profits may be derived from sources other than spatial preemption.
8. We have also ignored the possibility that network externalities may enhance the position of the first-mover firm. These externalities arise if there are incentives for interconnection or compatibility among users (see, for example, Farrell and Saloner, 1986 and Katz and Shapiro, 1986).
9. For example, see Weiss (1976). This finding applies to manufacturing operations only; greater scale economies may arise in distribution and advertising. Also, many retailing markets are geographically fragmented, leading to the possibility of spatial preemption of the sort described above. Such preemption requires the presence of some scale economies in the form of fixed costs.
10. One explanation of these findings is that physicians are price-insensitive because they do not actually pay the prescription costs. However, the Carpenter and Nakamoto (1986) experiments found that more typical consumers are also unwilling to switch to objectively similar 'me-too' brands, even at substantially lower prices.
11. Moreover, switching costs in industrial markets often dissipate over time as buyers become more knowledgeable about competing products (Cady, 1985).
12. A related point is that a late-mover may be able to take advantage of the first-mover's mistakes. For example, when Toyota was first planning to enter the U.S. market it interviewed owners of Volkswagens, the leading small car at that time. Information on what owners liked and disliked about the Volkswagen was incorporated in the design process for the new Toyota.
13. For first-movers, sunk costs are a two-edged sword: they lock the firm into a particular course of action but also provide commitment value that can help deter entry.
14. One example of the latter is Timex's introduction of the disposable watch. Timex introduced the disposable watch in drug stores and other mass channels, but the Swiss watch industry was unable to follow, for fear of offending the jewelry stores that were their prime mode of distribution (Porter, 1980).
15. One complication is that skill affects luck, and vice-versa. For instance, greater skill in research increases the probability of success in performing risky R&D. With repeated observation the proficiency level of the firm may be revealed by its mean success rate.
16. Rumelt (1987) calls profits generated by luck 'entrepreneurial rents.' His characterization differs slightly from our approach, since he ignores the potential for first-mover profits linked to proficiency.
17. Compounding this selection bias is the fact that if all potential entrants perceive net disadvantages to early entry, no entry will occur, and hence no pioneer will be observed. When this arises there may be an argument for public provision, as in the case of government funding of basic research projects.
18. Assume that R&D projects are drawn from some random distribution with a mean return of approximately zero, and that only successful projects with positive returns are introduced to the market. The average profit earned contingent on success rises with mean-preserving increases in risk. For a formal analysis along these lines, see Lippman and Rumelt (1982).
19. In this article we use the terms 'first-mover' and 'pioneer' interchangeably to refer to a unique firm within a given market.

However, a broader definition of 'pioneer' is often applied, as in the PIMS questionnaire which asks whether the business unit was 'one of the pioneers' at the time it entered the market. In the extreme, if market niches are defined narrowly enough, virtually all firms can be classified as 'pioneers.'

20. The only general source of such data is the PIMS data base, which has numerous limitations. For an assessment, see Anderson and Paine (1978).
21. For example, DuPont was the world's first commercial producer of cyclohexane, but exited when the firm was no longer able to compete with oil companies using refinery-based processes (Stobaugh, 1988).
22. The Carpenter and Nakamoto (1980) experiments suggest an elaboration of the 'me-too' product question. They found that 'me-too' brands tend to fail when positioned close to differentiated later entrants. A brand that mimics an entrenched pioneer usually finds it difficult to generate trial purchases, due to the dominant perceptual position of the pioneer. However, a brand positioned near a differentiated later entrant can make it easier for both to generate trial in competition with the pioneer. Thus, some 'me-too' positions may be superior to others (Carpenter, 1988).

Bibliography

Abegglen, J. C. and G. Stalk. *Kaisha, the Japanese Corporation*, Basic Books, New York, 1985.

Abell, D. F. "Strategic Windows," *Journal of Marketing*, 42, July 1978, pp. 21–26.

Abernathy, W. J. and K. Wayne. "Limits of the Learning Curve," *Harvard Business Review*, 52, 1974, pp. 109–19.

Anderson C. R. and F. T. Paine, "PIMS: A Reexamination," *Academy of Management Review*, 3, July 1978, pp. 602–12.

Arrow, K. "Economic Welfare and the Allocation of Resources to Innovation." In R. Nelson (ed.), *The Rate and Direction of Inventive Activity.* Universities-National Bureau Conference Series, No. 14, Arno Press, New York, 1962.

Baldwin, W. L. and G. L. Childs. "The Fast Second and Rivalry in Research and Development," *Southern Economic Journal*, 36, 1969, pp. 18–24.

Bevan, A. "The U.K. Potato Crisp Industry, 1960–72: A Study of New Entry Competition," *Journal of Industrial Economics*, XXII, June 1974, pp. 281–97.

Bond, R. S. and D. F. Lean. *Sales, Promotion and Product Differentiation in Two Prescription Drug Markets*. U.S. Federal Trade Commission, Washington, DC, 1977.

Boulding, W. and M. J. Moore. "Pioneering and Profitability: Structural Estimates from a Nonlinear Simultaneous Equations Model with Endogenous Pioneering." Research Paper, Fuqua School of Business, Duke University, May 1987.

Bresnahan, T. F. "Post-Entry Competition in the Plain Paper Copier Market," *American Economic Review*, 75, May 1985, pp. 15–19.

Bright, A. A. *The Electric Lamp Industry*, Macmillan, New York, 1949.

Brock, G. W. *The U.S. Computer Industry: A Study of Market Power*, Ballinger Publishing Company, Cambridge, MA, 1975.

Buzzell, R. D. and B. T. Gale. *The PIMS Principles: Linking Strategy to Performance*, Free Press, New York, 1987.

Cady, J. F. "Marketing Strategies in the Information Industry." In R. D. Buzzell (ed.), *Marketing in an Electronic Age*. Harvard Business School Press, Boston, 1985.

Carpenter, G. S. "Market Pioneering and Competitive Positioning Strategy," *Annales de Telecommunications* (forthcoming 1988).

Carpenter, G. S. and K. Nakamoto. "Market Pioneers, Consumer Learning, and Product Perceptions: A Theory of Persistent Competitive Advantage." Research Paper, Columbia University and University of California, November 1986.

Chandler, A. D., Jr. *The Visible Hand: The Managerial Revolution in American Business*. Belknap Press of Harvard University Press, Cambridge, MA, 1977.

Conner, K. R. "Strategies for Product Cannibalism," *Strategic Management Journal*, 9 (Special Issue), 1988, pp. 9–26.

Cooper, A. C. and D. Schendel. "Strategic Responses to Technological Threats," *Business Horizons*, 19, February 1976, pp. 61–9.

Davidson, J. H. "Why Most New Consumer Brands Fail," *Harvard Business Review*, 54, March–April 1976, pp. 117–22.

Dixit, A. "The Role of Investment in Entry Deterrence," *Economic Journal*, 90, 1980, pp. 95–106.

Eaton, B. C. and R. Lipsey. "The Theory of Market Preemption: The Persistence of Excess Capacity and Monopoly in Growing Spatial Markets," *Economica*, 46, 1979, pp. 149–58.

Eaton, B. C. and R. Lipsey. "Capital, Commitment and Entry Equilibrium," *Bell Journal of Economics*, 12, 1981, pp. 593–604.

Eaton, B. C. and R. Ware. "A Theory of Market Structure with Sequential Entry," *Rand Journal of Economics*, 18, Spring 1987, pp. 1–16.

Farrell, J. and G. Saloner. "Installed Base and Compatibility: Innovation, Product Preannouncements and Predation," *American Economic Review*, 76, December 1986, pp. 940–55.

Fast, N. "Lincoln Electric Company." Working Paper Case No. 376–028, Harvard Business School, 1975.

Foster, R. N. *Innovation: The Attacker's Advantage*. Summit Books, New York, 1986.

Fudenberg, D., R. Gilbert, J. Stiglitz and J. Tirole. "Preemption, Leapfrogging, and Competition in Patent Races," *European Economic Review*, 22, June 1983, pp. 3–31.

Fudenberg, D. and J. Tirole. "Capital as a Commitment: Strategic Investment to Deter Mobility," *Journal of Economic Theory*, 31, December 1983, pp. 227–50.

Fudenberg, D. and J. Tirole. "The Fat-Cat Effect, the Puppy-Dog Ploy, and the Lean and Hungry Look," *American Economic Review*, 74, May 1984, pp. 361–66.

Fudenberg, D. and J. Tirole. "Preemption and Rent Equalization in the Adoption of New Technology," *Review of Economic Studies*, LII , 1985, pp. 383–401.

Gal-Or, E. "First Mover and Second Mover Advantages," *International Economic Review*, 26, October 1985, pp. 649–53.

Ghemawat, P. "Capacity Expansion in the Titanium Dioxide Industry," *Journal of Industrial Economics*, XXXIII, December 1984, pp. 145–63.

Ghemawat, P. "Drastic Product Innovations Under Uncertainty." Working paper, Harvard Business School, 1986a.

Ghemawat, P. "Wal-Mart Stores" Discount Operations." Working Paper case No. 0–387–018, Harvard Business School, 1986b.

Ghemawat, P. and A. M. Spence. "Learning Curve Spillovers and Market Performance," *Quarterly Journal of Economics*, 100, 1985, pp. 839–52.

Gilbert, R. J. "Pre-emptive Competition." In J. E. Stiglitz and G. F. Mathewson (eds), *New Developments in the Analysis of Market Structure*. MIT Press, Cambridge, MA, 1986.

Gilbert, R. J. and R. G. Harris. "Investment Decisions with Economies of Scale and Learning," *American Economic Review*, 71, May 1981, pp. 172–77.

Gilbert, R. J. and R. G. Harris. "Competition with Lumpy Investment," *Rand Journal of Economics*, 15, Summer 1984, pp. 197–212.

Gilbert, R. J. and D. M. G. Newbery. "Preemptive Patenting and the Persistence of Monopoly," *American Economic Review*, 72, June 1982, pp. 514–26.

Glazer, A. "The Advantages of Being First," *American Economic Review*, 75, June 1985, pp. 473–80.

Guasch, J. L. and A. Weiss. "Adverse Selection of Markets and the Advantages of Being Late," *Quarterly Journal of Economics*, May 1980, pp. 453–66.

Hannan, M. T. and J. Freeman. "Structural Inertia and Organizational Change," *American Sociological Review*, 49, April 1984, pp. 149–64.

Harvard Business School. "Deere & Company: Industrial Equipment Operations," case no. 577–112, 1977.

Hirshleifer, J. "The Private and Social Value of Information and the Reward to Inventive Activity," *American Economic Review*, 61, 1971, pp. 561–74.

Jacobson, G. and J. Hillkirk. *Xerox: An American Samurai*, Macmillan, New York, 1986.

Johnson, R. N. and A. Parkman. "Spatial Monopoly, Non-Zero Profits and Entry Deterrence: The Case of Cement," *Review of Economics and Statistics*, 65, August 1983, pp. 431–38.

Judd, K. L. "Credible Spatial Preemption," *Rand Journal of Economics*, 16, Summer 1985, pp. 153–166.

Katz, M. L. and C. Shapiro. "Technology Adoption in the Presence of Network Externalities," *Journal of Political Economy*, 94, August 1986, pp. 822–41.

Klemperer, P. "Markets with Consumer Switching Costs." Ph.D. thesis, Graduate School of Business, Stanford University, 1986.

Lambkin, M. "Order of Entry and Performance in New Markets," *Strategic Management Journal*, 9 (Special Issue) 1988, pp. 127–40.

Levin, R., A. Klevorick, R. Nelson and S. G. Winter. "Survey Research on R&D Appropriability and Technical Opportunity —Part I: Appropriability." Working Paper, Yale University, July 1984.

Lieberman, M. "The Learning Curve, Pricing and Market Structure in the Chemical Processing Industries," Ph.D. thesis, Harvard University, 1982.

Lieberman, M. "The U.S. Magnesium Industry." Stanford University Business Case No. S-BP-231, 1983.

Lieberman, M. "Excess Capacity as a Barrier to Entry: An Empirical Appraisal," *Journal of Industrial Economics*, 35, June 1987a, pp. 607–27.

Lieberman, M. "The Learning Curve, Barriers to Entry, and Competitive Survival in the Chemical Processing Industries." Unpublished, Graduate School of Business, Stanford University, March 1987b.

Lieberman, M. "The Learning Curve, Diffusion and Competitive Strategy," *Strategic Management Journal*, 8, September–October 1987c, pp. 441–52.

Lippman, S. A. and Rumelt, R. P. "Uncertain Imitability: An Analysis of Interfirm Differences in Efficiency Under Competition," *Bell Journal of Economics*, 13, Autumn 1982, pp. 418–38.

MacMillan, I. C. "Preemptive Strategies," *Journal of Business Strategy*, 4, Fall 1983, pp. 16–26.

MacMillan, I. C. "Preemptive Strategies." In W. Guth (ed.), *Handbook of Business Strategy*, Warren, Gorham & Lamont, New York, 1984.

Main, 0. W. *The Canadian Nickel Industry*. University of Toronto Press, Toronto, 1955.

Mansfield, E. *Industrial Research and Technological Innovation: An Econometric Analysis*, W. W. Norton Company, New York, 1968.

Mansfield, E. "How Rapidly Does New Industrial Technology Leak Out?" *Journal of Industrial Economics*, XXXIV, December 1985, pp. 217–23.

Mansfield, E., M. Schwartz, and S. Wagner. "Imitation Costs and Patents: An Empirical Study," *Economic Journal*, 91, December 1981, pp, 907–18.

Montgomery, D. B. "New Product Distribution: An Analysis of Supermarket Buyer Decisions," *Journal of Marketing* Research, 12, August 1975, pp. 255–64.

Porter, M. *Interbrand Choice, Strategy and Bilateral Market Power*. Harvard University Press, Cambridge, MA, 1976.

Porter, M. *Competitive Strategy*. Free Press, New York, 1980.

Porter, M. "Strategic Interaction: Some Lessons from Industry Histories for Theory and Anti-Trust Policy." In S. Salop (ed.), *Strategy, Predation and Anti-Trust Analysis*. Washington: FTC, 1981.

Prescott, E. and M. Visscher. "Sequential Location Among Firms with Foresight," *Bell Journal of Economics*, 8, 1977, pp. 378–93.

Rao, R. and D. Rutenberg. "Pre-empting an Alert Rival: Strategic Timing of the First Plant by Analysis of Sophisticated Rivalry," *Bell Journal of Economics*, 10, 1979, pp. 412–28.

Reinganum, J. F. "Uncertain Innovation and the Persistence of Monopoly," *American Economic Review*, 73, September 1983, pp. 741–48.

Ries, A. and J. Trout. *Marketing Warfare*, McGraw-Hill, New York, 1986.

Robinson, W. T. "Sources of Market Pioneer Advantages: The Case of Industrial Goods Industries," *Journal of Marketing Research*, (forthcoming, September 1988).

Robinson, W. T. and C. Fornell. "The Sources of Market Pioneer Advantages in Consumer Goods Industries," *Journal of Marketing Research*, 22, August 1985, pp. 297–304.

Rumelt, R. "Theory, Strategy and Entrepreneurship." In D. Teece (ed.), *Strategy & Organization for Industrial Innovation and Renewal*. Ballinger, Cambridge, MA, 1987.

SECTION VI

Perspectives on Action Learning in Marketing

The final section is devoted to perspectives on action learning in marketing, and more particularly to questions frequently raised by students, professors, and observers regarding the validity and value of *Markstrat* as an educational tool.

The Role of Simulations

The first article in this section, by Professor Larréché, positions the simulation against the alternative educational approaches of readings, lectures, case studies, and practice. He argues that the traditional educational approaches based on readings and lectures provide an incomplete coverage of the learning process for action-oriented disciplines like strategic marketing. Case studies were the original method for overcoming this failure of traditional teaching methods. Simulations have become a recent edition to the educator's kit of tools. Like the case method, simulations emphasize the application of concepts in an action oriented environment. The author describes the use of simulations in research and teaching in both academic and business settings as a "simulated environment laboratory." He then concludes with a typology of simulated environment laboratories and describes where *Markstrat* is positioned within this typology.

Demand Functions in Marketing Simulations

Professor Lambert reviews and compares the behavior of eight different marketing simulations. The author's concern is that the sales behavior of a simulation should be reasonable and that students should not learn false or unsubstantiated principles. The fundamental issue is whether demand functions in marketing simulations are "compensatory functions" or "non-compensatory" functions. In compensatory functions a change in one element can be offset by a change in another element. This can lead to both unreasonable and unsubstantiated results. Of these various simulations compared in this paper, *Markstrat* is the only one with non-linear, non-compensatory demand functions. With this underlying structure, *Markstrat* produces reasonable behavior, regardless of the vagaries of student input. The lessons of *Markstrat* closely mirror the lessons of the real world in this regard.

Learning from Success and Failure

Learning to mediate and adapt to a complex, ambiguous, dynamic environment is an important determinant of the health and survival of an organization. Professors Lant and Montgomery review the process of organizational learning from strategic

success and failure in the *Markstrat* environment. This paper illustrates how the simulated environment laboratory can be used for study of organizational learning in a competitive market. The authors argue that attainment discrepancy, the difference between aspirational levels and actual performance, determines the level of ambition, the level of risk taking, and the extent of innovative search activity by an organization. For example, an organization performing well will want to maintain its position and thus will shun risky choices, while an organization performing poorly can only improve its position by taking some big risks. The authors document carefully the process by which organizations learn from their strategic success and failure.

Experiences in Strategic Marketing Education

Thousands of managers in executive programs worldwide have learned strategic marketing principles in the *Markstrat* environment. The next two articles in this section review the use and flexibility of *Markstrat* in executive education programs, and present the opinions and perceptions of hundreds of executives on the value and validity of *Markstrat* as a learning environment.

The experience of International Computers Limited (ICL) over a six-year period involving over 1700 managers and staff with *Markstrat* is described in the article by Harvey Dodgson. The author reviews the ability of *Markstrat* to adapt to widely different geographic regions in the world, very different management backgrounds and experience, a wide variety of learning styles, and every position in the learning cycle. The author also documents the robust theory base which is the foundation of the *Markstrat* environment.

Tom Kinnear and Sharon Klammer report on managers' opinions and perceptions of *Markstrat* as it is used in the General Electric Company at the core of its Advanced Marketing Management Seminar (AMMS). Their results were based upon a survey of nearly 200 participants in recent General Electric AMMS programs. The results of their survey produced a profile of opinions on *Markstrat*'s general value, and its specific characteristics. The authors include direct quotes on the value of the *Markstrat* experience from General Electric managers in all divisions of the company. This is the first study to explicitly measure the educational impact of *Markstrat* on a management audience. The power of *Markstrat* to teach important marketing concepts and reflect competitive realities in diverse businesses is documented in their results. *Markstrat* is truly a powerful teaching tool. The authors argue there is also a profound conclusion for academic researchers in these results. One of the problems of academic researchers who study strategic marketing is to find a manageable environment that is sufficiently real to provide external validity to their studies. The authors argue that *Markstrat* is such an environment. ■

37

On Simulations in Business Education & Research

Jean-Claude Larréché

With the development of the computer and telecommunications technology, simulations constitute the most action-oriented form of education. They will probably become the most effective, convenient, and economical form of education.

This article first reviews the history of business simulations and their use in education and research. The concept of a simulated environment laboratory is then proposed based on the experience in the development of the *Markstrat* simulation and in its use over a period of 10 years. Such a laboratory is composed of a simulation designed to provide a realistic environment irrespective of its potential use, as opposed to simulations aiming at specific educational or research applications. The design characteristics and a typology of such simulated environment laboratories are discussed.

A GAME IS A TOOL THAT ALLOWS individuals to use and develop their decision-making skills in a fictitious competitive environment. Gaming has been an important and long tradition in the history of humans. From the earlier games of go and chess to the relatively more recent monopoly, pacman and other electronic games, it has been an important activity of children and adults alike.

This gaming approach has also been adopted to train people in a number of areas as diverse as politics, the military, science, history, geography, languages, religion, or business [24]. Games played for leisure and for education share the emphasis placed on quality and speed of decision making, as well as the motivating aspects of competition and rapid feedback. A major difference, however, is that the fictitious environment of an educational game has to be a faithful, although simplified, representation of the real world for the area of study. Consequently, the educational game needs also to be a simulation, and the two words are often used interchangeably. The effectiveness of an educational game will depend largely on the quality of the simulation in representing the behavior of the real world under study.

The early business games were developed in the 1950s as one of the contributions of operations research. The American Management Association produced the Top Management Simulation in 1957 and Andlinger published a description of his manually rated business game in 1958 [2 in 43, 46] .In 1961, Cohen and Rhenman were already discussing in *Management Science* the role of management games in education *and* research [6]. In 1962, the first survey of marketing games was published in the *Journal of Marketing* [39]. It was in the early 1960s that some business games, such as the Carnegie Tech Management Game and INTOP [7, 53] became widely available. By 1968, virtually all business schools were using at least some form of game in their teaching programs [21]. By 1970, it was estimated that over 200 games were in existence and over 100,000 executives had been exposed to them [50].

Today, all business educators, researchers, and managers are aware of the existence of simulations and a good proportion of them has used at least one. The use of business simulations has considerably evolved in the last 10 years from both the demand and supply point of view. On the demand side, the higher level of management sophistication

Jean-Claude Larréché is Professor of Marketing, INSEAD, Fontainebleau, France.

and the greater intensity of competition have placed pressures on individuals and corporations to identify more effective training techniques. On the supply side, the increased availability of microcomputers has greatly facilitated the development and usage of computerized simulations. The *Markstrat* simulation that is used in the research projects presented in this special issue of *The Journal of Business Research* is an example of this evolution [32]. The *Markstrat* simulation is today regularly used by several hundred business schools and corporations in many countries. In several companies, more than 500 managers have been exposed to the simulation in training seminars and this number exceeds 1,000 in a few corporations. Several research projects, in addition to those reported in this issue, have used the simulation to test specific hypotheses.

We will first try to summarize some issues raised in the use of business simulations in teaching and research. The concept of a simulated environment laboratory will then be proposed and discussed on the basis of the 10 years of experience with the *Markstrat* simulation.

The Use of Simulations for Business Education

The traditional education paradigm considers education to be primarily concerned with the transmission of knowledge. Since humans first existed, knowledge has been passed from generation to generation first in a verbal way and then in written form. Today, students of all ages in schools of different levels assimilate knowledge in a wide variety of disciplines by reading books and articles and listening to lectures. Over the centuries, the educational approach has, in the main, not changed in terms of its objective (the transmission of knowledge) nor in terms of the tools employed (readings and lectures). The content of traditional disciplines has substantially changed and new ones have been added, but new approaches and tools have only had a marginal effect compared to the mainstream of educational activities.

The traditional educational approach is well adapted to disciplines that are uniquely concerned with knowledge. This is in particular the case of the older disciplines such as languages, history, geography, philosophy, or mathematics. In each of these areas, competence is directly related to knowledge. For instance, being or not being a good mathematician is directly related to knowing or not knowing mathematical formulae and logic.

This is in contrast to other disciplines where knowledge is a means to an end but not an end in itself. Competence in marketing is related to taking the right course of action. One may have read all existing articles on marketing and know all the theories and still be a poor marketing practitioner if this knowledge is not properly translated into action. This is true of many other action-oriented disciplines such as medicine, law, or aviation. An essential part of the learning process in these fields is actually to perform tasks in a real environment. The proper realization of these tasks is the real objective of education. Knowledge acquisition is also an important, and often early, phase of the learning process, but should not be the only one.

The traditional educational approach exclusively using readings and lectures provides an incomplete coverage of the learning process for action-oriented disciplines. As a result, only a small fraction of the knowledge acquired has an effective impact on performance. Most of the remaining knowledge is not translated into action and is progressively forgotten. At the other extreme, one can try to learn by doing, without having first developed an adequate knowledge base. While this approach is probably perceived to be effective by those who have survived the experience, it is almost certainly the most expensive one and clearly a luxury in today's highly competitive world.

In between these two extreme educational approaches, two methods have been increasingly used in action-oriented disciplines: case studies and simulations. They have attempted to bridge the gap between knowledge and action as illustrated in Figure 1.

The informal use of the case method concept is ancient, as debates on "how differently should they have done it" were apparently common features of most civilizations in politics, military, games, or sports. The first discipline to have used this tool systematically as part of a teaching approach was probably medicine. Either by observing actual patients brought to the classroom or by reading documents describing the conditions and reactions of such patients, generations of medical students have been exposed to many situations in which they had to make diagnoses and recommend courses of action. Case studies were then adopted by law schools, before being introduced to the field of business. Initially developed at the Harvard Business School, they have since been widely used by other business schools [38].

Simulations are much more recent than cases, and their first formal use for educational purposes probably occurred in the military with war games. They are now widely used in a number of action-oriented disciplines including pilot training and sports. The experience gained of simulations in business education is, however, much more limited to date than that of cases, and the lessons learned from the history of the case method apply here. Like the case method, simu-

Figure 1
Educational approaches

Learning Stage	Method	Approach
Knowledge ↓	Readings, Lectures	Traditional
	Case studies, Simulations	Action-oriented
Action	Doing	Practice

lations emphasize the application of concepts in an action-oriented approach. Simulations do go further into action as students will have to make decisions (as opposed to recommendations) and to live with their consequences. Over a number of iterations composed of simulated months, quarters, or years, students have to analyze situations, identify problems and opportunities, make decisions, and implement them. They have rapid feedback on the value of their decisions that, together with the motivating nature of the competitive situation, provides the context and the means for an effective learning experience [20, 25, 36].

Educators fall into different categories, from vigorous opponents to strong advocates of the simulation approach. The opponents doubt that learning of concepts can actually take place in the context of a simulation in which they believe the "gaming" aspects dominate. Advocates are convinced that simulations provide a valuable environment for the dynamic learning and application of concepts [16, 27, 51].

This divergence of opinion vis-à-vis the effectiveness of simulations as learning tools in business is basically due to the diversity of objectives and simulations. The objective of a simulation is to develop skills to effectively apply concepts through making decisions and taking appropriate courses of action. It complements other pedagogical approaches that focus simply on the transmission of knowledge as an objective [42]. If someone is concerned with knowledge only and not with the ability of students to put this knowledge into action, then a simulation, as a case, will have little marginal utility. In today's increasingly competitive environment, quality of action is crucial, and simulation is the approach that can best develop the ability to act effectively, short of real-life experience. This, however, requires simulations that can successfully represent realistic environments conducive to the application of relevant concepts.

The Use of Simulations for Business Research

As soon as business simulations became available, their potential use for research was identified. In the late 1950s, researchers started investigating the relationships between game performance and psychodemographic characteristics of participants (see, for instance, [23] and [45]). More than 20 years ago, the conclusion of an article entitled "The Potential of Business Gaming Methods in Research" was expressed as follows [3]:

> It is too early to make a final evaluation of business gaming as a research tool. But exploratory studies now available indicate substantial research potential in areas such as the role of information in complex decision making, profits to be gained by additional information, effect of organizational variables on decision making, and effect of various market structure, psychological, and related factors on individual and group behavior. Research in some of these difficult areas has probably been limited by available research tools.

The two main points of this conclusion are still valid in 1987: We are still at an early stage of research based on simulations, and we have had confirmation that there is a wide scope of research made possible by simulations.

Simulations provide an attractive experimental setting for research. If the simulation is sufficiently realistic, the decisions and the environment in which they are made represent real-world situations. Decisions are made successively over several simulated periods, allowing an explicit consideration of the time dimension. Measures of performance are readily available. Individual and group behavior can be observed and analyzed. Experimental conditions can be controlled relatively easily. The simulation is usually not explicitly administered for research purposes but for a more natural learning objective. Participants are motivated by the dynamic and competitive elements of the situation.

As a result of these attractive features of simulations as research tools, and with the increasing availability of various types of simulations, a substantial number of research projects have been developed in this area in the past 20 years [17]. The main topics of research can be grouped under three main categories:

Simulations as Teaching Tools

One of the first new avenues of research offered by the advent of business simulations was naturally to test the relative effectiveness of simulations as teaching tools. Several research projects have investigated specific issues such as the acquisition of international business knowledge [29], the effect of game complexity on learning [56], or the motivation of business-game participants [49]. A number of studies have attempted to measure the effectiveness of simulations in business-policy courses (see [57] for a review). The concept of effectiveness has progressively led to two separate notions of internal validity (meeting some short-term teaching objectives), and external validity (transferring academic insights into useful and effective real-world orientations, perceptions, and business career practices) [55]. External validity is obviously much more difficult to evaluate and most studies have addressed the issue of internal validity [44]. The main utility of this type of research is derived more from the development of evaluation methodologies than from the specific results obtained. Indeed, these results vary widely and particularly depend on the nature of the simulation, the learning situation, and the quality of the instructors.

Decision Making and Information Handling

Simulations provide a natural setting to analyze decision-making processes. Studies have, for instance, included investigations of consistency in decision making [22, 47], quality and speed of decisions [11], changes in risk behavior when decisions are made by groups instead of individuals [41], and the influence of aspiration levels on risk taking and innovation [31]. The presentation and use of information also can be effectively monitored within the context of a simulation. This has led to several projects on the relative effectiveness of various inquiry methods [10], the value of information [40], or the reactions to different information systems [12, 37].

Organization, Leadership, and Personality Traits

Simulations also create situations that are particularly appropriate for the study of group organization and leadership. Projects have explored the impact on performance of team size [58], organizational control [4], allocation of persons to tasks [15], and leadership style [48]. Negotiations and conflict within or between organizations also have been studied in controlled experiments based on simulations [1, 52]. The influence of personality [5, 26] and other individual traits [14] on various performance dimensions also have been investigated.

All the topics mentioned above relate broadly to *corporate behavior*, from the individual to the organizational level. Between the artificiality of a contrived experiment and the problem of isolating causal relationships in real situations, simulations offer an appropriate context in which to study the various facets of corporate behavior. In an increasingly competitive environment, more importance is given today to the analysis of *competitive behavior* within marketing.

There exists a great potential for the development of an experimentally based research field in marketing to study competitive behavior within the context of simulations. Such an area could at the same time build on the conceptual base of marketing strategy and the experimental tradition of consumer behavior. A number of important strategic issues relating to competitive behavior could be researched effectively in a simulated environment, such as barriers to entry, segmentation, competitive advantage [8], experience effects, or signalling. This direction presents great potential but, in order to be successful, depends on simulations that represent these strategic aspects with a high degree of realism.

The Concept of a Simulated Environment Laboratory

The dynamic qualities of simulations place them in a uniquely advantageous position for action-oriented education and for research into competitive behavior. Their potential contribution to teaching and research can, however, only be realized when they exhibit satisfactorily realistic behavior. In this respect, the most critical element of a business simulation concerns the interface between the firm, its competitors, and the market. The modeling of financial accounts or the flow of goods in manufacturing is a relatively deterministic process even if not always straightforward. The market and competitive interfaces cannot be completely specified by research, since they are specific to different business activities. These interfaces are of paramount importance as they drive the rest of the simulation.

The role of an advanced market simulation is to provide a realistic environment for a wide range of teaching and research applications that the designer is often unable to foresee. Therefore, the development of the simulation should be driven by the theoretical knowledge of market and competitive mechanisms and not by the pedagogical concepts it is designed to illustrate. If the body of knowledge available to the designer is coherent, the behavior of the simulation should automatically provide the context in which to apply the desired concepts, as well as many others known or unknown at the time of development. Such a tool can be called a *simulated environment laboratory.* It provides a general context for educational and research activities. It is the user, instructor, or researcher, who decides which concepts to apply in this environment, rather than this decision being dictated by the designer.

As illustrated in Figure 2, a simulated environment laboratory draws simultaneously from the academic and business worlds. Based mainly on academic research of market and competitive behavior, it should offer a realistic representation of the business world. It should exhibit both theoretical validity (being coherent with the existing body of knowledge) and behavioral validity (being coherent with the behavior of the real business environment).

It has been progressively realized that the *Markstrat* simulation was not only a marketing strategy game, but had the properties of a more general simulated environment laboratory. Its development was based on the integration of a diversity of known "microtheories" on market and competitive dynamics, rather than on narrow pedagogical objectives. This development philosophy was the basis of its theoretical validity. It has since been used for a wide variety of teaching and research purposes, many of which could not have been anticipated at the time of the design [8, 9, 19, 22,

Figure 2
The concept of a simulated environment laboratory.

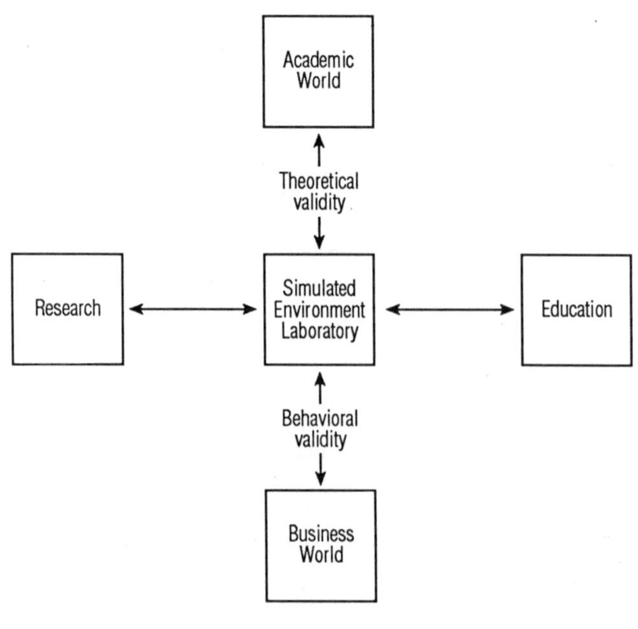

31, 47, 54]. Experienced business executives from diverse industries and countries have been exposed to the simulation and have found it to behave realistically. This positive feedback from experienced business executives over a 10-year period has established its behavioral validity [13, 28].

There are a number of elements explaining why, rather than being used simply as a strategic marketing game, *Markstrat* has been increasingly recognized as a simulated environment laboratory. Different users in both the academic and business worlds have in fact emphasized different contributing factors. Based on the experience gathered to date, the three most important dimensions appear to be the representation of a hierarchy of effects, the use of noncompensatory functions, and a satisfactory information load.

The Representation of a Hierarchy of Effects

The market and competitive models of most simulations are represented by a direct response function of sales or market share to marketing instruments such as price, advertising, or size of the sales force. Such an aggregate form is an extremely truncated view of reality. It does not provide much assistance to students when sales levels are inadequate, except pushing them to "cut price," "spend more on advertising," or "increase the sales force." In practice, these are too simplistic and often misleading pieces of advice. In the hierarchy-of-effects approach, a given marketing instrument will have an impact on a multitude of intermediate variables that, in turn, interact eventually to determine a proper market response.

For instance, advertising in *Markstrat* has an influence on brand awareness, the relative positioning of the product and competitive offerings, the evolution of market segments' needs, the primary demand at the market-segment level, barriers to entry, the motivation of the sales force, and the readiness of distributors to carry the product. As a result of all these interactions, advertising will have an impact on product sales. The nature of this impact is, however, not predetermined and will vary according to the situation [18]. It can even be negative in the case of a poorly positioned product. This hierarchy of effects not only provides a level of realism, but also a degree of learning that cannot be obtained by direct aggregate response functions.

The Use of Noncompensatory Functions

Most simulations are based on compensatory functions where the effect of one variable can be offset by the effect of another variable. In this context, a decrease in demand due to an increase in price can, for instance, be compensated by higher advertising expenditures. In a review of eight marketing simulations, Lambert remarked that *Markstrat* was the only one using noncompensatory functions, and had a reasonable behavior "regardless of the vagaries of student-input" [30]. Although a compensatory function can be specified and parameterized more easily, it cannot simulate a realistic behavior over a wide range of input values. On the other hand, noncompensatory functions can be defined so that they replicate realistic behavior over the whole range of possible input values. Their parameterization, however, is probably more delicate.

A Satisfactory Information Load

Research that preceded the development of the *Markstrat* simulation confirmed that individuals of different cognitive complexity process information differently when using marketing models [33]. There exists for each individual an optimum level of information. Below this level, more information would lead to better decisions. Above this level, decision-making processes tend to deteriorate because of information overload. In practice, individuals develop defense mechanisms such as selective filtering to protect themselves from information overload, or they can search and find additional information when required. In the context of a simulation, as information is imposed on participants, it is important that the level of information provided is appropriate for the target audience. In the case of the *Markstrat* simulation, it was planned to make available a significant amount of information to challenge the decision-making processes of even experienced executives. Some items that were found to add complexity without a proportionate increase in educational utility were then deleted. Most of the information is also provided on an optional basis so that participants decide themselves the amount of information they wish to consult.

It is this third design element, the existence of an optimum information load, rather than conceptual or technological limitations, which constrains the universality of a single simulated environment laboratory. For instance, more elements could be added to the *Markstrat* simulation either by further detailing the implementation of specific marketing activities or by including more complete models of the manufacturing or financial functions. This would probably lead to an information overload for the participants and a reduction in the educational effectiveness, unless these additions were to be compensated by a withdrawal of some of the current features in the simulation.

Simulated environment laboratories are thus necessary, and it is probable that they will become available over time. A possible typology is illustrated in Figure 3. It is based on three dimensions:

1. *Conceptual Scope*. Three levels of conceptual scope have been identified: marketing management, marketing strategy, and corporate strategy. A marketing management simulation deals only with marketing-mix decisions such as pricing, advertising, or selling for one or two products in one or two markets. It concentrates on the management of existing products. In addition to marketing-mix considerations, a marketing-strategy simulation gives the opportunity to make decisions on product portfolio, market segmentation, and product-positioning issues. It requires a segmentation of markets, an evolving product line with suppressions and introductions, and hence the develop-

Figure 3
A proposed typology of simulated environment laboratories

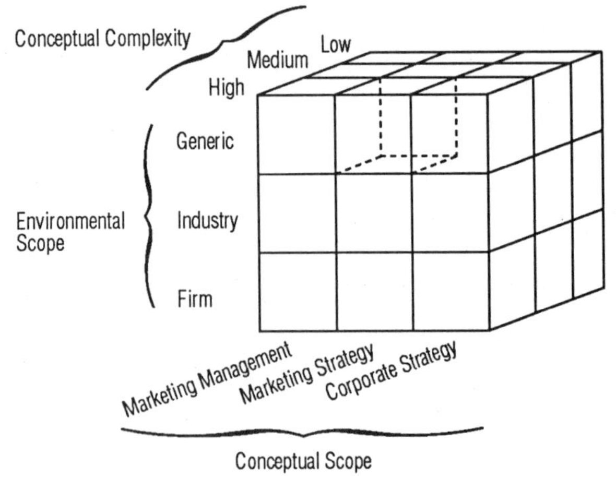

ment of nonmarketing functions such as research and development. A corporate-strategy simulation contains a broader coverage of many business functions such as manufacturing, finance, and marketing. It cannot, however, be as detailed in any of these functions as a specialized simulation.

2. *Conceptual Complexity.* To be consistent with the other dimensions, three levels of conceptual complexity are represented, although this scale is clearly continuous. The notion of conceptual complexity is linked mainly to the depth of the hierarchy of effects represented in the simulation. At one extreme, a simulation based on direct aggregate response functions has a very low conceptual complexity. At the other extreme, the depth of a hierarchy of effects is only limited by the resulting information load placed on participants.
3. *Environmental Scope.* The environmental scope of a simulation is generic when the concepts learned from using it are not limited to a specific environment. This approach is particularly appropriate with strategic concepts that are universal. A simulation can also be developed to represent the specificities of a given industry such as banking or distribution, or of a given firm. While the technology exists to design simulations with such a narrow environmental scope, their validity is limited to the specific firm for which they are developed.

In this typology, the *Markstrat* simulation corresponds to the following cell: marketing strategy, high conceptual complexity, and generic environmental scope. A number of simulations are available in the cells corresponding to low conceptual complexity both for marketing management and corporate strategy. In the area of marketing strategy in an industrial-goods environment, the *Industrat* and *Markops* simulations represent respectively high and medium levels of conceptual complexity [34, 35]. A number of development projects now in progress are aimed at other cells in this typology. Their development will better meet the diverse educational and research needs of the business and academic communities.

Conclusions

Simulations represent one of the most sophisticated and promising uses of technology in business education and research. At one end of the scale, progress made on the availability of large and fast computers has made possible the effective and convenient use of relatively complex models. At the other end, the proliferation of microcomputers allows participants to have direct access to part of the simulation, to develop decision aids and even simulations of a simulation. In each of the last three years, 150 management teams dispersed in different corporations all over Europe have, for instance, participated in an international *Markstrat* competition. In this distance learning event, each management team is in charge of a simulated firm and confronted with international competitors without having to leave the office. Each team has access to a microcomputer to process decisions and results contained on diskettes that are shipped between the teams and a central location. The development of telecommunications and networking will in the future provide opportunities for even more innovative and effective approaches.

With the development of the computer and telecommunications technology, simulations constitute the most action-oriented form of education. They will probably also become the most effective, convenient, and economical form of education. The efforts made today to better understand the use of simulations in teaching and research contribute to the development of more effective simulations. This turns their potential more and more into reality.

References

1. Ackelsberg, Robert, and Yukl, Gary, "Negotiated Transfer Pricing and Conflict Resolution in Organizations," *Decision Sciences*, 10 (July 1979), 387–398.
2. Andlinger, G. R., "Business Games-Play One," *Harvard Business Review*, 36 (March–April 1958), 115–125.
3. Babb, E. M., Leslie, M. A., and Van Slyke, M. D., "The Potential of Business-Gaming Methods in Research," *The Journal of Business*, 39 (1966), 465–472.
4. Baumler, John V., "Defined Criteria of Performance in Organizational Control," *Administrative Science Quarterly*, 16 (September 1971), 340–349.
5. Chanin, Michael N., and Schneer, Joy A., "A Study of the Relationship between Jungian Personality Dimensions and Conflict-Handling Behavior," *Human Relations*, 37 (October 1984), 863–879.
6. Cohen, Kalman J., and Rhenman, E., "The Role of Management Games in Education and Research," *Management Science*, 7 (July 1961), 131–166.
7. Cohen, Kalman J., Dill, William R., Kuehn, Alfred A., and Winters, Peter R., *The Carnegie Tech Management Game*. Richard D. Irwin, Homewood, IL, 1964.
8. Cook, Victor J. Jr., and Page, John R., "Assessing Marketing Risk," *Journal of Business Research*, 15 (1987).

9. Cook, Victor J. Jr., and Strong, Edward C., "Strategic Concepts in Markstrat." Working paper no. 85–1445–07, A. B. Freeman School of Business, Tulane University, December 1985.
10. Cosier, Richard A., and Rechner, Paula L., "Inquiry Method Effects on Performance in a Simulated Business Environment," *Organizational Behavior and Human Decision Processes*, 36 (August 1985), 79–95.
11. Davis, D. L., "Are Some Cognitive Types Better Decision Makers Than Others? An Empirical Investigation," *Human Systems Management*, 3 (1982), 165–172.
12. Dickson, Gary W., Senn, James A., and Chervany, Norman L., "Research in Management Information Systems: The Minnesota Experiments," *Management Science*, 23 (May 1977), 913–923.
13. Dodgson, Harvey, "Management Learning in *Markstrat*: The ICL Experience," *Journal of Business Research*, 15 (1987).
14. Eccles, A. J., and Wood, D., "How Do Managers Decide?" *The Journal of Management Studies*, 9 (October 1972), 291–302.
15. Etzion, Dalia, and Segev, Eli, "Competence and Task Allocation in a Simulated Work Environment," *Simulation & Games*, 15 (December 1984), 395–413.
16. Fripp, John, "Business Games Can Be Educational Too!" *Journal of European Industrial Training*, 8 (June 1984), 27–32.
17. Fripp, John, "Games for Research," *Journal of European Industrial Training*, 8 (August 1984), 17–22.
18. Gatignon, Hubert, "Strategic Studies in Markstrat," *Journal of Business Research*, 15 (1987).
19. Glazer, Rashi, Steckel, Joel, and Winer, Russell S., "Group Processes and Marketing Performance," *Journal of Business Research*, 15 (1987).
20. Gordon, Jack, "Games Managers Play," *Training*, 22 (July 1985), 30–47.
21. Graham, Robert G., and Gary, Clifford F., *Business Games Handbook*. American Management Association, New York, 1969.
22. Hogarth, Robin M., and Makridakis, Spyros, "The Value of Decision Making in a Complex Environment: An Experimental Approach," *Management Science*, 27 (January 1981), 93–107.
23. Hoggatt, A. C. "An Experimental Business Game," *Behavioral Science*, 4 (October 1959), 192–203.
24. Horn, Robert E., *The Guide to Simulations/Games for Education and Training*, 3rd ed. Didactic Systems, Cranford, NJ, 1977.
25. Hunter, Bill, and Price, Margaret, "Business Games: Underused Learning Tools?" *Industry Week*, August 18, 1980, pp. 52–56.
26. Jones, Robert E., and White, Charles S., "Relationships among Personality, Conflict Resolution Styles, and Task Effectiveness," *Group & Organization Studies*, 10 (June 1985), 152–167.
27. Keys, Bernard, "Improving Management Development through Simulation Gaming," *Journal of Management Development*, 5, 41–50.
28. Kinnear, Thomas C., and Klammer, Sharon, "Management Perspectives on Markstrat: The GE Experience and Beyond," *Journal of Business Research*, 15 (1987).
29. Klein, Ronald D., "Adding International Business to the Core Program via the Simulation Game," *Journal of International Business Studies*, 15 (Spring/Summer 1984), 151–159.
30. Lambert, David R., "On Compensatory Demand Functions in Marketing Simulations," in *Experimental Learning Enters the Eighties*. Daniel C. Brenenstuhl and William D. Biggs, eds., Proceedings of the 7th Annual Conference of the Association for Business Simulation and Experimental Learning, Dallas, Texas, April 9–12, 1980.
31. Lant, Theresa K., and Montgomery, David B., "Learning From Strategic Success and Failure," *Journal of Business Research*, 15 (1987).
32. Larréché, Jean-Claude, and Gatignon, Hubert, *Markstrat: A Marketing Strategy Game*. Palo Alto, CA, The Scientific Press, 1977.
33. Larréché, Jean-Claude, "Integrative Complexity and the Use of Marketing Models," in *The Implementation of Management Science*. Robert Doktor, Randall L. Schultz, and Dennis P. Slevin, eds., North Holland, Amsterdam, 1979, pp. 171–187.
34. Larréché, Jean-Claude, and Weinstein, David, *Industrat: A Strategic Industrial Marketing Simulation*. Prentice-Hall, Englewood Cliffs, NJ, in press.
35. Larréché, Jean-Claude, *Markops: A Simulation of Marketing Operations*. Strat*X, Boston, in press.
36. Lloyd, D. C. F., "An Introduction to Business Games," *Industrial and Commercial Training*, 10 (January 1978), 11–18.
37. Lucas, Henry C. Jr., and Nielsen, Norman R., "The Impact of the Mode of Information Presentation on Learning and Performance," *Management Science*, 26 (October 1980), 982–993.
38. McNair, Malcolm P., ed., *The Case Method at the Harvard Business School*. McGraw-Hill, New York, 1954.
39. McRaith, J. F., and Goeldner, C. R., "A Survey of Marketing Games," *Journal of Marketing*, 26 (July 1962), 69–72.
40. Mock, Theodore J., "The Value of Budget Information," *The Accounting Review*, 48 (July 1973), 520–534.
41. Muhs, William F., and Justis, Robert T., "Group Choices in a Simulated Management Game," *Simulation & Games*, 12 (December 1981), 451–465.
42. Neider, Linda L., "Training Effectiveness: Changing Attitudes," *Training and Development Journal* (December 1981), 24–28.
43. Neuhauser, John J., "Business Games Have Failed," *Academy of Management Review*, 1 (October 1976), 124–129.
44. Norris, Dwight R., and Snyder, Charles A., "External Validation of Simulation Games, *Simulation & Games*, 13 (March 1982), 73–85.
45. Purdy, M. M., "Management Decision-Making Simulation: A Study of Psychological Relationships." Unpublished Ph.D. dissertation, Purdue University, 1959.
46. Ricciardi, Frank M., et al., *Top Management Simulation: The A.M.A. Approach*. Elizabeth Marting, ed., American Management Association, 1957.
47. Ross, William T., "A Re-examination of the Results of Hogarth and Makridakis' 'The Value of Decision Making in a Complete Environment: An Experimental Approach,' " *Management Science*, 33 (February 1987), 288–296.
48. Rowland, K. M., and Gardner, D. M., "The Uses of Business Gaming in Education and Laboratory Research," *Decision Sciences*, 4 (April 1973), 268–283.
49. Schriesheim, Chester A., and Yaney, Joseph P., "The Motivation of Business Game Participants," *Training and Development Journal* (August 1975), 11–15.
50. Shim, Jae K., "Management Game Simulation: Survey and New Direction," *University of Michigan Business Review*, 30 (May 1978), 26–29.
51. Sims, Henry P. Jr., and Hand, Herbert H., "Simulation Gaming: The Confluence of Quantitative and Behavioral Theory," *Academy of Management Review*, 1 (July 1976), 109–113.

52. Slusher, E. Allen, Sims, Henry P. Jr., and Thiel, John, "Bargaining Behavior in a Business Simulation Game," *Decision Sciences*, 9 (April 1978), 310–321.
53. Thorelli, H. B., Graves, R. L., and Howells, L. T., "The International Operations Simulation at the University of Chicago," *Journal of Business*, 35 (July 1962).
54. Utsey, Marjorie F., "Profit Potential as a Martingale Process," *Journal of Business Research*, 15 (1987).
55. Wolfe, Joseph, "Correlates and Measures of the External Validity of Computer-Based Business Policy Decision-Making Environments," *Simulation & Games*, 7 (December 1976), 411–438.
56. Wolfe, Joseph, "The Effects of Game Complexity on the Acquisition of Business Policy Knowledge," *Decision Sciences*, 9 (January 1978), 143–155.
57. Wolfe, Joseph, "The Teaching Effectiveness of Games in Collegiate Business Courses," *Simulations & Games*, 16 (September 1985), 251–288.
58. Wolfe, Joseph, and Chacko, Thomas I., "Team-Size Effects on Business Game Performance and Decision-Making Behaviors," *Decision Sciences*, 14 (January 1983), 121–133.

On Compensatory Demand Functions in Marketing Simulations

David R. Lambert

Most marketing simulations can be coaxed into anomalous behavior. A major reason is the use of a compensatory demand function which does not adequately portray marketplace behavior.

Given the usual pedagogical environment in which simulations are used, the potential for teaching the wrong things through their use is very great, especially since it appears that most marketing simulations can be coaxed into anomalous behavior. It is argued in this paper that a major reason for this potentially anomalous behavior is the use of a compensatory demand function which, while possessing a desired level of algorithmic simplicity, does not adequately portray marketplace behavior. A general approach to a solution to this problem is suggested.

THE WIDESPREAD USE of computerized simulations as pedagogical aids in schools of management is seen as a positive sign that professors are interested in innovative ways to move beyond the traditional lecture format. Marketing has been a part of this trend to simulations in the classroom. The number of marketing simulations is increasing (albeit slowly), and presumably this reflects an increasing number of adoptions.[1] But it is important to recognize the large potential for teaching the wrong things when using simulations. Shubik singles-out a marketing cse to illustrate this point [12. p. 31]:

> A flagrant example of potential misuse has been in the modeling of advertising in business games. Even a brief glance at the literature on how advertising affects sales is sufficient to indicate that there is little substantiated theory on advertising, yet in many of the business games played both at universities and in business training programs, advertising has been thrown in as an *ad hoc* modification on demand with teaching results which could be damaging were it not for the basic skepticism of most of the players. It is important that players be warned against learning false or unsubstantiated principles.

David Lambert is Professor at San Francisco State University.

While Shubik's point is well taken concerning the lack of a theory of advertising, the modeling of the impact of advertising (and of other marketing mix elements) often does not even reflect the state of the art. While the lack of a comprehensive theory of the behavior of sales in response to marketing tactics is a handicap, still every effort must be made in designing these simulations to insure that sales behavior at least appears plausible.

Demand Functionsin Marketing Simulations

Broadly speaking, there are two approaches which might be taken to modeling the relationship between the demand for an individual firm's products and the firm's marketing mix: compensatory, or noncompensatory. This suggestion of a primary dichotomy of would-be demand functions borrows its terminology from psychological studies of human information processing [4]. Compensatory functions are those in which a change in one element can be offset by a change in another element. Noncompensatory functions, on the other hand, do not permit such trade-offs to be made. Both models may assume several different forms, a thorough discussion of which lies outside the scope of this paper.[2] A linear non-interactive compensatory function is typified by the familiar equation form:

$$Y = b_1X_1 + b_2X_2 + \cdots + b_iX_i \qquad (1)$$

And of course non-linearity and interactions may be added to this compensatory form through the use of exponents other than one, and the addition of one or more multiplicative terms. Noncompensatory functions were formulated originally as conceptual aids to the study of decision making and were not mathematically specified. More recently several of the noncompensatory forms have been defined mathematically [6].

If the commercially available marketing simulations are examined, one finds that almost all have compensatory demand functions. Eight simulations were considered for illustrative purposes for this paper. Of this group, all but one featured a compensatory demand function.[3]

Marketing Reality as Translated by Compensatory Demand Functions

Considering the nature of compensatory demand functions, it is evident that the marketplace impact of a given set of tactical decisions will be profoundly affected by the fact that these functions, by design, freely permit tactical element trade-offs to be made. Given a compensatory non-interactive demand function, it is possible, for example, to generate a reasonable level of demand with distribution set to zero if the other controllable elements are sufficiently high. Thus a product may sell well if enough is spent on advertising, price is (perhaps) low enough, and quality high enough, in spite of the fact that it is ostensively not available.

Interactive compensatory demand functions are more difficult to manipulate into anomalous behavior. One often seen method of implementing an interactive compensatory function is that of multiplicatively combining indices which represent a team's spending deviation from the mean for that element, where the mean is defined as one. The following is such a function:

$$DI_i = \prod_{j=1}^{n} I_{ij} \qquad (2)$$

where: DI_i = the demand index for firm i

I_{ij} = the expenditure index for element j for firm i

n = the number of controllable elements.

This approach handles situations such as the previous example of zero distribution very well (if the indices are not constrained). However, there are marketing mixes which are quite reasonable which will be penalized by this form of demand algorithm. Deviations in indices from the mean produce asymmetrical demand movements, such that a drop below unity in any index will produce a relatively larger decrease in demand than will be offset by a corresponding upward shift in another index. On the other hand, if all indices are greater than or equal to one, an increase in an index has a powerful upward impact upon the demand index. This can be illustrated by the following set of index numbers:

I_1	I_2	I_3	I_4	DI_i (equation 2)
1.0	1.0	1.0	1.0	1.00
1.0	1.0	0.8	1.2	0.96
1.0	1.0	0.2	1.8	0.36
1.0	1.0	1.3	0.7	0.91
1.0	1.0	1.5	1.0	1.50

Consider that I_3 is product quality, and I_4 price, where an increasing index number indicates increasing quality, or decreasing price. The second and third sets of indices are examples of a lower quality, lower price strategy. Neither of these sets of decisions is as effective in generating sales volume as is the first set of indices. In fact, before the third set of indices yields a demand index of one, the price index must be equal to five. In a similar fashion, we see that a high quality, high price strategy produces less demand—perhaps not unreasonable. The last example illustrates the direct impact of an above average element when the others are one. Thus we see that a demand function such as this one rapidly punishes those whose marketing mixes deviate by much from the mean, and provides pressures for "me too" strategies, and spending "wars." But rather than look at hypothetical sets of indices, let us consider the results of an experiment using actual marketing simulations.

Of the seven simulations examined for this paper which have compensatory demand functions, all but one have interactive compensatory formulations. Of this group (i.e. those with interactive compensatory functions), one was used to provide illustrative data; the selection of this particular simulation was based only upon its availability. In Table 1 the results of several trials are reported. The price shown is the mean price of a team's product mix; all other factors not shown in the table are held constant across all five teams.

The output of this simulation, summarized in Table 1, describe a strange circumstance. The product is not available,[4] yet sales are not too bad. The impact reduced demand makes in this instance may be eased a bit by increasing price 20% (trial 2), and the EPS discrepancy considerably reduced by eliminating advertising (trial 3). Since this particular simulation does not include advertising carryover effects, trial 3 is especially interesting. Admittedly these results were obtained with a knowledge of this simulation's operation, but the fact remains that the simulation should not behave in this fashion. This simulation performs in this manner because the marketing mix elements are constrained to non-zero lower limits, in an attempt to produce reasonable behavior in what the authors apparently believe to be a reasonable operating range. But artificially defining operating ranges, either through index limits or by non-linearities, does not eliminate the fundamental problem: a compensatory demand function.

A Suggested Solution

Obviously this paper is directed towards noncompensatory demand functions as a solution to the problem discussed. As

Table 1

		Mean Price	Total Salesforce	Total Advertising	Total Sales (in units)	EPS
Trial 1	Team Number 5	$330	0	$12,550,000	312,086	−$9.16
	Each Other Team	$330	1600	$12,550,000	682,437	−$ .22
Trial 2	Team Number 5	$397	0	$12,550,000	217,920	−$8.61
	Each Other Team	$330	1600	$12,550,000	672,535	−$ .72
Trial 3	Team Number 5	$330	0	$0	147,132	$ .72
	Each Other Team	$330	1600	$12,550,000	723,673	$1.34

noted earlier, some forms of noncompensatory (usually called configural) functions have been mathematically specified. Perhaps then all that needs to be done is to substitute one equation for another. For example, a conjunctive function (one of the configural forms) requires some minimum level on all elements to produce a non-zero demand. However the mathematical approximations of these configural functions often rely simply on particular non-linear interactive functions to generate a response surface corresponding to, for example, the conjunctive model. Simply substituting one non-linear compensatory equation for another will not solve the problem. Since these equations are compensatory approximations of noncompensatory systems, they can undoubtedly be coaxed into anomalous behavior.

One approach to modeling demand which offers promise as a solution is that of a two stage demand function: configural screening followed by a compensatory function. For example, the Keiser and Lupul simulation [9], features this two stage process in its handling of the distribution function. Without adequate distribution, this simulation severely restricts sales. What is needed to accomplish a configurally behaving demand function is not necessarily a pre-processing program as incorporated in the Keiser and Lupul game, but rather modeling each element of the marketing mix in terms of the state-of-the-art in marketing. For example, what does advertising do? Does it shift the demand function? In the economist's model this is advertising's impact on industry demand. But in marketing our view of the role of advertising is that of generating awareness and interest, affecting attitude and belief structures, and of interactively affecting responses to other marketing variables. At the very least, a product will not be too successful if the marketplace is unaware of it. Isn't this then the sort of process to model when attempting to simulate responses to marketing efforts? Such factors as brand awareness and product availability might be used as limiting (i.e. noncompensatory) factors in calculating sales potential.

Notes

1. For an estimate of the overall market for business simulations, and an overview of the problems in estimating this market, see [1].
2. The interested reader is referred to [13] for an overview of and literature references to these models.
3. The simulations reviewed were [2, 3, 5, 7, 8, 9, 10, 11]. The simulation with a noncompensatory demand function is *Markstrat* [10]. It is this simulation's reasonable behavior, regardless of the vagaries of student input, which inspired this paper.
4. In this simulation, the salesforce is responsible for servicing all existing accounts and cultivating new ones.

References

1. Biggs, William D. "Who is Using Computerized Business Games?: A View From the Publishers' Adoption Lists," In Samuel C. Certo and Daniel C. Brenenstuhl (eds.), *Insights into Experiential Pedagogy*, Proceedings of the Sixth Annual ABSEL Conference, 1979, pp. 202–206.
2. Boone, Louis E. and Edwin C. Hackleman, Jr., *Marketing Strategy: A Marketing Decision Game* (Columbus: Charles E. Merrill, 1975).
3. Bush, Ronald F. and Bob Brobst, *Marketing Simulation: Analysis for Decision Making* (New York: Harper and Row, 1979).
4. Coombs, C. H., *A Theory of Data* (New York: John Wiley and Sons, Inc., 1964).
5. Doddridge, Ben F. and J. Rodney Howard, *Operation Encounter: Marketing Decision Making in a Changing Environment* (Pacific Palisades, CA: Goodyear Publishing Company, 1975).
6. Einhorn, Hillel J. "Use of Nonlinear, Noncompensatory Models as a Function of Task and Amount of Information," *Organizational Behavior and Human Performance*, Vol. 6 (January 1971), pp. 1–27.
7. Faria, A. J., R. O. Nulsen, Jr., and J. L. Woznick, *Compete: A Dynamic Marketing Simulation* (Dallas, TX: Business Publications Inc., 1979).
8. Hinkle, Charles L. and Russell C. Koza, *Marketing Dynamics: Decision and Control* (New York: McGraw-Hill, 1975).
9. Keiser, Stephen K. and Max E. Lupul, *Marketing Interaction: A Decision Game* (Tulsa: PPC Books, 1977).
10. Larréché, Jean-Claude and Hubert Gatignon, *Markstrat: A Marketing Strategy Game* (Palo Alto, CA: The Scientific Press, 1977).
11. Ness, Thomas E. and Ralph L. Day, *Marketing in Action: A Decision Game* (Homewood, IL: Richard D. Irwin, 1978).
12. Shubik, Martin, *The Uses and Methods of Gaming* (New York: Elsevier, 1975).
13. Wright, Peter, "Consumer Choice Strategies: Simplifying vs. Optimizing," *Journal of Marketing Research*, Vol. 12 (February 1975), pp. 60–67.

39

Learning from Strategic Success & Failure

Theresa K. Lant & David B. Montgomery

Testing three models, this study has made significant steps toward the goal of contributing to our knowledge of decision making and learning in a complex and ambiguous setting.

Organizations facing complex, ambiguous, and dynamic environments find adaptive learning a key to survival and success. This study proposes three models of organization response in such environments: (1) A model of how aspiration levels or goals adapt over time, (2) a model of the riskiness of strategic choices made, and (3) a model of the innovativeness of search activities (R&D). In each model, the difference between performance and aspiration level is posited to be an important explanatory variable. Using the *Markstrat* game as a research environment, the data are consistent with all three models.

LEARNING TO MEDIATE and adapt to the environment are important determinants of organization health and even survival. Such learning occurs largely through organizational interaction with and observation of its environments. However, adaptive learning is difficult in the usual case where the relationship between an organization and its environment is complex, ambiguous, and dynamic. Thus, it is important for organizational theories of adaptation to address the question of how organizations learn in such situations.

The literature on organizational adaptation has typically addressed either of two questions. First, what type of decisions and behavior lead to adaptation? Second, how are such decisions made? The former question has been addressed, for example, by structural-contingencies theory [4, 18] and resource-dependence theory [31]. The latter has been addressed in the administrative theories of Barnard [1], Simon [35], and the organizational theories of March and Simon [25] and Cyert and March [6], and more recently by decision-process research, such as Weick [42], Cohen, March, and Olsen [5], and Dutton, Fahey, and Narayanan [8]. The present research addresses the latter issue by investigating the learning process that leads to decisions regarding strategic organizational adaptation. Specifically, we are concerned with how organizational goals and success in achieving these goals affect the setting of future goals, the riskiness of choices, and innovativeness of search activities.

The literatures that have delved into these issues include models of individual and organizational learning and adaptation, models of strategic decision making, cognitive and behavioral theories of individual decision making, and the work on human inference and attribution. The thread that ties these literatures together is evident in the typical situation facing a group of strategic decision makers. These decision makers take certain actions, monitor the activities of their organization and their environment, and then make future decisions concerning future organizational activities. It can generally be agreed that these individuals have the capability of learning from experience. Further, they enlist this ability when trying to adapt to their environments [6]. However, the relationships between individual, organizational, and environmental actions are often complex, ambiguous, and change rapidly [22]. Further, decision makers are subject to cognitive limitations, such as bounded rationality. This combination of factors creates barriers to effective, adaptive learning. How, then, do decision makers manage

Theresa K. Lant is Assistant Professor at the Leonard N. Stern School of Businedss, New York University. David B. Montgomery is the Robert A. Magowan Professor of Marketing at Stanford University.

under these circumstances? This issue is investigated by studying the decisions of several groups of players of the *Markstrat* marketing strategy game. *Markstrat* provides a complex and dynamic decision-making setting in which to study decision makers.

The Role of Aspirations in Organizational Learning

March and Simon [25] and Cyert and March [6] have suggested several mechanisms by which organizations can make decisions despite the complex situations that face them. March and Simon [25] have suggested that organizations set multiple operational goals rather than a general, nonoperational goal. Setting specific goals enables the organization to make concrete performance evaluations, which provide a basis for future action.

Cyert and March [6] model how organizational decision makers make basic operating and strategic decisions. Organizations face substantial complexity generated by the demands of multiple coalitions and interest groups that make up the organization and its environment. Response to this complexity involves attending to multiple goals and attempting to satisfice on each.

The present study explores whether goals, or aspiration levels, are attended to by decision makers, and if so, how performance relative to these aspirations affects the type of actions taken in trying to manage the organization-environment relationship. The aspiration levels of concern here are goals held by the dominant coalition regarding certain organizational outcomes, such as sales and market share. While early work on aspirations focused on individual behavior [20,34], later work has applied models of aspirations to the organizational domain [25,6]. Before discussing the possible effects of aspiration levels on behavior, it is important to understand the significance of aspiration levels alone to decision making. Specific attention to modeling organizational aspirations has been taken by Levinthal and March [19]. They developed a model of organizational learning and adaptation in which organizations set performance aspirations, compare actual performance to these aspirations, and modify future aspirations based on this comparison. Herriot, Levinthal, and March [10] extended this model to include organizational responses to other organizations in the environment. They added factors such as the diffusion of experience and the diffusion of aspirations across organizations. Thus, they modeled aspiration level as a function of the past performance of other organizations as well as the past performance of the focal organization.

The difference between the aspiration level for a period and the actual performance level is called *attainment discrepancy* [20]. Attainment discrepancy is calculated by subtracting aspiration level from actual performance achieved. The evaluation of new performance in light of one's attainment discrepancy generates a *feeling of success or failure*. Attainment discrepancy is used as a cue that determines the next aspiration level and affects other behavior. Thus, attainment discrepancy serves as a crucial piece of information that decision makers look for in assessing the organization-environment relationship, and that colors their perceptions of possibilities for action.

One key to the importance of attainment discrepancy is the degree of complexity and ambiguity that faces most decision makers. Concrete operational goals are set in organizations because they provide a concrete link to specific actions. A vague, nonoperational goal, such as maximizing long-term profit, provides little information for taking specific actions. The relationship between possible actions and this desired, but vague, outcome is ambiguous. A more concrete goal, about which one can receive concrete feedback, provides more information about which actions will lead to this goal, thus enhancing learning in this situation. Levinthal and March [19] found that organizations generally learned adaptively when there were strong, unambiguous signals. At the individual level, expectancy theory links environmental conditions, individual beliefs, and individual behavior. This research found that beneficial behavior was more likely when the links between components were clear [30,17]. Thompson and Tuden [38] classified organizational decision processes according to the certainty of cause-effect relations and the clarity of preferences. When there are clear preferences for goals, and the cause-effect relationship between means and goals is known, decisions can be made by computation. By setting concrete, agreed-upon goals, and gathering performance information, decision makers attempt to mold their ambiguous situation into one that approximates clear goal preferences and clear cause and effect relationships. There is substantial evidence that decision makers seek to simplify the decision situation facing them. For example, Payne [28] and Olshavsky [27] found that while simple tasks were evaluated holistically, more complex tasks were simplified by the use of decision rules that quickly eliminated large numbers of alternatives. Russo and Dosher [32] found that, even for simple tasks, subjects dimensionalized the task rather than examining it holistically.

Thus, in setting aspiration levels and comparing them with actual performance, decision makers are seeking clear signals about how they are doing. The value of attainment discrepancy is hypothesized to determine the level of aspiration set in the future, the level of risk taken in taking certain actions, and the extent of innovation in search activity.

Attainment Discrepancy and Riskiness of Choice

Several organization and cognitive psychology models have used aspiration levels as a key element. However, there has been little explicit use of the concept of attainment discrepancy, and little empirical work on setting aspirations and the effect of attainment discrepancy on behavior. In the cognitive psychology literature relating performance and risk taking, Payne, Laughunn, and Crum [29], Fishburn [9], and

Tversky and Kahneman [40] all suggest that aspiration levels, often conceptualized as a reference point or target return, serve as a cognitive frame of reference for decision makers, and thus should be incorporated as a concept in models of choice behavior. These researchers have found that individuals, rather than being uniformly risk averse or risk seeking, exhibit varying risk-taking behavior depending on their perceived performance position relative to some aspiration level.

Kahneman and Tversky's [12] prospect theory makes predictions about individual valuations of risky prospects. In simple terms, their theory states that, in contrast to the assumptions of expected utility theory, the carriers of value or utility are changes in wealth rather than final asset positions. The decision maker first simplifies the choice situation by coding the situation as either above or below the reference point. Then the decision maker determines how much he or she stands to lose or gain, relative to the reference point. One of prospect theory's predictions is that decision makers will exhibit risk-averse choices when faced with outcomes above their reference point, and risk-seeking choices when faced with outcomes below the reference point.

Several studies in the organization literature have also found that aspiration levels mediate the relationship between performance and risk. Consistent with a general prediction from prospect theory, Bowman [2] found that high average profit firms had lower risk over time. In a separate study [3], he found that individuals in a loss situation made more risk-seeking choices, and that firm performance was negatively related to the riskiness of decisions. In an early study of illegal business activity, Lane [15] found that poor performing firms were more likely to violate government regulations than other firms. Staw and Szwajkowski [36] found that firms cited for trade violations had significantly worse performance records than firms that were not cited. To the extent that illegal acts can be classified as high-risk activities, these findings support the predictions of organizational theory regarding performance and risk taking.

A common limitation, however, of the empirical work on the relationships between performance, aspirations, and risk taking is that aspiration levels have been assumed rather than measured directly. Also, in the organizational studies, risk tends to be measured post hoc. Research is needed in this area that measures aspirations and perceptions of risk as reported directly by decision makers. This study seeks to fill this gap.

The effect of context on risk taking in organizations is further explicated by March [21] in a model of variable risk preferences where aspirations adapt over time, and these changing aspirations form the context against which organizational decision makers make choices. March suggests that risk behavior varies depending on this contextual evaluation. An intelligent response to this contextual evaluation is to vary one's risk taking in the following way. An organization performing well wants to maintain its position, and thus will shun risky choices. However, an organization performing poorly will only have an opportunity to improve its position by taking some risks. Thus, the tendency to prefer risky alternatives when performance is poor and nonrisky alternatives when performance is good is shown to result in a lower probability of ruin than when risk preference remains stable across situations. This model also shows that when aspirations adapt over time, an organization with variable risk behavior will yield a higher average return than one with fixed risk behavior.

Attainment Discrepancy and Innovativeness of Search

Just as the desire for change, and thus the willingness to take risks, is evoked when performance is below a satisfactory level, search for substantial changes in current activities is likely to be evoked when performance associated with the status quo is unsatisfactory. Simon [35] introduced the idea that outcomes are coded by decision makers as either satisfactory or unsatisfactory, and that search for additional alternatives is a response to unsatisfactory outcomes. The original theory of satisficing implied that organizations would innovate when in trouble [23]. March and Simon [25] suggest that one implication of satisficing behavior is that no action or change is required as long as a satisfactory level of performance is met, where "no action" is defined as continuity of current activities, not a lack of activity.

Cyert and March [6] described two types of search that go on in organizations. *Problemistic* search was defined as search for small refinements in current activities and more efficient activities. Alternatives are searched for that are similar to what the organization is already doing. This type of activity can be seen as consistent with March and Simon's notion of continuity. *Innovative* search, on the other hand, was defined as search for new technologies such as new products, new processes, new goals, and so forth. It is activity directed at finding alternatives that are different from what the organization is already doing. Thus, this type of search is consistent with change. Given that refinement search is consistent with continuity, and innovative search is consistent with change, what would we expect to be the relationships between refinement, innovation, and attainment discrepancy? From the arguments of the satisficing literature, we would predict a positive relationship between attainment discrepancy and refinement, and a negative relationship between attainment discrepancy and innovation.

Research Hypotheses

While the concept of aspirations has played an important role in the organization literature, it still remains to be seen empirically if it is actually an important variable to organizational decision makers. That is, do they routinely set aspiration levels? Do they remember the targets they have set? Do they compare actual performance to these targets? Do they adjust their aspirations based on experience? Do they adjust their behavior based on the comparison of performance to aspiration level? The following three models will investigate these issues empirically. The first model addresses the question of whether decision makers behave as though they remember their aspirations and compare them to actual performance, and if they adjust their aspirations on the basis of this comparison. The second model addresses the question of whether the amount of risk taken in certain strategic decisions is affected by the comparison of performance to aspiration. The third model addresses the question of whether the extent of innovative and problemistic search is affected by this comparison.

Model 1

This model tests the prediction that decision makers will adapt their aspiration levels on the basis of their past aspiration level and their past performance relative to this aspiration level. That is,

$$\begin{aligned} Y_{it} &= \alpha_0 + \alpha_1 Y_{it-1} + \alpha_2 X_{it-1} + \epsilon_{it} \\ &= \alpha_0 + \alpha_1 Y_{it-1} + \alpha_2 (Z_{it-1} - Y_{it-1}) + \epsilon_{it-1} \end{aligned} \tag{1}$$

where Y_{it} = aspiration level for goal i in period t

$X_{it-1} = Z_{it-1} - Y_{it-1}$ = attainment discrepancy for goal i in period $t-1$

Z_{it-1} = actual performance on goal i in period $t-1$

ϵ_{it} = residual error

This is a more general model than the Levinthal and March [19] model that views aspiration level as an exponentially-weighted moving average of past performance. Model 1 is equivalent to the Levinthal and March model when $\alpha_0 = 0$ and $\alpha_1 = 1$.[1]

The hypotheses associated with Model 1 (as well as Models 2 and 3) are summarized in Table 1. Cyert and March [6] and Levinthal and March [19] suggest that aspirations adjust to changes in performance, but at a slower rate than changes in performance. Thus, there is some inertia in the adjustment of aspiration levels. Decision makers anchor on their prior target as a starting point from which to make adjustments, and are unlikely to make a full adjustment in a single time period to the level of performance achieved. The phenomenon of inadequate adjustment, or anchoring, to a past behavior or judgement has been well documented by the work of Tversky and Kahneman [39] and Nisbett and Ross [26]. A positive relationship between prior aspiration level and current aspiration level would indicate that decision makers do remember their past aspiration levels, and that these aspirations constrain the amount of adjustment that will be made in subsequent aspirations. Thus, Hypothesis H1.1 states that $\alpha_1 > 0$.

The literature on aspirations also suggests that decision makers adapt their aspirations to performance. This is modeled by suggesting that decision makers make a mental calculation of the discrepancy between their performance and the aspiration level they had set. They will adapt their aspirations in the direction of this discrepancy, and proportional to the size of the discrepancy. That is, if performance is above their aspiration level, they will adjust their aspiration upward. If performance is below their aspiration level, they will adjust their aspiration downward. The larger the discrepancy, the greater the extent of adjustment. Consequently, Hypotheses H1.2 holds that $\alpha_2 > 0$.

Table 1
Research Hypotheses

Model 1—The Adaptation of Aspiration Levels

H1.1 Aspiration level in the previous time period will have a positive effect on aspiration level in the current period. ($\alpha_1 > 0$)

H1.2 Attainment discrepancy will have a positive effect on aspiration level ($\alpha_2 > 0$)

Model 2—Riskiness of Choice

H2.1 Attainment discrepancy will have a negative effect on risk taking. ($\beta_1 < 0$)

H2.2 Prior risk taking will have a positive effect on current risk taking. ($\beta_2 > 0$)

Model 3—Innovativeness of Search

H3.1 Attainment discrepancy will have a negative effect on innovativeness of search. ($\gamma_1 < 0$)

H3.2 Proportion of successfully completed R&D projects will have a negative effect on the current innovativeness of search. ($\gamma_2 < 0$)

H3.3 Amount of resources available will have a positive effect on innovativeness of search. ($\gamma_3 > 0$)

H3.4 Innovativeness of search in the previous period will be positively associated with innovative search in the current period. ($\gamma_4 > 0$)

Model 2

This model predicts that decision makers will change their risk-taking behavior based on prior experience. Risk in the current period is modeled as a function of risk in the prior period, attainment discrepancy, and profit in the prior period. The specific equation is:

$$R_{it} = \beta_0 + \beta_1 X_{it-1} + \beta_2 P_{it-1} + \beta_3 R_{it-1} + \epsilon_{it} \tag{2}$$

where R_{it} is the amount of risk taken in the current period, R_{it-1} is the amount of risk taken in the previous period, X_{it-1} is the attainment discrepancy from the previous period, and P_{it-1} is the profit achieved in the previous period.[2]

The crucial piece of information from a decision maker's experience is their attainment discrepancy. Since prior theory suggests that performance below a certain target will lead decision makers to take more risks than performance above a target, negative attainment discrepancy should cause more risk-taking behavior to take place, and positive attainment discrepancy will result in less risk taking. Hence, Hypothesis H2.1 specifies $\beta_1 < 0$.

In addition to the predicted relationship between attainment discrepancy and risk, an anchoring effect similar to the one suggested in the aspiration level model is predicted. That is, the amount of risk taken in the previous period will have a constraining effect on risk in the current period. Thus, Hypothesis H2.2 states that $\beta_3 > 0$.

While the major argument has been that performance relative to an aspiration level is the causal mechanism at work, it is reasonable to allow for effects of performance that are not measured relative to an aspiration level. That is, absolute performance may serve as a cue that affects future behavior. Thus, a measure of profit has been included to control for this effect.

Model 3

This model proposes to test in part the relationship between the innovativeness of search and attainment discrepancy, past success, and amount of resources. Specifically,

$$I_{it} = \gamma_0 + \gamma_1 X_{it-1} + \gamma_2 D_{it-1} + \gamma_3 M_{it-1} + \gamma_4 I_{it-1} + \epsilon_{it} \quad (3)$$

where I_{it} is the innovativeness of search in the current period, I_{it-1} is the innovativeness of search in the prior period, X_{it-1} is the attainment discrepancy in the prior period, D_{it-1} is the proportion of R&D projects successfully completed in the prior period, and M_{it-1} is the amount of resources available in the prior period.

This model assumes that problemistic search is a form of continuity and innovative search is a form of change. Following the logic of satisficing theory, attainment discrepancy is predicted to be negatively related to the innovativeness of search. That is, change is more likely when performance is below expectations than when it is above. Hypothesis H3.1 specifies $\gamma_1 < 0$.

Attainment discrepancy is based on a measure of performance that is not directly related to search activity. It is based on a measure of performance for which decision makers are likely to set specific targets. The search activity in this study is research and development projects. It is likely that the degree of success of these projects, in terms of being successfully completed, will have an effect on the type of R&D conducted in the future. A similar satisficing effect is predicted. The greater the proportion of R&D projects successfully completed in the previous period, the less likely it is that more substantial changes in technology will be sought after immediately. Hypothesis H3.2 specifies $\gamma_2 < 0$.

Because different types of research projects may require more resources to pursue than others, it is important to control for the amount of resources available to the organization. Since it is most likely that innovative projects cost more than problemistically oriented projects, we expect there to be a positive relationship between innovativeness and resources. Thus, H3.3 specifies $\gamma_3 > 0$.

A lagged value of the innovativeness of search is also included as a control variable. Since it may take several periods for R&D projects to be completed, it is likely that the same projects will be pursued for multiple periods. Thus, the innovativeness of the projects pursued in the current period will be positively associated with the innovativeness of projects in the prior period. Consequently, H3.4 specifies $\gamma_4 > 0$.

The Empirical Setting

In order to test model predictions, it is necessary to find a decision-making setting in which similar decisions are made over multiple time periods, since the models are dynamic. It is also important to be able to track the specific decisions, actions, and performance of the decision makers. Further, the setting should be complex enough so that decisions that are made are similar to those that must be made in a real organization. The *Markstrat* marketing-strategy game [16] provides such a setting. *Markstrat* was written as a comprehensive model of marketing dynamics that incorporated knowledge from prior marketing research and real-world experience. Its realism has led to its being adopted as a pedagogical and research tool. Discussions with managers from a variety of large, successful corporations who use *Markstrat* for their in-house management training revealed that they feel the game has a great deal of external validity. *Markstrat* has also been used for research purposes [14, 41, 37], and specifically for research on decision making [11].

A typical play of *Markstrat* consists of five teams, each representing the marketing-profit center of an organization, who compete with each other in a single industry for up to 10 periods. The five competitors can produce and sell two types of consumer products—Sonites and Vodites. The teams are responsible for making strategic and resource-allocation decisions. Decisions are made regarding the types of products to market, product characteristics, advertising expenses, research and development projects, distribution channels, and size of sales force. Thus, this game offers the opportunity to observe teams of decision makers setting objectives, making strategic and resource-allocation decisions, and receiving feedback, over several periods of time.

The teams are also making decisions in a complex environment. The *Markstrat* game is controlled by complicated algorithms that simulate a competitive market. It is a multidimensional, interdependent world that is difficult to understand by observing organizational actions and environmental responses.

Operational Definitions

Data were gathered from a *Markstrat* industry comprised of five teams of Sloan Management Fellows at the Stanford Graduate School of Business. Three data sources were used: the actual decision forms filled out by the *Markstrat* players, the computer generated results, and questionnaires.[3] The teams played for seven periods, and data were collected for each period.

Model 1

The variables for Model 1 were measured as follows. Aspiration levels were measured using self-reports of unit sales goals from each team regarding each brand they were marketing in each period. These goals are reported by the teams in the questionnaire they fill out each week. In the course of planning their strategies, most *Markstrat* teams will set performance objectives. The questionnaires were used to insure that a systematic record of these objectives was kept. The actual performance achieved was measured as the corresponding unit sales associated with each brand, and was collected from the computer-generated results each week. Attainment discrepancy was then calculated simply as performance minus aspiration. The unit of analysis for Model 1 is at the brand level because the causal mechanisms are posited to work primarily at this level. The teams make their decisions specific to each individual brand they are marketing. They are trying to position each brand in a certain market segment, and are making brand-specific decisions in their attempt to do so. They set their performance targets at the brand level, and watch performance at the brand level. Thus, it is important to tap the decision-making process at the brand level.

Model 2

For Model 2, the dependent variable, riskiness of choice, was calculated from information gathered by the weekly questionnaire and from the decision forms. This model is concerned specifically with choices regarding brand marketing. A number of strategic actions (i) can be taken toward each brand (j) being marketed by each team in each period. The actions of interest are: (1) do nothing to change the brand from last period, (2) reposition the brand through advertising, (3) change the physical characteristics of an existing brand, (4) change the retail price of a brand, (5) introduce a new brand of Sonites, (6) introduce a new brand of Vodites, (7) withdraw a brand of Sonites, (8) withdraw a brand of Vodites. Each of these variables are coded 1 if the action was taken, 0 if it was not.

During each period when these decisions were made, each team reported the degree of risk they felt was associated with each of these actions. For each of the eight actions of interest, risk was subjectively scaled on a 1 to 10 scale anchored by very low and very high variance or uncertainty. These subjective perceptions of risk are combined with actual actions taken to determine the degree of risk taken in brand management. An index is created, whereby the value of each action variable (0,1) is multiplied by the corresponding risk rating. These values are then summed for each brand to yield a measure of the riskiness of activity associated with each brand. In summary: $Risk_j = \Sigma_i^8 = 1[(Sub_jRisk_i)(Action_{ij})]$.

For each brand marketed, a performance measure called gross marketing contribution is computed, which is the revenues generated less the costs associated with the brand. Thus, it is a measure of gross profit. It is used conceptually in the model as an "objective" measure of success for each brand, as opposed to the subjective measure of attainment discrepancy. The attainment discrepancy measure is the same as that used in model one.

Model 3

The search process being investigated is research and development. The innovativeness of R&D projects is measured by a self-report by each team in each period. They categorized their R&D projects as either pursuing cost reduction, brand modification, or new-product research. New-product research is defined as more innovative than brand modification, which, in turn, is more innovative than cost reduction.[4] Cost reduction is coded as 0, modification as 1, and introduction as 2. The average level of innovation across R&D projects (i) pursued is computed for each team in each period as $AvgInnov = [\Sigma_{i=1}^4 LevelInnov_i]/Number\ of\ Projects$. This calculation comprises the measure of innovativeness of search.

The past success of research and development is computed as the proportion of R&D projects successfully completed by a team in a given period. The proportion is simply the number of successful projects divided by the total number of projects attempted in that period. This information is collected from the computer-generated results. The amount of available resources is computed as the budget granted each team plus any exceptional budget items. It represents the amount of resources available to a team that they can use in resource-allocation decisions. Attainment discrepancy is basically the same measure used in the first two models, except that in this model it is the average attainment discrepancy across all brands being marketed by a team in a given period.

Results

The results for the three models are presented in Table 2. Use of the residual plots suggested by Draper and Smith [7] indicated that heteroskedacticity was not an apparent problem. However, both Model 1 and Model 2 indicated positively autocorrelated residuals[5]; consequently, these models were estimated using Cochrane-Orcutt Iterative Generalized Least Squares. Model 3 was estimated by OLS. In all cases, the differences in the parameter estimates were very small between OLS and GLS, and the conclusions from the hypothesis tests were identical.

Model 1

This model provides an excellent fit to the data with the coefficients of both variables highly significant in the predicted direction. Consequently, the results are consistent with Model 1, and hypotheses 1.1 and 1.2. Further, the simpler exponential smoothing model of Levinthal and March [19] is not consistent with the data since $\alpha_0 \neq 0$ and $\alpha_1 \neq 1$ at about the .05 level.

While this model fits the data well, it is important to consider that there may exist alternative models that better describe the true relationships at work. In order to test this idea, the model was compared to three other models that could be considered given past research on aspirations. The first alternative suggests that aspiration level is simply a

Table 2
Results

Explanatory Variable	Estimated Coefficient	Standard Error	T Statistic	Beta Weight
Model 1—Aspiration Levels				
α_0 Constant	31140.6	13282.1	2.345	
α_1 Aspiration level$_{t-1}$	1.0987	.0502	21.881	.8653
α_1 Attainment discrepancy$_{t-1}$	1.2571	.0935	13.439	.5288
Estimate of serial correlation = .300		F statistic (2,102) = 271.73		$p < .001$
$N = 105$				
Adjusted $R^2 = .8389$		Generalized Least Squares		
Model 2—Riskiness of Choice				
β_0 Constant	7.3745	1.3504	5.4609	
β_1 Attainment discrepancy$_{t-1}$	−.000012	.000005	−2.3436	−.1984
β_2 Profit$_{t-1}$	.0000087	.000026	.3398	.0289
β_3 Risk$_{t-1}$	.232218	.090952	2.5532	.2524
Estimate of serial correlation = .384		F statistic (3,97) = 3.986		$p < .01$
$N = 101$				
Adjusted $R^2 = .0822$		Generalized Least Squares		
Model 3—Innovativeness of Search				
γ_0 Constant	1.10082	.270742	4.0659	
γ_1 Attainment discrepancy$_{t-1}$	−.0000036	.0000018	−2.0310	−.2956
γ_2 R&D success$_{t-1}$	.754792	.235521	−3.2048	−.4546
γ_3 Resources$_{t-1}$	.000000006	.000000008	−.7475	−.1081
γ_4 Innovativeness$_{t-1}$	.323343	.138220	2.3393	.3325
$N = 30$		F statistic (4,25) = 6.394		$p < .001$
Durbin-Watson = 1.99				
Adjusted $R^2 = .4266$		Ordinary Least Squares		

function of past aspiration levels. As could have been guessed from the results of Model 1, past aspiration levels do go a long way in explaining current aspiration levels. However, the results of testing the first alternative suggest, not surprisingly, that a model that contains attainment discrepancy explains the behavior of aspiration levels much better.[6] The second alternative model suggests that the relationship between attainment discrepancy and aspirations is not linear. However, attainment discrepancy squared is not significant when added to the model. Finally, it is plausible that the causal relationship between aspiration level and attainment discrepancy is not a one-period lag. Again, attainment discrepancy lagged for two periods is not significant when added to the model.

Model 2

This model provides a significant fit to the data, albeit a much weaker one than for Model 1. The coefficients for attainment discrepancy (β_1) and lagged risk (β_3) are both significant in the directions predicted by the hypothesis in Table 1. Thus, hypotheses 2.1 and 2.2 are found to be consistent with the data. The profit covariate does not have a significant effect on the riskiness of choice.

As in Model 1, attainment discrepancy adds significant explanatory power to a model containing lagged risk only. Further, the linear form of attainment discrepancy seems to be preferable to a quadratic term in this variable.

Model 3

This model fits the data well. The coefficients of attainment discrepancy and R&D success are both significant in the predicted negative direction. The lagged coefficient of innovativeness of search is also significant in the predicted positive direction. Resources available did not turn out to be significantly related to innovativeness of search, and had the wrong sign. Consequently, hypothesis 3.1, 3.2, and 3.4 were confirmed, while hypothesis 3.3 did not receive support. Again, specification checks indicate that attainment discrepancy adds significant explanatory power to an autoregressive model in innovativeness of search, and a quadratic term in attainment discrepancy does not enhance the model.

Conclusions

The results of Model 1 strongly support the prediction that aspiration levels are a linear function of past aspiration levels and the discrepancy between prior aspiration and actual performance. Further, they suggest that the effect is summarized in a single-period lag. This study is perhaps the first to empirically test this model of the behavior of aspirations, using aspiration levels directly reported by the decision makers using them. Not only are aspirations shown to track the movement of actual performance, but the discrepancy between aspiration and performance is shown to be a distinct construct that can be used to predict the movement of aspiration levels.

Model 2 offers substantial support for the prediction that risk taking is a function of past risk and attainment discrepancy. Decision makers do seem to anchor on their past position of risk taking as would be predicted by the cognitive social psychology literature. They also exhibit an effect consistent with some of the predictions of Kahneman and Tversky [12] and March [21] .That is, they take more risks when performance is below aspiration level than when performance is above aspiration level.

A major contribution of the second model, beside the fact that attainment discrepancy is computed relative to self-perceived aspirations, is that the amount of risk taken is based on risk as perceived by the decision makers. The causal mechanism that is posited in this model is based on the idea that decision makers are cognizant of the discrepancy between their aspirations and performance, associate different levels of risk with different actions, will take fewer perceived risks when they are satisfied with their performance, and will take more perceived risks when they are dissatisfied with performance. Thus, it is important to tap both aspirations and risk from the decision maker's point of view.

The testing of Model 3 offers support for the satisficing predictions of the model. The greater the extent of previous success in search activities, the less innovative is the next set of search activities. The more negative one's attainment discrepancy, the more innovative one will be in subsequent search activity. These results are consistent with the notion that innovativeness of search represents a change in current activities, and will not be pursued unless current activities are unsatisfactory.

The testing of the three models in this study has made significant steps toward the goal of contributing to our knowledge of decision making and learning in a complex and ambiguous setting. It has provided evidence that decision makers pay attention to their aspirations, adjust their aspirations in response to experience, and use performance relative to their aspiration level as a cue that affects the nature of their future decisions. Understanding these processes will help us in studying the question of when the learning process is adaptive and when it is not. Better knowledge of these issues will help both researchers and managers improve their understanding of the managing of organization-environment relations.

Notes

1. The Levinthal and March model is $Y_{it} = (1 - \alpha_2)Y_{it-1} + \alpha_2 Z_{it-1}$ that is equivalent to (1) under the stated conditions.
2. This model posits a linear relationship, but, as has been suggested by March and Shapira [24], the relationship may not be constant over all levels of performance, and may exhibit nonlinearities, with a possible reversal of effect in the extreme positive and negative regions. Possible nonlinearities in the relationship will be explored in future research.
3. All data are at the team level. Decisions are made as a team, results are given for the team, and questionnaires are filled out by the team.
4. This categorization corresponds well to team reports of what constitutes innovative R&D.
5. The OLS estimates of Models 1 and 2 were tested for autocorrelation by comparison to d_{it}, which Kenkel [13] has shown to be quite accurate for models with lagged endogenous variables. Significance levels were determined from the extended tables of Savin and White [33].
6. Using GLS, the adjusted R^2 for the model using lagged aspirations only was .5799 versus an overall adjusted R^2 of .8389 when attainment discrepancy is added to the model. The result is highly significant.

References

1. Barnard, Chester I., *Functions of the Executive*. Harvard University Press, Cambridge, MA, 1938.
2. Bowman, E.H., "A Risk-Return Paradox for Strategic Management," *Sloan Management Review*, 21 (1980), 17–31.
3. Bowman, Edward H., "Risk Seeking by Troubled Firms," *Sloan Management Review* (Summer 1982), 33–42.
4. Burns, Tom, and Stalker, G.M., *The Management of Innovation*. Tavistock, London, 1961.
5. Cohen, Michael D., March, James G., and Olsen, Johan P., "A Garbage Can Model of Organizational Choice," *Administrative Science Quarterly*, 17 (March 1972), 1–25.
6. Cyert, Richard M., and March, James G., *A Behavioral Theory of the Firm*. Prentice-Hall, Englewood Cliffs, NJ, 1963.
7. Draper, N. R., and Smith, H., *Applied Regression Analysis*. Wiley, New York, 1966.
8. Dutton, Jane E., Fahey, Liam, and Narayanan, V. K., "Toward Understanding Strategic Issue Diagnosis," *Strategic Management Journal*, 4 (1983), 307–323.
9. Fishburn, P. C., "Mean Risk Analysis and Risk Associated with Below Target Returns," *American Economic Review*, 67 (1977), 116–126.
10. Herriott, Scott R., Levinthal, Daniel, and March, James G., "Learning from Experience in Organizations," *Proceedings of the American Economic Association* (May 1985).
11. Hogarth, Robin M., and Makridakis, Spyros, "The Value of Decision Making in a Complex Environment: An Experimental Approach," *Management Science*, 27 (1981), 93–107.
12. Kahneman, Daniel, and Tversky, Amos, "Prospect Theory: An Analysis of Decision Under Risk," *Econometrica*, 47 (March 1979), 263–292.
13. Kenkel, James L., "Some Small Sample Properties of Durbin's Tests for Serial Correlation in Regression Models Containing Lagged Dependent Variables," *Econometrica*, 42 (July 1974), 763–769.
14. Kinnear, Thomas C., "Problems and Opportunities in Using MARKSTRAT for Experimental Research in Marketing Management Decisions." Paper presented at Summer Marketing Educator's Conference, 1986.
15. Lane, R. E., "Why Businessmen Violate the Law," *Journal of Criminal Law, Criminology and Political Science*, 19 (July–August 1953), 151–165.
16. Larréché, Jean-Claude, and Gatignon, Hubert, *Markstrat: A Marketing Strategy Game*, The Scientific Press, Palo Alto, CA, 1977.
17. Lawler, Edward E., "Secrecy about Management Compensation: Are There Hidden Costs?" *Organizational Behavior and Human Performance*, 2 (1967), 182–189.
18. Lawrence, Paul R., and Lorsh, Jay W., *Organization and Environment*. Graduate School of Business Administration, Harvard University, Boston, 1967.
19. Levinthal, Daniel, and March, James G., "A Model of Adaptive Organizational Search," *Journal of Economic Behavior and Organization*, 2 (May 1981), 307–333.
20. Lewin, Kurt, Dembo, Tamara, Festinger, Leon, and Sears, Pauline Snedden, "Level of Aspiration," *Personality and the Behavior Disorders*, J. McV. Hunt, ed., The Ronald Press Company, New York, 1944.
21. March, James G., "Variable Risk Preferences, Succeeding, and Surviving." Unpublished, Stanford University, September 1985.
22. March, James G., and Olsen, Johan P., *Ambiguity and Choice in Organizations*. Universitetsforlaget, Bergen, 1976.
23. March, James G., and Shapira, Zur, "Behavioral Decision Theory and Organization Decision Theory," in *Decision Making: An Interdisciplinary Inquiry*. Gerardo R. Ungson and Daniel N. Braunstein, eds., Kent Publishing, Boston, 1982.
24. March, James G., and Shapira, Zur, "Managerial Perspectives on Risk and Risk Taking." Unpublished, Stanford University and Hebrew University, October 1986.
25. March, James G., and Simon, Herbert, *Organizations*. Wiley, New York, 1958.
26. Nisbett, T., Richard, and Ross, Lee, *Human Inference: Strategies and Shortcomings of Social Judgment*. Prentice-Hall, Englewood Cliffs, NJ, 1980.
27. Olshavsky, Richard W., "Task Complexity and Contingent Processing in Decision Making: A Replication and Extension,"

Organizational Behavior and Human Performance, 24 (1979), 300–316.

28. Payne, John W., "Task Complexity and Contingent Processing in Decision Making: An Information Search and Protocol Analysis," *Organizational Behavior and Human Performance*, 16 (1976), 366–387.
29. Payne, John W., Laughhunn, Dan J., and Crum, Roy, "Translation of Gambles and Aspiration Level Effects on Risky Choice Behavior," *Management Science*, 26 (1980), 1039–1060.
30. Peters, Lawrence H., "Cognitive Models of Motivation, Expectancy Theory and Effort: An Analysis and Empirical Test," *Organizational Behavior and Human Performance*, 20 (1977), 129–148.
31. Pfeffer, Jeffrey, and Salancik, Gerald R., *The External Control of Organizations: A Resource Dependency Perspective*. Harper & Row, New York, 1978.
32. Russo, Edward J., and Dosher, Barbara Anne, "Strategies for Multiattribute Binary Choice," *Journal of Experimental Psychology: Learning, Memory, and Cognition*, 9 (1983), 676–696.
33. Savin, N. E., and White, K. J., "The Durbin-Watson Test for Serial Correlation with Extreme Sample Sizes or Many Regressors," *Econometrica*, 45 (November 1977), 1989–1996.
34. Siegel, S., "Level of Aspiration and Decision Making," *Psychology Review*, 64 (1957), 253–262.
35. Simon, Herbert A., "A Behavioral Model of Rational Choice," in *Models of Man*. Herbert A. Simon, ed., Wiley, New York, 1957.
36. Staw, Barry M., and Szwajkowski, Eugene, "The Scarcity-Munificence Component of Organizational Environments and the Commission of Illegal Acts," *Administrative Science Quarterly*, 20 (September 1975), 345–354.
37. Strong, Edward C., and Nolan, Johannah J., "Any Number Can Play: A Cross-Sectional View of Marketing Strategies." Paper presented at Summer Marketing Educator's Conference, 1986.
38. Thompson, James D., and Tuden, Arthur, "Strategies, Structures, and Processes of Organizational Decision," in *Comparative Studies in Administration*. James D. Thompson, ed., University of Pittsburgh Press, 1959.
39. Tversky, Amos, and Kahneman, Daniel, "Judgment Under Uncertainty: Heuristics and Biases, *Science*, 185 (1974), 1124–1131.
40. Tversky, Amos, and Kahneman, Daniel, "The Framing of Decisions and the Psychology of Choice," *Science*, 211 (1981).
41. Utsey, Marjorie F., "Is Marketing a Martingale Process?" Paper presented at Summer Marketing Educator's Conference, 1986.
42. Weick, Karl E., *The Social Psychology of Organizing*. Addison-Wesley, Reading, 1979.

40

Management Learning in *Markstrat*: The ICL Experience

Harvey Dodgson

A manager in ICL France said on completion of *Markstrat* that the main benefit from the course is the ability to analyze market situations with the same terms of reference as ICL colleagues worldwide.

International Computers Limited, a $1.7 billion information-systems company, created a comprehensive marketing-development program to make its managers internationally competitive in industrial marketing. *Markstrat* contributed greatly to the success of this program. Its contribution was due partly to *Markstrat*'s ability to adapt to the widely different learning styles of managers and staff around the world, and partly to the ability of *Markstrat* to evolve dynamically as more demanding skill levels were required by participants. All of this was made possible by the robust theory base on which *Markstrat* is built.

THIS ARTICLE DESCRIBES the experiences of International Computers Limited, (ICL), operating in the information-systems marketplace in over 70 countries, in making radical changes to its marketing culture and processes. The article reviews the role that *Markstrat* played in a major marketing training program that involved participants from many different countries and backgrounds.

In the spring of 1982, following a serious downturn in the fortunes of ICL, the company began a comprehensive marketing-training program aimed at creating a skill base equal to the best of industrial marketing organizations worldwide. This training was part of a complete restructuring of ICL. It was accompanied by a significant repositioning that involved adding distributed and office-systems markets to the company's existing portfolio of mainframe product markets.

Markstrat played a key role in this comprehensive program of marketing development,[1] providing a learning environment that permitted the training of staff from a wide range of disciplines and cultural backgrounds. *Markstrat* was used by some 1,700 participants out of a total company population of just below 21,000. *Markstrat* also allowed the training to evolve to increasingly rigorous levels, as knowledge of the company's marketing practices increased, and provided a robust theory base on which to build.

The ICL marketing-development program has been an essential part of the company's recent recovery. ICL has moved from losses in 1981 of $199 million on sales of $1,066 million, to profits of $135 million on sales of $1,783 million in 1986.

The Mission

Embarking on a program of fundamental change in corporate culture is both a deliberate management decision and an act of faith. When the group marketing director of ICL, now the chairman and managing director, committed the company to a long-haul marketing-training program, he was setting the company's direction toward being market led, not product led. The direction and fundamental extent of the change were understood, but no detailed road maps existed for what became a unique corporate journey. Now, some five years later at the time of this writing, the new skills ICL management has acquired in the daily practice of industrial marketing have also increased our understanding of many of the underlying forces working during the change.

Harvey Dodgson is Director of Business Strategy at International Computers, Inc.

To understand the test to which *Markstrat* has been put within ICL, it is necessary to appreciate the context of the marketing program, and of ICL's needs. ICL operates in the competitive and dynamic market for information-management technology. The company mission statement declares: "ICL is an international company dedicated to applying information technology to provide profitable high value customer solutions for improved operational and management effectiveness."

This mission statement itself arose from the far-reaching effects of the change in company culture. During the 1970s, ICL had operated as a mainframe computer manufacturer, based in the United Kingdom, and trading in some 80 countries. Sales had grown on average 20% to 25% per annum. Profits reached $46 million on sales of $936 million in 1979, if pound sterling is converted to dollars at a constant rate of $1.50. The average number of employees was some 34,000 in 1979.

However, the cost base had grown on assumptions of continuing sales increases. Sales growth ceased between 1980 and 1981. Profits, within a single year, dropped from $46 million in 1979 to $9 million in 1980. The product/market portfolio of the company was badly unbalanced. First, it was limited to medium and large mainframe computers. Plans had not been made to adapt to the rapid emergence of a wider user community, partly created by the explosive growth of the personal computer market. Second, the redefinition of the "computer market" arising from the convergence of computing and telecommunications, exposed the company's narrow product base, making it additionally vulnerable to downturns in the market. Trading and extraordinary losses in 1981 made for a total loss of $199 million on sales on $1,066 million. ICL was restructured in 1980–1981 under the management of a new chairman, managing director, and group marketing director.

Against this background, in the spring of 1982, the author was commissioned by the group marketing director to begin a program for developing internationally competitive industrial marketing skills across the whole company. *Markstrat* was a key element in a six-course program, spanning 19 days of intensive management education.

The Participants

The marketing training program was initially targeted at full-time, senior marketing managers in business centers and countries. Figure 1 describes the number of key members of corporate management who were in the target population. It identifies the major roles in the ICL marketing organization, the key accountabilities of such a job holder, and the functional stream within the company from which such people are selected.

The chairman and every member of the board of directors as well as their direct reports completed the training program, including the *Markstrat* simulation. In ICL, the board consists primarily of senior-line management. This group numbered 35 in total.

Business centers form the core of ICL's corporate marketing network, linking functional management with country management. A "business center manager" has marketing and systems development accountabilities. Typically, in ICL, the center manager is sourced from a senior-sales management background, or from a senior product-development role. Each of the 18 business center managers participated in the training program and completed *Markstrat*.

The "segment marketing manager" is a new creation resulting specifically from the marketing program, and he or she is concerned with individual market segments. A segment manager's previous jobs in ICL may have been in a sales management, or in a customer-support management role. In all, 326 segment managers participated in the play of *Markstrat*.

Country marketing managers implement marketing strategy in local markets from Hong Kong to Paris, and from Sydney to New York. A country manager typically comes from a sales-management background. A total of 259 country marketing managers participated in the program to date.

Strategy managers are responsible for the fit between marketing and business strategies worldwide. Typically coming from sales-management and business-planning backgrounds, 90 strategy managers participated in the program.

Nearly 1,000 staff members from the diverse functional areas of finance, personnel, manufacturing, and technical development were introduced to the principles of marketing strategy in a short course with *Markstrat* as its mainspring.

Finally, the many different countries in which the participants were located included Australia, the Asia Pacific basin, India, the Middle East and Africa, South Africa, North America, and each of the countries of Western Europe.

The management-development problem was, thus, formidable. The diversity of management and staff backgrounds demanded that the program (1) adapt readily to the different learning styles of the participants, (2) dynamically adjust to the stages of the learning cycle, and (3) offer a

Figure 1

ICL *Markstrat* Participants

Role in Organization	Accountabilities	Source	Number
Business Center Manager	Management of marketing and development resource to achieve target profit in defined markets	Sales management Development management	13
Segment Marketing Manager	Management of marketing mix and life cycle	Same as above plus support management	283
Country Marketing Managers	Management of marketing resource to implement country marketing strategy	Sales management	375
Strategy Manager	Fit of marketing strategies to business strategies	Sales management Business planning	53
Staff	Finance, personnel, manufacturing, technical development		1000

Figure 2
Learning styles

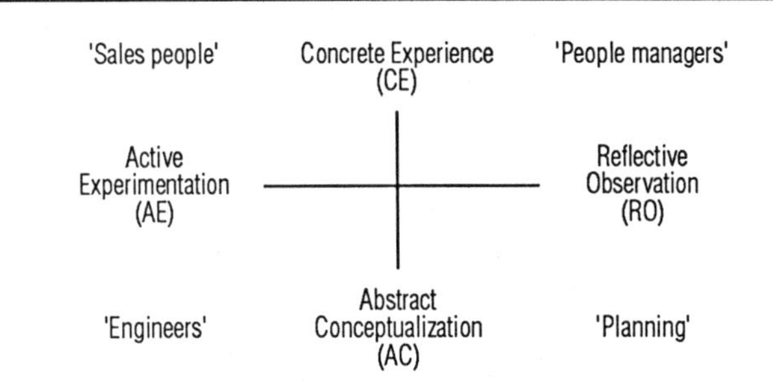

robust theory base capable of expanding with the level of marketing competence.

Learning Styles

Different individuals have acquired propensities to learn from different kinds of stimuli, often depending on their background and sometimes derived from unconscious preferences. To assess the individual's preference, the "learning style inventory" process was defined by Kolb [2].

Figure 2 illustrates the four learning styles identified by Kolb as a function of the two basic dimensions of learning. The vertical dimension in Figure 2 captures the need for "concrete experience" as compared with "abstract conceptualization" in the learning environment. The horizontal dimension reflects the need for "active experimentation" compared with "reflective observation."

Kolb identified people scoring highly on the "concrete experience" (CE) dimension as being receptive to experience-based learning. High CE individuals tend to be people oriented, to learn from specific examples, and from tangible feedback. Those with a high score on "abstract conceptualization" (AC) have an analytic approach, relying on logical thinking and rational evaluation. They learn best by "systematic planning, manipulation of abstract symbols, and quantitative analysis" [2, p. 34]. A high score on "active experimentation" (AE) denotes learning by doing—an active, extrovert approach to learning. "Reflective observation" (RO)-oriented individuals have a tentative, impartial, and reflective approach to learning. An effective training environment must be capable of adapting to each of these widely different learning styles.

ICL's experience in training design supports Kolb's observations. This basic paradigm was used by ICL in design of the marketing-development program. Those participants high on both AC and AE axis are to be found amongst our technical and engineering population. Kolb labeled these individuals "convergers." Kolb's "assimilators" are high on AC and RO, and are to be found in research and planning departments. The "divergers" tendency towards CE and RO is found among individuals with humanities and liberal-arts backgrounds. The "accommodator," with high CE and AE, is to be found in action-oriented jobs such as sales.

It was ICL's experience over the past five years that *Markstrat* does support a learning environment in which teams of mixed learning styles can find scope for individualized interaction with the model, yet within an integrated context. *Markstrat* also supports team building among individuals. The company reports produced in the play of *Markstrat* provide the "concrete experience" necessary. The "company" environment provides the people feedback. The underlying theory base provides material for "reflective observation." The need for players to project forward on a theory base provides "abstract conceptualization." Finally the dynamic simulation process itself supports an "active experimentation" environment. Nearly everyone can find a comfortable fit for their particular learning style within the *Markstrat* environment.

Learning Cycles

The marketing program must also adapt to evolution over time of individual management skills as the impact of the training deepens and broadens in its reach through the company. As the culture changes, so must the program adapt. This process is illustrated in Figure 3.

"Competence" in marketing strategy consists of both a knowledge base and a set of successful actions. These two components are essential, interactive and dynamic. Before the marketing-development program began, the vast majority of managers and staff were lacking in the knowledge base or the successful actions or both.

An individual, at any particular level of "competence," can be stimulated by external input to realize the need for further knowledge, or skill. This stimulus induces an awareness—the "conscious incompetence" phase. The individual progresses (A → B) in Figure 3. This first step is not easily achieved, especially among individuals who consider themselves "marketing professionals."

Figure 3
Learning cycles

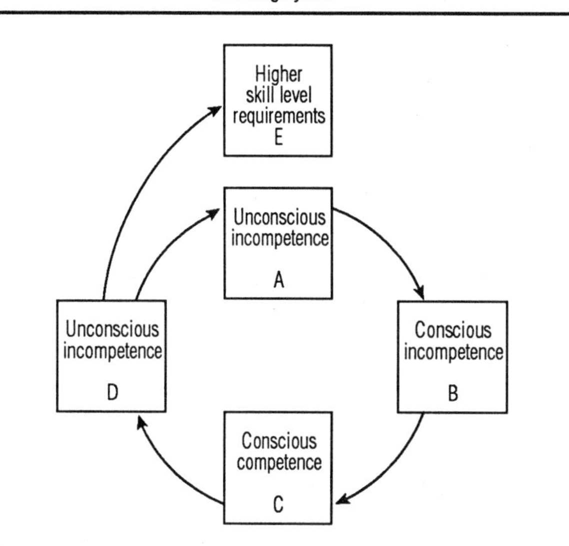

With acceptance of the need to progress, and with input, an individual can be made "competent," but at a level of competence requiring carefully deliberate thought processes (B → C). Recall, if you will, your early experiences in riding a bicycle. Finally, with practice, the person can "ride without thinking." The state of "unconscious competence" is achieved (C → D). Continued practice of such a useful skill gives rise to a state where the individual is ready to redo the cycle, to achieve a higher or different skill level (D → E). Lack of practice, or lack of reinforcement, can allow a reversion to the previous state of "unconscious incompetence" (D → A).

Just as individuals develop around this cycle, so by analogy, do collections of individuals, such as companies. The distribution of individuals within the cycle "conscious incompetence" through "unconscious competence" is influenced by the quality of the training program. In addition, the process is dynamic. The diffusion of marketing competence throughout an organization causes those new to the program to start with a higher level of competence.

Markstrat adjusts well to this dynamic learning cycle. During the unconscious incompetence phase, the game element of the simulation provides a compelling attraction. It is enjoyable and it appeals to the competitive nature of managers. *Markstrat's* built-in rule base resists the temptation of those having learning difficulties to doubt the simulated outcome. ICL's marketing manager, specialty stores, in the retail business center, wrote, after attending *Markstrat*, "Its major realism was, perhaps, to highlight a mismatch between one's own perceptions and those of the world."

Participants are now, in 1987, attending *Markstrat* with levels of diffused expertise, which puts their start point at a level of conscious competence, compared to their peers of 1983. In this circumstance, the model still provides a powerful training tool, but more of its intrinsic resources are called upon to sustain the teaching input. Instead of *Markstrat* having the appearance of a "game," it is seen more and more as a market simulation, with a realistic complexity, that calls for, and allows, a richness of management decision making. The rule structure, mirroring the real underlying competitive market forces, provides a challenging basis for managerial decision making. It provides the theory foundation for ICL's increasing use of the concept of differential advantage [4] to build targeted market share.

Robust Theory Base

A final feature of *Markstrat* found essential in the long-term marketing program begun by ICL is its robust theory base. The hierarchy of substantive theory that can be addressed in *Markstrat* appears on the vertical axis, with time in years on the horizontal axis. The rate at which ICL's marketing program has introduced successfully each successively more difficult element of theory within the *Markstrat* environment is represented by the curved line in Figure 4. The horizontal axis begins with the first running of *Markstrat* in early 1983.

Figure 4
Robust theory base

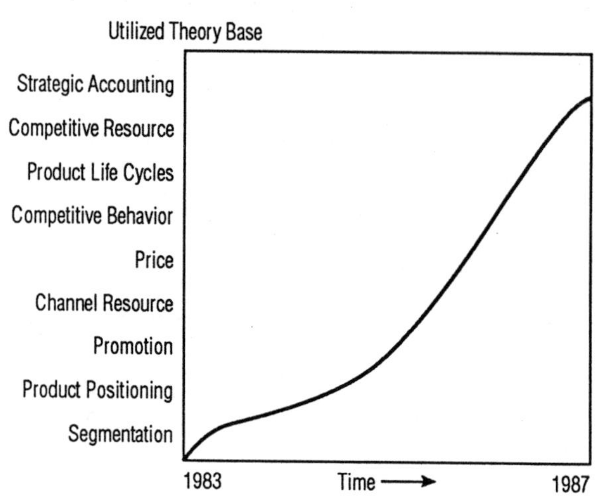

Individuals entering the course in 1983 would require the full course to master just the concepts and methods of market segmentation. Because the starting base of theoretical tools was so low in 1983, segmentation processes were the main elements of the course.

The theory base in *Markstrat* is sufficiently robust to develop as the principles diffuse throughout the organization. As in the beginning of a market life cycle, the participant's minimal skills allow appreciation of only simple product attributes, addressing clear market needs. As the diffusion of ideas proceeds and the market life cycle matures, so increased levels of competence allow for more sophisticated selection criteria. At this point, more complex aspects of competence in marketing strategy are both perceived and valued. This deeper need often demands refinements to the original program, or new, more sophisticated program development. In the case of ICL's experience with *Markstrat*, the original product had the deeper layers of capability embedded in its robust theory base. Thus, the company was able to extend the original product to reach the more knowledgeable students, without creating additional programs.

The participants using *Markstrat* for the first time in 1987, come prepared for segmentation and the concepts of product positioning. Their learning during the simulation now takes them much further along the path of internalizing the management of the full marketing mix. They now can move significantly toward a working grasp of the competitive resource implications of marketing strategy and the principles of accounting for strategic initiative.

Conclusions

ICL embedded *Markstrat* within a carefully constructed marketing-development program designed to change the company's culture from product to market led. *Markstrat* was selected as a key element in the program because of its ability to adapt to a wide variety of learning styles, adjust dynamically to the learning cycle over the long run, and because of its robust theory base. *Markstrat* provided a common learning environment to nearly 1,700 participants with a wide range of experiences, learning styles, job functions, and national and cultural backgrounds. As the manager in ICL France said on completion of *Markstrat*, "The main benefit I get from the *Markstrat* course is the ability to analyze market situations with the same terms of reference as my ICL colleagues worldwide." As reported in the *Financial Times* [4], the overall effect of these programs on ICL has been "a dramatic change in character . . . it has begun to focus its attention and resources to much more profitable effect."

Note

1. The marketing development program was designed and implemented by a team of professionals from International Computers, Ltd., working in close cooperation with Meyer Feldberg Associates, Chicago, Illinois.

References

1. Cook, Victor J., Jr., "Marketing Strategy and Differential Advantage," *Journal of Marketing Strategy* (Spring 1983), 68–75.
2. Kolb, David A., Rubin, Irwin M., and McIntyre, James., *Organizational Psychology: An Experiential Approach to Organizational Behavior*, 4th ed. Prentice-Hall, Englewood Cliffs, NJ, pp. 31–41.
3. Larréché, Jean-Claude, and Gatignon, Hubert, *MARKSTRAT: A Marketing Strategy Game*. The Scientific Press, Palo Alto, CA, 1977.
4. Lorenz, Christopher, "Corporate Renewal: Making It Happen," *Financial Times*, May 12, 1986.

41

Management Perspectives on *Markstrat*: The GE Experience & Beyond

Thomas C. Kinnear & Sharon K. Klammer

One of the great problems facing academic researchers who study marketing decision making is to find a manageable environment that is also real enough to provide external validity to the results of these studies. The results presented here indicate strongly that *Markstrat* is such an environment.

Markstrat has attained great success as an educational tool for marketing management. It is also a simulated environment in which academics are now conducting experimental studies on marketing variables and monitoring the impact in the *Markstrat* context. A most important question that arises in both these types of utilization of *Markstrat* is the degree to which it reflects the real world of marketing decision making. Do managers from diverse industry experience perceive that *Markstrat* reflects a real enough marketplace to be useful both as a teaching tool and as a research environment? This article reports the results of a study of this question in the General Electric Company, plus the perceptions of another set of managers drawn from a broad set of other companies. Overall results indicate that managers working in diverse industries believe that *Markstrat* does reflect a real environment useful for teaching and research.

MARKSTRAT IS a marketing-strategy simulation game in which five firms compete against each other. This competition is based upon the utilization of the classic marketing variables: product development and management, distribution, promotion, and price. Decision makers in competing firms utilize marketing research studies and develop strategies based upon effective segmentation and positioning. Their performance in the game is based upon such measures as market share, sales, contribution margin, and return on marketing investment (see [3]). In many respects, then, it is a classic strategic marketing situation that a real-world manager would face.

This perceived match between the context of *Markstrat* and the real world of the marketing manager is the prime reason for the great popularity of *Markstrat* in MBA and executive-education programs. Recently, because of this perceived match with reality, many academic researchers have begun to use the *Markstrat* simulation as an environment for studying marketing decision making and other aspects of marketing [1, 2, 4].

One problem with both the training and academic research aspects of utilizing *Markstrat* is that the true match between the real world of the marketing manager and the context of the simulation has never been tested empirically. The key question is: Do managers from diverse industry experiences perceive that *Markstrat* reflects a real enough environment to be a productive and useful learning experience? The purpose of this article is to present empirical results related to this question. To understand the results of this study, it is also necessary to describe the use of *Markstrat* within General Electric Company, the source of most of the data utilized in the study. This is the topic that will be discussed first.

Thomas C. Kinnear is a professor at the University of Michigan and Sharon K. Klammer is Manager of Business Education at General Electric.

Markstrat Within General Electric

General Electric is a $39 billion dollar company operating in diverse sectors of the world economy. Today, it includes, in addition to old-line manufacturing operations such as motors and contractor equipment and well-known consumer goods such as major appliances, high-tech operations such as medical systems and plastics and business-to-business services such as financing and information systems. Working within this diversity, GE's in-house management development center, known as "Crotonville," offers a prescribed sequence of general-management and functional courses to prepare rising executives for top management positions.

At Crotonville these days, the need for quality marketing/sales education is being emphasized as GE struggles for leadership in highly competitive world markets. Marketing courses at Crotonville include basic marketing management, technical sales training, product development, and the Advanced Marketing Management Seminar (AMMS). AMMS is the capstone course in GE's marketing education curriculum. It is in the AMMS course that *Markstrat* is used. AMMS is targeted at high-potential marketing and other functional managers in GE. AMMS participants typically have significant experience within GE and currently hold jobs that impact the marketplace. They are part of GE's corps d'elite, managers who are tracking toward top-level marketing or general-manager positions. AMMS utilizes cases, lectures, action learning, team problem solving, and the *Markstrat* simulation to immerse participants in three weeks of marketing decision making. The fundamental purpose of the *Markstrat* part of AMMS is to provide new strategic insight to the players. The typical class size of 50 is such that two industries of five teams with five participants per team play during each session.

Table 1

Number of GE AMMS participants surveyed	277	
Number of responses	177	(64%)
*Respondents' GE Business Affiliation**		
Technical equipment and services (Medical systems, transportation, power systems and services)		27%
Industrial flow goods (Construction equipment, motors, commercial and industrial lighting, GE supply company, plastics, specialty materials and manufacturing automation)		21%
Consumer products (Major appliance, consumer lighting, video and audio products)		16%
Defense (Aerospace and aircraft engine)		13%
Business-to-business services (Financial services and information systems)		14%
International		6%
Corporate		3%
		100%
Respondents' Functional Area		
Marketing		61%
Sales		20%
Finance		6%
Engineering		3%
Manufacturing		2%
General management		1%
Other		7%
		100%
Respondents' GE Work Experience		
Median length of GE service		11–15 years

*Grouped by go-to-market approach, not by formal company classification. These groupings are meant to be representative; not all company businesses are included.

The Study

In November 1986, a mail questionnaire was sent to participants of six different sessions of AMMS. These respondents had participated in the 1985 and 1986 plays of *Markstrat*, so their post-*Markstrat* job experience ranged from 1 to 18 months. The respondents had all used the distributed personal computer version of *Markstrat*, *Markstrat* D, with which GE combines customized Lotus 1-2-3 software to enhance players' analytical capability. A profile of the respondents by functional area and the GE business in which they work are presented in Table 1.

The results of Table 1 show the respondents to be a diverse group in terms of both their businesses and their functional areas. Only about 60% are strictly marketing people. Therefore, the sample is one of great relevance to test the question of interest in this article. However, in order to augment the results of this sample, an additional sample was drawn from *Markstrat* players from the University of Michigan's Advanced Strategic Marketing Planning seminar that also utilizes *Markstrat*. The participants in the latter program are drawn from such diverse industries as beer, automobiles, package delivery, pharmaceuticals, plastics, and industrial capital goods. The GE sample was asked both to indicate their attitudes toward *Markstrat* based on a multiple-choice basis, and to give their open-ended perceptions of the simulation. The Michigan sample was asked only for open-ended responses. The results of both samples are presented in this article.

The Results

Respondents from GE were first asked a series of questions designed to ascertain their attitudes about *Markstrat*'s relevance to the job environment in which they work (see Table 2). Their responses give insight into *Markstrat*'s general value. The most significant findings, which are summarized in Figure 1 are:

1. Ninety-four percent of respondents indicate that *Markstrat* has given them at least a few useful insights about their marketplace, while 26% indicate that they have gained many fresh and applicable new ideas. This outcome is consistent with the fact that AMMS participants are predominately seasoned GE managers with an average of 11 to 15 years of marketing and/or general business experience. One would not expect a high percentage of such a group to perceive that the simulation introduced them to totally new marketing ideas.

Table 2

Markstrat's General Value

Please indicate which of the following responses most nearly describes *Markstrat's* influence on the way you manage your business.

1. Since competing in the *Markstrat* simulation during AMMS, I think about my marketplace:

1. a. with many fresh and applicable new ideas
   b. with a few useful insights
   c. the same as before the simulation

2. The total *Markstrat* experience had the following effect on me: (please circle as many as apply)
   a. drove home valuable lessons in marketing strategy
   b. taught me new analytical skills and techniques
   c. reinforced what I already knew
   d. no effect

3. Since competing in *Markstrat* I can:
   a. identify changes in the way I think about my markets due to *Markstrat*
   b. name specific actions I have taken to improve my business's go-to-market strategy that were influenced by the simulation
   c. both (a) and (b)
   d. not think of any *Markstrat*-based changes in the way I approach marketing or business decision making

4. *Markstrat's* value to me can best be described as (please circle as many as apply):
   a. improving my ability to analyze marketing environment
   b. increasing my understanding of competitive market dynamics
   c. making me feel competent and confident in making key marketing and business decisions
   d. none of the above

5. In developing my subordinates, I would:
   a. recommend that they compete in *Markstrat*
   b. not recommend *Markstrat* as a good use of their time
   c. not applicable (e.g., respondent has no subordinates)

Markstrat's Specific Characteristics

Please indicate which response most nearly describes *Markstrat* as a teaching vehicle.

6. *Markstrat* is a realistic simulation of competitive market forces.
   a. agree b. agree somewhat c. disagree somewhat d. strongly disagree
7. *Markstrat* emphasizes the importance of accurate market segmentation and focused product positioning.
   a. agree b. agree somewhat c. disagree somewhat d. strongly disagree
8. *Markstrat* reinforces the importance of achieving dominance in well-defined market segments.
   a. agree b. agree somewhat c. disagree somewhat d. strongly disagree
9. *Markstrat* emphasizes the use of market research to anticipate customer needs.
   a. agree b. agree somewhat c. disagree somewhat d. strongly disagree
10. *Markstrat* stresses the strategic value of leapfrogging competition with new product introductions.
    a. agree b. agree somewhat c. disagree somewhat d. strongly disagree
11. *Markstrat* illustrates the value and limitations of advertising.
    a. agree b. agree somewhat c. disagree somewhat d. strongly disagree
12. *Markstrat* stresses the importance of being the low-cost producer (the experience curve effect).
    a. agree b. agree somewhat c. disagree somewhat d. strongly disagree
13. *Markstrat* emphasizes the linkages between focused product positioning, segment dominance, accurate pricing, and product profitability.
    a. agree b. agree somewhat c. disagree somewhat d. strongly disagree
14. *Markstrat* reinforces the necessity of exiting unprofitable market segments and/or eliminating low-share product.
    a. agree b. agree somewhat c. disagree somewhat d. strongly disagree
15. *Markstrat* stresses the importance of targeting resources such as new product development, advertising, promotion, sales, and distribution expenditures on those products/segments where you are best positioned to dominate.
    a. agree b. agree somewhat c. disagree somewhat d. strongly disagree

Markstrat's Impact on Marketing Decision Making

16. Describe specific marketing actions you initiated on your job based on your *Markstrat* experience.
17. What were the most important lessons you learned from *Markstrat?*
18. Identify analytical tools and techniques learned in *Markstrat* that you use on your job.
19. What would say is *Markstrat's* greatest strength?

2. Fifty-nine percent think that *Markstrat* drove home valuable lessons in marketing strategy, while 60% indicate that *Markstrat* has taught them new analytical skills and techniques.

3. Seventy percent can identify changes in the way they think about their markets since competing in *Markstrat*, and an impressive 39% can actually name specific actions they have taken to improve their businesses' go-to-market strategies based on what they learned from the simulation.

4. Seventy-seven percent see *Markstrat* as increasing their understanding of competitive market dynamics, while 43% thought that *Markstrat* had improved their ability to analyze their marketing environment. 25% think that the game has made them feel competent and confident in making key marketing and business decisions. These results are, again, consistent with the marketing background and experience level of AMMS participants.

5. Of those to whom the question applied, 91% see *Markstrat* as an experience that they would recommend for their subordinates as part of their development.

In addition, a series of questions about *Markstrat's* specific characteristics was asked in the GE survey. A summary of participant responses as shown in Figure 2 indicates:

6. Ninety-three percent agree that *Markstrat* is a realistic simulation of competitive market forces.

7. Ninety-nine percent of the participants think that *Markstrat* emphasizes the importance of accurate market segmentation and focused product positioning. This is an

Figure 1
Responses to survey questions 1-5

Markstrat's General Value *

Gave them a few useful insights. (1B) 94%
Would recommend for the development of their subordinates. (5A) 91%
Increased their understanding of competitive market dynamics. (4B) 77%
Could identify changes in their thinking about markets. (3A) 70%
Taught them new analytical skills and techniques. (2B) 60%
Drove home valuable lessons in marketing strategy. (2A) 50%
Improved their ability to analyze their marketing environment. (4A) 43%
Could name specific actions taken to improve their business' go-to-market strategy. (3B) 30%
Gained many fresh and applicable new ideas. (1A) 26%
Thought the game had made them feel competent and confident in making key marketing and business decisions. (4C) 25%

0 10 20 30 40 50 60 70 80 90 100

*Survey question numbers are indicated in ( ).

Figure 2
Responses to survey questions 6-15

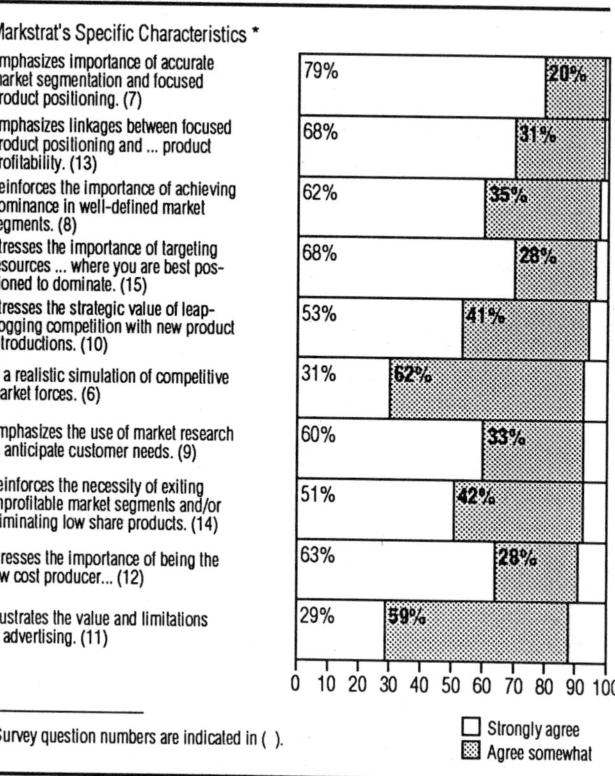

*Survey question numbers are indicated in ( ).

important result since the simulation was designed to teach these key marketing concepts.

8. Ninety-seven percent believe that the game reinforces the importance of achieving dominance in well-defined market segments.
9. Ninety-three percent indicate that the simulation emphasizes the use of market research to anticipate consumer needs.
10. Ninety-four percent see *Markstrat* as stressing the strategic value of leapfrogging competition with new product introductions,
11. Eighty-eight percent think that the game illustrates the value and limitations of advertising.
12. Ninety-one percent indicate that the simulation stresses the importance of being the low-cost producer.
13. Ninety-nine percent of respondents believe that *Markstrat* emphasizes the linkages between focused product positioning, segment dominance, accurate pricing, and product profitability.
14. Ninety-three percent think that the game reinforces the necessity of exiting unprofitable market segments and/or eliminating low-share products.
15. Ninety-six percent believe that *Markstrat* stresses the importance of targeting resources such as new product development, advertising, promotion, sales, and distribution expenditures on those product/segments where the firm is best positioned to dominate.

In summary, most participants surveyed believe that *Markstrat* emphasizes critical elements of marketing strategy. The fact that 50% or more of respondents strongly agree with 8 of the 10 statements in this section reinforces the simulation's value as a teaching vehicle. It is particularly impressive that 93% of those responding believe that *Markstrat* is a realistic simulation of competitive market forces with 31% strongly agreeing with this statement. When the diversity of businesses represented in the sample is considered, this outcome argues that *Markstrat* approaches the ideal of a truly generic simulation, relevant to virtually all go-to-market endeavors.

In addition to the scale-based results presented above, respondents were asked a series of open-ended questions to ascertain *Markstrat*'s impact on marketing decision making. The first of these questions dealt with the specific marketing actions that participants initiated on their jobs based on their *Markstrat* experience. Table 3 presents selected quotes of respondents. Overall, these responses indicate that the game has had a significant impact on these managers.

The second question asked respondents to name the most important lessons learned from *Markstrat*. Table 4 represents selected responses to this question. These quotes indicate that participants are learning the lessons that *Markstrat* is designed to teach.

The third area of interest was concerned with the specific analytical tools and techniques that were learned in *Markstrat* that are being used on the job. Although *Markstrat*'s main purpose is to teach strategic marketing thinking and

Table 3

Describe Specific Marketing Actions You Initiated on Your Job Based on Your *Markstrat* Experience

"I reviewed our marketing plans based on segment strengths and weaknesses. I then revised specific segment plans based on size of market estimate/strengths analysis."
(marketing manager, consumer electronics)

"I redefined our product plan '87 and revisited recent market research to pick up trends and improve our anticipation. I am now preparing the introduction of a product which does not currently exist in the marketplace."
(product manager, CAMCO, Canadian GE)

"I created a data base for competitive analysis. . . and redefined our business areas. . . ." (business development manager, aerospace)

"I did some product pruning to ensure targeted products and made some price modifications changing from cost based to value based pricing."
(manager, marketing analysis and support, commercial and industrial lighting)

"I initiated several research projects to evaluate competitive pricing and positioning. I then established a 'perceived value' comparison roughly based on a two-dimensional mapping of product quality versus product features. This led to cost improvements or major service lines and projects."
(manager, corporate systems marketing, GE Information Services, Inc.)

"I increased our advertising segmentation and our use of print advertising to target more finely." (product manager, consumer lighting)

"I compared one of our new products to competitors' products to properly position and price the new product . . . the *Markstrat* experience was a major asset in developing this positioning."
(specialist, magnetic resonance marketing, medical systems)

Table 4

What Were the Most Important Lessons You Learned from *Markstrat?*

"If you don't get to market first with the best product, you get hammered."
(manager, new business development, plastics)

"Segmentation commitment to a strategy based on thorough analysis."
(manager, operational planning, GE Financial Services, Inc.)

"——— Product positioning
——— Value of advertising
——— Identifying consumer needs
——— Importance of achieving low cost status in the marketplace."
(manager, financial analysis, major appliance)

"The need to focus resources selectively in product/markets in which you have competitive edge. Importance of matching product with consumer perceptions of what is required." (manager, financial planning, power systems)

"That market research information, when properly analyzed and correctly used, can be a powerful tool in developing new products and planning new business penetrations."
(manager, marketing, aerospace)

"Advertising and price strategies cannot overcome the deficiencies of a poorly designed product."
(manager, market research, commercial and industrial lighting)

"——— Pricing is a product attribute, not a consequence
——— Clearly analyze relevant costs vs. direct product costs
——— Find ways to maintain long-term advantage."
(services project manager, power systems)

"Leapfrog and low cost or you won't win."
(manager, manufacturing and equipment technology, contractor equipment)

not the development of specific analytical skills, many participants were able to identify tools and techniques that they are really using on the job based upon the *Markstrat* experience. Table 5 presents selected responses.

Also, respondents were asked to identify *Markstrat*'s greatest strength. Selected results are presented in Table 6. These comments serve as a useful summary of the great impact that *Markstrat* has as a teaching device and as a realistic laboratory setting for research.

As a final check on the impact of *Markstrat* on real managers, Table 7 presents selected results from the group of non-GE managers who played *Markstrat* at the University of Michigan program. The consistently powerful impact of the experience is again noted.

Discussion

Those who have used *Markstrat* as an educational device have consistently praised its impact on students and managers for years. The problem with this praise has been that it has been based upon general impressions and isolated comments of participants. This study is the first to explicitly measure the educational impact of *Markstrat* on a managerial audience. *Markstrat*'s power to teach important marketing concepts and reflect the marketplace and competitive realities of diverse businesses is well documented in the results presented here. What is even more impressive is that real managers take real action based upon their *Markstrat* experience. It is a truly powerful teaching tool.

There is also a profound conclusion for academic researchers in these results. One of the great problems facing academic researchers who study marketing decision making is to find a manageable environment that is also real enough to provide external validity to the results of these studies. The results presented indicate strongly that *Markstrat* is such an environment.

Table 5

Identify Analytical Tools and Techniques Learned in *Markstrat* That You Use on Your Job

"Monitoring competitive marketing actions."
(manager, pricing analysis, major appliance)

"——— Market research and competitor analysis techniques
——— Distribution channel analysis
——— Perceptual mapping."
(area manager, construction equipment)

"Competitive analysis based on perceptual mapping."
(manager, new business development and automotive sales, motors)

"Trend identification and prediction."
(manager, materials, manufacturing and quality technology marketing, aircraft engine)

"Enhanced spread sheet analysis, more 'what if' simulations and use of improved math models for forecasting." (manager, business operations, aircraft engine)

"Use of Lotus 1-2-3 as a management tool not just as a single spreadsheet."
(regional manager, GE Information Services, Inc.)

"I am now using Lotus 1-2-3 to keep track of all proposal/customer activity. I can sort the data to show types of applications, units, etc. This data shows me market trends."
(manager, industrial marketing support, power systems)

"I am using the PC for upfront analysis of sales programs, competitive price tracking, product line price tracking and price/share/volume trade-offs."
(regional manager, major appliance)

Table 6
What Would You Say Is *Markstrat*'s Greatest Strength?

"*Markstrat* brings you close to a real world situation . . . a very competitive marketing environment." (manager, business development, GE Mexico)

"Teaching me that the dynamics of competitive markets are driven both by consumer needs and product development." (manager, field market development, plastics)

"Changing my sales mind set to make me more aware of the positive value of advertising and competitive changes in the marketplace." (regional sales manager, GE Information Services, Inc.)

"Its realism in simulating the market environment with a large number of variables." (manager, advanced marketing, aerospace)

"Its ability to gain the player's undivided attention and interest. It didn't feel like a game." (manager, industrial product planning, motors)

"In a short period of time most, if not all, strategic market forces are utilized in a competitive, fun exercise." (financial analyst, factory automation)

"It is extremely lifelike. Even for the nonconsumer product portion of our Company the lessons are the same . . . we just have fewer but more powerful buyers." (manager, advanced engine system marketing, aircraft engine)

"It's like time lapse photography. It speeds up the product life cycle and simplifies the market so that you can clearly see the effects of your decisions." (service manager, power systems)

Table 7
Quotes from Non-GE Managers from Michigan Programs

"Good practical way to review/experience interaction of different parameters affecting business. Better understanding of interaction of marketing elements." (beer company sales and distribution vice-president)

"Confirmed a thinking process and reinforced awareness of the dynamic market process particularly the competitive activity. It also placed the marketing process in context and the relative importance of the various marketing mix elements. The experience emulated the real world and sharpened the senses." (international sales and promotion manager for major automobile company)

"I have begun to champion an on-going and informationally consistent market research effort. I now recognize that to be 'market driven' it is imperative to evaluate buyers and their motives. I enjoyed the 'adventure, chills and thrills' that ensued." (senior marketing manager for a major overnight delivery service)

"It took away the mystique of complex problem solving. It gave very good insight on how to look at a problem analytically and to break it down into segments that have meaning and direction." (market manager for a major industrial supplier of capital products)

"It helped paint a single picture of marketing strategy using all the elements at once. I've become more precise in my requests to market research. I also have begun to think more in terms of where the market will be tomorrow rather than where it is today." (senior product manager for a major ethical drug company)

"It came at a time in my career when the strategic market planning concept was being implemented by my company. It helped to clear my understanding of the concept and sharpen my skills." (director of distribution for a major plastics company)

"We have 'positions' for all new products based on the same basis learned." (advertising and merchandising manager for the truck division of a major automobile company)

References

1. Bovich, Edward, "The Impact of Marketing Decision Support Systems on Marketing Decision Making." Unpublished Ph.D. Dissertation, The University of Michigan, Ann Arbor, 1987.
2. Cook, Victor J. Jr., and Page, John R. "Assessing Marketing Risk," *Journal of Business Research*, 15 (1987).
3. Larréché, Jean-Claude, and Gatignon, Hubert, *MARKSTRAT. A Marketing Strategy Game*. The Scientific Press, Palo Alto, CA, 1977.
4. Utsey, Marjorie, F., "A study of the Achievement of Profit Potential in a Simulated Environment." Unpublished Ph. D. dissertation, Tulane University, New Orleans, 1985.